Praise for Felipe Fernández-Armesto

'Felipe Fernández-Armesto is one of the most brilliant historians currently at work. All his books are bravura displays of erudition, fizzing with seminal thoughts, original ideas and new syntheses of existing knowledge.'

Frank McLynn, *Independent*

'He makes history a smart art.'

Victoria Glendinning, *The Times*

'One of the most formidable political explicators of our time is undoubtedly Felipe Fernández-Armesto... His theses are never dull; indeed they are sometimes surprising and often memorably expressed.'

Jan Morris, *New Statesman*

'He is in a class of his own for serious scholarship.'

John Bayley, *Spectator*

'An Argonaut of an author, indefatigable and daring.'

Washington Post

'...he has written a book of travels not unlike those of Marco Polo or of Sir John Mandeville, filled with marvels and sensations, rich in description and replete with anecdote. *1492* is a compendium of delights. Felipe Fernández-Armesto is a global voyager on a cultural and intellectual odyssey through one year.'

Peter Ackroyd, *The Times*

'Fernández-Armesto's chapters on the western Mediterranean are models of how to write popular history: accessible, provocative and full of telling detail.'

Mail on Sunday* on *1492

'I cannot remember having read anything as intellectually deft on so ambitious a subject...an enthralling and delightful read.'

Lisa Jardine, *Independent*, on *Truth: A History*

'One of the most dazzlingly assured works of history I have read.'

Sunday Telegraph* on *Millennium

'A tour de force of compilation and writing... Its central thesis is provocative, its range immense.'

Financial Times* on *Millennium

'Startling comparisons and imaginative characterizations... Fernández-Armesto wanders around the globe and across 10,000 years of history putting things together that by conventional methods are always kept apart.'

J. R. McNeill, *New York Times Book Review*, on *Civilizations*

'A mix of deep learning and rigorous argument, beautifully written...delightful and indispensable.'

John Gray, *Literary Review*, on *A Foot in the River*

OUT OF OUR MINDS

What We Think and How We Came to Think It

FELIPE FERNÁNDEZ-ARMESTO

SIMON & SCHUSTER

London • New York • Sydney • Toronto • New Delhi

A CBS COMPANY

First published in Great Britain, the Republic of Ireland
and Australia by Oneworld Publications, 2019

Published in India by Simon & Schuster India, 2019
A CBS company

1 3 5 7 9 10 8 6 4 2

Simon & Schuster India
818, Indraprakash Building,
21, Barakhamba Road,
New Delhi 110001

www.simonandschuster.co.in

Hardback ISBN: 978-93-86797-58-2
eBook ISBN: 978-93-86797-59-9

Typeset in Tetragon, London

Printed and bound in India by Replika Press Pvt. Ltd.

MIX
Paper from
responsible sources
FSC® C016779

Simon & Schuster India is committed to sourcing paper that is made from wood grown in sustainable forests and support the Forest Stewardship Council,® the leading international forest certification organisation. Our books displaying the FS ®C logo are printed on FSC® certified paper.

And as thought is imperishable – as it leaves its stamp behind it in the natural world even when the thinker has passed out of this world – so the thought of the living may have power to rouse up and revive the thoughts of the dead – such as those thoughts were in life ...

E. BULWER-LYTTON
The Haunted and the Haunters

What is Mind? No matter.
What is Matter? Never mind.

Punch (1863)

Contents

Preface

The thoughts that come out of our minds can make us seem out of our minds.

Some of our most potent ideas reach beyond reason, received wisdom, and common sense. They lurk at chthonic levels, emerging from scientifically inaccessible, rationally unfathomable recesses. Bad memories distort them. So do warped understanding, maddening experience, magical fantasies, and sheer delusion. The history of ideas is patched with crazy paving. Is there a straight way through it – a single story that allows for all the tensions and contradictions and yet makes sense?

The effort to find one is worthwhile because ideas are the starting point of everything else in history. They shape the world we inhabit. Outside our control, impersonal forces set limits to what we can do: evolution, climate, heredity, chaos, the random mutations of microbes, the seismic convulsions of the Earth. But they cannot stop us reimagining our world and labouring to realize what we imagine. Ideas are more robust than anything organic. You can blast, burn, and bury thinkers, but their thoughts endure.

To understand our present and unlock possible futures, we need true accounts of what we think and of how and why we think it: the cognitive processes that trigger the reimaginings we call ideas; the individuals, schools, traditions, and networks that transmit them; the external influences from culture and nature that colour, condition, and tweak them. This book is an attempt to provide such an account. It is not meant to be comprehensive. It deals only with ideas from the past that are still around today, forming and informing our world, making and misleading it. By 'ideas' I mean thoughts that are products of imagination – exceeding experience and excelling mere anticipation. They are different from ordinary thoughts not only because they are new but because they involve seeing what has never before been seen. Those covered in this book may take the form of visions or inspiration, but are different from mental 'trips' – incoherent transports or ecstasies – or mental music (unless or until words are set to it) because they constitute models for changing the world. My subtitle, including 'What We Think', is meant seriously. Some historians will call this 'presentism' and deplore it, but I use it only as a principle of selection, not a lens through which to refract light from the past to fit the present. To avoid misunderstanding, I may have to say that by speaking of 'what we think' I do not mean to refer to all the mental occurrences or processes we call thoughts – only to the ideas from the past that we still think about: what we think in the sense of the mental armoury we have inherited for confronting enduring or new problems. 'We', to whom I refer, are not everyone. By using the word I mean to invoke ideas that have appealed beyond their places of origins and have been adopted by all – or nearly all – over the world, in all – or nearly all – cultures. They have dissenters as well as adherents, but you cannot dissent from an idea you have not thought about. Many, perhaps most people, are barely aware of and utterly uninterested in most of the selected ideas, which, however, are part of the background of shared wisdom or folly against which even the indifferent lead their lives.

In three respects, mine is unlike any previous writer's attempt to narrate the history of ideas. First, I include the underexplored problem of how and why we have ideas in the first place: why, by comparison with other, selectively similar animals, our imaginations bristle with so many novelties, probe so far beyond experience, and picture so many different versions of reality. I try to use revelations from cognitive science to expose the faculties that make us, among comparable species, exceptionally productive of ideas. Readers uninterested in theoretical pourparlers can skip to p. 33.

Second, instead of following the usual routine and relying only on written records, I start the story in deep layers of evidence, reconstructing thoughts of our Palaeolithic ancestors and even, in the limited degree the sources permit, reaching for ideas that came out of the minds of cognate or preceding species of hominins and hominids. Among revelations that will, I hope, surprise most readers are: the antiquity of much of the toolkit of ideas on which we rely; the subtlety and profundity of the thinking of early *Homo sapiens*; and how little we have added to the stock of ideas we inherited from the remote past.

Finally, I depart from the convention of writing the history of ideas as if it were a parade of the thoughts of individual thinkers. I cannot avoid mentioning Confucius and Christ, Einstein and Epicurus, Darwin and Diogenes. But in this book, the disembodied ideas are the heroes and the villains. I try to follow their migrations in and out of the minds that conceived and received them. I do not think that ideas are autonomous. On the contrary, they do not – because they cannot – operate outside minds. But they seem intelligible to me only if we acknowledge that genius is just part of the systems that encourage them, and that circumstances, cultural contexts, and environmental constraints, as well as people, play their parts in the story. And I am interested as much in the transmission of ideas, through media that sometimes pollute and mutate them, as in their parturition – which is never immaculate.

There is no one way of tracking ideas across time and cultures, because in pace, direction, and means their migrations are so various. Sometimes they spread like stains, getting fainter and shallower as they go; sometimes they creep like lice, drawing attention to themselves by irritating their hosts into awareness. Sometimes they seem to fall like leaves on a windless day, and rot for a while before they start anything new. Sometimes they get airborne, zooming in erratic swarms and alighting in unpredictable places, or they succumb to the wind and get blown where it listeth. Sometimes they behave like atomic particles, popping up simultaneously in mutually distant places in defiance of normal laws of motion.

The story matches the matrix of history in general, as ideas, like cultures, multiply and diverge, pullulate and perish, exchange and reconverge, without ever – in any sustained fashion – progressing or developing or evolving, or gaining in simplicity or complexity, or fitting any other formula.

In the early phases of the story, all the ideas we know about seem to be the common property of humankind, carried, unforgotten, from a single culture of origin over time and across migrants' changing environments. Increasingly, however, for reasons I try to explore, some regions and some cultures demonstrate peculiar inventiveness. The focus of the book therefore narrows, first to privileged parts of Eurasia, later to what we conventionally call the West. Toward the end of the book, other parts of the world figure mainly as receptors of ideas most of which originate in Europe and North America. I hope no reader mistakes this for myopia or prejudice: it is just a reflection of the way things were. Similarly, the globe-wide perspective and shifting focus of earlier chapters are the results not of political correctness or cultural relativism or anti-Eurocentrism, but of the reality of a world in which cultural exchanges happened in different directions. I hope readers will notice and credit the fact that throughout the book I explore non-Western contributions to ideas and intellectual movements commonly or properly regarded as Western in origin. I do so not for the sake of political correctness but in deference to the truth. Even in the long passages that focus on the West, the book is not primarily about Western ideas but about those that, wherever they originated, have spread so widely as to become fully intelligible, for good and ill, only as part of the intellectual heritage of humankind. Equally, obviously, most of the thinkers I mention were male, because the book is about one of the many areas of human endeavour in which one sex has been disproportionately preponderant. I hope and expect that historians of twenty-first-century ideas, when they get round to the subject with the benefits of hindsight, will properly be able to mention a lot of women.

In each chapter, I try to keep commonly conceived categories distinct, dealing separately with political and moral thinking, epistemology and science, religion and suprarational or subrational notions. In most contexts, the distinctions are, at best, only partly valid. Respecting them is a strategy of convenience and I have tried to make the interchanges, overlaps, and blurred edges apparent at every stage.

Compression and selection are necessary evils. Selection always leaves some readers fuming at the omission of whatever seems more important to them than to the author: I ask their indulgence. The ideas I identify and select will, at least at the margins, be different from those other historians might want to put into a book of this kind were they to try to write one: I rely on every writer's prerogative – which is not to have to write other writers' books for them. Compression is in some ways a self-defeating device, because the swifter the pace of a book, the more slowly readers must go to take in all of it. But it seems better to engage readers' time with concision than waste it with dilatation. I should make one further principle of selection clear: this book is about ideas, understood as merely mental events (or perhaps cerebral ones – though for reasons that will become clear I prefer not to use the term and wish to retain, at least provisionally, a distinction between mind and brain). Though I try to say something about why each idea is important, readers mainly interested in the technologies that ideas trigger or the movements they inspire need to look elsewhere.

The pages that follow garner a lot of work dispersed over many years: from various books I have written, dozens of articles in different journals or collaborative works, and scores of papers and lectures delivered at assorted academic venues. Because I have devoted a lot of attention in the past to environmental history and the history of material culture, it may look as if I have switched to a new approach, via the mind. But minds mediated or originated almost all the evidence we have about the human past. Mental behaviours shape our physical actions. Culture starts in the mind and takes shape when minds meet, in the learning and examples that transmit it across generations. I have always thought that ideas are literally primordial, and occasionally I have foregrounded them, especially in *Truth: A History* (1997), an attempt at a typology of techniques various cultures have relied on to tell truth from falsehood; *Ideas* (2003), a collection of very brief essays, of between 300 and 500 words each, in which I tried to isolate some important notions – 182 of them, almost all of which reappear in various ways in the present book; and *A Foot in the River* (2015), a comparison of biological and cultural explanations of cultural change. Though some readers of *Civilizations* (2001), in which I approached global history through biomes instead of using countries or communities or regions or civilizations as units of study, and of *The World: A History* (2007) have told me I am a materialist, ideas hover and swerve through those books, too, stirring the mixture, impelling events. Here, I put what I know of the history of ideas together in an unprecedented way, weaving strands into a global narrative, and threading among them mental events I have never touched before. The publisher's editors – Sam Carter, Jonathan Bentley-Smith, and Kathleen McCully – have helped a lot, as did four anonymous academic readers. At every stage, I have gathered advice and useful reactions from too many people to mention – especially from the undergraduates who over the last few years have followed my courses on the history of ideas at the University of Notre Dame, and have worked so hard to put me right. In combining the results, I benefited uniquely from Will Murphy's suggestions. 'I want you', he said, 'to write a history of the human imagination.' That still seems an unimaginably big imagination for me to picture. If such a history is possible, what follows is or includes a small contribution toward it.

FELIPE FERNÁNDEZ-ARMESTO

Notre Dame, IN, All Saints' Day, 2017

Chapter 1

Mind Out of Matter

The Mainspring of Ideas

I feel guilty, now that he is dead, because I could never bring myself to like him. Edgar was a senior colleague, to whom, when I was young, I had to defer. He had become a professor when universities were expanding unrestrainedly and jobs multiplied faster than the talent to fill them: competence rather than excellence and indifference rather than vocation were enough. Edgar concealed his inferiority behind complacency and self-congratulation. He bullied his students and patronized his peers. One of the ways in which he enjoyed annoying me was by deprecating my beloved dog. 'Imagine', he would say, 'how little goes on in that pea-sized brain – incapable of thought, just responding to nasty little stimuli from the scent of mouldering scraps and whiffs of other dogs' urine.'

'You can see how unintelligent he is', Edgar added, whenever the dog disobliged him by ignoring his commands.

Secretly and silently, I suspected that Edgar comforted himself by comparison with the dog only because his own mind would be wanting by any other standard. Gradually, however, I came to realize that his attitude reflected common prejudices and fallacies about the way we think. We humans tend to class ourselves as more intelligent than other species, even though the intelligences in question are of such different orders as to make any comparison largely meaningless: it would be no more intelligent, in a dog, to waste time devising an algorithm than for a human to sniff for a mate. We mistake for dumbness what is really dissent from or incomprehension of our priorities. My disappointment at my dog's unresponsiveness to my efforts to make him fetch for me, for instance, is, from his perspective, no more puzzling than my neglect of old bones or my inability to detect an interesting spoor. We call animals intelligent when they do our bidding, whereas if we encountered the same subservience in fellow humans we should despise it as evidence of lack of initiative or critical thought.

The matter is beyond proof, but a lifetime's observation of my own family's dogs has convinced me that they discriminate between commands on rational calculations of interest. Ivan Pavlov thought canine behaviour was conditioned – which, like rare instances of human behaviour, it sometimes is; but dogs defy expectations when they try to solve doggy problems, rather than humanly designed puzzles: problems, that is, conceived not to interest us but to involve them. I once saw my dog, for instance, devise a new squirrel-catching strategy, after many unsuccessful experiments, by stationing himself at right angles to the path between two trees at a point equidistant from both. The plan did not yield a squirrel, but it was, by any standards, intelligently thought out. In his own way, for his own purposes, as two of the most dedicated researchers on canine intelligence say, 'Your dog is a genius.'[1] René Descartes decided that his dog had no more thought or feeling than a machine (and supposedly concluded that he could punish him without moral qualms);[2] the dog, I suspect, recognized Descartes, by contrast, as a sentient, ratiocinative fellow-being. If so, which of the two showed more common sense or practical wisdom?

As with intelligence, most other ways of trying to measure humans' distance from other animals in capacities we share with them are doomed to failure. The claim that we have a special property of consciousness remains just a claim, because there is no satisfactory way of seeing that deeply into other creatures' minds. To know that humans are uniquely sensitive or empathetic, or existentially intuitive, or aware of time, or gifted by God or nature with a peculiar, privileged faculty – such as a 'language acquisition device',[3] or an aesthetic tic, or a moral sense, or a discriminating power of judgement, or an eternally redeemable rational soul, or a meta-mental level of thinking about thinking, or an unparalleled skill in inference capable of deducing universals from instances, or any of the other supposed possessions that humans congratulate themselves on collectively monopolizing – we would need to be able to talk it over with fellow-creatures in other species, or else craft objective tests that have so far eluded our efforts.

All that observation and experiment can guarantee, so far, is that humans' endowment of creative and imaginative mental properties that we share with other animals is palpably, visibly, stunningly enormous. It is proper to ask why and how the divergences in quantity arise, whether or not one suspects differences in quality, too.

This book is about what I think is the most conspicuous such divergence. Humans do exceed dogs and, as far as we know, all other animals, in ability of a peculiar and, to us, exciting and rewarding kind: the power to grasp (and even in some abnormally ingenious humans to generate) the imagined acts (or products of such acts) that we call ideas. The creativity gap between human animals and the rest is vastly greater than that in, say, tool use or self-awareness or theory of mind or effectiveness in communication. Only a human – I want to say – can imagine a canine Bach or a simian Poe or a 'literally' reptilian Plato or a cetacean Dostoevsky who insists that two times two might be five.[4] I am not fully authorized to say so, because a chimp or a dog or a bacillus may secretly harbour such imaginings; but if so, he or it does nothing about it, whereas humans declare their fantasies and project them onto the world, sometimes with revolutionary effects. With peculiar frequency and intensity, we can picture the world to ourselves differently from the way it looks, or responds to our senses. When that happens, we have an idea, as I understand the word.

The results of this capacity are startling, because we often go on to refashion the world in whatever way we have pictured it. Therefore we innovate more than any other species; we devise more ways of life, more diversity of culture, more tools and techniques, more arts and crafts, and more outright lies than other animals. A human can hear a note and compose a symphony; see a stick and turn it mentally into a missile; survey a landscape and envision a city; taste bread and wine and sense the presence of God; count and leap to infinity and eternity; endure frustration and conceive perfection; look at his chains and fancy himself free. We do not see similar outcomes from fancies other animals may have.

Anyone who wants to apply the words 'intelligence' or 'reason' to the faculty that enables ideas can, of course, do so. But the word that best denotes it is surely 'imagination' or perhaps 'creativity'. The degree to which humans are, as far as we know, uniquely creative seems vast by comparison with any of the other ways in which we have traditionally been said to excel other animals.[5] So the first questions for a history of ideas are, 'Where does active, powerful, teeming imagination come from?' and, 'Why are humans peculiarly imaginative animals?'

The questions have been strangely neglected, perhaps in part because of an unsatisfactory assumption: that imagination is just a cumulative product of intensive thinking and needs no special explanation (see p. 10). The nearest thing in the available literature to an evolutionary account of the origins of imagination credits sexual selection: imaginative behaviour, so goes the theory, is conspicuous exhibitionism, likely to attract mates – the human equivalent of unfolding a peacock's tail.[6] At most, the theory locates imagination in a class of evolved faculties, but fails to account for it: if imagination belongs among the results of sexual selection it occupies a pretty lowly place, compared with physical attractions and practical considerations. If only mental musculature were sexier than a six-pack, or a poet more recommendable as a mate than a plumber! I recall a story about one of Henry Kissinger's mistresses who reportedly said, when her sexual taste was questioned, 'Why have a body that can stop a tank when you can have a brain that can stop a war?' I make no comment on her judgement, her sincerity, or her representative value.

Neuroscientists, who like to make their own peacock-displays of brain scans, associating thoughts of every kind with neuronal activity, have not been able to trap a creature at a moment of especially imaginative thinking. In any case, brain scanning has limited powers of explanation: electrical and chemical changes in the brain show that mental events are happening, but are at least as likely to be effects as causes.[7] I do not mean that neurological evidence is contemptible: it helps us know when memory, for instance, is active, and helps us track constituents or ingredients of imagination at work. At present, however, no scientific narrative recounts satisfactorily how humans became imaginatively supercharged.

If we want to understand how humans generate the ideas that are the subject of this book, one good way of starting is by comparing our relevant resources with those of other animals: it can be no more than a starting point because humans are at least as different from all other animals as every non-human species is from all the others. But, in the absence of angels and extra-terrestrials, the creatures with whom we share the planet are our obvious subjects. Our usual assumptions about the relative excellence of humans' equipment are not entirely false, but the comparison, as we shall see, is less to our advantage than we commonly suppose. For present purposes I focus on the brain, not because I think mind and brain are synonymous or coterminous but because the brain is the organ in which our bodies register thoughts. Ideas may exist outside the material universe, but we have to look at the brain for evidence that we have them. As we study the evidence, a paradox will emerge: some of our relative deficiencies of brainpower contribute to making us richly imaginative, and therefore abundantly productive of ideas.

Evolution is an inescapable part of the background. Ideas, as far as we can tell at present, are probably psychic, not organic or material. Except for people who believe in 'memes' (the 'units of culture' Richard Dawkins dreamed up to behave like genes)[8] ideas are not themselves subject to evolutionary laws. But they work with our bodies: our brains process and manage them, our limbs and digits and muscles and speech organs apply and communicate them. Everything we do with our thoughts, and *a fortiori* with ideas, which are thoughts of a special kind or special order, has to deploy the equipment that evolution has given us.

In the pages that follow I intend to argue that evolution has endowed us with superabundant powers of anticipation, and relatively feeble memories; that imagination issues from the collision of those two faculties; that our fertility in producing ideas is a consequence; and that our ideas, in turn, are the sources of our mutable, volatile history as a species.[9]

Big Brains, Big Thoughts?

One of Edgar's widely shared fallacies was his conviction that the bigger your brain, the better you think.[10] I once read that Turgenev had an almost uniquely big brain, whereas Anatole France had an almost uniquely small one. I no longer recall where I learned this and have no means of verifying it, but *se non è vero è ben trovato*: both writers were great geniuses. Women have bigger brains, on average and relative to body size, than men; Neanderthals had bigger brains than *Homo sapiens*; Palaeolithic people exceeded moderns in the dimensions of their brains. Will anyone aver that these differences correspond to differences in power of thought? A few years ago, on the island of Flores in Indonesia, archaeologists discovered the remains of a creature with a brain smaller than a chimpanzee's, but with a toolkit comparable to what one might expect to find in excavations of our own ancestors of about forty thousand years ago, whose brains were, on average, bigger than ours.

Big brains are not necessary to big thoughts:[11] a microchip is big enough to do most of what most people's brains can achieve. Human brains are almost as much of an encumbrance as an amenity: to emulate the microchip they need more nourishment, process more blood, and use up a lot more energy than is necessary. As far as we know, most brain cells are dormant for most of the time. Neuroscientists have speculated about the purpose of the apparently inert astrocytes that vastly outnumber the measurably functional neurons – but no consensus has emerged on what most brain-volume is for or whether it is for anything at all.[12]

The size of human brains is not, therefore, a necessary condition for human-style thinking, but is probably what evolutionary jargon calls a 'spandrel' – a by-product of the evolution of the faculties that equip us to think.[13] Most of the human brain, to put it bluntly, is probably functionless junk, like tonsils and appendixes. To say that it would not be there unless it were useful – only we do not know how – is obviously fallacious or else an expression of over-confidence in the efficiency of evolution,[14] which, as Darwin acknowledged, perhaps in an unguarded moment, is no more consistently targeted than the wind.[15]

It is not hard to see how humans' brains might have become bigger than they would be if a conscious and competent designer were at work. Diet conditions brain growth: fruit is more nourishing and more demanding for foragers than leaves, and meat more so than fruit. As the most omnivorous of apes, our ancestors needed and nourished the biggest brains.[16] Or they may have added brain cells in order to live in larger groups than most other creatures. The bigger your group, the more data you have to handle; rather than starting over and designing a brain fit for purpose, nature grows the brain you already have, stuffing your skull with cortex, multiplying folds and caruncles, extruding lobules. That is perhaps why brain size among apes (though not primates generally) is roughly proportionate to group size.[17] Advantages accrue: in consequence, more neurons can interact in our brains than in those of other species; but more efficient compression could contrive the same effect. By other animals' standards, we have brains with a lot more room for thought; but all the functions we can identify – by seeing, for instance, what people can no longer do if parts of their brains fail or are excised – are part of the equipment of various species. Brain size, in short, helps explain why we do more thinking than other apes, but not why we do thinking of a different order.

The Galactic Overview

Instead, therefore, of complimenting ourselves for our big brains, or congratulating ourselves on the superiority of human intelligence, it may be helpful to focus on the exact cerebral functions or instances of intelligent behaviour in which our species seems peculiarly well endowed or most adept.

We have to face an immediate difficulty: most humans do not do much thinking. 'Oh', they implicitly echo Keats, 'for a life of sensation, not of thought!' Usually, humans' brains are seriously under-employed. Most of us leave others to do our thinking for us and never have thoughts beyond those that outsiders have put into our heads: hence the success of advertising and propaganda. Imitation, repetition, and follow-the-leader may, by some standards, be classed as intelligent behaviour. Why not obey the tyrant who feeds you? Why not ape those apparently wiser or stronger than yourself? For limited purposes, such as survival in a hostile environment, or ease in more amenable circumstances, these may be well-chosen strategies. But domesticated non-humans show plenty of intelligence of that kind – the fawning hound, the submissive sheep. If we want to identify uniquely human thinking we have to focus on the large minority of humans who do a lot of it: those who are responsible for the big, conspicuous differences between our lives and those of other creatures.

To understand what those differences are, we need to shift perspective. Difference-spotting is almost entirely a matter of perspective. If, for example, I ask members of one of my classes at the University of Notre Dame to identify the differences between classmates, they will point to small and often trivial details: Maura has more freckles than Elizabeth; Billy always wears long sleeves, whereas Armand is always in a T-shirt. Xiaoxing is a year younger than everyone else. An outsider, looking at the class with a degree of objectivity unattainable from the inside, will see the big picture and approach the question impersonally, looking for classifiable differences. 'Forty per cent are male', he or she will say, 'and the rest female. Most of your students are white, but three have features that look East Asian, two look as if they have South Asian origin, and two are black. The roster seems to have a surprisingly large number of names of Irish origin', and so on. Both perspectives yield true observations, but for present purposes we want data of the kind more easily visible to the outsider. To spot the big peculiarities of human thinking, compared with that of other animals, we have to try for a similar degree of objectivity.

A thought experiment will help. If I try to envisage the most objective standpoint accessible to my mind, I come up with a sort of cosmic crow's nest, where a lookout with godlike powers of vision can see the entire planet, and the whole history of every species on it, in a single glance, from an immense distance of time and space, like the onlooker who, in *The Aleph*, a short story by Jorge Luis Borges, perceived all the events of every creature's past simultaneously. How would such a privileged observer assess the difference between us and other animals? The cosmic lookout, I suspect, would say, 'Basically you're all the same – inefficient, short-lived arrangements of cells. But I notice some odd things about you humans. You do most of what all the other species do, but you do a lot more of it. As far as I can tell, you have more thoughts, tackle more tasks, penetrate more places, adopt more foods, and elaborate more political and social forms, with more stratification, more specialization, and more economic activities. You develop more lifeways, more rites, more technologies, more buildings, more aesthetic fancies, more modifications of the environment, more consumption and production, more arts and crafts, more means of communication; you devise more culture, and – in short – turn over more ideas with more speed and variety than any other creature I can see. As far as I can tell, you put more time and effort than other animals into self-contemplation, the identification of values, the attempt to generalize or analyse; you devote vast mental resources to telling stories previously untold, composing images of what no one ever saw, and making music no ear ever heard before. By comparison with most of your competitor-species you are torpid, weak, tailless, deficient in prowess, and poorly fitted with fangs and claws (though you are, luckily, good at throwing missiles and have agile hands). Yet, despite your ill-endowed, ill-shaped bodies, your capacity for responding to problems, exceeding minimal solutions, and rethinking your futures has given you a surprising degree of mastery on your planet.'

These observations might not make the lookout admire us. He or she would notice the uniqueness of every species and might not think ours was of an order superior to all the others'. But though we may not be unique in being innovative and creative (that would be another self-congratulatory claim, belied by evidence), our power to innovate and create seems unique in range and depth and abundance. In these respects, the differences between humans and non-humans carry us beyond culture, of which, as we shall see, many species are capable, to the uniquely human practice we call civilization, in which we reshape the world to suit ourselves.[18]

Becoming Imaginative

How could our brains have helped us to this improbable, unparalleled destination? The brain, like every evolved organ, is the way it is because conditions in the environment have favoured the survival and transmission of some genetic mutations over others. Its function is to respond to the world outside it – to solve the practical problems the world poses, to meet the exigencies it demands, to cope with the traps it lays and the constraints it tangles. The repertoire of thoughts that belongs in this book is of another kind, a different order. They constitute the sort of creativity enchantingly called '*fantasia*' in Italian, with resonances of fantasy that exceed what is real. They create worlds other than the ones we inhabit: worlds unverifiable outside our minds and unrealized in existing experience (such as refashioned futures and virtual pasts), or unrealizable (such as eternity or heaven or hell) with resources that we know, from experience or observation, that we command. V. S. Ramachandran, a neurologist who has hunted valiantly for differences between humans and other apes, puts it like this: 'How can a three-pound mass of jelly ... imagine angels, contemplate the meaning of infinity, and even question its own place in the cosmos?'[19]

There are two traditional answers: one popular in scientific tradition, the other in metaphysics. The strictly scientific answer is that quantity becomes quality when a critical threshold is crossed: humans' brains, according to this line of thinking, are so much bigger than those of other apes that they become different in kind. It is not necessary for the brain to have a specialized function for creativity or for the generation of ideas: those events ensue from the sheer abundance of thinking of more mundane kinds that emanates from big brains.

On the other hand, the metaphysical answer is to say that creativity is a function of an immaterial faculty, commonly called a mind or a rational soul, which is unique to humans, or of which humans possess a unique kind.

Either answer, though not both, may be true. But neither seems plausible to everyone. To accept the first, we need to be able to identify the threshold beyond which brains leap from responsiveness to creativity. To accept the second, we have to be metaphysically inclined. Mind, according to sceptics, is just a fancy word for functions of the brain that neurology cannot quite pin down in the present state of knowledge.

So how can we improve on the traditional answers? I propose reformulating the question to make it less vague, specifying the exact thought-generating function we want to explain. The term that best denotes what is special about human thinking is probably 'imagination' – which covers *fantasia*, innovation, creativity, re-crafting old thoughts, having new ones, and all the fruits of inspiration and ecstasy. Imagination is a big, daunting word, but it corresponds to an easily grasped reality: the power of seeing what is not there.

Historians, like me, for instance, have to reconfigure in imagination a vanished past. Visionaries who found religions must bring to mind unseen worlds. Storytellers must exceed experience to recount what never really happened. Painters and sculptors must, as Shakespeare said, 'surpass the life' and even photographers must capture unglimpsed perspectives or rearrange reality if they are going to produce art rather than record. Analysts must abstract conclusions otherwise invisible in the data. Inventors and entrepreneurs must think ahead beyond the world they inhabit to one they can remake. Statesmen and reformers must rethink possible futures and devise ways to realize better ones and forestall worse. At the heart of every idea worth the name is an act of imagination – experience excelled or transcended, reality reprocessed to generate something more than a snapshot or echo.

So what makes humans super-imaginative? Three faculties, I suggest, are the constituents of imagination. Two are unmistakably products of evolution. On the third, the jury is out.

First comes memory – one of the mental faculties we call on for inventiveness, starting, whenever we think or make something new, with what we remember of whatever we thought or made before. Most of us want our memories to be good – accurate, faithful to a real past, reliable as foundations for the future. But surprisingly, perhaps, bad memory turns out to be what helps most in the making of imagination.

Remembering Wrongly

Unsurprisingly, in most tests of how human thinking compares with that of other animals, humans score highly: after all, we devise the tests. Humans are relatively good at thinking about more than one thing at a time, divining what other creatures might be thinking about, and handling large repertoires of humanly selected symbols.[20] Memory, however, is one of the kinds of thinking at which, even by human standards, other animals can rival or outstrip us. Remembering information of relevant kinds is one of the most striking faculties in which non-humans can excel. Beau, my dog, beats me – metaphorically, not in the sense Descartes envisaged – in retaining memories of people and routes. He can reconstruct, unbidden, any walk he has ever been on. After six years without seeing an old friend of mine, he recognized her on her next visit, rushing off to present her with a toy that she had given him on the previous occasion. Beau makes me willing to believe Homer's story of how only the family dog recognized Odysseus when the hero returned from his wanderings. He retrieves toys or bones unerringly, while I waste my time seeking misfiled notes and errant reading glasses.

Anyone who has a pet or a non-human work-partner can match stories of their enviable powers of memory. Yet most people still echo Robert Burns's pitying address to his 'wee, sleekit, cow'rin', tim'rous' mouse, whom, he thought, 'the present only toucheth', as if the little beast were frozen in time and isolated from past and future.[21] But this sort of distinction between brutish and human memory is probably another example of unjustified human self-congratulation. We do not have to rely on anecdotal stories of dogs of suspected shagginess. Controlled studies confirm that in some respects our memories are feeble by other animals' standards.

Scrub-jays, for instance, know what food they hide and remember where and when they hide it. Even without food-inducements, rats retrace routes in complex labyrinths, whereas I get muddled in the simplest garden mazes. They recall the order in which they encounter smells. Clearly, therefore, they pass tests of what specialists call episodic memory: the supposedly human prerogative of travelling back, as it were, in time by recalling experiences in sequence.[22] Clive Wynne, the apostle of non-human minds, whose fame is founded on the vividness with which he can imagine what it would be like to be a bat, has summarized some relevant experiments. Pigeons, he points out, retain for months, without degradation, memories of hundreds of arbitrary visual patterns associable with food. They home in on their own lofts after long absences. Bees recall the whereabouts of food, and how to find it in a maze. Chimpanzees retrieve from apparently casually selected locations the stones they use as anvils for cracking nuts. In laboratories, challenged to perform for rewards, they remember the correct order in which to press keys on a computer screen or keyboard. And 'vampire bats can remember who has given them a blood donation in the past and use that information in deciding whether to respond to a petitioner who is begging for a little blood'.[23]

Belittlers of non-human memory can insist that many non-human animals' responses are no better, as evidence of thinking, than the fawning and cowering of Pavlov's dogs, who, back in the 1890s, started to salivate when they saw their feeder, not – according to the theory that became notorious as 'behaviourism' – because they remembered him but because the sight of him triggered psychic associations. The apparent memory feats of rats, bats, pigeons, and apes – any surviving behaviourist might claim – more resemble conditioned reflexes or reactions to stimuli than recollections retrieved from a permanent store. Apart from prejudice, we have no good grounds for making such a distinction. St Augustine, whom I revere as, in most other respects, a model of clear thinking, was a behaviourist *avant la lettre*. He thought that a horse could retrieve a path when he was following it, as each step triggered the next, but could not recall it back in his stable. Even the saint, however, cannot have been sure about that. No experiment can verify the assumption. Augustine's only basis for making it was a religious conviction: that God would hardly condescend to give horses minds resembling those of His chosen species. Equally dogmatic successors today make a similar mistake. Most psychologists have stopped believing that human behaviour can be controlled by conditioning: why retain the same discredited belief in trying to understand other animals? For material directly comparable with human experience we can turn to experiments with chimpanzees and gorillas. They resemble us in relevant ways. We can access their own accounts of their behaviour. We can converse with them – within the limited sphere our common interests permit – in humanly devised language. They do not have mouths and throats formed to make the same range of sounds that figure in humans' spoken languages but non-human apes are remarkably good at learning to use symbolic systems – that is, languages – of other kinds. By following examples and heeding instruction, just as human learners do or should do if they are good students, apes can deploy many of the manual signs and representative letters or images that humans use.

Panzee, for example, is an exceptionally dexterous symbol-juggling female chimpanzee at Georgia State University. She communicates with her carers via cards, which she brandishes, and keyboards, which she taps to access particular signs. In a typical experiment, while Panzee watched, researchers hid dozens of succulent fruits, toy snakes, balloons, and paper shapes. Without prompting, except by being shown the symbol for each object in turn, Panzee remembered where the little treasures were and could guide keepers to them. Even after relatively long intervals of up to sixteen hours she recalled the locations of more than ninety per cent. No 'cheating' was involved. Panzee had never had to obtain food by pointing to places outside her enclosure before. Her keepers could provide no help, conscious or unconscious, because they were not privy in advance to any information about the hiding-places. Panzee, therefore, did more than show that chimps have an instinct for finding food in the wild: she made it clear that they – or at least she – can remember unique events. As well as displaying what we might call retrospective prowess, she displays a kind of prospective skill, applying her memory to advantage in predicting the future by foreseeing where food will be found.[24] In another intriguing experiment, using her keyboard, she guided a carer to the whereabouts of concealed objects – peanuts, for preference, but including non-comestible items in which she had no active interest. The head of her lab, Charles Menzel, says, 'Animal memory systems have always been underestimated – the upper limits are not really known.'[25]

Among Panzee's rival rememberers is Ayuma, a quick-witted chimpanzee in a research facility in Kyoto. She became famous in 2008 as the star of a TV show, beating human contestants in a computerized memory game. Participants had to memorize numerals that appeared on a screen for a tiny fraction of a second. Ayuma recalled eighty per cent accurately. Her nine human rivals all scored zero.[26] With practice humans can ape Ayuma.[27] Evidence in chimpanzees' favour, however, has continued to accumulate. If one discounts uncharacteristic prodigies, typical humans can remember sequences of seven numbers; other apes can remember more and can learn them faster. *Ape Memory* is a video game for members of our species who want to try to reach simian levels of excellence. King, a gorilla resident of Monkey Jungle, Miami, Florida, inspired a version called *Gorilla Memory*. King is good at counting. He communicates with humans by waving and pointing to icons printed on cards. When primatologists picked on him for memory tests he was thirty years old – too well stricken with maturity, one might think, to be receptive in learning new tricks. But he knew human peculiarities from long experience. He showed that he could master past events in time, arraying them in order. With a level of performance significantly well above chance, he could recall each of three foods and could reverse, when asked to do so, the order in which he ate them.[28] He can connect individuals with foods they have given him, even when his keepers have forgotten who provided which treat, just as my dog can associate, in memory, his toys with the benefactors who bestowed them. Both King and Beau would, on these showings, make far better witnesses than most humans at a criminal identity parade. A team tested King by performing acts that were new to him, including physical jerks and charades – pretending to steal a phone, or playing 'air guitar'. When they asked King who had done which performance, he got the answer right sixty per cent of the time. The score may seem modest – but try getting humans to emulate it.[29]

Chimps can locate memories in time, arrange them in order, and use them to make predictions. The work of Gema Martin-Ordas at Leipzig Zoo stands out among experiments that have challenged claims that such faculties are uniquely human. In 2009, eight chimpanzees and four orang-utans watched her use a long stick to reach a banana. She then hid the stick and another, too short for the job, in different locations for the apes to find. Three years later, with no promptings in the interval, the sticks returned to their former places. A banana was suitably installed, too. Would the apes be able to get at it? All the participants, except for one orang-utan, recalled the location of the right stick without effort. Other apes, who had not taken part in the previous exercise, were unable to do so. To capture memories and store them for future use, therefore, is part of the cognitive equipment humans share with other apes.[30]

A more sophisticated experiment designed by psychologist Colin Camerer and primatologist Tetsuro Matsuzawa tested chimps' and humans' ability to project predictions from remembered events. Subjects from both species played a game in which they observed other individuals' moves on a touch screen and then had an opportunity to win rewards by predicting what they would choose next. Chimps proved, on average, better at detecting the patterns than their human rivals, apparently because they could remember longer sequences of moves. The game tests for superior memory and strategic capability: how well the players recall opponent's selections; how well they detect patterns in choice-making; how cleverly they make their own predictions. The results suggest that some chimps, at least, excel some humans in these skills.[31]

So Edgar was wrong, in the present connection, to belittle non-human intellects. I do not mean to suggest that human memories are incapable of prodigious feats. Preachers, performers, and examinees can often parade stupendous amounts of data. Vaudeville acts formerly hauled vast chains of facts before audiences, like Mr Memory in Hitchcock's version of *The Thirty-Nine Steps*. There are idiot-savants who can reel off the contents of the telephone directory. In some comparable functions, however, where memory is in play, non-human animals outclass us. Most people recoil when you tell them that human memories are not the best on our planet, but it is worth pausing to think about this counterintuitive notion. Humans have almost always assumed that any faculty that might justify us in classifying ourselves apart from other beasts must be a superior faculty. But maybe we should have been looking at what is inferior – at least, inferior in some respects – in us. Memory is not in every respect humans' most glorious gift, compared with that of other animals. Poverty, unreliability, deficiency, and distortions corrode it. We may not like to acknowledge the fact, because it is always hard to forfeit self-regard. We prize our memories and take pride in them because they seem so precious for our sense of self – something we are only just beginning to concede to other animals.

Literature – psychological, forensic, imaginative – is full of evidence of the weakness of most humans' recollections. Perhaps the most effective way of summoning up a sense of how badly memory works is to look at one of Salvador Dalí's most famous paintings – a bleak landscape scattered with disturbing, misshapen objects. He called the painting *The Persistence of Memory* but that is one of the artist's characteristic ironies: the real subject is how memory fades and warps. In the background is a westering sky, where the light is in retreat, over an indistinct sea, in which every feature seems to dissolve. Then comes a crumbling cliff, as if eroded, like memory, by the passage of time, and a blank slate, from which every impression has been erased. A dead, truncated tree, from which all life has withered, juts into the middle ground, over an almost traceless shore. Huge chronometers, stopped at different moments, sag and wilt, as if to proclaim the mutability time inflicts, the contradictions it unwinds. Bugs seem to eat away at the casing of another watch in the foreground, while in the centre of the composition a monstrous, menacing shape seems to have been transferred from some evil fantasy by Hieronymus Bosch. Memories do turn into monsters. Time does subvert recall. Recollections decay.

The inefficiencies of human memory bridge the difference between memory and imagination. The difference is not, in any case, very great. Memory, like imagination, is a faculty of seeing something that is not present to our senses. If imagination is, as defined above, the power to see what is not really there, memory enables us to see what is there no longer: it is, in a sense, a specialized form of imagination. Memory works by forming representations of facts and events – which is also what imagination does.

Mnemotechnics, the ancient 'art of memory' that Cicero used to deliver speeches in the Roman courts and senate, assigns a vivid image – which may not be a naturally suggestive symbol – to each point the speaker wants to make. A bloody hand might stand for a humdrum point of procedure, a lovely rose or a luscious fruit for the deplorable vices of the speaker's opponent.[32] Observations of how the brain works confirm the contiguity of memory and imagination: as far as we can tell, both 'happen' in overlapping areas. Almost identical electrical and chemical activity goes on in the brain when imagination and memory are at work.

Memory and imagination overlap. But some philosophers are reluctant to acknowledge that fact.[33] I blame Aristotle. He insisted, with his usual common sense, that memories must refer to the past – and the past, he pointed out, was fundamentally unlike imaginary events because it really happened. Sometimes, however, life traduces common sense. In practice, memories and imaginings fuse.

But memories are closest to imaginings when they are false. Their creative power consists in distorting recollections. Misremembering recasts reality as fantasy, experience as speculation. Every time we misremember something old, we are imagining something new. We mingle and mangle the past with features it never really had. Life would be unbearable otherwise. Daniel Schacter, the Harvard cognitive scientist who monitors what happens in the brain when memories are registered and retrieved, points out that evolution has given us bad memories to spare us from the burden of cluttering our minds. We have to make space in the lumber room, discarding relatively unimportant data to focus on what we really need.[34]

Women who remember faithfully the real pain of childbirth will be reluctant to repeat it. Socialites and networkers have to filter the names and faces of people they do not need. Soldiers would never return to the trenches, unless they suppressed or romanticized the horrors of war. Old men remember their feats – according to Shakespeare – 'with advantages'. To these self-interested modifications of memory, we add outright errors. We mistake our imaginatively transformed recollections for literal copies of the events we recall. The memories we think we 'recover' in hypnosis or psychotherapy can really be fantasies or distortions, but they have life-changing power for good and ill.

We can live with the quicksilver slips and slidings of our individual memories; but when we share and record them in enduring forms, the outcome is social memory: a received version of the past, which can reach back to times no individual can claim to remember. The same vices raddle it: self-interest, rose-tinting, and sins of transmission. Propaganda engraves falsehood on pedestals, copies it into textbooks, slaps it onto billboards, and insinuates it into ritual. In consequence, social memory is often unresponsive to facts or intractable to historical revision. If psychologists can detect false memory syndrome in individuals, historians can disclose it in entire societies.

Workers in jurisprudence may want to demur. The similarity of memory and imagination subverts the value of legal testimony. For law courts, it would be convenient to divide fanciful versions from real accounts. We know, however, that witness statements rarely tally in practice. The most widely cited text is fictional but true to life: *In a Grove*, a short story from 1922 by Ryūnosuke Akutagawa, inspired one of the great works of cinema, Akira Kurosawa's *Rashomon*. Witnesses to a murder give mutually contradictory evidence; a shaman releases the testimony of the victim's ghost. But the reader – or the audience of the movie version – remains unconvinced. Every trial, every comparison of testimony, confirms the unreliability of memory. 'You were all in gold', sings a reminiscent, ageing lover in the stage-musical version of *Gigi*. The lady corrects him: 'I was dressed in blue.' 'Oh yes', is his rejoinder. 'I remember it well.' In our various ways, we all remember equally badly.

Poorly functioning memory helps to make humans outstandingly imaginative. Every false memory is a glimpse of a possible new future that, if we so choose, we can try to fashion for ourselves.

Anticipating Accurately

The distortions of memory enlarge imagination but do not wholly account for it. We also need what the biomedical researcher Robert Arp calls 'scenario visualization': a fancy name for what one might more simply call practical imagination. Arp links it with a psychological adaptation that might have arisen – uniquely, he thinks – among our hominin ancestors in the course of making complicated tools, such as spear-throwing devices for hunting.[35] Among surviving species, no other creature has a mind's eye powerful enough to transform a stick into a javelin, and then, by a further imaginative leap, to add a throwing spear.

The test, expressed in these terms, may be unfair: other animals do re-envision sticks: chimpanzees, for instance, are capable of seeing them as means of fishing for termites or guiding floating objects towards a riverbank or smiting nuts or for wielding, for enhanced effect, in an aggression display. If they do not see them as potential spears, that may be because no other animal is as good at throwing as humans typically are.[36] Non-human apes, who do relatively little throwing to relatively little effect, find practical uses for sticks, all of which involve some 'scenario visualization' or capacity for imaginatively foreseeing a solution. Many animals, especially species with evolutionary pasts as predators or prey, deploy imagination in problem-solving. When a rat finds a way through a maze, it is reasonable to assume that the creature knows where he or she is going. When, by trial and error over a period of weeks, my dog in his youth developed his ingenious (though ultimately unavailing) strategy for catching squirrels (see p. 2), he displayed, in a small way, imaginative foresight.

Dogs also dream. So do cats. You can see them twitching in their sleep, scrabbling with their paws, and making noises consistent with wakeful states of excitement or anxiety. Their eyes revolve in sleep, matching the rapid eye-movement of dreaming humans.[37] In dreams pets may be rehearsing or relishing playfulness or reliving or anticipating adventures with prey or other food. This does not mean that when awake they can imagine unreality with the same freedom as human minds exhibit: sleep is a special, untypical form of consciousness that bestows exceptional licence. But in dreaming non-humans do share a visionary property of human minds.

They also help us envisage the circumstances in which our ancestors acquired the power of imagination. Like Arp's tool-makers, my dog hunts: indeed, dogs and humans have a long history of hunting together. A canine evolutionary psychologist, if there were such a thing, would identify a lot of behaviour, even in the most placid lapdog, as a product of predation: eviscerating a fluffy toy, mock-fighting in play, scratching at a scent in a rug as if trying to dig out a rabbit warren or foxhole. I do not want to invoke the concept of 'Man the Hunter', which feminist critique has impugned (although 'man', to me, is a word of common gender, unconfined to either sex). Because hunting is a form of foraging, 'The Human Forager' may be a better term in any case. Still, in species that prey and are preyed on, hunting genuinely stimulates the development of imagination in the long run. It does so, I suggest, because hunting and hunted creatures need to evolve an intermediate faculty, which I call anticipation.

If imagination is the power to see what is not there, and memory is the power to see what is there no longer, anticipation is of a similar sort: the property of being able to see what is not there yet, envisaging dangers or opportunities beyond the next rise or behind the next tree trunk, foreseeing where food might be found or peril might lurk. Like memory, therefore, anticipation is a faculty at the threshold of imagination – poised to cross, like an intrusive salesman or an importunate caller. Like memory, again, anticipation jostles with imagination in overlapping regions of the brain. All three faculties conjure absent scenes. Blend bad memory and good anticipation together: imagination results.

Anticipation is probably a product of evolution, a faculty selected for survival and encoded in heritable genes. The discovery of 'mirror neurons' – particles in the brains of some species, including our own, that respond similarly when we observe an action or perform it ourselves – excited expectations, about a quarter of a century ago, that they would disclose the roots of empathy and imitation; more remarkably, however, measurements of activity of these 'suculs' in macaques demonstrated powers of anticipation: in experiments in 2005, some monkeys only saw people move as if to grasp food; others witnessed the completed action. Both groups responded identically.[38]

Culture can encourage anticipation, but only if evolution supplies the material to work with. Predator and prey both need it, because each needs to anticipate the movements of the other.

Humans have a lot of it because we need a lot of it. We need more of it than our competitor-species, because we have so little of almost everything else that matters. We are slow in eluding predators, catching prey, and outrunning rivals in the race for food. Because we are clumsy in climbing, a lot of foods are effectively beyond our reach and a lot of refuge is denied us. We are not as sharp-eyed as most rival animals. Our skill in scenting prey or danger, or hearing from afar, has probably declined since hominid times, but is never likely to have matched canids, say, or felines. We have pitiably feeble fangs and claws. Our ancestors had to commit themselves to the hunt despite the way other species with superior equipment dominated the niche: hominin digestive equipment, from jaws to guts, was inadequate to deal with most plants; so carnivorism became compulsory, perhaps as much as three or four million years ago. First as scavengers and gradually, increasingly as hunters, in the line of evolution that produced us, hominins had to find ways of acquiring meat for food.

Evolution gave us few physical advantages to make up for our defects. Bipedalism freed hands and hoisted heads, but our overall agility remains laggard, and by becoming merely feet, our lowest extremities ceased to be available as useful extra hands. The biggest adjustment evolution made in our favour is that no species can challenge our average skill in throwing and in fashioning objects to throw and tools to throw them with; we can therefore deploy missiles against the prey we cannot catch and the predators who can catch us. To aim at moving objects, however, we need keenly developed anticipation, so as to predict how the target is likely to shift. Anticipation is the evolved skill that minimized our deficiencies and maximized our potential. A lot of the arguments that help to explain human anticipation apply to other primates. Indeed, all primates seem well endowed with the same faculty. Some of them even show potential, at least, for flights of imagination recognizably like those of humans. Some paint pictures (like Congo the chimp, whose canvases command thousands of dollars at auction), while some coin new words, as Washoe, the linguistically adept ape of the Yerkes Institute, did when she referred to a Brazil nut as a 'rock-berry' in American sign-language, and became the first ape to construct a term for an item her keepers had not labelled. She also devised 'water birds' to designate swans even when they were out of water. Other non-human apes invent technologies, introduce cultural practices, and change the way they look by adorning themselves with what seems to be a protean aesthetic sensibility – though they never take these practices anything like as far as humans.

What then makes us the most imaginative primates? In part, no doubt, the selectively superior memories we observe in chimpanzees and gorillas account for the difference: you need, as we have seen, a bad memory to be maximally imaginative. In part, too, we can point to differing levels of attainment in physical prowess: we need most anticipation, among primates, because we have least strength and agility. Evolutionary psychology – that divisive discipline, which pits disdainers against disciples – can supply the rest of the answer.

Uniquely, among extant primates, we humans have a long hunting history behind us. Our dependence on hunted foods is extreme. Chimpanzees hunt, as, to a lesser extent, do bonobos (who used to be classified as 'dwarf chimpanzees'). But it means much less to them than it does to us. They are stunningly proficient in tracking prey and positioning themselves for the kill, but no one observed them hunting until the 1960s: that may be a trick of the evidence, but the environmental stresses human encroachments inflicted on them may have forced them to develop new food sources by or at that time. In any case, hunting is a marginal activity for chimpanzees, whereas it was the foundation of the viability of human societies for ninety per cent of the time *Homo sapiens* has existed. Typically, hunting chimps get up to three per cent of the calorific content of their diet from the hunt; a study, on the other hand, of ten typical hunting peoples in tropical environments, similar to those favoured by chimps, yielded hugely higher figures. On average, the selected communities derived nearly sixty per cent of their intake from hunted meat.[39]

Overwhelmingly, moreover, chimpanzee carnivores focus on a narrow range of species, including wild pigs and small antelopes, with preference, at least in Gombe where most observations have been recorded, for colobus monkeys. Every human community, by contrast, has a rich variety of prey. Chiefly, perhaps, because hunting is still a relatively infrequent practice among chimpanzees, and the young have only occasional opportunities to learn, it takes up to twenty years to train a chimp to be a top-rated hunter, able to head off the fleeing colobus or block his route to trap him; novices begin, like beaters in humans' hunting, by springing the trap – scaring the prey into flight. Human youngsters, by contrast, can become proficient after a few expeditions.[40] Even in the course of their limited experience as hunters you can literally see chimpanzees cultivating a faculty of anticipation, estimating the likely path of prey and planning and concerting efforts to channel and block it with all the elegance of an American football defence tracking a runner or receiver. Hunting hones anticipation for every creature that practises it. But it is not surprising that *Homo sapiens* has a more developed faculty of anticipation than other, comparable creatures – even more than our most closely related surviving species.

Highly developed powers of anticipation are likely to precede fertile imaginations. When we anticipate, we imagine prey or predator behind the next obstacle. We guess in advance the way a threat or chance will spring. But imagination is more than anticipation. It is, in part, the consequence of a superabundant faculty of anticipation, because, once one can envisage enemies or victims or problems or outcomes ahead of their appearance, one can, presumably, envisage other, ever less probable objects, ending with what is unexperienced or invisible or metaphysical or impossible – such as a new species, a previously unsampled food, unheard music, fantastic stories, a new colour, or a monster, or a sprite, or a number greater than infinity, or God. We can even think of Nothing – perhaps the most defiant leap any imagination has ever made, since the idea of Nothing is, by definition, unexampled in experience and ungraspable in reality. That is how our power of anticipation leads us, through imagination, to ideas.

Imagination reaches beyond the range accessible to anticipation and memory; unlike normal products of evolution, it exceeds the demands of survival and confers no competitive edge. Culture stimulates it, partly by rewarding it and partly by enhancing it: we praise the bard, pay the piper, fear the shaman, obey the priest, revere the artist. We unlock visions with dance and drums and music and alcohol and excitants and narcotics. I hope, however, that readers will agree to see imagination as the outcome of two evolved faculties in combination: our bad memories, which distort experience so wildly that they become creative; and our overdeveloped powers of anticipation, which crowd our minds with images beyond those we need.

Any reader who remains unconvinced that memory and anticipation constitute imagination may like to try a thought experiment: try imagining what life would be like without them. Without recalling effects of memory, or looking ahead to a future bereft of memory, you cannot do it. Your best recourse is to refer – again, deploying memory – to a fictional character deficient in both faculties. To Sergeant Troy in *Far From the Madding Crowd*, 'memories were an encumbrance and anticipation a superfluity'. In consequence, his mental and emotional life was impoverished, without real empathy for others or admirable accomplishments for himself.

Thinking with Tongues

Alongside memory and anticipation, language is the last ingredient of imagination. By 'language' I mean a system of symbols: an agreed pattern or code of gestures and utterances with no necessarily obvious resemblance to the things signified. If you show me a picture of a pig, I get an idea of what you want to refer to, because a picture is representative, not symbolic. But if you say 'pig' to me, I do not know what you mean unless I know the code, because words are symbols. Language contributes to imagination to this extent: we need it to turn imaginings, which may take the form of images or noises, into communicable ideas.

Some people think or claim to think that you cannot conceive of anything unless you have a term for it. Jacob Bronowski was among them. He was one of the last great polymaths and believed passionately that imagination is a uniquely human gift. 'The ability', he said, shortly before his death in 1974, 'to conceive of things which are not present to the senses is crucial to the development of man. And this ability requires the existence of a symbol somewhere inside the mind for something that is not there.'[41] Some kinds of thinking do depend on language. Speakers of English or Dutch, for instance, understand the relationship between sex and gender differently from people who think in, say, Spanish or French, and who therefore have no words of common gender at their disposal, and yet who are used to designating male creatures by feminine terms and vice versa. Spanish feminists, in partial consequence, coin feminine terms to designate, for instance, female lawyers and ministers, while leaving other designations untouched, whereas their Anglophone counterparts, equally illogically, abjure such feminine words as they have, renouncing, for instance, 'actress' or 'authoress'.

Yet scholars used to exaggerate the extent to which the languages we speak have measurable effects on how we perceive the world.[42] On the basis of currently available evidence, it seems more commonly the case that we devise words to express our ideas, rather than the other way round. Experiments show, for instance, that human infants make systematic choices before they make symbolic utterances.[43] We may not be able to say how thought can happen without language, but it is at least possible to conceive of a thing first and invent a term or other symbol for it afterwards. 'Angels', as Umberto Eco once said, summarizing Dante, 'do not speak. For they understand each other through a sort of instantaneous mental reading, and they know everything they are allowed to know ... not by any use of language but by watching the Divine Mind.'[44] It makes just as good sense to say that language is the result of imagination as that it is a necessary precondition.

Symbols – and language is a system of symbols, in which utterances or other signs stand for their referents – resemble tools. If my case so far is valid, symbols and tools alike are results of a single property of the creatures that devise them: the ability to see what is not there – to fill gaps in vision, and to re-envisage one thing as if it were something else. That is how a stick can become a proxy for an absent limb or a lens transform an eye. Similarly, in language, sounds stand for emotions or objects and evoke absent entities. My wife and dog, as I write these lines, are four thousand miles away; but I can summon them symbolically by mentioning them. I have finished my cup of coffee, but because the image of it, brimming and steaming, is in my mind, I can conjure the phantasm of it in writing. Of course, once we have a repertoire of symbols the effect on imagination is freeing and fertilizing; and the more abundant the symbols, the more prolific the results. Language (or any symbolic system) and imagination nourish each other, but they may originate independently.

Language was, presumably, the first system of signs people developed. But how long ago did that happen? Fallacies – or, at least, unwarranted assumptions – underlie almost all our thinking about language. Disputes over the configuration of jaws and palates have dominated controversy about the dating of the first language; but vocal equipment is irrelevant: it can affect the kind of language you use but not the feasibility of language in general. In any case, we tend to assume that language is for communication and socialization, creating bonds of mutual understanding and facilitating collaboration: the human equivalent of monkeys picking at one another's lice or dogs exchanging sniffs and licks. But language may have started as mere self-expression, uttered to communicate one's pain or joy or frustration or fulfilment only to oneself. Our ancestors' first vocalizations were, presumably, physical effects of bodily convulsions, such as sneezes, coughs, yawns, expectorations, exhalations, farts. The first utterances with deeper significance might have been purrs of satisfaction, smacks of the lips, or pensive murmurs. And when people first consciously used noises or gestures or utterances to make a point, it is surely as likely to have been a hostile point, warning off predators or rivals with a snarl or scream or a display of prowess, as an attempt to set up a partnership of more than a merely sexual nature.

Besides, if language is for communication, it does not do its job very well. No symbol exactly matches what it signifies. Even signifiers specifically designed to resemble objects are often obscure or misleading. One day, I noticed a fellow-diner in search of the lavatory in a pretentious restaurant. He poised uncertainly for a moment between doors marked respectively with pictures of a strawberry and a banana, before realization dawned. I often blink uncomprehendingly at the icons designers scatter over my computer screen. I once read a perhaps fanciful newspaper report of the writer's attempt to buy a small gold cross pendant as a baptismal gift. 'Do you', the shop assistant asked, 'want one with a little man on it?' Since most of the signs language deploys are arbitrary, and have no resemblance to the object signified, the chances of misleading multiply.

Misunderstanding – which we usually condemn for breaking peace, marring marriage, occluding the classroom, and impeding efficiency – can be fruitful; it can make ideas multiply. Many new ideas are old ideas, misunderstood. Language contributes to the formulation of ideas and the flow of innovation, through distortions and disasters as well as through successful communication.

Producing Cultures

Memory and anticipation, then, with perhaps a little help from language, are the factories of imagination. Ideas, if my argument is right so far, are the end products of the process. So what? What difference do ideas make to the real world? Don't vast forces – climate and disease, evolution and environment, economic laws and historical determinants – shape it, beyond the reach of human power to change what is bound to happen anyway? You can't think your way out of the clockwork of the cosmos. Or can you? Can you escape the wheels without getting crushed among the cogs?

I propose that ideas, rather than impersonal forces, make the world; that almost everything we do starts in our minds, with reimagined worlds that we then try to construct in reality. We often fail, but even our failures impact on events and jar them into new patterns, new courses.

The oddness of our experience is obvious if, again, we compare ourselves with other animals. Plenty of other species have societies: they live in packs or herds or hives or anthills of varying complexity but – species by species and habitat for habitat – uniform patterning marks the way they live. As far as we can tell, instinct regulates their relationships and predicts their behaviour. Some species have culture – which I distinguish from non-cultural or pre-cultural kinds of socialization whenever creatures learn behaviours by experience and pass them on to subsequent generations by example, teaching, learning, and tradition.

The first discovery of non-human culture occurred in Japan in 1953, when primatologists observed a young female macaque monkey, whom they called Imo, behave in unprecedented ways. Until then, members of Imo's tribe prepared sweet potatoes for eating by scraping off the dirt. Imo discovered that you can wash them in a spring or the sea. Her fellow-macaques had difficulty separating food-grains from the sand that clung to them. Imo found that by plunging them in water you can separate them easily, scooping up the edible matter as the heavier sand sinks. Imo was not just a genius: she was also a teacher. Her mother, her siblings, and, little by little, the rest of the tribe learned to imitate her techniques. To this day, the monkeys continue her practices. They have become cultural in an unequivocal sense: rites practised for the sake of upholding tradition rather than for any practical effect. The monkeys still dip their sweet potatoes in the sea, even if you present them with ready-washed specimens.[45]

Over the last seven decades, science has revealed ever increasing instances of culture beyond the human sphere, first among primates, subsequently among dolphins and whales, crows and songbirds, elephants and rats. One researcher has even suggested that the capacity for culture is universal and detectible in bacteria so that, potentially, any species might develop it given time and appropriate environmental pressures or opportunities.[46] However that may be, on present evidence no animal has gone nearly so far along the cultural trajectory as *Homo sapiens*. We can measure how cultures diverge: the more variation, the greater the total amount of cultural change. But only humans display much material to study in this respect. Whales have pretty much the same social relationships wherever they graze and blow. So do most other social species. Chimpanzees exhibit divergence: in some places, for instance, they crack nuts with stones; in others they wield sticks to fish for termites. But human differences dwarf such instances. Baboons' mating habits cover an interesting range from monogamous unions to sultanic seraglio-gathering and serial polygamy, but again they seem unable to match the variety of humans' couplings.

Other animals' cultures are not stagnant – but they seem so by comparison with ours. There is now a whole academic sub-discipline devoted to chimpanzee archaeology. Julio Mercader of the University of Calgary and his colleagues and students dig up sites chimps have frequented for thousands of years; so far, however, they have found remarkable continuities in the selection and use of tools, but not much evidence of innovation since the animals first began to crack nuts with the help of stones. Chimpanzee politics, too, are a rich field of study. Frans de Waal of the Yerkes Institute has made a speciality of the study of what he calls Chimpanzee Machiavellianism.[47] And of course, chimp societies experience political change in the form of leadership contests, which often produce violent reversals of fortune for one alpha male or another, and for the gangs of toughs who surround and support candidates for the role of top ape.

Occasionally, we can glimpse chimps' potential for revolutionary change, when, for instance, an intelligent chimp usurps, for a while, the role of the alpha male. The classic case is that of Mike, a small and feeble but clever chimpanzee of Gombe, who seized power over his tribe in 1964. Enhancing his displays of aggression by clashing big cans that he filched from the primatologist's camp, he intimidated the alpha male into submission and remained in control for six years.[48] He was the first chimpanzee revolutionary we know of, who not only usurped leadership but changed the way a leader emerged. We can assume, therefore, that similar revolutions could occur deep in the hominid past. But even Mike was not clever enough to devise a way of passing power on without the intervention of another putsch by a resurgent alpha male.[49]

A remarkable transformation of political culture occurred among some baboons in 1986, when the entire elite was wiped out, perhaps as a result of eating poisonous trash from a human midden, perhaps because of tuberculosis. No new alpha male arose to take over: instead, a system of wide power-sharing emerged, with females playing major roles.[50] Chimpanzee tribes sometimes split when young males secede in the hope of finding mates outside the group. Wars between the secessionists and the *vieille garde* frequently ensue. But these fluctuations take place within an overall pattern of barely disturbed continuity. The structures of chimpanzee societies hardly alter. Compared with the rapid turnover and amazing diversity of human political systems, variation in other primates' politics is tiny.

The Power of Thought

So the problem historians are called on to solve is, 'Why does history happen at all?' Why is the story of humankind so crowded with change, so crammed with incident, whereas other social and cultural animals' lifeways diverge at most only a little from place to place and time to time?

Two theories are on the table: the first, that it is all to do with matter; the second, that it is all to do with mind. People used to think that mind and matter were very different types of thing. The satirist who coined the *Punch* joke that appears as an epigraph to this book expressed the perfect mutual exclusivity of the concepts – mind was no matter, and matter never mind. The distinction no longer seems reliable. Scholars and scientists reject what they call 'mind–body dualism'. We now know that when we have ideas, or, more generally, whenever thoughts arise in our minds, physical and chemical process accompany them in the brain. The way we think, moreover, is trapped in the physical world. We cannot escape the constraints of our environments and the pressures and stresses from outside ourselves that encroach on our freedom to think. We are prisoners of evolution – limited to the capacities with which nature has endowed us. Material drives – such as hunger, lust, fear – have measurable effects on our metabolisms and invade and warp our thoughts.

I do not think, however, that human behaviour can be explained only in terms of response to material exigencies, first, because the stresses that arise from the physical framework of life also affect other animals, and so cannot be invoked to explain what is peculiarly human; and, second, because the rhythms of change in evolution and environment tend to be relatively slow or fitful, whereas the turnover of new behaviour in humans is bewilderingly fast.

Instead, or additionally, I propose mind – by which I simply mean the property of producing ideas – as the chief cause of change: the place where human diversity starts. Mind in this sense is not the same thing as the brain, nor a part or particle embedded in it. It more resembles, perhaps, a process of interaction between cerebral functions – the creative flash and crash you see and hear when memory and anticipation spark and scrape against each other. The claim that we make our own world is frightening to those of us who fear the terrible responsibilities that flow from freedom. Superstitions ascribe our ideas to the promptings of imps or angels, demons or gods, or attribute our ancestors' innovations to extraterrestrial whisperers and manipulators. For Marxists and other historicists, our minds are the playthings of impersonal forces, doomed or destined by the course of history, to which we may as well assent as we cannot restrain or reverse it. For sociobiologists, we can think only what is in our genes. For memeticists, ideas are autonomous and evolve according to a dynamic of their own, invading our brains as viruses invade our bodies. All these evasions seem to me to fail to confront our real experience of ideas. We have ideas because we think them up, not thanks to any force outside ourselves. To seek to accumulate and juxtapose information may be an instinctive way we have of trying to make sense of it. There comes a point, however, when the 'sense' we make of knowledge transcends anything in our experience, or when the intellectual pleasure it gives us exceeds material need. At that point, an idea is born.

Human ways of life are volatile because they change in response to ideas. Our species' most extraordinary facility, compared with the rest of creation, is our capacity for generating ideas so powerful and persistent that they make us seek ways of applying them, altering our environs, and generating further change. Put it like this: we re-envision our world – imagining a shelter more efficient than nature provides, or a weapon stronger than our arms, or a greater abundance of possessions, or a city, or a different mate, or a dead enemy, or an afterlife. When we get those ideas we strive to realize them, if they seem desirable, or to frustrate them, if they inspire us with dread. Either way, we ignite change. That is why ideas are important: they really are the sources of most of the other kinds of change that distinguish human experience.

Chapter 2

Gathering Thoughts

Thinking Before Agriculture

If what I have said so far is right, the logical conclusion is that the history of thinking should include non-human creatures. We have, however, little or no access to the thoughts even of the other animals with whom we interact most closely. Extinct species of hominid predecessors or hominin ancestors, however, have left tantalizing evidence of their ideas.[1]

The Moral Cannibals: The Earliest Ideas?

The earliest instance I know of lies among the detritus of a cannibal feast eaten about 800,000 years ago in a cave in Atapuerca, Spain. Specialists bicker about how to classify the feasters, who probably belonged to a species ancestral to our own but preceding ours by so long an interval – of some 600,000 years – that anything they had in common with us seems astonishing. They split bones of their own species to suck out the marrow. But there was more to the feast than hunger or gluttony. These were thinking cannibals. We have trained ourselves to recoil from cannibalism and to see it as treason against our species: a form of sub-human savagery. The evidence, however, suggests the opposite: cannibalism is typically – you might almost say peculiarly, even definingly – human and cultural. Under the stones of every civilization lie human bones, snapped and sucked. Most of us nowadays, like chimpanzees beholding occasional cannibal aberrations among their peers, react uncomprehendingly. But in most human societies, for most of the past, we should have accepted cannibalism as normal – embedded in the way society works. No other mammals practise it so regularly or on such a large scale as we do: indeed, all others tend to avoid it except in extreme circumstances – which suggests that it did not come 'naturally' to our ancestors: they had to think about it.

It is consistent with just about everything we know about the nature of cannibalism to assume that the Atapuerca cannibals were performing a thoughtful ritual, underlain by an idea: an attempt to achieve an imagined effect, augmenting the eaters' powers or reshaping their natures. Cannibals sometimes eat people to survive famine or deprivation or top up protein-deficient diets.[2] Overwhelmingly, however, more reflective aims, moral or mental, aesthetic or social, inspire them: self-transformation, the appropriation of power, the ritualization of the eater's relationship with the eaten, revenge, or the ethic of victory. Normally, where it is normal, cannibalism occurs in war, as an act symbolizing dominance of the defeated. Or human meat is the gods' food and cannibalism a form of divine communion.

In a crazed frenzy, villagers of Hautefaye in the Dordogne in 1870 devoured one of their neighbours, whom a mad rumour misidentified as a 'Prussian' invader or spy, because nothing save cannibalism could satiate the fury they felt.[3] For the Orokaiva people of Papua, it – until the island authorities banned it in the 1960s – was their way of 'capturing spirits' in compensation for lost warriors. The Hua of New Guinea ate their dead to conserve vital fluids they believed to be non-renewable in nature. In the same highlands, Gimi women used to guarantee the renewal of their fertility by consuming dead menfolk. 'We would not leave a man to rot!' was their traditional cry. 'We take pity on him! Come to me, so you shall not rot on the ground: let your body dissolve inside me!'[4] They unconsciously echoed the Brahmins who, in an anecdote of Herodotus, defended cannibalism on the grounds that other ways of disposing of the dead were impious.[5] Until 'pacification' in the 1960s the Amazonian Huari ate their slaughtered enemies in revenge and their close kin in 'compassion' – to spare them the indignity of putrefaction. Aztec warriors ingested morsels of the bodies of battle-captives to acquire their virtue and valour.[6] The hominids of Atapuerca launched an adventure in thought.[7]

Theirs was the earliest recoverable idea – recorded deep in layers of cognitive stratigraphy: the idea that thinkers can change themselves, appropriate qualities not their own, become something other than what they are. All subsequent ideas echo from the cave-walls of Atapuerca: we are still trying to refashion ourselves and remake our world.

By about 300,000 years ago – still long before the advent of *Homo sapiens* – when a landslide sealed the cave-mouth and turned Atapuerca into a kind of time-capsule, the locals were stacking the bones of their dead in recognizable patterns. What the rite meant is unfathomable, but it was a rite. It had meaning. It suggests, at a minimum, another idea – the distinction between life and death – and perhaps a kind of religious sensibility that treats the dead as deserving of the honour or trouble of the living.

Inklings of Afterlife

There is similar but more easily interpreted evidence in burials of some forty thousand years ago: recent enough to coincide with *Homo sapiens* but actually belonging to the distinct species we call Neanderthals. There is in principle no good reason to suppose that Neanderthals were less imaginative or less productive of ideas than humans of our own species. Redating, according to uranium–thorium techniques newly applied to palaeoanthropological materials in 2018, has reassigned to the seventieth millennium BCE some of the representational and symbolic cave paintings in northern Spain (such as those examined in the previous section); they include sketches of animals, hand prints, and geometric designs of kinds formerly assigned to *Homo sapiens* artists of about thirty or forty thousand years ago.[8] The same dating techniques have yielded dates of over 115,000 years ago for artefacts made of shell and for pigments.[9] If the revisions are valid, the artists responsible were of a species that long predated the earliest known evidence of *Homo sapiens* in the regions, in a period when Neanderthals were already at home there. The evidence of active imaginations and powerful thinking in Neanderthal graves should not surprise us.

In a grave at La Ferrassie, France, for instance, two adults of different sexes lie curled in the foetal position typical of Neanderthal graves. Three children of between three and five years old and a newborn baby lie nearby among flint tools and fragments of animal bones. The remains of two foetuses were interred with equal dignity. Other dead Neanderthals were graced at burial with even more valuable grave goods: a pair of ibex horns accompanied one youth in death, a sprinkling of ochre bedecked another. At Shanidar, in what is now Iraq, an old man – who had survived in the care of his community for many years after the loss of the use of an arm, severe disablement to both legs, and blindness in one eye – lies with traces of flowers and medicinal herbs. Sceptical scholars have tried to 'explain away' these and many other cases of what look like ritual interments as the results of accident or fraud, but there are so many graves that the commonsense consensus acknowledges them as genuine. At the other extreme, irresponsible inferences credit Neanderthals with a broad concept of humanity, a system of social welfare, belief in the immortality of the soul, and a political system dominated by philosopher-gerontocrats.[10]

The burials do, however, disclose strenuous thinking, not just for such material ends as safeguarding the dead from scavengers, or masking putrescence, but also in order to differentiate life from death. The distinction is subtler than people commonly suppose. Apart from conception, which some people contest, no moment defines itself as the start of life. Impenetrable comas make it hard even today to say when it ends. But thirty or forty thousand years ago, Neanderthals made the same conceptual distinction as we make, marking it by rites of differentiation of the dead. Celebrations of death hallow life. Rites of burial are more than merely instinctive valuing of life. Those who undertake them make a display of their confidence that life deserves reverence, which is the basis of all human moral action.

It is tempting to treat ceremonial burial as evidence that people who practise it believe in an afterlife. But it might be no more than an act of commemoration or a mark of respect. Grave goods may be intended to work propitiatory magic in this world. On the other hand, by thirty-five to forty thousand years ago, complete survival kits – food, clothes, negotiable valuables, and the tools of one's trade – accompanied the dead all over the inhabited world, as if to equip life in or beyond the grave. Corpses from very modest levels of society had gifts of ochre, at least, in their graves; those of higher rank had tools and decorative objects presumably in accordance with status.

The idea that death could be survived probably came easily to those who first thought of it. The constant transformations we observe in our living bodies never seem to impair our individual identities. We survive puberty, menopause, and traumatic injury without ceasing to be ourselves. Death is just another, albeit the most radical, of such changes. Why expect it to mark our extinction? To judge from goods normally selected for burial, mourners expected the afterworld to resemble life familiar from experience. What mattered was survival of status, rather than of the soul. No change in that principle is detectable until the first millennium BCE, and then only in some parts of the world.[11]

Later refinements, however, modified the afterlife idea: expecting reward or punishment in the next world or imagining an opportunity for reincarnation or renewed presence on Earth. The threat or promise of the afterlife could then become a source of moral influence on this world and, in the right hands, a means of moulding society. If, for instance, it is right to see the Shanidar burial as evidence that a half-blind cripple survived thanks to the nurture of fellow-Neanderthals for years before he died, he belonged in a society that prescribed care for the weak: that implies either that the kind of costly moral code Social Democrats advocate today was already in place, or that his carers were trying to secure access to his wisdom or esoteric knowledge.

The Earliest Ethics

Everybody, at all times, can cite practical reasons for what they do. But why do we have scruples strong enough to override practical considerations? Where does the idea of a moral code – a systematic set of rules for distinguishing good from evil – come from? It is so common that it is likely to be of very great antiquity. In most societies' origins myths, moral discrimination figures among humans' earliest discoveries or revelations. In Genesis, it comes third – after acquiring language and society – among Adam's accomplishments: and 'knowledge of good and evil' is his most important step; it dominates the rest of the story.

In an attempt to trace the emergence of morality, we can scour the archaeological record for evidence of apparently disinterested actions. But calculations unrevealed in the record may have been involved; we might pay homage to Neanderthal altruism, for instance, in default of information about the Shanidar carers' quid pro quo. Many non-human animals, moreover, perform disinterested actions without, as far as we know, having a code of ethics (although they do sometimes get depressed if their efforts go unrewarded. There is a credible story about earthquake-rescue dogs demoralized after a long period with no one to save. Their keepers had to draft in actors to pretend to be survivors). Altruism may deceive us into inferring ethics: it may be just a survival mechanism that impels us to help each other for the sake of kickback or collaboration. Morals may be a form of self-interest and 'morality' a misleadingly high-minded term for covertly calculated advantage. We behave well, perhaps, not because we have thought up morality for ourselves, but because evolutionary determinants have forced it on us. Maybe the 'selfish gene' is making us altruistic to conserve our gene pool. Evidence of a distinction between right and wrong is never unequivocal in preliterate sources in any but a practical sense.

We are still equivocal about the difference. Right and wrong, according to a formidable philosophical tradition, are words we give to particular ratios between pleasure and pain. Good and evil, in a sceptical tradition, are elusive notions, both definable as aspects of the pursuit of self-interest. Even philosophers who grant morality the status of a sincerely espoused code sometimes argue that it is a source of weakness, which inhibits people from maximizing their power. More probably, however, goodness is like all great goals: rarely attained, but conducive to striving, discipline, and self-improvement.[12] The benefits are incidental: committed citizens in societies that loyalty and self-sacrifice enrich. We can get closer to the earliest identifiable thoughts about good and evil, as about almost everything else, if we turn to the explosion of evidence – or, at least, of evidence that survives – from about

170,000 years ago. It may seem recent by the standards of Atapuerca, but it is far longer ago than previous histories of ideas have dared to go.

Identifying the Early Thoughts of *Homo Sapiens*

The longer an idea has been around, the more time it has had to modify the world. To identify the most influential ideas, therefore, we have to start with the earliest past we can reconstruct or imagine. Ideas are hard to retrieve from remote antiquity, partly because evidence fades and partly because ideas and instincts are easily confused. Ideas arise in the mind. Instincts are there 'already': inborn, implanted, presumably, by evolution; or, according to some theories, occurring first as responses to environmental conditions or to accidental experiences – which is how Charles Lamb imagined the discovery of cooking, as a consequence of a pig partially immolated in a house-fire. Darwin depicted the beginnings of agriculture in the same way, when a 'wise old savage' noticed seeds sprouting from a midden (see p. 80).

In these, as in every early instance of emerging ideas, the judgements we make are bound to be imperfectly informed. Do we talk and write, for instance, because the idea of language – of symbols deployed systematically to mean things other than themselves – occurred to some ancestor or ancestors? Or is it because we are 'hard-wired' to express ourselves symbolically? Or because symbols are products of a collective human 'subconscious'?[13] Or because language evolved out of a propensity for gesture and grimace?[14] Do most of us clothe ourselves and adorn our environments because ancestors imagined a clothed and adorned world? Or is it because animal urges drive seekers of warmth and shelter to expedients of which art is a by-product? Some of our longest-standing notions may have originated 'naturally', without human contrivance.

The next tasks for this chapter are therefore to configure means for evaluating the evidence by establishing the antiquity of the earliest records of thinking, the usefulness of artefacts as clues to thought, and the applicability of anthropologists' recent observations of foragers. We can then go on to enumerate ideas that formed, frozen like icicles, in the depths of the last ice age.

The Clash of Symbols

The claim that we can start so far back may seem surprising, because a lot of people suppose that the obvious starting point for the history of ideas is no deeper in the past than the first millennium BCE, in ancient Greece.

Greeks of the eighth to the third centuries BCE or thereabouts have, no doubt, exerted influence out of all proportion to their numbers. Like Jews, Britons, Spaniards, at different times, and perhaps the Florentines of the Quattrocento, or nineteenth-century Mancunians, or Chicagoans in the twentieth century, ancient Greeks would probably feature in any historian's list of the most surprisingly impactful of the world's peoples. But their contribution came late in the human story. *Homo sapiens* had been around for nearly 200,000 years before Greeks came on the scene and, of course, a lot of thinking had already happened. Some of the best ideas in the world had appeared many millennia earlier.

Maybe, if we are looking for reliable records, we should start the story with the origins of writing. There are three reasons for doing so. All are bad.

First, people assume that only written evidence can disclose ideas. But in most societies, for most of the past, oral tradition has attracted more admiration than writing. Ideas have been inscribed in other ways. Archaeologists sieve them from fragmentary finds. Psychologists may exhume them from deep in the subconscious stratigraphy – the well-buried layers – of modern minds. Sometimes anthropologists elicit them from among the practices traditional societies have preserved from way back in the past. No other evidence is as good as evidence we can read in explicitly documented form, but most of the past happened without it. To foreclose on so much history would be an unwarrantable sacrifice. At least in patches, we can clarify the opacity of preliterate thinking by careful use of such data as we have.

Second, an impertinent assumption – which almost everyone in the West formerly shared – supposes that 'primitive' or 'savage' folk are befogged by myth, with few or no ideas worth noting.[15] 'Prelogical' thought or 'superstition' retards them or arrests their development. 'For the primitive mind', asserted Lucien Lévy-Bruhl, one of the founders of modern anthropology, in 1910, 'everything is a miracle, or rather nothing is; and therefore everything is credible and there is nothing either impossible or absurd.'[16] But no mind is literally primitive: all human communities have the same mental equipment, accumulated over the same amount of time; they think different things, but all in principle are equally likely to think clearly, to perceive truth, or to fall into error.[17] Savagery is not a property of the past – just a defect of some minds that forswear the priorities of the group or the needs or sensibilities of others.

Third, notions of progress can mislead. Even enquiries unprejudiced by contempt for our remote ancestors may be vulnerable to the doctrine that the best thoughts are the most recent, like the latest gizmo or the newest drug, or, at least, that whatever is newest and shiniest is best. Progress, however, even when it happens, does not invalidate all that is old. Knowledge accumulates, to be sure, and can perhaps pile up so high as to break through a formerly respected ceiling to new thoughts in, as it were, a previously unaccessed attic. As we shall see repeatedly in the course of this book, ideas multiply when people exchange views and experiences, so that some periods and places – like ancient Athens, or Renaissance Florence, or *Sezessionist* Vienna, or any crossroads of culture – are more productive of creativity than others. But it is false to suppose that thinking gets better as time unfolds or that its direction is always towards the future. Fashion gyrates. Revolutions and renaissances look back. Traditions revive. The forgotten is recovered with freshness more surprising than that of genuine innovations. The notion that there was ever a time when nothing was worth recalling is contrary to experience.

In any case, although nothing we can easily recognize as writing survives from the Ice Age, representative symbols do appear with unmistakable clarity in the art of twenty to thirty thousand years ago: a lexicon of human gestures and postures that recur so often that we can be sure that they meant something at the time – in the sense, at least, of evoking uniform responses in beholders.[18] Artworks of the time often parade what look like annotations, including dots and notches that suggest numbers, and puzzling but undeniably systematic conventional marks. No one can now read, for instance, a bone fragment from Lortet in France, with neat lozenges engraved over a dashingly executed relief of a reindeer crossing a ford; but perhaps the artist and his or her audience shared an understanding of what the marks once meant. A swirl that resembles a P occurs widely in 'cave art', attracting would-be decipherers who have noticed a resemblance to the hooplike curves the artists sketched to evoke the shapes of women's bodies. It may be fanciful to read the P-form as meaning 'female'; but to recognize it as a symbol is irresistible.

The idea that one thing can signify something else seems odd (though to us, who are so used to it, the oddness is elusive and demands a moment's self-transposition to a world without symbols, in which what you see is always exactly what you get and nothing more, like a library to an illiterate or a junkyard full of road signs but without a road). Presumably, the idea of a symbol is a development from association – the discovery that some events cue others, or that some objects advertise the proximity of others. Mental associations are products of thought, noises from rattled chains of ideas. When the idea of symbolic representation first occurred, the devisers of symbols had a means of conveying information and making it available for critical examination: it gave humans an advantage over rival species and, ultimately, a means of broadening communication and protracting some forms of memory.

The presence of a sign begs the question of its reliability: its conformity, that is, to the facts it is designed to represent. When we draw attention to an event or issue an alert at, say, the approach of a mastodon or a sabre-toothed tiger or the threat of fire or crack of ice, we detect what we think is real. We represent its reality in words (or gestures or grunts or grimaces or marks scarred on the surface of the world – on a patch of sand, perhaps, or the bark of a tree or the face of a rock). We 'name' it, as the first human did in so many myths of how he found his way round the dawning world. According to Genesis, naming was the first thing God did to light, darkness, sky, and sea after creating them. He then delegated the naming of living creatures to Adam. Danger or opportunity seem communicable without conscious intention on the part of an ululating or gesticulating animal. They can be apprehended, for instance, in a sensation or a noise or a pang of pain. In many species, instinct alone transmits awareness of danger between individuals.

A creature, however, who consciously wants to convey the reality of peril, pain, or pleasure to another has launched a search for truth:

for a means, that is, of expressing fact. We can properly ask of the first people, as of the greatest modern philosophical sophisticates, 'How did they separate truth from falsehood? How did they decide when and whether utterances were true?'

The Modern Stone Age: Foraging Minds

If ancient foragers' symbols resist interpretation, what else can help us detect their thoughts? Material artefacts, first, can yield readings to techniques specialists call 'cognitive archaeology'. Modern anthropological observations can provide further guidance.

Of truths uttered in jest, *The Flintstones* had some of the funniest. The Hanna-Barbera studio's 'modern Stone Age family' capered across the world's television screens in the early 1960s, reliving in their caves the everyday adventures of modern middle-class America. The concept was fantastic, the stories silly. But the series worked, partly because 'cave men' really were like us: with the same kinds of minds and many of the same kinds of thoughts.

In principle, therefore, there is no reason why people of the hunter-gatherer era should not have had ideas that anticipate our own. Their brains were at least as big, though, as we have seen, brain size and brainpower are only vaguely related. Over the entire history of our species, no evidence of any overall change is discernible, for better or worse, in the skill with which humans think. Maybe there was an era, long before the emergence of *Homo sapiens*, when life was 'poor, nasty, brutish and short' and hominids scavenged without leisure for ratiocination; but for hundreds of thousands of years thereafter all our ancestors, as far as we know, were relatively leisured foragers rather than relatively harried, hasty scavengers.[19] The artefacts they left are clues to creative minds. From about seventy thousand years ago, and abundantly from about forty thousand years later and onward, art displays a repertoire of symbols that hint at how Ice Age people reimagined what they saw.[20] Artworks are documents. If you want to know what people in the past thought, look at their art, even before you look at their writings, because their art literally pictures for us their world as they experienced it.

In alliance with art, a lot of digs yield material clues to what goes on in the mind. A simple test establishes the possibilities: if you look today at what people eat, how they embellish their bodies, and how they decorate their homes you can draw informed conclusions about their religions, for example, or ethics or their views on society, or politics, or nature. Do they have stuffed hunting trophies mounted on the walls and pelts as hearthrugs? Or do they like chintz and toile, or tapestry and oak mouldings, or tiling and Formica? Do they drive a Lincoln or a Lada? Palaeolithic tastes yield similar clues. For instance, the people who hunted mammoths to extinction on the Ice Age steppes of what is now southern Russia, over twenty thousand years ago, built dome-shaped dwellings of mammoth ivory. On a circular plan, typically twelve or fifteen feet in diameter, the bone-houses seem sublime triumphs of the imagination. The builders took mammoth nature and reconstructed it, humanly reimagined, perhaps to acquire the beasts' strength or to conjure magic power over them. To see a mammoth and imagine its bones transformed into a dwelling requires a commitment of creativity as dazzling as any innovation later ages came up with. People slept, ate, and enacted routines of family life inside the framework of bones. But no dwelling is purely practical. Your house reflects your ideas about your place in the world.

Alongside art and cognitive archaeology, comparative anthropology can also yield clues. By providing us with a means of measuring the antiquity of ideas, anthropologists can help interpret the evidence of the art and the other material remains. Strictly speaking, just as there are no primitive minds, there are no primitive peoples: we have all been on the planet for equally long; all our ancestors evolved into something recognizably human an equally long time ago. Some people, however, do, in one sense, have more primitive thoughts than others – not necessarily more retarded or more simplistic or more superstitious thoughts, or thoughts cruder or inferior or less abstract: just thoughts that first occurred earlier. Determinedly conservative societies, resistant to change, in close touch with their earliest traditions, are most likely to preserve their oldest thoughts. To check or explain the evidence of archaeological finds, we can use the practices and beliefs of the most consistently retrospective, most successfully conservative societies that survive in today's world: those that still live by hunting and gathering.

Of course, the fact that hunter-gatherer peoples today have certain ideas does not mean that people of similar culture anticipated them tens or scores or hundreds of thousands of years ago. But it raises the possibility. It helps make the archaeology intelligible. Broadly speaking, the more widely diffused an idea is, the older it is likely to be, because people communicated or carried it when they traded or migrated from elsewhere. The precept is not infallible, because, as we know from the wildfire of globalization in our own times, late ideas can spread by contagion, along with hamburgers 'leaping' from St Louis to Beijing, or IT initiatives from Silicon Valley to the Sunda Strait. We know a lot about how ideas spread in recent history, in the course of the worldwide transmission of culture by world-girdling technologies. We can identify the global popularity of jazz or jeans or soccer or coffee as the result of relatively recent events. But when we meet universal features of culture that predate well-documented periods, we can be fairly sure that they originated before *Homo sapiens* dispersed out of Africa and were transmitted by the migrants who peopled most of the world between about 15,000 and 100,000 years ago.

Cold Cases: Environment and Evidence of Ice Age Ideas

The migrations in question happened roughly during the last great ice age – a time from which enough symbolic notation and material clues survive, and for which modern anthropological observations are sufficiently applicable, for us to attempt to reconstruct a lot of thinking, sometimes in spectacular detail.

We need to know what made it conducive to creativity, and why a cold climate seems to have been mentally bracing. We can link the emergence of *Homo sapiens* with a cool period at about 150,000 to 200,000 years ago. Dispersal over an unprecedented swathe of the globe, from about 100,000 years ago, coincided with glaciation in the northern hemisphere as far south as the present lower courses of the Missouri and Ohio and deep into what are now the British Isles. Ice covered Scandinavia. About twenty thousand years ago, most of the rest of Europe was tundra or taiga. In central Eurasia, tundra reached almost to the present latitudes of the Black Sea. Steppes licked the shores of the Mediterranean. In the New World, tundra and taiga extended to where Virginia is today.

While ice crept over the world, migrants from humankind's East African 'cradle' carried artefacts we can associate with thoughts and sensibilities similar to our own: jewels made of shells; slabs of ochre incised with patterns. In Blombos Cave in South Africa, where migrants from East Africa were settling at the time, there are remnants of shell crucibles and spatulas for mixing pigments.[21] Of the same period are objects of art too delicate to be of much practical use: fragments of meticulously engraved ostrich eggshells, with geometric designs, from the Diepkloof rock shelter, 180 kilometres north of Cape Town. At about the same time, at Rhino Cave in the Tsodilo Hills of Botswana, decorators of spearheads ground pigments and collected colourful stones from many miles away. That people who made such objects had a 'theory of mind' – consciousness of their own consciousness – is a proposition that is hard to resist in the presence of so much evidence of imaginations so creative and so constructive. They had the mental equipment necessary to be able to reimagine themselves.[22] Otherwise, they would have remained, like most other surviving simians, in the environment in which their ancestors evolved, or in contiguous and broadly similar biomes, or in adjoining spaces where circumstances – such as conflict or predation or climate change – forced them to adapt. The arrivals at Blombos Cave did something far more inventive: they overleapt unfamiliar environments, as if able to anticipate changed circumstances. They saw a new world ahead of them and edged or strode towards it.

The cold they endured may not seem propitious to leisure – nowadays we associate cold with numbing effects, energy deficiencies, and demanding labour – but we have to rethink our image of the Ice Age and appreciate that, for people who experienced it, it was a productive time that supported specialized elites and plenty of inventive thinking and creative work.[23] Cold really suited some people. For hunters in the vast tundra that covered much of Eurasia, the edge of the ice was the best place to be: they could live off the slaughtered carcasses of big mammals that had adapted by efficiently storing their own body fat. Dietary fat has acquired a bad reputation, but for most of history, most people eagerly sought it. Animal fat is the world's most energy-giving source of food. It yields on average three times as much calorific reward per unit of bulk as any other form of intake. There were humanly exploitable small animals in parts of the tundra: easily trapped Arctic hare, for instance, or creatures vulnerable to the bows and arrows that appeared about twenty thousand years ago. More commonly, however, hunters of the Ice Age favoured big, fat species that could provide nourishment for many mouths over the long periods during which cold temperatures kept dead flesh fresh. Gregarious animals, such as mammoths and Arctic moose, oxen, and deer, were especially easy to garner. Hunters could kill them in large numbers by driving them over cliffs or into bogs or lakes.[24] For the killers, while stocks lasted, the result was a fat bonanza, achieved with a relatively modest expenditure of effort.

On average they were better nourished than most later populations. Daily, in some Ice Age communities, people ate about two kilograms of food. They absorbed five times the average intake of vitamin C of a US citizen today by gathering relatively large amounts of fruit and roots, though they did not neglect such starchy grains as they could get, ingesting plenty of ascorbic acid from animal organ meats and blood. High levels of nutrition and long days of leisure, unequalled in most subsequent societies, meant people had time to observe nature and think about what they saw.

Aesthetic, emotional, and intellectual choices reflected preferences in food. For Ice Age artists, fat was beautiful. At nearly thirty thousand years of age the Venus of Willendorf is one of the world's oldest artworks: a small, chubby carving of a bodacious female, named for the place in Germany where she was found. Rival classifiers have called her a goddess, or a ruler, or, because she looks as if she could be pregnant, a fertility-conjuring device. Her slightly more recent lookalike, however, the Venus of Laussel, who was carved in relief on a cave wall in France, perhaps about twenty-five thousand years ago, evidently got fat the way most of us do: by enjoying herself and indulging her fancy. She looks out from the cave wall, raising a horn – literally, a cornucopia, presumably full of food or drink.

In the depths of the Ice Age, a resourceful way of life took shape. Twenty to thirty thousand years ago cave painters crawled through twisting tunnels to work in secret under glimmering torchlight in deep caverns. They strained on laboriously erected scaffolding to fit their compositions to the contours of the rock. Their palette bore only three or four kinds of mud and dye. Their brushes were of twig and twine and bone and hair. Yet they drew freely and firmly, observing their subjects shrewdly, capturing them sensitively, and making the animals' looks and litheness spring to the mind. A mature tradition in practised, specialized hands produced these images. The result, according to Picasso and many other sensitive and well-informed modern beholders, was art unsurpassed in any later age.[25] Carvings of the same era – including realistic ivory sculptures in the round – are equally accomplished. Thirty-thousand-year-old horses from Vogelherd in southern Germany, for instance, arch their necks elegantly. In Brassempouy in France a portrait of a neatly coiffured beauty, from about five thousand years later, shows off her almond eyes, tip-tilted nose, and dimpled chin. In the same period creatures of the hunt were carved on cave walls or engraved on tools. A kiln twenty-seven thousand years old at Věstonice in the Czech Republic fired clay models of bears, dogs, and women. Other art, no doubt, in other places has faded from exposed rock faces on which it was painted, or perished with the bodies or hides on which it was daubed, or vanished with the wind from the dust in which it was scratched.

The function of Ice Age art is and probably always will be a subject of unresolved debate. But it surely told stories, accompanied rituals, and summoned magic. In some cave paintings animals' pictures were repeatedly scored or punctured, as if in symbolic sacrifice. Some look as if they were hunters' mnemonics: the artists' stock of images features the shapes of hooves, the spoor of the beasts, their seasonal habits and favoured foods. Footprints and handprints, denting sand or earth, may have been early sources of inspiration, for stencilling and hand-printing were commonplace Ice Age techniques. Handprints speckle cave walls, as if reaching for magic hidden in the rock. Stencils, twenty thousand years old, of human hands and tools fade today from a rock face in Kenniff, Australia. Yet the aesthetic effect, which communicates across the ages, transcends practical function. This was not, perhaps, art for art's sake, but it was surely art: a new kind of power, which, ever since, has been able to awaken spirits, capture imaginations, inspire actions, represent ideas, and mirror or challenge society.[26]

Distrusting the Senses: Undermining Dumb Materialism

The sources the artists have left us open windows into two kinds of thinking: religious and political. Take religion first. Surprisingly, perhaps, to modern sensibilities, religion starts with scepticism – doubts about the unique reality of matter, or, to put it in today's argot, about whether what you see is all you get. So we should start with early scepticism before turning, in the rest of this chapter, to ideas that ensued about spirits, magic, witchcraft, totems, mana, gods, and God.

What were the world's first sceptics sceptical about? Obviously, the prevailing orthodoxy. Less obviously, that the prevailing orthodoxy was probably materialist and the thinkers who challenged it were those who first entertained speculations about the supernatural. Nowadays, we tend to condemn such speculations as childish or superstitious (as if fairies only inhabit the minds of the fey), especially when they occur in the form of religious thinking that survives from a remote past. Powerful constituencies congratulate themselves on having escaped into science, especially proselytizing atheists, philosophical critics of traditional understandings of 'consciousness', neuroscientists dazzled by the chemical and electrical activity in the brain (which some of them mistake for thought), and enthusiasts for 'artificial intelligence' who favour a model of mind-as-machine formerly popularized by eighteenth- and early nineteenth-century materialists.[27] It is smart or, in some scientific vocabularies, 'bright',[28] to say that the mind is the same thing as the brain, that thoughts are electrochemical discharges, that emotions are neural effects, and that love is, as Denis Diderot said, 'an intestinal irritation'.[29]

Some of us, in short, think that it is modern to be materialist. But is it? It is more likely to be the oldest way of seeing the world – a grub's or reptile's way, composed of mud and slime, in which what can be sensed absorbs all available attention. Our hominin ancestors were necessarily materialist. Everything they knew was physical. Retinal impressions were their first thoughts. Their emotions started in tremors in the limbs and stirrings of the guts. For creatures with limited imaginations, materialism is common sense. Like disciples of scientism who reject metaphysics, they relied on the evidence of their senses, without recognizing other means to truth, and without realizing that there may be realities we cannot see or touch or hear or taste or smell.

Surfaces, however, rarely disclose what is within. 'Truth is in the depths', as Democritus of Abdera said, late in the fifth century.[30] It is impossible to say when an inkling that the senses are delusive first occurred. But it may have been around for at least as long as *Homo sapiens*: a creature typically concerned to compare experiences and to draw inferences from them is likely, therefore, to notice that one sense contradicts another, that senses accumulate perceptions by trial and error, and that we can never assume that we have reached the end of semblance.[31] A large block of balsa wood is surprisingly light; a sliver of mercury proves ungraspable. A refraction is deceptively angular. We mistake shapes at a distance. We succumb to a mirage. A distorted reflection intrigues or appals us. There are sweet poisons, bitter medicines. In extreme form, materialism is unconvincing: science since Einstein has made it hard to leave strictly immaterial forces, such as energy and antimatter, out of our picture of the universe. So maybe the first animists were, in this respect, more up-to-date than modern materialists. Maybe they anticipated current thinking better.

It took a wild stride of guesswork to exceed the reach of the senses and suppose there must be more to the world, or beyond it, than what we can eye up or finger or smell or taste. The idea that we do not have to confide in our senses alone was a master idea – a skeleton key to spiritual worlds. It opened up infinite panoramas of speculation – domains of thought that religions and philosophies subsequently colonized.

It is tempting to try to guess how thinkers first got to a theory more subtle than materialism. Did dreams suggest it? Did hallucinogens – wild gladiolus bulbs, for instance, 'sacred mushrooms', mescaline, and morning glory – confirm it? For the Tikopia of the Solomon Islands, dreams are 'intercourse with spirits'. Diviners are dreamers among the Lele of the Kasai in the Democratic Republic of the Congo.[32] The disappointments to which human imaginations are victim carry us beyond the limits of what is material: a hunter, for instance, who correctly envisions a successful outcome to a hunt may recall the imagined triumph as an experience of physical reality, like glimpsing the shadow of a presence ahead of its bulk. The hunter who fails, on the other hand, knows that what was in his mind never happened outside it. He becomes alert to the possibility of purely mental events. Ice Age painters, for whom, as we have seen, imagined events jostled with those observed and recalled, surely had such experiences.

Once the discoverers of unseen worlds began to subvert assumptions derived from sense perception and to suspect that sensed data may be illusory, they became philosophers. They broached the two supreme problems that have troubled philosophy ever since: the problems of how you tell truth from falsehood and how you tell right from wrong. Self-comparison with the animals that Ice Age artists admired may have helped, reinforcing awareness that humans have relatively feeble senses. Most of our animal competitors have hugely better organs for smelling; many of them see farther and more sharply than we do. Many can hear sounds way beyond our range. As we saw in chapter 1, we need to make up for our physical deficiencies in imaginative ways. Hence, maybe, our ancestors' realization that their minds might take them further than their senses. To mistrust the senses in favour of reliance on imaginative gifts was dangerous but alluring. It invited disaster but unlocked great achievements.

To judge from its ubiquity, the leap happened long ago. Anthropologists are always stumbling in unlikely places on people who reject materialism so thoroughly that they dismiss the world as an illusion. Traditional Maori, for instance, thought of the material universe as a kind of mirror that merely reflected the real world of the gods. Before Christianity influenced thinking on the North American plains, Dakota priests divined that the real sky was invisible: what we see is a blue projection of it. They evidently thought about the sky more searchingly than science textbook-writers who tell me that blue light is prevalent because it is easily refracted. When we behold earth and rock, the Dakota maintained, we see only their *tonwampi*, usually translated as 'divine semblance'.[33] The insight, which resembled Plato's thinking on the same subject, may not have been right, but it was more reflective and more profound than that of materialists who complacently contemplate the same earth and the same rock and seek nothing beyond them.

Discovering the Imperceptible

The idea of illusion freed minds to discover or guess that there are invisible, inaudible, untouchable – because immaterial – realities, inaccessible to the senses but attainable to humans by other means. A further possibility followed: that incorporeal beings animate the world or infest perceived things and make them lively.[34] Despite glib dismissals of spirit-belief as the maunderings of savage minds, it was an insightful early step in the history of ideas. Once you begin to reject the world of the senses, you can begin to suspect the presence of living forces that make winds quicken, daffodils dance, flames flicker, tides turn, leaves fade. Metaphorically, we still use the language of an animated universe – it is part of early thinkers' great legacy to us – and talk of it as if it were alive. Earth groans, fire leaps, brooks babble, stones bear witness.

To ascribe lively actions to spirits is probably false, but not crude or 'superstitious': rather, it is an inference, albeit not verifiable, from the way the world is. An active property is credible as the source of the restlessness of fire, say, or wave or wind, or the persistence of stone, or the growth of a tree. Thales, the sage of Miletus who was sufficiently scientific to predict the eclipse of 585 BCE, explained magnetism by crediting magnets with souls that excited attraction and provoked repulsion. 'Everything', he said, 'is full of gods.'[35] Thought, as well as observation, suggests the ubiquity of spirits. If some human qualities are immaterial – mind, say, or soul or personality or whatever makes us substantially ourselves – we can never be sure who or what else possesses them: other individuals, surely; people from outside the group we acknowledge as ours, perhaps; even, at a further remove of improbability, animals, plants, rocks. And, as the Brahmins ask in *A Passage to India*, what about 'oranges, cactuses, crystals and mud?' Get beyond materialism and the whole world can seem to come alive.

Science expelled spirits from what we call 'inanimate' matter: the epithet literally means 'non-spirited'. In the meantime, however, disembodied spirits or 'sprites', familiar in Western thought as fairies and demons, or less familiar as willies and kelpies, have proliferated. Even in scientifically sophisticated societies they still roam in some mindsets. Spirits, when first divined, were subtly and surprisingly conceived.

They represented a breakthrough in the prospects of life for those who were able to imagine them. Creatures previously submissive to the constraints of life in a material world could bask in the freedom of an infinitely protean, infinitely unpredictable future. A living environment is more stimulating than the humdrum universe materialists inhabit. It inspires poetry and invites reverence. It resists extinction and raises presumptions of immortality. You can quench fire, break waves, fell trees, smash rocks, but spirit lives. Spirit-belief makes people hesitate to intervene in nature: animists typically ask the victim's leave before they uproot a tree or kill a creature.

Ice Age thinkers knew, or thought they knew, the reality of creatures imperceptible to the senses when they painted and carved them. We can confirm this by calling again on the evidence of anthropologists' data. Analogy with rock- and cave-painters of later periods helps us understand that Ice Age art was a means of accessing worlds beyond the world, spirit beyond matter. It depicted an imagined realm, accessed in mystical trances, and inhabited by the spirits of the animals people needed and admired.[36] On the cave walls, we meet, in effigy, people set apart as special from the rest of the group. Animal masks – antlered or lion-like – transformed the wearers. Normally, in historically documented cases, masked shamans engage in efforts to communicate with the dead or with the gods. In the throes of psychotropic self-transformation, or with consciousness altered by dancing or drumming, they travel in spirit to extra-bodily encounters. When shamans disguise themselves as animals they hope to appropriate an alien species' speed or strength or else to identify with a totemic 'ancestor'. In any case, non-human animals are plausibly intelligible as closer than men to the gods: that would, for instance, account for their superior prowess or agility or sensory gifts. In states of extreme exaltation shamans become the mediums through which the spirits talk to this world. Their rites are those Virgil described so vividly in the sixth book of the *Æneid* in his account of the transports of the Sybil of Cumae, 'swell-seeming, sounding weird, somehow inhuman, as the god's breath blew within her ... Suddenly the tone of her rantings changed – her face, her colour, the kemptness of her hair. Her breast billowed. Wildly inside it spun her raving heart.'[37] Shamanic performances continue today in the same tradition in the grasslands of Eurasia, Japanese temples, dervish madrassas, and the boreal tundra, where the Chukchi of northern Siberia observe a way of life similar to that of Ice Age artists in an even colder climate. They are among the many societies in which shamans still experience visions as imagined journeys.

By combining clues such as these, we can build a picture of the world's first documented religion: the job of shamans, who still dance on cave walls, untired by the passage of time, was to be in touch with gods and ancestors who lodged deep in the rocks. From there the spirits emerged, leaving traces on cave walls, where painters enlivened their outlines and trapped their energy. Visitors pressed ochre-stained hands against nearby spots, perhaps because the ochre that adorned burials can be understood as 'blood for the ghosts' (such as Odysseus offered the dead at the gates of Hades). Clues to what may be another dimension of religion come from Ice Age sculpture, with stylized, steatopygous swaggerers, like the Venuses of Willendorf and Laussel: for many thousands of years, over widely spread locations, as far east as Siberia, sculptors imitated their bulbous bellies and spreading hips. Somewhere in the mental cosmos of the Ice Age, there were women of power or, perhaps, a goddess cult, represented in the big-hipped carvings.

Further evidence, which takes us beyond religion, strictly understood, into what we might call early philosophy, comes from anthropological fieldwork about how traditional peoples account for the nature and properties of things. The question 'What makes the objects of perception real?' sounds like a trap for an examinee in philosophy. So do the related questions of how you can change and still be yourself, or how an object can change and yet retain its identity, or how events can unfold without rupturing the continuity of the milieu in which they happen. But early humans asked all these questions, delving into the difference between what something is and the properties it has, appreciating that what it 'is' – its essence or 'substance' in philosophical jargon – is not the same as its 'accidence' or what it is 'like'. To explore the relationship between the two requires perseverant thinking. A distinction in Spanish makes the point: between the verbs *ser*, which denotes the essence of what is referred to, and *estar*, which is also translatable as 'to be' but which refers only to the mutable state of an object, or its transient characteristics. Yet even Spanish-speakers rarely grasp the importance of the distinction, which ought to make you aware, for instance, that your beauty (*ser*) can outlast your pretty appearance (*estar*) or coexist with your ugliness. Similarly, in principle, for instance, your mind might be separable from your brain, even though both are united in you.

So two questions arise: what makes a thing what it is? And what makes it what it is like? For the devisers of early animism, 'spirits' could be the answer to both. If such things exist, they may be everywhere – but to be everywhere is not quite the same as being universal. Spirits are peculiar to the objects they inhabit, but an idea of at least equal antiquity, well and widely attested in anthropological literature, is that one invisible presence infuses everything.

The notion arises rationally from asking, for instance, 'What makes sky blue, or water wet?' Blueness does not seem essential to sky, which does not cease to be sky when it changes colour. But what about the wetness of water? That seems different – a property that is essential because dry water would not be water. Maybe a single substance, which underlies all properties, can resolve the apparent tension. If you craft a spear or a fishing rod, you know it works. But if you go on to ask why it works, you are asking a deeply philosophical question about the nature of the object concerned. If anthropological evidence is anything to go by, one of the earliest answers was that the same single, invisible, universal force accounts for the nature of everything and makes all operations effective. To name this idea, anthropologists have borrowed the word 'mana' from South Sea languages.[38] The net's mana makes the catch. Fishes' mana makes fish catchable. The sword's mana inflicts wounds. The herb's makes them heal. A similar or identical concept is reported in other parts of the world, as a subject of stories and rituals, under various names, such as *arungquiltha* in parts of Australia or *wakan*, *orenda*, and *manitou* in parts of Native America.

If we are right about inferring antiquity from the scale of dispersal, the idea of mana is likely to be old. It would be mere guesswork, however, to try to date its first appearance. Archaeology cannot detect it; only traditions unrecorded until the fairly recent past can do so. Partisanship warps the debate because of the ferocity of controversy over whether spirits or mana came first. If the latter, animism seems a relatively 'developed' attitude to the world and looks more than merely 'primitive': later than magic and therefore more mature. Such questions can be left pending: spirit and mana could have been first imagined in any order, or simultaneously.

Magic and Witchcraft

A question commonly asked and effectively unanswerable is, 'Can you tweak, influence, or command mana?' Was it the starting point of magic, which originated in attempts to cajole or control it? Bronislaw Malinowski, the first occupant of the world's first chair of social anthropology, thought so. 'While science', he wrote, more than a hundred years ago, 'is based on the conception of natural forces, magic springs from the idea of a certain mystic, impersonal power ... called mana by some Melanesians ... a well-nigh universal idea wherever magic flourishes.'[39] Early humans knew nature so intimately that they could see how it is all interconnected. Whatever is systematic can be levered by controlling any of its parts. In the effort to manipulate nature in this way, magic was one of the earliest and most enduring methods people devised. 'The earliest scientists', according to two of the leading figures of early-twentieth-century anthropology, 'were magicians ... Magic issues by a thousand fissures from the mystical life ... It tends to the concrete, while religion tends to the abstract. Magic was essentially an art of doing things.'[40] Henri Hubert and Marcel Mauss were right: magic and science belong in a single continuum. Both set out to master nature intellectually so as to subject it to human control.[41]

The idea of magic comprises two distinct thoughts. First, effects can ensue from causes which senses cannot perceive but which minds can envision; second, the mind can invoke and apply such causes. You achieve power over the palpable by accessing the invisible. Magic is genuinely powerful – over humans, though not over the rest of nature; it recurs in every society. No amount of disappointment can shift it. It does not work; at least not so far. Yet despite their failures magicians have sparked hopes, fired fears, and drawn deference and rewards.

The prehistory of magic probably antedates the early evidence, in a slow process of mutual nourishment between observation and imagination, deep in the hominid past. When we look for evidence, we have to focus on what magicians aspire to: transformative processes that change one substance into another. Accidents can provoke apparently magical transformations. Tough, apparently inedible matter, for instance, turns digestible under the influence of benign bacteria. Fire colours food, caramelizes and crisps it. Wet clay becomes hard in heat. You may unreflectively seize a stick or bone, and it turns into a tool or weapon. Accidental transformations can be imitated. For other kinds, however, only radical acts of imagination will get them started. Take weaving, a miracle-working technology that combines fibres to achieve strength and breadth unattainable by a single strand. Chimpanzees do it in a rudimentary way when they twist branches or stalks and combine them into nests – evidence of a long, cumulative history that goes back to pre-human origins. In analogous cases, practical measures, extemporized to meet material needs, might stimulate magical thinking: those mammoth houses of the Ice Age steppes, for instance, seem magical in the way they transform bones into buildings grand enough to be temples. Though the time and context in which magic arose are irretrievably distant, Ice Age evidence is full of signs of it. Red ochre, the earliest substance (it seems) with a role in ritual, was perhaps the first magician's aid, to judge from finds adorned with criss-cross scorings, more than seventy thousand years old, in Blombos Cave (see p. 46). Ochre's vivid colour, which imitates blood, accompanied the dead perhaps as an offering from the living, perhaps to reinfuse cadavers with life.

In principle magic can be 'white' – good or morally indifferent – or black. But to someone who thinks that cause and effect are invisibly linked and magically manipulable a further idea is possible: that malign magic may cause ruin and ravage. If people can harness and change nature, they can do evil with it as well as good. They can – that is to say – be or try to be witches. Witchcraft is one of the world's most pervasive ideas. In some cultures it is everyone's first-choice explanation for every ill.[42] Pioneering anthropological fieldwork by E. E. Evans-Pritchard in the 1920s focused academic efforts to understand witchcraft on the Azande of the Sudan, whose practices and beliefs, however, are highly unusual.[43] For them, witchcraft is an inherited physical condition: literally, a hairy ball in the gut, which is the source of the witchcraft, not just a sign of it. No witch need consciously invoke its power: it is just there.

Autopsy reveals its presence. 'Poison oracles' reveal its action: when a victim or third party denounces a witch for some malignant act, the truth or falsehood of the accusation is tested by poison, forced down a chicken's throat. If the bird is spared, the presumed witch is absolved (and vice versa). In other cultures, common ways of detecting witches include physical peculiarities or deformities – Roald Dahl's toeless witches allude to such traditions – or ugliness, which some peoples see as the cause of a witch's propensity for evil.

New ideas about witchery have surfaced in every age.[44] In the world's earliest imaginative literature, from Mesopotamia in the second millennium BCE, incantations against it frequently invoke gods or fire or magical chemicals, such as salt and mercury; and only people and animals can be witches' victims, whereas Earth and heaven are exempt.[45] Ancient Roman witches, as surviving literature represents them, specialized in thwarting and emasculating males.[46] In fifteenth-century Europe, a diabolic compact supplied witches' supposed power. Modern scholarship shifts attention away from explaining witchcraft to explaining why people believe in it: as a survival of paganism, according to one theory, or as a means of social control,[47] or as a mere mental delusion.[48] The first theory is almost certainly false: though persecutors of witchcraft and paganism in the past often denounced both as 'devil worship', there is no evidence of any real connexion or overlap. The second theory was advanced by the innovative and egotistical physician, Paracelsus, in the sixteenth century. In the 1560s and 1570s the Dutch physician Johann Weyer published case histories of mentally aberrant patients who thought they were witches. In 1610 the Inquisitor Salazar confirmed the theory: working among alleged witches in the Basque country, he found that they were victims of their own fantasies. He came to doubt whether any such thing as witchcraft existed.[49] Yet in seventeenth-century Europe and America excessively zealous persecutors mistook many cases of crazed, hysterical, or overstimulated imagination.

More recently, historians have scrutinized and sometimes approved the theory that witchcraft is a social mechanism – a self-empowering device that marginal people deploy when institutions of justice fail them or are simply unavailable to them. In recognition that witchcraft is a delusion, other scholars focus rather on the persecution of alleged witches as a means to eradicate socially undesirable individuals – again in default of courts and laws capable of dealing with all the disputes that arise among neighbours. The distribution of witchcraft persecutions in the early modern West supports this explanation: they were intense in Protestant regions but relatively infrequent in Spain, where the Inquisition provided an alternative cheap recourse for poor or self-interested denouncers who wanted to launch vexatious proceedings against hated neighbours, masters, relatives, or rivals untouchable by due process. Persecutions indeed seem to have proliferated wherever judicial institutions were inadequate to resolve social tensions. In origin, however, witchcraft seems adequately explained as a perfectly reasonable inference from the idea of magic.

Is witchcraft a thing of the past? Self-styled practitioners and followers, allegedly a million strong in the United States, now claim to have recovered beneficent pagan 'Wicca'. Along a modern writer's odyssey through the pagan underground, she admires a body snatcher, visits 'Lesbianville', identifies witches' 'cognitive dissonance', and parties among lifestyle pagans with 'animal bones used as clever hairpins, waist-length hair and nipple-length beards'. A single joke, endlessly repeated, lightens the pathetic litany: every witch seems to have a comically incongruous day job, including tattoo artistry, belly dancing, and baking scones. Little else is characteristic among the witches, other than nudism (because of 'a belief that the human body can emanate raw power naked'), a faith in 'consecrating' sex, and the absurd claim that Wiccans uphold a pagan tradition unbroken since the Bronze Age.[50]

The variants, it seems, continue to multiply. But, understood at the most general level, as the ability of a person to do harm by supernatural means, belief in witchcraft is found in just about all societies – a fact that pushes its probable origins way back into the past.

Placed in Nature: Mana, God, and Totemism

Mana – for those who believe in it – is what makes the perceived world real. A further, deeper question is, 'Is it valid?' Not, 'Is the idea of mana the best way to understand nature?' but, 'Is it a way clever minds can reasonably have devised to match the facts?' It might help if we compare it with a modern paradigm that we use to explain the same facts. While we distinguish fundamentally between organic and inorganic matter, we do think of all matter as characterized by essentially similar relationships between particles. Quantum charges, because they are dynamic and formative, resemble mana in as much as they are a source of 'force' (though not of a purposeful kind, such as mana seems to be in most versions). In any event, on the basis of this chapter so far, mana is fairly described as an intellectually impressive concept.

A further question arises: what, if anything, did thinking about mana contribute to the origins of an idea we shall have to consider in due course (as it is among the most intriguing and, apparently, most persuasive in the world): the idea of a single, universal God? Missionaries in nineteenth-century North America and Polynesia thought God and mana were identical. It is tempting, at least, to say that mana could have been the idea – or one of the ideas – from which that of God developed. A closer parallel, however, is with some of the odd or esoteric beliefs that still seem ineradicable from modern minds: 'aura', for example, which figures in alternative-health-speak; or the elusive 'organic cosmic energy' that proponents of the East Asian-influenced 'new physics' detect everywhere in matter;[51] or vitalist philosophy, which intuits life as a quality inherent in living things.

These notions, which most people would probably class as broadly religious, and which are almost certainly false, are nevertheless also scientific, because they arise from real observations and reliable knowledge of the way things are in nature. Comparative anthropology discloses other equally or nearly equally ancient ideas that we can class as scientific in a slightly different sense, because they concern the relationship of humans to the rest of nature. Totemism, for instance, is the idea that an intimate relationship with plants or animals – usually expressed as common ancestry, sometimes as a form of incarnation – determines an individual human's place in nature. The idea is obviously scientific. Evolutionary theory, after all, says something similar: that all of us descend from other biota. Loosely, people speak of totemism to denote almost any thinking that binds humans and other natural objects (especially animals) closely together; in its most powerful form – considered here – the totem is a device for reimagining human social relationships. Those who share a totem form a group bound by shared identity and mutual obligations, and distinguishable from the rest of the society to which it belongs. People of shared ancestry, suppositious or genuine, can keep track of one another. The totem generates common ritual life. Members observe peculiar taboos, especially by abstaining from eating their totem. They may be obliged to marry within the group; so the totem serves to identify the range of potential partners. Totemism also makes it possible for people unlinked by ties of blood to behave towards one another as if they were: one can join a totemic 'clan' regardless of the circumstances of one's birth: in most totemic societies, dreams reveal (and recur to confirm) dreamers' totems, though how the connections really start, and what, if anything, the choice of totemic objects means, are subjects of inconclusive scholarly debate. All theories share a common and commonsense feature: totemism spans the difference between two early categories of thought: 'nature', which the totemic animals and plants represent, and 'culture' – the relationships that bind members of the group. Totemism, in short, is an early and effective idea for forging society.[52]

Despite animism, totemism, mana, and all the useful resources people have imagined for the practical conduct of life, distrust of sense perceptions carries dangers. It induces people to shift faith to sources of insight, such as visions, imaginings, and the delusions of madness and ecstasy, which seem convincing only because they cannot be tested. They often mislead, but they also always inspire. They open up possibilities that exceed experience and, therefore, paradoxical as it may seem, make progress possible. Even illusions can do good. They can help to launch notions that encourage endeavour in transcendence, magic, religion, and science. They nourish arts. They can help to make ideas unattainable by experience – such as eternity, infinity, and immortality – conceivable.

Imagining Order: Ice Age Political Thought

Visions also craft politics. The political thinking of the Ice Age is barely accessible, but it is possible to say something in turn about leadership, broader ideas of order, and what we might call Ice Age political economy.

Obviously, the societies of hominids, hominins, and early *Homo sapiens* had leaders. Presumably, by analogy with other apes, alpha males imposed rule by intimidation and violence (see p. 29). But political revolutions multiplied ways of assigning authority and selecting chiefs. Ice Age paintings and carvings disclose new political thinking – the emergence of new forms of leadership, in which visions empower visionaries and favour charisma over brute force, the spiritually gifted over the physically powerful.

The cave walls of Les Trois Frères in southern France are a good place to start reviewing the evidence. Priest-like figures in divine or animal disguises undertaking fantastic journeys or exerting menace as huntsmen are evidence of the rise of wielders of unprecedented power: that of getting in touch with the spirits, the gods, and the dead – the forces that are responsible for making the world the way it is. From another world in which ours is forged, shamans can get privileged access to inside information on what happens and will happen. They may even influence the gods and spirits to change their plans, inducing them to reorder the world to make it agreeable to humans: to cause rain, stop floods, or make the sun shine to ripen the harvest.

The shamans of the cave walls exercised tremendous social influence. For the favour of an elite in touch with the spirits, people would pay with gifts, deference, service, and obedience. The shaman's talent can be an awesome source of authority: the hoist that elevates him above alpha males or gerontocratic patriarchs. When we scan the caves, we see a knowledge class, armed with the gift of communicating with spirits, emerging alongside a prowess class, challenging or replacing the strong with the seer and the sage. Enthronement of the gift of communicating with spirits was clearly an early alternative – perhaps the earliest – to submission to a Leviathan distinguished by no feature more morally potent than physical strength.

In consequence, special access to the divine or the dead has been an important part of powerful and enduring forms of political legitimacy: prophets have used it to claim power. On the same basis churches have pretended to temporal supremacy. Kings have affected sacrality by the same means. In Mesopotamia of the second millennium BCE, gods were the nominal rulers of the cities where they took up their abodes. To their human stewards civic deities confided visions that conveyed commands: to launch a war, erect a temple, promulgate a law. The most graphic examples – albeit rather late – appear in Mayan art and epigraphy of the seventh, eighth and ninth centuries CE in what are now Guatemala and neighbouring lands. Rulers of eighth-century Yaxchilán, in what is now southern Mexico, can still be seen in carved reliefs, inhaling psychotropic smoke from bowls of drug-steeped, burning bark-paper, in which they gathered blood drawn from their tongues with spiked thongs (if they were queens) or by piercing their sexual organs with shell-knives or cactus spines. The rite induced visions of ancestral spirits typically issuing from a serpent's maw, with a summons to war.[53]

For the last millennium or so of the Ice Age, cognitive archaeology reveals the emergence of another new kind of leadership: heredity. All human societies face the problem of how to hand on power, wealth, and rank without stirring up strife. How do you stop every leadership contest from letting blood and unleashing civil war? More generally, how do you regulate inequalities at every level of society without class conflict or multiplying violent acts of individual resentment? Heredity, if a consensus in favour of it can be established, is a means of avoiding or limiting succession disputes. But there are no parallels in the animal kingdom, except as Disney represents it; and parental excellence is no guarantee of a person's merit, whereas leadership won in competition is objectively justifiable. Yet for most societies, for most of the past – indeed, until well into the twentieth century – heredity was the normal route to high levels of command. How and when did it start?

Although we cannot be sure about the nature of the hereditary Ice Age power class, we know it existed, because of glaring inequalities in the way people were buried. In a cemetery at Sunghir, near Moscow, perhaps as much as twenty-eight thousand years old, an elderly man lies buried with prodigious gifts: a cap sewn with fox's teeth, thousands of ivory beads formerly sewn onto his clothes, and about twenty ivory bracelets – rewards, perhaps, of an active life. Nearby, however, a boy and a girl, about eight or twelve years old, moulder alongside even more spectacular ornaments: animal carvings and beautifully wrought weapons, including spears of mammoth ivory, each over six feet long, as well as ivory bracelets, necklaces, and fox-tooth buttons. Over each child mourners sprinkled about 3,500 finely worked ivory beads. Such riches can hardly have been earned: the occupants of the grave were too young to accumulate trophies; at least one of them suffered from slight deformity of the lower limbs, which might have impeded her efficiency in physical tasks, or her general admirability as a physical specimen of her kind.[54] The evidence is therefore of a society that distributed riches according to criteria unlinked to objective merit; a system that marked leaders for greatness from childhood, at least.

It looks, therefore, as if heredity were already playing a part in the selection of high-status individuals. Genetic theory now provides sophisticated explanations for a matter of common observation: many mental and physical attributes are heritable, including, perhaps, some of those that make good rulers. A system that favours the children of self-made leaders is therefore rational. The instinct to nurture may play a part: parents who want to pass their property, including position, status, or office, to offspring are likely to endorse the hereditary principle. By creating disparities of leisure between classes, specialization frees parents in specialized roles to train their children to succeed them. Above all, in political contexts, the hereditary principle conduces to peace by deterring competition. It removes elites from conflictive arenas and corrupting hustings. For the sake of such advantages, some states still have hereditary heads of state (and, in the case of the United Kingdom, a partly hereditary legislature). If we must have leaders, heredity is, by practical standards, no bad way to choose them.[55]

In our attempt to understand where power lay in Ice Age societies, the final bits of evidence are crumbs from the tables of the rich. Though feasts can happen spontaneously when scavengers stumble on a carrion bonanza or hunters achieve a big kill, the usual focus is a political occasion, when a leader displays munificence to mediate power and forge allegiance. Because they involve a lot of effort and expense, feasts need justification: symbolic or magical, at one level, or practical at another. The earliest clear evidence is in the remains of deposits of plants and prey dropped by diners at Hallan Çemi Tepesi in Anatolia, about ten or eleven thousand years ago, among people who were beginning to produce food instead of relying wholly on hunting and gathering. But there are suggestive earlier concentrations of similar evidence at sites in northern Spain nearly twice as old as Hallan Çemi. At Altamira, for instance, archaeologists have found ashes from large-scale cooking and the calcified debris of food perhaps from as long as twenty-three thousand years ago, with records of what could be expenditure scratched on tally sticks. Analogies with modern hunting peoples suggest that alliances between communities may have been celebrated at such occasions. Male bonding was probably not the pretext: if it were the feasts would be served far from major dwelling sites to keep women and children at a distance. In early agrarian and pastoral societies, by contrast, chiefs used feasts to supervise the distribution of surplus production among the community, and so to enhance the feast-giver's power or status or clientage network, or to create ties of reciprocity between feasters, or to concentrate labour where feast-givers wanted it. In some instances, at a later stage, privileged feasts, with limited access, defined elites and provided them with opportunities to forge bonds.[56]

Cosmic Order: Time and Taboos

Specialized, privileged elites, who enjoyed the continuity of power that heredity guaranteed, had time to devote to thinking. We can detect some thoughts that occurred to them, as they scoured the heavens for the data they needed in their jobs. In the absence of other books, the sky made compelling reading for early humans. In some eyes, stars are pinpricks in the veil of the sky through which we glimpse light from an otherwise unapproachable heaven. Among the discoveries early searchers made there was a revolutionary idea of time.

Time was one of the great breakthrough ideas in the history of thought. Most people share St Augustine's despair at his inability to define it. (He knew what it was, he said, until someone asked him.) The best way to understand it is by thinking about change. No change, no time. You approach or reflect a sense of time whenever you calculate the possible effects of connected processes of change – when, for instance, you speed up to escape a pursuer or capture prey, or when you notice that a berry will be ripe for harvesting before a tuber. When you compare changes, you measure, in effect, their respective rates or pace. So we can define time as the rate at which one series of changes occurs, measured against another. A universal measure is not necessary. You can measure the passage of a raindrop across your windowpane against the movement of your clock – but in default of a clock you can do so by the drifting of a cloud or the crawling of a creature. As we shall see in chapter 4 (see p. 126), Nuer tribespeople calculate the passage of time according to the rate of growth of their cattle, while other cultures deploy all sorts of irregular measures, including changes of dynasty or of ruler or 'when Quirinius was governor of Syria'. The Lakota of North America traditionally used the occurrence of each year's first snowfall to start a new 'long count'.[57]

Still, if you want an unfailingly regular standard of measurement, look to the heavens. Congruities between the cycles of the heavens and other natural rhythms – especially those of our own bodies and of the ecosystems to which we belong – made the first systems of universal timekeeping possible. 'The sight of day and night', Plato said, 'and the months and the revolutions of the years have created number and have given us a conception of time.'[58] The cycle of the sun, for instance, suits the demands of sleep and wakefulness. The moon's matches the intervals of menstruation. Kine fatten with the march of the seasons, which in turn the sun determines. Celestial standards are so predictable that they can serve to time everything else. Star-time – the cycle of Venus, for instance, which occupies 584 years – is valued in cultures that favour long-term record-keeping and big-number arithmetic. Some societies, like ours, attempt elaborate reconciliations of the cycles of sun and moon, while others keep both sets of calculations going in imperfect tandem. As far as we know, all peoples keep track of the solar day and year, and the lunar month.

When the idea of using celestial motion as a universal standard of measurement first occurred, it revolutionized the lives of people who applied it. Humans now had a unique way of organizing memory and anticipation, prioritizing tasks, and co-ordinating collaborative endeavours. Ever since, they have used it as the basis for organizing all action and recording all experience. It remained the basis of timekeeping – and therefore of the co-ordination of all collaborative enterprise – until our own times (when we have replaced celestial observations with caesium-atomic timekeeping). It arose, of course, from observation: from awareness that some changes – especially those of the relative positions of celestial bodies – are regular, cyclical, and therefore predictable. The realization that they can be used as a standard against which to measure other such changes transcends observation: it was an act of commonplace genius, which has occurred in all human societies so long ago that – ironically – we are unable to date it.

The earliest known calendar-like artefact is a flat bone inscribed with a pattern of crescents and circles – suggestive of phases of the moon – about thirty thousand years ago in the Dordogne. Objects with regular incisions have often turned up at Mesolithic sites: but they could be 'doodles' or the vestiges of games or rites or ad hoc tallies. Then comes further evidence of calendrical computations: the horizon-marking devices left among megaliths of the fifth millennium BCE when people started erecting stones against which the sun cast finger-like shadows, or between which it gleamed towards strange sanctuaries. By mediating with the heavens, rulers became keepers of time. Political ideas are not only about the nature and functions of leaders, but also about how they regulate their followers' lives. How early can we detect the emergence of political thinking in this sense? The common life of early hominids presumably resembled primate bands, bound by kinship, force, and necessity. What were the first laws that turned them into new kinds of societies, regulated by ideas?

A working assumption is that a sense of cosmic order inspired early notions about how to organize society. Beneath or within the apparent chaos of nature, a bit of imagination can see an underpinning order. It may not require much thought to notice it. Even bugs, say, or bovines – creatures unpraised for their mental powers – can see connections between facts that are important to them: dead prey and available food, for instance, or the prospect of shelter at the approach of rain or cold.

Creatures endowed with sufficient memory can get further than bugs and bison. People connect the sporadic instances of order they notice in nature: the regularities, for instance, of the life cycle, the human metabolism, the seasons, and the revolutions of celestial spheres. The scaffolding on which early thinkers erected the idea of an orderly universe was composed of such observations. But awareness of orderly relationships is one thing. It takes a huge mental leap to get to the inference that order is universal. Most of the time, the world looks chaotic. Most events seem random. So imagination played a part in conjuring order. It takes a lively mind to see – as Einstein supposedly said – that 'God does not play dice.'

The idea of order is too old to be dated but once it occurred it made the cosmos imaginable. It summoned minds to make efforts to picture the entirety of everything in a single system. The earliest surviving cosmic diagrams – artistic or religious or magical – capture the consequences. A cave face, for instance, in Jaora in Madhya Pradesh, India, shows what the world looked like to the painter: divided among seven regions and circled with evocations of water and air. A four-thousand-year-old Egyptian bowl provides an alternative vision of a zigzag-surrounded world that resembles two pyramids caught between sunrise and sunset.

The 'dreamtime' of Australian aboriginals, in which the inseparable tissue of all the universe was spun, echoes early descriptions. So, in widespread locations, does rock painting or body art: the Caduveo of the Paraguay valley, for instance, whose image of the world is composed of four distinct and equipollent quarters, paint their faces with quarterings. A four-quartered world also appears on rocks that Dogon goatherds decorate in Mali. When potters in Kongo prepare rites of initiation in their craft, they paint vessels with their images of the cosmos. Without prior notions of cosmic order, arrayed in predictable and therefore perhaps manipulable sequences of cause and effect, it is hard to imagine how magic and oracular divination could have developed.[59]

In politics, order can mean different things to different people. But at a minimum we can detect it in all efforts to regulate society – to make people's behaviour conform to a model or pattern. It is possible to identify social regulations of great antiquity – so widespread that they probably predate the peopling of the world. The earliest are likely, from anthropological evidence, to have been of two kinds: food taboos and incest prohibitions.

Take food taboos first. Incontestably, they belong in the realm of ideas: humans are not likely to have been instinctively fastidious about food. It is obviously not natural to forgo nutrition. Yet all societies ban foods.

To help us understand why, the BaTlokwa, a pastoral people of Botswana, present the most instructive case. They forbid an incomparably vast and varied range of foods. No BaTlokwa is allowed aardvark or pork. Locally grown oranges are banned, but not those acquired by trade. Other foods are subject to restrictions according to the age and sex of potential eaters. Only the elderly can have honey, tortoise, and guinea fowl. Pregnancy disqualifies women from enjoying some kinds of beef offal. Some taboos only apply at certain seasons, others only in peculiar conditions, such as when sick children are present. In fieldwork-conversations, BaTlokwa give anthropologists unsystematic explanations, attributing variously to matters of health, hygiene, or taste prohibitions the complexity of which, though extreme, is representative of the range of food taboos worldwide.[60] All efforts to rationalize them have failed.

The classic case is that of the scruples encoded in one of the most famous ancient texts, the Hebrew scriptures. They defy analysis. The creatures on the forbidden list have nothing in common (except, paradoxically, that they are anomalous, as the anthropologist Mary Douglas pointed out, in some methods of classification, including, presumably, those of the ancient Hebrews). The same apparent senselessness makes all other cases intractable to comprehensive analysis. The best-known theories fail: in most known cases the claims of economics and of hygiene – that taboos exist to conserve valuable food-sources or to proscribe harmful substances – simply do not work.[61] Rational and material explanations fail because dietary restrictions are essentially suprarational. Meanings ascribed to food are, like all meanings, agreed conventions about usage. Food taboos bind those who respect them and brand those who break them. The rules are not meant to make sense. If they did, outsiders would follow them – but they exist precisely to exclude outsiders and give coherence to the group. Permitted foods feed identity; excluded foods help to define it.[62]

In the search for the first social regulations, incest prohibitions are the most likely alternative to food taboos. Every known human society has them, in a variety of forms almost as astonishing as the BaTlokwas' food-rules: in some cultures siblings can marry, but not cousins. Others allow marriages between cousins, but only across generations. Even where there are no blood ties, prohibitions sometimes apply, as in merely formal relationships between in-laws in canon law.

If we are to understand how incest prohibitions originated, we therefore have to take into account both their ubiquity and their variety. Mere revulsion – even if it were true that humans commonly feel it – would not, therefore, serve as an adequate explanation. 'One should try everything once', the composer Arnold Bax recommended, 'except incest and folk-dancing.' Neither activity, however, is abhorrent to everybody. Nor is it convincing to represent discrimination in controlling the sex urge as an instinct evolved to strengthen the species against the supposedly malign effects of inbreeding: in most known cases there are no such effects. Healthy children normally issue from incestuous alliances. Nor were primitive eugenics responsible: most people in most societies for most of the time have known little and cared less about the supposed genetic virtues of exogamy. Some societies impose prohibitions on remote kin who are unlikely to do badly as breeding stock. Some, on the other hand, authorize alliances of surprisingly close relatives among whom infelicitous genetic effects are more likely: Egyptian royal siblings, for instance; or Lot's daughters, whose duty was to 'lie with their father'. First cousins can contract lawful marriages with one another in twenty-six US states, where other forms of incest are prohibited. In contrast to most other Christians, Amish encourage cousins to marry. In some traditional Arabian societies, uncles have the right to claim their nieces as wives.

Claude Lévi-Strauss, writing in the 1940s, devised the most famous and plausible explanation of the ubiquity and complexity of incest rules. It came to him, he said, as a result of watching how fellow-Frenchmen overcame potential social embarrassment when they had to share a table in a crowded bistro. They exchanged identical glasses of the house wine. Neither luncher gained, in any material sense, from a superficially comical transaction, but, like all apparently disinterested exchanges of gifts, the mutual gesture created a relationship between the parties. From his observation in the bistro Lévi-Strauss developed an argument about incest: societies oblige their constituent families to exchange women. Potentially rival lineages are thereby linked and likely to co-operate. Societies of many families, in consequence, gain coherence and strength. Women are seen as valuable commodities (unhappily, most people in most societies function as commodities, exploitable and negotiable among exploiters), with magical bodies that echo the motions of the heavens and produce babies. Unless forced to exchange them, their menfolk would try to monopolize them. Like food taboos, sex taboos exist not because they make sense in themselves, but because they help build the group. By regulating incest societies became more collaborative, more united, bigger, and stronger. The reason why incest prohibitions are universal is, perhaps, that simple: without them societies would be poorly equipped for survival.[63]

Trading Ideas: The First Political Economy

If people's first thoughts about regulating society led to taboos on food and sex, what about regulations of relations between societies? Trade is the obvious context in which to look.

Economists have generally thought of commerce as a nicely calculated system for offloading surplus production. But when trade began, like controls on incest, in exchanges of gifts, it had more to do with ritual needs than with material convenience or mere profit. From archaeological evidence or anthropological inference, the earliest goods exchanged between communities seem to have included fire – which, perhaps because of ritual inhibitions, some peoples have never kindled but have preferred to acquire from outside the group – and ochre, the most widespread 'must-have' of Ice Age ritualists. Archaeologists whose predecessors regarded axe-heads of particular patterns or peculiarly knapped flints as evidence of the presence of their producers now recognize that even in the remotest traceable antiquity such artefacts could have been objects of commerce,[64] but not, perhaps, as, say, Walmart or Vitol might understand it: early traders exchanged goods for exclusively ritual purposes. As Karl Polanyi, one of the outstanding critics of capitalism, wrote in 1944:

> The outstanding discovery of recent historical and anthropological research is that man's economy, as a rule, is submerged in his social relationships. He does not act so as to safeguard his individual interest in the possession of material goods; he acts so as to safeguard his social standing, his social claims, his social assets. He values material goods only in so far as they serve this end.[65]

Not only are ritual goods part of well-established trading networks, but commerce itself, in much of the world, is practised as if it were a kind of rite.

In the 1920s anthropologists discovered and disseminated what became their standard example in the Solomon Sea, off eastern New Guinea, where the inhabitants laboriously carried polished shell ornaments and utensils from island to island, following routes hallowed by custom.[66] Tradition regulated the terms of payment. The goods existed for no purpose other than to be exchanged. The manufactures hardly varied from place to place in form or substance. Objectively there was no difference in value, except that antique items carried a premium. To each object, however, the system assigned a peculiar character and cost, on a scale apparently arbitrary but universally acknowledged. The 'Kula', as the system is called, shows how goods unremarkable for rarity or usefulness can become objects of trade. Globally ranging anthropological work by Mary W. Helms has demonstrated how commonly, in a great range of cultural environments, goods gain value with distance travelled, because they carry symbolic associations with divine horizons or with the sanctification of pilgrimage: the guardianship Hermes exercised over craftsmen, musicians, and athletes, extended to messengers, merchants, and 'professional boundary-crossers'.[67] In a feeble way, modern commercial practices retain some of this primitive aura. In the grocery around the corner from where I live, domestic parmesan is a third of the price of the product imported from Italy: I defy any gourmet to tell the difference once one has sprinkled it over one's spaghetti – but customers are happy to pay a premium for the added virtue of unquantifiable exoticism. 'Every man', wrote Adam Smith, 'becomes in some measure a merchant.'[68] But though we take it for granted, the idea that trade adds value to goods and can be practised for profit has not always been obvious to everybody. There was a time when it seemed a surprising innovation.

Despite the remoteness and opacity of much of the material, the lesson of this chapter is clear: before the Ice Age was over, some of the world's best ideas had already sprung into life and modified the world: symbolic communication, the distinction between life and death, the existence of more than a material cosmos, the accessibility of other worlds, spirits, mana, perhaps even God. Political thought had already produced various ways of choosing leaders – including by means of charisma and heredity, as well as prowess – and a range of devices for regulating society, including food- and sex-related taboos, and the ritualized exchange of goods. But what happened when the ice retreated and environments people had treasured disappeared? When global warming resumed, fitfully, between ten and twenty thousand years ago, threatening the familiar comfort of traditional ways of life, how did people respond? What new ideas arose in response or indifference to the changing environment?

Chapter 3

Settled Minds

'Civilized' Thinking

They felt a draft from inside the rockfall. Eliette Deschamps was thin enough to wriggle through as her fellow-speleologists widened the gap. Seeing a tunnel ahead, she called to Jean-Marie Chauvet and Christian Hillaire to join her. To get an echo, which would give them an idea of the cave's dimensions, they shouted into the darkness. Vast emptiness swallowed the sound.

They had stumbled on the biggest cavern ever discovered in the Ardèche in southern France, where caves and corridors honeycomb the limestone. In an adjoining chamber an even more astonishing sight awaited. A bear reared up, painted in red ochre, preserved for who knew how many thousands of years.[1]

Chauvet Cave, as they called the find they made in 1994, is one of world's earliest, best preserved, and most extensive collections of Ice Age art. It houses images some authorities reckon at well over thirty thousand years old.[2] On the walls, bison and aurochs storm, horses stampede, reindeer gaze and graze. There are running ibex, brooding rhinoceroses, and creatures that flee the hunt or fall victim to it. Previous scholarship assumed that art 'evolved' from early, 'primitive' scratchings into the sublime, long-familiar images of the late Ice Age at Lascaux in France; in technique and skill, however, some work at Chauvet is as accomplished as paintings done in similar environments millennia later. Evidence of the comparable antiquity of other artworks, which survive only in traces or fragments in caves as far apart as Spain and Sulawesi, makes the early dating at Chauvet credible. Yet some of the Chauvet scenes could be transferred, without seeming out of place, to unquestionably later studios in Lascaux, for instance, or Altamira in northern Spain. Had the Lascaux painters seen the work of predecessors at Chauvet, they might have been as astounded as we are by the similarities.

The Ice Age did not just support material abundance and leisured elites: it also favoured stable societies. If art is the mirror of society, the paintings display startling continuity. At the time, no doubt, such change as there was seemed dynamic. In hindsight, it hardly matches the fever and the fret of modern lives. We seem unable to sustain a fashion in art for ten minutes, let alone ten centuries or ten millennia. Ice Age people were resolutely conservative, valuing their culture too much to change it: on the basis of what we have already seen of the output of their minds, they did not stagnate for want of initiative; they maintained their lifeways and outlooks because they liked things as they were.

Climate change threatened their world. We can sympathize. We, too, inhabit a worryingly warming world. Fluctuations in the interim have brought protracted or profound cold spells; and human activities intensify current trends. On a long-term view, however, the warming that brought the Ice Age to an end is still going on. When the upward trend in global temperatures began, during an era of climatic instability ten to twenty thousand years ago, people responded – broadly speaking – in either of two ways. Some communities migrated in search of familiar environments. Others stayed put and tried to adapt.

After the Ice: The Mesolithic Mind

We can begin by following the migrants, tracing their halts and sites in search of the thinking along the way. Their routes accompanied or followed the retreat of fat, nourishing quadrupeds that lived on the ice edge. Hunting remained the basis of the migrants' ways of life, but we can retrieve evidence of at least one new idea that occurred to them as their circumstances changed.

In 1932 in northern Germany, Alfred Rust was digging campsites occupied by reindeer-hunters about ten thousand years ago. He found none of the great art he hoped for. In three lakes, however, he excavated remnants of thirty big, unbutchered beasts. Each had been ritually slashed to death and sunk with a big stone stuck between the ribs. There were no precedents for this kind of slaughter. Earlier ritual killings preceded feasts, or targeted lions and tigers or other rival predators. The lakeside deaths were different: the killers waived the food. They were practising pure sacrifice, entirely self-abnegatory, putting food at the feet of the gods but beyond the reach of the community. The remains Rust dug up were the first indications of new thinking about transcendence: the rise of gods jealous in their hunger and the emergence of religion apparently intended to appease them.

Usually, in later sacrifices, as far as we know, the sacrificers and the gods have shared the benefits more evenly. The community can consume the sacrificed matter, eating food the gods disdain, or inhabiting edifices erected to their glory, or exploiting labour offered in their honour. Anthropology has a convincing explanation: gifts commonly establish reciprocity and cement relationships between humans. A gift might also, therefore, improve relationships beyond humankind, binding gods or spirits to human suppliants, connecting deities to the profane world and alerting them to earthly needs and concerns. If sacrifice first occurred as a form of gift exchange with gods and spirits, it must have made sense to practitioners in the context of exchanges among themselves.

The idea of sacrifice probably first occurred much earlier than the earliest surviving evidence. It may not be too fanciful to connect it with reactions to the crisis of climate change and the rise of new kinds of religion, involving the development of permanent cult centres and of new, elaborate, propitiatory rituals. The first temple we know of – the first space demonstrably dedicated to worship – dates from even earlier than the sacrifice Rust identified: it measures about ten feet by twenty and lies deep under Jericho, in what is now the Palestinian portion of Israel. Two stone blocks, pierced to hold some vanished cult object, stand on ground that worshippers swept assiduously.

The idea of sacrifice appealed, perhaps, to potential practitioners because scapegoats divert potentially destructive violence into controllable channels.[3] Critics, especially in Judaism, Islam, and Protestantism, have reviled sacrifice as a quasi-magical attempt to manipulate God.

But they have not deterred most religions during the last ten millennia from adopting it. In the process, sacrifice has come to be understood in contrasting or complementary ways: as penance for sin, or thanksgiving, or homage to gods, or as a contribution to fuelling or harmonizing the universe; or as sacralized generosity – honouring or imitating God by giving to or for others.[4]

Thinking with Mud: The Minds of the First Agriculturists

The followers of the ice clung to their traditional means of livelihood in new latitudes. Other people, meanwhile, to whom we now turn, preferred to stay at home and adapt. They confronted climate change by changing with it. By stopping in one place, they heaped up layers of archaeologically detectable evidence. We can therefore say a lot about what was in their minds, starting with economic ideas; then, after an excursion among the professionals who did most of the thinking, we can turn to political and social thought before, finally, looking at deeper matters of morals and metaphysics.

Global warming opened new eco-niches for humans to exploit. After ice, there was mud. From easily worked soils the biggest, most enduring new economic idea of the era sprang: breeding to eat – domesticating, that is, plants and animals that are sources of food. Where water and sunshine were abundant and soils friable, people equipped with the rudimentary technology of dibblers and digging sticks could edge away from foraging and start farming. They did so independently, with various specializations, in widely separated parts of the world. Taro planting in New Guinea started at least seven, perhaps nine, thousand years ago.[5] Farming of wheat and barley in the Middle East, tubers in Peru, and rice in South-East Asia is of at least comparable antiquity. Cultivation of millet followed in China, as did that of barley in the Indus valley, and of a short-eared grain known as tef in Ethiopia. Over the next two or three millennia farming spread or began independently in almost every location where available technologies made it practicable. The invention of agriculture plunged the world into an alchemist's crucible, reversing millions of years of evolution. Previously natural selection had been the only means of diversifying creation. Now 'unnatural selection', by human agents for human purposes, produced new species.

I suspect that the first foodstuffs people selected and bred to improve their food stocks were snails and similar molluscs. To some extent, this is a logical guess: it makes better sense to start with a species that is easy to manage rather than with big, boisterous quadrupeds or laboriously tilled plants. Snails can be selected by hand, and contained with no technology more sophisticated than a ditch. You do not have to herd them or train dogs or lead animals to keep them in check. They come ready-packed in their own shells. A good deal of evidence supports the logic. In ancient middens all over the world, wherever ecological conditions favoured the multiplication of snail populations at the time, at deep stratigraphic levels, laid down some ten thousand years ago, you find shells, often at levels deeper than those of some hunted foods that demand sophisticated technology to catch.[6] The molluscs they housed belonged, in some cases, to varieties now extinct and bigger than any that survive – which suggests that people were selecting for size.

Farming was a revolution. But was it an idea? Should a practice so muddy and manual, so fleshy and physical, feature in an intellectual history of the world? Among theories that deny or belittle it, one says that farming happened 'naturally' in a gradual process of co-evolution, in which humans shared particular environments with other animals and plants, gradually developing a relationship of mutual dependence.[7] In some ways, the transition to agriculture does seem to have been a process too slow for a sudden mental spark to have ignited it. Foragers typically replant some crops, selecting as they go. Foraging aboriginals in Australia replant nardoo stalks in the soil. Papago in the California desert sow beans along their routes of transhumance. Anyone who observes them realizes that long continuities can link foraging and farming: one might transmute into the other without much mental input from practitioners. Hunting can edge into herding, as the hunters corral and cull their catches. New crops may develop spontaneously near human camps, in waste enriched by rubbish. Some animals became dependent on human care or vulnerable to human herding by virtue of sharing people's favoured habitats. In an exemplary co-evolutionary process, dogs and cats, perhaps, adopted humans for their own purposes – scavenging for tidbits, accompanying the hunt, or exploiting concentrations of small rodents which hung around human camps for waste and leftovers – rather than the other way round.[8]

A rival theory makes farming the outcome of environmental determinism: rising populations or diminishing resources require new food-generating strategies. Recent, historically documented times provided examples of foraging peoples who have adopted farming to survive.[9] But stress can hardly issue simultaneously from both population increase and the loss of resources: the latter would frustrate the former. And there is no evidence of either at relevant times in the history of the emergence of agriculture. On the contrary, in South-East Asia farming started at a time of abundance of traditional resources, which gave elites leisure to think of yet further ways of multiplying the sources of food.[10] Agriculture was an idea people thought of, not an involuntary twitch or an inescapable response.

According to a further, once-popular theory, farming began as an accident, when foragers carelessly dropped seeds in suitable soil. A woman – adepts of the theory tend to foreground a female, perhaps because of women's ascribed or adopted role as nurturers – or some 'wise old savage', as Charles Darwin thought, must have launched our ancestors' first experiments in agriculture, when, in Darwin's words, 'noticing a wild and unusually good variety of native plant ... he would transplant it and sow its seeds'. This narrative does make farming the product of an idea, but, as Darwin continued, 'hardly implies more forethought than might be expected at an early and rude period of civilization'.[11] One might put it on the level of new food strategies invented and diffused among communities of monkeys, like Imo's innovations with sweet potatoes among Japanese macaques (see p. 28).

Three intellectual contexts make the beginnings of tillage intelligible. Food and drink, after all, are for more than nourishing bodies and quenching thirst. They also alter mental states and confer power and prestige. They can symbolize identity and generate rituals. In hierarchically organized societies, elites nearly always demand more food than they can eat, not only to ensure their security but also to show off their wealth by squandering their waste.[12] Political, social, and religious influences on food strategies are therefore worth considering.

Feasts, for example, are political. They establish a relationship of power between those who supply the food and those who eat it. They celebrate collective identity or cement relations with other communities. In competitive feasting, of the kind that, as we have seen, people were already practising before farming began, leaders trade food for allegiance. The strategy is practicable only when large concentrations of food are available. Societies bound by feasting will therefore always favour intensive agriculture and the massive stockpiling of food. Even where forms of leadership are looser or decision making is collective, feasting can be a powerful incentive to use force, if necessary, to boost food production, and accumulate substantial stocks. In any event, the idea of agriculture is inseparable from the self-interest of directing minds.[13]

Equally, or alternatively, religion may have supplied part of the inspiration. In most cultures' myths the power to make food grow is a divine gift or curse, or a secret that a hero stole from the gods. Labour is a kind of sacrifice, which gods reward with nourishment. Planting as a fertility rite, or irrigation as libation, or enclosure as an act of reverence for a sacred plant are all imaginable notions. People have domesticated animals for use in sacrifice and prophecy as well as for food. Many societies cultivate plants for the altar rather than the table. Incense and ecstatic or hallucinatory drugs are among the examples, as are the sacrificial corn of some high Andean communities and the wheat that in orthodox Christian traditions is the only grain permitted for the Eucharist. If religion inspired agriculture, alcohol's ability to induce ecstasy might have added to its appeal of selecting plants suitable for fermentation. Ploughing or dibbling soil, sowing seeds, and irrigating plants might start as rites of birth and nurture of the god on whom you are going to feed. In short, where crops are gods, farming is worship. Agriculture may have been born in the minds of priestly guides, who may of course have doubled as secular leaders.

Finally, conservatism may have played a role, according to the archaeologist Martin Jones, who has suggested that in warming environments, settled foragers would be bound to take increasing care of climate-threatened crops. To preserve an existing way of life, people would weed them, tend them, water them, and winnow them, encouraging high-yielding specimens, channelling water to them, and even transplanting them to the most favourable spots. Similar practices, such as managing grazing ever more zealously, would conserve hunted species. Eventually humans and the species they ate became locked in mutual dependence – each unable to survive without the other. People who strove to keep their food sources intact in a changing climate were not seeking a new way of life. They wanted to perpetuate their old one. Agriculture was an unintended consequence. The process that brought it about was thoughtful, but directed to other ends.[14]

Farming did not suit everybody. Backbreaking work and unhealthy concentrations of people were among the malign consequences. Others included ecologically perilous increases of population, risks of famine from overreliance on limited crops, vitamin deficiencies where one or two staples monopolized ordinary diets, and new diseases in new eco-niches, where domestic animals formed – as they still form – reservoirs of infection. Yet where new ways of life took hold, new ideas accompanied them, and new forms of social and political organization followed, to which we can now turn.

Farmers' Politics: War and Work

Farming required more than just the right material conditions: it was also the product of an act of imagination – the realization that human hands could reshape land in the image of geometry, with cultivated fields, marked by straight edges and segmented by furrows and irrigation ditches. Minds fed by agriculture imagined monumental cities. Strong new states emerged to manage, regulate, and redistribute seasonal food surpluses. Chiefs gave way to kings. Specialized elites swarmed. Opportunities of patronage multiplied for artists and scholars, stimulating the cycle of ideas. Labour, organized on a massive scale, had to be submissive and warehouses had to be policed: the link between agriculture and tyranny is inescapable. Wars almost certainly got worse as sedentarists challenged each other for land. Armies grew and investment flowed to improve technologies of combat.

Rituals of exchange helped keep peace. But when they failed, war obliged participants to think up new kinds of behaviour. It has often been argued that humans are 'naturally' peaceful creatures, who had to be wrenched out of a golden age of universal peace by socially corrupting processes: war, according to the influential anthropologist Margaret

Mead, 'is an invention, not a biological necessity'.[15] Until recently, there was a dearth of evidence with which to combat this theory, because of the relatively scanty archaeological record of intercommunal conflict in Palaeolithic times. Now, however, it seems an indefensible point of view: evidence of the ubiquity of violence has heaped up, in studies of ape warfare, war in surviving forager societies, psychological aggression, and bloodshed and bone breaking in Stone Age archaeology.[16] This bears out Field Marshal Bernard Law Montgomery, who used to refer enquirers who asked about the causes of conflict to Maurice Maeterlinck's *The Life of the Ant*.[17]

So aggression is natural; violence comes easily.[18] As a way of gaining an advantage in competition for resources, war is older than humankind. But the idea of waging it to exterminate the enemy appeared surprisingly late. It takes little mental effort to wage war to gain or defend resources or assert authority or assuage fear or pre-empt attack by others: these are observable causes of violence among pack animals. But it takes an intellectual to think up a strategy of massacre. Massacre implies a visionary objective: a perfect world, an enemy-free utopia. Perfection is a hard idea to access, because it is so remote from real experience. Most people's accounts of perfection are humdrum: just more of the same, mere satiety or excess. Most visions of paradise seem cloying. But the first perpetrators of ethnocide and genocide, the first theorists of massacre, were truly radical utopians. In some versions of the fate of the Neanderthals, our species wiped them out. William Golding reimagined the encounter – romantically, but with an uncanny sense of what the beech forests of forty thousand years ago were like – in the novel he thought was his best, *The Inheritors*: his Neanderthals are simple, trusting folk, while the 'new people' resemble creepy, sinister alien invaders – incomprehensible, pitiless, strangely violent even in love-making. The Neanderthals seem incapable of suspecting the newcomers' strategy of extermination until it is too late.

The evidence is insufficient to support Golding's picture, or other claims that our ancestors plotted Neanderthal extinction. And smaller wars, of the kind chimpanzees wage against neighbouring tribes or secessionist groups who threaten to deplete their enemies' resources of food or females, are hard to identify in the archaeological record.[19] Warfare, no doubt, happened before evidence of it appeared: the first full-scale battle we know of was fought at Jebel Sahaba, some time between about eleven and thirteen thousand years ago, in a context where agriculture was in its infancy. The victims included women and children. Many were savaged by multiple wounds. One female was stabbed twenty-two times. The killers' motives are undetectable, but the agrarian setting raises the presumption that territory – the basic prerequisite of farmers' survival and prosperity – was valuable enough to fight over.[20] The twenty-seven men, women, and children, on the other hand, slaughtered at Nataruk in what is now Kenya, perhaps about eleven thousand years ago, were foragers: that did not save them from the arrows and clubs that pierced their flesh and crushed their bones.[21] The way farmers fortified their settlements points to intensification of conflict. So do the 'death pits' in which massacre victims were piled about in their hundreds, seven thousand years ago, at sites in what are now Germany and Austria.[22] Peoples who practise rudimentary agriculture today are often exponents of the strategy of massacre. When the Maring of New Guinea raid an enemy village, they normally try to wipe out the entire population. 'Advanced' societies often seem hardly different in this respect, except that their technologies of massacre tend to be more efficient.

New forms of work were among further consequences of the farming revolution. Work became a 'curse'. Farming needed heavy labour, while exploitative rulers proved adept in thinking up elaborate justifications for making other people toil. In the era of Stone Age affluence (see p. 43) two or three days' hunting and foraging every week were enough to feed most communities. Foragers did not, as far as we know, conceptualize their effort as a routine, but rather practised it as ritual, like the ceremonies and games that accompanied it. They had neither motive nor opportunity to separate leisure from work.

Agriculture seems to have changed all that by 'inventing' work and compartmentalizing it as a department of life distinct from leisure and pleasure. Many simple agrarian societies still exhibit the legacy of the hunters' approach. They treat tilling the soil as a collective rite and often as a form of fun.[23] Most early farmers, however, could not afford Palaeolithic levels of relaxation. Typically, soils they could work with rudimentary tools were either very dry or very wet. So they needed ditches for irrigation, laboriously dug, or mounds, tediously dredged, for elevation above the water-line. The hours of dedicated effort lengthened. Work became increasingly sensitive to the rhythms of seed time and harvest, and of daily tasks: weeding soil, tending ditches and dykes. By about four thousand years ago, 'hydraulic societies'[24] and 'agrarian despotisms' in ancient Mesopotamia, Egypt, the Indus, and China had reversed former ratios of work and leisure by organizing dense populations in unremitting food production, interrupted only, as season succeeded season, by massive public works undertaken to keep peasants and peons too busy to rebel.

An expanded, empowered leisure class arose. For workers, however, the political fallout was dire. Contrary to popular belief, 'work ethic' is not a modern invention of Protestantism or industrialization, but a code elites had to enforce when work ceased to be enjoyable. Ancient Chinese and Mesopotamian poets rhapsodized about unstinting effort in the fields. 'Six days shalt thou labour' was the curse of expulsees from Eden. Cain's grim vocation was to be a tiller of the soil.[25] Women seem to have been among the biggest losers, at least for a while: in hunting societies, men tend to specialize in relatively dangerous, physically demanding food-getting activities. In early agricultural work, on the other hand, women tended to be at least as good at dibbling and weeding and garnering as men. In consequence, as farming spread, women had to make additional contributions as providers without any relaxation of their inescapable roles in child-rearing and housekeeping. Sedentary life meant that they could breed, feed, and raise more babies than their nomadic forebears. Women probably withdrew from some work in the fields when managing heavy ploughs and recalcitrant draft animals was required, but in some ways, the curse of work has never abated for either sex. A paradox of 'developed' societies is that increasing leisure never liberates us. It makes work a chore and multiplies stress.

Civic Life

Agriculture imposed terrible problems but also ignited grand opportunities. The new leisured elites had more time than ever to devote to thinking. If agrarian societies suffered recurrent famines, the background was of routine abundance. Farming made cities possible. It could feed settlements big enough to encompass every form of specialized economic activity, where technologies could be refined and improved. 'A social instinct', Aristotle averred, 'is implanted in all men by Nature and yet he who first founded the city was the greatest of benefactors.'[26]

The city is the most radical means human minds have ever devised for altering the environment – smothering landscape with a new habitat, thoroughly reimagined, crafted for purposes only humans could devise. Of course, there was never a golden age of ecological innocence. As far as we know, people have always exploited their environment for what they can get. Ice Age hunters seem to have been willing to pursue to extinction the very species on which they depended. Farmers have always exhausted soils and dug dust bowls. Still, built environments represent to an extreme degree the idea of challenging nature – effectively, waging war on other species, reshaping the earth, remodelling the environment, re-crafting the ecosystem to suit human uses and match human imaginations. From as early as the tenth millennium BCE brick dwellings in Jericho seem to oppress the Earth with walls two feet thick and deep stone foundations. Early Jericho covered only ten acres. About three millennia later, Çatalhüyük, in what is now Turkey, was more than three times as big: a honeycomb of dwellings linked not by streets as we understand them but by walkways along the flat roofs. The houses were uniform, with standard shapes and sizes for panels, doorways, hearths, ovens, and even bricks of uniform scale and pattern. The painted streetscape of a similar city survives today on one of the walls.

Dwellers in such places may already have esteemed the city as the ideal setting for life. In the third millennium BCE, that was certainly the prevailing opinion in Mesopotamia, where received wisdom defined chaos as a time when 'a brick had not been laid ... a city had not been built'.[27] Ninety per cent of the population of southern Mesopotamia lived in cities by about 2000 BCE. Only now is the rest of the world catching up. It has taken that long for us to get close to overcoming the problems of health, security, and viability that cities unleash on their people. We are becoming a city-dwelling species but we do not know whether we can avoid the disasters that have overcome all city-building civilizations so far and made them one with Nineveh and Tyre.[28]

Leadership in Emerging States

As well as stimulating the city, agriculture solidified the state. The two effects were connected. To manage labour and police food stocks, communities strengthened rulers. The more food production increased, the more mouths there were to feed and more manpower to manage. Power and nutrition twisted like bindweed in a single upward spiral. Political scientists commonly distinguish 'chieftaincy' – the structure of political authority typical of foraging cultures – from 'the state', which herding and farming societies favour. In chieftaincies the functions of government are undivided: rulers discharge all of them, making laws, settling disputes, wielding justice, running lives. States, on the other hand, distribute the same functions among specialists. According to Aristotle, the state was a response to growing population: the first society was the family, then the tribe, then the village, then the state. The village represented a crucial phase: transition to sedentary life, the replacement of hunting and gathering by herding and agriculture. The state was the culmination: 'the union of families and villages in a perfect and self-sufficing life'.[29] We still rely on this sort of narrative of the unknowably distant past. In sociologists' and political scientists' usual model, chieftains ruled roving 'bands', but when people settled down, bands became states and chiefdoms became kingdoms.

However that may be, rival ideas of the state are discernible in political imagery from the third and second millennia BCE. In ancient Egypt, for instance, the commonest image of the state was as a flock, which the king tended in the role of a herdsman, reflecting, perhaps, a real difference between the political ideas of herders and foragers. Farming increases competition for space and therefore strengthens institutions of rulership, as disputes and wars multiply; in conflicts, elective leaders qualified by prowess or sagacity tend to shift patriarchs and elders out of supreme command. In such circumstances, 'primitive liberty', if it ever existed, would yield to a strong executive. Mesopotamian texts of the period enjoin obedience to draconian enforcers: to the vizier in the fields, the father in the household, the king in everything. 'The king's word is right', says a representative text, 'his word, like a god's, cannot be changed.'[30] The king towers over anyone else depicted in Mesopotamian reliefs, as he takes refreshment; he receives supplicants and tributaries, and hoists bricks to build cities and temples. It was the king's prerogative to form the first brick from the mud for any public edifice. State kilns stamped bricks with royal names. Royally effected magic transformed mud into civilization. Yet autocracy was there to serve the citizens: to mediate with the gods; to co-ordinate tillage and irrigation; to warehouse food against hard times and dole it out for the common good.

Even the most benign state tyrannizes somebody, because good citizenship requires adherence – sometimes by assent but always by force – to what political scientists call the social contract: the renunciation to the community of some of the liberties that a solitary individual might expect to enjoy. But no one has yet found a fairer or more practical way of regulating relationships among large numbers of people.[31]

Cosmologies and Power: Binarism and Monism

To control increasingly populous states, rulers needed new cadres of professional servants, and convincing ways of legitimizing their power. Their starting point was the world-picture farmers inherited from the foragers who preceded them. People in every age seek coherence: the understanding that comes from matching their feelings or perceptions with other information. A search for universal pattern – a meaningful scheme into which to fit all available information about the universe – ripples through the history of thought. The first idea people had for trying to make sense of everything was, as far as we know, to divide the cosmos in two. I call this idea binarism (traditionally called dualism – a name better avoided as, confusingly, it has also been used for a lot of other ideas).

Binarism envisages a universe in two parts, satisfyingly symmetrical and therefore orderly. In most models two conflicting or complementary principles are responsible for everything else. Balance between them regulates the system. Flow or flux makes it mutable. The idea probably arose in either or both of two experiences. First, as soon as you think of anything, you divide it from everything else: you therefore have two complementary and – between them – comprehensive categories. As soon as you conceive *x*, you imply a second class: call it not-x. As some wit once remarked, 'There are two classes of people in the world: those who think the world is divided between two classes of people, and those who don't.' Second, binarism arises from observation of life – which seems, on superficial examination, all to be either male or female – or the environment, all of which belongs either to earth or to air. The sexes interpenetrate. Sky and earth kiss and clash. The makings of binarism impress observant minds.

Binarism shapes the myths and morals of people who believe in it – and, to judge from anthropologists' records of common cosmologies, such people have been and are numerous, inhabiting a world envisaged by the remotest ancestors they know of. Among conflicting descriptions of the cosmos, one of the most frequently reported images is of uneasy equipoise or complementarity between dual forces, such as light and darkness or evil and good. A past generation of scholars interpreted the cave paintings of Ice Age Europe as evidence of a mentality in which everything the hunters saw was classified in two categories, according to gender[32] (though the phalli and vulvae they detected in the designs seem equally likely to be weapons and hoofprints, or part of some unknown code of symbols). Some of the earliest creation myths we know of represent the world as the result of an act of procreation between earth and sky. A picture of this sort of creative coupling was still influential in classical Athens. A character in a play of Euripides said that he 'had it from my mother: how heaven and earth were one form and when they were parted from one another, they gave birth to all things, and gave forth light, the trees, flying things, beasts, the nurslings of the salt sea and the human species'.[33] Although most of the new systems of thought that have claimed to describe the universe over the last three thousand years have rejected binarism, the exceptions include Taoism, which has had a formative influence on China and has made major contributions to the history of thought wherever Chinese influence has touched. In mainstream Judaism the universe is one, but God began to create it by dividing light from darkness. Christianity formally rejects binarism but has absorbed a lot of influence from it, including the notion or, at least, the imagery of angelic powers of light perpetually committed against satanic forces of darkness.

At an unknown date, a new cosmology challenged binarism: monism, the doctrine that there is really only one thing, which enfolds all the seeming diversity of the cosmos. In the first millennium BCE the idea became commonplace. Pre-Socratic sages who said the world was one probably meant it literally: everything is part of everything else. In the mid-sixth century BCE Anaximander of Miletus thought that there must be an infinite and ageless reality to 'encompass all worlds'.[34] A generation or two later, Parmenides, whom we shall meet again as an early exponent of pure rationalism, put it like this: 'There is and will be nothing beside what is ... It is all continuous, for what is sticks close to what is.'[35] According to this line of thinking, there are no numbers between one and infinity, which are equal to each other and share each other's boundaries, linking and lapping everything. All the numbers that supposedly intervene are illusory or are mere classificatory devices that we deploy for the sake of convenience. Two is one pair, three one trio, and so on. You can enumerate five flowers, but there is no such thing as 'five' independently of the flowers, or whatever else is in question. 'Fiveness' does not exist, whereas 'oneness' does. A satirist of about 400 BCE complained of the monists of his day, 'They say that whatever exists is one, being at the same time one and all – but they cannot agree what to call it.'[36] The monists seem, however, to have been indifferent to satire. Wherever ideas were documented, monism appeared. 'Identify yourself with non-distinction', said the legendary Taoist Zhuangzi.[37] 'Indiscriminately care for the myriad things: the universe is one', was how Hui Shi expressed the same sort of thought in the fourth century BCE.[38]

The monist idea was so prominent during the formative centuries of the history of Eurasian thought that it is tempting to suppose that it must already have been of great antiquity. The earliest evidence is in the Upanishads – documents notoriously difficult to date. The Kenopanishad is one of the earliest of them, enshrining traditions that may go back to the second millennium BCE. It tells the story of a cosmic rebellion. The powers of nature rebelled against nature itself. Lesser gods challenged the supremacy of Brahman. But the fire could not burn straw without Brahman. The wind could not blow the straw away without Brahman. On their own, these texts might suggest no more than the doctrine that God is omnipotent or that there is an omnipotent god: teaching similar to that of Judaism, Christianity, and Islam. In context, however, a more general, mystical conviction seems to be at work: of the oneness of the universe, infinite and eternal – a 'theory of everything', of a kind unprecedented in earlier civilizations. 'Brahman' is indeed clearly defined as the single reality that encompasses all in later Upanishads.

Perhaps from a birthplace in India, monism spread to Greece and China during the first millennium BCE. It became a major – one might even say the defining – doctrine of Hinduism. The oneness of everything and the equation 'infinity = one' have gone on exercising their fascination. Monism, in consequence, is one of those ancient ideas that never stopped being modern. Today, practical monism is called holism and consists in the belief that since everything is interconnected, no problem can be tackled in isolation. This is a recipe for never getting round to anything. A weak form of holism, however, has become extremely influential in modern problem-solving: everything is seen as part of a bigger, interconnected system, and every difficulty has to be addressed with reference to the systematic whole.[39] Don't tinker with the tax code, a modern holist might say, without taking the whole economy into account; don't extend the reach of the criminal code without thinking about the entire justice system; don't treat physical ailments without bearing psychic effects in mind.

Monism may not immediately have any obvious political, social, or economic consequences. It does, however, prompt other ideas about how the world works, with political consequences. If everything is interconnected, clues to events in one sphere must lie in another. If, for instance, bird flight, stars, weather, and individual fortunes are all linked, the links may be traceable. This is the thinking behind oracular divination.

Oracles and Kings: New Theories of Power

Intimacy with spirits gives mediums tremendous power. Most societies have therefore developed alternative means of communicating with the gods and the dead, searching for chinks in the wall of illusion, through which shafts of light penetrate from a world that feels more real – closer to truth – than our own. Of the new methods, the first we know of were oracles, legible 'in the book of Nature'. The Greeks' most ancient shrine was in a grove at Dodona, where they could hear the gods in the babble of the stream and the rustle of the leaves. Aberrations – departures from natural norms – could also encode messages. The world's earliest surviving literature, from Mesopotamia in the second millennium BCE, is full of allusions to omens: the gods revealed portents in anomalous weather or rare alignments of the celestial bodies. Similar irregularities typify other sources of oracular wisdom. Rare manifestations or mutations in the sky at night might be revelatory. So might swerves in the flight of birds or odd spots on the innards of sacrificed animals: to ancient Mesopotamians, sheep's livers were 'tablets of the gods'. Messages from the same divine source might bellow in volcanoes or earthquakes or flame in apparently spontaneous combustion. The behaviour of creatures specially designated for the purpose, such as the sacred geese of ancient Rome or the poisoned chickens of Zande witch-doctors in the Nilotic Sudan, might have prophecies to disclose. The Gypsy's tea leaves are the dregs of a tradition of libations to the gods.

Some early oracles have left records of their pronouncements. In China, for instance, hundreds of thousands of documents survive from the second millennium BCE in the silt of the great bend in the Yellow River: fragments of bone and shell heated to the breaking point at which they revealed their secrets, like messages scrawled in invisible ink. Forecasts made or memories confided by the ancestral spirits were legible in the shape of the cracks. Interpreters or their assistants often scratched interpretations alongside the fissures, as if in translation. Solutions of crimes appear, along with disclosures of hidden treasure, and the names of individuals whom the gods chose for office.

Most of these readings, like the celestial oracles of Mesopotamia, are official messages, evidently contrived to legitimate state policies. Such oracles were invaluable to contending parties in societies where rising state power challenged priestly elites for influence over subjects' lives. By breaking shamans' monopoly as spirit messengers, oracles diversified the sources of power and multiplied political competition. They were legible to specialist priests or secular rulers, who could find in oracles recommendations different from those the shamans claimed from the gods. Political authorities could control shrines and manipulate the messages. Just as Palaeolithic shamans danced and drummed their way to positions of command by virtue of their access to the spirit world, so kings in agrarian states appropriated the shamans' authority by usurping their functions. The rise of oracles could be considered one of the world's first great political revolutions. Empowered by oracles, states gradually withdrew patronage from spirit mediums, and subjected them to control or persecution. Shamans endured – and in China they continued to intervene in political decision making at the whims of particular emperors for as long as the empire lasted – but they increasingly withdrew or were excluded from politics. They became mediators or ministers of popular magic and the prophets of the poor.[40]

Divine Kings and Ideas of Empire

'The lips of the king', says one of the Old Testament Proverbs, 'speak as an oracle.' Rulers who acquired oracular roles occupied a pivotal position between men and gods. The relationship prompted a further claim: that a ruler is a god. Anthropologists and ancient historians have gathered hundreds, perhaps thousands, of examples. The device is a handy way of legitimating power and outlawing opposition. How did it come about?

Common sense suggests a likely sequence: gods came first; kings followed; kings then reclassified themselves as gods to shore up their power. Clearly, however, events do not always conform to common sense. Some historians think that rulers invented gods to dull and disarm opposition. That is what Voltaire hinted and Karl Marx believed. In some cases they seem to have been right. 'Listen to my words', says a typical pharaonic inscription, capturing, as do most early written ruler-statements, the timbre of speech, evoking the presence of the king. 'I speak to you. I tell you that I am the son of Re who issued from his own body. I sit upon his throne rejoicing. For he made me king.'[41] It is hard to make sense of what Egyptians meant when they said their king was a god. Because a pharaoh could bear the names and exercise the functions of many gods, there was no exact identity overlap with any one deity. A possible aid to understanding is the ancient Egyptian habit of making images and erecting shrines as places where gods, if they wished, could make themselves manifest. The image 'was' the god when the god chose to show himself by inhabiting the image. The supreme god, Isis, was, in some characterizations – perhaps including some of the oldest – his own deified throne. Pharaoh could be a god in the same sense: perhaps the writers of Genesis meant something similar when they called man the image of God.

The idea of the god-king genuinely made royal power more effective. In the ancient diplomatic correspondence known as the Amarna letters, the abject language of Egypt's tributaries is almost audible. 'To the king my lord and my Sun-god', wrote a ruler of Shechem in Canaan in the mid-fourteenth century BCE, 'I am Lab'ayu thy servant and the dirt whereon thou dost tread. At the feet of my king and my Sun-god seven times and seven times I fall.'[42] In about 1800 BCE, the treasurer Sehetep-ib-Re wrote 'a counsel of eternity and a manner of living aright' for his children. The king, he asserted, was the sun-god Re, only better. 'He illumines Egypt more than the sun, he makes the land greener than does the Nile.'[43]

Divine kingship on the Egyptian model became commonplace later. In its day, however, other forms of government prevailed in other civilizations. There is no surviving evidence of kings in the Indus valley, where collaborative groups, housed in dormitory-like palaces, ran the states. In China and Mesopotamia monarchs were not gods (though gods legitimated them and justified their wars). Rulers' skyward ascent helped them maintain enlarged horizons, as they mediated with heaven, maintained divine favour, and responded to such signs of the future as the gods were willing to confide. Gods adopted kings, elevating them not necessarily to divine rank but to representative status and the opportunity or obligation to assert divine rights in the world. Chosen rulers received not only their own inheritances but title to dominion over the world. In Mesopotamia, Sargon, king of Akkad around 2350 BCE, is commonly credited with the first empire universal in aspiration. From his upland fastnesses his armies poured downriver towards the Persian Gulf. 'Mighty mountains with axes of bronze I conquered',[44] he declared in a surviving chronicle fragment. He dared kings who come after him to do the same. In China during the second millennium BCE, the growth of the state outward from heartlands on the middle Yellow River stimulated political ambitions to become boundless.

Religion and philosophy conspired. The sky was a compelling deity: vast, apparently incorporeal, yet bulging with gifts of light and warmth and rain, and bristling with threats of storm and fire and flood. The limits of the sky were visible at the horizon, beckoning states to reach out to them and fulfil a kind of 'manifest destiny' – a reflection of divine order. Imperialism suited monism. A unified world would match the unity of the cosmos. By the time of the Middle Kingdom, Egyptians thought their state already encompassed all the world that mattered: there were only subhuman savages beyond their borders. In China, around the beginning of the first millennium BCE, the phrase 'mandate of heaven' came into use. In central Asia, the broad horizons, immense steppes, and wide skies encouraged similar thinking. Genghis Khan recalled an ancient tradition when he proclaimed, 'As the sky is one realm, so must the earth be one empire.'[45]

For hundreds, perhaps thousands of years, Eurasia's empires all aspired to universalism. Every conqueror who reunited a substantial part of China, India, or Europe after every dissolution, espoused the same programme. Some, such as Alexander the Great in the fourth century BCE or Attila in the fifth century CE, succeeded in achieving it, or at least in establishing empires that briefly overspilled traditional limits. Even after Rome and Persia collapsed, medieval Christendom and Islam inherited the ambition to encompass the world. In China, rulers accepted that there were 'barbarian' realms beyond their reach, but still asserted theoretical supremacy over them. Even today, when the bitter experience of the failed universalisms has left a politically plural planet as the only viable reality, idealists keep reviving 'world government' as part of a vision for the future. Its first proponents were rulers in antiquity, who intended to achieve it by conquest.

Enter the Professionals: Intellectuals and Legists in Early Agrarian States

States need intellectuals to run administrations, maximize resources, persuade subjects, negotiate with rival states, and bargain with rival sources of authority. We do not know the names of any political thinkers before the first millennium BCE (unless rulers did their own original thinking, which is not impossible, but would be unusual). We can detect some of their thoughts, thanks to a technology developed by professionals: systematic symbolic notation, or what we now call writing. It could inscribe royal commands and experiences on monuments, communicate them in missives, and make them immortal. It could extend a ruler's reach beyond the range of his physical presence. All other ideas that matter, ever since, have been expressed in writing.

Beyond the political sphere, most people subscribe to a romance of writing as one of the most inspiring and liberating ideas ever. Writing ignited the first information explosion. It conferred new powers of communication and self-expression. It extended communication. It started every subsequent revolution in thought. It could make memories unprecedentedly long (though not necessarily accurate). It helped knowledge accumulate. Without it progress would be stagnant or slow. Even amid emojis and telecom, we have found no better code. Writing was so powerful that most peoples' recorded myths of their origin ascribe it to the gods. Modern theories suggest that it originated with political or religious hierarchies, who needed secret codes to keep their hold on power and record their magic, their divinations, and their supposed communications with their gods.

The real origins of writing, however, were surprisingly humdrum.

Unromantically, it was a mundane invention, which started, as far as we can tell, among merchants between about five thousand and seven thousand years ago. If we set aside the systems of symbols we find in Palaeolithic art (see p. 26), the first examples appear on three clay discs buried over some seven thousand years ago in Romania, with no indication of what they were for. In most civilizations, the earliest known examples are unquestionably merchants' tags or tallies, or records kept by gatherers of taxes or tributes to record types, quantities, and prices of goods. In China, where the earliest known examples were recently discovered, the marks were made on pots; in Mesopotamia, formerly acclaimed as the birthplace of writing, wedge-like symbols were pressed into thin clay slabs; in the Indus valley, they were inscribed on stamps that were used to mark bales of produce. In short, writing started for trivial purposes. It recorded dull stuff that was not worth confiding to memory.

Great literature and important historical records were valuable enough to learn by heart and transmit by word of mouth. The masterpieces of bards and the wisdom of sages start as oral traditions;

centuries pass, typically, before admirers consign them to writing, as if the very act of penmanship were profanation. The Tuareg of the Sahara, who have their own script, still leave their best poems unwritten. When writing started, hierophants treated it with suspicion or contempt. In Plato's jokey account of the invention of writing, 'Here is an accomplishment, my King', said the priest Theuth, 'which will improve both the memory and wisdom of Egyptians.' 'No, Theuth', replied Thamus. '... Those who acquire it will cease to exercise their memory and will be forgetful. You have discovered a recipe for recollection, not memory.'[46] The reply anticipated complaints one often hears nowadays about computers and the Internet. Yet writing has been a universally irresistible technology. Most people who know how to write do so for every thought, feeling, or fact they want to conserve or communicate.[47]

The professionals who adapted writing to the needs of the state devised the idea of codifying law. The first codes have not survived. But they were probably generalizations from exemplary cases, transformed into precepts applicable to whole classes of cases. In Egypt, because the law remained in the mouth of the divine pharaoh, codification was unnecessary. The earliest known codes come from Mesopotamia, where, as we have seen, the king was not a god. Of the codes of Ur from the third millennium BCE only fragmentary lists of fines survive. But the code of King Lipit-Ishtar of Sumer and Akkad, of the early nineteenth century BCE, is an attempt at the comprehensive regulation of society. It expounds laws inspired and ordained 'in accordance with the word of' the god Enlil, in order to make 'children support the father and the father children ... abolish enmity and rebellion, cast out weeping and lamentation ... bring righteousness and truth and give well-being to Sumer and Akkad'.[48]

An accident has made Hammurabi, ruler of Babylon in the first half of the eighteenth century BCE, unduly celebrated: because his code was carried off as a war trophy to Persia, it survives intact, engraved in stone, surmounted by a relief showing the king receiving the text from the hands of a god. The epilogue makes clear the reason for writing it all down. 'Let any oppressed man who has a cause come into the presence of the statue of me, the king of justice, and then read carefully my inscribed stone, and give heed to my precious words. May my stone make his case clear to him.'[49] The code was there to substitute for the physical presence and utterance of the ruler.

The notion of a divine covenant was obviously present in these early law codes. The 'Laws of Moses', however – Hebrew codes of the first millennium BCE – had a novel feature: they were cast as a treaty that a human legislator negotiated with God. Even as Moses mediated it, law still depended on divine sanction for legitimacy. God wrote some commandments, at least, 'with his own finger', even deigning to issue, as it were, a second edition after Moses broke the original tablets. In chapter 24 of the Book of Exodus, in what may be an alternative version, or perhaps an account of the means of transmission of some other laws, God's amanuensis jotted down the rest at divine dictation. Elsewhere, the identification of law with divine will prevailed, everywhere we know about, until secular theories of jurisprudence emerged in China and Greece toward the middle of the first millennium BCE.

Down to our own times rival ideas have jostled with codified law: that law is a body of tradition, inherited from the ancestors, which codification might reduce and rigidify; or that law is an expression of justice, which can be applied and reapplied independently in every case, by reference to principles. In practice, codification has proved insuperable: it makes judges' decisions objectively verifiable, by means of comparison with the code; as circumstances require, it can be reviewed and revised; it suits democracies, because it shifts power from judges – who, in most societies are, in varying degrees, a self-electing elite – to legislators, who supposedly represent the people. Gradually, almost all laws have been codified. Even where principles of jurisprudence conflict – as in England and other places where, thanks to the way the British Empire shaped traditions of jurisprudence, equity and custom still have an entrenched place in judges' decision making – statutes tend to prevail over custom and principles in forming judicial decisions.

The Flock and the Shepherd: Social Thought

Law is a link between politics and society: the means by which rulers try to influence the way people behave towards each other. Among the same protean bureaucracies that wrote laws down, and produced new, sometimes terrifying justifications of state power, we can catch glimpses of new social thinking, too. By and large, the doctrines in question reflect the benign goals of many of the early law codes. Most concerned the problems of regulating relationships between classes, sexes, and generations.

The idea of the equality of all people is a case in point. We think of it as a modern ideal. Serious efforts to achieve it have been made in a sustained fashion only for the last two hundred years or so; but it crops up in every age. When did it start?

A doctrine of equality was first recorded in a famous Egyptian text from the mouth of Amun-Re: the god says he created 'every man like his fellow' and sent the winds 'that every man might breathe like his fellow' and floods 'that the poor man might have rights in them like the rich';[50] but evildoing had produced inequalities that were a purely human responsibility. The text appeared regularly on Egyptian coffins in the second millennium BCE. But it may have had a long prehistory. Some thinkers have argued that it was a sort of collective memory from an early phase, a 'golden age' of primitive innocence, when inequalities were slighter than in recorded times, or a pre-social past, such as Rousseau imagined, or a supposedly communitarian forager past. The notion has some impressive minds on its side. As a good Christian and a good Marxist, Joseph Needham, the unsurpassed historian of Chinese science, shared the hatred of landlords common in Chinese songs of the seventh century BCE. As one songster said of landlords, 'You do not sow. You do not reap. So where do you get the produce of those three hundred farms?'[51] Needham saw the songs as echoes from 'a stage of early society before ... bronze-age proto-feudalism and the institution of private property'.[52]

There never was such an age to remember. But it can have been imagined. Most cultures invoke a myth of good old days to denounce the vices of the present: 'the times that came after the gods', as ancient Egyptian proverbial wisdom called them, when 'books of wisdom were their pyramids: is there anyone here like [them]?'[53] In Mesopotamia in the second millennium BCE, *Gilgamesh*, the world's oldest surviving epic, sketched a time before canals, overseers, liars, sickness, and senectitude. The *Mahabharata*, reputedly the world's longest poem, condensed ancient Indian traditions on the same subject in the fourth or fifth century BCE: a world undivided between rich and poor, in which all were equally blessed.[54] Not long afterwards the Chinese book known as *Zhuangzi* depicted an ancient 'state of pure simplicity', when all men and all creatures were one, before sages, officials, and artists corrupted virtue and natural liberty.[55] In Ovid's summary of the corresponding Greek and Roman tradition, the first humans spent their lives in ease with only reason – the law encoded in their hearts – to rule them: hierarchy would have been pointless.[56]

The idea of equality originated in myth, extolled by many, believed by few. When, occasionally, idealists have taken it seriously, it has usually provoked violent rebellions of the underprivileged against the prevailing order. Equality is impracticable; but it is easier to massacre the rich and powerful than to elevate the poor and oppressed. We call successful rebellions 'revolutions': they have often proclaimed equality, especially in modern times, as we shall see at intervals in the rest of this book. But they have never achieved it for long.[57]

Egalitarians therefore usually strive only to diminish inequality or tackle it selectively. Women are among the people they seem commonly to exempt. Theories purporting to explain or justify female inferiority crop up often in sources that survive from the third and second millennia BCE in apparent tension with evidence, or at least frequent claims, that worship of a mother goddess was the – or a – primordial universal religion. Many feminists would like those claims to be true, but are they?

Palaeolithic hunters, as we have seen, carved female figures, in which it is tempting to see representations of a primeval Earth Mother. But they could have been talismans, or accessories in birthing rituals, or fertility offerings, or dildos. Early agrarian societies, on the other hand, clearly honoured female deities; in many surviving cases, depictions of goddesses display remarkably consistent features.

In what can fairly be called one of the earliest excavated urban sites, Çatalhüyük in Anatolia, a truly magnificent female, with pregnant belly, pendulous breasts, and steatopygous hips, sits naked except for a fillet or diadem on a leopard throne. Her hands rest on great cats' heads, while their tails curl around her shoulders. Similar images of a 'mistress of animals' survive from all over the Near East. At Tarxien in Malta, one of the world's earliest stone temples housed a similar embodiment of divine motherhood, attended by smaller female figures nicknamed 'sleeping beauties' by archaeologists. Mesopotamian texts of the second millennium BCE hailed a goddess as 'the mother-womb, the creatrix of men'.[58] Early thinkers do not seem to endorse Nietzsche's notorious view that 'woman was God's second mistake'.[59]

A single universal cult seems inherently improbable; but the evidence of a widespread way of understanding and venerating womanhood is incontrovertible. Even in cultures that had no known connections with each other, the same stylized, big-hipped body (familiar in today's art world to those who know the work of the Colombian artist Fernando Botero) appears in Native American and Australian aboriginal art. Goddess-archaeology has stimulated two influential but insecure theories: first, that men suppressed the goddess cult when they seized control of religion many thousands of years ago; second, that Christianity appropriated what survived of the goddess tradition and incorporated it in the cult of the Virgin.

However implausible those theories seem, men are likely to be responsible for the idea that women are inferior. It seems counter-intuitive. Women can do almost everything men can do. Except at the margins, where there are men more physically powerful than any women, they can do it all, on average, equally well. For their role in reproducing the species most men are strictly superfluous. Women are literally more precious, because a society can dispense with most of its men and still reproduce: that is why men are more commonly used as fodder for war. It has always been easy to take or mistake women as sacred because of the way their bodies echo the rhythms of the heavens. In the earliest kind of sexual economic specialization that assigned men mainly to hunting, women mainly to gathering, women's work was probably more productive in terms of calorific value per unit of energy expended. Yet the idea we now call sexism, which, in its extreme form, is the doctrine that women are inherently inferior, simply by virtue of being women, seems ineradicable in some minds. How did it start?

Three clues seem indicative: a shift to patrilineal from matrilineal descent systems (inheriting status from your father rather than mother); rapid rises in birth rates, which might tie women to child-rearing and eliminate them from competition for other roles; and art depicting them with servile status. Pouting, languid bronze dancing girls of the

Indus valley of the second millennium BCE are among the first. The one thing about female subordination on which everybody seems to agree is that men are responsible for it. A wife, says the Egyptian *Book of Instructions*, 'is a profitable field. Do not contend with her at law and keep her from gaining control.'[60] Eve and Pandora – both responsible, in their respective cultures, for all the ills of the world – are even more minatory: dallying with the devil in Eve's case, dog-headed and dishonest in Pandora's.[61] Sexism is one thing, misogyny another; but the latter probably sprang from the former, or at least may share common origins.

The earliest evidence of the idea of marriage as a contract in which the state is a partner or enforcer also comes from the second millennium BCE: an extremely detailed summary of what were evidently already long-standing traditions in the Code of Hammurabi. Marriage is defined as a relationship solemnized by written contract, dissolvable by either party in cases of infertility, desertion, and what nowadays we should call irretrievable breakdown. 'If a woman so hates her husband', the code enjoins, 'that she says, "You may not have me", the city council shall investigate ... and if she is not at fault ... she may take her dowry and return to her father's house.' Adultery by either sex is punishable by death.[62] This does not mean, of course, that before then no one formalized sexual partnerships.

Considered from one point of view, marriage is not an idea but an evolutionary mechanism: a species like ours, which is heavily information-dependent, has to devote plenty of time to nurturing and instructing its young. Unlike most other primate females, women typically raise more than one infant at a time. We therefore need long-term alliances between parents who collaborate in propagating the species and transmitting accumulated knowledge to the next generation. The functions of child-rearing are shared in various ways from place to place and time to time; but the 'nuclear family' – the couple specialized in bringing up its own children – has existed since the time of *Homo erectus*. Sex lives do not need the involvement of anyone outside the couple normally concerned; and no amount of solemnity guarantees partnerships against breakdown. Perhaps, however, as a side effect of the idea of the state, or partly in response to the complementarity of male and female roles in agrarian societies, the professionals who wrote the earliest surviving law codes seem to have devised a new idea: of marriage as more than a private arrangement, demanding the enforceable commitment of the contracting individuals and, in some sense, the assent of society. Laws now addressed problems that unenforceable contracts might leave dangling: what happens, for instance, if sexual partners disagree about the status of their relationship or their mutual obligations, or if they renounce responsibility for their children, or if the relationship ends or changes when a third or subsequent partner is introduced or substituted?

Marriage is a surprisingly robust institution. In most societies the power to control it has been keenly contested – especially, in the modern West, between Church and state. But the rationale that underlies it is problematical, except for people with religious convictions, who could, if they so wished, solemnize their unions according to their beliefs without reference to the secular world. It is hard to see why the state should privilege some sexual unions over others. State involvement in marriage is maintained in the modern world more, perhaps, by the inertia of tradition than by any abiding usefulness.

The subordination of women, some feminists suppose, was a meta-principle that governed other thinking – a master idea that went on shaping the patriarchies in which most people lived. But in many times and places women have been complicit in their own formal subjection, preferring, like one of the rival heroines of G. B. Shaw's feminist masterpiece, *Major Barbara*, to deploy informal power through their menfolk. Apron strings can dangle male puppets. Sexually differentiated roles suit societies in which children are a major resource, demanding a specialized, typically female labour force to breed them and nurture them. Nowadays, where children's economic value is slight – where their labour is outlawed, for instance, or their minds or bodies are too immature for efficiency, or where, as in most of the West today, they cost parents vast sums in care and nurture and education – women are not called on to produce them in large numbers. As with inanimate commodities, the law of supply and demand kicks in; supply of children slackens with demand. Hence men can divert women into other kinds of production. The liberation of women for what was formerly men's work in industrial and post-industrial society seems, in practice, to have suited men rather well and landed women with even more responsibility than previously. As women do more and work harder, men's relative contribution to household and family falls, and their leisure and egoism increase. Feminism is still searching for a formula that is fair to women and genuinely makes the best of their talents.[63]

Fruits of Leisure: Moral Thinking

The leisure class that thought up laws, defined the state, invented new notions of rulership, and assigned women and couples new roles and responsibilities obviously had time for less urgent speculations, such as we might classify as philosophical or religious. We can begin with three related notions, traceable to the second millennium BCE, all of which situate individuals in speculation about the cosmos: the ideas of fate, of immortality, and of eternal reward and punishment.

Take fate first. Common experience suggests that some events at least are predetermined in the sense that they are bound to happen sometime. Though we may retain limited power to expedite or delay some of them, decay, death, the round of the seasons, and other recurring rhythms of life are genuinely inescapable. Problems arise, which cannot have escaped the attention of thinkers in any age: how are inevitable changes related to one another? Does a single cause ordain them? (Most cultures answer, 'Yes', and call it fate or some equivalent name.) Where does the power come from that makes action irreversible? What are its limits? Does it control everything, or are some possibilities open to human endeavour, or left to chance? Can we conquer destiny, or at least temporarily master it or induce it to suspend its operations?

Broadly speaking, human nature rebels against fate. We want to curb it or deny it altogether: otherwise, we have little incentive for the constructive undertakings that seem typically human. Experience, on the other hand, is discouraging.

Among the earliest evidence are myths of heroes' struggles against fate. The Sumerian god Marduk, for instance, wrested from heaven the tablets on which history was inscribed in advance. The story is doubly interesting: it shows not only that fate, in the earliest known relevant myth, is the subject of a cosmic power struggle, but also that the power of fate is distinct from that of the gods. The same tension is a marked feature of ancient Greek myths, in which Zeus contends with the Fates, sometimes controlling them but more often submitting. In Egypt, early texts were buoyant with belief that destiny is manipulable but the conviction soon faded. In about the seventeenth century BCE, Egyptians became pessimistic about individuals' freedom to shape lives. 'One thing is the word man says, another is what fate does.' Or again: 'Fate and fortune are carved on man with the stylus of the god.' A Middle Kingdom maxim said, 'Cast not thy heart in pursuit of riches, for there is no ignoring fate or fortune. Invest no emotion in worldly achievements, for every man's hour must come.'[64]

The idea of fate cannot change the world on its own. But fatalism can, by deterring action. Claims that some cultures are more prone to fatalism than others often emerge in the course of efforts to explain different development rates. That 'oriental fatalism' retarded Muslim civilization was, for instance, a theme of what some scholars now call the Orientalist school of Western writings on Islam in the late nineteenth and early twentieth centuries. The young Winston Churchill, who, in this respect, perfectly reflected the spirit of what he read on the subject as much as the evidence of what he observed, traced the 'Improvident habits, slovenly systems of agriculture, sluggish methods of commerce, and insecurity of property' he detected among Muslims to 'fearful fatalistic apathy ... wherever the followers of the Prophet rule or live.'[65] Westerners' revulsion from supposed oriental passivity seems to have been the result of a genuine misunderstanding of the Muslim concept of 'the Decree of God'. This philosophical device exempts God, when he so wills, from constraint by the laws of science or logic. It does not mean that people forgo their divinely conferred gift of free will. *Inshallah* is no more to be taken literally in Islam than in Christendom, where no one treats seriously the habit of inserting the proverbial *Deo volente* into expressions of hope.[66]

Fatalism makes sense in a conception of time – probably false but widely espoused – in which every event is a cause and effect: an eternal braid makes everything, however transitory it seems, part of an everlasting pattern. This context helps to explain the popularity among ancient elites of a further idea: that of immortality. The Great Pyramid of Cheops, which exhibits it on a gigantic scale, is still the largest man-made structure and one of the most punctiliously planned. It contains about two million stones that weigh up to fifty tons each on a base so nearly perfectly square that the greatest error in the length of a side is less than 0.0001 inches. The pyramid's orientation on a north–south axis varies by less than a tenth of one degree. It still makes an impression of spiritual strength or – on susceptible minds – of magical energy as it shimmers in the desert haze: a mountain in a plain; colossal masonry amid sands; precision tooling with nothing sharper than copper. In its day, smooth, gleaming limestone sheathed the whole edifice, under a shining peak, probably of gold, at the summit.

What made Cheops want a monument of such numbing proportions in so original a shape? Nowadays we tend to suppose that artistic freedom is essential for great art. For most of history the opposite has been true. In most societies monumental achievements need the outrageous power and monstrous egotism of tyrants or oppressive elites to spark effort and mobilize resources. An inscription on a capstone made for a later pharaoh sums up the pyramid's purpose: 'May the face of the king be opened so that he may see the Lord of Heaven when he crosses the sky! May he cause the king to shine as a god, lord of eternity and indestructible!' Again, 'O King Unis', says a pyramid text of the twenty-fifth century BCE, 'thou hast not departed dead. Thou hast departed living.'[67] A form of idealism inspired and shaped most monumental building in remote antiquity: a desire to mirror and reach a transcendent and perfect world.

To the builders of the pyramids, death was the most important thing in life: Herodotus reports that Egyptians displayed coffins at dinner parties to remind revellers of eternity. The reason why pharaohs' tombs survive, while their palaces have perished, is that they built solidly for eternity, without wasting effort on flimsy dwellings for this transitory life. A pyramid hoisted its occupant heavenward, out of the imperfect, corruptible realm toward the unblemished, unchanging domain of the stars and the sun. No one who has seen a pyramid outlined in the westering light could fail to associate the sight with the words an immortalized pharaoh addressed to the sun: 'I have laid down for myself this sunshine of yours as a stairway under my feet.'[68]

Like the pharaohs, devisers of early ideas about an afterlife generally seem to have assumed that it would be, in some ways at least, a prolongation of this life. But the assumption proved questionable. Early grave goods, as we have seen, included cherished possessions and useful kit: tools of stone and bone, gifts of ochre, and strings of bone beads. Gravediggers expected the next world to replicate this one. A new idea of the afterlife emerged at an uncertain date: another world, called into existence to redress the imbalances of ours. Ancient Egyptian sources exemplify the shift: most of the Egyptian elite seem to have changed their attitude to the afterlife in the late third millennium BCE, between the Old and Middle Kingdom periods. Old Kingdom tombs are antechambers to a future for which this world is a practical training; for the dead of the Middle Kingdom the lives they led were moral, not practical, opportunities to prepare for the next life; their tombs were places of interrogation. On painted walls gods weigh the souls of the dead. Typically, jackal-headed Anubis, god of the underworld, supervises the scales: the deceased's heart lies in one scale; in the other is a feather. Balance is impossible except for a heart unweighted with evil. In accounts of the trials of the dead in the courts of the gods, the examined soul typically abjures a long list of sins of sacrilege, sexual perversion, and the abuse of power against the weak. Then the good deeds appear: obedience to human laws and divine will and acts of mercy: offerings for the gods and the ghosts, bread for the hungry, clothing for the naked, 'and a ferry for him who was marooned'.[69] New life awaits successful examinees in the company of Osiris, the sometime ruler of the cosmos. For those who fail, the punishment is extinction. Similar notions, albeit less graphically expressed, appear in proverbs. 'More acceptable', as one of them says, 'is the character of the man just of heart than the ox of the evildoer.'[70]

The idea of eternal reward and punishment is so appealing that it has cropped up independently in most major religions ever since. It is probably one of the ideas the Greeks got from the Egyptians, though they preferred to trace the teaching back to Orpheus – the legendary prophet whose sublime music gave him power over nature. The same idea provided ancient Hebrews with a convenient solution to the problem of how an omnipotent and benevolent God could allow injustice in this world: it would all come right in the end. Taoists in the same period – the first millennium BCE – imagined an afterworld elaborately compartmentalized, according to the virtues and vices of the soul, between torture and reward. Today, tourists on the Yangtze River can gawk at the gory sculptures of Fengdu 'Ghost City' where the scenes of the torture of the dead – sawn, clubbed, dangled from meathooks, and plunged in boiling vats – now gratify rather than terrify. For early Buddhists and Hindus, too, present wrong could be redressed beyond this world. The most amazing result of the idea of divine justice is that it has had so little result. Materialists have often claimed that political elites thought it up as a means of social control: using the threat of otherworldly retribution to supplement the feeble power of the states, and deploying hope to induce social responsibility and fear to cow dissent. If that is how the idea started, it seems to have been an almost total failure.[71]

Reading God's Dreams: Cosmogony and Science

Still, fate, immortality, and eternal punishment all seem to be ideas conceived to be socially useful. Two equally great but apparently useless thoughts, which we can look at in turn, seem to have issued from the same circles of professional intellectuals: the idea that the world is illusory, and the very notion that animates this book: the idea of the creative power of thought – an outcome of thinkers' perhaps self-interested respect for thinking.

It is one thing to realize that some perceptions are illusory, as – according to chapter 1 – Ice Age thinkers did; another to suspect that the whole world of experience is an illusion. A spiritual world in which matter is a mirage is one of the oldest and most insistent innovations of Indian thought. In the Upanishads and the ancient hymns that appear in the Rigveda, the realm of the senses is illusory: or, more exactly, the distinction between illusion and reality is misleading. The world is Brahman's dream: creation resembled a falling asleep. Sense organs can tell us nothing that is true. Speech is deceptive, since it relies on lips and tongues and ganglions; only the inarticulacy that later mystics call the dark night of the soul is real. Thought is untrustworthy, because it happens in or, at least, passes through the body. Most feelings are false, because nerves and guts register them. Truth can be glimpsed only in purely spiritual visions, or in kinds of emotions that do not have any physically registered feeling, such as selfless love and unspecific sadness.[72]

We are in the world, whether illusory or not. Except as an encouragement to inertia, the doctrine of all-pervading illusion therefore seems unlikely to have practical effects. Few people believe it. The suspicion, however, that it might be true is never wholly absent. It changes the way some people feel. It encourages mysticism and asceticism; it divides religions: Christian 'Gnostics' and a long series of successor heresies espoused it, provoking schisms, persecutions, and crusades. It alienates some thinkers from science and secularism.

It takes, of course, an intellectual or an idiot to perceive the deceptive power of thought. Its creative power, however, seems plausible to everybody once someone clever enough to notice it points it out. Everyday experience shows that thought is powerful as a stimulus to action. 'What is swifter than the wind?' the *Mahabharata* asks. 'The mind is swifter than the wind. What is more numerous than blades of grass? Thoughts are more numerous.'[73] The 'imagination' I credited with creative power in the first chapter of this book is or does a kind of thinking. The search for ways of harnessing thought power for action at a distance – trying to change things or bring them into being by thinking about them, or altering the world by concentrating on it – has inspired lots of efforts, most of them probably chimerical: positive thinking, willpower, transcendental meditation, and telepathy are among the examples. But how much creativity is thought capable of?

Thinkers in ancient Egypt and India seem to have been the first to see it as the starting point of creation – the power that brought everything else into being. A doctrine known as the Memphite Theology appears in an Egyptian document in the British Museum.[74] Although the surviving text dates only from about 700 BCE, its account of creation was allegedly thousands of years old when it was recorded: Ptah, chaos personified but endowed with the power of thought, 'gave birth to the gods'. He used his 'heart' – what we should call the mind, the throne of thought – to conceive the plan and his 'tongue' to realize it. 'Indeed', says the text, 'all the divine order really came into being through what the heart thought and the tongue commanded.'[75] The power of utterance was already familiar, but the priority of thought over utterance – creation by thought alone – is not found in any earlier known text. The *Mundaka*, one of the earliest and surely one of the most poetic of the Upanishads, which may go back to the late second millennium BCE, may mean something similar when it represents the world as an emission from Brahman – the one who is real, infinite, and eternal – like sparks from a flame or 'as a spider extrudes and weaves its thread, as the hairs sprout from a living body, so from that which is imperishable arises all that appears'.[76] Yet, attractive as it is, the idea of thought as creative of everything else is hard to make sense of. Something to think about or to think with – such as a mind and words – should surely be a prerequisite.[77]

In some ways, the professional intellectuals of the period covered in this chapter seem to have broached many philosophical or proto-philosophical problems – or, at least, they recorded them for the first time – while pondering a lot of new political and social thought. Yet, compared with later periods, the total output of ideas seems disappointingly small. Between the invention of agriculture and the collapse or transformation of the great farming civilizations that generated most of the evidence we have examined, something like eight or nine millennia unrolled. If we compare the ideas first conceived or recorded in that period with the tally of the next millennium, which is the subject of the next chapter, the turnover seems relatively torpid and timid. For little-understood reasons, the thinkers were remarkably retrospective, traditional, and static – even stagnant in their ideas. Perhaps the ecological fragility of early agriculture made them cautious, concentrating thinkers' minds on conservative strategies; but that explanation seems unsatisfactory, because Egypt and China included ecologically divergent regions and therefore acquired a measure of immunity from environmental disaster. Perhaps external threats induced defensive, restrictive mentalities: Egyptian and Mesopotamian states were often at loggerheads, and all the sedentary civilizations had to contend with the cupidity of the 'barbarian' peoples on their frontiers. But conflict and competition usually promote new thinking. In any case, we shall only have the measure of the conservatism of early agrarian minds if we move on to the era that followed and see how much more productive it was.

Chapter 4

The Great Sages

The First Named Thinkers

It was a bad time for civilization: in the late second millennium BCE a protracted climacteric – or 'crisis', in the contested argot of historians and archaeologists – afflicted regions that had formerly buzzed with new ideas. Still-mysterious catastrophes slowed or severed progress. Centralized economies, formerly controlled from palace labyrinths, vanished. Long-range trade faltered or ruptured. Settlements emptied. Monuments tumbled, sometimes to survive only in memories, like the walls of Troy and the labyrinth of Knossos, or in ruins, like the ziggurats of Mesopotamia, to inspire distant successors.

Natural disasters played a part. In the Indus valley, changing hydrography turned cities to dust. In Crete, volcanic ash and layers of bare pumice buried them. Traumatic migrations, which threatened Egypt with destruction, obliterated states in Anatolia and the Levant, sometimes with stunning suddenness: when the city-state of Ugarit in Syria was about to fall, never to be reoccupied, urgent, unfinished messages begged for seaborne reinforcements. No one knows where the migrants came from, but the sense of threat seems to have been very widespread. At Pylos in southern Greece, scenes of combat with skin-clad savages are painted on the walls of one of many shattered palaces. In Turkmenia, on the northern flank of the Iranian plateau, pastoralists overran fortified settlements where workshops in bronze and gold had once flourished.

Fortunes varied, of course. In China, around the beginning of the first millennium BCE, the Shang state, which had united the Yellow and Yangtze River valleys, dissolved, without, it seems, impairing the continuity of Chinese civilization: competition among warring courts actually multiplied the opportunities of royal sponsorship for wise men and literate officials. In Egypt the state survived but the new millennium was culturally and intellectually arid compared with what had gone before. In other affected regions, 'dark ages' of varying duration followed. In Greece and India, the art of writing was forgotten and had to be reinvented from scratch after a lapse of hundreds of years. As usual, when wars strike and states struggle, technological progress accelerated – hotter furnaces and harder, sharper weapons and tools. But there were no traceable innovations in ideas.

Revival, when and if it happened, was often in new places and among new peoples, after a long interval. Indian civilization, for instance, was displaced far from the Indus. Around the middle of the first millennium BCE logic, creative literature, mathematics, and speculative science re-emerged in the Ganges valley. At the margins of the Greek world, civilization crystallized in islands and offshoots around the Ionian Sea. In Persia the region of Fars, remote and previously inert, played the corresponding role.

The circumstances were inauspicious; but they made a fresh start possible. While the old civilizations lasted, they invested in continuity and the status quo. When they collapsed, their heirs could look ahead, and welcome novelty. Crisis and climacteric always prompt thinking about solutions. In the long run, as empires fragmented, new states favoured new intellectual cadres. Political contenders needed propagandists, arbiters, and envoys. Opportunities for professional training grew as states tried to educate their way out of disaster. In consequence, the first millennium before Christ was an age of schools and sages.

An Overview of the Age

In earlier periods, ideas arose anonymously. If pegged to a name, it was that of a god. By contrast, new ideas in the first millennium BCE were often the work of (or attributed to) famed individuals. Prophets and holy men emerged from ascetic lives to become authors or inspirers of sacred texts. Charismatic leaders shared visions and usually tried to impose them on everyone else. Professional intellectuals taught courses to candidates for public office or literate careers. Some of them sought the patronage of rulers or positions as political advisers.

They anticipated and influenced the way we think now. After all the technical and material progress of the last two thousand years, we still depend on the thought of a distant era, to which we have added surprisingly little. Probably no more than a dozen subsequent ideas compare, in their power to change the world, with those of the six centuries or so before the death of Christ. The sages scraped the grooves of logic and science in which we still live. They raised problems of human nature that still preoccupy us, and proposed solutions we still alternately deploy and discard. They founded religions of enduring power. Zoroastrianism, which still has devotees, appeared at an uncertain date probably in the first half of the millennium. Judaism and Christianity provided the teachings that later became the basis of Islam: about a third of the world's population today belongs to the 'Abrahamic' tradition the three religions comprise. Jainism and Buddhism were among other innovations of the age, as were most of the texts that furnished Hinduism with scriptures. In the sixth century BCE Confucius formulated teachings on politics and ethics that continue to influence the world. Taoism can be traced to around the turn of the fifth and fourth centuries BCE. In the same period, the achievements in science and philosophy of China's 'Hundred Schools' and of the Nyaya school of philosophers in India paralleled those of Greek sages. The whole of Western philosophy since the classical age of Athens is popularly apostrophized as 'footnotes to Plato'. Most of us still follow the rules for straight thinking that his pupil, Aristotle, devised.

If some of the people of the period seem instantly intelligible to us, it is because we think as they did, with the tools they bequeathed, the skills they developed, and the ideas they aired. But facts about their lives and circumstances are elusive. Heroic teachers inspired awestruck reverence that occludes them from our view. Followers recast them as supermen or even gods, and strew legends and lore across their reputations. To understand their work and why it proved so impactful, we have to begin by reconstructing the context: the means – networks, routes, links, texts – that communicated ideas and sometimes changed them along the way. We can then turn to sketching the formulators of the key ideas and, in turn, to their religious and secular wisdom and their moral and political nostrums.

The Eurasian Links

India, South-West Asia, China, and Greece were widely separated regions which produced comparable thinking about similar issues. More than mere coincidence was at work. People across Eurasia had access to each other's ideas.[1] Genius pullulates when intellectuals gather in institutions of education and research, where they can talk to each other. The broader the forum, the better. When cultures are in dialogue, ideas seem to breed, enriching each other and generating new thinking. That is why the central belt of the world – the densely populated arc of civilizations that stretched, with interruptions, across Eurasia – throbbed with so much genius in the millennium before Christ: contacts put its cultures in touch with one another.

The availability of written texts surely helped.[2] Many sages were indifferent or hostile to written teaching. The name of the Upanishads, which means something like 'the seat close to the master', recalls a time when wisdom, too holy and too worthy of memorization to be confided to writing, passed by word of mouth. Christ, as far as we know, wrote nothing, except words he traced in the dirt with his finger, to be dispelled by the wind. Only after the lapse of centuries were Buddhists driven to compile a supposedly ungarbled version of the teaching of the founder. Demand for quick-fix manuals arose, as it still does, from competition between gurus. All-purpose holy books, which purportedly contained all the truth the faithful needed, were among the consequences.

Supposedly divine revelations need human amanuenses. All scriptures are selected by tradition, modified by transmission, warped in translation, and misunderstood in reading. That they are or could be the unalloyed words of gods, 'inscribed', as the Bible says of the Ten Commandments, 'by the finger of God', must be a metaphor or a lie. They bring blights as well as blessings. Protestants of the Reformation thought they could replace the authority of the Church with the authority of Scripture, but demons lurk between the lines and pages of the

Bible, waiting for someone to open the book. To a rational, sensible reader, supposedly sacred texts can only be decoded tentatively, at the cost of enormous investment in scholarship. Anti-intellectual, literal-minded interpretations fuel fundamentalist movements, often with violent effects. Renegades, terrorists, tyrants, imperialists, and self-proclaimed messiahs abuse the texts. False prophets sanctify their own perverse readings of them. Yet some scriptures have been extraordinarily successful. We now take for granted the idea that writing is a suitable medium for sacred messages. Would-be gurus sell their wisdom as 'how-to' manuals. The great texts – the Upanishads, the Buddhist sutras, the Bible, and the later Qur'an – offer awe-inspiring guidance. They have become the basis of the religious beliefs and ritual lives of most people. They have deeply influenced the moral ideas even of those who reject religion. Other religions imitate them.

Texts cannot cross chasms on their own. They have to be carried. The sages' ideas spread around Eurasia along routes that bore Chinese silks to Athens, and to burial sites in what are now Hungary and Germany around the mid-first millennium BCE. Trade, diplomacy, war, and wandering took people far from home and brought networks into being. From about the third century of the millennium navigators and merchants carried narratives of Buddhahood to seekers of enlightenment around the shores of maritime Asia, where piloting a ship 'by knowledge of the stars' was deemed a godlike gift. In the tales, the Buddha protected sailors from goblin-seductresses in Sri Lanka. He rewarded a pious explorer with an unsinkable vessel. A guardian-deity saved shipwreck victims who piously combined commerce with pilgrimage or who 'worshipped their parents'.[3] Similar legends in Persian sources include the story of Jamshid, the shipbuilder-king who crossed oceans 'from region to region with great speed'.[4]

Behind such stories were accounts of genuine voyages of the mid-millennium, such as the naval mission that Darius I of Persia sent around Arabia from the northern tip of the Red Sea to the mouth of the Indus, or the commerce of what Greek merchants called the 'Erythraean Sea', from which they brought home frankincense, myrrh, and cassia (Arabia's ersatz cinnamon). Seaports for the Indian Ocean trade lined Arabia's shores. Thaj, protected by stone walls more than a mile and a half in circumference and fifteen feet thick, served as a good place to warehouse imports, such as the gold, rubies, and pearls that adorned a buried princess towards the end of the period. At Gerrha, merchants unloaded Indian manufactures. From a life-story engraved on a stone coffin of the third century BCE, we know that a merchant from Ma'in supplied Egyptian temples with incense.[5]

The regularity of the monsoonal wind system made the long seafaring, sea-daring tradition of the Indian Ocean possible. Above the equator, northeasterlies prevail until winter ends; air then warms and rises, sucking the wind toward the Asian landmass from the south and west. Seafarers can therefore be confident of a fair wind out and a fair wind home. Strange as it may seem to modern yachtsmen who love the breeze at their backs, most of history's maritime explorers have headed into the wind, in order to improve their chances of getting home. A monsoonal system frees navigators for adventure.

Compared with land routes, the sea always carries goods faster, more cheaply, and in greater variety and quantity. But long-range commerce, including that across Eurasia in antiquity, has always started on a small scale, with goods of high value, and limited bulk traded through markets and middlemen. So the land routes that traversed great stretches of the landmass also played a part in creating the networks of the first millennium BCE, bringing people from different cultures together, facilitating the flow of ideas, and transmitting the goods and artworks that changed taste and influenced lifestyles. When Alexander the Great marched along the Persian royal road as far as India, he was following established trade routes. The colonies he scattered as he went became emporia of ideas. Bactria was one of them. In about 139 BCE Zhang Qian went there as an ambassador from China. When he saw Chinese cloth on sale and 'asked how they obtained these things, the people told him their merchants bought them in India'. From the time of his mission, 'specimens of strange things began to arrive' in China 'from every direction'.[6] By the end of the millennium, Chinese manufactures flowed from the Caspian to the Black Sea, and into gold-rich kingdoms at the western end of the Eurasian steppe.

At Dunhuang, beyond China's western borders, in a region of desert and mountains, 'the roads to the western ocean' converged, according to a poem inscribed in a cave that sheltered travellers, like veins in a throat.[7] Here, a generation after Zhang Qian's mission, the victorious

Chinese general, Wudi, knelt before 'golden men' – captured idols taken, or perhaps mistaken, for Buddhas – to celebrate his success in obtaining horses from Fergana.[8] From Dunhuang, so-called Silk Roads skirted the Taklamakan Desert toward kingdoms beyond the Pamir, linking with routes that branched off into Tibet or India, or continued across the Iranian plateau. It took thirty days to cross the Taklamakan, clinging to the edges, where water drains from the heights. In Chinese accounts of the daunting journey, screaming demon drummers personified the ferocious winds, but at least the desert deterred bandits and the predatory nomads who lived beyond the surrounding mountains.

While travel and trade trawled a net across Eurasia, individual masters of thought, celebrities in their day, seemed to get caught in it. We can glimpse these big fish flashing briefly, then disappearing among shoals of usually unidentifiable disciples. Because they or their followers often travelled as pilgrims or missionaries or gatherers or disseminators of sacred texts, it makes sense to try to isolate the sages' religious thinking before we turn to secular topics.

New Religions?

To reach the sages' genuine thoughts, we have to acknowledge the unreliability of the sources. Texts attributed to the sages often date from generations after their deaths and survive only because followers lost confidence in the authenticity of oral transmission. Forgeries, pious or profiteering, abound. Chronologies are often vague. Zoroaster, who dominated mainstream thinking in Iran for a thousand years and influenced other Eurasian religions, is a case in point, insecurely dated to the late seventh and early sixth centuries BCE in Iran. Nothing solid can be said of his life or the background that produced him. Texts ascribed to him are so partial, corrupt, and obscure that we cannot reconstruct them with confidence.[9] According to tradition, he preached a doctrine that recalls the dualism of earlier traditions: contending forces of good and evil shaped the world; a good deity, Ahura Mazda, dwelt in fire and light. Rites in his honour summoned dawn and kindled fire, while night and darkness were the province of Ahriman, god of evil. Almost equally inaccessible is the sage Mahavira, purportedly a rich prince who renounced riches in revulsion from the world in the sixth century BCE: the earliest texts of Jainism, the religious tradition that venerates him as its founder, do not even mention him. Jainism is an ascetic way of life designed to free the soul from evil by means of chastity, detachment, truth, selflessness, and unstinting charity. Though it attracted lay followers and still commands millions of them, it is so demanding that it can only be practised with full rigour in religious communities: a religious Jain prefers starvation to ungenerous life and will sweep the ground as he walks rather than tread on a bug. Jainism never drew a following outside India except in migrant communities of Indian origin.

As well as acknowledging the imperfections of the evidence about new religions, we have to allow for the possibility that what seems religious to us might not have been so to the sages; we must also resist the assumption that religion, as we now understand it, launched every new intellectual departure of the age. In a period when no one recognized a hard-and-fast distinction between religion and secular life, it is still hard to say, for instance, whether Confucius founded a religion. While enjoining rites of veneration of gods and ancestors, he disclaimed interest in worlds other than our own. His dissenting admirer, Mozi, called for universal love on secular grounds (as we shall see), four hundred years before Christians' religious version. Like those of Confucius and Mozi, Siddhartha Gautama's doctrines were on the margins of what we usually think of as religion, as he ranged, teaching and wandering, over an uncertain swathe of eastern India, probably between the mid-sixth and early fourth centuries BCE (recent scholarship makes chronological precision impossible).[10] Like Mahavira, he wanted, it seems, to liberate devotees from the afflictions of this world. His disciples, who called him 'the Buddha' or 'the Enlightened One', learned to seek happiness by escaping desire. With varying intensity for different individuals according to their vocations in life, meditation, prayer, and unselfish behaviour could lead the most privileged practitioners to elude all sense of self in a mystical state called nirvana (or 'extinction of the flame'). The Buddha's language avoided echoes of conventionally religious terms. He seems never to have made any assertions about God. He decried the notion that there is anything essential or immutable about an individual person – which is why Buddhists now avoid the word 'soul'.

But the pull of religious thinking tugged at Buddhism. The notion that the self survives the death of the body, perhaps many such deaths in the course of a long cycle of death and rebirth, resounds in early Buddhist writings. In a famous text, recorded in eighth-century China, the Buddha promised that a righteous person can be born as an emperor for hundreds or thousands of aeons. This aim of self-liberation from the world, whether by individual self-refinement or by losing oneself in selflessness, was common in Indian religions: in any case it was likely to be a long job. The distinctive element in Buddhists' account of the process was that it was ethical: justice governed it. The soul would inhabit a 'higher' or 'lower' body in each successive life as the reward of virtue or the derogation due to vice.

The Buddha's devotees gathered in monasteries to help guide each other toward this rather indistinct form of enlightenment, but individuals in worldly settings could also achieve it, including, in many early Buddhist stories, merchants, seafarers, and rulers. This flexibility helped create powerful, rich, widespread constituencies for Buddhism – including, from the third century BCE onward, rulers willing to impose it, sometimes with scant attention to the Buddha's own pacifism, by force. In 260 BCE, for instance, the Indian emperor Ashoka expressed regret for the bloody consequences of his conquest of the kingdom of Kalinga: 150,000 deportees, 100,000 killed, 'and many times that number who perished ... The sound of the drum has become the sound of the Buddha's doctrine, showing the people displays of heavenly chariots, elephants, balls of fire, and other divine forms.'[11] In this respect, too, Buddhism resembles other religions, which may be meritorious but rarely succeed in making people good.

Some of the most unambiguously religious ideas, including those of the last of the great sages, whom we usually call Christ, emerged from among people later known as Jews (Hebrews, Israelites, and other names have had some currency at different periods for different writers): no group of comparable size has done more to shape the world. They and their descendants made transforming, long-term contributions to almost every aspect of the life of Western societies, and hence, by a kind of knock-on effect, to the rest of the world, especially in the arts and sciences, economic development, and, above all, religion. Jewish religious thinking shaped Christianity (which started as a

Jewish heresy and ultimately became the most widely diffused religion in the world). Later, Judaism deeply affected Islam. As we shall see, it pervaded Muhammad's mind. In the long run, Christianity and Islam spread Jewish influence throughout the world. It seems astonishing that some followers of the three traditions should think they are mutually inimical, or be unaware of their shared ground.

Christ, who died in about 33 CE, was an independent-minded Jewish rabbi, with a radical message. Some of his followers saw him as the culmination of Jewish tradition, embodying, renewing, and even replacing it. *Christ*, the name they gave him, is a corruption of a Greek attempt to translate the Hebrew term *ha-mashiad*, or Messiah, meaning 'the anointed', which Jews used to designate the king they awaited to bring heaven to earth, or, at least, to expel Roman conquerors from Jewish lands. Christ's adherents were virtually the only recorders of his life. Many of their stories about him cannot be taken literally, as they derive from pagan myths or Jewish prophecies. His teachings, however, are well attested, thanks to collections of his sayings recorded within thirty or forty years of his death. He made ferocious demands: a Jewish priesthood purged of corruption, the temple at Jerusalem 'cleansed' of moneymaking practices, and secular power forsaken for a 'kingdom not of this world'. He upended hierarchies, summoning the rich to repentance and praising the poor. Even more controversial was a doctrine some of his followers attributed to him: that humans could not gain divine favour by appealing to a kind of bargain with God – the 'Covenant' of Jewish tradition. According to Jewish orthodoxy, God responded to obedience to laws and rules; Christians preferred to think that, however righteously we behave, we remain dependent on God's freely bestowed grace. If Christ did say that, he broke new ground in ethics, expressing a truth that seems elusive until it is pointed out: goodness is only good if you expect no reward; otherwise, it is just disguised self-interest. No subsequent figure was so influential until Muhammad, the founder of Islam, who died six centuries later, and none thereafter for at least a thousand years.

Sceptics sometimes claim that the great sages prescribed old magic rather than new religion: that efforts to 'escape the world' or 'extinguish the self' or achieve 'union with Brahman' were high-sounding bids for immortality; that mystical practice was a kind of alternative medicine designed to prolong or enhance life; or that prayer and self-denial could be techniques for acquiring the shaman's power of self-transformation. The line between religion and magic is sometimes as blurred as that between science and sorcery. The Buddha called himself a healer as well as a teacher. Legends of the era associate founders of religions with what seem to be spells. Followers of Empedocles, for instance, who taught an obscure form of binarism in mid-fifth-century BCE Sicily, importuned him for magical remedies for sickness and bad weather.[12] Disciples often wrote of the sages, from Pythagoras to Christ, as miracle workers and though a miracle is not magic the one elides easily into the other in undiscriminating minds. Immortality, similarly, is not necessarily a worldly goal, but is conceivable in magic as the object of ensorcellment. Writings attributed to Laozi, who founded Taoism, make the point explicitly: the pursuit of immortality is a form of detachment from the world, amid the insecurities of life among the warring states. Disengagement would give the Taoist power over suffering – power, Laozi is supposed to have said, like that of water, which erodes even when it seems to yield: 'Nothing is softer or weaker, or better for attacking the hard and strong.'[13] Some of his readers strove to achieve immortality with potions and incantations.

However much the new religions owed to traditional magic, they proposed genuinely new ways to adjust humans' relationship with nature or with whatever was divine. Alongside formal rituals, they all upheld moral practice. Instead of just sacrificing prescribed offerings to God or gods, they demanded changes in adherents' ethics. They beckoned followers by trailing programmes of individual moral progress, rather than rites to appease nature. They promised the perfection of goodness, or 'deliverance from evil', whether in this world or, after death, by transformation at the end of time. They were religions of salvation, not just of survival. Their ideas about God are the best place to begin a detailed examination of the new thinking they inspired.

Nothing and God

God matters. If you believe in Him, He is the most important thing in or beyond the cosmos. If you don't, He matters because of the way belief in Him influences those who do. Among the volumes the sages added to previous thinking about Him, three new thoughts stand out: the idea of a divine creator responsible for everything else in the universe; the idea of a single God, uniquely divine or divine in a unique way; and the idea of an involved God, actively engaged in the life of the world he created. We can take them in turn.

In order to get your mind around the idea of creation, you have to start with the even more elusive idea of nothing. If creation happened, nothing preceded it. Nothing may seem uninteresting, but that, in a sense, is what is so interesting about it. It strains imagination more than any other idea in this book. It is an idea beyond experience, at the uttermost limits of thought. It is infuriatingly elusive. You cannot even ask what it is, because it isn't. As soon as you conceive of nothing, it ceases to be itself: it becomes something. People who have been taught basic numeracy are used to handling zero. But zero in mathematical notation does not imply a concept of nothing: it just means there are no tens or no units or whatever classes of numbers happen to be in question. In any case, it appeared surprisingly late in the history of arithmetic, first known in inscriptions of the seventh century CE in Cambodia. Real zero is a joker in arithmetic: indifferent or destructive to the functions in which it appears.[14]

Fittingly, perhaps, the origins of the idea of nothing are undetectable. The Upanishads spoke of a 'Great Void' and Chinese texts of around the middle of the first millennium BCE referred to a notion usually translated as 'emptiness'. But these seem to have been rather more than nothing: they were located in a space beyond the material universe, or in the interstices between the celestial spheres, where, moreover, in the Chinese writings, 'winds' stirred (though maybe we are meant to understand them metaphorically).

Nonetheless, we know that the sages of the Upanishads had a concept of nonbeing, because their texts repeatedly poured scorn on what they saw as its pretended coherence. 'How could it be', sneered one scripture, 'that being was produced from non-being?'[15] Or as King Lear said to his daughter in Shakespeare's play, 'Nothing will come of nothing: speak again!' Presumably, thinkers who postulated the 'void' were trying to explain motion, for how could anything move without resistance, except into nothingness? Most respondents rejected it for two reasons: first, the discovery of air in the gaps between objects cast doubt on the need to imagine the void; second, apparently invincible logic, as formulated in fifth-century BCE Greece by Leucippus, objected, 'The void is a non-being; and nothing of being is a non-being, for being, taken strictly speaking, is fully a being.'[16] Still, once you have got your head around the concept of nothing, anything is possible. You can eliminate awkward realities by classifying them as nonbeing, as Plato and other idealists did with all matter. Like some of the modern thinkers who are called existentialists, you can see nothingness as the be-all and end-all of existence; the source and destination of life and the context that makes it meaningful. The idea of nothing even makes it possible to imagine creation from nothing – or more exactly the creation of matter from non-matter: the key to a tradition of thought that is crucial to most modern people's religions.

Most of the creation narratives encountered in the last chapter are not really about creation; they just seek to explain how an existing but different material cosmos came to be the way it is. Until the first millennium BCE, as far as we know, most people who thought about it assumed that the universe had always existed. Ancient Egyptian myths we encountered in the last chapter describe a god who transformed inert chaos; but chaos was already there for him to work on. Brahman, as we saw, did not create the world out of nothing. He extruded it out of himself, as a spider spins its web. Though some ancient Greek poetry described genesis from nothing, most classical philosophy recoiled from the idea. Plato's Creator-god merely rearranged what was already available. The Big Bang Theory resembles these early cosmogonies: it describes infinitesimally compressed matter, already there before the Bang redistributed it, expanding into the recognizable universe. In more radical attempts to explain creation scientifically, some protoplasm is there to be moulded, or electrical charges or disembodied energy or random fluctuations in a vacuum or 'laws of emergence'.[17] Creation from nothing seems problematical, but so does eternal matter, which, because change cannot happen without time, would be unchanging in eternity and would require some other, equally problematical agent to make it dynamic. Very rarely anthropology encounters creation myths in which a purely spiritual or emotional or intellectual entity preceded the material world, and matter began spontaneously, or was summoned or crafted out of non-matter. According to the Winnebago people of North America, for instance, Earthmaker realized by experience that his feelings became things: in loneliness, he shed tears, which became the primeval waters.[18] On the face of it, the myth recalls the way Brahman produced the cosmos from himself, but we should not think of the tears literally: emotion in Winnebago lore was the source of the creative power that made the material world. For some ancient Greek sages, thought functioned in the same way. Indeed, feeling and thought can be defined in terms of each other: feeling is thought unformulated, thought is feeling, communicably expressed. The Gospel of St John borrowed from classical Greek philosophy to utter a mysterious notion of a world spawned by an intellectual act: 'In the beginning was the Logos' – literally, the thought, which English translations of the Bible usually render as 'the Word'.

The Gospel writer could fuse Greek and Jewish thinking, because the Old Testament (as commentators from the second half of the first millennium BCE onward understood it) presented the earliest and most challenging creation-account of this kind: the world is a product of thought – no more, no less – exerted in a realm without matter, beyond being and nothingness. This way of understanding creation has gradually convinced most people who have thought about creation, and has become the unthinking assumption of most who have not.[19]

Another new idea – of God as unique and creative – is inseparable from it. The chronology of the relationship is unclear. Neither idea was convincingly documented until the second half of the first millennium. We do not know whether the thinkers responsible started with the uniqueness of God and deduced creation out of nothing from it, or whether they started with a creation story and inferred God's uniqueness from that. In any case, the ideas were interdependent, because God was alone until he created everything else. It endowed Him with power over everything, because what we make we can remake and unmake. It made Him purely spiritual – or more than that, indescribable, unnameable, incomparable with anything else. This unique creator, Who made everything else out of nothing, and Who monopolizes power over nature, is so familiar nowadays that we can no longer sense how strange He must have seemed when first thought of. Pop atheism misrepresents God as an infantile idea, but it took a lot of strenuous thinking to achieve it. The simple-minded – who formerly, as always, as now, thought that only what is visible and tactile exists – responded, no doubt, with surprise. Even people who imagined an invisible world – beyond nature and controlling it – supposed that supernature was diverse: crowded with gods, as nature was crammed with creatures. Greeks arrayed gods in order. Persians, as we have seen, reduced them to two – one good, one evil. In Indian 'henotheism' multiple gods together represented divine unity. Hindus have generally responded to monotheism with a logical objection: if one god always existed, why not others? Most known kinds of unity are divisible. You can shatter a rock or refract light into the colours of the rainbow. Maybe, if God is unique, His uniqueness is of this kind. Or it could be a kind of comprehensiveness, like that of nature, the unique sum of everything else, including lots of other gods. Or other gods could be part of God's creation.

The most powerful formulation of divine uniqueness developed in the sacred writings of the Jews. At an unknown date, probably early in the first half of the millennium, Yahweh, their tribal deity, was, or became, their only God. 'You shall have no other gods to rival me', He proclaimed. Disillusionment with Him was, paradoxically, the starting point of Yahweh's further transformation into a singular and all-powerful being. After defeat in war and mass deportation from their homeland in the 580s BCE, Jews responded by seeing their sufferings as trials of faith, divine demands for uncompromising belief and worship. They began to call Yahweh 'jealous' – unwilling to allow divine status to any rival. Fierce enforcement of an exclusive right to worship was part of a supposed 'covenant', in which Yahweh promised favour in exchange for obedience and veneration. Not only was He the only God for His people; He was, by the end of the process, the only God there is.[20]

Along with God: Other Jewish Ideas

Among the side effects were three further notions that we still espouse: linear time, a loving God, and a hierarchical natural order divinely confided to human lords or stewards.

Typically, as we have seen, people model their ways of measuring time on the endless, repetitive revolutions of the heavens. In many cultures, however, instead of relating linear changes to cyclical ones – my (linear) age, say, to the (cyclical) behaviour of the sun – timekeepers compare two or more sequences of linear change. The Nuer of the Sudan, who, as we have seen, relate all events to the rates of growth of cattle or children are a case in point: the date of a famine, war, flood, or pestilence may be expressed as 'when my calf was so-high' or 'when such-and-such a generation was initiated into manhood'.[21] Annalists often juggle with both methods: in ancient Egypt and for most of the past in China they used sequences of reigns and dynasties as frameworks for measuring other changes. Every reader of the Old Testament will see how the writers tend to avoid astronomical cycles when they assign dates to events, preferring human generations as units of periodization.

Different measurement techniques can give rise to different concepts of time: is it cyclical and unending? Or is it like a line, with a single, unrepeatable trajectory?[22] In surviving texts, the earliest appearance of the linear concept is in the first book of the Hebrew Bible, with time unleashed in a unique act of creation. The Genesis story did not make a consistently linear narrative inescapable: time could begin like a loosed arrow or released clockwork and exhibit properties of both. The Jews, however, and everyone who adopted their scriptures, have stuck with a mainly linear model, with a beginning and, presumably, an end: some events may be echoed or repeated, but history as a whole is unique. Past and future could never look the same again.

Jewish input into Christendom and Islam ensured that the modern world inherited a sense of time as linear. For Christians a cyclical model is impossible, because the incarnation occurred once and Christ's sacrifice was sufficient for all time. His Second Coming will not be a repeat performance but a final curtain call at the end of everything. Linear time has proved inspiring as well as daunting. It has launched millenarian movements, galvanizing people into action in the belief that the world's end might be close at hand. It has nourished the conviction that history is progressive and that all its toils are worthwhile. Leaders and ideologues exhilarated by their sense of participating in the rush of history toward a goal or climax have ignited movements as various as the American and French Revolutions, Marxism, and Nazism.

Jews have rarely sought to impose their ideas on others: on the contrary, for most of history, they have treated their religion as a treasure too precious to share. Three developments, however, have made the God of the Jews the favourite God of the world.[23] First, the 'sacred' history of Jewish sacrifices and sufferings provided readers of the Old Testament with a compelling example of faith. Second, Christ founded a Jewish splinter group that opened its ranks to non-Jews and built up a vigorous and sometimes aggressive tradition of proselytization. Thanks in part to a compelling 'Gospel' of salvation, it became the world's most widely diffused religion. Finally, early in the seventh century CE, the prophet Muhammad, who had absorbed a lot of Judaism and Christianity, incorporated the Jewish understanding of God in the rival religion he founded, which by the end of the second millennium CE had attracted almost as many adherents as Christianity. Although Islam developed in ways removed from Jewish origins and Christian influences, the God of the three traditions remained – and remains to this day – recognizably one and the same. As Christians and Muslims conceived Him, God's cult demanded universal propagation and even universal assent. A long history of cultural conflicts and bloody wars followed. Moreover, in the legacy both religions got from Judaism, God required human compliance with strict moral demands that have often been in conflict with practical, worldly priorities. So the idea of God, thought up by the Jews in antiquity, has gone on shaping individual lives, collective codes of conduct, and intercommunal struggles. At an ever deeper level of sensibility, it has aroused inner conflicts of conscience and, perhaps in consequence, inspired great art in every society it has touched.

The idea that God (by most definitions) exists is perfectly reasonable. The idea that the universe is a divine creation is intellectually demanding, albeit not impossible. But He might have created the world capriciously, or by mistake, or for some reason, as inscrutable as Himself, which it is a waste of time to try to fathom. The notion that God should take an abiding interest in creation seems rashly speculative. Most Greek thinkers of the classical era ignored or repudiated it, including Aristotle, who described God as perfect and therefore in need of nothing else, with no uncompleted purposes, and no reason to feel or suffer. Yet thought – if it was responsible for creation – surely made creation purposeful.

Beyond that of a God interested in His creation, the further claim that His interest is specially focused on humankind is disquieting. That the cosmos is all about us – a puny species, clinging to a tiny speck – seems, for humans, suspiciously self-centred.[24] That God's interest in us should be one of love is stranger still. Love is the most human of emotions. It makes us weak, causes us suffering, and inspires us to self-sacrifice. In commonplace notions of omnipotence there is no room for such flaws. 'God is love, I dare say', joked Samuel Butler, 'but what a mischievous devil love is!'[25] Yet the image of a God of love has exerted amazing intellectual, as well as emotional, appeal.

Where does the idea come from? Who thought of it first? 'The peak of the West is merciful if one cries out to her'[26] was an Egyptian adage of the Middle Kingdom period, but it seems to have expressed divine justice rather than divine love. Chinese texts around the mid-first millennium BCE often mention 'the benevolence of heaven'; but the phrase seems to denote something a long way short of love. Mozi anticipated Christianity's summons to love more than four hundred years before Christ: as even his enemies admitted, he 'would wear out his whole being for the benefit of mankind'.[27] But his vision of humankind bound by love was not theologically inspired: rather, he had a romantic mental picture of a supposed golden age of 'Great Togetherness' in the primitive past. This was nothing like what Christ meant when he told his disciples to 'love one another with a pure heart perfectly'. Mozi recommended practical ethics, a useful strategy for a workable world, not a divine commandment, or a consequence of a desire to imitate God. His advice resembled the Golden Rule: if you love, he said, others' love in return will repay you. The Buddha's teaching on the subject was similar but distinctive and pliable into new shapes. Whereas Mozi advocated love for the sake of society, the Buddha enjoined it for one's own good. Teachers of the Buddhist tradition known as Mahayana took it further in the second century BCE. When they insisted that love was only meritorious if it was selfless and unrewarded, as a free gift of the enlightened toward all fellow humans, they came very close to Christ's doctrine of disinterested love. Many scholars suppose that

Buddhism influenced Christ; if so, he gave it a distinctive twist: by making disinterested love an attribute of God.

To understand the origins of the doctrine we should perhaps look beyond the catalogue of thinkers and the litany of their thoughts. Christ's own thinking started, presumably, from the ancient Jewish doctrine of creation. If God created the world, what was in it for Him? The Old Testament discloses no answer, but it does insist that God has a special relationship with His 'chosen people': occasionally, the compilers of scripture called this 'faithful, everlasting love', which they likened to a mother's feelings for her child. More usually, however, they spoke of a bargain or 'covenant' than of freely given love, but late in the first millennium BCE, as we know from fragmentary texts found in a cave near the Dead Sea in the 1950s, some Jewish groups were trying to redefine God. In their version, love displaced covenant. By invoking a powerful, spiritual, creative emotion, known to everyone from experience, they made God humanly intelligible. In identifying God with love, Christ and his followers adopted the same approach as the writers of the Dead Sea Scrolls. By making God's love universally embracing – rather than favouring a chosen race – they added universal appeal. They made creation expressible as an act of love consistent with God's nature.

The doctrine of a loving God solved a lot of problems but raised another: that of why He permits evil and suffering. Christians have produced ingenious responses. God's own nature is to suffer: suffering is part of a greater good uneasily fathomable by those immersed in it. Evil is the obverse of good, which is meaningless without it; bereft of evil, creation would not be good – it would be insipid. Freedom, including freedom to do evil, is – for reasons known only to God – the highest good. Suffering is doubly necessary: to chastise vice and perfect virtue, for goodness is only perfectly good if unrewarded. The rain raineth on the just.[28]

The idea of God's love for humankind had a further important but, in retrospect, seemingly ironic consequence: the idea that humankind is superior to the rest of creation. Humans' urge to differentiate themselves from the rest of nature is obviously part of human identity, but early humans seem to have felt – quite rightly – that they were part of the great animal continuum. They worshipped animals or zoomorphic gods, adopted totemic ancestors, and buried some animals with as much ceremony as humans. Most of their societies had, as far as we know, no large concept of humankind: they relegated everyone outside the tribe to the category of beasts or subhumans.[29] In Genesis, by contrast, God makes man as the climax of creation and gives him dominion over other animals. 'Fill the Earth and subdue it. Be masters of the fish of the sea, the birds of heaven, and all the living creatures that move on Earth' was God's first commandment. Similar ideas appear in texts from across Eurasia in the second half of the first millennium BCE. Aristotle schematized a hierarchy of living souls, in which man's was adjudged superior to those of plants and animals, because it had rational as well as vegetative and sensitive faculties. Buddhists, whose sensibilities extended to embrace all life, ranked humans as higher than others for purposes of reincarnation. The Chinese formula, as expressed, for example, by Xunzi early in the next century, was: 'Man has spirits, life, and perception, and in addition the sense of justice; therefore he is the noblest of earthly beings.'[30] Stronger creatures therefore rightfully submitted to humans. There were dissenting traditions. Mahavira thought that souls invest everything, and that humans' convictions of superiority imposed an obligation of care of the whole of the rest of creation; creatures with 'animal' souls had to be treated with special respect, because they most closely resembled people. His near-contemporary in southern Italy, Pythagoras, taught that 'all things that are born with life in them ought to be treated as kindred'.[31] So did human superiority mean human privilege or human responsibility? Lordship or stewardship? It was the start of a long, still-unresolved debate over how far humans should exploit other creatures for our benefit.[32]

Jesting with Pilate: Secular Means to Truth

Alongside the religious ideas of the first millennium BCE other notions arose, more easily classifiable as secular. At the time, I do not think anyone would have made such a distinction. The difficulty we still have today in classifying the doctrines of, say, the Buddha or Confucius testifies to that. But we shall never understand religion if we exaggerate its reach or its importance. It makes little or no difference to most lives – even those of people who call themselves religious. Unfortunately, except in spasms of conscience, most people ignore the injunctions of their gods and invoke religion only when they want to justify what they propose to do anyway – typically, war, mayhem, and persecution.

The great sages thought about God on their own time. In their day-jobs they were usually at the service of patrons, pupils, and public, who, like most of education's 'customers' today – alas! – wanted vocational courses and value for money. Some sages were rich enough to be independent or to teach for fun or for self-glorification. The Buddha and Mahavira came from princely families. Plato was a wealthy aristocrat who gave lavish endowments to his own academy. Most counterparts, however, were professionals, who had to foreground the practical thinking for which they were paid. Especially where the political world was also fissile and competitive, in Greece and in the China of the Hundred Schools, they prioritized rulers' needs: rules of argument to fortify ambassadors, or of persuasion to enhance propaganda, or of law to fortify commands, or of justice to guide elite decision making, or of rights to bolster rulers' claims. Plato, who could afford to be high-minded, denounced hirelings and flatterers who sold useful arts of rhetoric rather than courses designed to enhance virtue.

Inevitably, however, some sages carried their thinking beyond the limits of what customers deemed useful into areas of speculation that touched transcendence and truth. Being, Brahman, and reality, for instance, were the focus of the teachings collected in the Upanishads. 'From the unreal', as one of the prayers pleads, 'lead me into the real.'[33] Reflections on these matters were not disinterested: they probably started as investigations of rhetorical technique, designed to equip students with proficiency in detecting other people's falsehoods and masking their own. Anxiety about exposing falsehood focused thought on what seemed the most fundamental of problems: what is real? Did not access to knowledge of everything else – in this world and all others – depend on the answer?

The consequences included some of the most powerful ideas that still shape our world or, at least, the way we think about it: metaphysics, realism, relativism, pure rationalism, and logic – the subjects of this section; and the reaction represented by the ideas we shall turn to in the next: scepticism, science, and materialism.

Realism and Relativism

The starting point of all these developments was the idea that all the objects of sense perception, and even of thought, might be illusory. It was, as we have seen (p. 108), strongly expressed in the Upanishads and may have spread across Eurasia from India. It is such an elusive idea that one wonders how and when people first thought of it and how much difference it can really have made to them or to the successors who took it up.

Proponents of the notion of all-pervading illusion were contending with received wisdom. The intensity with which they argued shows that. In China in the mid-fourth century BCE, Zhuangzi, dreaming that he was a butterfly, woke to wonder whether he was really a butterfly dreaming of manhood. A little earlier, shadows that Plato saw on a cave wall aroused similar misgivings. 'Behold', he wrote, 'people dwelling in a cavern ... Like us, they see only their own shadows, or each other's shadows, which the fire throws onto the wall of their cave.'[34] We are mental troglodytes whose senses mislead. How can we get to see out of our cave?

To Plato and many other sages the best route seemed to lead through levels of generalization: you may be convinced, for instance, of the reality of a particular man, but what about 'Man'? How do you get from knowable, palpable particularities to vast concepts that are beyond sight and sense, such as being and Brahman? When you say, for instance, 'Man is mortal', you may merely be referring to all men individually: so said philosophers of the Nyaya school in fourth-century BCE India. But is 'Man' just a name for the set or class of men, or is there a sense in which Man is a reality that exists independently of its instances? Plato and most of his successors in the West believed that there is. Plato's visceral idealism, his revulsion from the scars and stains of ordinary experience, comes through his language. 'Think', he said, 'how the soul belongs to the divine and immortal and eternal and longs to be with them. Think what the soul might be if it reached for them, unrestrained. It would rise out of the mire of life.' He thought that only universals were real and that instances were imperfect projections, like the shades the firelight cast in the cave. 'Those who see the absolute and eternal and immutable', as he put it, 'may be said to have real knowledge and not mere opinion.'[35]

Most Chinese and Indian contributors to the debate agreed. In the third century BCE, however, Gongsun Long, a self-professed student of 'the ways of former kings', or, as we might now say, an historian, coined a startling apophthegm, 'A white horse is not a horse',[36] to express a profound problem: our senses, as far as they are reliable, assure us that the white horse exists, along with a lot of other particular creatures we call horses; but what about the horse referred to by the general term – the 'horse of a different colour', who is not grey or chestnut or palomino or differentiated by any of the particularities that mark one horse as different from others? Critics called Gongsun Long's paradox 'jousting with words', but it has unsettling implications. It suggests that maybe only the particular horse really exists and that general terms denote nothing real. The universe becomes incomprehensible, except patchily and piecemeal. Supposedly universal truths dissolve. Universal moral precepts crumble. Aspiringly universal empires teeter. The doctrine has inspired radicals in every age since its emergence. In the sixteenth and seventeenth centuries it helped Luther challenge the Church, and pitted individualists against old, organic notions of society. In the twentieth century, it has fed into existentialist and postmodern rebellion against the idea of a coherent system in which everyone has a place.

Nominalism, as the doctrine came to be called, showed how hard it is to formulate truth – to devise language that matches reality: so hard, indeed, that some sages proposed dodging it. Truth is an abstract idea, but a practical matter: we want decisions and actions to have a valid basis. But how do we choose between rival formulations? Protagoras became notorious in ancient Greece for dismissing the question on the grounds that there is no objective test. 'Man', he said, 'is the measure of all things, of the existence of the things that are, and the nonexistence of things that are not.' Socrates – the voice of wisdom in Plato's dialogues – knew exactly what this puzzling statement meant: relativism – the doctrine that truth for one person is different from truth for another.[37] There were relativists in ancient China, too. 'Monkeys prefer trees', Zhuangzi pointed out early in the third century BCE, 'so what habitat can be said to be absolutely right? Crows delight in mice, fish flee at the sight of women whom men deem lovely. Whose is the right taste absolutely?'[38]

Most thinkers have been unwilling to accept that although relativism may apply in matters of taste, it cannot be extended to matters of fact. The modern philosopher Roger Scruton put the key objection neatly: 'The man who says, "There is no truth" is asking you not to believe him. So don't', or in an equally amusing paradox of the Harvard logician, Hilary Putnam, 'Relativism just isn't true for me.'[39] Those who prefer, however, to stick with Protagoras have been able to embrace radical conclusions: everyone has his or her own reality, as if each individual embodied a separate universe; truth is just a rhetorical flourish, an accolade we give to utterances we approve, or a claim we make to suppress dissenters. All views are equally valueless. There are no proper arbiters of conflicts of opinion – not bishops, not kings, not judges, not technocrats. Populism is therefore the best politics. Sages who wanted to answer relativism often appealed to numbers: five flowers are real. What about five? Isn't that real, too? Wouldn't numbers exist even if there were nothing to count? To judge from tallies notched on sticks or scratched on cave walls in Palaeolithic times, counting came easily to humans as a way of organizing experience. But mathematics offered more: a key to an otherwise inaccessible world, more precious to those who glimpse it in thought than the world we perceive through our senses. Geometry showed how the mind can reach realities that the senses obscure or warp: a perfect circle and a line without magnitude are invisible and untouchable, yet real. Arithmetic and algebra disclosed unreachable numbers – zero and negative numbers, ratios that could never be exactly determined, yet which seemed to underpin the universe: π, for instance ($22 \div 7$), which determined the size of a circle, or what Greek mathematicians called the Golden Number ($[1 + \sqrt{5}] \div 2$), which seemed to represent perfection of proportion. Surds, such as the square root of two, were even more mysterious: they could not be expressed even as a ratio (and were therefore called irrational).

Pythagoras was a crucial figure in the history of the exploration of the world of numbers. Born on an Ionian island around the middle of the sixth century BCE, he spanned the Greek world, teaching, for most of his life, in a colony in Italy. He attracted stories: he communed with the gods; he had a golden thigh (perhaps a euphemism for an adjacent part of the anatomy). To his followers he was more than a mere man but a unique being, between human and divine. Two relatively trivial insights have made him famous to modern schoolchildren: that musical harmonies echo arithmetical ratios, and that the lengths of the sides of right-angled triangles are always in the same proportions. His real importance goes much deeper.

He was the first thinker, as far as we know, to say that numbers are real.[40] They are obviously ways we have of classifying objects – two flowers, three flies. But Pythagoras thought that numbers exist apart from the objects they enumerate. They are, so to speak, not just adjectives but nouns. He went further: numbers are the architecture by which the cosmos is constructed. They determine shapes and structures: we still speak of squares and cubes. Numerical proportions underlie all relationships. 'All things are numbers'[41] was how Pythagoras put it.

In his day civilization was still carving fields and streets from nature, stamping a geometric grid on the landscape. So Pythagoras's idea made sense. Not all sages shared his view: 'I sought the truth in measures and numbers', said Confucius, according to one of his followers, 'but after five years I still hadn't found it.'[42] But the reality of numbers became entrenched in the learned tradition that spread from ancient Greece to the whole of the Western world. In consequence, most people have accepted the possibility that other realities can be equally invisible, untouchable, and yet accessible to reason: this has been the basis of an uneasy but enduring alliance between science, reason, and religion.

Rationalism and Logic

If you do believe that numbers are real, you believe that there is a supersensible world. 'It is natural', as Bertrand Russell said, 'to go further and to argue that thought is nobler than sense, and the objects of thought more real than those of sense-perception.'[43] A perfect circle or triangle, for instance, or a perfectly straight line, is like God: no one has ever seen one, though crude man-made approximations are commonplace. The only triangles we know are in our thoughts, though the versions we draw on paper or blackboard merely help call them to mind, as a Van Gogh sky suggests starlight, or a toy soldier suggests a soldier. Maybe the same is true of everything. Trees may be like triangles. The real tree is the tree we think of, not the tree we see.

Thought needs no objects outside itself: it can make up its own – hence the creative power some sages credited it with. Reason is chaste rationalism, unravished by experience. That is what Hui Shi thought. He was China's most prolific writer of the fourth century BCE. His books filled cartloads. He uttered numbing, blinding paradoxes: 'Fire is not hot. Eyes do not see.'[44] He meant that the thought of fire is the only really hot thing we genuinely know about and that data act directly on the mind. Only then do we sense them. What we really see is a mental impression, not an external object. We encounter reality in our minds. Unaided reason is the sole guide to truth.

Of those we know by name, the first rationalist was Parmenides, who lived in a Greek colony of southern Italy in the early fifth century BCE, striving for self-expression in poetry and paradox. He endured – the way I imagine him – the agony of a great mind imprisoned in imperfect language, like an orator frustrated by a defective mike. He realized that what we can think limits what we can say, and is restricted in turn by the range of the language we can devise. On the only route to truth, we must bypass what is sensed in favour of what is thought. The consequences are disturbing. If, say, a pink rose is real by virtue of being a thought rather than a sensible object, then a blue rose is equally so. If you think of something, it really exists. You cannot speak of the nonexistence of anything.[45] Few rationalists are willing to go that far, but reason does seem to possess power that observation and experiment cannot attain. It can open those secret caverns in the mind, where truths lay buried, unblemished by the disfigurements on the walls of Plato's cave. The idea contributed all that was best and worst in the subsequent history of thought: best, because confidence in reason made people question dogma and anatomize lies; worst, because it sometimes inhibited science and encouraged self-indulgent speculation. Overall, the effects have probably been neutral. In theory, reason should inform laws, shape society, and improve the world. In practice, however, it has never had much appeal outside elites. It has rarely, if ever, contributed much to the way people behave. In history books, chapters on an 'Age of Reason' usually turn out to be about something else. Yet the renown of reason has helped to temper or restrain political systems founded on dogma or charisma or emotion or naked power. Alongside science, tradition, and intuition, reason has been part of our essential toolkit for discovering truths.

For some rationalists, reason became an escapist device – a way of overtrumping or belittling the irksome world we actually inhabit. The most extreme case of the use of reason to mock the cosmos was the paradox-enlivened mind of Zeno of Elea, who preceded Hui Shi's paradoxes with similar examples of his own. He travelled to Athens around the middle of the fifth century BCE to show off his technique, stun complacent Athenians, and confound critics of his master, Parmenides. He paraded, for example, the infuriating argument that an arrow in flight is always at rest, because it occupies a space equal to its own size. According to Zeno, a journey can never be completed, because half the remaining distance has always to be crossed before you get to the end. In an example startlingly like one of Hui Shi's – who pointed out that if a strip of bamboo is halved every day it will last forever – Zeno quipped that matter must be indivisible: 'If a rod is shortened every day by half its length, it will still have something left after ten thousand generations.'[46]

His impractical but impressive conclusions drove reason and experience apart. Other sages tried to plug the gap. The best representative of the attempt was Aristotle, a physician's son from northern Greece, who studied with Plato and, like all the best students, progressed by dissenting from his professor's teachings. Walter Guthrie, the Cambridge scholar whose knowledge of Greek philosophy no rival ever equalled, recalled how at school he was made to read Plato and Aristotle. Plato's prose impressed him equally for its beauty and unintelligibility. But even as a boy, he was amazed that he could understand Aristotle perfectly. He supposed that the thinker was 'ahead of his day', miraculously anticipating the thought of young Walter's own time. Only when Guthrie grew into maturity and wisdom did he realize the truth: it is not because Aristotle thought like us that we understand him, but because we think like Aristotle. Aristotle was not modern; rather, we moderns are Aristotelian.[47] He traced grooves of logic and science in which our own thoughts still circulate.

The process that led to logic started around the middle of the first millennium BCE, when teachers in India, Greece, and China were trying to devise courses in practical rhetoric: how to plead in courts, argue between embassies, persuade enemies, and extol patrons. Rules for the correct use of reason were a by-product of the persuaders' art. But, as Christopher Marlowe's Faustus put it, 'Is to dispute well logic's chiefest end? Affords this art no greater miracle?' Aristotle proposed purer ends and contrived a greater miracle: a system for sorting truth from falsehood, strapping common sense into practical rules. Valid arguments, he showed, can all be analysed in three phases: two premises, established by prior demonstration or agreement, lead, as if with a flourish of the conjurer's wand, to a necessary conclusion. In what has become the standard textbook example of a 'syllogism', if 'All men are mortal' and 'Socrates is a man', it follows that Socrates is mortal. The rules resembled mathematics: just as two and two make four, irrespective of whether they are two eggs and two irons, or two mice and two men, so logic yields the same results, whatever the subject matter; indeed, you can suppress the subject matter altogether and replace it with algebraic-style symbols. Meanwhile, in India, the Nyaya school of commentators on ancient texts were engaged on a similar project, analysing logical processes in five-stage breakdowns. In one fundamental way, however, they differed from Aristotle: they saw reason as a kind of extraordinary perception, conferred by God. Nor were they strict rationalists, for they believed that rather than arising in the mind, meaning derives from God, Who confers it on the objects of thought by way of tradition, or consensus. Clearly, logic is imperfect in as much as it relies on axioms: propositions deemed to be true, which cannot be tested within the system. But after Aristotle there seemed nothing much left for Western logicians to do, except refine his rules. Academic overkill set in. By the time the refiners had finished, they had classified all possible logical arguments into 256 distinct types.[48]

There should be no conflict between reason and observation or experience: they are complementary ways of establishing truth. But people take sides, some mistrusting 'science' and doubting the reliability of evidence, others rejecting logic in favour of experience. Science encourages distrust of reason by putting experiment first. As the senses are unreliable, according to rationalists' way of looking at things, observation and experience are inferior arts: the best laboratory is the mind and the best experiments are thoughts. Rationalism, on the other hand, in an uncompromisingly scientific mind, is metaphysical and unrooted in experience.

The Retreat from Pure Reason: Science, Scepticism, and Materialism

Thinkers of the first millennium BCE juggled science and reason in their efforts to get out of Plato's cave. In the conflicts that arose, we can discern the origins of the culture wars of our own time, which pit dogmatic science – 'scientism', as opponents call it – against spiritual styles of thinking. At the same time, sceptics cultivated doubts about whether any technique could expose the limits of falsehood. Between reason and science, a gap opened that has never been re-bridged.

In one sense, science begins with a form of scepticism: mistrust of the senses. It aims to penetrate surface appearances and expose underlying truths. The third-century encyclopaedia *Lushi Chunqiu* – one of the precious compendia of the time, designed to preserve Chinese learning from hard times and barbarian predators – points out instructive paradoxes. Metals that look soft can combine in hard alloys; lacquer feels liquid but the addition of another liquid turns it dry; apparently poisonous herbs can be mixed to make medicine. 'You cannot know the properties of a thing merely by knowing those of its components.'[49]

Nonetheless, like all text we class as scientific, *Lushi Chunqiu* focused on identifying what is reliable for practical purposes. The supernatural does not feature, not because it is false but because it is useless and unverifiable. When Aristotle demanded what he called facts, rather than mere thoughts, he was in intellectual rebellion against the arcane refinements of his teacher, Plato. But a deeper, older revulsion was also at work in the science of the era, which rejected appeals to invisible and undetectable spirits as the sources of the properties of objects and the behaviour of creatures (see pp. 55–6). Spirits inhibited science: they could be invoked to explain changes otherwise intelligible as the results of natural causes.

As far as we can tell, before the first millennium BCE no one drew a line between what is natural and what is supernatural: science was sacred, medicine magical. The earliest clear evidence of the distinction occurred in China in 679 BCE, when the sage Shenxu is said to have explained ghosts as exhalations of the fear and guilt of those who see them. Confucius, who deterred followers from thinking 'about the dead until you know the living',[50] recommended aloof respect for gods and demons. For Confucians, human affairs – politics and ethics – took precedence over the rest of nature; but whenever they practised what we call science they challenged what they regarded as superstition. They denied that inanimate substances could have feelings and wills. They disputed the notion that spirits infuse all matter. They derided the claim – which even some sophisticated thinkers advanced on grounds of cosmic interconnectedness – that the natural world is responsive to human sin or rectitude. 'If one does not know causes, it is as if one knew nothing,' says a Confucian text of about 239 BCE. 'The fact that water leaves the mountains is not due to any dislike on the part of the water but is the effect of height. The wheat has no desire to grow or be gathered into granaries. Therefore the sage does not enquire about goodness or badness but about reasons.'[51]

Natural causes, in varying degrees in different parts of Eurasia, displaced magic from the arena of nature in erudite discourse. Science could not, however, desacralize nature entirely: the withdrawal of spirits and demons left it, in most sages' minds, in the hands of God. Religion retained an irrepressible role in establishing humans' relations with their environments. In China, emperors still performed rites designed to maintain cosmic harmony. In the West, people still prayed for relief from natural disasters and imputed afflictions to sins. Science has never been perfectly separated from religion: indeed, each of these approaches to the world has impertinently colonized the other's territory. Even today, some hierophants try to tamper with the scientific curriculum, while some scientists advocate atheism as if it were a religion, evolution as if it were Providence, and Darwin as if he were a prophet.

For science to thrive, the idea of it was not enough. People needed to observe nature systematically, test the ensuing hypotheses, and classify the resulting data.[52] The method we call empiricism answered those needs. Where did it come from? We can detect intellectual origins in Taoist doctrines of nature, and early applications in medicine.

Magical and divinatory practices of early Taoism privileged observation and experiment. Confucians often dismiss Taoism as magical mumbo-jumbo, while Westerners often revere it as mystical, but the only Taoist word for a temple literally means 'watch-tower' – a platform from which to study nature. Commonplace observations launch Taoist teachings. Water, for instance, reflects the world, permeates every other substance, yields, embraces, changes shape at a touch, and yet erodes the hardest rock. Thus it becomes the symbol of all-shaping, all-encompassing, all-pervading Tao. In the Taoist image of a circle halved by a serpentine line, the cosmos is depicted like two waves mingling. For Taoists wisdom is attainable only through the accumulation of knowledge. They sideline magic by seeing nature as resembling any beast to be tamed or foe to be dominated: you must know her first. Taoism impels empirical habits, which probably reached the West from China. Chinese science has always been weak on theory, strong on technology, but it is probably no coincidence that the modern tradition of experimental science flourished in the West in the first millennium BCE, when ideas were travelling back and forth across Eurasia, and resumed – never again to be reversed – in the thirteenth century, at a time, as we shall see, of greatly multiplied contacts between the extremities of the landmass, when numerous Chinese ideas and inventions were reaching Europe across the steppelands and the Silk Roads.[53]

Some of the earliest evidence of empiricism in practice is identifiable in medical lore.[54] That all illness is physically explicable is unquestioned today but was a strange idea when it was first proposed. Like any abnormal state, including madness, illness could be the result of possession or infestation by a spirit. Some diseases could have material causes, others spiritual. Or a mixture of the two could be responsible. Or sickness could be divine retribution for sin. In China and Greece, from about the middle of the first millennium BCE professional healers tried to work out the balance. Controversy between magic and medicine arose in consequence; or was it just between rival forms of magic? In an incident in China, attributed by the chronicle that recorded it to 540 BCE, an official told his prince to rely on diet, work, and personal morale for bodily health, not the spirits of rivers, mountains, and stars. Nearly two hundred years later the Confucian scholar Xunzi scorned a man who, 'having got rheumatism from dampness, beats a drum and boils a suckling pig as an offering to the spirits'. Result: 'a worn-out drum and a lost pig, but he will not have the happiness of recovering from sickness'.[55] In Greece in the late fifth century BCE, secular physicians contended with rivals who were attached to temples. The lay school condemned patients to emetics, bloodletting, and capricious diets, because they thought that health was essentially a state of equilibrium between four substances in human bodies: blood, phlegm, and black and yellow bile. Adjust the balance and you alter the patient's state of health. The theory was wrong, but genuinely scientific, because its advocates based it on observation of the substances the body expels in pain or sickness. Epilepsy was assumed to be a form of divine possession until a treatise sometimes attributed to Hippocrates proposed a naturalistic explanation. The text advances a bizarre proof of its impressive conclusion: find a goat exhibiting symptoms like those of epilepsy. 'If you cut open the head, you will find that the brain is ... full of fluid and foul-smelling, convincing proof that the disease and not the deity is harming the body ... I do not believe', the Hippocratic writer went on, 'that the Sacred Disease is any more divine or sacred than any other disease but, on the contrary, has specific characteristics and a definite cause ... I believe that human bodies cannot be polluted by a god.'[56]

Temple healing survived alongside professional medicine. Religious explanations of disease retained adherents when the secular professionals were baffled – which they often were: folk medicine, homeopathy, faith healing, quackery, miracles, and psychoanalysis can all still help nowadays when conventional therapies fail. Nonetheless, medics of the first millennium BCE revolutionized healing, spoke and acted for science, and started a presumption that has gained ground ever since: nothing needs to be explained in divine terms. Biology, chemistry, and physics can – or, given a bit more time, will – account for everything.

Science finds purpose hard to detect. It raises suspicion that the world is purposeless – in which case, a lot of early orthodoxies crumble. If the world is a random event, it was not made for humans. We shrink to insignificance. What Aristotle called the final cause – the purpose of a thing, which explains its nature – becomes an incoherent notion. Materialist thinkers still assert with pride that the whole notion of purpose is superstitious and that it is pointless to ask why the world exists or why it is as it is. In around 200 BCE in China, the sage Liezi anticipated them. He used a small boy in an anecdote as a mouthpiece for purposelessness, presumably to evade orthodox critics of so dangerous an idea. When – so his story went – a pious host praised divine bounty for lavish provender, 'Mosquitoes', the little boy observed, 'suck human blood, and wolves devour human flesh, but we do not therefore assert that Heaven created man for their benefit.' About three hundred years later, the greatest-ever exponent of a purposeless cosmos, Wang Chong, expressed himself with greater freedom. Humans in the cosmos, he said, 'live like lice in the folds of a garment. You are unaware of fleas buzzing in your ear. So how could God even hear men, let alone concede their wishes?'[57]

In a purposeless universe, God is redundant. Atheism becomes conceivable.[58] 'The fool hath said in his heart', sang the psalmist, 'there is no God.' But what did this mean? Accusations of atheism in ancient times rarely amount to outright denial of God. Anaxagoras in the mid-fifth century BCE was the first philosopher prosecuted under the anti-atheism laws of Athens; but his creed was not atheism as we now know it. His only alleged offences were to call the sun a hot stone and say the moon was 'made of earth'. If Protagoras was an atheist, he wore agnosticism's mask. He supposedly said, 'Concerning the gods, I do not know whether they exist or not. For many are the obstacles to knowledge: the obscurity of the subject and the brevity of human life.'[59] Socrates was condemned for atheism only because the God he acknowledged was too subtle for popular Athenian taste. Diogenes of Sinope was an irrepressibly sceptical ascetic farceur, who supposedly exchanged witticisms with Alexander the Great and reputedly plucked a chicken to debunk Socrates's definition of man as a featherless biped. His hearers and readers in antiquity generally regarded his allusions to the gods as ironic.[60]

By about the end of the first century CE, Sextus Empiricus, who specialized in exploding other people's ideas, could express unambiguous rejection of belief. He is proof of how unoriginal Marx was in dismissing religion as the opiate of the masses. Quoting an adage already half a millennium old in his day, Sextus suggested, 'Some shrewd man invented fear of the gods' as a means of social control. Divine omnipotence and omniscience were bogies invented to suppress freedom of conscience. 'If they say', Sextus concluded, 'that God controls everything, they make him the author of evil. We speak of the gods but express no belief and avoid the evil of the dogmatizers.'[61]

Rejection of God is intelligible in broader contexts: retreat from rationalism, rehabilitation of sense perception as a guide to truth, recovery of materialism. Materialism is the default state of incurious minds and, as we have seen, predated most of the other -isms in this book (see pp. 49–50). Crudely simple-minded, and therefore, perhaps, long rejected, materialism was ripe for reassertion by the mid-first millennium BCE when the obscure but intriguing Indian sage, Ajita Kesakambala, revived it. Later, outraged denunciations by Buddhist critics are the only surviving sources; if they are reliable, Ajita denied the existence of any world beyond the here and now. Everything, he maintained, including humans, was physical, composed of earth, air, fire, and water. 'When the body dies', he asserted, 'fool and wise alike are cut off and perish. They do not survive after death.' When he said that there was no point in pious conduct and no real difference between 'good' and 'evil' deeds, he also perfectly anticipated a perhaps distinct but related tradition: a system of values that places quantifiable goods, such as wealth and physical pleasure, above morals or intellectual or aesthetic pleasures, or asserts that the latter are merely misunderstood manifestations of the former.[62] Mainstream Buddhists, Jains, and Hindus never fully suppressed Indian materialism.

Meanwhile, a similar materialist tradition persisted in Greece, represented and perhaps initiated by Democritus of Abdera, a wandering scholar whose life spanned the turn of the fifth and fourth centuries BCE. He generally gets the credit for being the first to deny that matter is continuous. He claimed instead that everything is made of tiny, discrete particles, which make substances different from each other by zooming around in different patterns, like specks of dust in a sunbeam. The doctrine was remarkable, because it so closely resembles the world modern science depicts; indeed, we think of atomic theory as model science: a reliable guide to the true nature of the universe. Yet Democritus and his collaborators achieved it by unaided contemplation. The argument they thought decisive was that because things move, there must be space between them, whereas, if matter were continuous, there would be no space. Not surprisingly, few opponents were convinced. The scientific consensus in the Western world remained hostile to the atomic theory for most of the next two and a half millennia.

Epicurus, who died in 270 BCE, was in the dissenting minority. His name is now indelibly linked with the pursuit of physical pleasure, which he recommended, though with far more restraint than in the popular image of Epicureanism as sinful self-indulgence. His interpretation of the atomic theory was more important in the history of ideas, because in the world he imagined – monopolized by atoms and voids – there is no room for spirits. Nor is there scope for fate, as atoms are subject to 'random swerves'. Nor can there be any such thing as an immortal soul, since atoms, which are perishable matter, comprise everything. Gods do not exist except in fantasies from which we have nothing to hope and nothing to fear. Materialists have never ceased to deploy Epicurus's formidable arguments.[63]

Materialists were simplifiers who sidelined big, unanswerable questions about the nature of reality. Other philosophers responded by focusing on practical issues. Pyrrho of Elis was among them. He was one of those great eccentrics who inspire anecdotes. Accompanying Alexander to India Pyrrho allegedly imitated the indifference of the naked sages he met there. He was absent-minded and accident-prone, which made him seem unworldly. On board ship on the way home, he admired and shared a pig's unpanicky response to a storm. He turned on reason with the same indifference. You can find, he said, equally good reasons on offer on both sides of any argument. The wise man, therefore, may as well resign from thinking and judge by appearances. He also pointed out that all reasoning starts from assumptions; therefore none of it is secure. Mozi had developed a similar insight in China around the beginning of the fourth century BCE: most problems, he averred, were matters of doubt, because no evidence was truly current. 'As for what we now know', he asked, 'is it not mostly derived from past experience?'[64] From such lines of thought scepticism proceeded: in its extreme form, the idea that nothing is knowable and that the very notion of knowledge is delusive.

Paradoxical as it may seem, science and scepticism throve together, since if reason and experience are equally unreliable one may as well prefer experience and the practical advantages it can teach. In second-century BCE China, for instance, *The Tao of the Huainan Masters* told of Yi the archer: on the advice of a sage he sought the herb of immortality in the far west, unaware that it was growing outside his door:

impractical wisdom is worthless, however well informed.[65] Among Taoist writers' favourite characters are craftsmen who know their work and rationalists who persuade them to do it otherwise, with ruinous results.

Morals and Politics

If the sages' efforts led to science and scepticism, a further strand encouraged thinking about ethics and politics: minds unconcerned about the distinction between truth and falsehood can turn to that between good and evil. To make men good, or constrain them from evil, one obvious resource is the state.

In Greece, for instance, after Plato and Aristotle had seemingly exhausted the interest of epistemology, philosophers turned to the problems of how to deliver the best practical choices for personal happiness or for the good of society. Altruism, moderation, and self-discipline were the components identified in stoicism. 'Show me', said Epictetus, an ex-slave who became a famous teacher in Nero's Rome, 'one who is sick and yet happy, in peril and yet happy, dying and yet happy, in exile or disgrace and yet happy. By the gods, I would see a Stoic!'[66] Happiness is hard to fit into a history of ideas because so many thinkers, and so many unreflective hedonists, have sought it and defined it in contrasting ways, but Stoics were its most effective partisans in the West: their thinking had an enormous effect on Christians, who esteemed a similar list of virtues and espoused a similar formula for happiness. Stoicism supplied, in effect, the source of the guiding principles of the ethics of most Western elites ever since its emergence. Further Stoic prescriptions, such as fatalism and indifference as a remedy for pain, were uncongenial in Christianity, but resembled teachings from the far end of Eurasia, especially those of the Buddha and his followers.[67]

Almost all the ideas covered in this chapter so far were spin-offs and sidelines from the sages' main job, as their patrons and pupils conceived it: politics. But all political thinking is shaped by moral and philosophical assumptions. You can predict thinkers' place in the political spectrum by looking at how optimistic or pessimistic they are about the human condition. On the one hand, optimists, who think human nature is good, want to liberate the human spirit to fulfil itself. Pessimists, who think humans are irremediably wicked or corrupt, prefer restraining or repressive institutions that keep people under control.

Humans like to claim they have a moral consciousness unique in the animal kingdom. The evidence lies in our awareness of good, and our willingness to do evil. So are we misguidedly benevolent, or inherently malign? It was a key question for the sages. We are still enmeshed in the consequences of their answers. Most of them thought human nature was essentially good. Confucius represented the optimists. He thought the purpose of the state was to help people fulfil their potential. 'Man', he said, 'is born for uprightness. If he lose it and yet live, it is merely luck.'[68] Hence the political doctrines of Confucianism, which demanded that the state should liberate subjects to fulfil their potential, and of Greek democracy, which entrusted citizens with a voice in affairs of state even if they were poor or ill-educated. On the other hand were the pessimists. 'The nature of man is evil – his goodness is only acquired by training', said Xunzi, for instance, in the mid-third century BCE. For him, humans emerged morally beslimed from a primeval swamp of violence. Slowly, painfully, progress cleansed and raised them. 'Hence the civilizing influence of teachers and laws, the guidance of rites and justice. Then courtesy appears, cultured behaviour is observed and good government is the consequence.'[69] Optimism and pessimism remain at the root of modern political responses to the problem of human nature. Liberalism and socialism emphasize freedom, to release human goodness; conservatism emphasizes law and order, to restrain human wickedness. So is man – understood as a noun of common gender – good or bad? The Book of Genesis offered a widely favoured but logically dodgy answer. God made us good and free; the abuse of freedom made us bad. But if man was good, how could he use freedom for evil? Optimism's apologists eluded the objection by adding a diabolical device. The serpent (or other devilish agents in other traditions) corrupted goodness. So even if humans are not inherently evil, we cannot rely on them to be good without coercion. Ever since, devisers of political systems have striven and failed to balance freedom and force.[70]

Pessimism and the Exaltation of Power

A strong state is one obvious remedy against individual evil. But as humans lead and manage states, most sages proposed to try to embody ethics in laws, which would bind rulers as well as subjects. Confucius pleaded for the priority of ethics over law in cases of conflict – a precept easier to utter than accomplish. Rules and rights are always in tension. In practice, law can function without respecting ethics. The thinkers known as legalists, who formed a school in fourth-century BCE China, therefore prioritized law and left ethics to look after themselves. They called ethics a 'gnawing worm' that would destroy the state. Goodness, they argued, is irrelevant. Morality is bunk. All society requires is obedience. As the most complete legalist spokesman, Han Fei, said in the early third century BCE, 'Benevolence, righteousness, love and generosity are useless, but severe punishments and dire penalties can keep the state in order.' Law and order are worth tyranny and injustice. The only good is the good of state.[71] This was a remarkable new twist: previous thinkers tried to make man-made law more moral by aligning it with 'divine' or 'natural' law. Law-givers, as we have seen, strove to write codes in line with principles of equity (see p. 97). The legalists overthrew tradition. They laughed off earlier sages' belief in the innate goodness of people. For them law served only order, not justice. The best penalties were the most severe: severance at the neck or waist, boring a hole in the skull, roasting alive, filleting out a wrongdoer's ribs or linking horse-drawn chariots to drag at his limbs and literally rend him apart.

The terrors of the times shaped legalism. After generations of disastrous feuding between the Warring States, during which the ethics-based thinking of the Confucians and Taoists did nothing to help, the legalists' ascendancy inflicted so much suffering that in China their doctrines were reviled for centuries. But, born in a time of great civil disaster, their doctrine, or something like it, has resurfaced in bad times ever since. Fascism, for instance, echoes ancient Chinese legalism in advocating and glorifying war, recommending economic self-sufficiency for the state, denouncing capitalism, extolling agriculture above commerce, and insisting on the need to suppress individualism in the interests of state unity.[72]

The legalists had a Western counterpart, albeit a relatively mild one, in Plato. No method of choosing rulers is proof against abuse; but he thought he could deliver his 'objective in the construction of the state: the greatest happiness of the whole, and not that of any one class'. He belonged to an Athenian 'brat pack' of rich, well-educated intellectuals, who resented democracy and felt qualified for power. Some of his friends and relations paid or staffed the death squads that helped keep oligarchs in office. His vocation was for theories of government, not for the bloody business of it, but when he wrote his prescriptions for the ideal state in *The Republic,* they came out harsh, reactionary, and illiberal. Censorship, repression, militarism, regimentation, extreme communism and collectivism, eugenics, austerity, rigid class structure, and active deception of the people by the state were among the objectionable features that had a baneful influence on later thinkers. But they were by the way: Plato's key idea was that all political power should be in the grip of a self-electing class of philosopher-rulers. Intellectual superiority would qualify these 'guardians' for office. Favourable heredity, refined by education in altruism, would make their private lives exemplary and give them a godlike vision of what was good for the citizens. 'There will be no end', Plato predicted, 'to the troubles of states, or indeed, of humanity ... until philosophers become kings in this world, or till those we now call kings and rulers really and truly become philosophers.'[73] The idea that rulers' education in philosophy will make them good is touching. Every teacher is susceptible to similar hubris. I go into every class, convinced that from my efforts to teach them how to unpick medieval palaeography or interpret Mesoamerican epigraphy they will emerge not only with mastery of such arcana, but also with enhanced moral value in themselves. Plato was so persuasive that his reasoning has continued to appeal to state-builders – and, no doubt, their teachers – ever since. His guardians are the prototypes of the elites, aristocracies, party apparatchiks, and self-appointed supermen whose justification for tyrannizing others has always been that they know best.[74]

Optimism and the Enemies of the State

Despite rulers' attraction toward legalism, and the power of Plato's arguments, optimists remained predominant. When Confucius summoned rulers and elites to the allegiance ordained by heaven, he meant that they should defer to the wants and wisdom of the people. 'Heaven', said Mencius, 'sees as the people see and hears as the people hear.'[75] Chinese and Indian thinkers of the time generally agreed that rulers should consult the people's interests and views, and should face, in case of tyranny, the subject's right of rebellion. They did not, however, go on to question the propriety of monarchy. Where the state was meant to reflect the cosmos, its unity could not be compromised.

On the other hand, the obvious way to maximize virtue and prowess in government is to multiply the number of people involved. So republican or aristocratic systems, and even democratic ones, as well as monarchy, had advocates and instances in antiquity. In Greece, where states were judged, unmystically, as practical mechanisms to be adjusted at need, political experiments unfolded in bewildering variety. Aristotle made a magisterial survey of them. He admitted that monarchy would be the best set-up if only it were possible to ensure that the best man were always in charge. Aristocratic government, shared among a manageable number of superior men, was more practical, but vulnerable to appropriation by plutocrats or hereditary cliques. Democracy, in which all the citizens shared, sustained a long, if fluctuating, record of success in Athens from early in the sixth century BCE. Aristotle denounced it as exploitable by demagogues and manipulable into mob rule.[76] In the best system, he thought, aristocracy would predominate, under the rule of law. Broadly speaking, the Roman state of the second half of the millennium embodied his recommendations. It became, in turn, the model for most republican survivals and revivals in Western history. Even when Rome abandoned republican government, and restored what was in effect a monarchical system under the rule of Augustus in 23 BCE, Romans still spoke of the state as a republic and the emperor as merely a 'magistrate' or 'chief' – *princeps* in Latin – of state. Greek and Roman models made republicanism permanently respectable in Western civilization.[77] Medieval city-republics of the Mediterranean imitated ancient Rome, as, in the late eighteenth century, did the United States and revolutionary France. Most new states of the nineteenth century were monarchies, but in the twentieth the spread of the republican ideal became one of the most conspicuous features of politics worldwide. By 1952, an ineradicable anecdote claims, the king of Egypt predicted there would soon be only five monarchs left in the world – and four of those would be in the pack of playing cards.[78]

The most optimistic political thinker of all, perhaps, was Christ, who thought human nature was redeemable by divine grace. He preached a subtle form of political subversion. A new commandment would replace all laws. The kingdom of Heaven mattered more than the empire of Rome. Christ cracked one of history's great jokes when Pharisees tried to tempt him into a political indiscretion by asking whether it was lawful for Jews to pay Roman taxes. 'Render unto Caesar the things which are Caesar's', he said, 'and unto God the things which are God's.' We have lost the sense of what made this funny. Every regime has taken it literally, and used it to justify tax demands. Charles I of England, fighting fiscally recalcitrant rebels, had 'Give Caesar His Due' embroidered on his battle flag. But Christ's auditors would have been rolling around, clutching their vitals in mirth at our Lord's rabbinical humour. To a Jew of Christ's day, nothing was properly Caesar's. Everything belonged to God. In denouncing taxes, and implying the illegitimacy of the Roman state, Christ was being characteristically demagogic. He welcomed outcasts, prostitutes, sinners, Samaritans, whom Christ's compatriots disdained, and tax collectors – the lowest form of life in his audience's eyes. He showed a bias toward the marginalized, the suffering, children, the sick, the lame, the blind, prisoners, and all the deadbeats and dropouts hallowed in the Beatitudes. With revolutionary violence, he lashed moneylenders and expelled them from the temple of Jerusalem. It is not surprising, against the background of this radical kind of politics, that Roman and Jewish authorities combined to put him to death. He was clear about where his political sympathies lay, but his message transcended politics. His followers turned away from political activism to espouse what I think was genuinely his main proposal: personal salvation in a kingdom not of this world.

Slavery

The antiquity of slavery as an institution is unfathomable. Most societies have practised slavery; many have depended on it and have regarded it – or some very similar system of forced labour – as entirely normal and morally unchallengeable. Our own society is anomalous in formally abjuring it, typical in perpetuating it in sweatshops and brothels and in the abuse of the labour of 'illegal' immigrants who are not free to change their jobs or challenge their conditions of work. Not even Christ questioned it, though he did promise that there would be neither bond nor free in heaven; Paul, the posthumously selected apostle, confided a missionary role to a slave, whose master was not obliged to free him, only to treat him as a beloved brother. Slavery is standard. Aristotle, however, did introduce a new idea about how to justify it. He saw the tension between enforced servility and such values as the independent worth of every human being and the moral value of happiness. But some people, he argued, are inherently inferior; for them, the best lot in life is to serve their betters. If natural inferiors resisted conquest, for instance, Greeks could capture and enslave them. In the course of developing the idea, Aristotle also formulated a doctrine of just war: some societies regarded war as normal, or even as an obligation of nature or the gods. Aristotle, however, rated wars as just if the victims of aggression were inferior people who ought to be ruled by their aggressors. At least this teaching made war a subject of moral scrutiny, but that would be little consolation to the victims of it.[79]

While slavery was unquestioned, Aristotle's doctrine seemed irrelevant; masters could admit, without prejudice to their own interests, that their slaves were their equals in everything except legal status. Jurists exhumed Aristotle's argument, however, in an attempt to respond to critics of the enslavement of Native Americans. 'Some men', wrote the Scots jurist John Mair in 1513, 'are by nature slaves and others by nature free. And it is just ... and fitting that one man should be master and another obey, for the quality of superiority is also inherent in the natural master.'[80] Because anyone who was a slave had to be classified as inferior, the doctrine proved to be a stimulus to racism.[81]

Chapter 5

Thinking Faiths

Ideas in a Religious Age

Religion should make you good, shouldn't it? It should transform your life. People who tell you it has transformed them sometimes talk about being born again. But when you look at the way they behave, the effects often seem minimal. Religious people, on average, seem to be as capable of wickedness as everyone else. I am assiduous in going to church, but I do little else that is virtuous. Inasmuch as religion is a device for improving people, why doesn't it work?

The answer to that question is elusive. I am sure, however, that while religion may not change our behaviour as much as we would like, it does affect the way we think. This chapter is about the great religions of the 1,500 years or so after the death of Christ: in particular, how innovative thinkers explored the relationship between reason, science, and revelation, and what they had to say about the problem of the relationship of religion to everyday life – what, if anything, it can do to make us good.

'Great religions' for present purposes are those that have transcended their cultures of origin to reach across the globe. Most religion is culturally specific and incapable of appealing to outsiders. So we have to begin by trying to understand why Christianity and Islam (and to a lesser extent Buddhism) have bucked the norm and demonstrated remarkable elasticity. We start with how they overcame early restraints.

Christianity, Islam, Buddhism: Facing the Checks

New religions opened the richest areas for new thinking: Christianity – new at the start of the period – and Islam, which appeared in the seventh century after Christ. Similar problems arose in both. Both owed a lot to Judaism. The disciples Christ acquired during his career as a freelance rabbi were Jews; he told a Samaritan woman that 'salvation comes from the Jews'; references to Jewish scriptures saturated his recorded teachings; his followers saw him as the Messiah whom Jewish prophets foretold and the Gospel writers reflected the prophecies in their versions of his life. Muhammad was not a Jew but he spent a formative part of his life alongside Jews; traditions locate him in Palestine, where, in Jerusalem, he made his storied ascent to heaven; every page of the Qur'an – the revelations an angel whispered into his ear – shows Jewish (and, to a lesser extent, Christian) influence. Christians and Muslims adopted key ideas of Judaism: the uniqueness of God and creation from nothing.[1]

Both religions, however, modified Jewish ethics: Christianity, by replacing law with grace as the means of salvation; Islam, by substituting laws of its own. While Christians thought Jewish tradition was too legalistic and tried to slim down or cut out the rules from religion, Muhammad had the idea of putting them back in, centrally. Reconfigured relationships between law and religion were among the consequences in both traditions. Christians and Muslims, moreover, came to occupy lands in and around the heartlands of Greek and Roman antiquity. A long series of debates followed about how to blend Jewish traditions with those of classical Greek and Roman learning, including the science and philosophies of the last chapter.

For Christians and Muslims alike, the social context made the task harder. Sneerers condemned Christianity as a religion of slaves and women, suitable only for victims of social exclusion. During Christianity's first two centuries, high-ranking converts faced a kind of derogation. The Gospels gave Christ divine and royal pedigrees, but insisted at the same time on the humility of his birth and of his human calling. He chose co-adjutors from among walks of life, lowly or despised, of provincial fishermen, fallen women, and – at what for

Jews at the time were even lower levels of degradation and moral pollution – tax-gatherers and collaborators with the Roman Empire. The vulgar language of Christians' holy books inhibited communication with the erudite. Early Islam faced similar problems in gaining respect among the elite in seventh-century Arabia. Muhammad came from a prosperous, urban, mercantile background, but he marginalized himself, excluding himself from the company of his own kind by embracing exile in the desert and adopting ascetic practices and a prophetic vocation. It was not in the civilized streets of Mecca and Medina that he found acceptance, but out among the nomadic Bedouin whom city dwellers despised. It took a long time for Christianity to become intellectually estimable. The talents and education of the Gospel writers invited learned contempt. Even the author of the Gospel of St John, who injected impressive intellectual content into the rather humdrum narratives of his predecessors, could not command the admiration of pedantic readers.

'The folly of God', said St Paul, 'is wiser than the wisdom of men.' Paul's writings – copious and brilliant as they were – came with embarrassing disfigurements, especially in the form of long sequences of participle phrases such as sophisticated rhetoricians abhorred. Despite being the most educated of the apostles, he was intellectually unimpressive to the snobs of his day and even of ours: when I was a boy, my teacher indicated my inept use of participles in Greek prose composition by writing a π for 'Pauline' in the margin. To a classically educated mind, the Old Testament was even more crudely embarrassing. In the pope's scriptorium in late-fourth-century Rome, Jerome, a fastidious, aristocratic translator, found the 'rudeness' of the prophets repellent, and the elegance of the pagan classics alluring. In a vision, he told Christ he was a Christian. 'You lie', said Christ. 'You are a follower of Cicero.'[2] Jerome vowed never to read good books again. When he translated the Bible into Latin (in the version that has remained the standard text of the Catholic Church to this day), he deliberately chose a vulgar, streetwise style, much inferior to the classical Latin he used and recommended in his own letters. At about the same time St Augustine found many classical texts distastefully erotic. 'But for this we should never have understood these words: the "golden shower", crotch, deceit.'[3]

The pagan elite, meanwhile, succumbed to Christianity almost as if a change of religion were a change of fashion in the unstable culture of the late Roman Empire, where neither the old gods nor the old learning seemed able to arrest economic decline or avert political crises.[4] Classical literature was too good to exclude from the curriculum, as St Basil acknowledged: 'into the life eternal the Holy Scriptures lead us ... But ... we exercise our spiritual perceptions upon profane writings, which are not altogether different, and in which we perceive the truth as it were in shadows and in mirrors',[5] and schoolboys were never entirely spared from the rigours of a classical education. Two hundred years after Jerome and Augustine, the turnaround in values, at least, was complete: Pope Gregory the Great denounced the use of the classics in teaching, since 'there is no room in the same mouth for both Christ and Jupiter'.[6] In the thirteenth century, followers of St Francis, who enjoined a life of poverty, renounced learning on the grounds that it was a kind of wealth: at least, so some of them said, though in practice they became stalwarts of the universities that were just beginning to organize Western learning at the time.

From the eleventh century onward, at least, a similar trend affected Islam, extolling popular wisdom and mystical insights above classical philosophy, 'abstract proofs and systematic classification ... Rather', wrote al-Ghazali, one of the great Muslim apologists for mysticism, 'belief is a light God bestows ... sometimes through an explainable conviction from within, sometimes by a dream, sometimes through a pious man ... sometimes through one's own state of bliss.'[7] The followers Muhammad gathered in his day, al-Ghazali pointed out, knew little and cared less about the classical logic and learning that later Muslim philosophers appreciated so admiringly.

In all these cases, it was an easy and obviously self-indulgent irony for learned men to affect mistrust of erudition; but their rhetoric had real effects, some of which were bad: to this day in the Western world you hear philistinism commended on grounds of honesty, and stupidity applauded for innocence or 'authenticity'. In Western politics, ignorance is no impediment. Some shorter-term effects of the turn towards popular wisdom were good: in the Middle Ages in Europe, jesters could always tell home truths to rulers and challenge society with satire.[8]

Meanwhile, the spread of the third great global faith, Buddhism, stuttered and stopped. One of the great unanswered questions is, 'Why?' In the third century BCE, when Buddhist scriptures were codified, Ashoka's empire (where, as we have seen, Buddhism was in effect the state religion) might have become a springboard for further expansion, just as the Roman Empire was for Christianity or the caliphate of the seventh and eighth centuries for Islam. During what we think of as the early Middle Ages, when Christendom and Islam stretched to gigantic proportions, Buddhism demonstrated similar elasticity. It became the major influence on the spirituality of Japan. It colonized much of South-East Asia. It acquired a huge following in China, where some emperors favoured it so much that it might have taken over the Chinese court and become an imperial religion in the world's mightiest state. Yet nothing of the sort happened. In China, Taoist and Confucian establishments kept Buddhism at bay. Buddhist clergy never captured the lasting allegiance of states, except eventually in relatively small, marginal places such as Burma, Thailand, and Tibet. Elsewhere, Buddhism continued to make big contributions to culture, but in much of India and parts of Indochina, Hinduism displaced or confined it, while in the rest of Asia, wherever new religions successfully challenged pagan traditions, Christianity and Islam grew where Buddhism stagnated or declined. Not until the late sixteenth century, thanks to the patronage of a Mongol khan, did Buddhism resume expansion in Central Asia.[9] Only in the twentieth century (for reasons we shall come to in their place) did it compete with Christianity and Islam worldwide.

The story of this chapter is therefore a Christian and Muslim story. It is Christian more than Muslim, because in the long run Christianity demonstrated greater cultural adaptability – greater flexibility in self-redefinition to suit different peoples at different times in different places. Islam, as apologists usually present it, is a way of life with strong prescriptions about society, politics, and law – highly suitable for some societies but unworkable in others. Recent migrations have extended the reach of Islam to previously untouched regions; in the case of North America, the rediscovery of their supposed Islamic roots by some people of slave ancestry has helped. For most of its past, however, Islam was largely confined to a fairly limited belt of the Old World, in a region of somewhat consistent cultures and environments, from the edges of the temperate zone of the northern hemisphere to the tropics.[10] Christianity is less prescriptive. Its more malleable code is better equipped to penetrate just about every kind of society in just about every habitable environment. Each adjustment has changed Christian tradition, admitting or arousing many new ideas.

Redefining God: The Unfolding of Christian Theology

The first task, or one of the first, for religious people who want to extend their creed's appeal is to propose a believable God, adjusted to the cultures of potential converts. Followers of Christ and Muhammad represented their teachings as divine: in Christ's case because he was God, in Muhammad's because God privileged him as the definitive prophet. Yet, if they were to grow and endure, both religions had to respond to earlier, pagan traditions, and win over elites schooled in classical learning. Both, therefore, faced the problem of reconciling immutable and unquestionable scriptures with other guides to truth, especially reason and science.

For Christian thinkers, the task of defining doctrine was especially demanding, because Christ, unlike Muhammad, left no writings of his own. The Acts of the Apostles and the letters that form most of the subsequent books of the New Testament show orthodoxy struggling for utterance: was the Church Jewish or universal? Was its doctrine confided to all the apostles or only some? Did Christians earn salvation, or was it conferred by God irrespective of personal virtue? Most religions misleadingly present adherents with a checklist of doctrines, which they usually ascribe to an authoritative founder, and invite or defy dissent. In reality, however – and manifestly in the case of Christianity – heresy normally comes first: orthodoxy is refined out of competing opinions.[11]

Some of the most contentious issues in early Christianity concerned the nature of God: a successful formula had to fit in God's three Persons, designated by the terms Father, Son, and Holy Spirit, without violating monotheism. Fudge was one way of getting round the problems, as in the creed of St Athanasius, which most Christians still endorse and which bafflingly defines the Persons of the Trinity as 'not three incomprehensibles but ... one incomprehensible'. On the face of it, other Christian doctrines of God seem equally inscrutable and absurd: that He should have, or in some sense be, a Son, born of a virgin; that the Son should be both fully God and fully human; that He should be omnipotent, yet self-sacrificing, and perfect, yet subject to suffering; that His sacrifice should be unique in time and yet perpetual; that He should have truly died and yet survived death; and that His earthly presence, in flesh and blood, should be embodied in the Church. Theologians took a long time to work out appropriate formulae that are consistent and, to most minds, on most of the contentious points, reasonable. The Gospel writers and St Paul seem to have sensed that Christ participated, in a profound and peculiar way, in the nature of God. St John's Gospel does not just tell the story of a human son of God or even of a man who represented God to perfection, but of the incarnate Logos: the thought or reason that existed before time began. Sonhood was a metaphor expressing the enfleshment of incorporeal divinity. But early Christians' efforts to explain this insight were ambiguous, vague, or clouded by affected mystery. Over the next two or three centuries, by making the incarnation intelligible, theology equipped Christianity with a God who was appealing (because human), sympathetic (because suffering), and convincing (because exemplified in everyone's experience of human contact, compassion, and love).

To understand how they did it, context helps. Christianity is definable as the religion that claims a particular, historic person as God incarnate. But the idea that a god might take flesh was well known for thousands of years before the time of Christ. Ancient shamans 'became' the gods whose attributes they donned. Egyptian pharaohs were gods, in the peculiar sense we have seen (see p. 93). Myths of divine kings and gods in human guise are common. The Buddha was more than human in the opinion of some of his followers: enlightenment elevated him to transcendence. Anthropologists with a sceptical attitude to Christianity, from Sir James Frazer in the nineteenth century to Edmund Leach in the late twentieth, have found scores of cases of incarnation, often culminating in a sacrifice of the man-god similar to Christ's own.[12] In the fourth century, a comparable Hindu idea surfaced: Vishnu had various human lives, encompassing conception, birth, suffering, and death. Islamic (or originally Islamic) sects, especially in Shiite traditions, have sometimes hailed Ali as a divine incarnation or adopted imams or heroes in the same role.[13] The Druzes of Lebanon hail as the living Messiah the mad eleventh-century Caliph al-Hakim, who called himself an incarnation of God. The Mughal emperor Akbar focused worship on himself in the religion he devised in the sixteenth century in an attempt to reconcile the feuding faiths of his realm.

So how new was the Christian idea? If it was ever unique, did it remain so?

In all the rival cases, as in the many reincarnations of gods and Buddhas that strew the history of South, East, and Central Asia, a spirit 'enters' a human body – variously before, at, and after birth. But in the Christian idea, the body itself was divinized: outside Christian tradition, all recorded incarnations either displace humanity from the divinized individual, or invest him or her with a parallel, godly nature. In Christ, on the other hand, human and divine natures fused, without mutual distinction, in one person. 'The Word was made flesh and dwelt among us', in the memorable formula of the opening chapter of St John's Gospel, 'and we have seen His glory ... full of grace and truth'.

Orthodox Christian theology has always insisted on this formula against heretics who want to make Christ merely divine, or merely human, or to keep his human and divine natures separate. The doctrine really is peculiarly Christian – which is why the Church has fought so hard to preserve it. The idea has inspired imitators: a constant stream of so-called Messiahs claimed the same attributes or were credited with them by their supporters. But the Christian understanding of the incarnation of God seems to be an un-recyclable idea. Since Christ, no claimant has ever convinced large numbers of people, all over the world.[14]

In the long run, Christian theologians were remarkably successful in alloying Jewish wisdom, which had percolated through Christianity's long pedigree, with ancient Greek and Roman ideas, crafting reasonable religion, which tempered the hard, brittle God of the Old Testament – remote, judgemental, 'jealous', and demanding – with supple philosophizing. The outcome encumbered the Church with one big disadvantage: a perplexingly complex theology, which excludes those who do not understand it and divides those who do. In the early fourth century, a council of bishops and theologians, under the chairmanship of a Roman emperor, devised a formula for overcoming that problem, or, at least, an idea which, without solving all the problems, established the framework in which they all had to fit. The Council of Nicaea formulated the creed to which most communities that call themselves Christian still subscribe. Its word for the relationship of Father and Son was homoousion, traditionally translated as 'consubstantial' and rather inaccurately rendered in some modern translations as 'of one being' or 'of one nature'. The formula ruled out suggestions that might weaken the Christian message: for instance, that Christ was God only in some metaphorical sense; or that his sonship should be taken literally; or that his humanity was imperfect or his suffering illusory. Christians continued to disagree about how the Holy Spirit should fit into the picture; but the homoousion idea effectively fixed the limits of debate on that issue, too. The shared identity of Father and Son had to embrace the Holy Spirit. 'The Divine Word', as Pope Dionysius had said in the late third century, 'must be one with the God of the Universe and the Holy Spirit must abide and dwell in God, and so it is necessary that the Divine Trinity be gathered and fused in unity.'[15]

Who thought of the homoousion idea? The word was one of many bandied about among theologians of the period. According to surviving accounts of the Council, the Roman emperor, Constantine, made the decision to adopt it officially and incontrovertibly. He called himself 'apostle-like' and, at his own insistence, presided over the council. He was a recent, theologically illiterate convert to Christianity. But he was an expert power broker who knew a successful negotiating formula when he saw one.

Preachers echoed the theologians, elaborating folksy images of the inseparably single nature of the persons of the Trinity. The most famous were St Patrick's shamrock – one plant, three leaves; one nature, three persons – and the clay brick, made of earth, water, and fire, that St Spyridon crushed in the sight of his congregation. It miraculously dissolved into its constituent elements. Most Christians have probably relied on such homely images for making sense of convoluted doctrines.[16]

Religions as Societies: Christian and Muslim Ideas

Theological subtleties, on the whole, do not put bums on seats. Most people do not rate intellect highly and do not, therefore, demand intellectually convincing religions: rather, they want a sense of belonging. Christ provided the Church with a way of responding. At supper on the eve of his death he left his fellow-diners with the idea that collectively they could perpetuate his presence on Earth. According to a tradition reliably recorded by St Paul soon after the event, and repeated in the Gospels, he suggested that he would be present in flesh and blood whenever his followers met to share a meal of bread and wine. In two ways the meal signified the founder's perpetual embodiment. First, in worship, the body and blood of Christ, respectively broken and spilled, were reunified when shared and ingested. Second, the members of the Church represented themselves as the body of Christ, spiritually reconstituted. He was, as he said, 'with you always' in the consecrated bread and in those who shared it.[17] 'As there is one bread', in St Paul's way of putting it, 'so we, although there are many of us, are one single body, for we all share in the one bread.' This was a new way of keeping a sage's tradition alive. Previously sages had nominated or adopted key initiates as privileged custodians of doctrine, or, in the case of the Jews, custodianship belonged to an entire but strictly limited 'chosen people'.

Christ used both these methods for transmitting teachings: he confided his message to a body of apostles, whom he selected, and to Jewish congregations who regarded him as the long-prophesied Messiah. Over the course of the first few Christian generations, however, the religion embraced increasing numbers of Gentiles. A new model was needed: that of the Church, which embodied Christ's continuing presence in the world and which spoke with his authority. Leaders, called overseers or (to use the anglicized word that means the same thing) bishops, were chosen by 'apostolic succession' to keep the idea of a tradition of apostleship alive. Rites of baptism, meanwhile, which guaranteed a place among God's elect (literally those chosen for salvation), sustained in Christian communities a sense of belonging to a chosen people. After the Romans destroyed the temple of Jerusalem in 70 CE, Christians strengthened their claim as stewards of Jewish tradition by adopting many of the temple rites of sacrifice: in some ways, you get more of a sense of what ancient Jewish worship was like in an old-fashioned church than in a modern synagogue.

In terms of appeal and durability, the Church has been one of the most successful institutions in the history of the world, surviving persecution from without and schisms and shortcomings from within. So the idea worked. But it was problematic. Baptism as a guarantee of preferential treatment in the eyes of God is hard to reconcile with the notion, equally Christian, or more so, of a universally benign deity who desires salvation for everybody. Theoretically, the Church was the united body of Christ; in practice Christians were always divided over how to interpret his will. Schismatics challenged and rejected efforts to preserve consensus. Many of the groups that seceded from the Church from the time of the Reformation onwards questioned or modified the notion of collective participation in sacraments of unity, sidestepping the Church with direct appeals to scripture, or emphasizing individual relationships with God, or insisting that the real Church consisted of the elect known to him alone.

In some ways, Islam's alternative seems more attractive to potential converts from most forms of paganism. A simple device, uncluttered with Christians' complicated theology and cumbersome creeds, signifies Muslims' common identity: the believer makes a one-line profession of faith and performs a few simple, albeit demanding, rituals. But demanding rites constitute encumbrances for Islam: circumcision, for instance, which is customary and, in most Islamic communities, effectively unavoidable, or exigent routines of prayer, or restrictive rules of dietary abstinence. Although Christianity and Islam have been competing on and off for nearly a millennium and a half, it is still too early to say which works better, in terms of ever-widening appeal. Despite phases of stupendous growth, Islam has never yet matched the global range of cultures and natural environments that have nourished Christianity.

Moral Problems

As a toolkit for spreading religion, theology and ecclesiology are incomplete: you also need a system of ethics strong enough to persuade audiences that you can benefit believers and improve the world. Christians and Muslims responded to the challenge in contrasting but effective ways.

Take Christian morals first. St Paul's most radical contribution to Christianity was also his most inspiring and most problematic idea. He has attracted praise or blame for creating or corrupting Christianity. The ways in which he developed doctrine might have surprised Christ.[18] But whether or not he captured his master's real thinking when he expressed the idea of grace (see p. 120), he projected an indelible legacy. God, he thought, grants salvation independently of recipients' deserts. 'It is through grace that you have been saved', he wrote to the Ephesians – not, as he constantly averred, through any merit of one's own. In an extreme form of the doctrine, which Paul seems to have favoured at some times and which the Church has always formally upheld, any good we do is the result of God's favour. 'No distinction is made', Paul wrote to the Romans. 'All have sinned and lack God's glory, and all are justified by the free gift of his grace.'

For some people the idea – or the way Paul puts it, with little or no place for human freedom – is bleak and emasculating. Most, however, find it appealingly liberating. No one can be self-damned by sin. No one is irredeemable if God chooses otherwise. The value of the way a life is lived is calibrated not by external compliance with rules and rites, but by the depth of the individual person's response to grace. A seventeenth-century play (*El condenado por desconfiado*, in which my actor-son once starred at London's National Theatre) by the worldly-wise monk, Tirso de Molina, makes the point vividly: a robber ascends to heaven at the climax, despite the many murders and rapes of which he boasts, because he echoes God's love in loving his own father; my son played the curmudgeonly, religiously scrupulous hermit, who has no trust in God, loves nobody, and is marked for hell. Confidence in grace can, however, be taken too far. 'A man's free will serves only to lead him into sin, if the way of truth be hidden from him',[19] St Augustine pointed out around the turn of the fourth and fifth centuries. St Paul hammered home his claim that God chose the recipients of grace 'before the world was made ... He decided beforehand who were the ones destined ... It was those so destined that He called, those that He called He justified.' This apparently premature decision on God's part makes the world seem pointless. Heretics treated the availability of grace as a licence to do what they liked: if they were in a state of grace, their crimes were no sin but holy and faultless; if not, their iniquities would make no difference to their damnation.

Some of Paul's fellow-apostles disapproved of a doctrine that apparently exonerated Christians from doing good. St James – a contender for leadership in the early Church whom contemporaries or near-contemporaries hailed as 'the Just' and 'the brother' of Christ – issued what modern spin doctors would call a clarification. He (or someone using his name) insisted that to love your neighbour as yourself was an ineluctable rule and that 'faith without deeds is useless'. A long controversy divided those who saw grace as a collaborative venture, in which the individual has an active role, from others, who refused to diminish God's omnipotence and love by conceding any initiative to the sinner. At the Reformation, the latter group dropped out of the Church, citing St Paul in support of their views. Further problems remained. Christ came to redeem sinners at a particular moment in time: so why then? And what about the sinners who missed out by living and dying previously? Even more perplexingly, if God is omniscient, he must know what we are going to do ahead of when we do it. So what becomes of the free will which is supposed to be one of God's precious gifts to us? And if he knew from before time began, as St Paul put it, who was bound for heaven, what about everyone else? How could God be just and righteous if the damned had no real chance of salvation? 'How can He ever blame anyone', St Paul imagined his correspondents asking, 'since no one can oppose His will?' The saint's own answer was chillingly logical: since everyone is sinful, justice demands damnation for all. God shows commendable forbearance by exempting the elect.

Christians who prized God for mercy, not justice, found this solution, which St Augustine approved, forbidding and unloving. A better answer arose by the way, from Augustine's efforts to solve the problem of time. At the end of the fourth century he wrote a remarkable dialogue with his own mind, in the course of which he confessed that he thought he knew what time was 'until anyone asks me'. He never ceased to be tentative on the point, but after much reflection he concluded 'that time is nothing else but a stretching out in length; but of what I know not and I marvel if it be not of the very mind'.[20] Time, Augustine said in effect, was not part of the real world, but what we should now call a mental construct: a way we devise for organizing experience. To understand it, think of a journey: travelling along the ground, you feel as if Washington, DC, or Moscow precedes, say, Kansas City or Berlin, which in turn precedes Austin and LA, or Amsterdam and Paris. From a godlike height, however, where you see the world as it really is, all these destinations appear simultaneously. In *Amadeus*, his play about the life of Mozart, Peter Shaffer imagined God hearing music in a similar fashion: 'millions of sounds ascending at once and mixing in His ear to become an unending music, unimaginable to us'. To God, time is like that: events are not arrayed in sequence. A couple of generations after Augustine, the philosopher Boethius, an old-fashioned Roman senator and bureaucrat in the service of a barbarian king, used the saint's insight to propose a solution to the problem of predestination, while he was in prison, waiting for his employer to put him to death on suspicion of plotting to restore the Roman Empire. God, Boethius appreciated, can see you, on what you think of as today, while you make a free choice on what you think of as tomorrow.

Other efforts at solving the problem have concentrated on separating foreknowledge from predestination. God knows in advance what your free will shall induce you to do. In *Paradise Lost*, John Milton's mid-seventeenth-century attempt 'to justify the ways of God to man', the poet puts into God's mouth a divine explanation of how Adam and Eve's fall was foreseeable, but not foreordained. 'If I foreknew,' says God, 'foreknowledge had no influence on their fault.' Milton's formula seems just about intelligible. In any case, it seems unnecessary to see human freedom as an infringement of God's omnipotence: free will could be a concession he chooses to make but has the power to revoke, like a police chief issuing a 'gun amnesty' or a general authorizing a ceasefire.

Thanks to such mental balancing acts, Christian thinking has always managed to keep free will and predestination in equilibrium between, on the one hand, an idealistic vision of human nature unpolluted by original sin, and, on the other, doom-fraught resignation in the face of inescapable damnation. Even so, extremists on one side or the other are always dropping out of communion with fellow-Christians: the Calvinists split with the Catholics in the sixteenth century and, in the seventeenth, the Arminians with the Calvinists over the scope of free will. Untold controversy over the same problem has riven Islam. As well as echoing all the Christian controversialists who have found ways to fit free will into a world regulated by an omniscient and omnipotent God, Shiites developed the fiercely contested idea of Bada' – the claim that God can change his judgement in favour of a repentant sinner.[21]

Christianity, meanwhile, faced a further high-minded challenge from thinkers intolerant of the world's imperfections. On balance, in the struggle of good and evil, creation seems to be on the Devil's side. When Plato looked on the world, he saw perfection's imperfect shadow. Some of his readers extended the thought beyond its logical conclusion and inferred that the world is bad. Zoroaster, Laozi, and many lesser thinkers of the first millennium BCE thought they could detect good and evil teetering in uneasy, all-encompassing balance across the cosmos – in which case, the sordid, sorrowful world must surely be on the evil side of the scale. Matter is, at best, corruptible; the body is prone to pollution and pain. The Prince of Darkness, in a tradition Jews, Christians, and Muslims shared, made the world his realm by invading Eden and inveigling humankind. It makes sense to see the world, the flesh, and the Devil as an immorally intimate threesome or a nastily discordant triad.[22]

People who thought so around the turn of the first millennium called their belief *gnosis* – literally, 'knowledge'. Christians tried and failed to twist it into the Church, or to chop at the Church to make a niche for gnosis. It was incompatible with the doctrine of the incarnation: the Devil might take flesh, but not God. Bloody, messy extrusion from a womb at one end of life, and coarse, crude crucifixion at the other, were undivine indignities. Just to be in the world was derogation for a pure, spiritual God. 'If any acknowledge the crucified Christ', in words St Irenaeus attributed to the Gnostic leader Basilides, 'he is a slave and subject to the demons who made our bodies.'[23] Gnostics engaged in impressive mental agility to dodge or duck the difficulties: Christ's body was an illusion; he only seemed to be crucified; he did not really suffer on the cross but substituted a scapegoat or a simulacrum. For extreme Gnostics, God could not have created anything as wicked as the world: a 'demiurge' or rival god must have made it. But if God was not a universal creator, he was not himself. If he did not wholly embrace human nature, including the burdens of the body and the strains and sufferings of flesh, Christianity was pointless.

But the Church, while rejecting Gnosticism, retained some Gnostic influence. Catholic tradition has always been fastidious about the body. Ascetic Christians have hated their bodies to the point of mistreating them: punishing them with dirt, scourging them with the lash, starving them with fasting, and irritating them with hair shirts, not just for reasons of discipline but in real revulsion from the flesh. The early Church, which might have encouraged procreation to boost numbers, nourished a surprising prejudice in favour of celibacy, which remains a requirement for a formally religious life. Throughout the Middle Ages, heretics perpetuated the influence of Gnosticism by reviving the prejudice and making it a precept: don't acknowledge the urgings of the flesh; don't engender recruits for the Devil. The cult of martyrdom also seems indebted to Gnostic distaste for the world as a burden and the body a cell for the soul. As Gerard Manley Hopkins put it, 'Man's mounting spirit in his bone-house, mean house, dwells.' Martyrdom is an escape from a prison in which Satan is the warder.

In reaction, mainstream Catholic Christianity emphasized the perception of the body as a temple, of nature as lovely, of sex as selectively sanctified, of martyrdom as unwelcome sacrifice, of celibacy as restricted to the religious life. This surely helps to explain the stunning appeal of a religion that gradually became the most popular in the world.

Nonetheless, an equivocal attitude to sex lingered in Christian tradition. People are equivocal about sex for many reasons: it is best kept private and functional; it activates anxieties about hygiene, health, mess, morals, and social control. But why are some people's objections religious? Fertility obsessions dominate many cults and it is tempting to assert that most religions recommend sex. Some celebrate it, as in Tantric exhortations to supposedly sanctifying copulation or Hindu instructions maximizing the pleasures and varieties of karma, or the Taoist tradition of fang-chungshu, in which 'arts of the inner chamber' confer immortality. Christianity is among religions that condone and even commend physical love under licence as, for instance, a metaphor for the mutual love of God and creation or Christ and the

Church. Almost all religions prescribe conventions for regulating sexual conduct in ways supposedly favourable to the community: this accounts for why so many religions condemn particular sexual practices; masturbation and homosexuality, for instance, attract objections because they are infertile; incest is antisocial; promiscuity and sexual infidelity are objectionable because they subvert institutions, such as marriage, that are designed for the nurture of the young. Conversely, celibacy and virginity may be valued for positive qualities, as sacrifices made to God, rather than in recoil from sex. St Augustine introduced – or at least, clearly formulated – a new objection to sex as such on the grounds that we cannot control our sex urges, which therefore infringe the free will God gave us. So the Devil must be to blame. A modern way of putting it might be to say that because sex is instinctive, and therefore animal, we enhance our humanity when we resist its temptations. In his youth, before his conversion to Catholic Christianity, Augustine had been a Manichaean – a follower of the teaching that all matter is evil. Manichaeans despised reproduction as a means of perpetuating diabolic power and had a correspondingly negative estimation of sex. 'Out of the squalid yearnings of my flesh', reads one of his self-reproaches, 'bubbled up the clouds and scum of puberty ... so that I could not tell the serenity of love from the swamp of lust.'[24] This may be why Western morality has been so heavily preoccupied with sex ever since. It is possible that the Church would in any case have adopted a highly interventionist attitude to people's sex lives: it is, after all, a matter of great importance to most people and therefore of great power to anyone who can control it. The struggle between churches and states in the modern West over who should have the right to license and register marriages might well have happened even if Augustine had never turned his mind to the problem of sex.[25]

In moral thinking, as in most respects, Islam, which literally means something like 'submission' or 'resignation', produced simpler, more practical formulations than Christianity. Christ invited individuals to respond to grace, but Muhammad, more straightforwardly, called them to obey God's laws. He was a ruler as well as a prophet and produced a blueprint for a state as well as a religion. One consequence was that where Christ had proclaimed a sharp distinction between the secular and the spiritual, Muslims acknowledged no difference. Islam was both a way of worship and a way of life. The responsibilities of the caliph – literally, the 'successor' of Muhammad – covered both. Whereas Moses legislated for a chosen people and Christ for an other-worldly kingdom, Muhammad aimed at a universal code of behaviour covering every department of life: the sharia – literally, 'the camel's way to water'. 'We gave you a sharia in religion', he said. 'So follow it and do not follow the passions of those who do not know.' He failed, however, to leave a code that was anything like comprehensive. Schools of jurisprudence, founded by masters of the eighth and ninth centuries, set out to fill in the gaps, starting with such utterances as Muhammad was said to have made in his lifetime, and generalizing from them, with help, in some cases from reason, common sense, or custom. The masters differed, but the followers of each treated his interpretations as divinely guided and therefore immutable. Trainees in each tradition guarded, as zealously as any genealogist, the record of the succession of masters through whom the teachings of the founder were preserved – back, for instance, to Abu Hanifa, who tried to incorporate reason, or bin Malik, who blended in ancient customary law, or Ibn Hanbal, who tried to purge both influences and get to the root of what Muhammad wanted.

The practical problems were as great as in Christendom, but different. Rival approaches had to be reconciled; the opportunities of development that arose in consequence led to hundreds of schisms and sub-divisions. Incompatible methods of electing the caliph cleft Islam between claimants. The rift that opened within a generation of Muhammad's death never healed. Schisms widened and multiplied. Eventually, in most of Islam, rulers or states arrogated caliphal or quasi-caliphal authority to themselves. Whenever they lapsed in observance of the sharia by self-serving practices or, in recent times, by 'modernizing' or 'westernizing tendencies', revolutionaries – with increasing frequency – could impugn 'apostate' rulers by waving the Prophet's mantle as a flag and his book as a weapon.[26] Like any system, sharia has to adapt to changes in social context and consensus – not least today, in an increasingly interconnected world, where common understanding of human rights owes much to Christian and humanist influence. But even Muslims who see the need to reinterpret sharia cannot agree on who should do the job. Theocrats gain power in states that prioritize Islam in making and enforcing laws; Islamist movements or terrorist fanatics menace modernizers.

Aesthetic Reflections by Christian and Muslim Thinkers

Christians and Muslims inherited revulsion from 'graven images' along with the rest of Jewish law. They differed about how to respond. Codes the Bible dated to the time of Moses proscribed religious imagery on the grounds that God is too holy or too remote from what is knowable even to be named, let alone represented. Idolatry, moreover, in some minds, is incompatible with the unity of God: even if he alone is represented, the worship of several images of him compromises his unique status. This may be one of the reasons why Jews, who have been eminent in so many learned and aesthetic accomplishments, are less well represented in visual arts than in music or letters.

If sayings ascribed to him after his death can be trusted, part of what Muhammad took from Jewish teachers was a perception of statues as abominable. Supposedly, he threatened image makers with reckoning on the Day of Judgement. Early Islam did not, however, oppose all representational art. Realistic pictures adorn an early caliph's hunting lodge, where you can still see the somewhat lubricious scenes of naked women that entertained Walid I in his bath.[27] In the tenth century, Abu 'Ali al-Farisi turned back to the unglossed Qur'an to interpret Muhammad's supposed strictures accurately, as prohibiting images of deities in order to forestall idolatry, not to ban all depictions of the natural world and its creatures. In some medieval Muslim art, notably in surviving fourteenth-century paintings from Iran, Muhammad appears in person in scenes of his life, including his birth, unmistakably modelled on the Christian iconography of the nativity of Christ. In a manuscript of Rashid al-Din's Universal History, made in Tabriz in 1307, the angels croon over little Muhammad, while magi bow and Joseph hovers discreetly in his place.[28] Most Muslims, however, acknowledged realism as sacrilege; Muslim artists, in consequence, have tended to stick to nonrepresentational subjects.

Christians might have taken the same line: indeed, sometimes, in some places, they did so. In Byzantium in 726 the emperor Leo III, who still claimed nominal authority throughout Christendom, banned images of Christ and the Virgin and ordered existing examples to be destroyed – perhaps in literal-minded response to biblical prohibitions, perhaps in order to protect worshippers from the heresy that Christ's human person could be depicted apart from his divine nature. In the twelfth century in the West, rival monastic orders bickered over whether artworks were a good use of the Church's money. In the sixteenth and seventeenth centuries, some Protestants destroyed or defaced every image they could reach, while others merely outlawed practices they linked with 'that most detestable offence of idolatry' – such as kissing images or offering them candles or ex-votos. Most Christians, however, have been content with common sense: images are useful, as long as they do not become idols. Pictures function as aids to devotion in a way similar to that of relics. They can even be relics. The most precious relic of the medieval cathedral of Constantinople was a portrait of the Virgin 'not made with human hands' but painted by an angel for St Luke while he rested.[29] Under-educated congregations in Western churches could remedy illiteracy by looking at paintings on the walls – the 'books of the unlettered', which made the deeds of the inhabitants of heaven memorable. Because 'the honour paid to the image passes to the original', worshippers could, without idolatry, channel adoration and reverence through pictures and sculptures.[30] The argument anticipated by Plotinus, the third-century philosopher who seems to have revered Plato more than Christ, was unanswerable: 'Those who look on art ... are deeply stirred by recognizing the presentation of what lies in the idea, and so are called to recognition of the truth – the very experience out of which Love rises.'[31]

Such thinking made the Church the biggest patron of art in Christendom – almost the only source for much of the time. Medieval artists took part, in a small way, in the nature of priests and saints, for they brought people to a sense of what heaven was like and of how its inhabitants enhanced the Earth. No work of St Relindis of Maaseik survives, but the embroideries she made in the eighth century were inspired enough for sanctity. The tombstone of Petrus Petri, the chief architect of the cathedral of Toledo, assures onlookers that 'thanks to the admirable building he made, he will not feel God's wrath'. St Catherine of Bologna and Blessed James Grissinger were subjects of popular devotion long before their formal elevation. When Franciscan artists began to paint landscape in the thirteenth century, devotion, not romanticism, inspired them. To glorify God by depicting creation was a purpose almost inconceivable to a Muslim or Jew.

Expanding Faith's Intellectual Frontiers

Equipped with practical ethics, a believable God, and coherent ways of representing him, Christians and Muslims still had to face major intellectual difficulties: fitting their religions into potentially rival systems, such as science and personal faith in individuals' religious experience; adjusting them to diverse and mutable political contexts; and working out strategies of evangelization in a violent world where hearts and minds are more susceptible to coercion than conviction. We can look at how they coped with each of these tasks in turn.

Christian thinkers' synthesis of classical and Jewish ideas seems to have reached a tipping point after 325, when the Church proclaimed the doctrine of homoousion or consubstantiality – the essential sameness – of Father and Son. The social and intellectual respectability of Christianity became unquestionable, except by pagan diehards. The elite produced ever increasing numbers of converts. Emperor Julian 'the apostate', who struggled to reverse the trend, died in 363, allegedly conceding victory to Christ. By the time of the definitive adoption of Christianity as the emperors' only religion in 380, paganism seemed provincial and old-fashioned. In the mounting chaos of the fifth century, however, the world in which Christ and the classics met seemed under threat. Religious zealots menaced the survival of ancient secular learning. So did barbarian incursions, the withdrawal of traditional elites from public life, the impoverishment and abandonment of the old pagan educational institutions. In China in the third century BCE compilers instructed invaders. So the Roman world needed compendia of the wisdom of antiquity to keep learning alive under siege.

Boethius, whom we have met as a mediator of Augustine's views on time and predestination, and who never even alluded to the differences between pagan and Christian thinking, produced a vital contribution: his guide – a duffer's guide, one could almost say – to Aristotle's logic. Throughout the Middle Ages, it remained the prime resource for Christian thinkers, who gradually embellished it and made it ever more complicated. About a hundred years after Boethius, St Isidore of Seville compiled scientific precepts from ancient sources that were in danger of extinction. With successive enhancements, his work fed into that of Christian encyclopaedists for the following thousand years. In the parts of the Roman Empire that Muslims conquered over the next hundred years or so, the survival of classical culture seemed doomed, at first, to obliteration by desert-born fanatics. But Muslim leaders rapidly recognized the usefulness of existing elites and of the learning they wielded from the Greek and Roman past. In Islam, therefore, scholars collected and collated texts and passed them on to Christian counterparts. Part of the effect was the 'Renaissance' of the twelfth and thirteenth centuries in the West, when exchanges between Christendom and Islam were prolific. Renewed contacts, meanwhile, by way of trade and travel across the steppes, Silk Roads, and monsoonal corridors of Eurasia, enriched thinking as in the first millennium BCE.

In consequence, some Christian and Muslim thinkers of the time were so familiar with the reason and science of antiquity that they naturally thought of secular and religious learning not just as compatible but also mutually reflective and symbiotic. Two examples will have to do service as illustrations of what became possible in the West. Consistently with the sentiments of our own times, Peter Abelard is now most celebrated for his love affair with his pupil Heloise; they exchanged some of the most moving letters that survive from the Middle Ages. He was lesser in love than his paramour, whose letters – painful in their despair, mild in their reproaches, candid in their sentiments – record moving insights into how affective feelings trump conventional morals. In logic, however, Abelard was insuperable. Castration by the outraged uncle confined him to a teacher's proper sphere, while Heloise became an ornament of the religious life. He exposed tensions between reason and religion in a stunning set of paradoxes: the evident purpose of his long, self-exculpatory preface is that, with proper humility and caution, students can identify errors in apparently venerable traditions. Abelard's older contemporary St Anselm also recorded thoughts about God, using reason as his only guide, without having to defer to Scripture or to tradition or to the authority of the Church. He is often credited with 'proving' the existence of God, but that was not his purpose. Rather, he helped to show that belief in God is reasonable. He vindicated Catholicism's claim that divinely conferred powers of reason make God discoverable. He started from Aristotle's assumption that ideas must originate in perceptions of realities – an assumption that other thinkers questioned but which is at least stimulating: if you have an idea unsampled in experience, where do you get it from? Anselm's argument, as simply – perhaps excessively so – as I can put it, was that absolute perfection, if you can imagine it, must exist, because if it did not, you could imagine a degree of perfection that exceeds it – which is impossible. In much of the rest of his work, Anselm went on to show that God, if he does exist, is intelligible as Christian teaching depicts him: human, loving, suffering. It bears thinking about: if God's nature is not human and suffering, why is the human condition so tortured, and the world as wicked as it is?

There were Christian thinkers who were equally brilliant at making Christianity rational and scientific. The century and a half after the period of Anselm and Abelard was a vibrant time of scientific and technological innovation in western Europe. Towards the end of the period, St Thomas Aquinas, sticking to reason as a guide to God, summed up the learning of the age with amazing range and clarity.[32] Among his demonstrations that the existence of God is a reasonable hypothesis, none resonated in later literature more than his claim that creation is the best explanation for the existence of the natural world. Critics have oversimplified his doctrine to the point of absurdity, supposing that he thought that everything that exists must have a cause. Really, he said the opposite: that nothing would exist at all if everything real has to be contingent, as our existence, say, is contingent on that of the parents who engendered and bore us. There must be an uncreated reality, which might be the universe itself, but which might equally well be prior to and beyond contingent nature. We can call it God.

Like Anselm, Aquinas was more concerned with understanding what God might be like once we acknowledge the possibility that the deity exists. In particular, he confronted the problem of how far the laws of logic and science could extend into the realm of a creator. He bound God's omnipotence in thongs of logic when he decided there were some things God could not do, because they were incompatible with divine will. God could not, for instance, make illogicalities logical or inconsistencies consistent. He could not command evil. He could not change the rules of arithmetic so as to make two times three equal anything other than six. He could not extinguish himself. Or at least, perhaps, if theoretically he could do such things, he would not, because he wants us to use his gifts of reason and science and – while allowing us liberty to get things wrong – will never delude us or subvert truths of his own making. Aquinas insisted that 'what is divinely taught to us by faith cannot be contrary to what we learn by nature: ... since we have both from God, He would be the cause of our error, which is impossible'.[33]

Aquinas was part of what can properly be called a scientific movement – perhaps even a scientific revolution or renaissance – in high-medieval Europe. He followed the precepts of one of its luminaries – his own teacher, St Albertus Magnus, whose statue stares from the door-frame of a science building at my university and who claimed that God worked primarily by and through scientific laws, or 'natural causes' in the terminology of the time. Empiricism was all the rage, perhaps because intensified cultural exchange with Islam reintroduced texts of Aristotle and other scientifically minded ancients, and perhaps because renewed contacts with China, thanks to exceptionally peaceful conditions in central Asia, restored the circumstances of the last great age of Western empiricism in the mid-first millennium BCE, when, as we have seen (p. 140), trans-Eurasian routes were busy with traders, travellers, and warriors. Confidence in experimentation verged on or even veered beyond the absurd in the mid-thirteenth century, as the work of Frederick II, ruler of Germany and Sicily, shows. He was a science buff of an extreme kind and the most relentless experimenter of the age. Investigating the effects of sleep and exercise on the digestion, he had – so it was said – two men disembowelled. Entering a debate about the nature of humans' 'original' or 'natural' language, he had children brought up in silence 'in order to settle the question ... But he labored in vain', said a contemporary narrator, writing more, perhaps, for éclat than enlightenment, 'because all the children died.'[34]

Parisian teachers in the third quarter of the thirteenth century developed a sort of theology of science. Nature was God's work; science, therefore, was a sacred obligation, disclosing the wonder of creation, and therefore unveiling God. An inescapable question was therefore whether science and reason, when they were in agreement, trumped scripture or tradition or the authority of the Church as a means of disclosing God's mind. Siger of Brabant and Boethius of Dacia, colleagues at the University of Paris, who collaborated in the 1260s and 1270s, pointed out that the doctrines of the Church on the creation and the nature of the soul were in conflict with classical philosophy and empirical evidence. 'Every disputable question', they argued, 'must be determined by rational arguments.' The proposition was both compelling and disturbing. Some thinkers – at least according to critics who damned or derided them – took refuge in an evasive idea: 'double truth', according to which things true in faith could be false in philosophy and vice versa. In 1277 the Bishop of Paris, taking the opportunity to interfere in the business of the university, condemned this doctrine (along with a miscellany of magic, superstition, and quotations from Muslim and pagan authors).[35]

Meanwhile, another professor at the University of Paris, Roger Bacon, was serving the cause of science by condemning excessive deference to authority – including ancestral wisdom, custom, and consensus – as a cause of ignorance. Experience, by contrast, was a reliable source of knowledge. Bacon was a Franciscan friar, whose enthusiasm for science was linked, perhaps, with St Francis's rehabilitation of nature: the world was worth observing, because it made 'the lord of all creatures' manifest. Bacon insisted that science could help to validate scripture or improve our understanding of sacred texts. Medical experiments, he pointed out, could increase knowledge and save life. He even claimed that science could cow and convert infidels, citing the examples of the lenses with which Archimedes set fire to a Roman fleet during the siege of Syracuse.

Friars may seem odd heralds of a scientific dawn. But St Francis himself, properly understood, can hardly be bettered as an instance. Superficial students and devotees look at him and see only a man of faith so intense and complete as to make reason seem irrelevant and evidence otiose. His irrationality was theatrical. He turned his renunciation of possessions into a performance when he stripped naked in the public square of his native town. He preached to ravens to display his discontent with human audiences. He abjured great wealth to be a beggar. He affected the role of an anti-intellectual, denouncing learning as a kind of riches and a source of pride. He acted the holy fool. He proclaimed a faith so otherworldly that knowledge of this world could be of no help. On the other hand, nature really mattered to Francis. He opened his eyes – and ours – to the godliness of God's creation, even the apparently crude, sometimes squalid blear and smear of the world and the creatures in it. His contribution to the history of sensibilities alerted us to the wonder of all things bright and beautiful: the loveliness of landscape, the potential of animals, the fraternity of the sun and the sorority of the moon. His scrupulous, realistic image of nature was part of the scientific trend of his time. Observation and understanding mattered to him as to the scientists. You can see Francis's priorities in the art he inspired: the realism of the paintings Franciscans made or commissioned for their churches, the new sense of landscape that fills backgrounds formerly smothered with gilding, the scenes of sacred history relocated in nature.

The high-medieval spirit of experiment, the new mistrust of untested authority, has long been thought to be the basis of the great leap forward in science, which, in the long run, helped to equip Western civilization with knowledge and technology superior to those of its rivals.[36] In fact other influences seem to have been more important: the voyages of discovery of the fifteenth century onwards opened European eyes to intriguing visions of the world and crammed with the raw material of science – samples and specimens, images and maps – the wonder chambers of knowledge that European rulers in the sixteenth and seventeenth centuries compiled. The magical quest for power over nature overspilled into science: the lust for learning of the magi of the Renaissance, symbolized by Dr Faustus, the fictional character who sold his soul to the Devil in exchange for knowledge, fused with every kind of enquiry. Successive renaissances reacquainted European elites with ancient empiricism. A 'military revolution' displaced aristocracies from the battlefield, liberating the curriculum from the exercise of arms, and noble fortunes for the practice of science.

Nevertheless, the ideas of Roger Bacon and other scientific thinkers of the thirteenth century were important for the reaction they provoked. 'How can the supernatural conform to the laws of nature?' critics asked. If God's work has to be intelligible to science, what becomes of miracles? In part, recoil took the form of rejection of reason and science. A God reducible to logic, accessible to reason, aloof from revelation, is, to some sensibilities, a God not worth believing in – passionless and abstract, removed from the flesh and blood, the pain and patience that Christ embodied. Reason confines God. If he has to be logical, the effect is to limit his omnipotence.

Many of the philosophers in Aquinas's shadow hated what they called 'Greek necessitarianism' – the idea of a God bound by logic. They felt that by reconciling Christianity with classical philosophy, Aquinas had polluted it. The teacher William of Ockham, who died in 1347, led a strong movement of that kind. He denounced the logicians and apostles of reason for forcing God's behaviour into channels logic permitted. He coined frightening paradoxes. God, he said, can command you to perform a murder if he so wishes, such is the measure of his omnipotence, and 'God can reward good with evil': Ockham did not, of course, mean that literally, but uttered the thought to show the limitations of logic. For a time, the teaching of Aristotle was suspended pending 'purgation' of his errors.[37] Suspicion of reason subverts one of our main means of establishing agreement with each other. It undermines the belief – which was and remains strong in the Catholic tradition – that religion has to be reasonable. It fortifies dogma and makes it difficult to argue with opinionated people. It nourishes fundamentalism, which is essentially and explicitly irrational. Many of the Protestants of the Reformation rejected reason as well as authority in turning back to Scripture as the only basis of faith. The extreme position was attained by the eighteenth-century sect known as the Muggletonians, who thought reason was a diabolic subterfuge to mislead humankind: the serpent's apple that God had warned us to resist.

Meanwhile, the Church – formerly a patron of science – began a long relationship of suspicion with it. Except in medical schools, late-medieval universities abandoned interest in science. Although some religious orders – especially the Jesuits in the seventeenth and eighteenth centuries – continued to sponsor important scientific work, innovations tended to be repudiated at first and accepted with reluctance. Fr Ted Hesburgh, the legendary president of my university, who trained as an astronaut in order to be the first celebrant of the Mass in space, and who represented the Holy See on the International Atomic Energy Commission, used to say that if science and religion seemed to be in conflict, there must be something wrong with the science, or with the religion, or both. The idea that science and religion are enemies is false: they concern distinct, if overlapping, spheres of human experience. But the presumption has proved extremely hard to overcome.

The Frontier of Mysticism

Apart from rejecting reason and science, other thinkers in the Middle Ages sought ways around them – better approaches to truth. Their big recourse was what we call mysticism, or, to put it more mildly, the belief that by inducing abnormal mental states – ecstasy or trance or visionary fervour – you can achieve a sense of union with God, an emotional self-identification with his loving nature. You can apprehend God directly through a sort of hotline. To those of us who have not had them, mystical experiences are hard to express, understand, and appreciate. It may help, however, to approach the problems through the experiences of a fellow-non-mystic: St Augustine, who, although he befriended logic, mastered classical learning, and was a thinker more subtle and supple than almost any other in the history of thought, contributed profoundly to the history of Christian mysticism. As far as we can tell, he never had a mystical experience. He did once, by his own account, have a vision, perhaps better described as a dream: he was puzzling over the doctrine of the Trinity when a little boy, digging on the beach, confronted him. When Augustine asked the purpose of the hole, the child replied that he proposed to drain the sea into it. Augustine pointed out that the laws of physics would make that impossible. 'You have as much chance of understanding the Trinity', replied the digger.[38] This charming story hardly qualifies its author as a visionary. The whole trajectory of Augustine's own life, rather than any sudden event, shaped his thinking. In his *Confessions*, he described his journey from childish feelings of guilt at selfishness and pubescent dilemmas at the onset of sensuality toward dependence on God.

Nevertheless, perhaps his biggest contribution to the history of ideas was what scholars call his doctrine of illumination: the claim that there are truths known by direct apprehension from God. Augustine said that mathematical axioms, for instance, and the idea of beauty, and maybe the existence of God himself are ideas of that kind, together with all facts inaccessible to reason, sense perception, revelation, or recollection. He realized that there must be some other source of validation for such knowledge, 'in that inward house of my thoughts', as he put it, 'without help of the mouth or the tongue, without any sound of syllables'.[39] His language is a clue to his thinking: deepening self-awareness came to him through the habit – unusual at the time – of silent reading. His personality helped. Selective humility, which afflicts many people of genius, made him diffident about discerning all the dark mysteries of life without divine flashes of illumination.[40] His thinking in this respect bears comparison with the ancient Greek belief that knowledge is accessed from within the self, not acquired by input from outside. The Greek word for truth is *aletheia* – literally, 'things unforgotten'. Knowledge is innate – Plato said as much. Education reminds us of it. Recollection makes us aware of it. We retrieve it from within ourselves. In St Augustine's notion, by contrast, we rely on impressions from outside. Mysticism had been practised among Christians from the time of the apostles: St Paul twice describes what seem like mystical experiences. Before Augustine pronounced on the subject, however, mystics were – as it were – on their own, compelled to make their messages convincing without a general theory to fall back on in self-justification. Augustine supplied the justification. He licensed mystics to represent raptures as revelations. For Christians he opened up a new means to knowledge: mysticism joined reason, experience, scripture, and tradition. The consequences were serious. Western mysticism became largely a matter of introspective meditation. The alternative – nature-mysticism or the contemplation of the external world in an effort to arouse a mystical response – remained a marginal pursuit. More serious were the inducements mysticism gave to heresy. Mystics can transcend reason, overleap science, bypass Scripture, and dodge the Church.

Augustine's idea of illumination has affinities with the tradition in Buddhism that we know by its Japanese name, Zen. As we have seen (see p. 132), traditions about the illusory nature of perceptions – Zen's starting point – were common in India and China in the first millennium BCE. Nagarjuna, whom most students and initiates regard as the intellectual progenitor of the tradition that led to Zen, systematized them in the early second century CE. 'As dream or as the lightning flash', he suggested, 'so should one look at all things, which are only relative.'[41] Over the next couple of hundred years his followers pursued his advice unremittingly, even so far as to embrace an apparently self-defeating paradox by doubting the reality, or at least the individuality, of the doubting mind: strictly speaking (as Descartes later pointed out – see p. 213) it is logically impossible for you to doubt your own doubts. Zen, however, delights in paradox. To achieve perfect Buddhist enlightenment, you have to suspend thought, forgo language, and obliterate all sense of reality. There are commendable consequences: if you forgo consciousness, you escape subjectivism. If you renounce language, you can engage the ineffable. When the teacher Bodhidharma arrived in China in the early sixth century, he announced that enlightenment was literally inexplicable. A twelfth-century Japanese text defines his doctrine with a formula that fits the way Augustine wrote about illumination, as 'a special transmission, outside the scriptures, not founded on words or letters, which allows one to penetrate the nature of things by pointing directly to the mind'.[42]

In traditional tales of Zen masters from Bodhidharma onwards, they baffled their pupils into enlightenment, answering questions with apparently irrelevant rejoinders, or meaningless noises, or enigmatic gestures. They might offer the same answer to different questions. A single question might elicit mutually contradictory answers or no response at all. Zen is popular in the West today with revellers in uncertainty, because it makes every perspective seem evanescent and none objectively correct.[43] It is therefore more appealing than the indifference of ancient Greek and Roman sceptics, who professed contentment with things as they seemed, on the grounds that appearances could do duty for truths no one can know (see p. 139). By contrast, Zen's 'forgetfulness of the sky, retirement from the wind' represents radical withdrawal from perceived reality – a consequence of self-extinction, the inertia of nonbeing, beyond thought and language. Zen is a bid by mere humans for the reality and objectivity of a clod or a rock. You have 'no wandering desires at all', says Robert Pirsig, author of *Zen and the Art of Motorcycle Maintenance*, 'but simply perform the acts of ... life without desire'.[44]

Zen does not sound like an attempt to be practical. But it had enormous practical consequences: by encouraging practitioners in discipline, self-abnegation, and willingness to embrace extinction it contributed to the martial ethos of medieval and modern Japan; the art Zen helped to inspire included gardens of meditation and mystical poems; and in the late twentieth century, as we shall see (p. 363) the appeal of Zen was among the influences from East and South Asia that reshaped the mental worlds of Western intellectuals.

Faith and Politics

Religious thinkers did a good and conscientious but imperfect job of reconciling reason and science. What about the further problems of reconciling religion 'not of this world' with real life? Thinkers of the period contributed world-changing ideas in this connection in two ways. First, thinking about the state – how you make the state holy, how you legitimize authority by appealing to divine investiture of the powers that be, or even how you sanctify war – and second, thinking about the problem that opened this chapter: how you devise ways of applying religion to improve behaviour.

Take political thinking first. We have seen how tradition misinterpreted Christ's humour (p. 151). The command 'Render unto Caesar the things that are Caesar's, and unto God the things that are God's' has not only been misapplied to reinforce taxation, but also abused more generally to mean, 'Respect the distinction between the secular and spiritual realms.' But is this what Christ meant? It is not surprising that Christ should have been radically misunderstood – irony is the hardest form of humour to penetrate across chasms of time and culture.

The Church has always tended to emphasize the second half of Christ's sentence and to insist that 'things of God' are not subject to the state: so the clergy have enjoyed immunity under the law, in some

Christian states, or the right to be tried by their own courts; church property has often secured exemption from taxation or, at least, privileged fiscal status. The long history of dispute over these liberties started in Milan in the late fourth century, when the bishop, Ambrose, refused to surrender a church to imperial expropriators. 'I answered that if the emperor asked of me what was mine I would not refuse it. But things which are God's are not subject to the emperor.'[45] A power struggle was under way. Pope Boniface VIII, who contended as fiercely as any cleric, summed it up toward the end of the thirteenth century: 'That laymen have been hostile to the Church has been clear from antiquity ... Nor do they realize that power over the clergy is forbidden to them.'[46]

Alternatively, religious people with no stomach for such squabbles have shut themselves off from the world. In the mid-third century, the theologian and church historian Origen thought Christ's words obliged the people of God to withdraw from the state, passively obeying it at most; many others have continued to think the same. Early in the fifth century, St Augustine drew a distinction between two worlds – or cities as he called them: God's and the state, the latter of which was of little concern to Christians. Ascetics literally withdrew – to found hermitages in the desert or on remote islands: this was the beginning of Christian monasticism. But Church and state always seemed to get entangled. Because of their purity and objectivity, holy men were not allowed to escape the world: people brought them their troubles. Monks became magistrates; anchorites, administrators; and popes, in effect, came to do the jobs of emperors.[47]

So Christ – to the evident disappointment of some of his followers – tried to steer clear of politics; in some parts of the world where Christians are a minority and in most of the Orthodox world, churches have managed to stay that way. In western Europe, as the Roman Empire dissolved, the Church took on ever more of the functions of the state. Bishops ran administrations that bureaucrats abandoned. Holy men replaced judges and professional arbitrators where the system of justice broke down.[48] For much of what we now think of as the early Middle Ages, the popes had the best chancery in Europe – and therefore, in effect, the most wide-ranging network of intelligence and influence. Government needed the Church: this was where learned and disinterested personnel could be recruited. The Church wanted influence over government: laws that conduced to the salvation of souls, agreements that kept peace within Christendom, crusades that deflected aggression against the infidel.

Theorists responded to this practical environment with arguments in favour of a politically committed Church and – ultimately – with the idea that the Church should rule the world. The fifth-century pope Gelasius proposed the image of Two Swords: when Christ told Peter to sheathe his sword, it was still ready for action. The Church had a residual right to rule. In the eighth century, the forgers of the Donation of Constantine went a stage further and claimed that imperial power had been surrendered to the pope at the time of the conversion of the first Christian Roman emperor. In the thirteenth century, Pope Innocent III devised a new image: the Church was the sun and the state the moon, disposing only of reflected power. In 1302, Pope Boniface VIII delivered the most trenchant utterance yet in this tradition:

> Truly he who denies that the temporal sword is in the power of Peter misunderstands the words of the Lord ... Both swords are in the power of the Church, the spiritual and the material. The latter is to be used by kings and captains, only at the will and with the permission of priests ... Temporal authority should be subject to spiritual.[49]

The position was unsustainable in practice: states simply had bigger battalions than churches. But Christianity remained enmeshed in politics. The pope was useful as an arbiter in the power struggles of states, imposing truces, organizing crusades, setting disputed frontiers. In modern times, churches continued to interfere in politics, supporting political parties or movements, organizing trade unions, and publicly endorsing or condemning policies according to how well they conform to the Gospel or suit the interests or prejudices of Christians.[50]

The story is not yet over. 'How many divisions has the pope?' sneered Joseph Stalin, and papal impotence or pusillanimity in the face of the great dictators during the Second World War seemed to show that the Church was indeed a spent force in secular politics. Yet in the long and dramatic pontificate of John Paul II, which straddled the twentieth and twenty-first centuries, the Church re-entered the political arena with new confidence. Partly, political re-involvement was the result of the pope's own initiatives in subverting communist regimes, challenging capitalist ones, reinvigorating the papal diplomatic service, and renewing the papacy's roles in international arbitration. Partly, it was a grass-roots initiative by religiously committed political activists – sometimes under papal disapproval – such as the Latin American revolutionaries inspired by 'liberation theology' to demand rights for poor peasants and underprivileged native communities. Partly, too, a resurgently political Church was the result of voters in democratic countries seeking a 'third way' in place of discredited communism and insensitive capitalism – and finding it in the Catholic social tradition.

In conflicts with the Church, secular rulers had, for most of the Middle Ages, a serious disadvantage: they depended on the Church to educate and often to pay the men they employed to run their administrations, write their propaganda, and formulate their own claims to legitimacy. 'The powers that be are ordained of God', said St Paul, but how did his legitimation get transmitted? Did it descend from heaven upon his anointed, or did it arise via the people by popular election – 'the voice of God'? Everyone in the medieval West, and every devout Catholic to this day, continually hears politically revolutionary sentiments uttered in the prayer of the Church to a God who hath put down the mighty, exalted the meek, and shattereth kings in the day of wrath. The Church, however, generally left the revolutionary implications to heresiarchs and millenarians and sought a practical way of reconciling God's bias to the poor with the world's preference for the mighty.

In thirteenth-century Latin Christendom, this dilemma was resolved in practice by borrowing a model from classical antiquity: 'mixed' government, originally recommended by Aristotle,[51] modified to combine monarchical, aristocratic, and popular elements. 'The state', in Aristotle's opinion, 'is better inasmuch as it is made up of more numerous elements.'[52] Typically, medieval monarchs consulted 'the community of the realm' through representative assemblies in which magnates, who were the king's natural advisers and his companions, joined deputies of other 'estates' – usually the clergy and the common people (who were variously defined, from country to country).

Early in the fourteenth century, at a time when the papacy was in conflict with kings over power and money, Marsilius of Padua worked as a propagandist against Rome. He lived in a world of Italian city-republics that resembled Aristotle's polities: small states where citizens and senates ruled. Marsilius thought it was not just Aristotle's choice but God's: God chose the people; the people chose their delegates, who might be assemblies or monarchs. Marsilius applied the mixed-government model to the Church, too, advocating collegiality among the bishops, in which the pope is unprivileged or merely presides. He even raised the question of whether bishops should be popularly elected. These recommendations were obviously the self-interested programme of a particular party. But they responded to a deeply democratic tradition in Christianity, which went back to the teachings of Christ: He came to call publicans and sinners, summoned the rich to poverty, and welcomed the discipleship of fishers and prostitutes. And for Christ, no one was too lowly for God's love.

Every step in the popes' progress to unique power in the Church has therefore had to be ratified by the bishops collegially, and has been protected from reversal only by the tradition that 'ecumenical' decisions are divinely inspired and therefore irreversible. Conciliarism is alive and well today, reinvigorated by the use that recent popes have made of councils of the Church in launching and guiding their own reform programmes. The arguments of Marsilius were taken up by reformers who wanted only to improve Church government, not confide it to secular rulers, though the Reformation seemed to show that the pope was a necessary guarantee of the independence of the Church: wherever Luther's message was successful, secular states usurped the pope's traditional functions. Conciliarism, which originated as the appropriation of a secular model for the Church, influenced secular political thought in its turn. This started, in a very obvious way, in the fifteenth century in the German Empire, where the great princes claimed a role analogous to bishops in the Church. It continued with the rise of representative institutions in many European states, claiming equality with kings in making laws and raising taxes. In the long run, developments of this sort fed into and sped the ideas that have shaped modern politics: popular sovereignty and democracy.[53]

Early in the fifteenth century, the Church was the main focus of the political thought of Jean Gerson; his concern was to justify the view that the bishops collectively, rather than the pope in particular, exercised the authority of Christ on earth. In the course, however, of comparing secular and ecclesiastical government, he developed a theory of the origins of the state that has affected politics in the Western world ever since. The state arose because of sin: outside Eden, there was no limit to iniquity except that which men established by agreement to pool resources and bind liberty in the interests of peace. The process was natural and reasonable. The agreement of the citizens is the only legitimate foundation of the state. In contrast to the Church, which is God-given, the state is a creation of human free will, made by a historic contract and sustained by the implicit renewal of that contract. In the case of a monarchy, the power of the ruler owes nothing to God, everything to the contract by which the people entrust their rights to his keeping.

The ruler is simply the minister of this historic contract and the trustee of rights that he cannot abrogate or annul. The sovereign power remains with the people: the ruler merely exercises it on their behalf. They can recover it in cases where the ruler breaks or abuses the contract. He is not above the community, but part of it. He has no rights over the society, or its members, or their property, except by common consent. An 'absolute' ruler, who claims to be entitled to change the law at his own prompting, or to dispose of the lives or property of subjects, cannot be a lawful ruler: the people have the right to eject him.

For anyone who values freedom or thinks collaboration in civil society is natural for our species, the state is a limitation or even an almost inexplicable burden. The problems of explaining and justifying it came together in social contract theory. The idea of the contractual foundation of the state has nourished constitutionalism and democracy. By providing a justification for the state without reference to God, it has been particularly useful in the modern, secular world. There were, however, critical weaknesses in the idea as Gerson devised it: he made the ruler party to the contract – leaving open the possible objection that the ruler was actually outside it and not bound by its terms (see p. 252); and he made challengeable assumptions about the clauses of the contract: apologists for absolutism could argue that the other parties surrendered their rights to the state, rather than merely placing them in trusteeship.[54]

The idea that the ruler is absolute has a certain logic on its side: how can the lawmaker be bound by law? But it had to be reasserted for the modern West after the Middle Ages effectively suppressed it. The sovereign power of medieval rulers was limited in theory in four ways: first, it was conceived essentially as a matter of jurisdiction – the administration of justice. Legislation, the right to make and unmake laws, which we now think of as the defining feature of sovereignty, was a relatively minor area of activity, in which tradition, custom, divine law, and natural law covered the field and left little scope for innovation. Second, royal power was limited, as we have seen, by the notion of a community of Christendom, in which the king of a particular country was not the ultimate authority: the pope had, at least, a parallel supremacy. Next, the notion persisted that the Roman Empire had never come to an end and that the authority of the emperor over Christendom continued to repose in the person of the pope or the elected head of the German Reich, who was actually called 'Roman emperor'. Finally, kings were lords among lords and were obliged to consult their so-called natural counsellors – that is, the nobles who in some cases derived their power from royal favour but, in others, sometimes also claimed to get it directly from God.

In the late Middle Ages, kings challenged these limitations systematically. Fourteenth-century French and Castilian kings, and a sixteenth-century English one, called their own kingdoms their empires and proposed that they were 'emperors in their own realms'. The imagery of majesty surrounded them – ideological strategies devised by propagandists. The French king's office was miraculous, endowed by God with 'such a virtue that you perform miracles in your own lifetime'.[55] The earliest recognizable portrait of a French king – that of John the Good, done in the mid-fourteenth century – resembles the depiction of a Roman emperor on a medallion and of a saint in a nimbus of glory. Richard II of England had himself painted staring in majesty from a field of gold, and receiving the body of Christ from the hands of the Virgin. The idea never quite took hold in practice. 'You have the power to do what you like', said President Guillart of the Parlement of Paris, addressing King Francis I early in the sixteenth century. 'But you do not or should not wish to do it.'[56] Nevertheless, with occasional setbacks, kings did gain power progressively from the fourteenth to the eighteenth centuries in most of Europe, at the expense of other traditional sources of authority: the Church, aristocracies, and city patriciates.[57]

Social Thought in Christianity and Islam: Faith, War, and Ideas of Nobility

One reason moral philosophers have for putting a lot of effort into political thinking is the ancient assumption, which Aristotle endorsed and made almost unquestionable, that the purpose of the state is to facilitate or promote virtue. In practice, however, states seem no better at this than religions. Medieval thinkers therefore addressed directly the problem of how to influence individual behaviour for the better. Christ's whole life and work show an unflinching desire to sanctify real life and make people's lives in this world conform to what he called the kingdom of Heaven. On the whole, however, his teachings were honoured in the breach: even his most enthusiastic followers found it hard to practise love of others, meekness, humility, cheerful suffering, marital fidelity, and 'hunger and thirst after righteousness'. As Christ recognized, the difficulty of behaving well increases with wealth, which clogs the eye of a needle, and power, which corrupts. So the problem of human behaviour generally was a problem for elites in particular. How do you stop them exploiting the people, oppressing vassals, and exchanging with each other, as aristocrats did in warfare, the abhorrent levels of violence that scar the bones archaeologists excavate from medieval battlefields?

The best answer anyone came up with was chivalry. The religious model suggested the idea that the lay life could be sanctified – like those of monks and nuns – by obedience to rules. The first such rules or codes of chivalry appeared in the twelfth century. Three writers formulated them: St Bernard, the austere abbot who excoriated rich and lazy clergy; Pope Eugenius II, who was always looking for ways to mobilize lay manpower for the Church; and the pious nobleman Hugh de Payens. They realized that warriors tended to savagery in the heat of battle, the adrenaline of fear, and the euphoria of victory. Knights needed civilizing. Discipline could save them. The earliest rules reflected religious vows of chastity, poverty, and obedience, but lay virtues gathered prominence. The prowess that fortified the knight against fear could be adapted to confront temptations, and practical virtues could be turned against deadly sins: largesse against greed, equanimity against anger, loyalty against lies and lust.[58]

Chivalry became the great common aristocratic ethos of the age. In the popular pulp fiction of the late Middle Ages, heroes of the kingship of a pre-chivalric age, including Alexander, Arthur, Pericles, and Brutus of Troy, were transformed into exemplars of chivalric values. Even the Bible was ransacked for recruits, and King David and Judas Maccabeus joined the canon. Maccabeus appeared in illuminations and wall paintings as an exponent of the art of jousting.[59] Ritual jousts and accolades became foci of political display in every princely court.

Chivalry was a powerful force. It could not, perhaps, make men good, as it was intended to do. It could, however, win wars and mould political relationships. It was probably the main ingredient in Europe's unique culture of overseas expansion, making Christendom a more dynamic society, more far-going in exploration and out-thrust than better-equipped neighbours to the east, such as Islam and China. It inspired venturers such as Christopher Columbus and Henry 'the Navigator', in search of the denouements of their own romances of chivalry.[60] Ethos is more powerful than ideology in shaping behaviour, because it supplies individuals with standards by which to adjust and appraise their actions. Chivalry did that job for medieval Europe. It has continued as a spur to Western actions and self-perceptions ever since. In the nineteenth century, it could cram Victorian gentlemen into their creaking reproduction armour. 'The Age of Chivalry is never past', remarked that great sentimentalist, Charles Kingsley, 'so long as there is a wrong left unredressed on earth.'[61] In the twentieth century, chivalric soubriquets could still compensate the 'knights of the air' of the Battle of Britain for their generally modest social origins. It could still shape the heroics of the golden age of Hollywood. It has dwindled almost to nothing today.[62]

Chivalry was, in a sense, an apology for war: it provided an escape route to salvation for professional warriors who had to present themselves bloodstained at the gates of heaven. But chivalry could not justify war: that needed separate attention from the thinkers.

War as a religious obligation was enshrined in the sacred history of the ancient Jews, whose God heaped high the bodies and scattered heads far and wide. As we have seen, the third-century BCE Indian emperor Ashoka even justified wars 'for Buddhism'. But it was one thing to use religion to justify war, another to make war seem good. Islamic and Christian traditions produced justifications of war so sweeping and sanctifying that they have had frightening consequences ever after.

Jihad literally means 'striving'. 'Those who believe with the Prophet', says the Qur'an, 'strive with their wealth and lives. Allah hath made ready for them gardens where rivers flow ... That is the supreme triumph.' Muhammad used the word in two contexts: first, to mean the inner struggle against evil that Muslims must wage for themselves; second, to denote real war, fought against the enemies of Islam. These have to be genuine enemies, evincing a genuine threat. But since in Muhammad's day the community he led was frequently at war, these terms of reference have always been quite generously interpreted. Chapter 9 of the Qur'an seems to legitimate war against all polytheists and idolaters. After the Prophet's death, the doctrine was turned against the apostates who left the camp, believing their obligations to the leader had lapsed at his demise. It was then used to proclaim a series of highly successful wars of aggression against Arabian states and the Roman and Persian empires. The rhetoric of *jihad* has often been abused by Muslims to justify their wars against each other. It is used to this day to dignify shabby squabbles, like those of tribal strongmen in Afghanistan and of terrorists against innocent people in areas singled out for enmity by self-appointed Islamist leaders.

Nevertheless, the term 'holy war' seems an appropriate translation for *jihad*: the enterprise is sanctified by obedience to what are thought to be the Prophet's commands and rewarded by the promise of martyrdom.[63] According to a saying traditionally ascribed to Muhammad, the martyr in battle goes straight to the highest rank of paradise, nearest to the throne of God, and has the right to intercede for the souls of his own loved ones. It is worth observing, however, that most Islamic legal traditions lay down strict laws of war, which ought surely to define a *jihad*, including indemnity for the lives and property of non-belligerents, women, infants, the sick, and non-resisters. These limitations effectively outlaw all terrorism and most state violence.

Abuses apart, the idea of *jihad* has been influential in two main ways. First, and more importantly, it fortified Muslim warriors, especially in the early generations of the expansion of Islam. In the hundred years or so after the death of Muhammad, it is hard to imagine how Islam could have achieved its successes of scale – which turned most of the Mediterranean into a Muslim lake – without it. Second, the *jihad* idea came to be copied in Christendom. Christians started the crusades with two comparable notions: one of just war, waged to recover lands allegedly usurped by their Muslim occupants, and another of armed pilgrimage, undertaken as a religious obligation to do penance for sin. Until crusaders began to see themselves in terms analogous to those applied to Islamic warriors – as potential martyrs for whom, as *The Song of Roland* said, 'the blood of the Saracens washes away sins' – there was no idea of holy war, though the objective was hallowed in the sense that the disputed territory had borne the blood and footprints of Christ and the saints.[64]

In the late Middle Ages in the West, as crusading waned and politics and law increasingly provided new routes to power and wealth, the notion of nobility became detached from war. Firepower gradually diminished the need for a warrior aristocracy, expensively trained in horseborne combat with sword and lance. A society of opportunity could never develop freely where ancient riches or ancient blood determined rank and the elites were impenetrable except by individuals of exceptional prowess, virtue, or genius. China, in this as so many respects, was way ahead of the West in the Middle Ages, because the imperial elite was selected by examination in an arduous, humanistic curriculum; clans could club together to pay for the training of intelligent poor relations. In the West, where no such system existed, government was revolutionized in the fourteenth and fifteenth centuries by the use first of paper, then of printing. Princes' commands could be cheaply and speedily transmitted to the farthest corners of every state. The consequent bureaucratization added another avenue of social advancement to the traditional routes via the Church, war, commerce, and adventure. The magnate ranks of Western countries were everywhere supplemented – and in some areas almost entirely replaced – with new men. To suit their self-perceptions, Western moralists embarked on the redefinition of nobility.

'Only virtue is true nobility', proclaimed a Venetian ambassador's coat of arms. A Parisian academic in 1306 declared that intellectual vigour equipped a man best for power over others. A German mystic a few years later dismissed carnal nobility among qualifications for office, as inferior to the nobility of the soul. Letters, according to a Spanish humanist of the fifteenth century, ennobled a man more thoroughly than arms. Gian Galeazzo Visconti, the strong-arm man who seized Milan in 1395, could be flattered by an inapposite comparison with the exemplary self-made hero of humanists, Cicero. Antonio de Ferraris, a humanist of Otranto whose very obscurity is a guarantee that he was typical, declared that neither the wealth of Croesus nor the antiquity of Priam's blood could replace reason as the prime ingredient of nobility. 'Virtue solely', declared Marlowe's Tamburlaine, 'is the sum of glory and fashions men with true nobility.'[65]

This doctrine, however, was resisted in eastern Europe. In Bohemia, nobility was simply ancient blood. In the Kingdom of Hungary, only nobles constituted the nation; their privileges were justified by their presumed descent from Huns and Scythians whose right to rule was founded on the right of conquest; other classes were tainted with disgraceful ancestry from natural slaves who had surrendered their rights. Even here, however, the doctrine was tempered by the influence of humanism. István Werböczy, the early-sixteenth-century chancellor of the kingdom, who was the great apologist of aristocratic rule, admitted that nobility was acquired not only by 'the exercise of martial discipline' but also by 'other gifts of mind and body', including learning. But he saw this as a means of recruitment to what was essentially a caste – not, as in the thought of Western humanists, a method of opening up an estate of society.[66] This bifurcation of Europe had important consequences. The term 'eastern Europe' came to have a pejorative sense in the West, denoting a laggard land of arrested social development, held back during a protracted feudal age, with a servile peasantry and a tightly closed elite.[67]

Spiritual Conquest

As holy wars failed – at least for Christian practitioners expelled from the Holy Land – and aristocracies diversified, a new idea arose. We might call it spiritual conquest. One of the conspicuous trends of modern history has been the rise of Christianity to become the world's most successful proselytizing religion. To judge from the appeal of the Hebrew God, Judaism could have anticipated or trumped it to become a great world religion; the numbers of adherents, however, remained small because Jews generally shunned proselytization. Islam grew slowly to its present massive dimensions: Richard W. Bulliet, who has devised the only method of computation that has so far achieved anything like wide scholarly approval, calculates for Iran that 2.5% of the population were converted to Islam by 695, 13.5% between 695 and 762, 34% between 762 and 820, another 34% from 820 to 875, and the remainder between 875 and 1009.[68] As well as being slow-growing, Islam, as we have seen, has remained culturally specific: extremely popular in a belt of the world that stretches across a broad but limited band, and virtually unable to penetrate elsewhere except by migration. Buddhism seems infinitely elastic, to judge from the worldwide appeal it demonstrates today, but was checked for a long time. Early Christendom flamed with missionary zeal, which flagged after the eleventh century CE. The crusades produced few converts.

The idea of spiritual conquest was instrumental in reviving evangelization. Christ's own reported words were, perhaps, the key source of inspiration. 'Go into the highways and byways and compel them to come in' was the master's injunction to his servants in the parable of the wedding feast. The words called for reinterpretation in the late Middle Ages, when a new sense of mission grew in the Church: a new conviction of the obligations of the godly elite to spread a more active, committed, and dogmatically informed Christian awareness to parts of society and places in the world where, so far, evangelization had hardly reached or only superficially penetrated.

A new conversion strategy was the result, addressed to two constituencies. First came the unevangelized and under-evangelized masses inside Christendom: the poor, the rootless, the neglected country folk, the dwellers in forest, bog, and mountain, beyond the candle-glow of the Church, and the deracinated masses of growing cities, cut off from the discipline and solidarity of rural parish life. Then there was the vast, infidel world revealed or suggested by exploration and improved geographical learning. The rise of the mendicant orders, with their special vocations for missions to the poor, the unbelieving, and the under-catechized, helped the trend along. So did the growing interest in a restoration of apostolic habits to the Church, which was a prominent theme from the time of the rise of the friars to the Reformation. The outward drive revived thanks to a new idea of what conversion meant, formulated at the end of the thirteenth century and in the early years of the fourteenth by the Majorcan Ramon Llull. He realized that proselytization had to be culturally adjusted. You need to know the culture you are converting people from and make appropriate compromises. Above all, you have to address people in their own terms. So he instituted language schooling for missionaries. Indifferent elements of native culture could be left undisturbed. There was an apostolic precedent: St Paul decided Gentile converts could elude circumcision; St Peter decreed that they could waive Jewish dietary laws. In consequence, the Christianity of converted societies normally exhibits original features, which are best understood as examples of two-way cultural exchange.[69]

The period was alive with popular preachers and prophets who made insurrection holy and sanctified the poor in their often violent response to the oppression of the elite. At the end of time, God would put right all the inequalities of society. For revolutionaries the millennium meant something more immediate. The poor could precipitate it by taking matters into their own hands and trying to realize God's objectives for the world here and now. The problems of monstrous, menacing inequalities were insoluble by such means. The next age would take a fresh look and propose new answers.

Chapter 6

Return to the Future

Thinking Through Plague and Cold

Intellectuals ruled – to judge from the episodes traditionally highlighted in histories of the sixteenth and seventeenth centuries. Renaissance, Reformation, and Scientific Revolution succeeded each other, marking the world more deeply than changes of dynasty and fortunes of war. Even 'the Age of Expansion' – the conventional name for the era as a whole – was the product of expanding minds: 'the discovery of the world and of man'. In the background, of course, other forces were also at work: recurrent plagues; dispiriting cold; and transmutations and relocations of life forms ('biota' in the scientists' lexicon) unendowed with mind – plants, animals, microbes – amounting to a global ecological revolution.

The shifts of biota changed the face of the planet more than any innovation since the invention of agriculture. Rather as farming modified evolution by introducing what we might call unnatural selection – but more so – changes that began in the sixteenth century went further, reversing a long-standing evolutionary pattern. Since something like 150 million years ago, when Pangea split apart, and oceans began to sever the continents from one another, life forms in the separate landmasses became ever more distinct. Eventually the New World came to breed species unknown elsewhere. Australian flora and fauna became unique, unexampled in the Americas or Afro-Eurasia. With extraordinary suddenness, 150 million years of evolutionary divergence yielded to a convergent trend, which has dominated the last few centuries, spreading similar life forms across the planet. Now there are llamas and wallabies in English country parks, and kiwi fruit are an important part of the economy of my corner of Spain. The 'native' cuisines of Italy and Sichuan, Bengal and Kenya, rely on plants of American origin – chillies, potatoes, 'Indian' corn, tomatoes – while the mealtimes of much of America would be unrecognizable without the wine and kine that came from Europe, the coffee from Arabia, or Asian rice or sugar. A single disease environment covers the planet: you can catch any communicable illness just about anywhere.

The world-girdling journeys of European colonizers and explorers gave biota a ride across the oceans. In some cases planters and ranchers transferred breeds deliberately in an attempt to exploit new soils or create new varieties. To that extent, the revolution conformed to the argument of this book: people reimagined the world and worked to realize the idea. But many vital seeds, germs, insects, predators, and stowaway pets made what Disney might call 'incredible journeys' in people's seams and pockets, or in ships' stores or bilges, to new environments where their effects were transforming.[1]

Meanwhile, an age of plague afflicted the world.[2] It began in the fourteenth century, when the Black Death wiped out great swathes of people – a third of the population in the worst-affected regions – in Eurasia and North Africa. For the next three hundred years, baffling plagues recurred frequently in all these areas. The DNA of the bacillus that seems to have been responsible was almost identical to the agent that causes what we now call bubonic plague. But there was a crucial difference: bubonic plague likes hot environments. The world of the fourteenth century to the eighteenth was exceptionally cold. Climate historians call it the Little Ice Age.[3] The most virulent plagues often coincided with intensely cold spells. The wintry landscapes Dutch artists painted in the late sixteenth and seventeenth centuries, when the cold was at its sharpest, convey a sense of what it looked and felt like. In the sixteenth century, moreover, some Old World diseases, especially smallpox, spread to the Americas, killing off about ninety per cent of the indigenous population in areas where the effects were most concentrated.

So this was an age when environment exceeded intellect in its impact on the world. No one has ever explained the obvious paradox: why did so much progress – or what we think of as progress – happen in such unpropitious circumstances? How did the victims of plague and cold launch the movements we call the Renaissance and the Scientific Revolution? How did they explore the world and reunite sundered continents? Maybe it was a case of what the great but now unfashionable historian Arnold Toynbee called 'challenge and response'. Maybe no general explanation will serve, and we must look separately at the particular circumstances of each new initiative. In any case, even in a time when impersonal forces put terrible constraints on human creativity, the power of minds could evidently still imagine transformed worlds, issue world-changing ideas, and generate transmutative initiatives. Indeed, in some places the output of innovative thinking seems to have been faster than ever – certainly faster than in any earlier period that is comparably well documented.

New ideas were concentrated, disproportionately, in Europe. Partly because of this intellectual fertility, and partly because of the export of European ideas by European trade and imperialism, the age of plague and cold was also a long period of gradual but unmistakable shift in the worldwide balance of inventiveness, innovation, and influential thinking. For thousands of years, historical initiative – the power, that is, of some human groups to influence others – had been concentrated in the civilizations of Asia, such as India, the world of Islam, and, above all, China. In technology, China had generated most of the world's most impressive inventions: paper and printing were the foundation of modern communications; paper money was the basis of capitalism; gunpowder ignited modern warfare; in the blast furnace modern industrial society was forged; the compass, rudder, and separable bulkhead were the making of modern shipping and maritime endeavour. In the meantime, glassmaking was the only key technology in which the West possessed clear superiority (except perhaps for mechanical clock-making, which was maybe a Chinese invention but certainly a Western speciality).[4]

By the late seventeenth century, however, the signs were accumulating that Chinese supremacy was under strain from European competition. The representative event – perhaps it would not be excessive to call it a turning point – occurred in 1674, when the Chinese emperor took control of the imperial astronomical observatory out of the hands of native scholars and handed it over to the Jesuits. Throughout the period and, in some respects, into the nineteenth century, Europeans continued to look to China for exemplars in aesthetics and philosophy and to 'take our models from the wise Chinese'.[5] Chinese economic superiority, meanwhile, measured by the balance of trade across Eurasia in China's favour, was not reversed until about the 1860s. It was increasingly evident, however, that the big new ideas that challenged habits and changed societies were beginning to come overwhelmingly from the West. If the Little Ice Age, the Columbian Exchange, and the end of the age of plague were the first three conspicuous features of the early modern world, Europe's great leap forward was the fourth.

Europe is therefore the place to start trawling for the key ideas of the time. We can begin with the didactic, philosophical, and aesthetic ideas we usually bundle together and label 'the Renaissance', which preceded and perhaps helped to shape the Scientific Revolution.

We must start by identifying what the Renaissance was and was not, and locating where it happened and where it came from, before turning, in the following section, to the problem of where it went.

Forward to the Past: The Renaissance

If I had my way, we would drop the word 'Renaissance' from our historical lexicon. It was invented in 1855 by Jules Michelet, a French historian who wanted to emphasize the recovery or 'rebirth' of ancient learning, classical texts, and the artistic heritage of Greece and Rome in the way people thought about and pictured the world. Michelet was a writer of immense gifts, but, like many historians, he got his inspiration by reflecting on his own time; he tended to use history to explain the present rather than the past. In 1855, a renaissance really was under way. More boys learned Latin – and innumerably more learned Greek – than ever before. Scholarship was making ancient texts available in good editions on an unprecedented scale. The stories and characters they disclosed were the subjects of art and the inspiration of writers. Michelet detected in his own times an affinity with fifteenth-century Italy. He thought the modernity he saw there had been transmitted to France as a result of the passage to and fro of armies during the wars that took French invaders into Italy repeatedly from the 1490s to the

1550s. His theory became textbook orthodoxy, and successor historians elaborated on it, tracing everything they thought 'modern' back to the same era and the same part of the world. I recall my own teacher, when I was a little boy, chalking on the board, in his slow, round writing, '1494: Modern Times Begin'. Critics, meanwhile, have been chipping away at this powerful orthodoxy, demonstrating that classical aesthetics were a minority taste in most of Italy in the fifteenth century. Even in Florence, where most people look for the heartland of the Renaissance, patrons preferred the gaudy, gemlike painting of Gozzoli and Baldovinetti, whose work resembles the glories of medieval miniaturists, bright with costly pigments, to classicizing art. Much of what Florentine artists thought was classical in their city was bogus: the Baptistery was really early medieval. The Basilica of San Miniato, which the cognoscenti thought was a Roman temple, had been built in the eleventh century. Almost everything I – and probably you, dear reader – learned about the Renaissance in school was false or misleading.[6]

For instance: 'It inaugurated modern times.' No: every generation has its own modernity, which grows out of the past. 'It was unprecedented.' No: scholarship has detected many prior renaissances. 'It was secular' or 'It was pagan.' Not entirely: the Church remained the patron of most art and scholarship. 'It was art for art's sake.' No: politicians and plutocrats manipulated it. 'Its art was realistic in a new way.' Not altogether: perspective was a new technique, but much pre-Renaissance art was realistic in depicting emotions and anatomies. 'The Renaissance elevated the artist.' Yes, but only in a sense: medieval artists might achieve sainthood; the wealth and worldly titles some Renaissance artists received were derogatory by comparison. 'It dethroned scholasticism and inaugurated humanism.' No: Renaissance humanism grew out of medieval scholastic humanism. 'It was Platonist and Hellenophile.' No: there were patches of Platonism, as there had been before, but few scholars did more than dabble in Greek. 'It rediscovered lost antiquity.' Not really: antiquity had never been lost and classical inspiration never withered (though there was an upsurge in the fifteenth century). 'It discovered nature.' Hardly: there was no pure landscape painting in Europe previously, but nature achieved cult status in the thirteenth century, when St Francis discovered God outdoors. 'It was scientific.' No: for every scientist, as we shall see, there was a sorcerer.[7]

Still, there really was an acceleration of long-standing or intermittent interest in reviving the supposed glories of antiquity in the medieval West, and I daresay we must go on calling it the Renaissance, even though researchers have discovered or asserted revivals of classical ideas, style, and imagery in just about every century from the fifth to the fifteenth. There was, for instance, a 'renaissance' of classical architecture among basilica builders in Rome even before the last Western Roman Emperor died. Historians often speak of a Visigothic renaissance in seventh-century Spain, a Northumbrian renaissance in eighth-century England, a Carolingian renaissance in ninth-century France, an Ottonian renaissance in tenth- and eleventh-century Germany, and so on. The 'renaissance of the twelfth century' is recognized in the routine lexicon of historians of Latin Christendom.

In some ways, the classical tradition never needed revival: writers and artists almost always exploited classical texts and models where and when they could get them.[8] Consular diptychs inspired the decorator of a church in eighth-century Oviedo. In eleventh-century Frómista, in northern Spain, the carver of a capital had no example of the famous ancient Greek representation of Laocoön to hand, but he based his work on Pliny's description of it. Florentine builders of the same period copied a Roman temple sufficiently well to deceive Brunelleschi. A sculptor in thirteenth-century Orvieto made a creditable imitation of a Roman sarcophagus. What we usually call 'Gothic' architecture of the high Middle Ages was often decorated with classicizing sculpture. Throughout the period these examples cover, writers of moral and natural philosophy continued to echo such works of Plato and Aristotle as they could get hold of, and prose stylists often sought the most nearly classical models they could find.

As renaissances multiply in the literature in the West, so they appear with increasing frequency in scholars' accounts of episodes of the revival of antique values elsewhere.[9] Unsurprisingly, renaissances have become part of the vocabulary of historians of Byzantium, too, especially in the context of the revival of humanist scholarship and retrospective arts in Constantinople in the late eleventh century. Byzantine ivory-workers, who usually avoided pagan and lubricious subjects, were able in a brief dawn to make such delicate confections as the Veroli casket, where the themes are all of savagery tamed by art, love, and beauty. Hercules settles to play the lyre, attended by cavorting putti. Centaurs play for the Maenads' dance. Europa poses prettily on her bull's back, pouting at pursuers and archly waving her flimsy stole.[10] Transmissions of classical models came from eastern Christendom, especially through Syriac translations of classical texts and via Byzantine art and scholarship, from regions around the eastern Mediterranean where the classical tradition was easier to sustain than in the West.

Muslims occupied much of the heartland of classical antiquity in the Hellenistic world and the former Roman Empire. They therefore had access to the same legacy as Latin Christians: indeed, the availability of texts and intact monuments from Greco-Roman antiquity was superior in Islam, which covered relatively less despoiled and ravaged parts of the region. So not only is it reasonable, in principle, to look for renaissances in the Islamic world; it would be surprising if there were none. Indeed, some of the texts with which Latin Christendom renewed acquaintance in the Renaissance had formerly passed through Muslim hands and Arabic translations, from which Western copyists and retranslators recovered them.

Renaissance-hunters can find them in China, where neo-Confucian revivals happened at intervals during what we think of as the Middle Ages and the early modern period in the West. One might without much more contrivance also cite retrospective scholarship in seventeenth-century Edo, reconstructing classic texts, rediscovering forgotten values, and searching for authentic versions of Shinto poems, half-a-millennium old, which became the basis of a born-again Shintoism, stripped of the accretions of the intervening centuries.

The Renaissance mattered less for reviving what was old – for that was a commonplace activity – than for inaugurating what was new. In art, this meant working out principles that, by the seventeenth century, were called 'classical' and were enforced as rules by artistic academies. The rules included mathematical proportion, which made music harmonious, as the secret of how to contrive beauty. Accordingly, architects and archaeologists privileged shapes that varied from time to time and school to school: the circle, the triangle, and the square in the fifteenth and sixteenth centuries; from the sixteenth century onwards the 'golden' rectangle (with short sides two-thirds the length of the long ones); and, later, the spiral and the 'serpentine line'. Other rules enjoined the observation of mathematically calculated perspective (first explained by Leon Battista Alberti in a work of 1418); the embodiment of ancient philosophical ideas, such as Plato's of the ideal form or Aristotle's of the inner substance that a work of art should seem to wrest from whatever part of nature it represented; the demand that an artist should, as Shakespeare said, 'surpass life' in depicting perfection; and, above all, the rule that realism should mean more than the mere imitation of nature – rather, it should be an attempt to reach transcendent reality. 'It is not only Nature', said J. J. Winckelmann, who codified classicism in a work of 1755, in his first translator's version, 'which the votaries of the Greeks find in their works, but still something more, something superior to Nature; ideal beauties, brain-born images'.[11]

In learning, similarly, what was new in the late-medieval West was not so much a renaissance as a genuinely new departure. Schools in France and northern Italy in the late fourteenth and fifteenth centuries shifted the curriculum toward a family of subjects called 'humanist', concentrating on 'humane' subjects, rather than the abstractions of formal logic or the superhuman horizon of theology and metaphysics, or the infrahuman objects of the natural sciences. The humanist curriculum privileged moral philosophy, history, poetry, and language. These were the studies Francis Bacon had in mind when he said that they were not only for ornament but also for use.[12] The aim was to equip students for eloquence and argument – saleable skills in a continent full of emulous states and a peninsula full of rival cities, just as they had been in the China of the Warring States, or the Greece of competing cities.

There were consequences for the way scholars beheld the world. To humanists, a historical point of view came easily: an awareness that culture changes. To understand old texts – the classics, say, or the Bible – you have to take into account the way the meanings of words and the web of cultural references have changed in the meantime. Humanists' interests in the origins of language and the development of societies turned their researches outward, to the new worlds and remote cultures the explorers of the period disclosed. Boccaccio cannibalized travellers' lexica of new languages. Marsilio Ficino, a Florentine priest and physician who worked for the Medici, pored uncomprehendingly over Egyptian hieroglyphs. Both wanted to know what language Adam spoke in Eden, and where the first writing came from.

The Renaissance did not spring fully armed in Italy or any part of the West. It is necessary to insist on this point, because academic Eurocentrism – the assertion of uniqueness of Western achievements and their unparalleled impact on the rest of the world – makes the Renaissance one of the West's gifts to the rest. Great cultural movements do not usually happen by parthenogenesis. Cross-fertilization nearly always helps and is usually vital. We have seen how much trans-Eurasian contacts contributed to the new ideas of the first millennium BCE. It is hard to accept that the high-medieval fluorescence of ideas and technologies in western Europe was unstimulated by influences that flowed with the 'Mongol Peace'. As we shall see in the next chapter, the Enlightenment of the eighteenth century borrowed aesthetic and political models from China, India, and Japan, and relied on contacts with remoter cultures, in the Americas and the Pacific, for some new ideas. If the Renaissance happened in Europe without comparable external influences, the anomaly would be startling.

Nonetheless, the case for seeing the Renaissance as an event severed from extra-European sources of influence is, on the face of it, strong.[13] Trans-Eurasian contacts collapsed just as the Renaissance was becoming discernible in the work of Petrarch and Boccaccio and in the art of Sienese and Florentine successors of Giotto and Duccio. In the 1340s, Ambrogio Lorenzetti included Chinese onlookers in a scene of Franciscan martyrdom. At about the same time, Francesco Balducci Pegolotti wrote a guidebook for Italian merchants along the Silk Roads. An Italian miniature of the same period in the British Library shows a plausible Mongol khan banqueting while musicians play and dogs beg. Less than a generation later, Andrea da Ferrara depicted the Dominican order spreading the Gospel over what Westerners then knew of the world, with what seem to have been intended for Chinese and Indian participants in the scene. Then, however, the collapse of the Yuan dynasty in 1368 ended the Mongol Peace, or at least shortened the routes it policed. Rome lost touch with the Franciscan mission in China, which seems to have withered by the 1390s, as its existing staff died out. The West was largely isolated during the formative period of the Renaissance, with few or none of the enriching contacts with China, Central Asia, and India that had inseminated earlier movements with exotic notions and representations or equipped them with useful knowledge and technology or inspiring ideas. When Columbus set out for China in 1492, his royal masters' information about that country was so out of date that they furnished him with diplomatic credentials addressed to the Grand Khan, who had not ruled in China for a century and a quarter.

Despite the interruption of former trans-Eurasian contacts, some transmissions did happen across Eurasia, or substantial parts of it, in the fifteenth century by credible, documented means, via Islam. The Muslim world filled and to some degree bridged the gap between Europe and South and East Asia. Chinese and Indian artefacts, which became models for European imitators, arrived in European courts as diplomatic gifts with embassies from Muslim potentates. Qait Bey, the late-fifteenth-century ruler of Egypt, was prolific with gifts of porcelain. So a few, privileged Europeans could behold Chinese scenes. Islamic ceramics transmitted some images vicariously. And without influence from Islam generally, in the transmission of classical texts, in the communication of scientific knowledge and practice, especially in astronomy, in introducing Western artists to Islamic art through textiles, carpets, glassware, and pottery, and in the exchange of craftsmen, the arts and books of Renaissance Europe would have looked and read very differently and been less rich.

Spreading the Renaissance: Exploration and Ideas

However much or little the Renaissance owed to influences from outside Christendom, we can say unequivocally that, in its effects, it was the first global intellectual movement in the history of ideas: the first, that is, to resonate effects on both hemispheres and to penetrate deep into continental interiors on both sides of the equator. The Renaissance could be borne – like the biota of the Columbian Exchange – to new destinations. Derived from the study of or the desire to imitate classical antiquity, Westerners' ways of understanding language, representing reality, and modelling life accompanied the humanist curriculum around the world. Ancient Greek and Roman values and aesthetics became more widely available than any previously devised repertoire of texts, objects, and images.

On the flyleaf of his copy of Vitruvius's work on architecture – a text that taught Renaissance architects most of what they knew about classical models – Antonio de Mendoza, first viceroy of New Spain, recorded that he 'read this book in the city of Mexico' in April 1539. At the time, Franciscan professors in the nearby College of Santa Cruz de Tlatelolco were teaching young Aztec nobles to write like Cicero, and Mexico City was taking shape around the viceroy as a grid-planned exemplum of Vitruvius's principles of urban planning. Later in the same century, Jesuits presented Akbar the Great with prints by Albrecht Dürer for Mogul court artists to copy. Within little more than a generation's span, the Italian missionary Matteo Ricci introduced Chinese mandarins to Renaissance rhetoric, philosophy, astronomy, geography, and mnemotechnics as well as to the Christian message. The Renaissance, a headline writer might say, 'went global'. Nowadays, we are used to cultural globalization. Fashion, food, games, images, thoughts, and even gestures cross frontiers with the speed of light. At the time, however, the success of the Renaissance in penetrating remote parts of the world was strictly without precedent.

Exploration made possible the projection of European influence across the world. Explorers also laid out the routes along which the global ecological exchange happened. The way Columbus imagined the world – small and therefore comprehensively navigable with the technology at his disposal – therefore has some claim to be an exceptionally influential idea. Until then, knowledge of how big the world was deterred exploration. By imagining a small world, Columbus inspired efforts to put a girdle round the Earth. 'The world is small', he insisted in one of his late retrospects on his life. 'Experience has now proved it. And I have written the proof down ... with citations from Holy Scripture ... I say the world is not as big as commonly supposed ... as sure as I stand here.'[14] But his was the most productive example ever of how a wrong idea changed the world. Eratosthenes, a librarian in Alexandria, had worked out the size of the globe with remarkable accuracy in around 200 BCE, using a mixture of trigonometry, which was infallible, and measurement, which left room for doubt. Controversy remained academic until Columbus proposed new calculations, according to which the world seemed about twenty-five per cent smaller than it really is. His figures were all hopelessly wrong but they convinced him that the ocean that lapped western Europe must be narrower than was generally believed. This was the basis of his belief that he could cross it.

He was saved from disaster only because an unexpected hemisphere lay in his way: if America had not been there, he would have faced an unnavigably long journey. His miscalculation led to the exploration of a previously untravelled route linking the New World to Europe. Previously, Europeans had been unable to reach the western hemisphere, except by the unprofitable Viking seaway, current-assisted, around the edge of the Arctic, from Norway or Iceland to Newfoundland. Columbus's route was wind-assisted, therefore fast, and it linked economically exploitable regions that had large populations, ample resources, and big markets. The consequences, which of course included the beginnings of intercontinental ecological exchange, reversed other great historical trends, too. The world balance of economic power, which had long favoured China, began gradually to shift in favour of western Europeans, once they got their hands on the resources and opportunities of the Americas. Missionaries and migrants revolutionized the world balance of religious allegiance by making the New World largely Christian. Before, Christendom was a beleaguered corner; henceforth, Christianity became the biggest religion. Vast migrations occurred – some forced, like those of black slaves from Africa, some voluntary, like those of the settlers whose descendants founded and fought for the states of the modern Americas. A false idea about the size of the globe was the starting point for all these processes. The effects are still resonating as the influence of the New World on the Old becomes ever more thorough and profound.[15]

Historians, who tend to overrate academic pursuits, have exaggerated the extent to which Columbus was a scholar and even a humanist. He did read some of the classical geographical texts that the Renaissance discovered or diffused – but there is no evidence that he got round to most of them until after he had made his first transatlantic voyage and he needed learned support for his claim to have proved his theories. The reading that really influenced him was old-fashioned enough: the Bible, hagiography, and the equivalent of station-bookstall pulp fiction in his day: adventure stories of seaborne derring-do, in which, typically, a noble or royal hero, cheated of his birthright, takes to the sea, discovers islands, wrests them from monsters or ogres, and achieves exalted rank. That was the very trajectory Columbus sought in his own life.

His indifference to textual authority made him, in effect, a harbinger of the Scientific Revolution, because, like modern scientists, he preferred observed evidence over written authority. He was always exclaiming with pride how he had proved Ptolemy wrong. Humanism impelled some scholars toward science by encouraging a critical approach to textual work, but that was not enough to provoke a scientific revolution.[16] Further inducement came, in part, in the form of knowledge that accumulated from the extended reach of exploration in Columbus's wake. Explorers brought home reports of previously unknown regions and unexperienced environments, cratefuls of samples of flora and fauna, and ethnographic specimens and data: from Columbus's first transatlantic voyage onward, explorers kidnapped human exhibits to parade at home. By the seventeenth century, it became normal for explorers to make maps of the lands they visited and drawings of the landscape. Two vivid kinds of evidence display the effects: world maps, transformed in the period from devotional objects, designed not to convey what the world is really like, but to evoke awe at creation; and *Wunderkammern*, or cabinets of curiosities – the rooms where elite collectors gathered samples explorers brought home, and where the idea of the museum was born. So we come to science – the field or group of fields in which Western thinkers made their most conspicuous great leap forward in the seventeenth century, first to parity with and then, in some respects, to preponderance over their counterparts in Asia, who had so long exercised their superiority.

Scientific Revolution

The extraordinary acceleration of scientific activity in the West in the late sixteenth and seventeenth centuries – roughly, say, from Copernicus's publication of the heliocentric theory of the universe in 1543 to the death of Newton in 1727 – raises a problem similar to that of the Renaissance. Was the scientific revolution a home-grown Western achievement? It depended on access to a wider world: it was precisely owing to the contents of *Wunderkammern* and the records and maps of long-range expeditions that Western scientists were uniquely advantaged at the time. But Europeans inspired and led the voyages in question. The 'curiosities' and observations that constituted the raw material of scientific enquiry in the West were identified by Western minds and gathered by Western hands. The revolution occurred at a time of renewed trans-Eurasian contacts: indeed, the opening of direct seaborne communications between Europe and China in the second decade of the sixteenth century greatly increased the scope of potential exchange. Efforts to demonstrate that such contacts informed Western science in any important measure have failed. There were some exchanges where the fringes of Islam and Christendom brushed against each other, in the Levant, where Christian scholars sought the Ur-text of the Book of Job or lost texts of Pythagoras and picked up Arabic learning on medicine or astronomy.[17] Copernicus may have been aware of and probably adapted earlier Muslim astronomers' speculations about the shape of the cosmos.[18] Western optics also benefited from the incorporation of Muslims' work.[19] But the input is conspicuous by its paucity. And though Leibniz thought he detected Chinese parallels with his work on binomial theory, the evidence of Chinese or other far-flung oriental influence on Western science is utterly lacking.[20] The Scientific Revolution was remarkable not only for the accelerated accumulation of useful and reliable knowledge but also for the shift of initiative it represented in the balance of potential power and wealth across Eurasia: the seventeenth century was a kind of 'tipping point' in the relationship of China and Europe. The previously complacent giant of the East had to take notice of the formerly despised barbarians who, like climbers up a beanstalk, arose to demonstrate unsuspected superiority: in 1674 the Chinese emperor turned the imperial astronomical observatory over to Jesuits. Five years later, when Leibniz summarized the evidence of Chinese learning that Jesuit scholars had reported, the great polymath concluded that China and Latin Christendom were equipollent civilizations, with much to learn from each other, but that the West was ahead in physics and mathematics.[21]

Social changes, which increased the amount of leisure, investment, and learned manpower available for science, were a further part of the background in the West.[22] Most medieval practitioners, as we have seen, were clergy. Others were artisans (or artists, whose social status was not much better). In the seventeenth century, however, science became a respectable occupation for lay gentlemen, as the economic activities of aristocracies diversified. As we saw in the previous chapter, war no longer occupied them, partly thanks to the development of firepower, which anyone could wield effectively with a little training: the need to keep a costly class available for the lifelong exercise of arms vanished. Education became a route to ennoblement. The multiplication of commercial means to wealth, as explorers opened global trade routes, liberated bourgeois generations for the kinds of service in which aristocrats had formerly specialized and therefore, indirectly, aristocrats for science. Robert Boyle, a nobleman, could devote his life to science without derogation. For Isaac Newton, a tenant farmer's son, the same vocation could become a stepway to a knighthood.

The strictly intellectual origins of the Scientific Revolution lay partly in a tradition of empirical thinking that accumulated gradually or fitfully after its re-emergence in the high-medieval West (see p. 176). Of at least equal importance was growing interest in and practice of magic. We have already seen plenty of links between the science and magic of earlier eras. Those links were still strong. Astronomy overlapped with astrology, chemistry with alchemy. Dr Faustus was a fictional character, but a representative case of how yearners after learning were exposed to temptation. He sold his soul to the Devil in exchange for magical access to knowledge. If wisdom was God's gift to Solomon, occult knowledge was Satan's gift to Faust. More brainpower was expended on magic in the Renaissance than perhaps ever before or since.

Unearthing magical texts of late antiquity, scholars thought they could discover a great age of sorcerers in the pre-classical – but perhaps retrievable – past: incantations of Orpheus for the cure of the sick; talismans from pharaonic Egypt to bring statues to life or resuscitate mummies in a style later popularized by Hollywood; methods ancient Jewish cabbalists devised to invoke powers normally reserved to God. Ficino was the foremost of the many Renaissance writers who argued that magic was good if it served the needs of the sick or contributed to knowledge of nature. Ancient magical texts, formerly condemned as nonsensical or impious, became lawful reading for Christians.

In the search for wisdom more ancient than that of the Greeks, Egypt's lure was irresistible and its lore unverifiable. Hieroglyphics were indecipherable; archaeology was jejune. With no reliable source of knowledge, students did, however, have a bogus and beguiling source of insights: the corpus under the name of Hermes Trismegistos, claimed as ancient Egyptian but actually the work of an unidentified Byzantine forger. Ficino found it in a consignment of books bought from Macedonia for the Medici Library in 1460. As an alternative to the austere rationalism of classical learning it provoked a sensation.

In the last years of the sixteenth century and early in the seventeenth, the 'New Hermes' was the title magi bestowed on the Holy Roman Emperor Rudolf II (1552–1612), who patronized esoteric arts in his castle in Prague. Here astrologers and alchemists and cabbalists gathered to elicit secrets from nature and to practise what they called pansophy – the attempt to classify knowledge and so unlock access to mastery of the universe.[23] The distinction between magic and science as means of attempting to control nature almost vanished. Many of the great figures of the Scientific Revolution in the Western world of the sixteenth and seventeenth centuries either started with magic or maintained an interest in it. Johannes Kepler was one of Rudolf's protégés. Newton was a part-time alchemist. Gottfried Wilhelm Leibniz was a student of hieroglyphs and cabbalistic notation. Historians used to think that Western science grew out of the rationalism and empiricism of the Western tradition. That may be, but it also owed a lot to Renaissance magic.[24]

None of the magic worked, but the effort to manipulate it was not wasted. Alchemy spilled into chemistry, astrology into astronomy, cabbalism into mathematics, and pansophy into the classification of nature. The magi constructed what they called 'theatres of the world', in which all knowledge could be compartmentalized, along with *Wunderkammern* for the display of everything in nature – or as much, at least, as explorers could furnish: the outcome included methods of classification for life forms and languages that we still use today.

After magic, or alongside it, the work of Aristotle – who remained *hors de pair* among the objects of Western intellectuals' respect – encouraged confidence in observation and experiment as means to truth. Aristotle's effect was paradoxical: by inspiring attempts to outflank authority he encouraged experimenters to try to prove him wrong. Francis Bacon, in most accounts, represented this strand in scientific thinking and perfectly expressed the scientific temper of the early seventeenth century. He was an unlikely revolutionary: a lawyer who rose to be Lord Chancellor of England. His life was mired in bureaucracy, from which his philosophical enquiries were a brilliant diversion, until at the age of sixty he was arraigned for corruption. His defence – that he was uninfluenced by the bribes he took – was typical of his robust, uncluttered mind. He is credited with the phrase 'Knowledge is power', and his contributions to science reflect a magician's ambition to seize nature's keys as well as a lord chancellor's natural desire to know her laws. He prized observation above tradition and was said to have died a martyr to science when he caught a chill while testing the effects of low-temperature 'induration' on a chicken. This seemed an appropriate end for a scientist who recommended that 'instances of cold should be collected with all diligence'.[25]

Bacon devised the method by which scientists turn observations into general laws: induction, by which a general inference is made from a series of uniform observations, then tested. The result, if it works, is a scientific law, which can be used to make predictions.

For over three hundred years after Bacon's time, scientists claimed, on the whole, to work inductively. 'The great tragedy of science', as Darwin's henchman, Thomas Huxley, later put it, 'is the slaying of a beautiful hypothesis by an ugly fact.'[26] The reality is very different from the claim: no one ever really begins to make observations without already having a hypothesis to test. The best criterion for whether a proposition is scientific was identified by Karl Popper, who argued that scientists start with a theory, then try to prove it false. The theory is scientific if a test exists capable of proving it false; it becomes a scientific law if the test fails.[27]

Experience, to Bacon, was a better guide than reason. With the Dutch scientist J. B. van Helmont, he shared the trenchant motto 'Logic is useless for making scientific discoveries.'[28] This was consistent with the growing tension between reason and science we observed in late-medieval thought. But a final strand in the thinking of the time helped to reconcile them. René Descartes made doubt the key to the only possible certainty. Striving to escape from the suspicion that all appearances are delusive, he reasoned that the reality of his mind was proved by its own self-doubts.[29] In some ways, Descartes was an even more improbable hero than Bacon. Laziness kept him abed until noon. He claimed (falsely) to avoid reading in order not to alloy his brilliance or clutter his mind with the inferior thoughts of other authors. Scholars point to suspicious resemblances between his supposedly most original thinking and texts St Anselm wrote half a millennium earlier. The starting point, for Descartes, was the age-old problem of epistemology: how do we know that we know? How do we distinguish truth from falsehood? Suppose, he said, 'some evil genius has deployed all his energies in deceiving me.' It might then be that 'there is nothing in the world that is certain.' But, he noted, 'without doubt I exist also if he deceives me, and let him deceive me as much as he will, he will never cause me to be nothing so long as I think that I am something.' Descartes's doctrine is usually apostrophized as, 'I think, therefore I am.' It would be more helpful to reformulate it as, 'I doubt, therefore I am.' By doubting one's own existence, one proves that one exists. This left a further problem: 'What then am I? A thing which thinks. What is a thing which thinks? It is a thing which doubts, understands, conceives, affirms, denies, wills, refuses, which also imagines and feels.'[30]

Thought proceeding from such a conviction was bound to be subjective. When, for instance, Descartes inferred the existence of the soul and of God, he did so on the grounds, for the former, that he could doubt the reality of his body but not that of his thoughts, and for the latter that his knowledge of perfection must have been implanted 'by a Being truly more perfect than I'. Political and social prescriptions developed from Descartes therefore tended to be individualistic. While organic notions of society and the state never disappeared from Europe, Western civilization, by comparison with other cultures, has been the home of individualism. Descartes deserves much of the praise or blame. Determinism remained attractive to constructors of cosmic systems: in the generations after Descartes, Baruch Spinoza, the Jewish materialist and intellectual provocateur who achieved the distinction of censure by Catholic and Jewish authorities alike, implicitly denied free will. Even Leibniz, who devoted much effort to refuting Spinoza, eliminated free will from his secret thoughts, and suspected that God, in his goodness, allowed us only the illusion that we have it. But in the following century, determinism became a marginalized heresy in an age that made freedom its highest value among a strictly limited range of 'self-evident truths'. Descartes, moreover, contributed something even more sacred to our modernity: by rehabilitating reason alongside science, his era left us an apparently complete toolkit for thinking – science and reason realigned.

Beyond or beneath this mental apparatus, much of the new science that explorers triggered was to do with the Earth. Locating the Earth in the cosmos was a task inextricably entwined with the rapidly unfolding technology of maps. When texts by Ptolemy, the great second-century BCE Alexandrian geographer, began to circulate in the West in the fifteenth century, they came to dominate the way the learned pictured the world. Even before Latin translations began to circulate, Western mapmakers imbibed one of Ptolemy's big ideas: constructing maps on the basis of co-ordinates of longitude and latitude. Latitude turned cartographers' eyes toward the heavens, because a relatively easy way to fix it was by observation of the sun and the Pole Star. Longitude did so, too, because it demanded minute and complicated celestial observations. Meanwhile, astronomical data remained of major importance in two traditional fields: astrology and meteorology. In partial consequence, the technology of astronomy improved; from the early seventeenth century, the telescope made visible previously unglimpsed parts of the heavens. Increasingly accurate clockwork helped record celestial motion. Hence, in part, the advantage Jesuit astronomers established over local practitioners when they got to China. The Chinese knew about glassware, but, preferring porcelain, had not bothered to develop it. They knew about clockwork, but had no use for timing mechanisms that were independent of the sun and stars. Westerners, by contrast, needed the technologies China neglected for devotional reasons: glass, to rim churches with light-transmuting, image-bearing windows; clocks to regularize the hours of monastic prayer.[31]

The era's biggest new idea in cosmology, however, owed nothing to technical innovations and everything to rethinking traditional data with an open mind. It arose in 1543, when the Polish astronomer Nicolaus Copernicus proposed reclassifying the Earth as one of several planets revolving around the sun. Until then, the prevailing mental picture of the cosmos was unresolved. On the one hand, the vastness of God dwarfed the material universe, as eternity dwarfed time. On the other, our planet and therefore our species was at the heart of observable space, and the other planets, sun, and stars seemed to surround it as courtiers surround a sovereign or shelters a hearth. Ancient Greeks had debated the geocentric model, but most upheld it. In the most influential synthesis of ancient astronomy, Ptolemy ensured that geocentrism would be the orthodoxy of the next thousand years. Toward the end of the tenth century, Al-Biruni, the great Persian geographer, questioned it, as did subsequent theorists writing in Arabic (some of whose work Copernicus almost certainly knew).[32] In the fourteenth century, in Paris, Nicolas of Oresme thought the arguments finely balanced. By the sixteenth century, so many contrary observations had accumulated that a new theory seemed essential.

Copernicus's suggestion was formulated tentatively, propagated discreetly, and spread slowly. He received the first printing of his great book on the heavens when he lay on his deathbed, half paralysed, his mind and memory wrecked. It took nearly a hundred years to recast people's vision of the universe in a Copernican mould. In combination with Johannes Kepler's early-seventeenth-century work on the mapping of orbits around the sun, the Copernican revolution expanded the limits of the observable heavens, substituted a dynamic for a static system, and wrenched the perceived universe into a new shape around the elliptical paths of the planets.[33]

This shift of focus from the Earth to the sun was a strain on eyes adjusted to a geocentric galactic outlook. It would be mistaken, however, to suppose that the 'medieval mind' was focused on humans. The centre of the total composition was God. The world was tiny compared to heaven. The part of creation inhabited by man was a tiny blob in a corner of an image of God at work on creation: Earth and firmament together were a small disc trapped between God's dividers, like a bit of fluff trapped in a pair of tweezers. Yet humans were at least as puny in a heliocentric universe as they had seemed formerly in the hands of God: perhaps more so, because Copernicus displaced the planet we live on from its central position. Every subsequent revelation of astronomy has reduced the relative dimensions of our dwelling place and ground its apparent significance into tinier fragments.

God is easy to fit around the cosmos. The problem for religion is where to fit man inside it. Like every new scientific paradigm, heliocentrism challenged the Church to adjust. Religion often seems to go with the notion that everything was made for us and that human beings have a privileged rank in divine order. Science has made such a cosmos incredible. Therefore – it is tempting to conclude – religion is now purposeless and incapable of surviving the findings of science. So how did the Christian understanding of human beings' value survive heliocentrism?

Religion, I suspect, is not necessarily an inference from the order of the universe: it can be a reaction against chaos, an act of defiance of muddle. So the challenge of Copernicanism, which made better sense of the order of the cosmos, was not hard to accommodate. The illusion that it conflicts with Christianity arose from the peculiar circumstances of a much-misunderstood case. Galileo Galilei, the first effective wielder of the telescope for astronomical observation, was an eloquent teacher of the heliocentric theory. He exposed himself to inquisitorial persecution in the course of what was really an academic demarcation dispute. Galileo presumed to take part in the textual criticism of Scripture, deploying Copernican theory to elucidate a text from Exodus, in which Joshua's prayers make the sun halt in its heavenly course. He was forbidden to return to the subject; but there was, as Galileo himself maintained, nothing unorthodox in Copernicanism, and other scholars, including clerics and even some inquisitors, continued to teach it. In the 1620s, Pope Urban VIII, who did not hesitate to acknowledge that Copernicus was right about the solar system, encouraged Galileo to break his silence and publish a work reconciling the heliocentric and geocentric pictures with recourse to the old paradigm of two kinds of truth – scientific and religious. The treatise the scientist produced, however, made no such concessions to geocentrism. Meanwhile, papal court politics alerted rival factions, especially within the Jesuit order, to the potential for exploiting astronomical debate, as Copernicans were heavily overrepresented in one faction. Galileo was caught in the crossfire, condemned in 1633, and confined to his home, while suspicion of heresy tainted heliocentrism. Everyone who thought seriously about it, however, realized that the Copernican synthesis was the best available description of the observed universe.[34] The pop version of the episode – benighted religion tormenting bright science – is drivel.

After the work of Galileo and Kepler, the cosmos seemed more complicated than before, but no less divine and no more disorderly. Gravity, which Isaac Newton discovered in a bout of furious thinking and experimenting, beginning in the 1660s, reinforced the appearance of order. It seemed to confirm the idea of an engineered universe that reflected the creator's mind. It was, to those who perceived it, the underlying, permeating secret, which had eluded the Renaissance magi. Newton imagined the cosmos as a mechanical contrivance – like the wind-up orreries, in brass and gleaming wood, that became popular toys for gentlemen's libraries. A celestial engineer tuned it. A ubiquitous force turned and stabilized it. You could see God at work in the swing of a pendulum or the fall of an apple, as well as in the motions of moons and planets.

Newton was a traditional figure: an old-fashioned humanist and an encyclopaedist, a biblical scholar obsessed by sacred chronology – even, in his wilder fantasies, a magus hunting down the secret of a systematic universe, or an alchemist seeking the Philosopher's Stone. He was also a representative figure of a trend in the thought of his time: empiricism, the doctrine beloved in England and Scotland in his day, that reality is observable and verifiable by sense perception. The universe, as empiricists saw it, consisted of events 'cemented' by causation, of which Newton found a scientific description and exposed the laws. 'Nature's Laws', according to the epitaph Alexander Pope wrote, 'lay hid in Night' until 'God said, "Let Newton be!" and there was Light.' It turned out to be an act of divine self-effacement. Newton thought gravity was God's way of holding the universe together. Many of his followers did not agree on that point. Deism throve in the eighteenth century in Europe, partly because the mechanical universe could dispense with the divine Watchmaker after he had given it its initial winding. By the end of the eighteenth century, Pierre-Simon Laplace, who interpreted almost every known physical phenomenon in terms of the attraction and repulsion of particles, could boast that he had reduced God to 'an unnecessary hypothesis'. According to Newton's description of himself, 'I seem only to have been like a boy playing on the sea-shore ... while the great ocean of truth lay all undiscovered before me.' As we shall see in future chapters, the navigators who followed him onto it were not bound to steer by his course.[35]

Political Thought

New political thinking in the age of the Renaissance and the Scientific Revolution followed a similar trajectory to that of science, beginning with reverence for antiquity, adjusting to the impact of new discoveries, and ending in revolution.

People started by looking back to the Greeks and Romans but invented new ideas in response to new problems: the rise of sovereign states and of unprecedented new empires forced thinking into new patterns. The new worlds that exploration revealed stimulated political as well as scientific imaginations. Ideal lands, imagined in order to make implicit criticisms of real countries, had always figured in political thoughts. In Plato's imaginary ideal society, arts were outlawed and infants exposed. The *Liezi*, a work complete by about 200 BCE, featured a perfumed land discovered by a legendary emperor, who was also a great explorer, where 'people were gentle, following Nature without strife',[36] practising free love, and devoted to music. Zhou Kangyuan in the thirteenth century told a tale of travellers returning, satiated from paradise, to find the real world empty and desolate. Most peoples have golden age myths of harmony, amity, and plenty. Some humanists responded to Columbus's accounts of his discoveries by supposing that he had stumbled on a golden age, such as classical poets sang of, that survived, uncorrupted from a remote past in fortunate isles. The people Columbus reported seemed almost prelapsarian. They were naked, as if in evocation of Eden and of utter dependence on God. They exchanged gold for worthless trinkets. They were 'docile' – Columbus's code for easily enslaved – and naturally reverent.

The model work that gave the utopia genre its name was Thomas More's *Utopia* of 1529. 'There is hardly a scheme of political or social reform', according to Sidney Lee, a critic who spoke for most of More's interpreters, 'of which there is no definite adumbration in More's pages.'[37] But Utopia was a strangely cheerless place, where there were gold chamber pots and no pubs, and the classless, communistic regime delivered education without emotion, religion without love, and contentment without happiness. A string of other wonderlands followed, inspired by the real-life El Dorados explorers were disclosing at the time. They seemed to get ever less appealing. In Tommaso Campanella's *La città del sole* of 1580, sexual couplings had to be licensed by astrologers. Milton's Paradise would have bored any lively denizen to death. Louis-Antoine de Bougainville thought he had found a real-life sexual utopia in eighteenth-century Tahiti and found on departure that his ships' crews were raddled with venereal disease. In the following century, in Charles Fourier's projected settlement, which he called Harmony, orgies were to be organized with a degree of bureaucratic particularity such as seems certain to kill passion. In America, as John Adolphus Etzler proposed to remodel it in 1833, mountains are flattened and forests 'ground to dust' to make cement for building: something like this has actually happened in parts of modern America. In Icaria, the utopia Étienne Cabet launched in Texas in 1849, clothes had to be made of elastic to make the principle of equality 'suit people of different sizes'. In Elizabeth Corbett's feminist utopia, the empowered women get terribly pleased with cures for wrinkles.[38]

In individual Western imaginations, in short, most utopias have turned out to be dystopias in disguise: deeply repellent, albeit advocated with impressive sincerity. All utopianists evince misplaced faith in the power of society to improve citizens. They all want us to defer to fantasy father-figures who would surely make life wretched: guardians, proletarian dictators, intrusive computers, know-all theocrats, or paternalistic sages who do your thinking for you, overregulate your life, and crush or stretch you into comfortless conformity. Every utopia is an empire of Procrustes. The nearest approximations to lasting realizations of utopian visions in the real world were built in the twentieth century by Bolsheviks and Nazis. The search for an ideal society is like the pursuit of happiness: it is better to travel hopefully, because arrival breeds disillusionment.

Niccolò Machiavelli's realism is usually seen as a perfect contrast with More's fantasy. But Machiavelli's was the more inventive imagination. He traduced all previous Western thinking about government. The purpose of the state – ancient moralists decreed – is to make its citizens good. Political theorists of antiquity and the Middle Ages recommended various kinds of state, but they all agreed that the state must have a moral purpose: to increase virtue or happiness or both. Even the legalist school in ancient China advocated oppression in the wider interest of the oppressed. When Machiavelli wrote *The Prince*, his rules for rulers, in 1513, the book seemed shocking to readers not just because the author recommended lying, cheating, ruthlessness, and injustice, but because he did so with no apparent concession to morality. Machiavelli cut all references to God out of his descriptions of politics and made only mocking references to religion. Politics was a savage, lawless wilderness, where 'a ruler ... must be a fox to recognize traps and a lion to frighten off wolves'.[39] The only basis of decision making was the ruler's own interest, and his only responsibility was to keep hold of his power. He should keep faith – only when it suits him. He should feign virtue. He should affect to be religious. Later thinking borrowed two influences from this: first, the doctrine of realpolitik: the state is not subject to moral laws and serves only itself; second, the claim that the end justifies the means and that any excesses are permissible for the survival of the state, or public safety, as some later formulations put it. Meanwhile, 'Machiavel' became a term of abuse in English and the Devil was apostrophized as 'Old Nic'.

But did Machiavelli really mean what he said? He was a master of irony who wrote plays about behaviour so revoltingly immoral that they could make men good. His book for rulers is full of contemporary examples of monarchs of ill repute, whom many readers would have despised: yet they are portrayed as models to imitate with deadpan insouciance. The hero of the book is Cesare Borgia, a bungling adventurer who failed to carve out a state for himself, and whose failure Machiavelli excuses on grounds of bad luck. The catalogue of immoralities seems as suited to condemn the princes who practise them as to constitute rules of conduct for imitators. The real message of the book is perhaps concealed in a colophon, in which Machiavelli appeals to fame as an end worth striving for and demands the unification of Italy, with the expulsion of the French and Spanish 'barbarians' who had conquered parts of the country. It is significant that *The Prince* explicitly deals only with monarchies. In the rest of his oeuvre, the author clearly preferred republics and thought monarchies were suited only to degenerate periods in what he saw as a cyclical history of civilization. Republics were best because a sovereign people was wiser and more faithful than monarchs. Yet, if *The Prince* was meant to be ironic, a greater irony followed: it was taken seriously by almost everyone who read it, and started two traditions that have remained influential to this day: a Machiavellian tradition, which exalts the interests of the state, and an anti-Machiavellian quest to put morals back into politics. All our debates about how far the state is responsible for welfare, health, and education go back to whether it is responsible for goodness.[40]

More, perhaps, than Machiavellianism, Machiavelli's great contribution to history was *The Art of War*, in which he proposed that citizen armies were best. There was only one thing wrong with this idea: it was impracticable. The reason why states relied on mercenaries and professional soldiers was that soldiering was a highly technical business; weapons were hard to handle well; experience was essential seasoning for battle. Gonzalo de Córdoba, the 'Great Captain' of the Spanish armies that conquered much of Italy, invited Machiavelli to instruct his troops: the result was a hopeless parade-ground tangle. Still, the citizen might be a superior soldier in some ways: cheaper, more committed, and more reliable than the mercenaries, who avoided battle and protracted wars in order to extend their employment. The result was a 'Machiavellian moment' in the history of the Western world, where yeomanries and militias of dubious efficacy were maintained for essentially ideological reasons, alongside regular, professional forces.

Machiavelli's influence in this respect contributed to political instability in the early modern West: armed citizenries could and sometimes did provide cannon fodder for revolution. By the late eighteenth century, however, the game had changed. Technically simple firearms could be effective even in ill-instructed hands. The impact of large masses of troops and intense firepower counted for more than expertise. The American Revolutionary War was a transitional conflict: militias defended the revolution with help from professional French forces. By the time of the French Revolution, newly liberated 'citizens' had to do all their fighting for themselves. 'The Nation in Arms' won most of its battles, and the era of mass conscription began. It lasted until the late twentieth century, when rapid technical developments made large conscript forces redundant, though some countries kept 'national service' going in order to maintain a reservoir of manpower for defence or in the belief that military discipline is good for young people. Another, apparently ineradicable relic of the Machiavellian moment is that peculiar institution of the United States: the loose gun laws, which are usually justified on the grounds that tight regulation of the gun trade would infringe the citizen's constitutional right to bear arms. Few US citizens today realize that they are admiring a doctrine of Machiavelli's when they cite with satisfaction the Second Amendment to the Constitution: 'A well-regulated militia being necessary to the security of a free state, the right of the people to keep and bear arms shall not be infringed.'[41]

Machiavelli was, in one respect, a faithful monitor of his own times: the power of states and of rulers within states was increasing. The ideal of Western political unity faded as states solidified their political independence and exerted more control over their inhabitants. In the Middle Ages, hopes of such unity had focused on the prospect of reviving the unity of the ancient Roman Empire. The term 'Roman Empire' survived in the formal name of the group of mainly German states – the Holy Roman Empire of the German Nation. When the king of Spain was elected to be Emperor Charles V in 1519, the outlook for uniting Europe seemed favourable. Through inheritance from his father, Charles was already ruler of the Low Countries, Austria, and much of Central Europe. His propagandists speculated that he or his son would be the 'Last World Emperor' foretold by prophecy, whose reign would inaugurate the final age of the world before the Second Coming of Christ. Naturally, however, most other states resisted this idea, or tried to claim the role for their own rulers. Charles V's attempt to impose religious uniformity on his empire failed, demonstrating the limits of his real power. After his abdication in 1556, no one ever again convincingly reasserted the prospect of a durable universal state in the tradition of Rome.

Meanwhile, rulers eclipsed rivals to their authority and boosted their power over their own citizens. Though most European states experienced civil wars in the sixteenth and seventeenth centuries, monarchs usually won them. Cities and churches surrendered most of their privileges of self-government. The Reformation was, in this respect as in most others, a sideshow: Church yielded to state, irrespective of where heresy or schism struck. Aristocracies – their personnel transformed as old families died out and rulers elevated new families to noble status – became close collaborators in royal power, rather than rivals to it, as aristocrats had been so often in the past. Offices under the crown became increasingly profitable additions to the income that aristocrats earned from their inherited estates.

Countries that had been difficult or impossible to rule before their civil wars became easy to govern when their violent and restless elements had been exhausted or became dependent on royal rewards and appointments. Ease of government is measurable in yields from taxation. Louis XIV of France turned his nobles into courtiers, dispensed with representative institutions, treated taxation as 'plucking the goose with minimal hissing', and proclaimed, 'I am the state.' England and Scotland had been particularly hard for their monarchs to tax in the sixteenth and early seventeenth centuries. The so-called Glorious Revolution of 1688–9, which its aristocratic leaders represented as a blow against royal tyranny, actually turned Britain into Europe's most fiscally efficient state. In place of a dynasty committed to peace, the revolution installed rulers who fought expensive wars. Taxation trebled during the reign of the monarchs crowned by the British revolutionaries.

Along with the growth of the power of the state, the way people thought about politics changed. Traditionally, law was a body of wisdom handed down from the past (see pp. 97, 189). Now it came to be seen as a code that kings and parliaments could endlessly change and recreate. Legislation replaced jurisdiction as the main function of government: in Lithuania a statute of 1588 actually redefined the nature of sovereignty in those terms. In other countries, the change simply happened without formal declaration, though a French political philosopher, Jean Bodin, formulated the new doctrine of sovereignty in 1576. Sovereignty defined the state, which had the sole right to make laws and distribute justice to its subjects. Sovereignty could not be shared. There was no portion of it for the Church, or any sectional interest, or any outside power. In a flood of statutes, states' power submerged vast new areas of public life and common welfare: labour relations, wages, prices, forms of land tenure, markets, the food supply, livestock breeding, and even, in some cases, what personal adornments people could wear.

Historians often search for the origins of the 'modern state', in which the authority of the aristocracy shrank to insignificance, the crown enforced an effective monopoly of government jurisdiction, the independence of towns withered, the Church submitted to royal control, and sovereignty became increasingly identified with supreme legislative power, as laws multiplied. Instead of scouring Europe for a model of this kind of modernity, it might make better sense to look further afield, in the terrains of experiment that overseas imperialism laid at European rulers' feet. The New World really was new. The Spanish experience there was one of the biggest surprises of history: the creation of the first great world empire of land and sea, and the only one, on a comparable scale, erected without the aid of industrial technology. A new political environment took shape. Great nobles were generally absent from the Spanish colonial administration, which was staffed by professional, university-trained bureaucrats whom the crown appointed and paid. Town councils were largely composed of royal nominees. Church patronage was exclusively at the disposal of the crown. With a few exceptions, feudal tenure – combining the right to try cases at law along with land ownership – was banned. Though Spaniards with rights to Native American labour or tribute pretended to enjoy a sort of fantasy feudalism, speaking loosely of their 'vassals', they were usually denied formal legal rights to govern or administer justice, and the vassals in question were subject only to the king. Meanwhile, a stream of legislation regulated – or, with varying effectiveness, was supposed to regulate – the new society in the Americas. The Spanish Empire was never efficient, because of the vast distances royal authority had to cover. One should not demand, as Dr Johnson recommended of a dog walking on its hind legs, that it be well done, but applaud the fact that it could happen at all. Remote administrators in American hinterlands and Pacific islands could and did ignore royal commands. In emergencies, locals extemporized *sui generis* methods of government based on ties of kinship or of shared rewards. But if one looks at the Spanish Empire overall it resembles a modern state because it was a bureaucratic state and a state governed by laws.

China already displayed some of the same features – and had done for centuries, with a tame aristocracy, subordinate clergies, a professional administrative class, a remarkably uniform bureaucracy, and a law code at the emperor's disposal. These features anticipated modernity but did not guarantee efficiency: magistrates' jurisdictions were usually so large that a lot of power remained effectively in local hands; administration was so costly that corruption was rife. In the mid-seventeenth century, China fell to Manchu invaders – a mixture of foresters and plainsmen, whom the Chinese despised as barbarians. The shock made Chinese intellectuals re-evaluate the way they understood political legitimacy. A doctrine of the sovereignty of the people emerged, similar to those we have seen circulating in the late Middle Ages in Europe. Huang Zongxi, a rigid moralist who devoted much of his career to avenging his father's judicial murder at the hands of political enemies, fled into exile rather than endure foreign rule. He postulated a state of nature where 'each man looked to himself' until benevolent individuals created the empire. Corruption set in and 'the ruler's self-interest took the place of the common good ... The ruler takes the very marrow from people's bones and takes daughters and sons to serve his debauchery.'[42] Lü Liuliang, his younger fellow exile, whose distaste for barbarians dominated his thinking, went further: 'The common man and the emperor', he said, 'are rooted in the same nature ... It might seem as though social order was projected downwards to the common man' but, from the perspective of heaven, 'the principle originates with the people and reaches up to the ruler'. He added, 'Heaven's order and Heaven's justice are not things rulers and ministers can take and make their own.'[43]

In the West, this sort of thinking helped to justify republics and generate revolutions. Nothing comparable happened in China, however, until the twentieth century, when a great deal of Western influence had done its work. There were plenty of peasant rebellions in the interim, but, as throughout the Chinese past, they aimed to renew the empire, replacing the dynasty, not ending the system by transferring the Mandate of Heaven from monarch to people. Unlike the West, China had no examples of republicanism or democracy to look to in history or idealize in myth. Still, the work of Huang, Lü, and the theorists who accompanied and followed them was not without practical consequences: it passed into Confucian tradition, served to keep radical criticism of the imperial system alive, and helped to prepare Chinese minds for the later reception of Western revolutionary ideas.[44]

Nor did Chinese scholars need to think about international law, which, as we shall see in a moment, became a focus of obsessive concern in the early modern West. 'Middle Kingdom', or 'Central Country', is one of the most persistent names Chinese have given their land. In a sense, it is a modest designation, since it implicitly acknowledges a world beyond China, as certain alternative names – 'All under Heaven', 'All Within the Four Seas' – do not. But it conveys unmistakable connotations of superiority: a vision of the world in which the barbarian rim is undeserving of the benefits and unrewarding of the bother of Chinese conquest. 'Who', asked Ouyang Xiu, an eminent Confucian of the eleventh century, 'would exhaust China's resources to quarrel with serpents and swine?'[45] Orthodox Confucianism expected barbarians to be attracted to Chinese rule by example: awareness of China's manifest superiority would induce them to submit without the use of force. To some extent, this improbable formula worked. Chinese culture did attract neighbouring peoples: Koreans and Japanese largely adopted it; many Central and South-East Asian peoples were deeply influenced by it. Conquerors of China from the outside have always been seduced by it.

The Zhou dynasty, which seized control of China towards the end of the second millennium BCE, is generally said first to have adopted the term 'Middle Kingdom'. By then, China constituted all the world that counted; other humans, in Chinese estimations, were outsiders, clinging to the edges of civilization, or envying it from beyond. From time to time the picture might be modified; barbarian kingdoms might be ranked in greater or lesser proximity to China's unique perfection. At intervals, powerful barbarian rulers exacted treaties on equal terms or attracted titles of equal resonance. From Chinese emperors willing to purchase security in response to threats, foreign powers could often extort tribute due to patrons of equal or even superior status, though the Chinese clung to the convenient fiction that they paid such remittances merely as acts of condescension.

In what we think of as the Middle Ages, the name of the Middle Kingdom reflected a world picture, with Mount Chongshan in Henan Province at the exact centre, the true nature of which was much disputed among scholars. In the twelfth century, for instance, the prevailing opinion was that, since the world was spherical, its centre was a purely metaphorical expression. In the most detailed surviving maps of the twelfth century the world was divided between China and the barbarian residue; the image persisted. Although in 1610 Matteo Ricci, the visiting Jesuit who introduced Western science to China, was criticized for failing to place China centrally in his 'Great Map of Ten Thousand Countries', this did not mean that Chinese scholars had an unrealistic world view, only that the symbolic nature of China's centrality had to be acknowledged in representations of the world. Cartographic conventions do, however, tell us something about the self-perception of those who devise them: like the fixing of the Greenwich meridian, which makes one's distance from the capital of the British Empire one's place in the world, or Mercator's projection, which exaggerates the importance of northerly countries.[46]

Japanese political thought was heavily dependent on the influence of Chinese texts and doctrines, and was therefore also largely indifferent to the problems of how to regulate interstate relations. From the first great era of Chinese influence in Japan in the seventh century CE, Japanese intellectuals submitted to Chinese cultural superiority, as Western barbarians did to that of ancient Rome. They absorbed Buddhism and Confucianism from China, adopted Chinese characters for their language, and chose Chinese as the language of the literature they wrote. But they never accepted that these forms of flattery implied political deference. The Japanese world picture was twofold. First, in part, it was Buddhist and the traditional world map was borrowed from Indian cosmography: India was in the middle, with Mount Meru – perhaps a stylized representation of the Himalayas – as the focal point of the world. China was one of the outer continents and Japan consisted of 'scattered grains at the edge of the field'. Yet at the same time, this gave Japan a critical advantage: because Buddhism arrived late, Japan was the home of its most mature phase, where, so Japanese Buddhists thought, purified doctrines were nourished.[47]

Second, there was an indigenous tradition of the Japanese as the offspring of a divine progenitrix. In 1339, Kitabatake Chikafusa began the tradition of calling Japan 'divine country', claiming for his homeland a limited superiority: proximity to China made it superior to all other barbarian lands. Japanese replies to tribute demands in the Ming period challenged Chinese assumptions with an alternative vision of a politically plural cosmos and a concept of territorial sovereignty: 'Heaven and earth are vast; they are not monopolized by one ruler. The universe is great and wide, and the various countries are created each to have a share in ruling it.'[48] By the 1590s, the Japanese military dictator

Hideyoshi could dream of 'crushing China like an egg' and 'teaching the Chinese Japanese customs'.[49] This was a remarkable (though not a sustained) reversal of previous norms.

The traditions were summarized and taken to a further stage by the Confucian astronomer Nishikawa Joken (1648–1724), guided by contacts with the West and informed by the vastness of the world that Western cartography disclosed. He pointed out that no country was literally central in a round world, but that Japan was genuinely divine and inherently superior on allegedly scientific grounds: the climate was best there, which was proof of heaven's favour. From the time of the Meiji restoration in 1868, a state-building ideology recycled traditional elements in a myth of modern concoction, representing all Japanese as descendants of the sun goddess. The emperor is her senior descendant by the direct line. His authority is that of a head of family. The 1889 constitution called him 'sacred and inviolable', the product of a continuity of succession 'unbroken for eternal ages'. The most influential commentary on the constitution averred that 'the Sacred Throne was established when the heavens and earth separated. The Emperor is Heaven, descended, divine and sacred.'[50] Acknowledging defeat after the Second World War, Emperor Hirohito repudiated, according to the translation deemed official by the US occupying forces, 'the false conception that the Emperor is divine, and that the Japanese people are superior to other races'. But allusions to the divinity of emperor and people continually resurface in political discourse, popular culture, religious rhetoric, and the comic books that, in Japan, are respectable adult entertainments.[51]

In the West, once the notion of a universal empire had collapsed, even as a theoretical ideal, it was impossible to take as narrow a view of interstate relations as in China or Japan. In Europe's teeming state system, a way of escape from chaotic, anarchic international relations was essential. When Thomas Aquinas summarized the traditional state of thinking in the Western world in the thirteenth century, he distinguished the laws of individual states from what, following traditional usage, he called the *ius gentium*, the Law of Nations, which all states must obey and which governs the relationships between them. Yet he never said what where or how this *ius gentium* could be codified. It was not the same as the basic, universal principles of justice, because these excluded slavery and private property, both of which the Law of Nations recognized. Many other jurists assumed it was identical with natural law, which, however, is also hard to identify in complex cases. In the late sixteenth century, the Jesuit theologian Francisco Suárez (1548–1617) solved the problem in a radical way: the Law of Nations 'differs in an absolute sense', he said, 'from natural law' and 'is simply a kind of positive human law': that is, it says whatever people agree it should say.[52]

This formula made it possible to construct an international order along lines first proposed earlier in the sixteenth century by one of Suárez's predecessors at the University of Salamanca, the Dominican Francisco de Vitoria, who advocated laws 'created by the authority of the whole world' – not just pacts or agreements between states. In 1625 the Dutch jurist Hugo Grotius worked out the system that prevailed until the late twentieth century. His aim was peace. He deplored the use of war as a kind of default system in which states declared hostilities with trigger-happy abandon, with 'no reverence left for human or divine law, exactly as if a single edict had released a sudden madness'. Natural law, he argued, obliged states to respect each other's sovereignty; their relations were regulated by the mercantile and maritime laws that they formerly ratified or traditionally embraced, and by treaties they made between themselves, which had the force of contracts and which could be enforced by war. This system did not need ideological concurrence to back it. It could embrace the world beyond Christendom. It would remain valid, Grotius said, even if God did not exist.[53]

It lasted reasonably well, but not as enduringly as Grotius's claims might have led his readers to hope. His system was fairly successful in helping to limit bloodshed in the eighteenth century. For a while, law seemed to have filleted savagery out of warfare. The great compiler of the laws of war, Emer de Vattel, thought combat could be civilized. 'A man of exalted soul', he wrote, 'no longer feels any emotions but those of compassion towards a conquered enemy who has submitted to his arms ... Let us never forget that our enemies are men. Though reduced to the disagreeable necessity of prosecuting our right by force of arms, let us not divest ourselves of that charity which connects us with all mankind.' Such pieties did not protect all victims of combat, especially in guerrilla warfare and in aggression against non-European enemies.

But law did make battle more humane. For much of the nineteenth century, when generals abandoned all notions of restraint in pursuit of 'total war', Grotius's principles still contributed to and maintained peace – at least in Europe. The horrors of the twentieth century, however, and especially the genocidal massacres that came to seem routine, made reform urgent. At first, when US governments proposed a 'new international order' after the Second World War, most people assumed there would be a collaborative system in which international relations would be brokered and enforced by the United Nations. In practice, however, it meant the hegemony of a single superpower, acting as a global policeman. Exercised by the United States, the role proved unsustainable because, although American policy was generally benign, it could not be immune to the distortions of self-interest or escape the outrage of those who felt unfairly treated. By the twenty-first century, it was obvious that the US monopoly of superpower status was coming to an end. The power of the United States – measured as a proportion of the wealth of the world – was in decline. Today, the search is on for an international system that will succeed American guardianship, and no solution is in sight.[54] Grotius left another still redolent, relevant legacy: he tried to divide the oceans of the world, which were arenas of ever intensifying conflict among rival European maritime empires, into zones of free and restricted movement. His initiative was designed to favour the Dutch Empire over others, and was rejected by legists in most other countries, but it laid down terms of debate which still animate controversies over whether the Internet is like the ocean – a free zone everywhere, or a partible resource for sovereign states to control if they can or divide if they wish.[55]

Redefining Humanity

In the sixteenth century, a further consequence of the construction of extra-European empires was to turn political thought back to wider considerations that transcended the limits of states. 'All the peoples of humankind are human', said the Spanish moral reformer Bartolomé de Las Casas in the mid-sixteenth century.[56] It sounds like a truism, but it was an attempt to express one of the most novel and powerful ideas of modern times: the unity of humankind. The recognition that everyone we now call human belonged to a single species was by no means a foregone conclusion. To insist, as Las Casas did, that we all belong to a single moral community was visionary.

For in most cultures, in most periods, no such concept existed. Legendary monsters, often mistaken for products of teeming imaginations, are really the opposite: evidence of people's mental limitations – their inability to conceive of strangers in the same terms as themselves. Most languages have no term for 'human' that comprehends those outside the group: most peoples refer to outsiders by their name for 'beasts' or 'demons'.[57] There is, as it were, no middle term between 'brother' and 'other'. Although sages of the first millennium BCE had expatiated on the unity of humankind, and Christianity had made belief in our common descent a religious orthodoxy, no one was ever sure where to draw the line between humans and supposed subspecies. Medieval biology imagined a 'chain of being' in which, between humans and brute beasts, lay an intermediate, monstrous category of *similitudines hominis* – creatures resembling men but not fully human. Some of them appeared vividly to the imaginations of mapmakers and illuminators, because the Roman naturalist Pliny catalogued them, in a work of the mid-first century CE, which Renaissance readers treated with all the credulity an ancient text was thought to deserve. He listed dog-headed men, and Nasamones, who wrapped themselves in their enormous ears, Sciapods who bounced around on one leg, pygmies and giants, people with backward-turned, eight-toed feet, and others who took nourishment by inhaling for want of mouths, or had tails or lacked eyes, sea-green men who battled griffins, hairy folk, and Amazons, as well as 'the Anthropophagi and men whose heads do grow beneath their shoulders' who were among the adversaries Shakespeare's Othello faced.

Medieval artists made the images of these creatures familiar. Should they be classed as beasts or men or something in between? On the portico of the twelfth-century monastery church of Vézelay many of them appear in procession, approaching Christ to be judged at the Last Trump; so the monks clearly thought the weird creatures capable of salvation, but other scrutineers, with the authority of St Albertus Magnus, denied that such aberrations could possess rational souls or qualify for eternal bliss. Naturally, explorers were always on the lookout for such creatures. It took a papal bull to convince some people that Native Americans were truly human (even then some Protestants denied it, suggesting that there must have been a second creation of a different species or a demonic engendering of deceptively human-like creatures in America). Similar doubts were raised concerning blacks, Hottentots, Pygmies, Australian aboriginals, and every other odd or surprising discovery exploration brought to light. There was a protracted debate concerning apes in the eighteenth century, and the Scots jurisprudentialist Lord Monboddo championed the orang-utan's claim to be considered human.[58] One should not condemn people who had difficulty recognizing their kinship with other humans or deride those who sensed humanity in apes: the evidence on which we base our classifications took a long time to accumulate, and the boundaries of species are mutable.

The question of where to draw the frontiers of humankind is of vital importance: ask those who, unfairly classified, would lose human rights. Although over the last couple of hundred years we have drawn the limits of humankind ever wider, the process may not yet be over. Darwin complicated it. 'The difference', he said, 'between savage and civilized man ... is greater than between a wild and domesticated animal.'[59] The theory of evolution suggested that no rupture of the line of descent divides humans from the rest of creation. Campaigners for animal rights concluded that even our present broad category of humankind is in one respect too inelastic. How far should our moral community, or at least our list of creatures with selective rights, stretch beyond our species to accommodate other animals?

Another problem arises: how far back should we project our human category? What about Neanderthals? What about early hominids? We may never meet a Neanderthal or a *Homo erectus* on the bus, but from their tombs they admonish us to interrogate the limits of our moral communities. Even today, when we set the frontiers of humanity more generously, perhaps, than at any time in the past, we have really only shifted the terms of the debate: there are no Neanderthals on the bus, but there are analogous cases – the unborn in wombs, the moribund in care – that are more immediately challenging, because they belong unquestionably to our own species. But do they share human rights? Do they have the right to life – without which all other rights are meaningless? If not, why not? What is the moral difference between humans at different stages of life? Can one detect such a difference more readily or objectively than between humans, say, with different pigmentation, or variously long noses?

A large view of humankind; a narrow view of the moral responsibilities of the state; shaky confidence in sovereign states as a workable basis for the world, without overarching empires or theocracies; classicizing values and aesthetics; and faith in science and reason as allied means to truth: these were the ideas that made the world the Renaissance and Scientific Revolution bequeathed to the eighteenth century: the world in which the Enlightenment happened.

Chapter 7

Global Enlightenments

Joined-Up Thinking in a Joined-Up World

Reflected and refracted among the rocks and ice, the dazzle made the Arctic 'a place for fairies and spirits',[1] according to the diary of Pierre Louis Moreau de Maupertuis, who pitched camp at Kittis in northern Finland, in August 1736. He was engaged in the most elaborate and expensive scientific experiment ever conducted. Since antiquity, Western scientists had assumed that the Earth was a perfect sphere. Seventeenth-century theorists broached doubts. Isaac Newton reasoned that just as the thrust you sense on the edge of a circle in motion tends to fling you off a merry-go-round, centrifugal force must distend the Earth at the equator and flatten it at the poles. More than a basketball, it must resemble a slightly squashed orange. Meanwhile, mapmakers working on a survey of France demurred. Their observations made the world seem egg-shaped – distended toward the poles. The French Royal Academy of Sciences proposed to resolve debate by sending Maupertuis to the edge of the Arctic and a simultaneous expedition to the equator to measure the length of a degree along the surface of the circumference of the Earth. If measurements at the end of the world matched those at the middle, the globe would be spherical. Any difference between them either way would indicate where the world bulged.

In December 1736, Maupertuis began work 'in cold so extreme that whenever we would take a little brandy, the only thing that could be kept liquid, our tongues and lips froze to the cup and came away bloody'. The chill 'congealed the extremities of the body, while the rest, through excessive toil, was bathed in sweat'.[2] Total accuracy was impossible under such conditions, but the Arctic expedition made readings that were overestimated by less than a third of one per cent. They helped to convince the world that the planet was shaped as Newton predicted – squashed at the poles and bulging at the equator. On the front page of his collected works, Maupertuis appears in a fur cap and collar over a eulogy that reads, 'It was his destiny to determine the shape of the world.'[3]

Seared by experience, however, Maupertuis, like many scientific explorers, discovered the limits of science and the grandeur of nature. He set off as an empiricist and ended as a mystic. In his youth he believed that every truth was quantifiable and that every fact could be sensed. By the time of his death in 1759, 'You cannot chase God in the immensity of the heavens', he averred, 'or the depths of the oceans or the chasms of the Earth. Maybe it is not yet time to understand the world systematically – time only to behold it and be amazed.' In 1752 he published *Letters on the Progress of the Sciences*, predicting that the next topic for science to tackle would be dreams. With the aid of psychotropic drugs – 'certain potions of the Indies' – experimenters might learn what lay beyond the universe. Perhaps, he speculated, the perceived world is illusory. Maybe only God exists, and perceptions are only properties of a mind 'alone in the universe'.[4]

An Overview of the Age

Maupertuis's mental pilgrimage between certainty and doubt, science and speculation, rationalism and religious revelation, reproduced in miniature the history of European thought in the eighteenth century.

First, a great flare of optimism lit up confidence in the perfectibility of man, the infallibility of reason, the reality of the observed world, and the sufficiency of science. In the second half of the century, Enlightenment flickered: intellectuals elevated feelings over reason and sensations over thoughts. Finally, revolutionary bloodshed and war seemed for a while to dowse the torch completely. But embers remained: enduring faith that freedom can energize human goodness, that happiness is worth pursuing in this life, and that science and reason – despite their limitations – can unlock progress and enhance lives.

Environmental changes favoured optimism. The Little Ice Age ended, as sunspot activity, which had been wayward in the seventeenth century, resumed its normal cycles.[5] Between 1700 and the 1760s, all the world's glaciers for which measurements survive began to shrink. For reasons, still obscure, which must, I suspect, be traceable to renewed global warming, the world of microbial evolution changed to the advantage of humankind. Plagues retreated. Population boomed almost everywhere, especially in some of the former plague trouble spots, such as Europe and China. Traditionally, historians have ascribed the demographic bounce to human cleverness: better food, hygiene, and medical science depriving the deadly microbes of eco-niches in which to pullulate. Now, however, awareness is spreading that this explanation will not do: areas of poor food, medicine, and hygiene benefited almost as much as those that were most advanced in these respects. Where the Industrial Revolution threw up slums and warrens that were ideal environments for germs to breed, the death rate declined nonetheless. The number of people continued relentlessly upward. The main explanation lies with the microbes themselves, which seem to have diminished in virulence or deserted human hosts.[6]

The political and commercial state of the world, meanwhile, was conducive to innovation. Europe was in closer contact with more cultures than ever, as explorers put just about every habitable coast in the world in touch with all the others. Western Europe was perfectly placed to receive and radiate new ideas: the region was the emporium of global trade and the place where worldwide flows of influence focused and radiated. As never before, Europe generated initiative – the power of influencing the rest of the world. But Westerners would not have had a world-reshaping role were it not for the reciprocity of impact. China exerted more influence than ever, partly owing to a growing trade gap in Europe's disfavour, as new levels of trade in tea, for instance, porcelain, and rhubarb – which may no longer be a world-stopping medicament but was in much demand as an early modern prophylactic – added new near-monopolies to China's traditional advantages. The eighteenth was, in one historian's apostrophization, the world's 'Chinese century'.[7] Jesuits, ambassadors, and merchants transmitted images of China and processed Chinese models of thought, art, and life for Western consumption. In 1679, Leibniz, whose contributions to science included calculus and binomial theory, reflected on the new proximity of the extremities of Eurasia in *Novissima Sinica,* his digest of news from China compiled mainly from Jesuit sources. 'Perhaps', he mused, 'Supreme Providence has ordained such an arrangement, so that, as the most cultivated and distant peoples stretch out their arms to each other, those in between may gradually be brought to a better way of life.'[8]

Elite taste in Europe changed under China's spell. A fashion for Chinese-style decorative schemes started with Jean-Antoine Watteau's designs for an apartment for Louis XIV. It spread through all the palaces of the Bourbon dynasty, where rooms encased in porcelain and smothered in Chinese motifs still abound. From Bourbon courts, the Chinese look spread throughout Europe. In England, King George II's son, the Duke of Cumberland, sailed at his ease on a fake Chinese pleasure boat when not justifying his soubriquet of 'Bloody Butcher' by massacring political opponents. William Halfpenny's *Chinese and Gothic Architecture* (1752) was the first of many books to treat Chinese art as equivalent to Europe's. Sir William Chambers, the most fashionable British architect of the day, designed a pagoda for Kew Gardens in London and Chinese furniture for aristocratic homes, while 'Chinese' – as contemporaries nicknamed him – Thomas Chippendale, England's leading cabinetmaker, popularized Chinese themes for furniture. By mid-century, engravings of Chinese scenes hung even in middle-class French and Dutch homes. In gardens and interiors, everyone of taste wanted to be surrounded by images of China.

Eurocentric Thought: The Idea of Europe

By almost every measure of success – economic and demographic buoyancy, urban development, technical progress, industrial productivity – China had dwarfed Europe for perhaps a millennium and a half.[9] But if the eighteenth was the Chinese century, it was also a time of opportunity and innovation in the West. In some respects Europe replaced China to become again, in the famous opening phrase of Edward Gibbon's

History of the Decline and Fall of the Roman Empire – 'the fairest part of the Earth', housing 'the most civilized portion of mankind'.[10] In a sense, 'Europe' itself was a new or newly revived idea. It was a familiar geographical name among ancient Greeks for the vast hinterland they admired to their north and west. 'I must begin with Europe', wrote Strabo about half a century before the birth of Christ, anticipating the self-congratulation of later Europeans, 'because it is both varied in form and admirably adapted by nature for the development of excellence in men and governments.'[11] Near oblivion followed, however, over a long period when the Roman Empire waned while contacts within and across Europe weakened. People in different regions had too little to do with each other to foster or maintain common identity. The Mediterranean and Atlantic seaboards, which the Roman Empire had united, drew apart in obedience to the dictates of geography, for a vast watershed of mountains and marshes divides them, stretching from the Spanish tablelands across the Pyrenees, the Massif Central, the Alps, and the Carpathians to the Pripet Marshes. The breakwater has always been hard to cross. The Latin Church ensured that pilgrims, scholars, and clerics traversed much of the western end of the continent, and kept a single language of worship and learning alive; but to those who tried to cross them the frontiers between vernacular tongues were alienating. The Latin Church spread north and east only slowly. Scandinavia and Hungary remained beyond its reach until the eleventh century, Lithuania and the east shore of the Baltic until the fourteenth. It got no further.

The name and idea of Europe revived between the fifteenth and eighteenth centuries, as European self-confidence recovered. The divisions of Europe did not heal (rather, they got worse, as the Reformation and fragmentation among mutually hostile or, at least, emulous sovereign states multiplied hatreds). Agreement about where the frontiers of the region lay was never achieved. Yet the sense of belonging to a European community and sharing a Europe-wide culture gradually became typical of elites, who got to know each other in person and print. The uniformity of enlightened taste in the eighteenth century made it possible to glide between widely separated frontiers with little more cultural dislocation than a modern traveller feels in a succession of airport lounges. Gibbon – Strabo's devoted reader who made his stepmother send him his copy to study while he was at a militia training camp – was midway through his *History of the Decline and Fall of the Roman Empire* when he formulated a European idea: 'It is the duty of a patriot to prefer and promote the exclusive interest of his native country: but a philosopher may be permitted to enlarge his views, and to consider Europe as one great republic, whose various inhabitants have attained almost to the same level of politeness and cultivation.'[12] A few years later, the British statesman Edmund Burke, whom we shall meet again shortly as an influential thinker on the relationship between liberty and order, echoed the thought. 'No European can be a complete exile in any part of Europe.'[13]

Like Strabo's, Gibbon's belief in common European culture was inseparable from a conviction of European superiority, 'distinguished above the rest of mankind'. The re-emergence of the idea of Europe was fraught with menace for the rest of the world. Yet the overseas empires founded or extended from Europe in the eighteenth and nineteenth centuries proved fragile; their moral records were not good enough to sustain the notion of European superiority. In the first half of the twentieth century, the idea of a single Europe dissolved in wars and subsided in the fissures of ideological quakes. It became commonplace to acknowledge the fact that 'Europe' is an elastic term, a mental construction that corresponds to no objective geographical reality and has no natural frontiers. Europe, said Paul Valéry, was merely 'a promontory of Asia'. The form in which the idea was revived in the European Union movement of the late twentieth century would have been unrecognizable to Gibbon: its unifying principles were democracy and a free internal market, but its member states' choice of how to define Europe and whom to exclude from its benefits remained as self-interested as ever.[14]

The Enlightenment: The Work of the Philosophes

For understanding the context of new thinking, the *Encyclopédie* was the key work: the secular bible of the *philosophes* – as the enlightened intellectuals of France were called – who, for a while, mainly in the third quarter of the eighteenth century, dictated intellectual taste to the rest of Europe's elite. Seventeen volumes of text and eleven of accompanying plates appeared over a period of twenty years from 1751. By 1779, twenty-five thousand copies had been sold. The number may seem small, but, by way of circulation and detailed report, it was big enough to reach the entire intelligentsia of Europe. Countless spinoff works, abstracts, reviews, and imitations made the *Encyclopédie* widely known, loftily respected, and, in conservative and clerical circles, deeply feared.

It had perhaps the most helpful subtitle in the history of publishing: *Reasoned Dictionary of the Sciences, Arts, and Trades*. The phrase disclosed the authors' priorities: the reference to a dictionary evokes the notion of arraying knowledge in order, while the list of topics encompasses abstract and useful knowledge in a single conspectus. According to the editor-in-chief, Denis Diderot, a Parisian radical who combined fame as a thinker, efficiency as a project-manager, mordancy as a satirist, and skill as a pornographer, the goal was to 'start from and return to man'. He contrived, as he put it in the article on encyclopaedias in the homonymous work, 'to assemble knowledge scattered across the face of the Earth, that we may not die without having deserved well of humanity'. The emphasis was practical – on commerce and technology, how things work and how they add value. 'There is more intellect, wisdom and consequence', Diderot declared, 'in a machine for making stockings than in a system of metaphysics.'[15] The idea of the machine was at the heart of the Enlightenment, not just because it delivered usefulness, but also because it was a metaphor for the cosmos – like the dramatically lit clockwork model in Joseph Wright's painting of the early to mid-1760s, in which moons and planets, made of gleaming brass, revolve predictably according to a perfect, unvarying pattern.

The authors of the *Encyclopédie* largely concurred on the primacy of the machine and the mechanical nature of the cosmos. They also shared a conviction that reason and science were allies. English and Scots philosophers of the previous two generations had convinced most of their fellow intellectuals in the rest of Europe that those twin means to truth were compatible. The *Encyclopédie*'s allegorical frontispiece depicted Reason plucking a veil from the eyes of Truth. The writers were united in their hostility, as in their enthusiasms: they were, on the whole, critical of monarchs, and aristocrats, drawing on the writings of an English apologist for revolution, John Locke, who, around the turn of the seventeenth and eighteenth centuries, extolled the value of constitutional guarantees of freedom against the state. Exceptions vitiated Locke's principles: he believed in freedom of religion, but not for Catholics; freedom of labour, but not for blacks; and rights of property, but not for Native Americans. Still, the *philosophes* adhered more to his principles than to his exceptions.

More even than monarchs and aristocrats, the authors of the *Encyclopédie* distrusted the Church. Insisting on the average moral superiority of atheists and the superior beneficence of science over grace, Diderot proclaimed that 'mankind will not be free until the last king is strangled with the entrails of the last priest'.[16] Voltaire, a persistent voice of anticlericalism, was the best-connected man of the eighteenth century. He corresponded with Catherine the Great, corrected the King of Prussia's poetry, and influenced monarchs and statesmen all over Europe. His works were read in Sicily and Transylvania, plagiarized in Vienna, and translated into Swedish. Voltaire erected his own temple to 'the architect of the universe, the great geometrician', but regarded Christianity as an 'infamous superstition to be eradicated – I do not say among the rabble, who are not worthy of being enlightened and who are apt for every yoke, but among the civilized and those who wish to think.'[17] The progress of the Enlightenment can be measured in anticlerical acts: the expulsion of the Jesuits from Portugal in 1759; the tsar's secularization of a great portfolio of Church property in 1761; the abolition of the Jesuit order in most of the rest of the West between 1764 and 1773; the thirty-eight thousand victims forced out of religious houses into lay life in Europe in the 1780s. In 1790 the King of Prussia proclaimed absolute authority over clergy in his realm. In 1795 a Spanish minister proposed the forfeiture of most of the Church's remaining land. Meanwhile, at the most rarefied levels of the European elite, the cult of reason took on the characteristics of an alternative religion. In the rites of Freemasonry, a profane hierarchy celebrated the purity of its own wisdom, which Mozart brilliantly evoked in *The Magic Flute*, first performed in 1791. In 1793 revolutionary committees banned Christian worship in some parts of France and erected signs proclaiming 'Death Is an Eternal Sleep' over cemetery gates. Briefly, in the summer of 1794, the government in Paris tried to replace

Christianity with a new religion, the worship of a Supreme Being of supposed 'social utility'.

The enemies of Christianity did not prevail – at least, not exclusively or for long. In the second half of the eighteenth century, religious revivals saw off the threat. Churches survived and in many ways recovered, usually by appealing to ordinary people and affective emotions in, for instance, the stirring hymns of Charles Wesley in England, or the poignant cult of the Sacred Heart in Catholic Europe, or the tear-jerking charisma of revivalist preaching, or the therapeutic value of quiet prayer and of submission to God's love. Elite anticlericalism, however, remained a feature of European politics. In particular, the claim that in order to be liberal and progressive a state must be secular has maintained an ineradicable hold – so much so that one cannot wear a veil in school in *la France laïque* or a crucifix over a nurse's uniform in an NHS hospital, or say prayers in a US state school. On the other hand – if we continue to look ahead for a moment – we can see that modern attempts to rehabilitate Christianity in politics, such as Social Catholicism, the Social Gospel, and the Christian Democrat movement, have had some electoral success and have influenced political rhetoric without reversing the effects of the Enlightenment. Indeed, the country where Christian rhetoric is loudest in politics is the one with the most rigorously secular constitution and public institutions and the political tradition most closely representative of the Enlightenment: the United States of America.[18]

Confidence in Progress

Back in the eighteenth century, a progressive outlook or habit of mind underpinned the *philosophe* temper. The *encyclopédistes* could proclaim radicalism in the face of the powers that be in state and Church, thanks to their underlying belief in progress. To challenge the status quo, you must believe that things will get better. Otherwise, you will cry, with the archconservative, 'Reform? Reform? Aren't things bad enough already?'

It was easy for eighteenth-century observers to convince themselves that evidence of progress surrounded them. As global temperatures rose, plague retreated, and ecological exchange increased the amount and variety of available food, prosperity seemed to pile up. The rate of innovation, as we shall see, in science and technology unveiled lengthening vistas of knowledge and provided powerful new tools with which to exploit it. When the institution that more than any other embodied the Enlightenment in England was founded in 1754, it was called the Royal Society for the Encouragement of Arts, Manufactures and Commerce. The name captured the practical, useful, technical values of the age. James Barry painted a series of canvases entitled *The Progress of Human Culture* for the walls of the Society's premises, starting with the invention of music, ascribed to Orpheus, and proceeding through ancient Greek agriculture. Scenes followed of the ascent of modern Great Britain to equivalence with ancient Greece, culminating in views of the London of Barry's day and a final vision of a new Elysium, in which heroes of arts, manufactures, and commerce (most of them, as it happened, English) enjoy ethereal bliss.

Yet the idea that in general, allowing for fluctuations, everything is always – and perhaps necessarily – getting better is contrary to common experience. For most of the past, people have stuck to the evidence and assumed they were living in times of decline or in a world of decay – or, at best, of indifferent change, where history is just one damned thing after another. Or, like ancient sages who thought change was illusory (see p. 137), they have denied the evidence and asserted that reality is immutable. In the eighteenth century, even believers in progress feared that it might be merely a phase; their own times enjoyed it, but were exceptional by the standards of history in general. The Marquis de Condorcet, for instance, thought he could see 'the human race ... advancing with a sure step along the path of truth, virtue and happiness' only because political and intellectual revolutions had subverted the crippling effects of religion and tyranny on the human spirit, 'emancipated from its shackles' and 'released from the empire of fate'.[19] Ironically, he wrote his endorsement of progress while under sentence of death from the French revolutionary authorities.

Yet the idea of progress survived the guillotine. In the nineteenth century it strengthened and fed on the 'march of improvement' – the history of industrialization, the multiplication of wealth and muscle power, the insecure but encouraging victories of constitutionalism against tyranny. It became possible to believe that progress was irreversible, irrespective of human failings, because it was programmed into nature by evolution. It took the horrors of the late nineteenth and twentieth centuries – a catalogue of famines, failures, inhumanities, and genocidal conflicts – to unpick the idea from most people's minds.

This does not mean that the idea of progress was just a mental image of the good times in which it prevailed. It had remote origins in two ancient ideas: of human goodness and of a providential deity who looks after creation. Both these ideas implied progress of a sort: confidence that, despite the periodic interventions of evil, goodness was bound to triumph in the end – perhaps literally in the end, in some millennial climax.[20] But millenarianism was not enough on its own to make the idea of progress possible: after all, everything might (and in some prophets' expectations would) get worse before the final redemption. Confidence in progress relied in turn on an even deeper property of the mind. Optimism was the key. You had to be an optimist to embark on a project as long, daunting, laborious, and dangerous as the *Encyclopédie*.

Because it is hard to be an optimist in confrontation with the woes of the world, someone had to think up a way of comprehending evil to make progress credible. Misery and disaster had somehow to seem for the best. Theologians shouldered the task, but never satisfied atheists with answers to the question, 'If God is good, why is there evil?' Possible answers (see p. 129) include recognition that suffering is good (a proposition most people who experience it reject), or that God's own nature is to suffer (which many feel is inadequate consolation), or that evil is needed to make good meaningful (in which case, dissenters say, we might be better off with a more favourable balance or a morally neutral world), or that freedom, which is the highest good, entails freedom for ill (but some people say they would rather forgo freedom). In the seventeenth century, the growth of atheism made the theologians' task seem urgent. Secular philosophy was no better at discharging it, because a secular notion of progress is as hard to square with disasters and reversals as is providentialism. 'To justify the ways of God to man' was the objective Milton set himself in his great verse epic, *Paradise Lost*. But it is one thing to be poetically convincing, quite another to produce a reasoned argument.

In 1710, Leibniz did so. He was the most wide-ranging polymath of his day, combining outstanding contributions to philosophy, theology, mathematics, linguistics, physics, and jurisprudence with his role as a courtier in Hanover. He started from a truth traditionally expressed and witnessed in everyday experience: good and evil are inseparable. Freedom, for example, is good, but must include freedom to do evil; altruism is good only if selfishness is an option. But of all logically conceivable worlds, ours has, by divine decree, said Leibniz, the greatest possible surplus of good over evil. So – in the phrase Voltaire used to lampoon this theory – 'all is for the best in the best of all possible worlds'. In Voltaire's satirical picaresque novel, *Candide*, Leibniz is represented by the character of Dr Pangloss, the hero's tutor, whose infuriating optimism is equal to every disaster.

Leibniz formulated his argument in an attempt to show that God's love was compatible with human suffering. It was not his purpose to endorse progress, and his 'best world' could have been interpreted as one of static equilibrium, in which the ideal amount of evil was inbuilt. But, in alliance with the conviction of human goodness, which most thinkers of the Enlightenment shared, Leibniz's claims validated optimism. They made a secular millennium possible, toward which people could work by using their freedom to adjust the balance, bit by bit, in favour of goodness.[21]

Economic Thought

Optimism breeds radicalism. As we saw when exploring the political thought of the first millennium BCE (see p. 146), belief in goodness commonly precedes belief in freedom, liberating people to exhibit their natural good qualities. If they are naturally good, they are best left free. Or do they need a strong state to redeem them from natural wickedness? In the eighteenth century, it proved hard to get a consensus about the value of freedom in politics. In economics it was an easier sell.

The previous two centuries of economic thinking in the West, however, had first to be overturned. The orthodoxy known as mercantilism was a major obstacle. A Spanish moralist, Tomás de Mercado, formulated it in 1569: 'One of the principal requisites', he wrote, 'for the prosperity and happiness of a kingdom is always to hold within itself a great quantity of money and an abundance of gold and silver.'[22] The theory made sense in the light of the history people were aware of. For centuries, at least since Pliny made the first relevant calculations in the first century BCE, European economies laboured under the burden of an adverse balance of payments with China, India, and the Near East. It was a matter of concern in ancient Rome. It drove late-medieval explorers to cross oceans for new sources of gold and silver. By the sixteenth century, when European travellers were able, in relatively large numbers, to cast envious eyes on the riches of the East, the adverse balance of payments induced two obsessions in Western minds: that bullion is the basis of wealth, and that to grow rich an economy must behave like a business and sell more than it buys.

According to Mercado, what 'destroys ... abundance and causes poverty is the export of money'.[23] All European governments came to believe this. In consequence, they tried to evade impoverishment by hoarding bullion, trapping cash inside the realm, limiting imports and exports, regulating prices, defying the laws of supply and demand, and founding empires to create controllable markets. The consequences were woeful. Overseas investment, except in imperial ventures or in purchases for onward sale, was unknown. Protection of trade nourished inefficiency. Resources had to be squandered on policing. Competition for protected markets caused wars and, consequently, waste. Money drained out of circulation. Two concerns from the mercantilist era abide. The first, which few economists treat as an infallible index of economic propriety, is with the balance of payments between what an economy earns from other economies and what is paid out to external suppliers of goods and services. The second is with 'sound money', no longer pegged to gold and silver in the coinage or in promises printed on promissory notes, but rather – in fiscally responsible governments – to the total performance of the economy.[24] We still unthinkingly overvalue gold – which is really rather a useless material, undeserving of its privileged position as the commodity in terms of which all other commodities, including money, are still commonly reckoned. But it is hard to say whether this is a relic of mercantilism or of gold's ancient, magical reputation as an untarnishable substance.[25]

Even while mercantilism reigned, some thinkers advocated an alternative way of understanding wealth, in terms of goods rather than specie. The idea that price is a function of money supply was the starting point among theologians known as the School of Salamanca in the mid-sixteenth century. Domingo de Soto and Martín de Azpilcueta Navarro were particularly interested in what we might now call problems of the morality of capitalism. While studying business methods, they noticed a connection between the flow of gold and silver from the New World and the inflation of prices in Spain. 'In Spain', observed Navarro, 'in times when money was scarcer, saleable goods and labour were given for very much less than after the discovery of the Indies, which flooded the country with gold and silver. The reason for this is that money is worth more where and when it is scarce than where and when it is abundant.'[26] In 1568 the same observation was made in France by Jean Bodin: he thought he was the first but the Salamanca theorists anticipated him by some years. Three explanations were current for the phenomenon they observed: that value was a purely mental construct, reflecting the irrationally different esteem the market applied to intrinsically equivalent products in different times and places; or that price depended on the supply and demand of goods rather than of money; or that 'just' value was fixed by nature and that price fluctuation was the result of greed.

The Salmantine thinkers showed that money is like other commodities. You can trade it, as Navarro put it, for a moderate profit without dishonour. 'All merchandise', wrote Navarro, 'becomes dearer when it is in great demand and short supply, and ... money ... is merchandise, and therefore also becomes dearer when it is in great demand and short supply.'[27] At the same time, the theory reinforced ancient moral prejudices about money: you can have too much of it; it is the root of evil; the wealth of a nation consists in goods produced, not cash collected. Today's disquiet over the way services displace manufactures and financial finagling seems to beggar factories and mines is an echo of such thinking. In the sixteenth century critics denounced empire, not only for injustice against indigenous peoples but also for impoverishing Spain by flooding the country with money. Martín González de Cellorigo, one of the subtlest economists of the period, coined a famous paradox:

> The reason why there is no money, gold or silver in Spain is that there is too much, and Spain is poor because she is rich ... Wealth has been and still is riding upon the wind in the form of papers and contracts ... silver and gold, instead of in goods that ... by virtue of their added value attract to themselves riches from abroad, thus sustaining our people at home.[28]

Ironically, economic historians now mistrust the observations of the School of Salamanca and suspect that sixteenth-century inflation was rather the result of increasing demand than of the growth of the money supply. The theory, however, irrespective of the soundness of its foundations, has been immensely influential. Modern capitalism would hardly be imaginable without awareness that money is subject to laws of supply and demand. In the late eighteenth century, the doctrine helped to displace mercantilism as the key common assumption of economic theorists, thanks in part to the influence the School of Salamanca exerted on a Scots professor of moral philosophy, Adam Smith, whose name has been linked with the cause of economic freedom ever since he published *The Wealth of Nations* in 1776.

Smith had a lofty view of the importance of the relationship between supply and demand. He believed that it affected more than the market. 'The natural effort of every individual to better his own condition'[29] was the foundation of all political, economic, and moral systems. Taxation was more or less an evil: first, as an infringement of liberty; second, as a source of distortion in the market. 'There is no art which one government sooner learns of another than that of draining money from the pockets of the people.'[30] Self-interest could be trusted to serve the common good. 'It is not from the benevolence of the butcher, the brewer or the baker that we expect our dinner, but from their regard to their own interest ... In spite of their natural selfishness and rapacity', Smith declared, the rich 'are led by an invisible hand to make nearly the same distribution of the necessaries of life which would have been made, had the earth been divided into equal portions among all its inhabitants.'[31] In the long run, this expectation has proved false: the Industrial Revolution of the nineteenth century and the knowledge economy of the twentieth have opened glaring wealth gaps between classes and countries. It was formerly possible to believe that the market could correct wealth gaps, just as it could adjust supply to demand, because for a long time in the twentieth century the gaps shrank; it was as if bosses realized that prosperous workers were in business's best interests, or that they sensed that only by being fair could they avert the menace of proletarian revolt. It seems, however, that capitalists are incapable of long-term restraint: war, not market forces, was responsible for the temporary trend towards fair rewards and in the late twentieth and early twenty-first centuries the wealth gap widened anew to levels unknown since before the First World War.[32]

In his day, of course, Smith's predictions could not be falsified. To his contemporary admirers, as Francis Hirst observed, Smith 'issued from the seclusion of a professorship of morals ... to sit in the council-chamber of princes'.[33] His word was 'proclaimed by the agitator, conned by the statesman, and printed in a thousand statutes'. For a long time, Smith's formula seemed only slightly exaggerated: the rich of the industrializing era, for instance, increased their workers' wages to stimulate demand; for a while, economists seriously hoped to eliminate poverty, as medical researchers hoped to eliminate disease.

The Wealth of Nations appeared in the year of the US Declaration of Independence and should be counted among that nation's founding documents. It encouraged the revolution, for Smith said that government regulations limiting the freedom of colonies to engage in manufacture or trade were 'a manifest violation of the most sacred rights of mankind'. The United States has remained the homeland of economic liberalism ever since and an only mildly tarnished example of how laissez-faire can work. Meanwhile, wherever planning, government regulation, or the command economy have displaced Smith's doctrines, economic progress has failed. Capitalism, to judge from the evidence available so far, is the worst economic system, except for all the others.

Or is it? In most respects Smith's influence was benign. On the other hand, to represent self-interest as enlightened is like speaking of greed as good. Smith made no place for altruism in economics. He thought that merchants and usurers served their fellow men by buying cheap and selling dear. This was one defect of his thought. The other was to assume that people can be relied on to predict their own best interests in the marketplace. In reality, people act irrationally and impulsively far more often than rationally or consistently. The market is more like a betting ring than a magic circle. Its unpredictability breeds lurches and crashes, insecurities and fears. Smith's principles, strictly interpreted, would leave even education, religion, medicine, infrastructure, and the environment at the mercy of the market. In some respects, especially in the United States, this has come to pass. Gurus have become entrepreneurs, so-called universities now resemble businesses, conservation is costed, highways are 'sponsored', and you can buy health even in systems expressly designed to treat it as a right. The world is still seeking a 'third way' between unregulated and overregulated markets.[34]

Political Philosophies: The Origins of the State

The benefits of economic freedom always seem easier to project convincingly than those of political liberty – as we see in our own day in China and Russia, where illiberal politics have persisted despite the relaxation of economic controls. Smith's doctrine was widely acceptable because it could appeal equally to liberators, who believed in human goodness, and restrainers, who mistrusted human nature. His argument, after all, was that economic efficiency arises from self-interest: the morals of economic actors are irrelevant.

In the political sphere, such doctrines do not work. Freeing people makes sense only if one confides in their basic benevolence. And in the sixteenth and seventeenth centuries in Europe, unfolding evidence accumulated to subvert such confidence. Discoveries of explorers and reports of ethnographers in the Americas and the Pacific suggested to some readers, as to many of the colonists who found an alien adversary baffling, that 'natural man' was, as Shakespeare put it, just 'a bare, fork'd animal' who could not be relied on to conform to the behaviour empires demanded. Revelations of previously unknown or little-known realms in Asia, meanwhile, introduced Europeans to new models of political power. The best path through the material starts with the effects of the new evidence on thinking about the origins of states; then on how Chinese and other Asian models affected notions of power and founded new schools of absolutism; then on the contrary effects of the discovery of peoples Europeans called savages, whose sometimes surprisingly impressive attainments encouraged radical, even revolutionary ideas, culminating in arguments for equality, universal rights, and democracy.

From the assumption that the state originated in a contract – a tradition that, as we have seen, became strong in the West in the late Middle Ages – presumptions arose about how and why people needed the state in the first place. The condition of humankind in the remote past must have been extremely grim, or so the comfortable European literati supposed: misery induced people to get together and sacrifice freedom for the common good. Early in the second half of the seventeenth century, reflections of these kinds came together in the mind of Thomas Hobbes, who was an extreme royalist in politics and an extreme materialist in philosophy. His natural inclinations were authoritarian: after living through the bloodshed and anarchy of the English Civil War, he retained a strong preference for order over freedom. He imagined the state of nature that preceded the political state as 'a war of every man against every man' where 'force and fraud are the two cardinal virtues'.

This picture, which he confided in 1651 to the most famous passages of his classic *Leviathan*, contrasted with that of traditional political theory, in which the natural state was simply a time, presumed to have prevailed in the remote past, when man-made legislation was otiose: the laws of nature or the rule of reason supplied all needful regulation. Hobbes provided a refreshing contrast to the myth of a golden age of primitive innocence when people lived harmoniously, uncorrupted by civilization. He believed that, unlike ants and bees, which form society instinctively, people had to grope towards the only workable way out of insecurity. They agreed with one another to forfeit their freedom to an enforcer, who would compel observance of the contract but who would not be a party to it. Instead of a compact between rulers and ruled, the founding covenant of the state became a promise of obedience. By virtue of belonging to the state, subjects renounced liberty. As for rights, self-preservation was the only one subjects retained: they never had any others to renounce in the first place, for in the state of nature there was no property, no justice. People had only what they could grab by force. There was some support for this view in the work of Aristotle, who admitted that 'man when perfected is the best of animals but when separated from law and justice he is the worst of them all'.[35]

Hobbes's idea changed the language of politics forever. Contract theory lost its hold over the power of the state: the sovereign (whether a man or 'an assembly of men'), in minds Hobbes convinced or enlarged, was outside the contract and so was not bound to keep it. Humans could be equal – indeed, Hobbes assumed that all were naturally equal – and yet be at the mercy of the state: equality of subjection is a fate familiar to subjects of many egalitarian regimes. Hobbes's doctrine had chilling implications, finally, for international politics: governments were in a state of nature with respect to each other. There were no constraints on their capacity to inflict mutual harm, except the limitations of their own power. From one point of view, this justified wars of aggression; from another, it necessitated some contractual arrangement – proposals for which we shall encounter in future chapters – to ensure peace.

Asian Influences and the Formulation of Rival Kinds of Despotism

For most of the eighteenth century, debate seemed poised between liberators and restrainers: evidence on the goodness or malevolence of human nature was equivocal. Instead, therefore, of arguing about an unverifiably remote past, contenders focused on the examples of other cultures disclosed by the long-range exchanges of the time. China was the most conspicuous example. Admirers of China advocated limits to freedom and an elite empowered to lead, while enthusiasts for freedom rejected the notion that China could be a model for Western states. Voltaire was, for much of his life, a leading Sinophile.[36] Confucianism attracted him as a philosophical alternative to organized religion, which he detested. And he sympathized with the Chinese conviction that the universe is orderly, rational, and intelligible through observation. In the Chinese habit of political deference to scholars, he saw an endorsement of the power of the class of professional intellectuals to which he belonged. In the absolute power of the Chinese state, he saw a force for good.

Not everyone in Europe's intellectual elite agreed. In 1748, in *The Spirit of Laws*, a work that inspired constitutional reformers all over Europe, the Baron de Montesquieu claimed that 'the cudgel governs

China' – a claim endorsed by Jesuit accounts of Chinese habits of harsh justice and judicial torture. He condemned China as 'a despotic state, whose principle is fear'. Indeed, a fundamental difference of opinion divided Montesquieu and Voltaire. Montesquieu advocated the rule of law and recommended that constitutional safeguards should limit rulers. Voltaire never really trusted the people and favoured strong, well-advised governments. Montesquieu, moreover, developed an influential theory, according to which Western political traditions were benign and tended toward liberty, whereas Asian states concentrated power in the hands of tyrants. 'This', he wrote, 'is the great reason for the weakness of Asia and the strength of Europe; for the liberty of Europe and the slavery of Asia.' 'Oriental despotism' became a standard term of abuse in Western political writing.[37]

While Diderot echoed and even exceeded Montesquieu in favour of the subject against the state, François Quesnay, Voltaire's colleague, echoed the idealization of China. 'Enlightened despotism', he thought, would favour the people rather than elites. In their day, Quesnay's ideas were more influential than Montesquieu's. He even persuaded the heir to the French throne to imitate a Chinese imperial rite by ploughing land in person as an example to agrarian improvers. In Spain, dramatists provided the court with exemplars of good kingship, translated or imitated from Chinese texts.[38] 'Enlightened despotism' entered the political vocabulary along with 'oriental despotism', and many European rulers in the second half of the eighteenth century sought to embody it. One way or another, Chinese models seemed to be shaping European political thought.

The result was a bifurcation in Western politics. Reforming rulers followed the principles of enlightened despotism, while the radical enlightenment of Montesquieu influenced revolutionaries. Both traditions, however, could only lead to revolution from above, crafted or inflicted by despots or by a Platonic guardian class of the Enlightenment who would, as one of them said, 'force men to be free'. The Abbé Raynal, a hero of the *philosophes*, assured the 'wise of the Earth, philosophers of all nations, it is for you alone to make the laws, by indicating to other citizens what is needed, by enlightening your brothers'.[39] So how did real, bloody, uncontrolled revolution, red in tooth and claw, happen? What induced part of the elite to relax control and confide in the risky and unpredictable behaviour of the 'common man'? New influences arose in the eighteenth century to make some *philosophes* challenge the established order so thoroughly as even to question their own hold over it.

The Noble Savage and the Common Man

The subversive ideas had a long history behind them. Civilization has always had its discontents. Moralists have always berated each other with examples of virtuous outsiders, or of natural virtues that make up for deficient education, or of the goodness of the simple life corrupted by commerce and comfort. In the fifteenth and early sixteenth centuries, European overseas exploration had begun to accumulate examples of ways of life supposedly close to those of natural man – naked, untutored, dedicated to foraging, dependent on God. At first, they seemed disappointing. The golden age of primitive innocence was nowhere to be found. But clever scrutineers could find redeeming features in 'savages'. In the mid-sixteenth century, the sceptic Michel de Montaigne argued that even so repugnant a practice as cannibalism had moral lessons for Europeans, whose mutual barbarities were much worse. In the seventeenth century, missionaries believed they really had found the good savage of legend among the Hurons, who practised appalling barbarities, torturing human-sacrifice victims; yet their egalitarian values and technical proficiency, compared with other, meaner neighbours, combined to make them seem full of natural wisdom. In the early eighteenth century, Louis-Armand de Lahontan – an embittered, dispossessed aristocrat who sought escape in Canada from derogation at home – made an imaginary Huron a spokesman for his own anticlerical radicalism. Voltaire made a hero of an 'ingenuous Huron' who criticized kings and priests. Joseph-François Lafitau praised the Huron for practising free love. In a comedy based on Voltaire's work and performed in Paris in 1768, a Huron hero led a storming of the Bastille. From the noble savage the philosophers hailed, it was but a short step to the common man whom revolutionaries idolized.[40]

The socially inebriant potential of the Huron myth grew as more noble savages appeared during the exploration of the South Seas, a voluptuary's paradise of liberty and licence.[41] Feral children, with whom enlightened thinkers became obsessed as specimens of unsocialized primitivism, provided supposedly supporting evidence. Carl Linnaeus – the Swedish botanist who devised the modern method of classifying species – supposed wild children were a distinct species of the genus *Homo*. Plucked from whatever woods they were found in, wrenched from the dugs of vulpine surrogates, they became experiments in civilization. Savants tried to teach them language and manners. All the efforts failed. Boys supposedly raised by bears in seventeenth-century Poland continued to prefer the company of bears. Peter the Wild Boy, whom rival members of the English royal family struggled to possess as a pet in the 1720s, and whose portrait stares blankly from the stairway frescoes of Kensington Palace, hated clothes and beds and never learned to talk. The 'savage girl' kidnapped from the woods near Songi in 1731 liked to eat fresh frogs and rejected the viands of the kitchen of the Château d'Epinoy. For a long time she was better at imitating birdsong than speaking French. The most famous case of all was that of the Wild Boy of Aveyron, who, kidnapped for civilization in 1798, learned to dress and dine elegantly, but never to speak or to like what had happened to him. His tutor described him drinking fastidiously after dinner in the window of the room, 'as if in this moment of happiness this child of nature tries to unite the only two good things which have survived the loss of his liberty – a drink of limpid water and the sight of sun and country'.[42]

The savage Eden, meanwhile, proved full of serpents. The Huron died out, ravaged by European diseases. Commerce and contagion corrupted the South Seas. Yet, despite the disappointments, in some philosophical minds the noble savage blended into the common man, and the idea of natural wisdom legitimated that of popular sovereignty. Without the Huron, the South Sea Islander, and the wolf-child, perhaps, the French Revolution would have been unthinkable.[43]

Among the consequences was the impetus the noble savage gave to an old but newly influential idea: natural equality. 'The same law for all' was a principle ancient Stoics advocated. Their justifications were that men were naturally equal, that inequalities were historical accidents, and that the state should try to redress them. Plenty of ancient religious thinking, well articulated in early Christianity, lighted on the notions that all people were equal in divine eyes and that society was bound, by allegiance to God, to try to match the vision. Some thinkers and – sporadically and briefly – some societies have gone further in demanding equality of opportunity, or of power, or of material well-being. In practice, communism tends to ensue, since communal ownership is the only absolute guarantee against the unequal distribution of property.

From the fifteenth to the nineteenth centuries, many projects were launched to create egalitarian utopias in Europe and America, usually by religious fanatics in a Christian tradition. Most went seriously wrong. When, for instance, the Anabaptist prophet Jan of Leiden set out to start a utopia of his own devising in Münster in 1525, the corruption of power transformed him into a monstrous tyrant, who acquired a harem, licensed orgies, and massacred enemies. Violence was a typical consummation. When the Levellers took advantage of the English Civil War to recreate what they imagined was apostolic equality, their project ended in bloody suppression. Other efforts merely subsided under their own impracticality. The backwoods utopias socialists constructed in the US Midwest in the nineteenth century lie in ruins today. Gilbert and Sullivan convincingly lampooned egalitarianism in their comic opera *The Gondoliers*:

> The earl, the marquis and the duke,
> the groom, the butler and the cook,
> the aristocrat who banks with Coutts,
> the aristocrat who cleans the boots ...
> all shall equal be.

No one has seriously recommended equalizing age or brainpower or beauty or stature or fatness or physical prowess or luck: some inequalities genuinely are natural. It is noble to try to remedy their effects, but nobility in pursuit of equality tends always to be condescending.

Still, there was a moment in the eighteenth century when equality seemed deliverable, if the state were to guarantee it. In some ways, the notion was reasonable: the state always tackles gross inequalities, so why not all inequalities? For those who believe in the natural equality of all, the state is there to enforce it; for those who do not, government has a moral role, levelling the 'playing field', redressing the imbalances between the strong and the weak, the rich and the poor. It is a dangerous idea, because equality enforced at the expense of liberty can be tyrannous.

The idea that this function of the state exceeds all others in importance is no older than the thought of Jean-Jacques Rousseau. Of the thinkers who broke with the outlook of the *Encyclopédie* in the second half of the eighteenth century, Rousseau was the most influential. He was a restless supertramp who loved low life and gutter pleasures. He changed his formal religious allegiance twice without once appearing sincere. He betrayed his mistresses, quarrelled with his friends, and abandoned his children. He shaped his life in addiction to his own sensibilities. In 1750, in the prize-winning essay that made his name, he repudiated one of the most sacred principles of the Enlightenment – 'that the Arts and Sciences have benefited Mankind'. That the topic could be proposed at all shows how far disillusionment with enlightened optimism had already gone. Rousseau denounced property and the state. He offered nothing in their place except an assertion of the goodness of humans' natural, primeval condition. Voltaire loathed Rousseau's ideas. After reading them, 'one wants to walk on all fours', he said. Rousseau abjured other Enlightenment shibboleths, including progress. 'I dared to strip man's nature naked', he claimed, 'and showed that his supposed improvement was the fount of all his miseries.'[44] He anticipated the post-Enlightenment sensibility of romantics who would value feelings and intuition, in some respects, above reason. He was the hero par excellence of the makers and mob of the French Revolution, who paraded his effigy around the ruins of the Bastille, invoked his 'holy name', and engraved his portrait over revolutionary allegories.[45]

Rousseau regarded the state as a corporation, or even a sort of organism, in which individual identities are submerged. Inspired by naturalists' reports of the habits of orang-utans (whom Rousseau called gorillas, and whom, like many equally under-informed commentators, he classified in the genus *Homo*), he imagined a pre-social state of nature, in which humans were solitary rovers.[46] At an irrecoverable moment, he thought, the act occurred 'by which people become a people ... the real foundation of society. The people becomes one single being ... Each of us puts his person and all his power in common under the supreme direction of the general will.' Citizenship is fraternity – a bond as organic as blood. Anyone constrained to obey the general will is 'forced to be free ... Whoever refuses to obey the general will shall be compelled to do so by the whole body.'[47] Rousseau was vague about how to vindicate morally this obviously dangerous doctrine. Towards the end of the century Immanuel Kant provided a precise justification. He was averse to change, as solitary as an orang-utan, and, reputedly a creature of boringly predictable habits, rarely stirring from his accustomed paths around his home town of Königsberg. His thinking, however, was restless and boundless. Reason, he suggested, replacing individual will or interests, can identify objective goals, whose merit everyone can see.

Submission to the general will limits one's freedom in deference to the freedom of others. In theory, the 'general will' is different from unanimity or sectional interests or individual preferences. In practice, however, it just means the tyranny of the majority: 'The votes of the greatest number always bind the rest', as Rousseau admitted. He wanted to outlaw political parties because 'there should be no partial society within the state'.[48] Rousseau's logic, which would forbid trade unions, religious communions, and reformist movements, was a licence for totalitarianism. All the movements or governments it influenced – the French Jacobins and Communards, the Russian Bolsheviks, the modern fascists and Nazis, the advocates of tyranny by plebiscite – have suppressed individual liberty. Yet the passion with which Rousseau invoked freedom made it hard for many of his readers to see how illiberal his thought really was. Revolutionaries adopted the opening words of his essay of 1762: 'Man is born free and everywhere he is in chains!' They loosed the slogan more easily than the chains.

Universal Rights

Rousseau did share one of the axioms of the enlightened mainstream: the doctrine, as we now say, of human rights, inferred from natural equality. Here was the alchemy that could turn subjects into citizens. In the course of defending American rebels against the British crown, Thomas Paine, a publicist for every radical cause, formulated the idea that there are liberties beyond the state's reach, rights too important for the state to overrule. Paine's assertion was the climax of a long search by radical thinkers for ways of limiting rulers' absolute power over their subjects. Revolutionaries in France and America seized on the idea. But it is easier to assert human rights than to say what they are. The US Declaration of Independence named them as 'life, liberty and the pursuit of happiness'. All states ignored the first: they continued to put people to death when it suited them. The second and third rights seemed, at first, too vague to change the course of history; they could be ignored on the specious grounds that different people had conflicting claims to liberty and happiness. In France revolutionaries enthusiastically echoed the US Declaration. Illiberal governments, however, repeatedly sidelined, until well into the twentieth century, the rights the document proclaimed. Napoleon set something of a pattern: he managed to practise tyranny – including judicial murders, arbitrary manipulation of laws, and bloody conquests – while embodying revolutionary principles in his admirers' eyes: to this day, hardly a liberal's study seems well furnished without his bust in bronze. Even in America, slaves and their black descendants were long denied the rights that, according to the founding Declaration, were universal.

The idea of rights with which all people are endowed acted unexpectedly on the world. In the late nineteenth and twentieth centuries, it became the basis of the American dream, according to which everyone in America could pursue purported happiness, in the form of material prosperity, with encouragement (instead of the usual interference) from the state. In partial consequence, the United States became the richest and, therefore, the most powerful country. By the turn of the millennium, the United States was a model most of the world acknowledged, copying institutions – a free market, a democratic constitution, and the rule of law – that made the American dream deliverable.[49]

In the same period, an agreement, to which most states signed up, with varying degrees of sincerity and commitment in the 'Helsinki Process' of 1975–83, defined further human rights: of immunity from arbitrary arrest, torture, and expropriation; of family integrity; of peaceful association for cultural, religious, and economic purposes; of participation in politics, with a right of self-expression within limits required by public order; of immunity from persecution on grounds of race, sex, creed, sickness, or disability; of education; and of a basic level of shelter, health, and subsistence. Life and liberty, however – the other choice ingredients of the US founding fathers' formula – remained problematic: life, because of abiding disputes over whether criminals, the unborn, and euthanasia victims deserve inclusion; liberty, because of disparities of power. Neither right could be secure against predatory states, criminal organizations, and rich corporations. The rhetoric of human rights triumphed almost everywhere, but the reality lagged. Female workers are still routinely short-changed; children's rights to live with their families are commonly alienated, often to the state, as are those of parents to bring up their children; immigrants are unable to sell their labour at its true value or even to escape effective servitude if they are without the documents that states unblinkingly deny them. Employees without access to collective bargaining, which laws often forbid, are often not much better off. Targets of crime commonly get protection or redress in proportion to their wealth or clout. Above all, it is no good prating about human rights to the lifeless victims of war, fatal neglect, abortion, euthanasia, and capital punishment.

French revolutionaries often referred to inalienable rights as 'the rights of man and the citizen'. A by-product was a new focus on the rights and citizenship of women. Condorcet's wife ran a salon in revolutionary Paris, where guests declaimed rather than debated the doctrine that women collectively constitute a class of society, historically oppressed and deserving of emancipation. Olympe de Gouges and Mary Wollstonecraft launched a tradition, recognizable in feminism today, in two works of 1792, *Déclaration des droits de la femme et de la citoyenne* and *A Vindication of the Rights of Women*. Both authors struggled to earn their livings; both led irregular sex lives; both ended tragically. De Gouges was guillotined for defending the king of France; Wollstonecraft died in childbirth. Both rejected the entire previous tradition of female championship, which eulogized supposedly female virtues. Instead, de Gouges and Wollstonecraft admitted to vices and blamed male oppression. They rejected adulation in favour of equality. 'Women may mount the scaffold', de Gouges observed. 'They should also be able to ascend the bench.'[50]

At first, the impact was barely perceptible. Gradually, however, in the nineteenth and twentieth centuries, growing numbers of men grew to like feminism as a justification for reincorporating women into the labour market and so exploiting their productivity more effectively. After two world wars had demonstrated the need for and efficacy of contributions by the sex in realms formerly reserved or privileged for men, it became fashionable for people of both sexes to extol viragos and acclaim women's suitability for what was still thought of as 'men's work' in demanding jobs. Simone de Beauvoir, Jean-Paul Sartre's undomesticable paramour, had launched a new message one day in 1946, when, she said, 'I began to reflect about myself and it struck me with a sort of surprise that the first thing I had to say was, "I am a woman".'[51] In the second half of the century, at least in the West and among communities elsewhere whom Western intellectual fashions influenced, the idea became current that women could discharge the responsibilities of leadership in every field, not because they were like men, but because they were human – or even, in the minds of feminists we might call extremists, because they were female.

Some feminists claimed to be able to force men to change the rules in women's favour. More commonly, they addressed women, whom they urged to make the most of changes and opportunities that would have occurred anyway. Unintended effects followed: by competing with men, women gave up some traditional advantages – male deference and much informal power; by joining the workforce, they added another level of exploitation to their roles as homemakers and mothers, with consequent stress and overwork. Some women, who wanted to remain at home and dedicate themselves to their husbands and children, found themselves doubly disadvantaged: exploited by men and pilloried by 'sisters'. Society still needs to strike the right balance: liberating all women to lead the lives they want, without having to conform to roles devised for them by intellectuals of either sex.

Gropings toward Democracy

Popular sovereignty, equality, universal rights, general will: the logical conclusion of the Enlightenment, in these respects, was democracy. Briefly, in 1793, revolutionary France had a democratic constitution, largely drafted by Condorcet. Universal male suffrage (Condorcet wanted to include women but yielded to colleagues' alarms) with frequent elections and provision for a plebiscite were the essential ingredients. But, in democracy, in Diderot's words, 'the people may be mad but is always master'.[52] Madness and mastery make a daunting combination. Democracy without the rule of law is tyranny. Even before France's revolutionary constitution came into effect, a coup brought Maximilien de Robespierre to power. In emergency conditions of war and terror, virtue – Robespierre's word for brute force – supplied the decisive direction that reason could not provide. The Constitution was suspended after barely four months. Terror doused the Enlightenment in blood. It took nearly a hundred years for most European elites to overcome the abhorrence the very name of democracy inspired. The fate of revolutionary democracy in France foreshadowed twentieth-century examples: the electoral successes of fascism, Nazism, communism, and charismatic embodiments of personality-cults, the abuse of plebiscite and referendum, the miseries of living in 'people's democracies'.

America, however, was relatively isolated from the horrors that extinguished the Enlightenment in Europe. The US Constitution was constructed along principles rather like those Condorcet followed, with a similar degree of indebtedness to the Enlightenment. With little violence, except in the slave states, progressive extensions of the franchise could and did genuinely turn the United States into a democracy. Eventually, most of the rest of the world came to follow this reassuring model, which seemed to show that the common man could take power without dealing it to dictators or dipping it in blood. The democracy we know today – representative government elected by universal or near-universal suffrage under the rule of law – was a US invention. Attempts to trace it from the ancient Greek system of the same name or from the French Revolution are delusively romantic. What made it peculiarly American is much disputed. Radical Protestantism, which throve more in the United States than in the old countries from which radicals fled, may have contributed traditions of communal decision making and the rejection of hierarchy;[53] the frontier, where escapees from authority accumulated and communities had to regulate themselves, may have helped.[54] Surely decisive was the fact that the Enlightenment, with its respect for popular sovereignty and folk wisdom, survived in the United States when it failed in Europe.

While democracy matured in America, almost everyone in Europe decried it. Prudent thinkers hesitated to recommend a system Plato and Aristotle had condemned. Rousseau detested it. As soon as representatives are elected, he thought, 'the people is enslaved ... If there were a nation of gods, it would govern itself democratically. A government so perfect is not suited to men.'[55] Edmund Burke – the voice of political morality in late-eighteenth-century England – called the system 'the most shameless in the world'.[56] Even Immanuel Kant, who was once an advocate, reneged on democracy in 1795, branding it as the despotism of the majority. The political history of Europe in the nineteenth century is of 'mouldering edifices' propped up and democracy deferred, where the elite felt the terror of the tumbril and the menace of the mob.

In the US, by contrast, democracy 'just growed': it took European visitors to observe it, refine the idea, and recommend it convincingly to readers back home. By the time the sagacious French observer, Alexis de Tocqueville, went to America to research democracy in the 1830s, the United States had, for the time, an exemplary democratic franchise (except in Rhode Island, where property qualifications for voters were still fairly stringent) in the sense that almost all adult white males had the vote. Tocqueville was wise enough, however, to realize that democracy meant something deeper and subtler than a wide franchise: 'a society which all, regarding the law as their work, would love and submit to without trouble', where 'a manly confidence and a sort of reciprocal condescension between the classes would be established, as far from haughtiness as from baseness'. Meanwhile, 'the free association of citizens' would 'shelter the state from both tyranny and licence'. Democracy, he concluded, was inevitable. 'The same democracy reigning in American societies' was 'advancing rapidly toward power in Europe', and the obligation of the old ruling class was to adapt accordingly: 'to instruct democracy, reanimate its beliefs, purify its mores, regulate its movements' – in short, to tame it without destroying it.[57]

America never perfectly exemplified the theory. Tocqueville was frank about the shortcomings, some of which are still evident: government's high costs and low efficiency; the venality and ignorance of many public officials; inflated levels of political bombast; the tendency for conformism to counterbalance individualism; the menace of an intellectually feeble pantheism; the peril of the tyranny of the majority; the tension between crass materialism and religious enthusiasm; the threat from a rising, power-hungry plutocracy. James Bryce, Oxford's Professor of Jurisprudence, reinforced Tocqueville's message in the 1880s. He pointed out further defects, such as the way the system corrupted judges and sheriffs by making them bargain for votes, but he recommended the US model as both inevitable and desirable. The advantages of democracy outweighed the defects. They could be computed in dollars and cents, and measured in splendid monuments erected in newly transformed wildernesses. Achievements included the strength of civic spirit, the spread of respect of law, the prospect of material progress, and, above all, the liberation of effort and energy that results from equality of opportunity. In the last three decades of the nineteenth century and the first of the twentieth, constitutional reforms would edge most European states and others in Japan and in former European colonies towards democracy on the representative lines the United States embodied.[58]

Revolutionary disillusionment made it plain that liberty and equality were hard to combine. Equality impedes liberty. Liberty produces unequal results. Science, meanwhile, exposed another contradiction at the heart of the Enlightenment: freedom was at odds with the mechanistic view of the universe. While political thinkers released chaotic freedoms in societies and economies, scientists sought order in the universe and tried to decode the workings of the machine: a well-regulated system, in which, if one knew its principles, one could make accurate predictions and even control outcomes.

Truth and Science

Until the eighteenth century, most work in the sciences started with the assumption that external realities act on the mind, which registers data perceived through the senses. The limitations of this theory were obvious to thinkers in antiquity. We find it hard to challenge the evidence of our senses, because we have nothing else to go on. But senses may be the only reality there is. Why suppose that something beyond them is responsible for activating them? Toward the end of the seventeenth century, John Locke dismissed such objections or, rather, refused to take them seriously. He helped found a tradition of British empiricism that asserts simply that what is sensed is real. He summed his view up: 'No man's knowledge here' – by which Locke meant in the world we inhabit – 'can go beyond his experience.'[59]

For most people the tradition has developed into an attitude of commonsensical deference to evidence: instead of starting with the conviction of our own reality and doubting everything else, we should start from the assumption that the world exists. We then have a chance of making sense of it. Does empiricism imply that we can know nothing except by experience? Locke thought so; but it is possible to have a moderately empirical attitude, and hold that while experience is a sound test for knowledge, there may be facts beyond the reach of such a test. Locke's way of formulating the theory dominated eighteenth-century thinking about how to distinguish truth from falsehood. It jostled and survived among competing notions in the nineteenth. In the twentieth, Locke's philosophy enjoyed a new vogue, especially among Logical Positivists, whose school, founded in Vienna in the 1920s, demanded verification by sense-data for any claim deemed meaningful. The main influence, however, of the tradition Locke launched has been on science rather than philosophy: the eighteenth-century leap forward in science was boosted by the respect sense-data commanded. Scientists have generally favoured an empirical (in Locke's sense) approach to knowledge ever since.[60]

Science extended the reach of the senses to what had formerly been too remote or too occluded. Galileo spotted the moons of Jupiter through his telescope. Tracking the speed of sound, Marin Mersenne heard harmonics that no one had previously noticed. Robert Hooke sniffed 'nitre-air' in the acridity of vapour from a lighted wick, before Antoine Lavoisier proved the existence of oxygen by isolating it and setting it on fire. Antonie van Leeuwenhoek saw microbes through his microscope. Newton could wrest the rainbow from a shaft of light or detect the force that bound the cosmos in the weight of an apple. Luigi Galvani felt the thrill of electricity in his fingertips and made corpses twitch at the touch of current. Friedrich Mesmer thought hypnotism was a kind of measurable 'animal magnetism'. Through life-threatening demonstrations with kite and keys, Benjamin Franklin (1706–90) showed that lightning is a kind of electricity. Their triumphs made credible the cry of empiricist philosophers: 'Nothing unsensed can be present to the mind!'

Scientific commitment and practical common sense were part of the background of the so-called 'Industrial Revolution' – the movement to develop mechanical methods of production and mobilize energy from new sources of power. Although industrialization was not an idea, mechanization, in some sense, was. In part, its origins lie in the surprising human ability to imagine slight sources of power generating enormous force, just as threadlike sinews convey the strength of the body. Steam, the first such power-source in nature to be 'harnessed' to replace muscles, was a fairly obvious case: you can see it and feel its heat, even though it takes some imagination to believe that it can work machinery and impel locomotion. In the 1760s James Watt applied a discovery of 'pure' science – atmospheric pressure, which is invisible and undetectable except by experiment – to make steam power exploitable.[61]

Germs were perhaps the most astonishing of the previously invisible agents that the new science uncovered. Germ theory was an idea equally serviceable to theology and science. It made the origins of life mysterious, but illuminated the causes of decay and disease. Life, if God didn't devise it, must have arisen from spontaneous generation. At least, that was what everybody – as far as we know – thought for thousands of years, if they thought about it at all. For ancient Egyptians, life came out of the slime of the Nile's first flood. The standard Mesopotamian narrative resembles the account favoured by many modern scientists: life took shape spontaneously in a swirling primeval soup of cloud and condensation mixed with a mineral element, salt. To envisage the 'gods begotten by the waters', Sumerian poets turned to the image of the teeming alluvial mud that flooded up from the Tigris and Euphrates: the language is sacral, the concept scientific. Challenged by theology, common sense continued to suggest that the mould and worms of putrescence generate spontaneously.

When microbes became visible under the microscope of Antonie van Leeuwenhoek, it hardly, therefore, seemed worth asking where they come from. The microbial world, with its apparent evidence of spontaneous generation, cheered atheists. The very existence of

God – or at least, the validity of claims about his unique power to create life – was at stake. Then, in 1799, with the aid of a powerful microscope, Lazzaro Spallanzani observed fission: cells reproduced by splitting. He demonstrated that if bacteria – or animalculi, to use the term favoured at the time, or germs, as he called them – were killed by heating, they could not reappear in a sealed environment. 'It appeared', as Louis Pasteur later put it, 'that the ferments, properly so-called, are living beings, that the germs of microscopic organisms abound in the surface of all objects, in the air and in water; that the theory of spontaneous generation is chimerical.'[62] Spallanzani concluded that living organisms did not appear from nowhere: they could only germinate in an environment where they were already present. No known case of spontaneous generation of life was left in the world.

Science is still grappling with the consequences. As far as we know, the one-celled life forms called archaea were the first on our planet. The earliest evidence of them dates from at least half a billion years after the planet began. They were not always around. So where did they come from? Egyptian and Sumerian science postulated a chemical accident. Scrutineers are still looking for the evidence, but, so far, without avail.

Germ theory also had enormous practical consequences: almost at once, it transformed the food industry by suggesting a new way of preserving foods in sealed containers. In the longer term, it opened the way for the conquest of many diseases. Germs, it became clear, sickened bodies as well as corrupting food.[63]

To some extent, the success of science encouraged mistrust of religion. The evidence of the senses was all true. Real objects caused it (with exceptions that concerned sound and colour and that experiments could confirm). Jangling, for instance, is proof of the bell, as heat is of the proximity of fire, or stench of the presence of gas. From Locke, eighteenth-century radicals inherited the conviction that it was 'fiddling' to waste time thinking about what, if anything, lay beyond the scientifically observed world. But this attitude, which we would now call scientism, did not satisfy all its practitioners. The Scottish philosopher David Hume, born a few years after Locke's death, agreed that it is nonsense to speak of the reality of anything imperceptible, but pointed out that sensations are not really evidence of anything except themselves – that objects cause them is an unverifiable assumption. In the 1730s the renowned London preacher, Isaac Watts, adapted Locke's work for religious readers, exalting wordless 'judgement' – detectable in feeling yet inexpressible in thought – alongside material perceptions. Towards the end of the century, Kant inferred that the structure of the mind, rather than any reality outside it, determines the only world we can know. Meanwhile, many scientists, like Maupertuis, drifted back from atheism toward religion, or became more interested in speculation about truths beyond the reach of science. Spallanzani's work restored to God a place in launching life. Churches, moreover, knew how to defeat unbelievers. Censorship did not work. But appeals, over the intellectuals' heads, to ordinary people did. Despite the hostility of the Enlightenment, the eighteenth century was a time of tremendous religious revival in the West.

Religious and Romantic Reactions

Christianity reached a new public. In 1722, Nikolaus Ludwig, Count von Zinzendorf, experienced an unusual sense of vocation. On his estate in eastern Germany he built the village of Herrnhut ('the Lord's keeping') as a refuge where persecuted Christians could share a sense of the love of God. It became a centre from which radiated evangelical fervour – or 'enthusiasm', as they called it. Zinzendorf's was only one of innumerable movements in the eighteenth century to offer ordinary people an affective, unintellectual solution to the problems of life: proof that, in their way, feelings are stronger than reason and that for some people religion is more satisfying than science. As one of the great inspirers of Christian revivalism, Jonathan Edwards of Massachusetts, said, 'Our people do not so much need ... heads stored, as ... hearts touched.' His congregations purged their emotions in ways intellectuals found repellent. 'There was a great moaning', observed a witness to one of Edwards's sermons, 'so that the minister was obliged to desist – the shrieks and cries were piercing and amazing.'[64]

Preaching was the information technology of all these movements. In 1738, with a 'heart strangely warmed', John Wesley launched a mission to workers in England and Wales. He travelled eight thousand miles a year and preached to congregations of thousands at a time in the open air. He communicated a mood rather than a message – a sense of how Jesus can change lives by imparting love. Isaac Watts's friend George Whitfield held meetings in Britain's American colonies, where 'many wept enthusiastically like persons that were hungering and thirsting after righteousness' and made Boston seem 'the gate of heaven'.[65] Catholic evangelism adopted similar means to target the same enemies: materialism, rationalism, apathy, and formalized religion. Among the poor in Naples Alfonso Maria de Liguori seemed like a biblical prophet. In 1765 the pope authorized devotion to the Sacred Heart of Jesus – a bleeding symbol of divine love. Cynically, some European monarchs collaborated with religious revival as a means to distract people from politics and to exploit churches as agents of social control. King Frederick the Great of Prussia, a freethinker who liked to have philosophers at his dinner table, favoured religion for his people and his troops. In founding hundreds of military chaplaincies and requiring religious teaching in schools, he was applying the recommendation of his sometime friend, Voltaire: 'If God did not exist, it would be necessary to invent him.' Voltaire was more concerned that God should constrain kings than commoners, but to 'leave hopes and fear intact' was, he realized, the best formula for social peace.[66]

Music helped to quieten rationalism, partly because it evokes emotion without expressing clear meaning. In the eighteenth century, God seemed to have all the best tunes. Isaac Watts's moving hymns made singers pour contempt on pride. John Wesley's brother Charles made congregations sense the joy of heaven in love. The settings of Christ's passion by Johann Sebastian Bach stirred hearers of all religious traditions and none. In 1741 one of the Bible texts that George Frideric Handel set to music made an effective reply to sceptics: God was 'despised and rejected of men', but 'I know that my Redeemer liveth, and though worms destroy this body, yet in my flesh shall I see God'. Mozart was a better servant of the Church than of Masonry. He died in 1791 while at work on his great *Requiem Mass* – his own triumph over death.

You need understand nothing, intellectually, in order to appreciate music. For most of the eighteenth century, of course, composers reflected Enlightenment values in mathematically precise counterpoint, for example, or rational harmonics. But music was about to triumph as a kind of universal language, thanks to deeper currents of cultural and intellectual history. Mozart lay almost unmourned in a pauper's grave, whereas when Ludwig van Beethoven died in 1834, scores of thousands thronged his funeral, and he was buried with pomp that would hardly have disgraced a prince.[67] In the interim, romanticism had challenged enlightened sensibilities.

The eighteenth century in Europe was supposedly 'the Age of Reason'. But its failures – its wars, its oppressive regimes, its disappointment with itself – showed that reason alone was not enough. Intuition was at least its equal. Feelings were as good as thought. Nature still had lessons to teach civilization. Christians and their enemies could agree about nature, which seemed more beautiful and more terrible than any construction of the human intellect. In 1755 an earthquake centred near Lisbon shook even Voltaire's faith in progress. One of Europe's greatest cities, home to nearly 200,000 people, was reduced to ruins. As an alternative to God, radical philosophers responded to the call to 'return to nature' that Baron d'Holbach, one of the most prominent *encyclopédistes,* uttered in 1770: 'She will ... drive out from your heart the fears that hobble you ... the hatreds that separate you from man, whom you ought to love.'[68] 'Sensibility' became a buzzword for responsiveness to feelings, which were valued even more than reason.

It is worth remembering that exploration in the eighteenth century was constantly revealing new marvels of nature that dwarfed the constructions of human minds and hands. New World landscapes inspired responses that eighteenth-century people called 'romantic'. Modern scholars seem unable to agree about what this term really meant. But in the second half of the eighteenth century it became increasingly frequent, audible, and insistent in Europe, and increasingly dominant in the world thereafter. Romantic values included imagination, intuition, emotion, inspiration, and even passion, alongside – or in extreme cases, ahead of – reason and scientific knowledge as guides to truth and conduct. Romantics professed to prefer nature to art, or, at least, wanted art to demonstrate sympathy with nature. The connection with global exploration and with the disclosure of new wonders was apparent in the engravings that illustrated the published reports of two young Spanish explorers, Jorge Juan and Antonio de Ulloa, who straddled the equator in the 1730s as part of the same project as took Maupertuis to the

Arctic: determining the shape of the Earth. They combined scientific diagrams with images of awestruck reverence for untamed nature. Their drawing, for instance, of Mount Cotopaxi erupting in Ecuador, with the phenomenon, depicted in the background, of arcs of light on the mountain slopes, combines precision with rugged romance. Ironically, a scientific illustration was among the first artworks of romanticism.

The merging of science and romance is apparent, too, in the work of one of the greatest scientists of the age, Alexander von Humboldt, who aimed 'to see Nature in all her variety of grandeur and splendour'. The high point of his endeavours came in 1802, when he tried to climb Mount Chimborazo – Cotopaxi's twin peak. Chimborazo was thought to be the highest mountain in the world – the untouched summit of creation. Humboldt had almost reached the top, when, sickened by altitude, racked by cold, bleeding copiously from nose and lips, he had to turn back. His story of suffering and frustration was just the sort of subject romantic writers were beginning to celebrate in Europe. The English poet John Keats hymned the lover who 'canst never have thy bliss'. In 1800 the introspective but influential German poet Novalis created one of romanticism's most potent symbols, the *blaue Blume*, the elusive flower that can never be plucked and that has symbolized romantic yearning ever since. The cult of the unattainable – an unfulfillable yearning – lay at the heart of romanticism: in one of Humboldt's illustrations of his American adventures, he stoops to pick a flower at the foot of Chimborazo. His engravings of the scenery he encountered inspired romantic painters in the new century.[69]

Romanticism was not just a reaction against informally deified reason and classicism: it was also a re-blending of popular sensibilities into the values and tastes of educated people. Its poetry was, as Wordsworth and Coleridge claimed, 'the language of ordinary men'. Its grandeur was rustic – of solitude rather than cities, mountains rather than mansions. Its aesthetics were sublime and picturesque, rather than urbane and restrained. Its religion was 'enthusiasm', which was a dirty word in the salons of the *ancien régime* but which drew crowds of thousands to popular preachers. The music of romanticism ransacked traditional airs for melodies. Its theatre and opera borrowed from the charivari of street mummers. Its prophet was Johann Gottfried Herder, who collected folk tales and praised the moral power of the 'true poetry' of 'those whom we call savages'. '*Das Volk dichtet*', he said: the people make poetry. Romanticism's educational values taught the superiority of untutored passions over contrived refinement. Its portraiture showed society ladies in peasant dress in gardens landscaped to look natural, reinvaded by romance. 'The people' had arrived in European history as a creative force and would now begin to remould their masters in their own image: culture, at least some culture, could start bubbling up from below, instead of just trickling down from the aristocracy and high bourgeoisie. The nineteenth century – the century of romanticism – would awaken democracy, socialism, industrialization, total war, and 'the masses' backed, by far-seeing members of the elite, 'against the classes'.[70]

Chapter 8

The Climacteric of Progress

Nineteenth-Century Certainties

The common man resorted to bloodshed. The noble savage reverted to type. The French Revolution streaked the Enlightenment with shadows. In Paris in 1798, Étienne-Gaspard Robert's freak light show made monstrous shapes loom from a screen, or flicker weirdly through billowing smoke. Meanwhile, in demonstrations of the new power of galvanization, Frankenstein's real-life precursors made corpses twitch to give audiences a thrill. Francisco Goya drew creatures of the night screaming and flapping in nightmares while reason slept, but monsters could emerge in reason's most watchful hours. Prefigurations of how monstrous modernity could be appeared amid the hideous issue of scientific experimentation or in minds tortured by 'crimes committed in the name of liberty'.

The transformation of an entire culture was audible in the discords that invaded Beethoven's music and visible in the deformations that distorted Goya's paintings. After the Enlightenment – rational, passionless, detached, precise, complacent, ordered, and self-assertive – the prevailing mood in nineteenth-century Europe was romantic, sentimental, enthusiastic, numinous, nostalgic, chaotic, and self-critical. Bloodied but unbowed, belief in progress persisted, but now with sights trained desperately on the future rather than complacently on the present. With Enlightenment dimmed, progress was discernible but indistinct. Some sixty years after Barry's paintings of progress for the Royal Society of Arts in London, Thomas Cole conceived a similar series on 'The Course of Empire' to illustrate lines from Lord Byron:

> There is the moral of all human tales;
> 'Tis but the same rehearsal of the past.
> First freedom and then Glory – when that fails,
> Wealth, vice, corruption – barbarism at last.

Whereas Barry's sequence had climaxed in Elysium, Cole's proceeded from savagery through civilization and decadent opulence to desolation.

An Overview of the Age

Instead of a golden age of the past – the normal locus of utopias in earlier periods – the perfectibilians of the nineteenth century thought the golden age was still to come. They could no longer rely on reason to produce progress. The collapse of the Enlightenment brought down the house of reason, exposing human violence and irrationality. All that remained were 'crooked timbers' with which 'nothing straight' could be made: the language is that of the great transitional figure who, between Enlightenment and romanticism, 'critiqued' reason and lauded intuition: Immanuel Kant.[1]

In place of reason, vast impersonal forces seemed to drive improvement: laws of nature, of history, of economics, of biology, of 'blood and iron'. The result was a mechanized and brutalized world picture. Staggering conquests in science and technology sustained the illusion of progress. Steam-driven industrialization immeasurably multiplied the power of muscle. Science continued to reveal formerly unseen truths, teasing microbes into view, manipulating gases, measuring previously ill-known forces, such as magnetism, electricity, and atmospheric pressure, perceiving links between species, exposing fossils, and so disclosing the antiquity of the Earth. English journalists and politicians levered, cranked, and puffed progress as 'the march of improvement' – their misleading name for the noise and confusion of unregulated industries. Every advance was adaptable for evil: for war or exploitation. Intellect and morality registered none of the expected improvements, which were all material and largely confined to privileged people and places. Like the Enlightenment that preceded it, the nineteenth-century 'age of progress' dissolved in blood: in the cataclysm of the First World War and the horrors of the twentieth century.

Those horrors flowed from nineteenth-century ideas: nationalism, militarism, the value of violence, the rootedness of race, the sufficiency of science, the irresistibility of history, the cult of the state. A chilling fact about the ideas in this chapter is that most of them generated appalling effects. They shaped the future, even if they had little influence at the time. That is not surprising: there is always a time lag between the birth of an idea and the engendering of its progeny. Factories went up in what was still a Renaissance world, as far as the elite were concerned; as William Hazlitt observed, they were 'always talking about the Greeks and Romans'.[2] Inspired, curious, high-minded, nineteenth-century scientists resembled artists or practitioners of higher mathematics: few had practical vocations. Science, as we have seen, could nourish industry. But the inventors of the processes that made industrialization possible – of coke smelting, mechanized spinning, steam pumping, and the steam-driven loom – were heroes of self-help: self-taught artisans and engineers with little or no scientific formation. Science was eventually hijacked for the aims of industry – bought by money for 'useful research', diverted by dogmas of social responsibility – but not until the nineteenth century was nearly over.

All the technical innovations that reforged the nineteenth-century world started in the West. So did initiatives in almost every other field. Those that arose in Asia were responses or adjustments to the white man's unaccustomed power – receptions or rejections of his exhortations or examples. At the start of the nineteenth century, William Blake could still draw Europe as a Grace among equals in the dance of the continents, supported, arm in arm, by Africa and America. But she reduced her sister-continents to emulation or servility. Though they sometimes took a long time to effect change in extra-European societies, Western ideas, exemplified or imposed, spread rapidly, symbolizing and cementing a growing advantage in war and wares. European cultural influence and business imperialism extended the reach of political hegemony. Unprecedented demographic, industrial, and technical strides opened new gaps. Industrialized and industrializing regions drew apart and ahead. Although Europe's hegemony was brief, European miracles were the most conspicuous feature of the nineteenth century:

the culmination of long commercial out-thrust, imperial initiatives, and scientific achievements.

Demography and Social Thought

Demographic changes are the proper starting place, because they underpinned all the others. A brief summary of the demographic facts will also help explain the theories with which observers responded.

Despite mechanization, manpower remained the most useful and adaptable of natural resources. In the nineteenth century, the fastest growth of population was in Europe and North America – 'the West', as people came to say, or 'Atlantic civilization', which embraced its home ocean, its '*mare nostrum*', just as the Roman Empire clung to its middle sea. Between about 1750 and about 1850, the population of China doubled; that of Europe nearly doubled; that of the Americas doubled and doubled again. For war and work, people mattered most, though the West outpaced everywhere else in mobilizing other resources, too, especially in growing food and mining mineral wealth.

Everyone realizes that the shift in the global distribution of population favoured the West. But no one has been able to show how it affected industrialization. Historians and economists compete to identify the circumstances that made industrialization possible. They usually refer to propitious financial institutions, a conducive political environment, a commercially minded elite, and access to coal for smelting and making steam. These were all relevant and perhaps decisive. None of the widely supported theories, however, confronts the great paradox of mechanization: why did it happen where and when population was booming? Why bother with the cost and trouble of machines when labour was plentiful and should, therefore, have been cheapened by glut? Population was key, I think, because of the relationship between labour and demand. Beyond a still-unspecifiable threshold, abundant labour inhibits mechanization: the most industrious, productive economies of the preindustrial world, in China and India, were like that. But below the threshold, I suggest, the growth of population generates excess demand for goods, relative to the manpower available to produce them. A propitious balance between labour supply and demand for goods is the essential condition for industrialization. Britain was the first country to meet it, followed, in the course of the nineteenth century, by Belgium and some other parts of Europe, and then the United States and Japan.

Although relatively concentrated in the West, population growth of unprecedented magnitude happened worldwide. Acceleration had begun in the eighteenth century, when the transoceanic, intercontinental exchange of edible biota hugely boosted the world's food supplies, while, for obscure reasons, probably traceable to random mutations in the microbial world, the global disease environment changed in favour of humans. At first the effects were hard to discern. Many late-eighteenth-century analysts were convinced that the statistical drift was adverse, perhaps because they noticed rural depopulation – a sort of epiphenomenon that was the result of the relatively faster growth of towns. Even those who spotted the trend early did not know what would happen in the long run and wrestled with conflicting responses to their own bafflement. Among the consequences was one of the most influential instances ever of a mistaken idea that proved immensely powerful: the idea of overpopulation.

Too many people? No one believed there could be any such thing until an English parson, Thomas Malthus, formulated the idea in 1798. Previously, increased human numbers promised more economic activity, more wealth, more manpower, more strength. Malthus's was a voice crying for the want of a wilderness. He peered with anxious charity into a grave new world, where only disaster would temper overpopulation. The statistics he used in *An Essay on the Principle of Population* came from the work of the Marquis de Condorcet, who cited increasing population as evidence of progress. Whereas Condorcet was an arch-optimist, Malthus re-filtered the same statistics through a lens dusty with gloom. He concluded that humankind was bound for disaster because the number of people was rising much faster than the amount of food. 'The power of population is indefinitely greater than the power in the earth to produce subsistence for man ... Population, when unchecked, increases in a geometrical ratio. Subsistence only increases in an arithmetical ratio.'[3] Only 'natural checks' – an apocalyptic array of famine, plague, war, and catastrophe – could keep numbers down to a level at which the world could be fed.

Malthus wrote so convincingly that the elites of the world panicked into believing him. His view, according to William Hazlitt, was 'a ground on which to fix the levers that may move the world'.[4] Among the disastrous consequences were wars and imperial ventures, provoked by people's fear of running out of space: the drive for German *Lebensraum*, and the 'colonizing' as 'the only means to salvation' that the demographer Patrick Colquhoun urged on Britain in 1814. The results were again disastrous when a new wave of Malthusian apprehension hit the world in the mid-twentieth century as world population surged forward. The so-called 'green revolution' of the 1960s onward spattered the world with pesticides and chemical fertilizers in an attempt to grow more food. 'Factory farming' made grocers' shelves groan with cruelly raised, poorly fed, over-medicated carcasses. Some countries introduced compulsory family-limitation policies, effectively encouraging infanticide, and including sterilization programmes and cheap or free abortions; contraceptive research attracted enormous investments, which produced dubious moral and medical side effects.

Malthusian anxieties have proved false: demographic statistics fluctuate. Trends are never sustained for long. Overpopulation is extremely rare; experience suggests that as an ever higher proportion of the world's population attains prosperity, people breed less.[5] But in the nineteenth century, Malthus's doom-fraught oracles seemed reasonable, his facts incontrovertible, his predictions plausible. Every thinker read Malthus and almost all took something from him. Some adopted his apocalyptic anxieties; others appropriated his materialist assumptions, his statistical methods, his environmental determinism, or his model of the struggle of life as competitive or conflictive. At the broadest level, he challenged confidence in the inevitability of progress. The political thought of the West, and therefore of the world, in the nineteenth century was a series of responses to the problem of how to sustain progress: how to avert or survive disaster, or perhaps to welcome it as a purgative or as a chance to make a new start.

Right and left were equally inventive. At the extremes, they came to seem hardly distinguishable, for politics are horseshoe-shaped and the extremities almost touch. At the outer edges, convinced ideologues may have contrasting views but they tend to adopt the same methods of forcing them on others. So we start with conservatism and liberalism before tackling socialism, but tack between left and right as we review the doctrines of confiders in the state and the anarchists and Christian political thinkers who opposed them, before turning to the emergence of nationalisms that trumped, in appeal and effects, all other political ideas of the period.

Conservatisms and Liberalism

Even conservatism, which proved paradoxically fertile in new thinking, was part of an insecurely forward-looking world. Conservatism is best understood stratigraphically – detectable in three layers of depth. It usually issues from a pessimistic outlook: unwillingness to tamper radically with things as they are, in case they get worse. At a deep level, where humans seem irremediably bad and in need of restraint, pessimism inspired another kind of conservatism – authoritarianism that values order above liberty and the power of the state above the freedom of the subject. There is also, overlappingly, a conservative tradition that values the state, or some other community (such as 'race' or 'nation'), above the individual, generally on the grounds that one's own identity is imperfect except as part of a collective identity.

These constructions, however, were not what the Anglo-Irish statesman, Edmund Burke, envisaged in 1790. Like mainstream conservatism ever since, his concerns were to safeguard progress and to reform in order to survive. Burke had radical sympathies with victims and underdogs but recoiled from the excesses of the French Revolution. Time is 'the grand instructor', he said, and custom or tradition the source of stability.[6] Order is essential, but not for its own sake: rather, to equalize all subjects' opportunities to exercise liberty. A state must be willing to reform itself when necessary; otherwise revolution, with all its evils, will ensue. When Robert Peel founded the British Conservative Party in 1834, he enshrined this balance. The programme of the party was to reform what needed reforming and to conserve what did not – a formula with flexibility to endure change. '*Plus ça change, plus c'est la même chose*' is how the French apostle of conservatism, Alphonse Karr, put it in 1849, after a series of frustrated revolutions alarmed the European elite. Most successful governments in modern times adopted broadly conservative strategies, although they did not always admit as much. Those that opted for revolution or reaction rarely lasted long.

Conservatism started as a way of managing nature, especially human nature, for the common good: not very far, therefore, from agendas we now think of as social-democratic, which deploy modest amounts of regulation to protect otherwise free markets from distortion by corruption, profiteering, exploitation, gross inequalities of income or privilege, and other abuses of freedom. Distrust of ideology is another feature Burke transmitted to modern conservatism. He declared peace better than truth. 'Metaphysical distinctions' he deplored as 'a Serbonian bog', and theorizing as a 'sure symptom of an ill-conducted state'.[7]

Conservatism has never pretended to be scientific – based, that is on verifiable data and delivering predictable effects. Malthus's statistical approach, however, made a science of society imaginable: policies based on infallible facts could yield guaranteed outcomes. The search could be literally maddening: Auguste Comte, the pioneer of what he called 'sociology' or 'social science' was, for a while, interned in a madhouse. In lectures he began to publish in 1830, when he was struggling with self-diagnosed insanity and a stagnating academic career, he predicted a new synthesis of scientific and humanistic thinking, though he was unsure about how to frame or forge it. As it developed during the rest of the century, sociology was favoured on the right as was an attempt to make social change controllable. Only in the long run did sociologists become synonymous in popular mythology with the hairy, baggy, elbow-patched stereotypes of the intellectual left.

In the meantime, however, an English philosopher, Jeremy Bentham, thought of a way of achieving in policy-making a synthesis similar to that for which Comte yearned. Bentham is now treated as a kind of secular saint, as befits the founder of a college without a chapel – 'an angel without wings'.[8] His body is exhibited there, in University College London, as encouragement to students. His 'utilitarianism' was a creed for the irreligious. He devised a sort of calculus of happiness. He defined good as a surplus of happiness over unhappiness. The object he set for the state was 'the greatest happiness of the greatest number'. This was not liberalism as most people understood the word at the time, because Bentham rated social 'utility' above individual liberty; but his philosophy was radical, because it proposed a new way of evaluating social institutions without reference or deference to their antiquity or authority or past record of success. The doctrine was purposely godless and materialist: Bentham's standard of happiness was pleasure; his index of evil was pain.

Benthamism was instantly influential. His British admirers reorganized the state, purging the penal code of pointless pain, while inflicting new kinds of pain on the supposedly undeserving in what came to be called 'the public interest'. Poor laws sought to cut the numbers of vagrants and outcasts by making their misfortunes unbearable. Britain's bureaucracy was re-staffed with good examinees. Even under nominally right-wing governments libertarian prejudices could never quite excise public interest from legislators' priorities. Until well into the twentieth century, the radical tradition in Britain was preponderantly Benthamite, even when it called itself socialist.[9]

Bentham was the most eloquent member of a British ruling class engaged in a retreat from romanticism. He and his friends tried to think austerely, rationally, and scientifically about how to run society. The greatest happiness of the greatest number, however, always means sacrifices for some. It is strictly incompatible with human rights, because the interest of the greatest number leaves some individuals bereft. Nor were Benthamites alone in willingness to sacrifice liberty to supposedly greater good. As we shall see, German worshippers of will and supermen shared the same disposition. Thomas Carlyle, Britain's most influential moralist until his death in 1881, who fed German thinking to English believers in the essential unity of an 'Anglo-Saxon race', thought it made good sense to 'coerce human swine'.[10]

Nonetheless, the right in Britain remained 'civilized' – unwilling, on the whole, to cudgel liberty or cripple individualism. Bentham's most effective and devoted disciple, John Stuart Mill, helped keep freedom in conservatives' focus. Mill never ceased to recommend aspects of utilitarian philosophy, perhaps because he could not forget a lesson from his father, who had long served virtually as Bentham's amanuensis: 'The most effectual mode of doing good', Mill senior explained, 'is ... to attach honour to actions solely in proportion to their tendency to increase the sum of happiness, lessen the sum of misery.'[11]

His formula describes the way philanthropy still works in the United States, rewarding millionaires with veneration in exchange for private investment in public benefits.

Yet young John Stuart Mill could not quite escape romantic yearnings. At the age of twenty he began to lose faith in his father's guru, when he experienced a vision of a perfect world, in which all Bentham's prescriptions had been adopted. He recoiled in horror from the prospect. Modifying, then rejecting utilitarianism, Mill ended by putting freedom at the top of his scale of values. For Bentham's greatest number, he substituted a universal category: the individual. 'Over himself, over his own body and mind, the individual is sovereign.' An individual's liberty, Mill decided, must be absolute, unless it impinges on the liberty of others. 'The liberty of the individual', he averred, 'must thus far be limited: he must not make himself a nuisance to other people ... The only purpose for which power can be rightfully exercised over any member of a civilized community, against his will, is to prevent harm to others' – not 'to make him happier' or 'because, in the opinions of others, to do so would be wise or even right'.[12] If we now think of nineteenth-century Britain as a great liberal society – liberal in the original, European sense of a word that started in Spain and properly means 'focused on the freedom of the individual' – it was largely Mill's influence that made it so. For Lord Asquith (the wartime prime minister whom admirers praised for patience and enemies condemned for procrastination), Mill was 'the purveyor-general of thought for the early Victorians'.[13]

Mill's individualism, however, never undervalued social needs. 'Society', he wrote, 'is not founded on a contract, and ... no good purpose is answered by inventing a contract in order to deduce social obligations from it.' But 'for the protection of society', the citizen 'owes a return for the benefit'; he must therefore respect others' rights and contribute a reasonable share of taxes and services to the state.[14] Nor was Mill's liberalism perfect. At times he veered wildly between extremes of rejection and praise for socialism. In consequence of his influence, the British political elite adopted what might be called a modified liberal tradition, which responded undogmatically to change and helped to make the country surprisingly impervious to the violent revolutions that convulsed most other European states.[15]

'Women and Children First': New Categories of Social Thought

The clash of Bentham against Mill illustrates contradictions in industrializing societies. On the one hand, inventors of machines need to be free, as do devisers of economic and commercial strategies, or organizers of business for maximum efficiency. Workers, too, need liberation for leisure, in order to compensate for drudgery and routine. On the other hand, capitalism must be disciplined for the common good or, at least, for the good of 'the greatest number'. Industry is, paradoxically, both the fruit of capitalism and an emblem of the priority of community over individuals: factories slot individuals in a larger whole; markets work by pooling investment. Machines do not function without cogs. By analogy with industry, society can follow dirigible courses, like assembly lines or business algorithms. Mechanical processes become models for human relationships. As we shall see, much new nineteenth-century thought and language submerged individuals in 'masses' and 'classes' and, on a wider scale, in talk of 'races'.

Before we explore those sweeping and delusive categories it is worth pausing for two real groups of people whom the systematizing minds of the era tended to overlook: women and children. Under the impact of industrialization, both demanded re-evaluation. The exploitation of children's and women's labour was one of the scandals of the early phases; gradually, however, mechanization took these marginally efficient groups out of the labour market. Men transferred womanhood to a pedestal. Adults treated children no longer as little adults but as a distinct rank of society, almost a subspecies of humankind. Women and children, deified by artists and advertisers, were confined to shrines in the home: 'women and children' became, in a famous line from E. M. Forster's *A Passage to India*, 'the phrase that exempts the male from sanity'. European idealizations, enviable in artists' images of delicately nurtured femininity or cherubic childhood, were barely intelligible in cultures where women and children were still men's partners in production.

There were disadvantages in being idealized. Societies that freed children from the workplace tried to confine them inside schools. Sweeps did not naturally change into the water-babies that Charles

Kingsley mawkishly imagined; the romantic ideal of childhood was more often coerced than coaxed into being. In 1879 Henrik Ibsen captured the plight of women in his most famous play, *A Doll's House*, casting them in a role that resembled that of children. For women the fall from the pedestal could be bruising, as for the adulteress pictured by Augustus Egg in three terrible stages of decline and destitution, or for sexually louche operatic heroines, such as Manon and Violetta. The fallen woman, *la traviata*, became a favourite topos of the age. *Doll's House* and Frances Hodgson Burnett's *Secret Garden* proved, in practice, to be oppressive pens from which the women and children of twentieth-century Europe struggled to escape.[16]

New thinking, however, about women and children was little remarked. They were indistinguishably immersed, like male individuals, in the categories of class and mass on which most intellectuals focused. The clash of political visions in nineteenth-century Europe was the echo of a mightier clash of rival philosophies of humankind. Was 'man' ape or angel?[17] Was he the image of God or the heir of Adam? Would the goodness inside him emerge in freedom or was it corroded with evil that had to be controlled? Politics of fear and hope collided. In the rest of this section, we shall be in the great arena of their collisions: that of socialism and kindred thinking.

Socialism was an extreme form of optimism. In Milan in 1899, Giuseppe Pellizza, a convert from a guilt-ridden bourgeois background, began his vast symbolic painting on the subject. In *Il quarto stato* he depicted a vast crowd of workers, advancing, the artist said, 'like a torrent, overthrowing every obstacle in its path, thirsty for justice'.[18] Their pace is relentless, their focus unwavering, their solidarity intimidating. But, except for a madonna-like woman in the foreground, who seems bent on a personal project as she appeals to one of the rugged leaders at the head of the march, they are individually characterless. They move like parts of a giant automaton, with a mechanical rhythm, slow and pounding.

No work of art could better express the grandeur and grind at the heart of socialism: noble humanity, mobilized by dreary determinism. In the history of socialism, the nobility and humanity came first. Radicals apostrophized them as 'equality and fraternity'; early socialist communities tried to embody the same qualities in practices of sharing and co-operating (see p. 220). In Icaria, envy, crime, anger, rivalry, and lust would – so the founder hoped – disappear with the abolition of property. The sexual orgies Charles Fourier planned would be organized on egalitarian principles.[19]

Such experiments failed, but the idea of reforming society as a whole on socialist lines appealed to people who felt under-rewarded or outraged by the unequal distribution of wealth. Icarus came down to earth, with the 'accountants' socialism' of Thomas Hodgskin. He endorsed the view of David Ricardo, whom we shall come to in a moment, that workers' labour added the greater part of most commodities' value; so they should get the lion's share of the profits. This was a capitalist's kind of socialism, in which ideals carried a price tag. Once socialist economics had become conventional, Louis Blanc made its politics conventional, too. Blanc, who in 1839 coined the phrase 'from each according to his abilities, to each according to his needs', convinced most socialists that the state could be trusted to impose their ideals on society. John Ruskin, the self-tortured art critic and arbiter of Victorian taste, echoed these arguments in England. For him, 'the first duty of a state is to see that every child born therein shall be well housed, clothed, fed and educated'.[20] Increased state power could surely only help the needy. Meanwhile, Karl Marx predicted socialism's inevitable triumph through a cycle of class conflicts; as economic power passed from capital to labour, so workers, degraded and inflamed by exploitative employers, would seize power. Early socialist experiments had been peaceful, with no land to conquer except in the open spaces of the wilderness, no human adversaries except selfishness and greed. Now, transformed by language of conflict and coercion, socialism became an ideology of violence, to be resisted uncompromisingly by those who valued property above fraternity and liberty above equality.[21]

In some ways, socialists were still pursuing, by new methods, the ancient Greek ideal of a state that served to make men virtuous. Wherever it was tried, however, socialism failed to achieve any noticeably positive moral effects. 'As with the Christian religion', as the sceptical leftist George Orwell observed in his account of his travels through the England of the 1930s along *The Road to Wigan Pier*, 'the worst advertisement for socialism is its adherents'. Advocates thought they could appeal to factual evidence – economic or historical – and represent their doctrine as 'scientific'. The work of David Ricardo, who was never a socialist but who tried, without prejudice, to identify economic laws by analogy with laws of nature, produced the supposed economic evidence. In 1817 he recognized a principle of economics – that labour adds value to a product – and turned it into a law.[22]

'Labor', Ricardo contended, is 'the foundation of all value', with 'the relative quantity of labor ... almost exclusively determining the relative value of commodities'.[23] In its crude form, the theory is wrong. Capital affects the value at which goods are exchanged, and capital is not always just stored-up labour, since extremely valuable natural assets can be almost instantly realized for cash. The way goods are perceived or presented affects what people will pay for them (Ricardo did recognize rarity value, but only as a short-term distorter, citing objects of art and 'wines of a peculiar quality'). Still, Ricardo's principle was right. He drew from it counterintuitive and mutually contradictory conclusions. If labour makes the biggest contribution to profits, one would expect wages to be high; Ricardo therefore opined that wages could 'be left to the fair and free competition of the market, and should never be controlled by the interference of the legislature'. On the other hand he expected that capitalists would keep wages low to maximize profits. 'There can be no rise in the value of labor without a fall in profits.'[24]

Karl Marx believed Ricardo, but events proved both wrong, at least until the early twenty-first century. I used to think that this was because capitalists also recognized that it was in their interests to pay workers well, not only to secure industrial peace and avert revolution, but also to improve productivity and increase demand. It seems more likely, however, that the terrible, menacing wars of the twentieth century imposed social responsibility on entrepreneurs or obliged them to accept close regulation by government in the interests of social cohesion and national survival.[25]

Still, an idea does not have to be right to be influential. The essential features of Ricardo's thoughts on labour – the labour theory of value and the idea of a permanent conflict of interest between capital and labour – passed via Marx to animate revolutionary unrest in late-nineteenth-century Europe and the twentieth-century world.

Marx claimed to base his social and political prescriptions on scientific economics. But his study of history counted for more in shaping his thoughts. According to Marx's theory of historical change, every instance of progress is the synthesis of two preceding, conflicting events or tendencies. He got his starting point from G. W. F. Hegel, a Protestant ex-seminarian who rose spectacularly in the extemporized university hierarchy of early-nineteenth-century Prussia. Everything, according to Hegel, is part of something else; so if x is part of y, you have to understand y in order to think coherently about x, and then to know $x + y$ – the synthesis that alone makes perfect sense. This seems unimpressive: a recipe for never being able to think coherently about anything in isolation. As well as dialectical, Marx's scheme was materialist: change was economically driven (not, as Hegel thought, by spirit or ideas). Political power, Marx predicted, would end up with whoever held the sources of wealth. Under feudalism, for instance, land was the means of production; so landowners ruled. Under capitalism, money counted for most; so financiers ran states. Under industrialism, as Ricardo had shown, labour added value; workers would therefore rule the society of the future in a 'dictatorship of the proletariat'. Marx vaguely delineated a further, final synthesis: in a classless society, the state would 'wither'; everybody would share wealth equally; property would be common.

Apart from this improbable consummation, each of the transitions that Marx imagined from one type of society to the next would inevitably be violent: the ruling class would always struggle to retain power, while the rising class would strive to wrest it. Because Marx accepted Ricardo's argument that employers would exploit workers for all they were worth, he expected a violent reaction to follow. 'Not only', Marx wrote, 'has the bourgeoisie forged the weapons that bring death to itself: it has also called into existence the men who are to wield those weapons – the modern working class, the proletarians.'[26] Marx therefore tended to agree with the thinkers of his day who saw conflict as good and conducive to progress. He helped to inspire revolutionary violence, which sometimes succeeded in changing society, but never brought the communist utopia into being or even into sight.

All his predictions have proved false – so far, at least. If he had been right, the first great proletarian revolution ought to have happened in America, the vanguard society of capitalism. In fact, America remained the country where Marxism never happened on any great scale, while the great revolutions of the early twentieth century were traditional peasant rebellions in the largely unindustrialized environments of China and Mexico. Russia, which Marxists saw, for a while, as an exemplary case of Marxism in action, was only very patchily and partially industrialized in 1917, when the state was seized by revolutionary followers of Marx. But even there, the master's principles were honoured in the breach: it became a dictatorship, but not of the proletariat. The ruling class was replaced, but only by a ruling party; instead of discarding nationalism and promoting internationalism, Russia's new rulers soon reverted to traditional policy-making based on the interests of the state. Mother Russia mattered more than Mother Courage. When bourgeois exploitation of workers ended, state oppression of almost everybody ensued.[27]

The Apostles of the State

The state Marx hoped to see 'wither' was, for most of his contemporaries, the best means of maintaining progress. To some extent, empowerment of the state happened outside the realm of ideas: material contingencies made it unstoppable. Population growth manned armies and police forces; new technologies transmitted orders quickly and enforced them ruthlessly. Taxes, statistics, and intelligence accumulated. Means of punishment multiplied. Violence became increasingly a privilege (ultimately, almost a monopoly) of the state, which outgunned and outspent individuals, traditional institutions, associations, and regional power structures. The state triumphed in almost all its nineteenth-century confrontations with rival sources of authority – tribes, clans, and other kinship groups; the Church and other theocratic alternatives to secular power; aristocracies and patriciates; trade syndicates; local and regional particularisms; bandit chiefs and extra-legal mafias and freemasonries. In the civil wars of Germany, Japan, Italy, and the United States early in the second half of the nineteenth century, centralizers won.

Thinkers were on hand with support for the way things were going, or arguments for driving state power further, or assertions of the desirability or inevitability of absolute sovereignty, proclaiming the idea that the State Can Do No Wrong. We can consider their contributions in turn, starting with Hegel, before turning in the next section to the ideas of dissenters from and opponents (or, perhaps, in the case of the Church, rivals) of the state.

Hegel devised the philosophical starting point for state-worship, as for so much mainstream nineteenth-century thinking: the philosophy he called idealism. It would be easier to understand, perhaps, if it were renamed 'idea-ism', because in everyday language, 'idealism' means an approach to life targeted on lofty aspirations, whereas Hegel's idea was different: that only ideas exist. Philosophers in ancient India, China, and Greece anticipated him. Some people have used the term 'idealism' to denote Plato's superficially similar theory that only ideal forms are real (see p. 149). Plato influenced Hegel, but the latter's immediate source of inspiration was Bishop George Berkeley, whose sinecure in the early-eighteenth-century Church of Ireland provided plenty of leisure to think. Berkeley wanted to assert metaphysics against materialism and God against Locke. He began by examining the commonsense assumption that material objects are real, which derives, he reasoned, from the way we register them in our minds. But mentally registered perceptions are the only realities of which we have evidence. Therefore, we cannot know that there are real things outside our minds, 'nor is it possible that they should have any existence, out of the minds ... which perceive them'. There may be no such thing as a rock – just the idea of it. Samuel Johnson claimed to be able to refute this theory by kicking the rock.[28]

Idealism, however, was not so easily kicked. Hegel took Berkeley's thinking further. In his typical, defiantly tortuous language, he commended 'the notion of the Idea ... whose object is the Idea as such ... the absolute and all truth, the Idea which thinks itself'.[29] Hegel adopted a strategy unlikely to communicate yet calculated to impress: he made his thought hard to follow and his language hard to understand. Would-be intellectuals often overrate obscurity and even exalt unintelligibility. We all feel tempted to mistake complexity for profundity. Bertrand Russell told the story of how the council of his old Cambridge college consulted him about whether to renew the fellowship of Ludwig Wittgenstein, the cutting-edge philosopher, as they could not understand his work. Russell replied that he could not understand it, either. He therefore recommended renewal to be on the safe side. An anecdote popular in academia is of two researchers who gave the same lectures twice, once in intelligible and once in unintelligible English. They waited with clipboards to get the audience's ratings of the rival versions, with depressingly predictable results. Hegel's meaning can be simply expressed: we know what is in our minds. The only verifiable experience is mental experience. What is outside the mind is only inferred.

How did an apparently innocuous and practically irrelevant reflection about the nature of ideas affect politics and real life? Hegel provoked a sometimes furious and still-unresolved debate among philosophers: is it possible to distinguish 'things-in-themselves' from the ideas of them that we have in our minds? As with many of the theoretical debates of the past – over theological arcana in antiquity, for instance, or the proper dress for clergymen in the seventeenth century – it seems hard to see, at first glance, what the fuss was and is about, since, as a working hypothesis, the assumption that perceptions reflect realities beyond themselves seems ineluctable. The debate matters, however, because of its serious implications for the organization and conduct of society. Denial of the existence of anything outside our own minds is a desperate cul-de-sac into which anarchists (see p. 297), subjectivists, and other extreme individualists crowd. To escape the cul-de-sac, some philosophers proposed, in effect, the annihilation of the concept of self: to be real, ideas had to be collective. The claim fed corporate and totalitarian doctrines of society and the state. Ultimately, idealism led some of its proponents into a kind of modern monism according to which the only reality is 'the absolute' – the consciousness that we all share. Self is part of everything else.

The doctrine sounds benevolent, but can be appropriated by power-seekers who claim to embody or represent absolute consciousness. Hegel assigned a special kind of mandate over reality to the state. 'The State', he said, using capital letters with even greater profligacy than was usual in the German language of his day, 'is the Divine Idea as it exists on Earth.'[30] Hegel really meant this, although it sounds like overblown rhetoric. What the state wills, he thought – in practice, what the elite or ruler wills – is the 'general will' that Rousseau had claimed to identify (see p. 258). It trumps what individual citizens want, or even what they all want. Hegel saw no sense in speaking of individuals. Margaret

Thatcher, the conservative heroine of the late twentieth century, is supposed to have said, 'There is no such thing as society', meaning that only the individuals who compose it count. Hegel took the opposite view: individuals are incomplete except in the contexts of the political communities to which they belong. The State, however, with a capital 'S', is perfect. The assertion was imperfectly logical, because states are part of an even wider community, that of the entire world; but Hegel overlooked the point.[31]

His claims proved strangely attractive to contemporaries and successors, perhaps because he confirmed the trend, already under way, towards unlimited state power. Traditionally, institutions independent of the state – such as the Church in medieval Europe – had been able to constrain the state by dispensing natural or divine laws. But by Hegel's time, 'positive law' – the law the state made for itself – was supreme and effectively unchallengeable.

Hegel thought most people were incapable of worthwhile achievement and that we are all the playthings of history and of vast, impersonal, inescapable forces that control our lives. Occasionally, however, 'world-historical individuals' of extraordinary wisdom or prowess could embody the 'spirit of the times' and force the pace of history, without being able to alter its course. Accordingly, self-appointed 'heroes' and 'supermen' came forward to interpret the absolute on behalf of everyone else. It is hard for twenty-first-century intellectuals, who tend to prefer anti-heroes, to appreciate that the nineteenth century was an age of hero-worship. Carlyle, who did much of his thinking under a German spell, thought history was little more than the record of the achievements of great men. He advocated hero-worship as a kind of secular religion of self-improvement. 'The history of what man has accomplished in this world', he wrote, 'is at bottom the History of the Great Men who have worked here ... Worship of a Hero is transcendent admiration of a Great Man ... There is, at bottom, nothing else admirable ... Society is founded on hero-worship.'[32] Its bases are loyalty and 'submissive admiration for the truly great'. Time does not make greatness; the great make it for themselves. History does not make heroes; heroes make history. Even the liberal-minded historian Jacob Burckhardt, whose views on the Renaissance echo in almost every thought his successors had on aesthetic matters, agreed that 'great men' shaped the stories of their times by the power of their wills.[33]

Such ideas were hard to reconcile with the burgeoning democracy of the late nineteenth century. Such supermen never existed, so most scholars think, outside the minds of their admirers. That 'the history of the world is but the biography of great men' now seems an antiquated claim, quaint or queer or querulous, according to how seriously one fears despots or bullies. Carlyle evokes pity, derision, or detestation when we read, 'We cannot look, however imperfectly, upon a great man, without gaining something by him. He is the living light-fountain, which it is good and pleasant to be near. The light which enlightens, which has enlightened the darkness of the world ... a natural luminary shining by the gift of Heaven.'[34] Democracy, which Carlyle defined as 'despair of ever finding any heroes to govern you',[35] has made heroes seem superannuated. Nowadays we are likely to endorse Herbert Spencer's riposte to Carlyle: 'You must admit that the genesis of a great man depends on the long series of complex influences which has produced the race in which he appears, and the social state into which that race has slowly grown ... Before he can make his society, his society must make him.'[36]

In the nineteenth century, however, personality cults reshaped whole cultures. English schoolboys imitated the Duke of Wellington. Otto von Bismarck became a role model for Germans. Louis-Napoléon Bonaparte was unknown at the time of his election as president of the French Republic, but the echoes of heroism in his name inspired reverence. In the Americas, myth stripped George Washington and Simón Bolívar of their human failings. Hegel's own hero-worship was of blood-soaked despots. Heroes serve groups – parties, nations, movements. Only saints embody virtues for all the world. As heroes displaced saints in popular estimation, the world got worse.[37] In the belief that great men could save society, democracies entrusted ever more power to their leaders, becoming, in many cases in the twentieth century, self-surrendered to demagogy and dictators.[38]

The dangers of superman worship should have been apparent in the work of Friedrich Nietzsche, a frustrated provincial professor of philosophy, who spent much of the second half of the century subverting or inverting all the conventional thinking he detested, until his critical faculty elided into contrariety, his embitterment into paranoia, and his genius into delusion – signified in letters he wrote reporting his own crucifixion, summoning the Kaiser to self-immolation, and urging Europe to war. He thought 'the anarchical collapse of our civilization' was a small price to pay for such a superman as Napoleon – the selfsame hero who inspired the young Hegel by marching into the seminarian's home city as a conqueror. 'The misfortunes of ... small folk', Nietzsche added, 'do not count for anything except in the feelings of men of might.' He thought the 'artist-tyrant' was the noblest type of man, and that 'spiritualized and intensified cruelty' was the highest form of culture. This sounds like ironic provocation, especially as Nero was the proverbial embodiment of both qualities: the madly egotistical Roman emperor, who became a byword for refined forms of sadism, was said to have regretted his own death because of the loss it represented for art. Nietzsche, however, was entirely sincere. 'I teach you the Overman', he declared. 'The human is something that shall be overcome.'[39]

Nietzsche's moral philosophy seemed to invite power-hungry exploiters to abuse it. His 'master morality' was simple: he solved the problem of truth by denying that it exists: one interpretation should be preferred to another only if it is more self-fulfilling to the chooser; the same principle applied to morals. All moral systems, Nietzsche proposed, are tyrannies. 'Consider any morality with this in mind: [it] ... teaches hatred of the *laisser-aller*, of any all-too-great freedom, and implants the need for limited horizons and the nearest tasks – teaching the narrowing of our perspective and thus in a certain sense stupidity.' Love of neighbour was just a Christian euphemism for fear of neighbour. 'All these moralities', he asked, 'what are they but ... recipes against the passions?' Nietzsche was alone in his day but ominously representative of the future.[40]

In works mainly of the 1880s, he called for the reclassification of revenge, anger, and lust as virtues; among his recommendations were slavery, the subjection of women to 'the whip', the refinement of the human race by gloriously bloody wars, the extermination of millions of inferior people, the eradication of Christianity with its contemptible bias to the weak, and an ethic of 'might makes right'. He claimed scientific justification, on the grounds that conquerors are necessarily superior to their victims. 'I ... entertain', he wrote, 'the hope that life may one day become more full of evil and suffering than it has ever been.'[41] All this made Nietzsche Hitler's favourite philosopher. Yet Hitler misunderstood him. Nietzsche's hatreds were broad enough to encompass the state; individual strength was what he admired and state-imposed morality the kind he most detested. Like that of so many great thinkers misread by Hitler, his work became twisted and pressed into the service of Nazism.[42]

In the mid-nineteenth century a further contribution from moral philosophy fuelled the superman cult: the notion of the autonomy and primacy of the 'will' – a suprarational zone of the mind, where urgings coalesced that were morally superior to those of reason or conscience. The spokesman for this savagery hardly embodied it. Arthur Schopenhauer was reclusive, self-indulgent, and inclined to mysticism. Like so many other philosophers, he wanted to isolate something – anything – that was indisputably real: matter, spirit, the self, the soul, thought, God. Schopenhauer hit on 'the will'. The meaning of the term was elusive, perhaps even to him, but he obviously thought he could tell it apart from reason or morals. By 'subterranean passage and secret complicity akin to treachery' it led him to self-knowledge so distinct as to be convincing. The purpose he identified for life, the destiny the will sought, was, to most tastes, unencouraging: the extinction of everything – which, Schopenhauer claimed, was what the Buddha meant by nirvana. Usually only the alienated, the resentful, and the failed advocate unqualified nihilism. Schopenhauer did not mean it literally: his aim was mystical ascent akin to that of other mystics, starting with the abnegation of the external world, toward ecstatic self-realization (which, of course, eluded his sour, curmudgeonly soul); some readers, however, responded with lust for destruction, like the amoral nihilist in G. K. Chesterton's 'The Wrong Shape'. '*I* want nothing', he declares. 'I *want* nothing. I want *nothing*.' The shifts of emphasis signpost the route from egotism, to will, to nihilism.

Nietzsche mediated Schopenhauer's message to the would-be supermen who rose to power in the twentieth century. He also mutated it along the way, suggesting that will included the urge to struggle. Resolution could come only through the victory and domination of some over others. 'The world is the will to power', Nietzsche cried, addressing potential supermen, 'and nothing beside! And you are also this will to power – and nothing beside!'[43] To minds like Hitler's or Benito Mussolini's, this was a justification for imperialism and wars of aggression. *Triumph of the Will*, the name Leni Riefenstahl gave to a notorious propaganda film she made for Hitler, was her tribute to the nineteenth-century genealogy of the Führer's self-image.[44]

Public Enemies: Beyond and Against the State

Neither Nietzsche nor Schopenhauer intended – nor even foresaw – the way their doctrines would be manipulated to bolster state power. Every change that hoisted states and supermen above the law multiplied the prospects of injustice. This outcome often occurred in democracies; in dictatorships it was normal. Understandably, therefore, with varying degrees of rejection, some nineteenth-century thinkers reacted against doctrines that idolized or idealized the state.

Anarchism, for instance, was an uncomputably ancient ideal, which began, like all political thought, with assumptions about human nature. If humans are naturally moral and reasonable, they should be able to get along together without the state. From the moment when Aristotle first exalted the state as an agent of virtue, anarchy had a bad name in the Western tradition. In eighteenth-century Europe, however, belief in progress and improvement made a stateless world seem realizable. In 1793, Mary Wollstonecraft's future husband, William Godwin, proposed to abolish all laws, on the grounds that they derived from ancient compromises botched in a state of savagery, which progress rendered obsolete. Small, autonomous communities could resolve all conflicts by face-to-face discussion. Pierre-Joseph Proudhon, whose job as a printer fed his inordinate appetite for books, took the next step. In 1840 he invented the term 'anarchism' to mean a society run on principles of reciprocity, like a mutual or co-operative society. Many experimental communities of this sort followed, but none on a scale to rival the conventional state. Meanwhile, advocates of state power captured the socialist mainstream: social democrats, who proposed to capture the state by mobilizing the masses; and followers of Louis Blanc, a bourgeois intellectual, with bureaucrats in his ancestry, who put his faith in a strong, regulatory state to realize revolutionary ambitions. Anarchists became marginalized as leftist heretics; under the influence of the writings of Mikhail Bakunin, who crisscrossed Europe animating anarchist movements from the 1840s to the 1870s, they turned increasingly to what seemed the only practical alternative revolutionary programme: violence by terrorist cells.

Among revolutionary advocates of partisan warfare in the early nineteenth century, Carlo Bianco stands out, advocating 'cold terrorism of the brain, not the heart',[45] in defence of the victims of oppression. But most revolutionaries of his day were idealists whom terror repelled. They wanted insurrection to be ethical: targeting the armed forces of the enemy, sparing indifferent or innocent civilians. Johann Most, the apostle of 'propaganda of the deed', demurred. The entire elite – the 'reptile brood' of aristocrats, priests, and capitalists – with their families, servants, and all who did business with them, were, for him, legitimate victims, to be killed without compunction. Anyone caught in the crossfire was a sacrifice in a good cause. In 1884 Most published a handbook on how to make bombs explode in churches, ballrooms, and public places. He also advocated exterminating policemen on the grounds that these 'pigs' were not fully human. Cop haters and cop killers too dumb to read Most, and too ill-educated to have heard of him, have gone on using his lexicon ever since.[46]

Most called himself a socialist, but chiefly nationalist terrorists adopted his methods. The first movement to make terror its main tactic (the Internal Macedonian Revolutionary Organization, as it eventually came to be known) started in 1893. Damjan Gruev, one of its founders, summed up the justification: 'For great effect', he wrote, 'great force is necessary. Liberty is a great thing: it requires great sacrifices.' Gruev's weasel words masked the main fact: a lot of innocent people would be bombed to death. His slogan was, 'Better a horrible end than endless horror.'[47] The Macedonian revolutionaries anticipated and exemplified the methods of subsequent terrorists: murder, looting, and rapine intimidated communities into bankrolling, sheltering, and supplying them.[48]

The idea of terrorism has continued to reverberate. 'Liberation struggles' routinely morph into ill-targeted violence. Criminals – drug-traffickers and extortionists, especially – emulate terrorists, affecting political postures and masquerading as revolutionaries. In the late-twentieth-century drug wars of Colombia and Northern Ireland it was hard to distinguish criminal from political motives. The ideological posture of the team that destroyed New York's World Trade Center in 2001 seemed confused, at best: some of the supposed martyrs against Westernization led consumerist lives and prepared for their feat by heavy drinking. Nihilism is not a political creed but a psychological aberration; suicide bombers seem the prey, not the protagonists, of the causes they represent. For practitioners, terrorism seems to satisfy psychic cravings for violence, secrecy, self-importance, and defiance, rather than intellectual or practical needs.

After contributing reckless idealism and, sometimes, frenzied violence to the ideological struggles of the earlier twentieth century, anarchism seceded from the political forefront. Peter Kropotkin was its last great theorist. His *Mutual Aid* (1902) was a cogent riposte to social Darwinism, arguing that collaboration, not competition, is natural to humankind, and that the evolutionary advantage of our species consists in our collaborative nature. 'As the human mind frees itself', Kropotkin explained, 'from ideas inculcated by minorities of priests, military chiefs and judges, striving to establish their domination, and of scientists paid to perpetuate it, a conception of society arises, in which there is no longer room for those dominating minorities.'[49] Social coercion is unnecessary and counterproductive.

Anarchism's last great battles were defensive, fought against authoritarianism of left and right alike, in the Spanish Civil War of 1936–9. They ended in defeat. The anarchists' legacy to the student revolutionary movements of 1968 involved much rhetoric with little result. Nevertheless it is possible – though unproved – that lingering anarchist tradition helps to account for a conspicuous development of the late twentieth century: the growing strength of concern for freedom on the political left in Europe. Most analysts have credited the influence of the libertarian right on leftist thinking, but anarchism may have contributed at least as much. Certainly a preference for human-scale, 'communitarian' solutions to social problems, rather than the grand planning advocated by communists and socialists of the past, has become a major theme of the modern left.[50]

In any case, nonviolent challenges to the power of the state seem, in the long run, to be more practical and perhaps more effective. The idea of civil disobedience arose in the 1840s in the mind of Henry David Thoreau. He was an utterly impractical man, an incurable romantic who advocated and, for a long time, practised economic self-sufficiency 'in the woods'; yet his thought reshaped the world. His disciples included some of the dynamic figures of the twentieth century: Mohandas Gandhi, Emma Goldman, Martin Luther King. Thoreau wrote his most important essay on politics in revulsion from the two great injustices of the antebellum United States: slavery, which belaboured blacks, and warmongering, which dismembered Mexico. Thoreau decided that he would 'quietly declare war with the state', renounce allegiance, and refuse to pay for the oppression or dispossession of innocent people. If all just men did likewise, he reasoned, the state would be compelled to change. 'If the alternative is to keep all just men in prison, or give up war and slavery, the State will not hesitate which to choose.'[51] Thoreau went to gaol for withholding taxes, but 'someone interfered, and paid'. He was let out after a single night of incarceration.

He commended what was good in the US system: 'Even this state and this American government are in many respects very admirable and rare things, to be thankful for.' He recognized, moreover, that the citizen was under an obligation to do 'the good the state demands of me'. But he had identified a limitation of democracy: the citizen alienates power to the state. Conscience, however, remains his or her individual responsibility, which cannot be delegated to an elected representative. It was better, Thoreau thought, to dissolve the state than to preserve it in injustice. 'This people must cease to hold slaves and to make war on Mexico, though it cost them their existence as a people.'

Thoreau insisted on assent to two propositions. The first, that, in case of injustice, civil disobedience was a duty, reflecting the long Christian tradition of just resistance to tyrants. Under evil and oppressive rulers, Aquinas approved the people's right to rebellion and the individual's right to tyrannicide. The seventeenth-century English judge John Bradshaw had invoked the maxim 'Rebellion to tyrants is obedience to God' in vindication of the revolt that launched the English Civil War. Benjamin Franklin appropriated the phrase for the Great Seal of the United States, and Thomas Jefferson adopted it as his own motto. Thoreau's second proposition, however, was new. Political disobedience, he insisted, had to be nonviolent and prejudicial only to those who opt for resistance. Thoreau's stipulations were the basis of Gandhi's campaign of 'moral resistance' to British rule in India and Martin Luther King's civil-rights activism of 'nonviolent noncooperation' in the United States. Both succeeded without recourse to violence. John Rawls, one of the world's most respected political philosophers of the early twenty-first century, endorsed and extended the doctrine. Civil disobedience of the kind Thoreau urged is justified in a democracy, he said, if a majority denies equal rights to a minority.[52]

Anarchism and civil disobedience could succeed only against states insufficiently ruthless to repress them. Nor has it proved possible to create institutions within the state that can be relied on to guarantee liberty without violence. Judicatures, for instance, can be suborned, overruled, or sacked, as in the Venezuela of Nicolás Maduro. Unelected elites or heads of state can be as abusive as any disproportionately empowered minority. Where armed forces guarantee constitutions, countries often topple into the power of military dictators. Political parties often engage in cosy conspiracies to outflank their electorates by sharing power in turn or in coalition. Trade unions typically start by being independent or even defiant, if they amass sufficient support and wealth to challenge incumbent elites, but most states have dealt with them by incorporation, emasculation, or abolition. Some constitutions forestall tyranny by devolving and diffusing power among federal, regional, and local authorities. But devolved regional administrators can become tyrannous in turn. The dangers became apparent, for instance, in Catalonia in 2015, when a minority government defied the majority of voters in the province in an attempt to suspend the constitution, appropriate taxes, and arrogate the sole right to make and unmake law in the territory. In 2017 a Catalan regional government, elected by a minority of votes, tried to transfer sovereignty into its own hands by mobilizing its supporters in a referendum, mounting, in effect, a civil coup d'état. To counter the danger of merely multiplying tyranny and creating lots of little tin-pot despotisms, Catholic political tradition invented the notion of 'subsidiarity', according to which the only legitimate political decisions are those taken as close as practically possible to the communities affected. In practice, however, the disparity of resources means that rich and well-armed institutions will almost always triumph in cases of conflict.

Christian Politics

When all other checks on tyranny have been discounted, the Church remains. The Church did restrain rulers in the Middle Ages. But the Reformation created churches collusive with or run by states, and thereafter, even in Catholic countries, almost every confrontation ended with restrictions and compromises that transferred authority to secular hands. In the late twentieth century, the exceptional charisma and personal moral authority of Pope John Paul II gave him the opportunity to play a part in toppling communism in his native Poland and challenging authoritarian rule generally. But it is doubtful whether his achievement is repeatable. Today, even in countries with large congregations, the Church can no longer command sufficient obedience to prevail in conflicts over matters of supreme value to Christian consciences, including the protection of inviolable life and sacred matrimony.

In the nineteenth century, however, Catholic thinkers persisted in the search for new ways of conceptualizing the Church's aspirations for influence in the world. The result was a great deal of new thinking, involving radical reformulation of the Church's place in increasingly secular, increasingly plural societies. Leo XIII came to the papacy in 1878 with prestige immensely advanced by his predecessor's defiance of the world. Pius IX would neither submit to force nor defer to change. He had condemned almost every social and political innovation of his day. In retreat from the armies of the secular Italian state he made a virtual bunker of the Vatican. For his admirers and for many uncommitted onlookers, his intransigence resembled a godly vocation unprofaned by compromise. His fellow bishops rewarded him by proclaiming papal infallibility. Leo inherited this unique advantage and exploited it to manoeuvre into a position from which he could work with governments to minimize damage from the dangers Pius had condemned. Leo wanted, he said, 'to carry through a great policy' – in effect, updating apostleship in what came to be called *Aggiornamento*. He triumphed in spite of himself: he promoted modernization without understanding it or even liking it very much. He seems, however, to have realized that the vast Catholic laity was the Church's most valuable ally in an increasingly democratic age. He disliked republicanism, but made the clergy co-operate with it. He could not deny the validity of slavery in past centuries when the Church had allowed it, but he proscribed it for the future. He feared the power of trade unions, but he authorized them and encouraged Catholics to found their own. He could not abjure property – the Church had too much of it for that – but he could remind socialists that Christians, too, were called to social responsibility. He would not endorse socialism, but he did condemn naked individualism. Leo's was a church of practical charity without moral cowardice. After his death, the political fashion changed in Rome, and there were always clergy who sensed that they could not control change and so tried to frustrate it. Some of them, in the twentieth century, were willing to collaborate with repression and authoritarianism on the political right. *Aggiornamento*, however, was inextinguishable. The tradition Leo launched prevailed in the long run. The Church has gone on adjusting to worldly changes, and adhering to eternal verities.[53]

As usual in the history of the Church, Catholic thinkers outpaced the pope, christianizing socialism and producing, along with Protestant advocates of the so-called social gospel, a politically unsettling Christian social doctrine. They challenged the state to embody justice and follow the God whom the Virgin Mary praised because He 'hath filled the hungry with good things and the rich He hath sent empty away'. Early Christianity abjured the state. Medieval Christianity erected an alternative church-state. The challenge for modern Christianity in a secularizing age has been to find a way of influencing politics without getting engaged and perhaps corrupted. Potentially, Christians have something to contribute to all the major political tendencies represented in modern industrial democracies. Christianity is conservative, because it preaches absolute morality. It is liberal, in the true sense of the word, because it stresses the supreme value of the individual and affirms the sovereignty of conscience. It is socialist, because it demands service to the community, displays 'bias to the poor', and recommends the shared life of the apostles and early Church. It is therefore a possible source of the 'third way' eagerly sought nowadays in a world that has rejected communism but finds capitalism uncongenial.

A convincing, or at least plausible, route to a third way lies through the nineteenth-century programme of combining the communitarian values of socialism with insistence on individual moral responsibility.

For the movement known as 'Christian socialism' in the Anglican tradition, or 'the social gospel' in some Protestant traditions, and 'Catholic syndicalism' or 'social Catholicism' in the Catholic Church, the 1840s were a decisive decade. Wherever industrialization and urbanization flung unevangelized workers together, committed priests and bishops founded new parishes. The Anglican priest F. D. Maurice canvassed the term 'Christian socialism' – and was driven out of his job in the University of London for his pains. In Paris, meanwhile, the Catholic Sisters of Charity exercised a practical mission among the poor. Archbishop Affre died at the barricades in the revolution of 1848, waving an ineffectual olive branch.

After Leo XIII made the Church's peace with the modern world, it was easier for Catholic priests to take part in workers' political movements, with encouragement from bishops who hoped to 'save' workers from communism. Inexorably, however, Catholic political groups and trade unions multiplied under lay leadership. Some became mass movements and electorally successful parties. Social Catholicism, however, was still a minority interest in the Church. Not until the 1960s did it conquer orthodoxy, under the leadership of Pope John XXIII. In his encyclical of 1961, *Mater et Magistra,* he outlined a vision of the state that would enhance freedom by assuming social responsibilities and 'enabling the individual to exercise personal rights'. He approved a role for the state in health, education, housing, work, and subsidizing creative and constructive leisure. Subsidiarity is not the only current political buzzword from Catholic social theory: 'common good' is another. As secular socialist parties fade, politics in a Christian tradition may be due for revival.[54]

Nationalism (and Its American Variant)

Most of the thinking that strengthened state power in the nineteenth century – Hegel's idealism, Schopenhauer's 'will', Rousseau's 'general will', and the superman imagery of Nietzsche – now seems foolish or foul. In the late twentieth century, the state began to ebb – at least in respect of economic controls. Five trends were responsible: pooled sovereignty in an ever closer-knit world; the resistance of citizens and historic communities to intrusive government; the rise of new, non-territorial allegiances, especially in cyber-ghettoes of the Internet; the indifference of many religious and philanthropic organizations to state boundaries in the spirit, one might say, of 'médecins sans frontières'; and, as we shall see in the next chapter, new political and economic ideas that linked prosperity with circumscribed government. One nineteenth-century source of intellectual support for the legitimacy of states has, however, proved amazingly robust: the idea of nationalism.

Even the most impassioned nationalists disagree about what a nation is, and no two analysts' lists of nations ever quite match. Herder, who is usually credited with starting the modern tradition of nationalist thought, spoke of 'peoples' for want of a means of distinguishing them from nations in the German of his day. More recent nationalists have used 'nation' as a synonym for various entities: states, historic communities, races. Herder's concept was that a people who shared the same language, historic experience, and sense of identity constituted an indissoluble unit, linked (to quote the Finnish nationalist A. I. Arwidsson) by 'ties of mind and soul mightier and firmer than every external bond'.[55] Hegel saw the *Volk* as an ideal – a transcendent, immutable reality. Though validated – in some advocates' claims – by history and science, nationalism was usually couched in mystical or romantic language apparently ill-adapted to practical ends. Infected by romantic yearning for the unattainable, it was doomed to self-frustration. Indeed, like the passion of the lover on Keats's Grecian urn, it would have been killed by consummation. German nationalism throve on unfulfilled ambitions to unite all German-speakers in a single Reich. That of Serbs was nourished by inexhaustible grievances. Even in France – the land of 'chauvinism', which proclaimed, more or less, 'My country, right or wrong' – nationalism would have been weakened if the French had ever attained frontiers that satisfied their rulers.

Because nationalism was a state of romantic yearning rather than a coherent political programme, music expressed it best. *Má Vlast* by Bedřich Smetana in the Czech lands or *Finlandia* by Jean Sibelius have outlasted their era as no nationalist literature has done. Verdi's longing, lilting slaves' chorus in *Nabucco* probably did more, in the long run, to make Italians feel for a 'fatherland, so lovely and so lost' than all the urgings of statesmen and journalists. Nationalism belonged to the values of 'sensation, not thought', proclaimed by romantic poets. Nationalist rhetoric throbbed with mysticism. 'The voice of God' told Giuseppe Mazzini – the republican fighter for Italian unification – that the nation supplied individuals with the framework of potential moral perfection. Simón Bolívar supposedly experienced a 'delirium' on Mount Chimborazo, when 'the God of Colombia possessed me' ignited 'by strange and superior fire'.[56]

Nationalists insisted that everyone must belong to a nation of this kind, and that every nation had, collectively, to assert its identity, pursue its destiny, and defend its rights. None of this made much sense. Nationalism is obviously false: there is no innate spiritual bond between people who happen to share elements of common background or language; their community is simply what they choose to make of it. One of the most assiduous students of nationalism concluded that 'nations as a natural, God-given way of classifying men, as an inherent though long-delayed political destiny, are a myth ... Nationalism often obliterates pre-existing cultures.'[57] Even if a nation were a coherent category, belonging to it would not necessarily confer any obligations. Still, it was a kind of nonsense people were disposed to believe; some still are.

For an idea so incoherent, nationalism had astounding effects. It played a part in justifying most of the wars of the nineteenth and twentieth centuries and inspiring people to fight in them in combination with the doctrine of 'national self-determination'. It reshaped Europe after the First World War, and the entire world after the retreat of European empires. Nationalism ought to be irrelevant today, in a world of globalization and internationalization. Some politicians, however, clinging to supreme power in their own states, and some electorates, reaching for the comfort of old identities, have rediscovered it. Impatience with internationalization, immigration, and multiculturalism has made nationalist parties popular again in Europe, threatening cultural pluralism and clouding the prospects of European unification. We should not be surprised. Agglutinative processes that draw or drive people into ever larger empires or confederations always provoke fissile reactions. Hence, in late-twentieth-century and early-twenty-first-century Europe, secessionists have sought or erected states of their own, shattering Yugoslavia and the Soviet Union, splitting Serbia and

Czechoslovakia, putting Spain, Belgium, and the United Kingdom in jeopardy, and even raising questions about the futures of Italy, Finland, France, and Germany.[58] In other parts of the world, new-kid nationalisms, not always well founded historically, have shaken or shattered superstates that were the residue of decolonization. Iraq, Syria, and Libya look fragile. Secession from Indonesia, Somalia, and Sudan respectively has not stabilized East Timor, Somaliland, or South Sudan.

In practice, states that misrepresent themselves as national seem doomed to compete with each other. They must be assertive in self-justification or self-differentiation, or aggressive in defiance of real or feared aggression by other states. In the opening years of the nineteenth century French and Russian boots stamped across Germany. Fear and resentment provoked nationalist bravado: claims that, like all history's best victims, Germans were really superior to their conquerors. Germany, in many Germans' opinion, had to unite, organize, and fight back. Nationalist philosophers formulated the programme. In the early years of the nineteenth century the first rector of the University of Berlin, Johann Gottlieb Fichte, proclaimed German identity eternal and unchanging in his *Addresses to the German Nation*. 'To have character and be German' were 'undoubtedly one and the same thing'. The *Volksgeist* – the 'spirit of the nation' – was essentially good and insuperably civilizing. Hegel thought that the Germans had replaced the Greeks and Romans as the final phase in 'the historical development of Spirit ... The German spirit is the spirit of the new world. Its aim is the realization of absolute Truth as the unlimited self-determination of freedom.'[59] This sounds very grand and a bit scary. There was no good reason behind it except for intellectual fashion.

Nationalists' rhetoric never faced a basic problem: who belonged to the German nation? The poet Ernst Moritz Arndt was among many who proposed a linguistic definition: 'Germany is there wherever the German language resounds and sings to God in heaven.'[60] The hyperbole did not satisfy advocates of racial definitions, which, as we shall see, became increasingly popular in the course of the century. Many – at times, perhaps, most – Germans came to think that Jews and Slavs were indelibly alien, even when they spoke German with eloquence and elegance. Yet it was equally common to assume that the German state had the right to rule wherever German was spoken, even if only by a minority. The implications were explosive: centuries of migration had sprinkled German-speaking minorities along the Danube and into the southern Volga valley; Germanophone communities had seeped across all borders, including those of France and Belgium. Nationalism was an idea that incited violence; the nation-state was an idea that guaranteed it.[61]

Britain had even less coherence as a nation than Germany. But that did not frustrate formulators of doctrines of British (or often, in effect, English) superiority from coming up with equally illusory ideas. Thomas Babington Macaulay – who, as a statesman, helped design the British Raj and, as an historian, helped forge the myth of British history as a story of progress – belonged, in his own estimation, to 'the greatest and most highly civilized people that ever the world saw'.[62] As he sat in his study in November 1848, he measured his country's superiority in terms of the blood revolutionaries shed elsewhere in the Europe of his day, 'the houses dented with bullets, the gutters foaming with blood'. He was haunted by nightmares of a Europe engulfed, like the declining Roman Empire, in a new barbarism, inflicted by under-civilized masses. At the same time, he was confident of the reality of progress and the long-term perfectibility of man. Britain's destiny was to pioneer progress and approach perfectibility: the whole of British history, as Macaulay saw it, had been leading up to such a consummation, ever since the Anglo-Saxons had brought a tradition of liberty, born in the Germanic woods, to Britannia, where liberty blended with the civilizing influences of the Roman Empire and Christian religion. Britain's neighbours were simply laggard along the road of progress. Britain had pre-enacted the struggles between constitutionalism and absolutism that convulsed other countries at the time. Britons had settled them, a century and a half before, in favour of 'the popular element in the English polity'. Seventeenth-century revolutions had established that the right of kings to rule differed not one jot 'from the right by which freeholders chose knights of the shire or from the right by which judges granted writs of habeas corpus'.[63] Macaulay made a further error, which his US followers have often repeated: he assumed that political systems induce economic outcomes. Constitutionalism, he thought, had made Britain the 'workshop of the world', the 'mother-country' of the world's most extensive empire, and the cynosure of the world. Towards the end of the century, Cecil Rhodes offered a different but widely shared analysis, echoed in countless volumes of inspiringly imperialist schoolboy stories and pulp fictions: 'The British race is sound to the core and ... dry rot and dust are strangers to it.'[64]

One could multiply examples like those of Britain and Germany for other European countries, but in the long run the world's most impactful nationalism was that of the United States – a place where nationalist theorists had to work exceptionally hard to knead or pound that essentially plural land of heterogeneous immigrants into a mixture with a plausibly national character, and see it, in Israel Zangwill's words, as 'God's Crucible'.[65]

Ideas sometimes take a long time to get out of heads and into the world. Even while the United States was experiencing a founding revolution, some Americans began to imagine a single union filling the whole hemisphere, but it seemed a vision impossible to realize in practice. At first, it seemed hardly more realistic to hope to extend westwards across a continent that exploration had revealed as untraversibly immense. Colonial projectors had confidently claimed strips of territory from the Atlantic to the Pacific because they had been incapable of grasping the real dimensions of America. Such illusions were no longer tenable by 1793, when Alexander Mackenzie crossed North America, in latitudes still under British sovereignty: thereafter the fledgling republic had to hurry to reach across the continent. The Louisiana Purchase made it a theoretical possibility; a transcontinental expedition in 1803 sketched out a route. First, however, Mexicans and Indians had to be swept out of the way. During the decades of feverish hostility and war against Mexico in the 1830s and 1840s, the journalist John L. O'Sullivan heard a divine summons 'to overspread the continent allotted by Providence for the free development of our yearly multiplying millions'. Manifest destiny would embrace the breadth of the hemisphere from sea to shining sea in a single republican 'empire': people were happy to call it that in the early years of the United States. It was the idea from which America's future as a superpower sprang. According to the *United States Journal* in 1845, 'We, the American people, are the most independent, intelligent, moral and happy people on the face of the earth.' The self-congratulation resembled that of Germans and British.

A hostile environment remained to be traversed. Because the North American Midwest never experienced the long period of glaciation that preceded the forests and shaped the soil elsewhere, the so-called Great American Desert occupied most of the region between the exploitable lands of the Mississippi basin and the Pacific-side territories. Virtually nothing humanly digestible grew there; except in small patches, tough soils would not yield to pre-industrial dibblers and ploughs. To James Fenimore Cooper, it seemed a place without a future, 'a vast country, incapable of sustaining a dense population'. Then steel ploughs began to bite into the sod. Rifled guns freed up land for colonization by driving off the natives and killing off the buffalo. Balloon-framed, 'Chicago-built' cities rose in treeless places thanks to machined planks and cheap nails. From labour-lite grain elevators, introduced in 1850, railroads carried grain to giant flour mills that processed it into marketable wares. Wheat, a form of humanly edible grass, took over from the grasses the buffalo grazed. The most underexploited of North America's resources – space – was put to productive use, sucking up migrants. The prairie became the granary of the world and an arena of cities, the United States a demographic giant. The wealth generated helped to put and keep the country economically ahead of all rivals. The United States and, to a lesser extent, Canada became continent-wide countries and real world powers, with power over the price of food.[66]

US exceptionalism complemented US nationalism. Neither was complete without the other. Exceptionalism appealed to nineteenth-century enquirers, puzzling over why demographic, economic, and military growth in the United States exceeded that of other countries. But the idea of a unique country, beyond comparison with others, started earlier in America, with the 'pioneer spirit' – shining-faced enthusiasm for a promised land for chosen people. Nineteenth-century experience matched some of the hope and hype. The United States became, successively, a model republic, an exemplary democracy, a burgeoning empire, a magnet for migrants, a precocious industrializer, and a great power.

The Catholic reformer, Fr Isaac Hecker, formulated an extreme form of exceptionalism. Religious cant had always lurked in the undergrowth of the idea: Puritan ambitions for a City on a Hill, Mormon fantasies about land hallowed by Jesus's footfall. Hecker gave exceptionalism a Catholic twist. He argued that because progressive enrichment of divine grace accompanied modern progress, Christian perfection was more easily attainable in the United States than elsewhere. Leo XIII condemned this 'Americanism' as an arrogant attempt to devise a special form of Catholicism for the United States, painting the Church red, white, and blue. It undermined Americans' awareness of dependence on God and made the Church redundant as a guide for the soul.

The pope's suspicions were understandable. Two related heresies have helped shaped US self-images: I call them the Lone Ranger heresy and the Donald Duck heresy. According to the first, American heroes, from Natty Bumppo to Rambo, are outsiders, whom society needs but who do not need society: they do what a man's gotta do, saving society from the margins, with a loner's indifference to shootouts and showdowns. The Donald Duck heresy, meanwhile, sanctifies impulses as evidence of natural goodness, or of that over-valued American virtue of 'authenticity', feeding the self-righteous convictions that so often got Donald into trouble.[67] The American dream of individual liberation is only justifiable if one believes in the goodness of man – or, in Donald's case, of duck. Donald is at bottom warm, friendly, and well-disposed, despite embodying the vices of individualist excess – irrational self-reliance, opinionated noisiness, trigger-happy gun-toting, fits of temper, and irritating self-belief. The same vices, and the same sort of obedience to impulse, makes American policymakers, for instance, bomb people from time to time, but always with good intentions. The feel-good society, where personal guilt dissolves and self-satisfaction stalks, is among the other consequences. Therapy replaces confession. Self-discovery smothers self-reproach. US-watchers frequently notice myopic patriotism, morbid religiosity, and conflictive insistence on one's rights. The virtues we think of as characteristically American – civic-mindedness, neighbourly values, genuine love of freedom and democracy – are human virtues, intensely celebrated in America. In any case, if the United States was ever exceptional, it is so no longer, as the rest of the world strives to imitate its success.[68]

Anti-Americanism is the converse of US exceptionalism. People who see themselves as uniquely good invite characterization as uniquely bad. As US power grew to eclipse that of other powers, resentment grew with it. After the Second World War, US strength was felt as far as the frontiers of communism; Uncle Sam interfered in other people's empires, treated much of the world as his backyard, and legitimized illiberal regimes in US interests. The magnetism of the trashy culture of hot dog and hard rock was as resented as it was irresistible. GIs, irksome reminders of European impotence, were 'overpaid, oversexed, and over here'. Benign policies, such as support for war-weak European economies, elicited little gratitude.[69]

From 1958, the hero and spokesman of anti-Americanism was the French president Charles de Gaulle: a Samson in Dagon's temple, pushing at the pillars and striving to expel the philistines. Because he was an unruly client of the United States, his critique was more effective than the propaganda of self-interested enemies who issued their denunciations from behind the Iron Curtain. More convincing still – and more disturbing from an American point of view – was the growing clamour from morally committed, politically neutral quarters. Challenges came first from the liberal West, and especially from America itself, becoming strident during the Vietnam War; protests from the 'Third World' followed. In the 1970s, as America began to get over the trauma of Vietnam, an exiled Iranian mullah, Ayatollah Khomeini, became the loudest critic. While hating other forms of modernization, he was a master of mass communication. His conviction of self-righteousness was almost insane. His simple message was that the world was divided between oppressors and dispossessed. America was the Great Satan, corrupting humankind with materialist temptations, suborning the species with crude force.

As the self-proclaimed champion of capitalism in successful global confrontations with rival ideologies, the United States invited this caricature. Moreover, US society had undeniable defects, as its critics from within well knew. 'Trash capitalism' defied the canons of taste with ugly urban sprawl and cheap, tawdry products that made money in mass markets. US values elevated vulgar celebrities above sages and saints and has elected one of them as president. The country exhibited, without shame, excessive privileges of wealth, selective illiberalism, dumbed-down popular culture, stagnant politics, and conflictive insistence on individual rights, with the tetchiness and ignorance that veil the United States. The world seemed to forget that these are vices other communities also have in abundance, and America's virtues greatly outweigh them: the people's genuine emotional investment in freedom; the amazing restraint and relative disinterest with which the state discharges its superpower role. It is hard to imagine any of the other contenders for domination of the twentieth-century world – Stalinists, Maoists, militarists, Nazis – behaving in victory with similar magnanimity. Yet every American foreign-policy error and injudicious operation of global policing makes anti-Americanism worse. 'The "rogue state" has ... effectively declared war on the world', announced Harold Pinter, the world's most admired playwright in the late twentieth century. 'It knows only one language – bombs and death.'[70] The adverse image of the United States has nourished resentment and recruited terrorists.

Effects beyond the West: China, Japan, India, and the Islamic World

For people at the receiving end of Western influence anti-Americanism is a device to cope with and appropriate aggressive, ethnocentric thinking. In the nineteenth century, thinkers in China, Japan, India, and the Dar al-Islam – cultures with assertive traditions of their own – struggled to adjust by projecting quasi-nationalisms of their own.

China was psychologically unprepared for the experience of European superiority, first in war, then in wealth. When the nineteenth century began, the confidence of the 'central country' with a divine mandate was still intact. The world's biggest population was booming; the world's biggest economy enjoyed a favourable balance of trade with the rest of the world; the world's oldest empire was undefeated. Western 'barbarians' had demonstrated exploitable technical cleverness and had won wars elsewhere in the world; but in China they were still cowed, co-operative, and confined to a single waterfront in Canton by gracious permission of the emperor. The menace of Western industrialization was not yet apparent. The only danger to the invulnerability of the Chinese economy was the one product for which foreign traders had found a market big enough to affect the overall balance of trade: opium. When China tried to ban imports of the drug, British fleets and armies crushed resistance. China seemed stunned into backwardness, from which it is only beginning to re-emerge today.

In November 1861, Wei Mu-ting, an imperial censor with a taste for history, wrote a memorandum that laid out the principles of what came to be called self-strengthening. He stressed the need to learn from and catch up with the latest 'barbarian' weaponry, but pointed out that Western firepower derived from gunpowder – a technology the foreigners borrowed from the Mongols, who had picked it up in China. His view became a commonplace of Chinese literature on the subject for the rest of the century. Domestically unexploited Chinese prototypes, Wei continued, were the source of most of the military and maritime technology of which China was the victim. His argument is curiously reminiscent of the terms in which Western apologists nowadays denounce Japanese 'imitations' of Western technology. It is also probably true: Western historians of the diffusion of Chinese technology are now saying something similar themselves. Once China had recovered its lost sciences, Wei Mu-ting believed, it would again resume its customary supremacy.

The essence of self-strengthening as it was understood in China was that superficial technical lessons could be learned from the West, without prejudice to the essential verities on which Chinese tradition was based. New arsenals, shipyards, and technical schools teetered precariously on the edges of traditional society. Zeng Guofan, the model administrator widely credited with the key role in suppressing the Taiping Rebellion in the 1860s, uttered the language of Western conservatism. 'The mistakes inherited from the past we can correct. What the past ignored, we can inaugurate.'[71] He insisted, however, that imperial rule and rites were perfect; political decline was a product of moral degeneracy. 'Propriety and righteousness' came above 'expediency and ingenuity'.[72]

In the 1850s, Japan, too, was forced into opening its markets and exposing its culture to Western intruders. But the Japanese response was positive: the rhetoric was resentful, but the reception was enthusiastic. In 1868 successful revolutionaries promised to 'expel the barbarians, enrich the country, and strengthen the army', while restoring a supposedly ancient order of imperial government.[73] In practice, however, Okubo Toshimichi, the main author of the new policies, turned to Western models. The new ruling classes confirmed foreign treaties, unknotted their hair, rode in carriages, flourished umbrellas, and invested in railways and heavy industries. Military reform on Western lines mobilized conscript masses to subvert the samurai – the hereditary warrior class – to the advantage of central government bureaucrats. Japan became the Britain or Prussia of the East.[74]

'Asia', according to Rudyard Kipling, 'is not going to be civilized after the methods of the West. There is too much of Asia and she is too old.'[75] Even in his day, his prediction seemed insecure. Today's Asian Renaissance – the hectic development of Pacific-side China; the prominence of Japan; the rise of 'tiger economies' in South Korea, Singapore, and Hong Kong; the new profile of India as a potential major power; and the pace of economic activity in many parts of South-East Asia – is the latest phase of self-strengthening. The watchwords are unchanged: selective Westernization, defence of 'Asian values', and a determination to rival or eclipse Westerners at their own games of economic power.

Adjustment to Western hegemony has always been selective. In early-nineteenth-century India, for instance, Raja Ram Mohan Roy was the reputed paragon of Westernization. His West was Enlightenment Europe. He idealized human nature, prescribed Voltaire for his pupils, and replied, when the Bishop of Calcutta mistakenly congratulated him on converting to Christianity, that he had not 'laid down one superstition to take up another'.[76] Yet he was no mere mimic of Western ways. The roots of his rationalism and liberalism in Islamic and Persian traditions predated his introduction to Western literature. He knew about Aristotle from Arabic translations before he encountered the original works. The movement he founded in 1829, which became known as Brahmo Samaj, was a model of modernization for societies stranded by the headlong progress of the industrializing West, but eager to catch up without forfeiting traditions or identities.

Cultural cross-fertilization was normal in nineteenth-century India, where babus quoted Shakespeare to one another under the Athenian stoa of Hindu College, Calcutta, while British officials 'went native' and scoured Sanskrit scriptures for wisdom unavailable in the West. The next great figure in Roy's tradition, Isvar Chandra Vidyasagar (1820–91), did not learn English until he was on the verge of middle age. He did not hold up the West as a model to be imitated, but marshalled ancient Indian texts in support of his arguments for widow remarriage or against polygamy, or when he advocated relaxing caste discrimination in the allocation of school places. On the other hand, he dismissed the claims of some pious Brahmins who insisted that every Western idea had an Indian origin. He resigned the secretaryship of the Sanskrit College of Calcutta in 1846 because pundits opposed his projected new curriculum, which would include 'the science and civilization of the West'. His commitment to reform, however, was, in his mind, part of a drive to revitalize native Bengali tradition. 'If the students be made familiar with English literature', he claimed, 'they will prove the best and ablest contributors to an enlightened Bengali renaissance.'[77] This sounded like capitulation to the imperial project Macaulay had espoused when he was Britain's minister responsible for the government of India: to make English the learned language of India, as Latin had been for earlier generations of Englishmen. But Vidyasagar was right. In the next generation, the Bengali renaissance, like its earlier European counterpart, generated a vernacular revival.

Like many foreign, barbarian conquerors before them, the British in India added a layer of culture to the long-accumulated sediments of the subcontinent's past. In India, more than in China and Japan, Western traditions could be absorbed without a sense of submission, because the myth of the 'Aryan race' – the supposed original speakers of Indo-European languages, who spread across Eurasia thousands of years ago – created the possibility of thinking of Indian and European cultures as kindred, sprung from the same origin. The great advocate of the equipollence of Indian and European thought, Swami Vivekananda, called Plato and Aristotle gurus. In consequence, India could accept selective Westernization without sacrifice of identity or dignity.[78]

Western influence was harder to accept in the Islamic world. From the 1830s to the 1870s Egypt tried to imitate industrialization and imperialism, coveting an empire of its own in the African interior, but, owing in part to protective counter-strategies by Western industrialists, ended bankrupt and in virtual pawn to French and English business. One of the great founding figures of Islam's intellectual 'awakening' in the late nineteenth century, Jamal al-Din al-Afghani, faced, with typical uncertainty, the problems of assimilating Western thought. His life moved to the rhythm of exile and expulsion, as he fell out with his hosts in each asylum in turn. The fabric of his thought and behaviour was a tissue of contradictions. In Egypt he was a government pensioner who demanded subversion of the constitution. To his British patrons in India, he was both a foe and a consultant. His exile in Persia in the service of his shah ended when he was accused of plotting with assassins against his master. He founded the Egyptian Freemasons, but upheld religion as the only sound basis of society. He wanted Muslims to be abreast of modern science, but denounced Darwin for godlessness and materialism. His talk entertained the brilliant café society of Cairo from his spacious corner table in the Café de la Poste, and his sermons aroused worshippers in Hyderabad and Calcutta. He advocated parliamentary democracy but insisted on the sufficiency of the political lessons of the Qur'an. Muslim leaders have faced similar dilemmas ever since. It is probably true that traditional Islamic law and society can coexist with technical progress and scientific advance. Rational Muslims are always saying so. Yet the demon of modernization is always twisting the 'path of the Prophet' into a detour pointing west.[79]

Struggle and Survival: Evolutionary Thinking and Its Aftermath

So far, the political thinkers we have identified started from history or philosophy in formulating their prescriptions for society. The scientific basis Auguste Comte had sought remained elusive. In 1859 the publication of a biologist's study on the origin of species seemed to enhance the prospects of genuinely scientific sociology.

Charles Darwin had no such ambitious outcome in mind. Organic life absorbed his attention. By the mid-nineteenth century, most scientists already believed that life had evolved from, at most, a few primitive forms. But what Darwin called 'the mystery of mysteries' remained: how new species arose. Comprehensive schemes for classifying the world were legion. George Eliot satirized them in the obsessions of characters in *Middlemarch*, her novel of 1871–2: Mr Casaubon's 'key to all mythologies', Dr Lydgate's search for 'the common basis of all living tissues'. Darwin seems to have taken his first unmistakable step toward his similarly comprehensive linkage of all organic life when he was in Tierra del Fuego in 1832. There he encountered 'man in his lowest and most savage state'. The natives taught him, first, that a human is an animal like other animals – for the Fuegians seemed bereft of human reason, foul, naked, and snuffling with no inkling of the divine. 'The difference', Darwin found, 'between savage and civilized man is greater than between a wild and a domesticated animal.'[80] The Fuegians' second lesson was that the environment moulds us. The islanders adapted to their icy climate so perfectly that they could endure it naked. A little later, in the Galapagos Islands, Darwin observed how small environmental differences cause marked biological mutations. Back home in England, among game birds, racing pigeons, and farm stock, he realized that nature selects strains, as breeders do. The specimens best adapted to their environments survive to pass on their characteristics. The struggle of nature seemed awesome to Darwin partly because his own sickly offspring were the victims of it. He wrote, in effect, an epitaph for Annie, his favourite daughter, who died when she was ten years old: survivors would be more healthy and most able to enjoy life. 'From the war of nature', according to *On the Origin of Species*, 'from famine and from death, the production of higher animals directly follows.'[81] Natural selection does not account for every fact of evolution. Random mutations happen – they are the raw material natural selection works with, but they occur beyond its reach. Functionless adaptations survive, unsieved by struggle. Mating habits can be capricious and unsubmissive to natural selection's supposed laws. The theory of evolution has been abused by exploiters and idolized by admirers. But, with all these qualifications and grounds of caution, it is true. Species originate naturally, and divine intervention does not have to be evoked to explain the differences between them.[82]

As Darwin's theories became accepted, other thinkers proposed refinements that later came to be known as 'social Darwinism': the idea that societies, like species, evolve or vanish according to whether they adapt successfully in mutual competition in a given environment. Three probably misleading assumptions underpinned sociologists' appropriation of evolution: first, that society is subject to the same laws of inheritance as living creatures, because it has a life like an organism's, growing from infancy through maturity and senescence to death, passing characteristics to successor-societies as if by descent; second, that, like some plants and animals, some societies get more complex over time (which, though broadly true, is not necessarily the result of any natural law or inevitable dynamic); and finally, that what Darwin called 'the struggle for survival' favours what one of his most influential readers called 'the survival of fittest'. Herbert Spencer, who coined the phrase, explained it like this:

> The forces which are working out the great scheme of human happiness, taking no account of incidental suffering, exterminate such sections of mankind as stand in their way with the same sternness that they exterminate beasts of prey and useless ruminants. Be he human being or be he brute, the hindrance must be got rid of.[83]

Spencer claimed to have anticipated Darwin, not to have followed him;[84] the claim was false, but its effect in any case was to align the two thinkers, in whatever order, in the leading ranks of social Darwinism.[85] Spencer practised compassion and praised peace – but only in acknowledgement of the overwhelming power of morally indifferent nature. He had little formal academic training and was never encumbered by the need to specialize. He fancied himself as a scientist – his rather exiguous professional training was in engineering – and he ranged in his writings over science, sociology, and philosophy with all the assurance, and all the indiscipline, of an inveterate polymath. But he achieved vast influence, perhaps because contemporaries welcomed his comfortingly confident assertions of the inevitability of progress. He hoped to effect the synthesis Comte had sought, fusing science and humanism in 'social science'. Spencer's aim, he often said, was – recalling Comte's search for a science that would 'reorganize' society – to inform social policy grounded in biological truths.

Instead, he encouraged political leaders and policymakers in dangerous extrapolations from Darwinism. Warmongers relished the idea, for instance, that conflict is natural, and – because it promotes the survival of the fittest – progressive. There were potential justifications for massacre in further implications of Spencer's work: that society is well served by the elimination of antisocial or weak specimens and that 'inferior' races are therefore justly exterminated. Thanks to Spencer's disciple Edward Moore, who spent most of his career teaching in Japan, these principles became indelibly associated with the teaching of evolution in East, Central, South, and South-East Asia. From 1879 Moore's version of Darwinism began to appear in Japanese:[86] the work mediated the doctrines to readers in nearby regions. Meanwhile, Cesare Lombroso, who pioneered the science of criminology, convinced most of the world that criminality was heritable and detectable in the atavistic features of throwbacks – criminal types who, he argued, typically had primitive, neo-simian faces and bodies, which selective breeding could eliminate.[87] Louis Agassiz, the Harvard professor who dominated anthropology in the United States in the late nineteenth century, thought that evolution was driving races to become separate species, and that the offspring of interracial unions must suffer from reduced fertility and inherent feebleness of body and mind.[88] Hitler made the last turn in this twisted tradition: 'War is the prerequisite for the natural selection of the strong and the elimination of the weak.'[89]

It would be unfair to blame Darwin for this. On the contrary, by advocating the unity of creation, he implicitly defended the unity of mankind. He abhorred slavery. Yet he could hardly escape all the intellectual traps of his time; everyone in the nineteenth-century West had to fit into a world sliced and stacked according to race. Darwin thought blacks would have evolved into a separate species if imperialism had not ended their isolation; as it was they were doomed to extinction. 'When two races of men meet', he wrote, 'they act precisely like two species of animals. They fight, eat each other ... But then comes the more deadly struggle, namely which have the best-fitted organization or instincts ... to gain the day.'[90] He also thought people of weak physique, character, or intellect should refrain from breeding in the interests of strengthening the human lineage (see p. 323). There was no clear dividing line between social Darwinism and scientific Darwinism: Darwin fathered both.

Projected from biology onto society, the theory of natural selection was a good fit for three trends of the time in Western political thought: on war, on imperialism, and on race. The notion of the positive effects of the struggle for survival, for instance, seemed to confirm what apologists for war had always supposed: conflict is good. When Emer de Vattel wrote the mid-eighteenth century's great textbook on the laws of war, he assumed that his readers would agree that war is a disagreeable necessity, restrained by the norms of civilization and the obligations of charity.[91] Hegel disagreed. War, he thought, makes us realize that trivia, such as goods and individual lives, matter little. 'Through its agency', he observed, long before anyone could appropriate Darwin's theory in support of the same conclusion, 'the ethical health of nations is preserved.'[92] The beneficence of war was an idea with ancient roots, in the myth of the warrior-state of Sparta, which Aristotle, Plato, and most of the other classical authors on ethics and politics professed to admire for the austerity and selflessness of its citizens. The medieval tradition of chivalry – in which the profession of warrior was represented as a qualification for heaven – may have contributed, as, no doubt, did the religious traditions that made war for some faith or other seem holy (see pp. 190, 192, 194).

Surprisingly, perhaps, the idea that war is good also had a liberal pedigree in the tradition of a citizen militia, enhanced by military training, with experience of mutual responsibility and commitment to the state. The Continental Army in the American Revolutionary War embodied the tradition. In the same spirit, the French Revolution introduced mass conscription. Henceforth, war was for 'the Nation in Arms' to wage, not just a professional elite. Napoleon, who thought war was 'beautiful and simple', mobilized populations on a scale unseen in Europe since antiquity. His battles were of unrestrained violence, unlike the relatively gentlemanly encounters of the previous century, when generals were more concerned to conserve their forces than to destroy hecatombs of enemies. Total war – waged actively between entire societies, in which there is no such thing as a non-combatant or an illegitimate target – inverted the usual order of events: it was a practice before it was an idea.

Carl von Clausewitz formulated it as 'absolute war', in *On War*, posthumously published in 1832. Having risen through the ranks of the Prussian army, fighting against French revolutionary and Napoleonic armies, he assumed that states' interest in advancing at each other's expense made them irreversibly disposed to fight each other. Rational action was action adjusted to its ends. So the only rational way to wage war is 'as an act of violence pursued to the utmost bounds'. It is a mistake, Clausewitz suggested, to spare lives, for 'he who uses force unsparingly, without reference to the bloodshed involved, must obtain a superiority'. He advocated 'wearing down' the enemy by attrition and general destruction. The doctrine led ultimately to the shelling and bombing of cities to subvert civilian morale. The ultimate objective (though, to be fair to Clausewitz, he did point out that this was not always necessary) was to leave the enemy permanently disarmed. Belligerents who believed him, and who included the entire military and political establishment of Europe and America for the century and a half after publication of his book, demanded unconditional surrender when they were winning, resisted it obstinately when they were losing, and imposed vindictive and burdensome terms if they won. His influence made war worse, multiplying the victims, spreading the destruction, and encouraging pre-emptive attacks.[93]

Clausewitz, however, shared one aim with Grotius (see p. 230): he was willing to feed the dogs of war with unlimited meat once unleashed, but insisted on a prior condition: that war should not be for its own sake, but for political objectives otherwise unrealizable. 'War is a mere continuation of policy by other means' was his most famous utterance.[94] In practice, however, he was convinced that war was ubiquitous and inevitable. Hegel's view, meanwhile, encouraged a new wave of war worship in Europe.[95] When his country attacked France in 1870, the Prussian chief of staff, General Helmuth von Moltke, denounced 'everlasting peace' as 'a dream, and not even a pleasant one. War is a necessary part of God's order.'[96] In 1910 the founders of Futurism – the artistic movement that idealized machines, speed, danger, sleeplessness, 'violence, cruelty, and injustice' – promised to use art to 'glorify war – the world's only hygiene'.[97] War alone, wrote Mussolini, who owed much of his style and some of his thought to the Futurists, 'raises all human energy to the highest pitch and stamps with nobility the people who have the courage to face it'.[98]

By overspilling the battlefield and threatening entire societies with destruction, war provoked a pacifist reaction. The 1860s were the key cautionary decade. Around two-thirds of the adult male population of Paraguay perished in war against neighbouring countries. Observers in China put the total number lost in the Taiping Rebellion at twenty million. Over three-quarters of a million people died in the American Civil War, and over half a million, on the French side, in the Franco-Prussian War of 1870. Photography and battlefield reporting made the horrors of war graphic and vivid. The peace movements, however, were small, uninfluential, and bereft of practical remedies, save for an idea proposed by one of the late nineteenth century's most successful armaments manufacturers, Alfred Nobel. Most of his fellow-pacifists hoped to promote peace by honing international law; others, more crankily, proposed to ameliorate human nature by education or eugenics – filleting out or repressing people's instinct for violence. Nobel disagreed. War would 'stop short, instantly', he promised during a congress in Paris in 1890, if it were made 'as death-dealing to the civilian population at home as to the troops at the front'.[99] Consistently with his vocation as an explosives expert – and perhaps in an effort to assuage his own conscience – he dreamed of a super-weapon so terrible that it would frighten people into peace. When he founded the Peace Prize, he was hoping to reward the inventor. The idea seems counterintuitive, but it is the logical consequence of the old adage 'Who wants peace prepares for war.'

Nobel reckoned without lunatics or fanatics for whom no destruction is a deterrent and no weapon too woeful. Still, against the balance of probabilities, atomic bombs did contribute to the equipoise of 'mutually assured destruction' in the second half of the twentieth century. Nuclear proliferation has now revived insecurity. It may be that regionally balanced power, with, say, Israel and Iran or India and Pakistan deterring each other, will reproduce in miniature the peace that prevailed between the United States and the Soviet Union; but the prospect of a rogue state or terrorist network starting a nuclear war is unnerving.[100]

Late-nineteenth-century advocates of war had plenty of arguments in its favour before Darwin added one that seemed decisive. But the theory of evolution, as we have seen, could shape social thought. Darwin's influence on eugenics is a case in point. Not that eugenics as such was anything new. Plato thought that only perfect individuals could make up a perfect society: the best citizens should breed; the dim and deformed be exterminated. No such programme could work: there is no lasting agreement about desirable mental or physical qualities; an individual's worth depends on other, incalculable ingredients. Environmental conditions mingle with inherited characteristics to make us the way we are. Heredity is obviously important: as we saw above (p. 63) observers noticed it at work for tens of thousands of years before genetic theory produced a convincing explanation of why – for example – some looks, skills, quiddities, diseases, and deficiencies run in families.

Plato's candid but cruel recommendation was shelved. In nineteenth-century Europe and North America, however, it revived. A form of Darwinism boosted eugenics by suggesting that human agency might stimulate the supposed advantages of natural selection. In 1885, Darwin's cousin, Francis Galton, proposed what he called eugenics: by selectively controlling fertility to filter out undesirable mental and moral qualities, the human species could be perfected. 'If a twentieth part', he suggested, 'of the cost and pains were spent on measures for the improvement of the human race that is spent on the improvement of the breed of horses and cattle, what a galaxy of genius might we not create!' Eugenics, he insisted in 1904, 'co-operates with ... Nature by securing that humanity shall be represented by the fittest races'.[101]

Within a couple of decades, eugenics became orthodoxy. In early Soviet Russia and parts of the United States, people officially classified as feebleminded, criminal, and even (in some cases) alcoholic lost the right to marry. By 1926 nearly half the states in America had made the sterilization of people in some of these categories compulsory. The eugenic idea was most zealously adopted in Nazi Germany, where law followed its precepts: the best way to stop people breeding is to kill them. The road to utopia lay through the extermination of everyone in categories the state deemed genetically inferior, including Jews, Gypsies, and homosexuals. Meanwhile, Hitler tried to perfect what he thought would be a master race by what would now be called 'designer breeding' – matching sperm and wombs supposedly of the purest German physical type. Big, strong, blue-eyed, blond-haired human guinea pigs did not, on average, seem to produce children any better or any worse qualified for citizenship, leadership, or strenuous walks of life than other people.

Revulsion from Nazism made eugenics unpopular for generations. But the concept is now back in a new guise: genetic engineering can now reproduce individuals of socially approved types. Males allegedly of special prowess or talent have long supplied commercially available semen to potential mothers willing to shop for a genetically superior source of insemination. Theoretically, thanks to the isolation of genes, 'undesirable' characteristics can now be eliminated from the genetic material that goes into a baby at conception. The consequences are incalculable, but the human record so far suggests that every technological advance is exploitable for evil.[102]

Eugenics and racism were closely allied. Racism is a much abused term. I use it to denote the doctrine that some people are inescapably inferior to others by virtue of belonging to a group with racially heritable deficiencies of character. In weaker senses of the word – prejudice against alterity, revulsion from 'impure blood', hypersensitivity to differences of pigmentation, commitment to a narrowly circumscribed moral community of the like, and, in a current variant, mere willingness to assign individuals to racially defined units of speech or study – racism is untrackably ancient.[103] In the nineteenth century, however, a new kind emerged, based on supposedly objective, quantifiable, scientifically verifiable differences. In some ways, it was an unintended consequence of Enlightenment science, with its obsession with classification and measurement. Botanical taxonomy supplied racists with a model. Various methods of classification were proposed – according to pigmentation, hair type, the shape of noses, blood types (once the development of serology made this possible), and, above all, cranial measurements. Late-eighteenth-century efforts to devise a classification of humankind according to cranial size and shape threw up data that seemed to link mental capacity with pigmentation (see p. 255). The late-eighteenth-century Leiden anatomist, Petrus Camper, arranged his collection of skulls 'in regular succession', with 'apes, orangs, and negroes' at one end and Central Asians and Europeans at the other. Camper never subscribed to racism, but there was obviously an underlying agenda in his method: a desire not only to classify humans according to outward or physical characteristics, but also to rank them in terms of superiority and inferiority. In 1774 an apologist of the Jamaica plantations, Edward Long, had justified the subjection of blacks on the grounds of their 'narrow intellect' and 'bestial smell'. Henry Home in the same year went further: humans constituted a genus; blacks and whites belonged to different species. Now there was scientific backing for the claim. In the 1790s, Charles White produced an index of 'brutal inferiority to man', which placed monkeys only a little below blacks, and especially the group he called

'Hottentots', whom he ranked 'lowest' among those who were admissibly human. More generally, he found that 'in whatever respect the African differs from the European, the particularity brings him nearer to the ape'.[104]

Nineteenth-century science piled up more purported evidence in support of racism. Arthur, Comte de Gobineau, who died in the same year as Darwin, worked out a ranking of races in which 'Aryans' came out on top and blacks at the bottom. Gregor Mendel, the kind and gentle Austrian monk who discovered genetics in the course of experiments with peas, died two years later. The implications of his work were not followed up until the end of the century, but, when drawn, they were abused. With the contributions of Darwin and Gobineau, they helped to complete a supposedly scientific justification of racism. Genetics provided an explanation of how inferiority could be transmitted in a lineage across generations. Just when white power was at its most penetrative and most pervasive, scientific theory was driving it home. Inferior races were doomed to extinction by natural selection, or could be actively exterminated in the interests of progress.

It might be objected that racism is timeless and universal. In most languages – it is worth recalling (see p. 232) – the word for 'human being' denotes only members of the tribe or group: outsiders are classed as beasts or demons. Contempt is a common mechanism for excluding the stranger. What the nineteenth century called 'race' had been covered earlier by terms like 'lineage' and 'purity of blood'. None of these prefigurations of racism, however, had the persuasive might of science behind them, nor the power to cause so much oppression and so many deaths.[105]

Blacks were not the only victims. Anti-Semitism acquired new virulence in the nineteenth century. It is an odd doctrine, hard to understand in view of the beneficence of Jews' contributions to humankind, especially in spirituality, arts, and sciences. Christian anti-Semitism is especially perplexing, as Christ, his mother, the apostles, and all the starting points of Christian belief and devotion were Jewish. Nietzsche, indeed, often expressed admiration for Jewish achievements, but Jews' input into Christianity showed him that they were 'a people born for slavery', whose appeal from Earth to heaven marked, for him, 'the beginning of the slave rebellion in morals'.[106] A well-supported view is that anti-Semitism originated in Christianity and developed in the Middle Ages, when Jews – together with some other 'outsider' groups and ghetto dwellers in Europe – experienced persecution of increasing pace and virulence. But, though not completely emancipated, Jews benefited from the eighteenth-century Enlightenment, getting a share of the 'rights of man' and, in many cases, emerging from the ghettos into the social mainstream. In any case, the anti-Semitism that emerged in the nineteenth century was new. The tolerance of host societies cracked as Jewish numbers grew. Anti-Semitic violence, sporadic in the early part of the century, became commonplace in Russia from the 1870s and Poland from the 1880s; partly under pressure of the numbers of refugees, it spread to Germany and even, in the 1890s, to France, where Jews had previously seemed well integrated and established at every level of society.

Economic hard times always exacerbate the miseries of minorities. In the economically afflicted Europe of the 1920s and 1930s, anti-Semitism became an uncontainable contagion. Politicians exploited it. Some of them seem to have believed their own rhetoric and genuinely to have seen Jews as imperilling welfare or security. For demagogues of the right Jews were indelibly communist; for those of the left they were incurably capitalist. Anti-Semitic regimes had always tried to 'solve' the Jewish 'problem' by eliminating it – usually through hermetic sealing in ghettos, forced conversion, or mass expulsion. The Nazi 'final solution' for eliminating the Jews by extermination was an extreme development of a long tradition. About six million Jews perished in one of the most purposeful campaigns of genocide in history. Throughout Europe west of the Soviet border, fewer than two million survived. It was an act of European self-amputation of a community that had always contributed disproportionately to the life of the mind, to the arts, and to wealth creation.[107]

The Balance of Progress

Early in the nineteenth century, as Napoleon's career drew to a close and the world emerged from the horrors of revolution and the disasters of war, Thomas Love Peacock – one of the funniest novelists ever in

England and, therefore, in the world – wrote his first book. *Headlong Hall* is a dialogue among characters representative of rival trends in the thinking of the time. At the start of the tale, we learn,

> Chosen guests had, from different parts of the metropolis, ensconced themselves in the four corners of the Holyhead mail. These four persons were, Mr Foster, the perfectibilian; Mr Escot, the deteriorationist; Mr Jenkison, the statu-quo-ite; and the Reverend Doctor Gaster, who, though of course neither a philosopher nor a man of taste, had so won on the Squire's fancy, by a learned dissertation on the art of stuffing a turkey, that ... no Christmas party would be complete without him.

For Mr Foster, 'everything we look on attests the progress of mankind in all the arts of life and demonstrates their gradual advancement towards a state of unlimited perfection'. Mr Foster, in whom Malthus was savagely satirized, spoke consistently against the illusion of progress: 'Your improvements proceed in a simple ratio, while the factious wants and unnatural appetites they engender proceed in a compound one ... till the whole species must at length be exterminated by its own infinite imbecility and vileness.'

At the end of the century, their debate remained unresolved. The world was, perhaps, a machine, but was it a factory of progress, or was it grinding toward stasis, like the mills of God? Did material progress corrupt eternal values? Did enhanced technology merely increase the range of evil? Were vast, impersonal forces leading the world to ends beyond the reach of freedom, and, if so, for good or ill?

For a while, God looked like one of the casualties of progress. At the start of the century, Pierre-Simon Laplace, who had formulated ways of interpreting every known phenomenon of the physical world in terms of the attraction and repulsion of particles, boasted that he had reduced God to an unnecessary hypothesis. On Dover Beach, around the midpoint of the century, the poet Matthew Arnold heard with regret the 'long, withdrawing roar' of the 'Sea of Faith'. Evolution made God's role as an originator of new species redundant. In 1890 the anthropologist James Frazer published *The Golden Bough* – achieving, it seemed, in fact the fictional 'key to all mythologies' that Mr

Casaubon had sought. Frazer treated Christianity as unremarkably mythical – a set of myths among others – and predicted, in effect, the replacement of religion by science. Appeals to reason and science have justified atheism in every age. Even for believers, confidence or resignation that humans can or must manage without divine help has always been a practical recourse from our inability to harness God for our purposes. Only in the nineteenth century, however, did the idea arise of combining these strands and inaugurating a quasi-religion of atheists to rival real religions.

An early sign was the Cult of the Supreme Being, launched in revolutionary France (see p. 242). Despite its short life and risible failure the cult showed that it was possible to start an anti-Christian religious-style movement from scratch. It took over half a century more, however, for Auguste Comte to propose 'a religion of humanity' with a calendar of secular saints that included Adam Smith and Frederick the Great. Increasingly, Christian evangelists' success in industrial workers' slums alerted proselytizing atheists to the need and opportunity to fight back. Meanwhile, from within Christian ranks, Unitarians, whose radical form of Protestantism denied the divinity of Christ, spawned dissenting congregations that took scepticism beyond old limits; in dedication to social welfare they discovered an ethos that could outlive faith. Finally, Darwinism stepped into the mix, suggesting how the impersonal force of evolution might replace the majesty of providence. If science could explain a problem as mysterious – to use a term Darwin used himself – as the diversity of species, it might yet, for those susceptible to a new kind of faith, explain everything else.

The most influential of the new, quasi-religious movements was that of the Ethical Societies, which Felix Adler launched in New York in 1876 as a 'new religion'. His aim was to base moral conduct on humane values rather than on models of God, or on dogmas or commandments. Morality, he said, 'is the law which is the basis of true religion'.[108] A renegade Unitarian minister, Moncure Conway, took the movement to England. The more its influence extended, the less it came to resemble a religion, although a US high court decision of 1957 granted Ethical Societies the rights and status of religion, and British Humanists campaign for equal broadcasting time with the religions privileged in BBC schedules.[109]

A word to the wise may be in order. The modern humanist tradition had nothing to do with the so-called Renaissance curriculum that displaced theology and logic in favour of 'human subjects' (rhetoric, grammar, history, literature, and moral philosophy). The popularity of this 'Renaissance humanism' owed nothing to supposedly encroaching secularism (see p. 330). It was a response to increasing demand for training suitable for civil lawyers and civil servants.[110] Nor should the humanism of the repudiators of religion be confused with the 'New Humanism', which is properly the name of a movement of reaffirmation of belief in the value and moral nature of human beings after the horrors of the mid-twentieth century.

Reports of God's death have always been premature. As in the previous century, late-nineteenth-century revivalism in just about every tradition responded to atheism and secular religion. In 1896 Anton Bruckner died while composing his Ninth Symphony, out-noising religious doubts in a glorious finale of resurgent faith. Meanwhile, a new kind of religion imitated science by asserting certainties that, in the next century, as we are about to see, would prove to be delusive. Charles Hodge, who ran the Presbyterian seminary in Princeton, had written a reply to Darwin, not dismissing evolution but recommending literal readings of the Bible as similar and superior to scientific laws. In 1886, Dwight L. Moody founded a seminary in Chicago on the same basis. Nature, he admitted, could disclose truths about God, but the Bible overtrumped other evidence. The divines who followed Hodge and Moody in Princeton and Chicago tried to root the study of God in incontrovertible facts, in imitation of the methods of the observatory and the lab.[111] No one succeeded in the search for certainty, but the search was still on. Almost at the very end of the century, however, science strayed onto experimental terrain where its predictions began to break down, and where we must now follow.

Chapter 9

The Revenge of Chaos

Unstitching Certainty

Historians, I find when I join my fellow professionals in projects, colloquia, or conferences, are often escapists. Revulsion from the present and fear of the future drives them to the past. 'When in the past would you most like to have lived?' is a tempting question with which to start a game for players to outbid each other in ever more bizarre and self-revelatory choices of eras barbarous or bloody, glorious or gaudy. What period, dear Reader, would you choose? For someone with intellectual proclivities, who loves ferment, finds innovative thinking exciting, and relishes the bewilderment of confrontation with subversive ideas, the best time, I think, would be the decade and a half or so before the outbreak of the First World War.

The early years of the twentieth century were a graveyard and a cradle: a graveyard of longstanding certainties; the cradle of a different, diffident civilization. An astonishing, unsettling succession of new thoughts and discoveries challenged assumptions that had supported preponderant cultural trends of the previous couple of centuries in the West and therefore, by extension, in the world: ways of life, attitudes of mind, distributions of power and wealth. A sudden intellectual counter-revolution dethroned certainties inherited from the Enlightenment and scientific tradition. By 1914 the world seemed atomized, chaotic, seething with rebellion, raw-emotioned, sex-mad, and equipped with terrible technologies. Yet, although thinkers of the first decade and a half anticipated most of the great themes of the rest of the century, in politics none of the new ideas of the new age was powerful enough entirely to dissolve the legacy of the last. The ideological confrontations that rent the twentieth-century world between fascism and communism, authoritarianism and democracy, scientism and sensibility, reason and dogma, were battles among ideas of nineteenth-century origin.

Most history books treat the years preceding the First World War as a period of inertia when nothing much happened – a golden afterglow of the romantic era, which turned blood-red. It was as if the trenches of the Great War were channels for everything that followed. Thinking had to start anew in a scarred and blighted world, because the old order was invisible among the twists of barbed wire or from inside the foxholes and bomb craters. In consequence, it is hard to look back across the trenches and see the early twentieth century in its true light, as the most startlingly intense era ever in the output of revolutionary thought. We have, therefore, to start in or around the year 1900, looking at scientific ideas first, because science set the agenda for other disciplines and dominated the hierarchy of ideas.

Understanding the theory of relativity is the key to everything else because of the way Einstein's ideas reshaped the thinking that followed: the subversive consequences during the years in which he perfected his thinking; the reaction in favour of what turned out to be spurious certainty and menacing order; the overlap between relativity and relativism. Relativity, its context, and its effects are worth a short chapter of their own: the prelude to the rest of twentieth-century thinking in the final chapter of this book. Starting with science and mathematics, then turning to philosophy, linguistics, anthropology, psychology, and art, we shall end by broaching the political reaction that, surprisingly perhaps, some artists helped to lead. Einstein's essential predecessors, without whom his work would have been unthinkable, or, at least, unconvincing, come first: Henri Bergson and Henri Poincaré.

Relativity in Context

Nineteenth-century certainties began to unwind almost as soon as the new century opened, when Henri Bergson, who was born in the year Darwin published *On the Origin of Species*, tried to trump Darwin's thinking. As a schoolboy, Bergson seems to have been one of those annoyingly precocious young people who give the impression of being born middle-aged. He had studious habits, encumbering spectacles, and mature good manners. He kept himself mysteriously aloof from his contemporaries and classmates. His cerebral priorities bulged from an alarmingly big forehead.[1] Every intellectual assignment seemed to suit him. His maths teachers felt betrayed when he opted for philosophy. His mastery of Latin and Greek empowered him, he claimed, to read and think beyond the confines of the language of his day. Like all French professional intellectuals, he had to undergo punishingly protracted education and endure professorial apprenticeship in secondary schools. At last, he fulfilled his promise and became the great celebrity-guru of his era.

Bergson imbibed British pragmatism. Though he thought in abstruse, metaphysical French, he liked to have hard, scientific data to work with. He began his study of mind, for instance, with observations of the persistence of memory in severely brain-damaged patients – victims of industrial accidents and wars; the evidence led him, however, to conclude that mind is a metaphysical entity, better than the brain. He trusted intuition as a source of truth but grounded it in experience. He had a connoisseur's eye and often adduced art as evidence of how perceptions transform reality. Not surprisingly, he loved impressionism, which replaces distinct facts, such as our senses register, with subtle forms abstracted in the mind. He preferred questions to answers and hated to spoil good problems with cut-and-dried solutions that truncate thought.[2]

He became one of the most admired philosophers of his day. His books sold in tens of thousands, which seemed a lot at the time. At the École Normale or the Collège de France impatient audiences turned up early to be sure of their seats ahead of his classes. When some American ladies arrived late for a lecture after crossing the Atlantic to hear him, they professed themselves content with the aura of a hall in which he had spoken. Theodore Roosevelt could understand little of his readings in Bergson's work, which was notoriously difficult, but demanded that the genius be his guest at breakfast.

In the work generally considered his masterpiece, *L'Évolution créatrice*, Bergson characterized and christened the motive force of the universe. He called it *élan vital*. It did not command nature from within, like evolution, nor from without, like God. It was a spiritual force with the power to reorder matter. How it differed from the 'World-soul' that some romantics and magicians had sought was never clear, perhaps not even to Bergson. He invoked it in order to express the freedom we retain to make a future different from that which science predicts. He dismissed the claim that evolution was a scientific law and redefined it as an expression of the creative will of living entities, which change because they want to change.

Critics accused Bergson of irrationalism on the grounds that he was attacking science, representing objective realities as mental constructs, and ascribing purpose to unthinking creation. His thinking was welcome, however, to people who found scientific determinism constraining, inhibiting, or menacing. He comforted, for example, everyone who feared or doubted the standard threats of the seers of the time, who forecast allegedly inevitable proletarian revolution, or Aryan supremacy, or immolation by entropy. Bergson was the century's first prophet of the resurgence of chaos, the first architect of disorder, because he described a world in which agents were free to do anything. 'Intellect', he said, 'is life ... putting itself outside itself, adopting the ways of unorganised nature ... in order to direct them in fact.'[3]

If Bergson's version of evolution seems rather mystical, a further idea of his, which he called 'duration', proved more impactful, albeit almost equally unintelligible – baffling partly because his definition was opaque: 'the shape taken by the succession of our states of consciousness when our inner self lets itself live ... when it abstains from establishing a separation between its present states and the preceding states'.[4] This seemingly abstruse idea also affected real life by vindicating freedom, countering the determinism that prevailed among social and scientific theorizers, and restoring faith in free will. Duration becomes intelligible when we peer inside Bergson's mind and unpick the process by which he thought it up and of which, fortunately, he provided a narrative. His account begins with his early efforts to teach schoolboys about the Eleatics and about Zeno's paradoxes in particular (see p. 137). He suddenly realized – at least, he represented his insight as the result of a sudden intuition, rather like a religious convert describing a 'Damascus moment' – that in Zeno's imaginary races and journeys and arrow flights, or in any passage of time or episode of change, moments are not separable or successive. They are continuous. They constitute time rather in the way points form a line. When we speak of time as if it were made of moments – like matter, made of individual atoms – our thinking is 'contorted and debased by association with space'. Time is not a 'brief history' of atomized events, but a mental construct. 'I admit', Bergson conceded:

> that we routinely locate ourselves in time conceived as analogous to space. We've no wish to hear the ceaseless hum and buzz of deep life. But that's the level at which real duration lies ... Whether it's inside us or outside us, whether in me or in external objects, it's the continuous changing (*la mobilité*) that is the reality.

People who need to cling to fixed points, he suggested, may find the idea 'vertiginous'. Bergson, however, found it reassuring, because it resolved the paradoxes with which Zeno confounded the world.[5] Up to this point Bergson's idea of time resembled and may have reflected St Augustine's, a millennium and a half before (see p. 165). But Bergson went further. More exactly, he suggested, time is a product of memory, which is different from perception and therefore 'a power independent of matter. If, then, spirit is a reality, it is here, in the phenomena of memory, that we may come into touch with it experimentally.' Constructing time, according to Bergson, is not just a human proclivity. All creatures do it: 'Wherever anything lives, there is open, somewhere, a register in which time is being inscribed.'[6] The future, one might be tempted to say, is only the past we have not yet experienced. To those who understood duration, or who thought they did, it seemed a useful concept. As we shall see, it helped shape the revolution in our understanding of language, pioneered by Ferdinand de Saussure, who in lectures he gave in 1907 proposed that text is a kind of verbal duration, in which terms, like moments, are inseparable. Many creative writers, who got the same sort of idea directly from Bergson, felt liberated in narration from the discipline of chronology. Novels in the 'stream of consciousness' – a term William James coined after reading Bergson – were among the result.[7]

Bergson insisted on further insights that helped shape mainstream thinking for much of the twentieth century. He observed, for instance, that reality and experience are identical. 'There is change', he said, 'but there are no "things" that change', just as a melody is independent of the strings that play it or the stave on which it is written. Change exists, but only because we experience it. And experience, Bergson argued, in common with most philosophers and in defiance of materialists, is a mental process. Our senses transmit it; our brains register it; but it happens elsewhere in a transcendent part of the self that we call 'mind'. Even more significantly for the future, Bergson prepared the way for Einstein and made his paths straight. It is hard to imagine a theory as subversive as that of relativity penetrating undisarmed minds. Bergson accustomed his readers to the idea that time might not be the absolute, external reality scientists and philosophers had formerly supposed. It might be 'all in the mind'. In a world jarred by Bergson's thinking, Einstein's idea that time could change with the speed of the observer was only a little more shocking. Bergson also anticipated many of the inessential tics of Einstein's thinking, down to his fondness for analogies with trains. Explaining duration, for instance, he pointed out that we tend 'to think of change as a series of states that succeed each other', like travellers in a train who think they have stopped, because another train is passing at the same speed in the opposite direction. A false perception seems to arrest a continuous process.

A young French mathematician, Henri Poincaré, who was Bergson's ally in the exposure of chaos, supplied the link that led to Einstein. Poincaré shook the underpinnings of the Newtonian cosmos when, in the late 1890s, he sketched the beginnings of a new scientific paradigm. He was working on one of the problems modern science had been unable to solve: how to model the motions of more than two interdependent celestial bodies. His solution exposed the inadequacy of Newtonian assumptions. He proposed a double wave bending infinitely back on itself and intersecting infinitely. He prefigured the way science came to represent the cosmos more than half a century after his time, in the 1960s and 1970s, when, as we shall see, chaos theory and work on fractals recalled Poincaré's discovery with stunning immediacy. Poincaré nudged science towards complex, recursive, and chaotic pictures of how nature works.

He went on to question the basic assumption of scientific method: the link between hypothesis and evidence. He pointed out that scientists have their own agendas. Any number of hypotheses could fit experimental results. Scientists chose among them by convention, or even according to 'the idiosyncrasies of the individual'.[8] Poincaré cited Newton's laws, among examples, including the traditional notions of space and time. To impugn Newton was shocking enough. To call out space and time was even more perplexing, because they had pretty much always been accepted as part of the fixtures and fittings of the universe. For St Augustine, constant time was the framework of creation. Newton assumed that the same chronometers and yardsticks could measure time and space all over the universe. When Kant developed his theory of intuition at the beginning of the nineteenth century (see p. 276), his key examples of what we know to be true, independently of reason, were the absolute nature of time and space. Like a heretic picking apart a creed, Poincaré provided reasons for doubting everything formerly regarded as demonstrable. He likened Newton to 'an embarrassed theologian ... chained' to contradictory propositions.[9]

He became an international celebrity, widely sought, widely reported. His books sold in scores of thousands. He frequented popular stages, like a modern-day tele-expert haunting the chat shows. As usual when a subtle thinker becomes a public darling, audiences seemed to hear more than he said. Unsurprisingly, in consequence, he claimed to be misunderstood. Readers misinterpreted Poincaré to mean – to quote his own disavowal – that 'scientific fact was created by the scientist' and that 'science consists only of conventions ... Science therefore can teach us nothing of the truth; it can only serve us as a rule of action.'[10] Science, reverberating in the eardrums of Poincaré's audiences, seemed to yield insights no more verifiable than, say, poetry or myth. But the history of science is full of fruitful misunderstandings: Poincaré was important for how people read him, not for what he failed to communicate. Between them, Bergson and Poincaré startled the world into uncertainty and softened resistance to radical responses. One of the beneficiaries of the new mood was Albert Einstein.

Poincaré published his critique of traditional scientific thinking in 1902. Three years later, Einstein emerged from the obscurity of his dead-end job, like a burrower from a mine, to detonate a terrible charge. He worked as a second-class technical officer in the Swiss Patent Office. Donnish jealousy had excluded him from an academic career.

This was perhaps just as well. Einstein owed no debts to sycophancy and felt no obligation to defend established professors' mistakes. Independence from academic constraints freed him to be original. In the world Bergson and Poincaré created he was assured of an audience.

The theory of relativity changed the world by changing the way we picture it. In the 1890s, experiments had detected perplexing anomalies in the behaviour of light: measured against moving objects, the speed of light never seemed to vary, no matter how fast or slow the motion of the source from which it was beamed. Most interpreters blamed rogue results. If you release a missile, its speed increases with the force of propulsion; so how could light evade the same variability? Einstein produced a theoretical solution: if the speed of light is constant, he inferred, time and distance must be relative to it. At speeds approaching that of light, time slows, distances shorten. The inference was logical, but it was so counterintuitive and so different from what almost everyone formerly thought that it might have been dodged or dismissed had Poincaré not opened minds up to the possibility of thinking about space and time in fresh ways. Even so, Einstein's claim was hugely defiant and its success hugely disturbing. He exposed as assumptions what had previously seemed unquestionable truths: the assumption that space and time are absolute had prevailed only because, compared with time, we never go very fast. Einstein's most graphic example was a paradox he extemporized in reply to a question from the floor at one of his public lectures: a twin who left on an ultra-fast journey would return home younger than the one who stayed behind.

In Einstein's universe every appearance deceived. Mass and energy were mutually convertible. Parallel lines met. Notions of order that had prevailed since Newton turned out to be misleading. Commonsense perceptions vanished as if down a rabbit hole to Wonderland. Yet every experiment Einstein's theory inspired seemed to confirm its validity. According to C. P. Snow, who did as much as anyone to make cutting-edge science universally intelligible, 'Einstein ... sprang into public consciousness ... as the symbol of science, the master of the twentieth-century intellect ... the spokesman of hope.'[11] He transformed the way people perceived reality and measured the universe. For good and ill, he made possible practical research in the conversion of mass into energy. Nuclear power was among the long-term results.[12]

Relativity helped, moreover, to unlock new paradoxes. While Einstein reimagined the big picture of the cosmos, other scientists worked on the minutiae that make it up. In work published in 1911, Ernest Rutherford dissected the atom, revealing even tinier particles and exhibiting their dynamism, which earlier atomic explorers had barely suspected: the electrons that seem to slide erratically around a nucleus in patterns impossible to track or predict with the physics of the past. Physicists were already struggling to cope with the apparently dual nature of light: did it consist of waves or particles? The only way to comprehend all the evidence was to admit that it behaved as if it were both. The new discourse of 'quantum mechanics' dispelled old notions of coherence. The Danish Nobel Prize winner Niels Bohr described quanta as sharing the apparently self-contradictory nature of light.

From Relativity to Relativism

While relativity warped the world-picture, philosophical malaise eroded confidence in the traditional framework of every kind of thought: notions about language, reality, and the links between them. The drift to relativism began, however, with a self-subverting doctrine in the service of certainty: pragmatism.

In everyday language, 'pragmatism' just means a practical approach to life. In late-nineteenth-century America, William James elevated practical efficiency to be a criterion not just of usefulness, but of morality and truth. Along with Bergson and Poincaré, he became one of the most widely read intellectuals of the first decade of the twentieth century. From an enterprising grandfather James's father inherited more wealth than was good for him, dabbling in mysticism and socialism, and taking long naps in London at the Athenaeum, in an armchair of smooth green leather, next to Herbert Spencer's. Like his father, James was a contemplative and, like his grandfather, a capitalist. He felt guilty when he was not earning his own living. He wanted a distinctively American philosophy, reflecting the values of business and hustle and bustle. The Anglophilia for which his novelist brother, Henry, was famous – or notorious – bothered William. He recommended patriotism, resisted

Henry's attempts to Europeanize him, and always skedaddled back thankfully to 'my own country'.

He was a polymath who could not stick to any vocation. He qualified as a physician but recoiled from practice, succumbing to his own sickliness and denouncing medicine as quackery. He achieved renown as a psychologist, while struggling against self-diagnosed symptoms of insanity. He tried painting but bad eyesight obliged him to give it up. He was a workaholic who knew he could only be saved by rest. He advocated 'tough-minded' philosophy but flirted with Christian Science, engaged in psychical research, wrote rhapsodical prose, and indulged in spasms of mysticism. He extolled reason and paraded sentiment, but preferred fact. On the rebound from the sublime and ineffable, he turned to the grimy world of Mr Gradgrind, 'to fact, nothing more'. Pragmatism, which incorporated a lot of his prejudices, including Americanism, practicality, vague religiosity, and deference to facts, was as close as he came to a consistent view of the world. In his bestseller of 1907 he developed and popularized 'old ways of thinking' first formulated in the 1870s by Charles Sanders Peirce: philosophy should be useful. Usefulness, said James in effect, makes truth true and rightness right. 'A pragmatist turns ... towards concreteness and adequacy, towards facts, towards action, and towards power.'[13] Bergson hailed him for discovering 'the philosophy of the future'.[14]

James never wanted to be a radical. He was looking for reasons to believe in God, arguing that 'if the hypothesis of God works satisfactorily in the widest sense of the word, it is true'.[15] But what works for one individual or group may be useless to others. By reducing truth to conformity with a particular purpose, James abjured what, until then, had been the agreed basis of all knowledge: the assumption that truth and reality match. He set out to vindicate Christianity; in the end he subverted it by relativizing truth.[16]

Almost in secret, at first, without publicity, even without publication, linguistics took a similar route away from solid ground onto intellectual quicksand. For those of us who want to tell the truth, language is our attempt to refer to reality. Developments in twentieth-century linguistics, however, seemed to suggest, at least for a while, that the attempt is doomed. In lectures he began in Geneva in January 1907, the year James published *Pragmatism*, Ferdinand de Saussure shoved linguistics in a new direction. He introduced the distinction between social speech – the *parole* addressed to others – and subjective language: the *langue* known only to thought. His character affected the way he communicated. He lectured like Aristotle, notelessly, with an engaging air of spontaneity. His students' notes are the only surviving record of what he said, leaving experts room to bicker over their accuracy. Generally, his audience understood him to claim that the effect of language arises from the relationships of each term in a text or speech with all other terms. Particular terms have no significance except in combination with each other. What gives language sense are the structures of their relationships, which extend beyond any particular text into the rest of language. Meaning therefore is beyond authorial control. It is never complete, because language is always changing and relationships between terms are always re-forming. Meaning is constructed by culture, not rooted in reality. Readers are autonomous and can re-forge and distort text as they process it between page and memory. It took a long time for Saussure's thinking to get beyond the classroom into print and pedagogy, but it gradually became linguistic orthodoxy. Most readers reached his work through a series of editorial reconstructions – the scholarly equivalent of Chinese whispers. As we shall see in the next chapter, the message they usually got was that language does not say anything reliable about reality, or about anything except itself.[17]

Put this reading of Saussure together with popular interpretations of Poincaré, Bergson, William James, Einstein, and quantum mechanics: there is no fixed space or time; you cannot rely on scientific claims; the basic matter of the universe behaves in unpredictable and inexplicable fashion; truth is relative; and language is divorced from reality. While certainty unravelled, relativism and relativity entwined.

Science and philosophy between them undermined inherited orthodoxy. Anthropology and psychology, meanwhile, produced equally devastating heresies. The revolution in anthropology spread gradually from America, where Franz Boas started it. This undersung hero of the Western liberal tradition was a German Jew who became the doyen and presiding spirit of anthropology in America. He overturned an assumption in which scientists invested belief, empires effort, and financiers cash: the superior evolutionary status of some peoples and some societies. Like Darwin, he learned from people Westerners dismissed as primitive. But whereas the Fuegians disgusted Darwin, the Inuit inspired Boas. Working among them on Baffin Island in the 1880s, he came to appreciate their practical wisdom and creative imaginations. He turned his insight into a precept for fieldworkers, which also works well as a rule of life: empathy is the heart of understanding. In order to see the intriguing peculiarities of different cultures, anthropologists must strive to share the outlook of people among whom they are imbedded. Determinism of every kind then becomes unappealing and risky generalizations unconvincing, because no single explanation seems adequate to account for the observed divergences.

Boas was a fieldworker who became a museum curator, always in touch with the people and artefacts he sought to understand. He sent pupils to study Native American peoples along the railway lines that stretched westwards from his classroom in New York. The results proved that there was no such thing as what earlier and contemporary anthropologists called 'the savage mind'. We all share the same kind of mental equipment, irrespective of the material conditions, technological prowess, social complexity, or sophistication that surround us. Jared Diamond has a neat way of putting it: 'there are as many geniuses in New Guinea as New York'.[18] Boas exposed the fallacies of racist craniology – which alleged that some races had skulls better adapted for intelligence than others. From the biggest, fastest-growing, and most influential national school of anthropologists in the world, he outlawed the notion that peoples could be ranked according to how 'developed' their thinking supposedly was. People, he concluded, think differently in different cultures not because some have better brainpower, but because every mind reflects the traditions it inherits, the society that surrounds it, and the environment to which it is exposed. In lectures he gave in 1911, Boas summarized the findings of the research he conducted or supervised:

> The mental attitude of individuals who ... develop the beliefs of a tribe is exactly that of the civilized philosopher ... The value which we attribute to our own civilization is due to the

> fact that we participate in this civilization, and that it has been controlling all our actions since the time of our birth; but it is certainly conceivable that there may be other civilizations, based perhaps on different traditions and on a different equilibrium of emotion and reason, which are of no less value than ours, although it may be impossible for us to appreciate their values without having grown up under their influence ... The general theory of valuation of human activities, as developed by anthropological research teaches us a higher tolerance than the one we now profess.[19]

That was putting it mildly. It became impossible to make the traditional case for racism or imperialism – that race condemned some people to inescapable inferiority or that empires were custodianships like those of parents over children or guardians over imbeciles. Conversely, Boas made it possible to re-evaluate relationships between cultures. Cultural relativism, as we now call it, became the only credible basis on which a serious study of human societies could be pursued. Some cultures may be better than others, but such a judgement can only be made when the compared cultures share similar values. This is a rarely fulfilled condition. Every culture, says cultural relativism, has to be judged on its own terms.

Anthropological fieldwork reinforced the relativistic tendency by piling up enormous quantities of diverse data, intractable to the crudely hierarchical schemes of the nineteenth century, but cultural relativism took a while to spread beyond the circles Boas directly influenced. British anthropologists were the first foreigners to absorb his lessons, as early as the first decade of the century. France, where anthropologists commanded the greatest worldwide prestige, soon began to respond positively, and relativism radiated from there. It helped to undermine empires and build multicultural societies, but it threw up intellectual and practical problems that remain unsolved. If no culture is objectively better than another, what happens when their understandings of morality conflict? Can cannibalism, infanticide, widow burning, gender discrimination, headhunting, incest, abortion, female circumcision, and arranged marriage all shelter under the rubric of cultural relativism? How and where does one draw the line?[20]

The Tyranny of the Unconscious

While Boas and his pupils were at work, the autonomy of culture got a curious, unintended boost from the psychology of Sigmund Freud. This is surprising, because Freud was not well attuned to cultural differences. He aimed to explain individual behaviour by uncovering universal urges. Crucially, however, by concentrating on universals and individuals, Freud left culture in a gap between them, to explain itself. The spread of Freudian psychology, which claimed to expose the world of the subconscious, questioned conventional ideas of experience and, in particular, of sex and childhood.

Freud became a model and mentor of the twentieth century. He was even more subversive of scientific orthodoxy than Boas, because his discoveries or claims reached beyond the relationships between societies to challenge the individuals' understanding of the self. Freud's claim that much human motivation is subconscious defied traditional assumptions about responsibility, identity, personality, conscience, and mentality. His journey into the subconscious began in an experiment he conducted on himself in 1896, when he exposed his own 'Oedipus complex', as he called it: a supposed, suppressed urge, which he believed all male children shared, to supplant one's father. It was the first of a series of unconscious desires he identified as the stuff of the human psyche. In succeeding years, he developed a technique he called psychoanalysis, designed to make patients aware of subconscious impulses: by hypnosis or by triggering the mnemonic effects of free association, which were Freud's preferred methods, psychoanalysts could help patients retrieve repressed feelings and ease nervous symptoms. Patients rose from Freud's couch – or from that of his mentor, Josef Breuer – and walked more freely than before. Women who only a few years previously would have been dismissed as hysterical malingerers became instructive case studies, with benign effects on the re-evaluation of the role of women in society.

Freud's 'science' seemed to work, but failed to pass the most rigorous tests: when Karl Popper asked how to distinguish someone who did not have an Oedipus complex, the psychoanalytic fraternity bucked the question. They behaved like a religious sect or fringe political movement, denouncing each other's errors and expelling dissenters from their self-elected bodies. In any case, Freud surely underestimated the effects of culture in shaping psyches and varying the impact of experience in different times and places. 'Freud, Froid', said G. K. Chesterton. 'I pronounce it, "Fraud".' Psychoanalysis is not, by any strict definition, science.[21] Still, the efficacy of analysis for some patients mattered more than the approval of scientific peers. Freud's genius for communicating ideas in compelling prose helped spread his fame. He seemed able, from the evidence of a few burgesses of pre-war Vienna, to illuminate the human condition. His claims were shocking not only because they were candid about sexual urges most people had preferred to leave unmentioned in polite society, but also, more radically, because he was telling people, in effect, 'You do not and cannot know why you behave as you do, without my help, because your sources of motivation are unconscious.' He claimed to show that every child experienced, before puberty, common phases of sexual development, and that every adult repressed similar fantasies or experiences. Freud even seemed to supply enemies of religion with one of their own chief objects of desire: a scientific explanation for God. 'At bottom', he wrote, in one of his most influential texts, *Totem and Taboo*, 'God is nothing more than an exalted father.'[22] Potential moral consequences of Freud's thinking are alarming: if we cannot know for ourselves the reasons for our behaviour, our power of self-reformation is limited. The very notion of individual moral responsibility is questionable. We can liquidate guilt, and blame our defects and misdemeanours on our upbringing.

Under Freud's influence, introspection became a rite in the modern West, defining our culture, as dance or codes of gesture might define another. Repression became the demon of our days, with the analyst as exorcist. The 'feel-good society', which silences guilt, shame, self-doubt, and self-reproach, is among the consequences. So is the habit of sexual candour. So is the practice – prevalent for much of the twentieth century and still widespread among psychiatrists – to treat metabolic or chemical imbalances in the brain as if they were deep-rooted psychic disorders. The revolution in values Freud initiated – the struggle against repression, the exaltation of frankness, the relaxation of inhibitions – has outlived his own esteem. The balance of good and evil effects is hard to calculate. Psychoanalysis and other, sub-Freudian schools of therapy have helped millions and tortured millions – releasing some people from repressions and condemning others to illusions or unhelpful treatments.[23]

Freud's emphasis on the subconscious effects of childhood experience made education a psychologists' playground, even though, as Isaac Bashevis Singer said, 'Children have no use for psychology.' The Swedish feminist Ellen Key announced the rediscovery of childhood in 1909: children were different from adults. This apparent truism reflected the state of the idea of childhood as it had developed in the nineteenth-century West (see p. 285). Changing patterns of childhood mortality, however, stimulated new initiatives in research. I recall how moved I felt, when I was a schoolteacher in England, wandering through the old cloister, lined with memorials to troublingly large numbers of boys who had died at the school in the nineteenth century. In those days, it would have made little sense to invest heavily in such evanescent lives. But as childhood disease spared more of them for longer lives, children became suitable objects for the bestowal of time and emotion and study.[24] The most influential researcher was the Swiss polymath, Jean Piaget. You can trace the evidence of his impact across generations of schoolchildren, deprived of challenging tasks because Piaget said they were incapable of them. He was a child prodigy himself, but like many easily disillusioned specialists in education, his opinion of children was low. He made what he thought was a breakthrough in 1920, while helping to process results of early experiments in intelligence testing. Children's errors seemed to him to show that their mental processes were peculiar and structurally different from his own. The theory he devised to explain this was strikingly similar to the doctrine of stages of mental development that anthropologists had rejected on the strength of the evidence compiled by Boas. Piaget was better read in the work of Freud and Key than of Boas. 'Mental development', as he saw it, pertained to individuals, rather than societies. It occurred in predictable, universal stages, as people grow up. He was probably wrong. Most of what he took to be universal is culturally conditioned. What we acquire as we grow up are habits refined by experience and imposed by culture. There is increasing recognition that children do not come in standard packages.

Nonetheless, Piaget was so persuasive that even today school curricula bear his stamp, classifying children according to age and prescribing the same sorts of lessons, at the same levels of supposed difficulty, in much the same subjects, for everybody at each stage. The effect can be retarding or alienating for some individuals whose talents, if allowed to mature at their own pace, might benefit society generally. Some schools and colleges have come to realize this and now make special arrangements for children who are 'severely gifted', switching them to classes with older peers at higher standards than those of their contemporaries. Except in such exceptional cases, the prevailing system is inherently unfair to children because it provides a dubious theoretical basis for treating them as inherently inferior to grown-ups; this is hardly more just than the corresponding historic generalizations about the supposed inferiority of racially defined groups. Some children exhibit far more laudable characteristics, including those usually associated with maturity, than many adults.[25]

Innovation in Take-off Mode

New departures in other fields accompanied the new ideas that teemed and tumbled in the science, philosophy, linguistics, anthropology, and psychology of the early twentieth century. A bigger phenomenon was under way: unprecedentedly rapid change in every measurable field. Statistics of every kind – demographic and economic – leaped. Technology – the characteristic science of the century – hurtled into a new phase. The twentieth century would be an electric age, much as the nineteenth had been an age of steam. In 1901, Marconi broadcast by wireless. In 1903, the Wright brothers took flight. Plastic was invented in 1907. Other essentials of fulfilled twentieth-century lifestyles – the atom-smasher, the ferroconcrete skyscraper frame, even the hamburger and Coca-Cola – were all in place before the First World War broke out. The curiosities of late-nineteenth-century inventiveness, such as the telephone, the car, the typewriter, all became commonplace.

In politics, too, the new century opened with striking novelties. The world's first fully fledged democracies – fully fledged in the sense that women had equal political rights with men – appeared in Norway and New Zealand in 1901. In 1904, Japanese victories over Russia confirmed what ought to have been obvious, had the evidence – of Maori resistance against Britain, and Ethiopian success against Italy – not been mistrusted or suppressed: white empires were beatable. Encouraged by Japan's example, independence movements leapt into action. Eventually Japan would make British, French, and Dutch imperialism unsustainable in most of Asia. Meanwhile, militants took new heart in the struggle for equality among races. In 1911 the first great 'rebellions of the masses' began: the Mexican and Chinese revolutions – seismic convulsions that, in the long run, made the communist revolutions of later in the century look like a short-term blip. China's revolution toppled a dynasty that had ruled for two and a half centuries and ended thousands of years of political continuity. The main victims of the Mexican revolution were almost equally firmly established engrossers: landowners and the Church.

The unsettling effect of the early-twentieth-century shake-up of the world can be seen – literally seen – in the work of painters. In the twentieth century, painters have tended, to an unprecedented degree, to paint not what they see directly, but what science and philosophy depict. The revolutions of art have registered the jolts and shocks that science and philosophy administered. In 1907 cubism held up images of a shattered world, as if in a shivered mirror. Pablo Picasso and Georges Braque, the originators of the movement, seemed to confirm the vision that atomic theory suggested – of an ill-ordered, uncontrollable world, composed of poorly fitting fragments. They denied they had ever heard of Einstein. But they knew about relativity from the press. When they tried to capture elusive reality from different perspectives, they reflected anxieties typical of their decade: of the dissolution of a familiar world-picture. Even Piet Mondrian, whose paintings so perfectly captured the sharp angles of modern taste that he represented boogie-woogie rhythms as a rectilinear grid and Manhattan's Broadway as a straight line, had a shivered-mirror phase in the early years of the second decade of the century. Formerly, he painted riverbanks of his native Holland with romantic fidelity. Now he splayed and atomized them. In 1911, Wassily Kandinsky read Rutherford's description of the atom 'with frightful force, as if the end of the world had come. All things become transparent, without strength or certainty.'[26] The effects fed into a new style, which suppressed every reminiscence of real objects. The tradition Kandinsky launched, of entirely 'abstract' art, depicting objects unrecognizably or not at all, became dominant for the rest of the century. In France Marcel Duchamp denounced his own expertise in science as mere smattering, but he, too, tried to represent Einstein's world. His notes on his sculptural masterpiece *Large Glass* revealed how closely he had studied relativity. His painting of 1912, *Nude Descending a Staircase*, where reality seems to expand like the folds of a concertina, was, he said, an expression of 'time and space through the abstract presentation of motion'. Meanwhile, the syncopations of jazz and the apparently patternless noises of atonal music – which Arnold Schoenberg developed in Vienna from 1908 onward – subverted the harmonies of the past as surely as quantum mechanics reshuffled ideas of order. The effects of anthropology on the art of the time are even more explicit than those of science, as artists replaced the traditional lumber of their imaginations – Greek statuary, old masters – with bric-a-brac from ethnographic collections and illustrations. Picasso, Braque, Constantin Brancusi, and members of the Blue Rider School in Kandinsky's circle copied 'primitive' sculptures of the Pacific and Africa, demonstrating the validity of alien aesthetics, and drawing inspiration from minds formerly despised as 'savage'. Some of the faces Picasso painted seem forced into the shapes, angular or elongated, of Fang masks. André Derain traduced the bathing beauties of traditional beach-portraiture by making his *baigneuses* look like crudely carved fetishes. Some of the primitivists' models came from the loot of empire, displayed in galleries and museums, some from retrospective exhibitions that followed the death, in 1903, of Paul Gauguin, whose years of self-exile in Tahiti in the 1890s had inspired erotic essays in sculptured and painted exoticism too real to be romantic. The range of influences broadened, as connoisseurs in the Americas and Australia rediscovered 'native' arts.

Reaction: The Politics of Order

Reaction was predictable. Frenzied change menaces everyone with anything to lose. After the seismic thinking of the early twentieth century, the big question in disrupted minds was how to dispel chaos and retrieve reassurance. An early and effective response came from

Filippo Tommaso Marinetti – Italian dandy, *méchant*, and intellectual tease. In 1909 he published a manifesto for fellow artists. At the time, most artists professed 'modernism': the doctrine that the new excels the old. Marinetti wanted to go further. He thought, as it were, that the next must exceed the now. He therefore proclaimed 'futurism'. He believed that it was not enough to surpass the legacy of the past. Futurists must repudiate tradition, obliterate its residue, trample its tracks. 'The future has begun', Marinetti announced. It sounds like nonsense or, if not nonsense, a platitude, but, in a way, he was right. He had devised a telling metaphor for the pace of the changes that went on accelerating for the rest of the century.

Marinetti rejected all the obvious sources of comfort that people might normally crave in a disrupted environment: coherence, harmony, freedom, received morals, and conventional language. To him comfort was artistically sterile. Instead, Futurism glorified war, power, chaos, and destruction – ways of forcing humankind into novelty. Futurists celebrated the beauty of machines, the morals of might, and the syntax of babble. Old-fashioned values, including sensitivity, kindness, and fragility, they dismissed in favour of ruthlessness, candour, strength. They painted 'lines of force' – symbols of coercion – and machines in madcap motion. Earlier artists had tried and failed to capture the speed and rhythm of industrial energy: Turner's steam engine is a blur, Van Gogh's depressingly static. But the Futurists excelled them by breaking motion into its constituent elements, like physicists splitting atoms, and copying the way cinema reflected movement in split-second sequences of successive frames. The excitement of speed – attained by the new-fangled internal combustion engine – represented the spirit of the age, speeding away from the past.

Futurism united adherents of the most radical politics of the twentieth century: fascists, for whom the state should serve the strong, and communists, who hoped to incinerate tradition in revolution. Fascists and communists hated each other and relished their battles, first in the streets and later, when they took over states, in wars bigger and more terrible than any the world had ever seen. But they agreed that the function of progress was to destroy the past. It is often said that leaders 'foundered' or blundered into the First World War. That is so. But the surprising, shocking feature of the descent into war is how passionately the apostles of destruction worshipped and welcomed it.

Wars nearly always urge events in the direction in which they are already heading. Accordingly, the First World War quickened technologies and undermined elites. The better part of a generation of the natural leaders of Europe perished. Disruption and discontinuity in European history were therefore guaranteed. Destruction and despair leave citizens stakeless, with no investment in tranquillity and no allegiance amid wreckage; so the terrible expenditure of money and mortality bought not peace but political revolutions. Twelve new sovereign, or virtually sovereign, states emerged in Europe or on its borders. Superstates tumbled. Frontiers shifted. Overseas colonies were swivelled and swapped. The war felled Russian, German, Austro-Hungarian, and Ottoman empires at a stroke. Even the United Kingdom lost a limb: the revolt and civil war that broke out in Ireland in 1916 ended with independence, in effect, for most of the island six years later. Huge migrations redistributed peoples. After the war, more than one million Turks and Greeks shunted to safety across frantically redrawn borders. Excited by the discomfiture of their masters, the peoples of European empires elsewhere in the world licked their lips and awaited the next European war. 'Then is our time', are the last words of the hero of *A Passage to India*. 'We shall drive every blasted Englishman into the sea.'

Postwar poverty favoured extremisms. The financial disasters of Europe and the Americas in the 1920s and 1930s seemed to show that the West was wormwood. The rot went deeper than the corrosive politics that caused wars and blighted peace. An age of fault finding with Western civilization began. Anti-Semites blamed Jews for the world's hard times, on the mythic grounds that 'international Jewry' controlled the world's economies and exploited Gentiles for their own enrichment. Advocates of eugenics alleged that unscientific breeding was responsible for the woes of the world: it weakened society by encouraging 'inferior' classes and races and 'feeble' or 'mentally defective' individuals to spawn children as weak and useless as their parents. Anticlericals blamed the Church for supposedly subverting science, emasculating the masses, and encouraging the weak. Communists blamed capitalists. Capitalists blamed communists. Some of the things people blamed were so fantastic as to be rationally incredible – but rabble-rousers were noisy enough to drown out reason. Impoverished and miserable millions were ready to believe their claims. The politics of the megaphone – the appeal of shrill rhetoric, oversimplification, prophetic fantasy, and facile name-calling – appealed to constituencies hungry for solutions, however simplistic, strident, or supposedly 'final'. Revenge is the easiest form of righteousness and a scapegoat is a welcome substitute for self-sacrifice.

According to the most widespread analysis, the right place to lay blame was with what people called 'the system'. Marx's predictions seemed to be coming true. The poor were getting poorer. The failures of capitalism would drive them to revolution. Democracy was a disaster. Authoritarian leaders were needed to force people to collaborate for the common good. Perhaps only totalitarian governments could deliver justice, extending their responsibility over every department of life, including the production and distribution of goods. Cometh the hour, cometh the ideology.

Fascism was a political bias in favour of might, order, the state, and war, with a system of values that put the group before the individual, authority before freedom, cohesion before diversity, revenge before reconciliation, retribution before compassion, the supremacy of the strong before the defence of the weak. Fascism justified revocation of the rights of dissenters, dissidents, misfits, and subversives. Inasmuch as it was intellectual at all, it was a heap of ideas crushed into coherence like scrap iron in a junkyard compressor: an ideological fabrication, knocked together out of many insecurely interlocking bits of corporate, authoritarian, and totalitarian traditions. Whether fascists were splinters of socialism has been a matter of passionate debate. They mobilized proletarians and petty bourgeois by advocating policies that one might crudely summarize as 'socialism without expropriation'. Their creed could be classified as an independently evolved doctrine, or as a state of mind in search of an ideology, or merely as a slick name for unprincipled opportunism. In ancient Rome, a *fasces* was a bundle of sticks with an axe in the middle of it, carried before magistrates as a symbol of their power to scourge and behead people. Benito Mussolini adopted this icon of bloodstained law enforcement as what would now be called the 'logo' of his party, to express the essence of fascism: the weal of the rod and the gash of the axe. The colours of its street-troopers' shirtings might change or fade; the forms of its rites and the angles of its salutes might be altered or dropped. But you could tell it by effects you could feel: the sweat of the fear of it, the stamp of its heel. The magical lilt of fascist mumbo-jumbo could beguile even people who hated or feared it. 'Fascism is not a new order', said Aneurin Bevan, the British socialist leader, who was notorious for wrapping utterances in gnomic obscurity, like Sam Goldwyn or Yogi Berra without the humour, 'it is the future refusing to be born.'[27]

Nazism shared all these characteristics but was something more than fascism. Whereas fascists were routinely anticlerical, Nazis actively imitated religion. They replaced providence with history. For Nazis, history was an impersonal, powerful, thrusting force with a 'course' no one could dam. Human lives were playthings, like snakes to a mongoose or rats to a cat. History demanded human sacrifices, like a hungry goddess, strengthening herself by devouring profane races. The framework and language of millenarianism (see p. 245) suited Nazis. The fulfilment of history would be a 'thousand-year Reich'. Well-orchestrated ceremonial, shrines and sanctuaries, icons and saints, processions and ecstasies, hymns and chants completed the cult-life and liturgy of the quasi-religion. Like every irrational dogma, Nazism demanded unthinking assent from its followers: submission to the infallibility of the Führer. Nazis fantasized about replacing Christianity by restoring ancient folk-paganism. Some of them turned *Heimatschutz* – 'the homeland quest' – into a mystic trail that led through stone circles to Wewelsburg Castle, where, Heinrich Himmler believed, ley lines met at the centre of Germany and the world.[28]

Ideologies of order, at the sacrifice of humanity and pity, summed up the contradictions of modernity: technology progressed; morality regressed or, at best, seemed to stagnate. Sometimes, where bourgeois intellectuals like me gather, at dinner parties or academic conferences, I am surprised to hear expressions of confidence in moral progress: fluctuations in reported violence in developed countries, for instance, are often mistaken for evidence that educators' efforts yield dividends. Really, however, they just show that violence has been displaced to evidential black holes that don't show up in the statistics – to state coercion, for instance, and 'terminating' the elderly or unborn. Or the *bien-pensants* take comfort in the tolerance we properly accord to an ever wider range of traditionally proscribed behaviours – especially in matters of taste and dress; but the sum total of intolerance, and of the rage it nurtures, probably does not diminish. The noisy little men failed in the Second World War, but the allure of final solutions has not entirely faded. As the chaos and complexities of society get more intractable, the pace of change more threatening, electorates are reverting to authoritarian options: tougher policing, tighter gaols, torture for terrorists, walls and expulsions and exclusions, and national self-seclusion outside international organizations. In some ways, authoritarianism has become an ideology capable of transcending traditional rivalries. As I write, Vladimir Putin, the ex-KGB boss, seems to have become the idol of backwoods republicans in the United States and the darling of Donald Trump. Confused by chaos, infantilized by ignorance, refugees from complexity flee to fanaticism and dogma. Totalitarianism may not have exhausted its appeal.

Chapter 10

The Age of Uncertainty

Twentieth-Century Hesitancies

What happens inside minds reflects what happens outside them. The acceleration of change in the external world since the end of the nineteenth century has had convulsive effects on thinking: unrealistic hopes in some minds, intimidating fears in others, and puzzle and perplexity everywhere. We used to count in aeons, millennia, centuries, or generations when measuring change. A week is now a long time, not just in politics (as Harold Wilson supposedly said), but in every kind of culture. As change hurtles, the past seems less trackable, the future more unpredictable, the present less intelligible. Uncertainty unsettles. Voters turn in despair to demagogues with Twitter-adapted fixes, and snake-oil statesmen with slick and simplistic placebos for social problems.

The context of change is unavoidable for anyone who wants to understand the ideas that arose in response. First, for the biggest single indicator of acceleration in the recent past, look at global consumption. It increased nearly twentyfold in the course of the twentieth century. Population meanwhile merely quadrupled. Industrialization and urbanization made consumption hurtle uncontrollably, perhaps unsustainably. It is worth pausing to reflect on the facts: increased consumption per capita, not increase of population, is overwhelmingly responsible for humanly induced stresses in the environment. Madcap consumption is mainly the fault of the rich; recent population growth has been mainly among the poor. Production, meanwhile, inescapably, has risen in line with consumption; the range of products at rich consumers' disposal has multiplied bewilderingly, especially in pursuit of technological innovations, medical services and remedies, and financial and commercial instruments. World population growth has reignited Malthusian apprehensions and prompted, at intervals, in some countries, intrusive programmes of population control.[1] But the numbers – especially of the poor – are not to blame for most of the problems laid to their account. We could accommodate more people if we gave up some of our greed.[2]

In regions suitably equipped with physically unstrenuous means of livelihood and death-defying medical technology, lives lengthened unprecedentedly in the twentieth century. (We should not expect the lengthening to last – much less to lengthen further: the survivors of the century's wars were toughened in adversity; their children and grandchildren may turn out to be less durable.) Unlike most long-drawn-out experiences, lengthened life did not seem to slow down. To the ageing, events zoomed by, like hedgerows blurred into indistinguishability through the window of a bullet train. When I was a boy, sci-fi's favourite voyagers struggled to adjust in unfamiliar worlds far removed in time, and therefore in customs, from their own. By the time I was old, the BBC was featuring a hero projected back only about four decades. For young viewers early in the twenty-first century the 1970s were depicted as an almost unmanageably primitive era, without such apparently indispensable gadgets as home computers, video game consoles, or mobile phones. The show made me feel like a time traveller myself. Now, everyone resembles Rip Van Winkle, except that we need hardly go to sleep for more than a night to share his experience. We wake almost daily to unrecognizably changed manners, fashions, attitudes, surroundings, values, and even morals.

In a volatile world, victims of instability suffer from 'future shock'.[3] Fear, bewilderment, and resentment erode their security, well-being, and confidence in the future. When people feel the threat of change, they reach for the familiar, like a child clenching a comforter. When they do not understand what befalls them, they panic. The *locus classicus* was rural France in the summer of 1789, when peasants, convulsed by *grande peur*, turned their pitchforks and brands on suspected grain-hoarders. The contemporary equivalent is to turn on refugees, migrants, and minorities, or to clutch at the delusive reassurance of religious fanaticism or political extremism. Intellectuals, meanwhile, take refuge in 'postmodern' strategies: indifference, anomie, moral relativism and scientific indeterminacy, the embrace of chaos, *je-m'en-foutisme*.

This chapter is like a pioneering explorer's voyage through uncertain seas. It starts with the thoughts that – further or additional to pre-First World War relativisms – undermined traditional certainties. We then turn to twentieth-century philosophies and outlooks expressive of the new hesitancy, or representative of a search for alternatives – malleable but serviceable – to the discarded, hard-edged worldviews of the past. We unfold them – existentialism and postmodernism – along with a surprising companion or consequence: the increasing receptivity of Western minds to influences from Asia. After looking at the political and economic thinking of minds unable to persevere in ideological certainty, we shall end the chapter with a review of some largely unsuccessful but still-unextinguished attempts to reassert dogma and recover former assuredness in the company of surprising bedfellows: scientism and religious fundamentalism.

The Undeterminable World

Toward the end of the nineteenth century, every measurable kind of change leapt off the graph paper. Contemporaries noticed. Franz Boas's student, Alexander Goldenweiser, who studied totems and feared robots, suggested that cultural change 'comes with a spurt' in surges between inert phases – rather as Stephen Jay Gould thought evolution happens, 'punctuating' long periods of equilibrium. Boas himself noted that 'the rapidity of change has grown at an ever-increasing rate'.[4] 'The nature of our epoch', commented the fashionable poet Hugo von Hofmannsthal in 1905, 'is multiplicity and indeterminacy ... Foundations that other generations thought firm are really just sliding.'[5] In 1917 another of Boas's pupils, Robert Lowie, postulated a 'threshold', beyond which, after 'exceedingly slow growth', culture 'darts forward, gathering momentum'.[6] By 1919 'the spirit of unrest' – the *New York Times* could say – had 'invaded science'.[7]

Further contradictions piled up in the world of quanta. Electron-spotters noticed that subatomic particles moved between positions seemingly irreconcilable with their momentum, at rates apparently different from their measurable speed, to end up where it was impossible for them to be. Working in collaborative tension, Niels Bohr and his German colleague Werner Heisenberg coined a term for the phenomenon: 'uncertainty' or 'indeterminacy'. The debate they started provoked a revolution in thought. Scientists who thought about it realized that, because the world of big objects is continuous with the subatomic world, indeterminacy vitiates experiments in both spheres. The observer is part of every experiment and there is no level of observation at which his findings are objective. Scientists were back on par with their predecessors, the alchemists, who, working with impractically complex distillations under the wavering influence of the stars, could never repeat the conditions of an experiment and, therefore, never foresee its results.

When scientists acknowledged their uncertainty, they inspired practitioners of other disciplines to do the same. Academics in humanities and social studies look up to science, which gets more attention, commands more prestige, and mobilizes more research money. Science is a benchmark of the objectivity others crave as a guarantee of the truthfulness of their work. In the twentieth century philosophers, historians, anthropologists, sociologists, economists, linguists, and even some students of literature and theology proclaimed their intention to escape their status as subjects. They began to call themselves scientists in affectation of objectivity. The project turned out to be delusive. What they had in common with scientists, strictly so-called, was the opposite of what they had hoped: they were all implicated in their own findings. Objectivity was a chimera.

We usually strive to retrieve or replace lost confidence. Surely, people said in the twenties, there must still be reliable signposts to help us avoid the pits we have dug in the graveyard of certainty. Logic, for instance: was that not still an infallible guide? What about mathematics? Numbers, surely, were beyond corruption by change, and unaffected by quantum contradictions. Bertrand Russell and Alfred North Whitehead thought so. Before the First World War, they demonstrated to their own satisfaction, and that of almost everyone else who thought about it, that logic and mathematics were essentially similar and perfectly commensurable systems.

In 1931, however, Kurt Gödel proved them wrong when he proposed the theorem that bears his name. Maths and logic may be complete, or they may be consistent, but they cannot be both. They include, inescapably, unprovable claims. To illustrate Gödel's thinking, the brilliant enthusiast for artificial intelligence, Douglas R. Hofstadter, has pointed to drawings by the ingenious graphic designer, M. C. Escher, who, in search of ways of representing complex dimensions on flat surfaces, began to read mathematical works in the 1930s. The subjects in which he came to specialize were self-entangled structures, in which he veiled – to use his own word – impossible systems: stairways that led only to themselves; waterfalls that were their own sources; pairs of hands drawing each other.[8]

Gödel believed in mathematics, but the effect of his work was to undermine the faith of others. He felt certain – as certain as Plato or Pythagoras – that numbers exist as objective entities, independent of thought. They would still be there, even if there were no one to count them. Gödel's theorem, however, reinforced the opposite belief. He accepted Kant's view that numbers were known by apprehension, but he helped inspire others to doubt it. He excited doubts as to whether numbers were known at all, rather than just assumed. A wonderful skit by George Boolos purports to summarize Gödel's arguments 'in words of one syllable', concluding that 'it can't be proved that it can't be proved that two plus two is five'. This elusive computation showed that 'math is not a lot of bunk'.[9] Some readers concluded that it was.

As well as undermining Russell's and Whitehead's traditional way of understanding the mutual mappability of arithmetic and logic, Gödel provoked a final, unintended effect: philosophers of mathematics began to devise new arithmetics in defiance of logic – rather as non-Euclidean geometries had been devised in defiance of traditional physics. Intuitionist mathematics came close, at the extremes, to saying that every man has his own mathematics. To one mind or group of minds a proof may be momentarily satisfactory but permanently insecure. Paradigms or assumptions change.

Poincaré had already made such new departures imaginable by pointing out the transience of agreement about all kinds of knowledge. But he left most readers' convictions about the reality of number intact. One of the earliest and most influential intuitionists, for instance,

L. E. J. Brouwer of Amsterdam, thought he could intuit the existence of numbers from the passage of time: each successive moment added to the tally. If, as we have seen, Bergson's re-interpretation of time as a mental construct was irreconcilable with Brouwer's insight, Gödel's work was even more subversive. It challenged Plato's confidence that the study of numbers 'obviously compels the mind to use pure thought in order to get at the truth'. Now neither the purity nor the truth of arithmetic could be assumed; 'that which puts its trust in measurement and reckoning', Plato continued, 'must be the best part of the soul',[10] but that trust now seemed misplaced. To lose the trust and forgo the compulsion was a terrible forfeiture. The effect of Gödel's demonstrations on the way the world thinks was comparable to that of termites in a vessel formerly treated as watertight by those aboard it: the shock of the obvious. If maths and logic were leaky, the world was a ship of fools. Infuriatingly, for him, he was 'admired because misunderstood'. Self-styled followers ignored his deepest convictions and embraced his licence for chaos.[11]

For anyone who wanted to go on believing in the tottering or fallen idols of the past – progress, reason, certainty – the 1930s were a bad time. The Western world, where such beliefs had once seemed sensible, lurched through apparently random, unpredictable crises: crash, slump, Dust Bowl, social violence, mounting crime, the menace of recurrent war, and, above all, perhaps, the conflict of irreconcilable ideologies that fought each other into extinction.

With the Second World War, ideas that were already slithering out of touch became untenable. It dwarfed the destructiveness of every earlier war. Bombs incinerated huge cities. Ideological and racial bloodlust provoked deliberate massacres. The deaths mounted to over thirty million. Industry produced machines for mass killing. Science twisted into racial pseudo-science. Evolution evolved into a justification for winnowing the weak and unwanted. Old ideals morphed murderously. Progress now took the form of racial hygiene; utopia was a paradise from which enemies were gutted and flung; nationalism turned into a pretext for sanctifying hatred and vindicating war; socialism turned, too, like a mangle for squeezing and crushing individuals.

Nazis, who blamed Jews for the ills of society, set out calculatingly to get rid of them, herding them into death camps, driving them into sealed rooms, and gassing them to death. Pointless cruelty accompanied the Holocaust: millions enslaved, starved, and tortured in so-called scientific experiments. War or fear ignited hatred and numbed compassion. Scientists and physicians in Germany and Japan experimented on human guinea pigs to discover more efficient methods of killing. The atrocities showed that the most civilized societies, the best educated populations, and the most highly disciplined armies were unimmunized against barbarism. No case of genocide quite matched the Nazi campaign against the Jews, but that was not for want of other attempts. Experience of the Nazi death camps was too horrific for art or language to convey, though one gets, perhaps, a faint sense of the evil from photographs that show death-camp guards heaping up brutalized, emaciated corpses in the last weeks of the war: it was a desperate attempt to exterminate the survivors and destroy the evidence before the Allies arrived. They dismantled the incinerators, leaving starved, typhus-ridden cadavers to litter the ground or rot in shallow graves. Primo Levi, author of one of the most vivid memoirs, tried to encode memories of mass murder in sketches of individual suffering – of a woman, for instance, 'like a frog in winter, with no hair, no name, eyes empty, cold womb'. He begged readers to carve his images 'in your hearts, at home, in the street, going to bed, rising. Repeat them to your children.'[12]

Governments and institutions of public education joined the struggle to keep the memory of the Holocaust and other atrocities alive. We know how deficient human memories are (see p. 16), except, perhaps, in being adept at forgetting. The strange psychological quirk known as 'Holocaust denial' became widespread in the late-twentieth-century West: a refusal to accept the rationally incontrovertible evidence of the scale of Nazi evil. Many European countries tried to control the deniers by outlawing their utterances. Most people who thought about it drew obvious lessons from obvious facts: civilization could be savage. Progress was, at best, unreliable. Science had no positive effect on morals. The defeat of Nazism hardly seemed to make the world better. Revealed bit by gruesome bit, the even more massive scale of inhumanity in Stalin's Russia undermined faith in communism, too, as a solution to the world's problems.

Meanwhile, science had a redemptive claim to stake: it helped to bring the war against Japan to an end. In August 1945, American planes dropped atom bombs on Hiroshima and Nagasaki, virtually obliterating them, killing over 220,000 people, and poisoning the survivors with radiation. But how much credit did science deserve? The individuals who took part in making and 'delivering' the bomb struggled with conscience – including William P. Reynolds, the Catholic pilot commemorated in the chair I occupy at the University of Notre Dame, and J. Robert Oppenheimer, the mastermind of atomic war research, who retreated into mysticism.[13] A gap glared between technology's power to deliver evil and people's moral incapacity to resist it.

From Existentialism to Postmodernism

New or 'alternative' ideas offered refuge for the disillusioned. Oppenheimer turned to readings in Hindu texts. He set, as we shall see, a trend for the rest of the century in the West. To most seekers of relief from failed doctrines, existentialism was even more attractive. It was an old but newly fashionable philosophy that thinkers in Frankfurt – the 'Frankfurt School' in current academic shorthand – had developed in the 1930s and 1940s, as they struggled to find alternatives to Marxism and capitalism. They identified 'alienation' as the great problem of society, as economic rivalries and short-sighted materialism sundered communities, and left restless, unrooted individuals. Martin Heidegger, the tutelary genius of the University of Marburg, proposed that we can cope by accepting our existence between birth and death as the only immutable thing about us; life could then be tackled as a project of self-realization, of 'becoming'. Who we are changes as the project unfolds. Individuals, Heidegger contended, are the shepherds, not the creators or engineers, of their own identity. By 1945, however, Heidegger had become tainted by his support for Nazism, and his sensible observations were largely ignored. It fell to Jean-Paul Sartre to relaunch existentialism as a 'new creed' for the postwar era.

'Man', Sartre said, 'is only a situation' or 'nothing else but what he makes of himself ... the being who hurls himself toward a future and who is conscious of imagining himself as being in the future.' Self-modelling was not just a matter of individual choice: every individual action was 'an exemplary act', a statement about the sort of species we want humans to be. Yet, according to Sartre, no such statement can ever be objective. God does not exist; everything is permissible, and 'as a result man is forlorn, without anything to cling to ... If existence really does precede essence, there is no explaining things away by reference to a fixed ... human nature. In other words, there is no determinism, man is free, man is freedom.' No ethic is justifiable except acknowledgement of the rightness of this.[14] In the 1950s and 1960s, Sartre's version of existentialism fed the common assumptions of the educated young Westerners whom the Second World War left in command of the future. Existentialists could barricade themselves in self-contemplation: a kind of security in revulsion from an uglified world. Critics who denounced them for decadence were not far wrong in practice: we who were young then used existentialism to justify every form of self-indulgence as part of a project of 'becoming' oneself – sexual promiscuity, revolutionary violence, indifference to manners, drug abuse, and defiance of the law were characteristic existentialist vices. Without existentialism, ways of life adopted or imitated by millions, such as beat culture and 1960s permissiveness, would have been unthinkable. So, perhaps, would the late twentieth century's libertarian reaction against social planning.[15]

Of course, not every thinker cowered in egotism, succumbed to philosophies of disillusionment, or surrendered faith in objectively verifiable certainties. Survivors and disciples of the Frankfurt School's pre-war Viennese rivals were pre-eminent among the enemies of doubt. They fought a long rearguard action on behalf of what they called 'logical positivism', which amounted to reaffirmed faith in empirical knowledge and, therefore, in science. I recall watching Freddie Ayer, the Oxford don who was the public face and voice of logical positivism, denouncing the vacuity of metaphysics on television (which was still, in those days, an intelligent and educational medium). In the United States, John Dewey and his followers tried to revive pragmatism as a practical way of getting on with the world, reformulating it in an attempt to fillet out the corrosive relativism in William James's version (see p. 339).

A challenge to positivism came from one of its heretical disciples. 'Van' Quine was a Midwesterner who detested nonsense. He inherited some of the pragmatism that made the United States great: he wanted philosophy to work in the real, physical, or as he said 'natural' world. He penetrated Plato's cave, as all philosophy students do, and left it without seeing anything except vapid speculations about unverifiable claims. He was typical of the 1930s, when he started as a professional philosopher: he bowed to science as the queen of the academy and wanted philosophy to be scientific, rather in the way many historians and sociologists wanted to practise 'social sciences'; like other venerators of scientific means to truth Quine reeled from indeterminacy and recoiled from intuitive thinking. He talked a pared-down vocabulary, from which words he thought toxically vague, such as 'belief' and 'thought', were cut like cancers, or preserved, like bacilli in dishes or jars, for use as figures of speech. Ideally, one feels, he would have liked to limit communication to sentences expressible in symbolic logical notation. Positivism attracted him, perhaps, because it exalted demonstrable facts and empirical tests. He likened 'the flicker of a thought' to 'the flutter of an eyelid' and 'states of belief' to 'states of nerves'.[16] But the positivists were too indulgent, for his taste, of supposed truths unsusceptible to scientific testing. In two papers he read to fellow-philosophers in 1950 he demolished the basis on which positivists had admitted universal propositions: that, though they could not be proven, they were matters of definition, or usage, or 'meaning' – another term he deplored. In the classic example, you can assent to 'All bachelors are unmarried' because of what the words mean, whereas you cannot assent to 'Cliff Richard is a bachelor' without evidence. Quine condemned the distinction as false. At the core of his argument was his dismissal of 'meaning': 'bachelor' is a term that stands for 'unmarried man' in the sentence in question but is meaningless on its own.

Why did Quine's argument matter? It led him to a new way of thinking about how to test the truth of any proposition by relating it to the whole of experience and judging whether it makes sense in or helps us understand the material world. Few readers, however, followed the later stages of his journey. Most inferred one of two mutually contradictory conclusions. Some turned to science to justify such universal statements as can be subjected to sufficient if not conclusive tests, such as the laws of physics or the axioms of mathematics. Others abandoned metaphysics altogether on the grounds that Quine had shown the impossibility of formulating a proposition that is necessarily or inherently true. Either way, science seemed to take over philosophy, like a monopolist cornering the market in truth.[17]

Philosophers of language, however, made the projects of positivism and its offshoots seem shallow and unsatisfactory. Ludwig Wittgenstein's work was emblematic. He was an unruly disciple of Bertrand Russell. He staked his claim to independence in Russell's seminar at Cambridge University by refusing to admit that there was 'no hippopotamus under the table'.[18] Russell found his intellectual perversity exasperating but admirable. It was a young contrarian's way of abjuring logical positivism. Wittgenstein went on to evince brilliance unalloyed by knowledge: his method was to think problems out without encumbering his mind by reading the works of the reputable dead.

In 1953, Wittgenstein published his *Philosophical Investigations*. The printed pages still have the flavour of lecture notes. But unlike Aristotle and Saussure, Wittgenstein was his own recorder, as if in distrust of his students' ability to catch his meaning accurately. He left unanswered questions he anticipated from the audience and many dangling prompts and queries to himself. A potentially annihilating virus infected his work. 'My aim', Wittgenstein told students, 'is to teach you to pass from a piece of disguised nonsense to something that is patent nonsense.' He argued convincingly that we understand language not because it corresponds to reality but because it obeys rules of usage. Wittgenstein imagined a student asking, 'So you are saying that human agreement decides what is true and what is false?' And again, 'Aren't you at bottom really saying that everything except human behaviour is a fiction?' These were forms of scepticism William James and Ferdinand de Saussure had anticipated. Wittgenstein tried to distance himself from them: 'If I do speak of a fiction, it is of a grammatical fiction.' As we have seen, however, with Poincaré and Gödel, the impact of a writer's work often exceeds his intention. When Wittgenstein drove a wedge into what he called 'the model of object and name', he parted language from meaning.[19]

A few years later, Jacques Derrida became Saussure's most radical interpreter. He was an ingenious thinker whom provincial exile in an unprestigious position turned into a *méchant*, if not an *enragé*. In Derrida's version of Saussure, reading and misreading, interpretation and misinterpretation are indistinguishable twins. The terms of language refer not to any reality that lies beyond them but only to themselves. Because meanings are culturally generated, we get trapped in the cultural assumptions that give meaning to the language we use. In the interests of political correctness, strident programmes of linguistic reform accompanied or followed Derrida's insight: demands, for instance, to forgo, even in allusion to historical sources, historically abused terms or epithets, such as 'cripple' or 'negro' or 'midget' or 'mad'; or to impose neologisms, such as 'differently abled' or 'persons of restricted growth'; or the feminist campaign to eliminate terms of common gender (like 'man' and 'he') on the grounds that they resemble those of masculine gender and imply a prejudice in favour of the male sex.[20]

What came to be called postmodernism was more, however, than a 'linguistic turn'. Language malaise combined with scientific uncertainty to foment distrust in the accessibility – and even the reality – of knowledge. Distressing events and new opportunities provoked revulsion from modernism: the war, genocide, Stalinism, Hiroshima, the tawdry utopias created by the architectural modern movements, the dreariness of the overplanned societies Europeans inhabited in the postwar years. The alienated had to reclaim culture: the breakneck technology of electronically generated entertainment helped them do it.

In part, against this background, postmodernism looks like a generational effect. The baby boomers could repudiate a failed generation and embrace sensibilities suited to a postcolonial, multicultural, pluralistic era. The contiguities and fragility of life in a crowded world and a global village encouraged or demanded multiple perspectives, as neighbours adopted or sampled each other's points of view. Hierarchies of value had to be avoided, not because they are false but because they are conflictive. A postmodern sensibility responds to the elusive, the uncertain, the absent, the undefined, the fugitive, the silent, the inexpressible, the meaningless, the unclassifiable, the unquantifiable, the intuitive, the ironic, the inexplicit, the random, the transmutative or transgressive, the incoherent, the ambiguous, the chaotic, the plural, the prismatic: whatever hard-edged modern sensibilities cannot enclose. Postmodernism, according to this approach, arose in accordance with its own predictions about other 'hegemonic' ways of thought: it was the socially constructed, culturally engineered formula imposed by our own historical context. In famous lines, Charles Baudelaire defined the modern as 'the ephemeral, the fugitive, the contingent, the half of art whose other half is the eternal and the immutable'. It is tempting to adapt this phrase and say that the postmodern is the ephemeral, fugitive, and contingent half of the modern, whose other half is the eternal and the immutable.[21]

Specific events of the 1960s helped postmodernism crystallize. Students became aware that the prevailing scientific picture of the cosmos was riven by contradictions and that, for example, relativity theory and quantum theory – the most prized intellectual achievements of our century – could not both be correct. The work of Jane Jacobs voiced disillusionment with the modern vision of utopia, embodied in architecture and urban planning.[22] Thomas Kuhn and chaos theory completed the scientific counter-revolution of our century. The ordered image of the universe inherited from the past was replaced by the image we live with today: chaotic, contradictory, full of unobservable events, untrackable particles, untraceable causes, and unpredictable effects. The contribution of the Catholic Church – the world's biggest and most influential communion – is not often acknowledged. But in the Second Vatican Council, the formerly most confident human repository of confidence dropped its guard: the Church licensed liturgical pluralism, showed unprecedented deference to multiplicity of belief, and compromised its structures of authority by elevating bishops closer to the pope and the laity closer to the priesthood.

The result of this combination of traditions and circumstances was a brief postmodern age, which convulsed and coloured the worlds of academia and the arts and – in as far as civilization belongs to intellectuals and artists – deserved to be inserted into the roll call of periods into which we divide our history. And yet, if there has been a postmodern age, it seems to have been suitably evanescent. In the 1990s and after, the world passed rapidly from postmodernism to 'postmortemism'. Ihab Hassan, the literary critic whom postmodernists hailed as a guru, recoiled in ennui and denounced his admirers for taking 'the wrong turn'.[23] Jean-François Lyotard, the Derrida disciple and philosophical farceur who was another postmodernist hero, turned with a shrug or a moue, telling us – ironically, no doubt – that it was all a joke. Derrida himself rediscovered the virtues of Marxism and embraced its 'spectres'. Redefinitions of postmodernism by the astonishing polymath Charles Jencks (whose work as a theorist and practitioner of architecture helped popularize the term in the 1970s) gutted some supposedly defining features: he proposed reconstruction to replace deconstruction, excoriated pastiche, and rehabilitated canonical modernists in art, architecture, and literature. Many postmodernists seem to have yielded something to 'the return of the real'.[24]

The Crisis of Science

Disenchantment with science deepened. 'Modern societies', according to the French geneticist Jacques Monod in 1970, 'have become as dependent on science as an addict on his drug.'[25] Addicts can break their habits. In the late twentieth century, a breaking point approached.

For most of the century, science set the agenda for other academic disciplines, for politics, and even for religions. Whereas previously scientists had responded to the demands of patrons or populace, developments in science now drove change in every field, without deferring to any other agenda. Scientists' disclosures about life and the cosmos commanded admiration and radiated prestige. As we saw in the last chapter, however, counter-currents kept scepticism and suspicion flowing: a new scientific and philosophical climate eroded confidence in traditional ideas about language, reality, and the links between them. Nonetheless, ever larger and costlier scientific establishments in universities and research institutes guided their paymasters – governments and big business – or gained enough wealth and independence to set their own objectives and pursue their own programmes.

The consequences were equivocal. New technologies raised as many problems as they solved: moral questions, as science expanded human power over life and death; practical questions, as technologies multiplied. Science seemed to replace genies with genes. Primatology and genetics blurred the boundaries between humans and other animals; robotics and AI research battered the barriers between humans and machines. Moral choices dwindled to evolutionary accidents or surrendered to genetically determined outcomes. Science turned human beings into subjects of experimentation. Ruthless regimes abused biology to justify racism and psychiatry to imprison dissidents. Scientism denied all non-scientific values and became, in its own way, as dogmatic as any religion. As the power of science grew, people came to fear it. 'Science anxiety' almost qualified as a recognized syndrome of neurotic sickness.[26]

Increasingly, under the impact of these events, science proved strangely self-undermining. Ordinary people and non-scientific intellectuals lost confidence in scientists, downgrading expectations that they could solve the problems of the world and reveal the secrets of the cosmos. Practical failures further eroded awe. Though science achieved wonders for the world, especially in medicine and communications, consumers never seemed satisfied. Every advance unleashed side effects. Machines aggravated wars, depleted environments, and darkened life under the shadow of the bomb. They penetrated the heavens and contaminated the Earth. Science seemed superb at engineering destruction, and inconsistent in enhancing life and increasing happiness. It did nothing to make people good. Rather, it expanded their ability to behave worse than ever before. Instead of a universal benefit to humanity, it was a symptom or cause of disproportionate Western power. The search for underlying or overarching order seemed only to disclose a chaotic cosmos, in which effects were hard to predict and interventions regularly went wrong. Even medical improvements brought equivocal effects. Treatments intended to prolong the survival of patients boosted the strength of pathogens. Health became a purchasable commodity, exacerbating inequalities. Costs sometimes exceeded benefits. Medical provision buckled, in prosperous countries, under the weight of public expectations and the burden of public demand. 'Life is scientific', says Piggy, the doomed hero of William Golding's novel of 1959, *Lord of the Flies*. The rest of the characters prove him wrong by killing him and reverting to instinct and savagery.

Toward the end of the twentieth century, divisions – sometimes called culture wars – opened between apologists of science and advocates of alternatives. Quantum science encouraged a revival of mysticism – a 're-enchantment' of science, according to a phrase the American theologian David Griffin coined.[27] An antiscientific reaction arose, generating conflict between those who stuck to Piggy's opinion and those who returned to God, or turned to gurus and demagogues. Especially in the West, scepticism or indifference trumped the appeal of all self-appointed saviours.

Environmentalism, Chaos, and Eastern Wisdom

Environmentalism, despite its reliance on scientific ecology, was part of this reaction against scientistic complacency. Malign effects of science, in the form of chemical fertilizers and pesticides, poisoned people and polluted land. As a result, environmentalism turned into a mass movement with relative suddenness in the 1960s. As an idea, however, it had a long pedigree. All societies practise what we might call practical environmentalism: they exploit their environments and fix rational norms to conserve such resources as they know they need. Even idealistic environmentalism, which embraces the idea that nature is worth conserving for its own sake apart from its human uses, has been around for a long time. It forms part of ancient religious traditions in which nature is sacralized: Jainism, Buddhism, Hinduism, and Taoism, for example, and classical Western paganism. Sacred ecology – to coin a term – in which humans accepted an unlordly place in nature and deferred to and even worshipped other animals, trees, and rocks – was part of some of the earliest thinking we can detect in humans and hominids (see pp. 33–67). In modern times environmental priorities resurfaced in the sensibilities of late-eighteenth-century romantics, who revered nature as a book of secular morality (see p. 271). It developed in the same period among European imperialists awestruck at the custodianship of far-flung Edens.[28]

The mood survived in the nineteenth century, especially among lovers of hunting who wanted to preserve grounds for killing and species to kill, and among escapees from the noxious towns, mines, and factories of early industrialization. Love of 'wilderness' inspired John Wesley Powell to explore the Grand Canyon and Theodore Roosevelt to call for national parks. But global industrialization was too greedy for food and fuel to be conservationist. Madcap consumerism, however, was bound to provoke reaction, if only in anxiety at the prospect of exhausting the Earth. The twentieth century experienced 'something new under the sun' – environmental destruction so unremitting and extensive that the biosphere seemed unable to survive it.[29] An early monitor or prophet of the menace was the great Jesuit polymath, Pierre Teilhard de Chardin, who died in 1955, little known and hardly echoed. By then scientific publications were beginning to reveal causes for concern, but environmentalism had a bad reputation as a quirk of dewy-eyed romantics, or – what was worse – a mania of some prominent Nazis, who nourished bizarre doctrines about the relationship of mutual purity of 'blood and soil'.[30] To animate politics, raise money, launch a movement, and wield some power, environmentalism needed a whistle-blower with gifts as a publicist. In 1962, she emerged: Rachel Carson.

Industrialization and intensive agriculture were still spreading across the world: enemies of nature too familiar, to most people, to seem threatening. Two new circumstances combined to exacerbate menace and change minds. First, decolonization in underexploited parts of the world empowered elites who were anxious to imitate the industrialized West, and to catch up with the big, bloated economic giants. Second, world population was hurtling upward. To meet increased demands new farming methods saturated the fields with chemical fertilizers and pesticides. *Silent Spring* (1962) was Carson's denunciation of pesticide profligacy. She directly addressed America, but her influence reached around the world, as she imagined a spring 'unheralded by the return of the birds', with 'strangely silent' dawns.

Environmentalism fed on pollution and throve in the climate debate. It became the orthodoxy of scientists and the rhetoric of politicians. Mystics and cranky prophets espoused it. Ordinary people recoiled from exaggerated, doom-fraught predictions. Interests vested in environmental damage, in fossil fuels, agrochemicals, and factory farms, sprayed scorn. Despite efforts by activists and academics to interest the global public in deep – that is, disinterested – ecology, most environmentalism remains of a traditional kind, more anxious to serve man than nature. Conservation is popular, it seems, only when our own species needs it. Yet some harmful practices have been curtailed or arrested, such as dam building, 'greenhouse gas' emissions, unsustainable forestry, unregulated urbanization, and inadequate testing of chemical pollutants. The biosphere seems more resilient, resources more abundant, and technology more responsive to need than in the gloomiest scenarios. Dire oracles may come true – catastrophic warming, a new ice age, a new age of plague, the exhaustion of some traditional sources of energy – but probably not as a result of human agency alone.[31]

The erosion of popular confidence in any prospect of scientific certainty climaxed in the 1960s, partly thanks to Carson and partly in response to the work of the philosopher of science, Thomas Kuhn. In 1960, in one of the most influential works ever written about the history of science, he argued that scientific revolutions were not the result of new data, but were identifiable with what he called paradigm shifts: changing ways of looking at the world and new imagery or language in which to describe it. Kuhn gave the world a further injection of a sceptical serum similar to Poincaré's. Like his predecessor, he always repudiated the inference that most people drew: that the findings of science depended not on the objective facts but on the perspective of the enquirer. But in the world of shifting paradigms, further uncertainty softened the formerly hard facts of science.[32]

Chaos theory unleashed more complications. Scientists' oldest aim has been to learn 'nature's laws' (see pp. 49, 218) so as to predict (and maybe therefore to manage) the way the world works. In the 1980s, chaos theory inspired them with awe and, in some cases, despair by making unpredictability scientific; the predictability quest suddenly seemed misconceived. Chaos stirred first in meteorology. The weather has always eluded prediction and subjected practitioners to anguish and frustration. The data are never decisive. A fact they disclose, however, is that small causes can have huge consequences. In an image that captured the imagination of the world, the flap of a butterfly's wings could set off a series of events leading ultimately to a typhoon or tidal wave: chaos theory uncovered a level of analysis at which causes seem untraceable and effects untrackable. The model seemed universally applicable: added to a critical mass, a straw can break a camel's back or a dust particle start an avalanche. Sudden, effectively inexplicable fluctuations can disrupt markets, wreck ecosystems, upturn political stability, shatter civilizations, invalidate the search for order in the universe, and invade the sanctuaries of traditional science since Newton's day: the oscillations of a pendulum and the operations of gravity. To late-twentieth-century victims, chaotic distortions seemed to be functions of complexity: the more a system depends on multifarious and interconnected parts, the more likely it is to collapse as a result of some small, deeply imbedded, perhaps invisible changes. The idea resonated. Chaos became one of the few topics in science most people heard of and might even claim to understand.

In science the effect was paradoxical. Chaos inspired a search for a deeper or higher level of coherence at which chaos would resemble one of the short stories of José Luis Sampedro, in which a galactic traveller, visiting Madrid, mistakes a football match for a rite in imitation of the cosmos, in which the interventions of the referee represent random disturbances in the order of the system. If the observer had stayed for long enough, or read the rules of football, he would have realized that the ref is an important part of the system. Similarly, rightly understood chaos might be a law of nature, predictable in its turn. On the other hand, the discovery of chaos has raised the presumption that nature really is ultimately uncontrollable.

Other recent discoveries and speculations incite the same suspicion. As the Nobel Prize winner Philip Anderson has pointed out, there seems to be no universally applicable order of nature: 'When you have a good general principle at one level', you must not expect 'that it's going to work at all levels ... Science seems self-undermined and the faster its progress, the more questions emerge about its own competence. And the less faith most people have in it.'[33] To understand the pace of evolution, for instance, we have to acknowledge that not all events have causes; they can and do occur at random. What is random, strictly speaking, precludes explanation. Random mutations just happen: that is what makes them random. Without such mutations, evolution could not occur. Other observations abound that are inexplicable in the present state of our knowledge. Quantum physics can only be described with formulations that are strictly self-contradictory. Subatomic particles defy what were formerly thought to be laws of motion. What mathematicians now call fractals distort what were once thought to be patterns – such as the structures of snowflakes or spiders' webs or, indeed, of butterflies' wings: engravings of M. C. Escher seemed to predict this impressive fact.

In the decades that followed the Second World War, while scientism unravelled, the West rediscovered other options: 'Eastern wisdom', alternative medicine, and the traditional science of non-Western peoples. Traditions that Western influence had displaced or eclipsed revived, weakening Western preponderance in science. One of the first signs occurred in 1947, when Niels Bohr chose a Taoist symbol for the coat of arms he acquired when the King of Denmark knighted him. He adopted the wave-shaped division of light and darkness by double curve, interpenetrated by dots, because, as a description of the universe, it seemed to prefigure the quantum physics of which he was the leading practitioner. 'Opposites', according to the motto on his coat of arms, 'are complementary.' At about the same time, in a West disillusioned by the horrors of war, Oppenheimer, whose case we encountered above (p. 362), was only one of many Western scientists who turned eastward, to ancient Indian texts in Oppenheimer's case, for consolation and insights.

Then, in another case of a book momentous enough to change minds, came a real shift in Western perceptions of the rest of the world – especially of China. The author was a biochemist with a strong Christian faith and a troubled social conscience: Joseph Needham, who had served as director of scientific co-operation between the British and their Chinese allies during the Second World War. In 1956 he began to publish, in the first of many volumes, *Science and Civilisation in China*, in which he showed not only that, despite the poor reputation of Chinese science in modern times, China had a scientific tradition of its own, but also that Westerners had learned from China the basis of most of their achievements in technology until the seventeenth century. Most, indeed, of what we Westerners think of as Western gifts to the world reached us from China or depended on originally Chinese innovations or transmissions. Contemplate some key instances: modern communications relied on Chinese inventions – paper and printing – until the advent of electronic messaging. Western firepower, which forced the rest of the world into temporary submission in the nineteenth century, relied on gunpowder, which Chinese technicians may not have invented but certainly developed long before it appeared in the West. Modern infrastructure depended on Chinese bridging and engineering techniques. Western maritime supremacy would have been unthinkable without the compass, rudder, and separable bulkhead, all of which were part of Chinese nautical tradition long before Westerners acquired them. The Industrial Revolution could not have happened had Western industrialists not appropriated Chinese blast-furnace technology. Capitalism would be inconceivable without paper money, which astonished Western travellers to medieval China. Even empiricism, the theoretical basis of Western science, has a longer and more continuous history in China than in the West. Indian scientists, meanwhile, made similar claims for the antiquity – if not the global influence – of scientific thinking in their own country.

In the first half of the twentieth century, the rest of the world could only endure Western supremacy or attempt to imitate it. In the 1960s, the pattern shifted. India became a favoured destination for young Western tourists and pilgrims in search of values different from those of their own cultures. The Beatles sat at the feet of Maharishi Mahesh Yogi and tried to add the sitar to their range of musical instruments. So assiduous were the bourgeois youth of Western Europe in travelling to India at the time that I felt as though I were the only member of my generation to stay at home. Taoist descriptions of nature provided some Westerners, including, in one of the more fanciful representations, Winnie the Pooh,[34] with 'alternative' – that was the buzzword of the time – models for interpreting the universe.

Even medicine was affected, the showpiece science of Western supremacy in the early twentieth century. Doctors who travelled with Western armies and 'civilizing missions' learned from 'native' healers. Ethnobotany became fashionable, as the pharmacopoeia of Amazonian forest dwellers, Chinese peasants, and Himalayan shamans surprised Westerners by working. A remarkable reversal of the direction of influence accompanied the vogue for 'alternative' lifestyle in the late twentieth century. Alternative medical treatments turned Western patients toward Indian herbalism and Chinese acupuncture, just as at the beginning of the century, under the influence of an earlier fashion, Asian students had headed west for their medical education. Now, Chinese and Indian physicians were almost as likely to travel to Europe or America to practise their arts as to learn those of their hosts. In the 1980s, the World Health Organization discovered the value of traditional healers in delivering healthcare to disadvantaged people in Africa. Governments eager to disavow colonialism concurred. In 1985 Nigeria introduced alternative programmes in hospitals and healthcare centres. South Africa and other African countries followed.

Political and Economic Thought after Ideology

Science was not the only source of failure or focus of disenchantment. Politics and economics failed, too, as surviving ideologies crumbled and confident nostrums proved disastrous. Ideologies of the extreme right, after the wars they provoked, could only attract crackpots and psychotics. But some thinkers were slow to abandon hope on the extreme left. The British master spy Anthony Blunt continued to serve Stalin from deep inside the British establishment until the 1970s: he was keeper of the Queen's art collection. The iconic historian Eric Hobsbawm, who survived into the twenty-first century, would never admit he had been wrong to put his faith in Soviet benevolence.

In the 1950s, great red hopes focused on the Chinese ideologue Mao Zedong (or Tse-tung, according to traditional methods of transliteration, which sinologists have unhelpfully abandoned but which linger in the literature to confuse uninstructed readers). To most scrutineers, the Mexican and Chinese revolutions of 1911 showed that Marx was right about one thing: revolutions dependent on peasant manpower in unindustrialized societies would not produce the outcomes Marxists yearned for. Mao thought otherwise. Perhaps because, unlike most of his fellow-communists, he had read little by Marx and understood less, he could propose a new strategy of peasant revolution, independent of the Russian model, defiant of Russian advice, and unprejudiced by Marxist orthodoxy. It was, Stalin said, 'as if he doesn't understand the most elementary Marxist truths – or maybe he doesn't want to understand them'.[35] Like Descartes and Hobbes, Mao confided in his own brilliance, uncluttered by knowledge. 'To read too many books', he said, 'is harmful.'[36] His strategy suited China. He summed it up in a much-quoted slogan: 'When the enemy advances, we retreat; when he halts, we harass; when he retreats, we pursue.'[37] Through decades of limited success as a vagabond warlord leader, he survived and ultimately triumphed by dogged perseverance (which he later misrepresented as military genius). He throve in conditions of emergency and from 1949, when he controlled the whole of mainland China, Mao provoked endless new crises to keep his regime going. He had run out of ideas but had lots of what he called thoughts. From time to time he launched capricious campaigns of mass destruction against rightists and leftists, bourgeois deviationists, alleged class enemies, and even at different times against dogs and sparrows. Official crime rates were low, but habitual punishment was more brutalizing than occasional crime. Propaganda occluded the evils and failures. Mao suckered Westerners anxious for a philosophy they could rely on. Teenagers of my generation marched in demonstrations against wars and injustices, naively waving copies of the 'Little Red Book' of Mao's thoughts, as if the text contained a remedy.

Some of Mao's revolutionary principles were dazzlingly reactionary: he thought class enmity was hereditary. He outlawed romantic love, along with, at one time, grass and flowers. He wrecked agriculture by taking seriously and applying rigorously the ancient role of the state as a hoarder and distributor of food. His most catastrophic expedient was the class war he called the 'Great Proletarian Cultural Revolution' of the sixties. Children denounced parents and students beat teachers. The ignorant were encouraged in the slaughter of intellectuals, while the educated were reassigned to menial work. Antiquities were smashed, books burned, beauty despised, study subverted, work stopped. The limbs of the economy got broken in the beatings. While an efficient propaganda machine generated fake statistics and images of progress, the truth gradually seeped out. The resumption of China's normal status as one of the world's most prosperous, powerful countries, and as an exemplary civilization, was postponed. The signs of recovery are only beginning to be apparent in the early years of the twenty-first century. In the meantime Mao's influence held back the world, blighting many new, backward, economically underdeveloped states with a malignant example, encouraging experiments with economically ruinous and morally corrupting programmes of political authoritarianism and command economics.[38]

In the absence of credible ideology, the economic and political consensus in the West fell back on modest expectations: delivering economic growth and social welfare. The thinker who did most to shape the consensus was John Maynard Keynes, who, unusually for a professional economist, was good at handling money, and turned his studies of probability into shrewd investments. Privileged by his education and friendships in England's social acceptance-world and political establishment, he embodied self-assurance and projected his own self-assurance into optimistic formulae for ensuring the future prosperity of the world.

Keynesianism was a reaction against the capitalist complacency of the 1920s in industrialized economies. Automobiles became articles of mass consumption. Construction flung 'towers up to the sun'.[39] Pyramids of millions of shareholders were controlled by a few 'pharaohs'.[40] A booming market held out prospects of literally universal riches. In 1929 the world's major markets crashed and banking systems failed or tottered. The world entered the most abject and protracted recession of modern times. The obvious suddenly became visible: capitalism needed to be controlled, exorcized, or discarded. In America, President Franklin D. Roosevelt proposed a 'New Deal' for government initiatives in the marketplace. Opponents denounced the scheme as socialistic, but it was really a kind of patchwork that covered up the fraying but left capitalism intact.

Keynes did the comprehensive rethinking that informed every subsequent reform of capitalism. He challenged the idea that the unaided market produces the levels of production and employment society needs. Savings, he explained, immobilize some wealth and some economic potential; false expectations, moreover, skew the market: people overspend in optimism and underspend when they get the jitters. By borrowing to finance utilities and infrastructure, governments and institutions could get unemployed people back into work while also building up economic potential, which, when realized, would yield tax revenues to cover the costs of the projects retrospectively. This idea appeared in Keynes's *General Theory of Employment, Interest and Money* in 1936. For a long time, Keynesianism seemed to work for every government that tried it. It became orthodoxy, justifying ever higher levels of public expenditure all over the world.

Economics, however, is a volatile science and few of its laws last for long. In the second half of the twentieth century, prevailing economic policy in the developed world tacked between 'planning' and 'the market' as rival panaceas. Public expenditure turned out to be no more rational than the market. It saved societies that tried it in the emergency conditions of the thirties, but in more settled times it caused waste, inhibited production, and stifled enterprise. In the

1980s, Keynesianism became a victim of a widespread desire to 'claw back the state', deregulate economies, and reliberate the market. An era of trash capitalism, market volatility, and obscene wealth gaps followed, when some of the lessons of Keynesianism had to be relearned. Our learning still seems laggard. In 2008 deregulation helped precipitate a new global crash – 'meltdown' was the preferred term. Though US administrations adopted a broadly Keynesian response, borrowing and spending their way out of the crisis, most other governments preferred pre-Keynesian programmes of 'austerity', squeezing spending, restricting borrowing, and bidding for financial security. The world had hardly begun to recover when, in 2016, a US presidential election installed a government resolved to deregulate again (albeit also, paradoxically, making a commitment to splurging on infrastructure).[41]

The future that radicals imagined never happened. Expectations dissolved in the bloodiest wars ever experienced. Even in states such as the United States or the French republic, founded in revolutions and regulated by genuinely democratic institutions, ordinary people never achieved power over their own lives or over the societies they formed. How much good, after so much disappointment, could a modestly benevolent state do? Managing economies in recession and manipulating society for war suggested that states had not exhausted their potential. Power, like appetite according to one of Molière's characters, *vient en mangeant*, and some politicians saw opportunities to use it for good or, at least, to preserve social peace in their own interest. Perhaps, even if they could not deliver the virtue ancient philosophers dreamed of (see pp. 146–51), they could at least become instruments of welfare. Germany had introduced a government-managed insurance scheme in the 1880s, but the welfare state was a more radical idea, proposed by the Cambridge economist Arthur Pigou in the 1920s: the state could tax the rich to provide benefits for the poor, rather as ancient despotisms enforced redistribution to guarantee the food supply. Keynes's arguments in favour of regenerating moribund economies by huge injections of public spending were in line with this sort of thinking. Its most effective exponent was William Beveridge.

During the Second World War the British government commissioned him to draft plans for an improved social insurance scheme.

Beveridge went further, imagining 'a better new world', in which a mixture of national insurance contributions and taxation would fund universal healthcare, unemployment benefits, and retirement pensions. 'The purpose of victory', he declared, 'is to live in a better world than the old world.'[42] Few government reports have been so widely welcomed at home or so influential abroad. The idea encouraged President Roosevelt to proclaim a future 'free from want'. Denizens of Hitler's bunker admired it. Postwar British governments adopted it with near cross-party unanimity.[43]

It became hard to call a society modern or just without a scheme broadly of the kind Beveridge devised; but the limits of the role of the state in redistributing wealth, alleviating poverty, and guaranteeing healthcare have been and are still fiercely contested in the name of freedom and in deference to the market. On the one hand, universal benefits deliver security and justice in individual lives and make society more stable and cohesive; on the other, they are expensive. In the late twentieth and early twenty-first centuries two circumstances threatened welfare states, even where they were best established in Western Europe, Canada, Australia, and New Zealand. First, inflation made the future insecure, as each successive generation struggled to provide for the costs of care for its elders. Second, even when inflation came under something like control, the demographic balance of developed societies began to shift alarmingly. The workforce got older, the proportion of retired people began to look unfundable, and it became apparent that there would not be enough young, productive people to pay the escalating costs of social welfare. Governments have tried various ways of coping, without dismantling the welfare state; despite sporadic efforts by presidents and legislators from the 1960s onward, the United States never introduced a comprehensive system of state-run healthcare. Even President Obama's scheme, implemented in the teeth of conservative mordancy, left some of the poorest citizens uncovered and kept the state off the health insurance industry's turf. Obamacare's problems were intelligible against the background of a general drift back to an insurance-based concept of welfare, in which most individuals reassume responsibility for their own retirement and, to some extent, for their own healthcare costs and unemployment provision. The state mops up marginal cases.

The travails of state welfare were part of a bigger problem: the deficiencies and inefficiencies of states generally. States that built homes erected dreary dystopias. When industries were nationalized, productivity usually fell. Regulated markets inhibited growth. Overplanned societies worked badly. State efforts to manage the environment generally led to waste and degradation. For much of the second half of the twentieth century, command economies in Eastern Europe, China, and Cuba largely failed. The mixed economies of Scandinavia, with a high degree of state involvement, fared only a little better: they aimed at universal well-being, but produced suicidal utopias of frustrated and alienated individuals. History condemned other options – anarchism, libertarianism, the unrestricted market.

Conservatism had a poor reputation. 'I do not know', said Keynes, 'which makes a man more conservative: to know nothing but the present, or nothing but the past.'[44] Nonetheless, the tradition that inspired the most promising new thinking in politics and economics in the second half of the twentieth century came from the right. F. A. Hayek initiated most of it. He deftly adjusted the balancing act – between liberty and social justice – that usually topples political conservatism. As Edmund Burke (see p. 281) observed, initiating, toward the end of the eighteenth century, the tradition Hayek fulfilled, 'to temper together these opposite elements of liberty and restraint in one consistent work, requires much thought, deep reflection, in a sagacious, powerful and combining mind'.[45] Hayek's was the mind that met those conditions. He came close to stating the best case for conservatism: most government policies are benign in intention, malign in effect. That government, therefore, is best which governs least. Since efforts to improve society usually end up making it worse, the wisest course is to tackle the imperfections modestly, bit by bit. Hayek shared, moreover, traditional Christian prejudice in favour of individualism. Sin and charity demand individual responsibility, whereas 'social justice' diminishes it. *The Road to Serfdom* of 1944 proclaimed Hayek's key idea: 'spontaneous social order' is not produced by conscious planning but emerges out of a long history – a richness of experience and adjustment that short-term government intervention cannot reproduce. Social order, he suggested (bypassing the need to postulate a 'social contract'), arose spontaneously, and when it did so law was its essence: 'part of the natural history of mankind ... coeval with society' and therefore prior to the state. 'It is not the creation of any governmental authority', Hayek said, 'and it is certainly not the command of the sovereign.'[46] The rule of law overrides the dictates of rulers – a recommendation highly traditional and constantly urged (though rarely observed) in the Western tradition since Aristotle. Only law can set proper limits to freedom. 'If', Hayek opined, 'individuals are to be free to use their own knowledge and resources to best advantage, they must do so in a context of known and predictable rules governed by law.'[47] For doctrines of this kind the fatal problem is, 'Who says what these natural laws are, if not the state?' Religious supremos, as in the Islamic Republic of Iran? Unelected jurists, such as were empowered in the late twentieth century by the rise of an international body of law connected with human rights?

During the overplanned years, Hayek's was a voice unheard in the wilderness. In the 1970s, however, he re-emerged as the theorist of a 'conservative turn' that seemed to conquer the world, as the political mainstream in developed countries drifted rightward in the last two decades of the twentieth century. His major impact was on economic life, thanks to the admirers he began to attract among economists of the Chicago School, when he taught briefly at the University of Chicago in the 1950s. The university was well endowed and therefore a law unto itself. It was isolated in a marginal suburb of its own city, where professors were thrown on each other's company. It was out of touch with most of the academic world, variously envious and aloof. So it was a good place for heretics to nurture dissidence. Chicago economists, of whom Milton Friedman was the most vocal and the most persuasive, could defy economic orthodoxy. They rehabilitated the free market as an insuperable way of delivering prosperity. In the 1970s they became the recourse of governments in retreat from regulation and in despair at the failures of planning.[48]

The Retrenchment of Science

When chaos and coherence compete, both thrive. Uncertainty makes people want to escape back into a predictable cosmos. Advocates of every kind of determinism therefore found the postmodern world paradoxically congenial. Attempts were rife to invoke machines and organisms as models for simplifying the complexities of thought or behaviour, and replacing honest bafflement with affected assurance. One method was to try to eliminate mind in favour of brain – seeking chemical, electrical, and mechanical patterns that could make the vagaries of thought intelligible and predictable.

To understand artificial intelligence – as people came to call the object of these attempts – an excursion into its nineteenth-century background is necessary. One of the great quests of modern technology – for a machine that can do humans' thinking for them – has been inspired by the notion that minds are kinds of machine and thought is a mechanical business. George Boole belonged in that category of Victorian savants whom we have already met (see p. 317) and who sought to systematize knowledge – in his case, by exposing 'laws of thought'. His formal education was patchy and poor, and he lived in relative isolation in Ireland; most of the mathematical discoveries he thought he made for himself were already familiar to the rest of the world. Yet he was an uninstructed genius. In his teens he started suggestive work on binary notation – counting with two digits instead of the ten we usually use in the modern world. His efforts put a new idea into the head of Charles Babbage.

From 1828 Babbage occupied the Cambridge chair held formerly by Newton and later by Stephen Hawking. When he encountered Boole's work, he was trying to eliminate human error from astronomical tables by calculating them mechanically. Commercially viable machines already existed to perform simple arithmetical functions. Babbage hoped to use something like them for complex trigonometric operations, not by improving the machines but by simplifying the trigonometry. Transformed into addition and subtraction it could be confided to cogs and wheels. If successful, his work might revolutionize navigation and imperial mapping by making astronomical tables reliable. In 1833, Boole's data made Babbage abandon work on the relatively simple 'difference engine' he had in mind, and broach plans for what he called an 'analytical engine'. Though operated mechanically, it would anticipate the modern computer, by using the binary system for computations of amazing range and speed. Holes punched in cards controlled the operations of Babbage's device, as in early electronic computers. His new scheme was better than the old, but with the habitual myopia of bureaucracies, the British government withdrew its sponsorship. Babbage had to spend his own fortune.

Despite the assistance of the gifted amateur mathematician Ada Lovelace, Byron's daughter, Babbage could not perfect his machine. The power of electricity was needed to realize its full potential; the early specimens made in Manchester and Harvard were the size of small ballrooms and therefore of limited usefulness, but computers developed rapidly in combination with microtechnology, which shrank them, and telecommunications technology, which linked them along telephone lines and by radio signals, so that they could exchange data. By the early twenty-first century, computer screens opened onto a global village, with virtually instant mutual contact. The advantages and disadvantages are nicely weighed: information overkill has glutted minds and, perhaps, dulled a generation, but the Internet has multiplied useful work, diffused knowledge, and served freedom.

The speed and reach of the computer revolution raised the question of how much further it could go. Hopes and fears intensified of machines that might emulate human minds. Controversy grew over whether artificial intelligence was a threat or a promise. Smart robots excited boundless expectations. In 1950, Alan Turing, the master cryptographer whom artificial intelligence researchers revere, wrote, 'I believe that at the end of the century the use of words and general educated opinion will have altered so much that one will be able to speak of machines thinking without expecting to be contradicted.'[49] The conditions Turing predicted have not yet been met, and may be unrealistic. Human intelligence is probably fundamentally unmechanical: there is a ghost in the human machine. But even without replacing human thought, computers can affect and infect it. Do they corrode memory, or extend its access? Do they erode knowledge when they multiply information? Do they expand networks or trap sociopaths? Do they subvert attention spans or enable multi-tasking? Do they encourage new arts or undermine old ones? Do they squeeze sympathies or broaden minds? If they do all these things, where does the balance lie? We have hardly begun to see how cyberspace can change the psyche.[50]

Humans may not be machines, but they are organisms, subject to the laws of evolution. Is that all they are? Genetics filled in a gap in Darwin's description of evolution. It was already obvious to any rational and objective student that Darwin's account of the origin of species was essentially right but no one could say how the mutations that differentiate one lineage from another get passed across the generations. Gregor Mendel, raising peas in a monastery garden in Austria, supplied the explanation; T. H. Morgan, rearing fruit flies in a lab in downtown New York in the early nineteenth century, confirmed and communicated it. Genes filled what it is tempting to call a missing link in the way evolution works: an explanation of how offspring can inherit parental traits. The discovery made evolution unchallengeable, except by ill-informed obscurantists. It also encouraged enthusiasts to expect too much of the theory, stretching it to cover kinds of change – intellectual and cultural – for which it was ill designed.

In the second half of the twentieth century, the decoding of DNA stimulated the trend, profoundly affecting human self-perceptions along the way. Erwin Schrödinger started the revolution, pondering the nature of genes in lectures in Dublin in 1944. Schrödinger expected a sort of protein, whereas DNA turned out to be a kind of acid, but his speculations about what it might look like proved prophetic. He predicted that it would resemble a chain of basic units, connected like the elements of a code. The search was on for the 'basic building blocks' of life, not least in Francis Crick's lab in Cambridge in England. James Watson, who had read Schrödinger's work as a biology student in Chicago, joined Crick's team. He realized that it would be possible to discover the structure Schrödinger had predicted when he saw X-ray pictures of DNA. In a partner laboratory in London, Rosalind Franklin contributed vital criticisms of Crick's and Watson's unfolding ideas and helped build up the picture of how strands of DNA intertwined. The Cambridge team incurred criticism on moral grounds for dealing with Franklin unfairly, but there was no denying the validity of their findings. The results were exciting. Realization that genes in individual genetic codes were responsible for some diseases opened new pathways for therapy and prevention. Even more revolutionary was the possibility that many, perhaps all, kinds of behaviour could be regulated by changing the genetic code. The power of genes suggested new thinking about human nature, controlled by an unbreakable code, determined by genetic patterning.

Character, in consequence, seemed computable. At the very least, genetic research seemed to confirm that more of our makeup is inherited than anyone traditionally supposed. Personality could be arrayed as a strand of molecules, and features swapped like walnut shells in a game of Find the Lady. Cognitive scientists expedited materialist thinking of a similar kind by subjecting human brains to ever more searching analysis. Neurological research revealed an electrochemical process, in which synapses fire and proteins are released, alongside thinking. It should be obvious that what such measurements show could be effects, or side effects, rather than causes or constituents of thought. But they made it possible, at least, to claim that everything traditionally classed as a function of mind might take place within the brain. It has become increasingly hard to find room for nonmaterial ingredients, such as mind and soul. 'The soul has vanished', Francis Crick announced.[51]

Meanwhile, experimenters modified the genetic codes of non-human species to obtain results that suit us: producing bigger plant foods, for instance, or animals designed to be more beneficial, more docile, more palatable, or more packageable for human food. Work in these fields has been spectacularly successful, raising the spectre of a world re-crafted, as if by Frankenstein or Dr Moreau. Humans have warped evolution in the past: by inventing agriculture (see p. 78) and shifting biota around the planet (p. 197). They now have the power to make their biggest intervention yet, selecting 'unnaturally' not according to what is best adapted to its environment, but according to what best matches agendas of human devising. We know, for example, that there is a market for 'designer babies'. Sperm banks already cash in. Well-intentioned robo-obstetrics modifies babies to order in cases where genetically transmitted diseases can be prevented. It is most unusual for technologies, once devised, to be unapplied. Some societies (and some individuals elsewhere) will engineer human beings along the lines that eugenics prescribed in former times (see p. 324). Morally dubious visionaries are already talking about a world from which disease and deviancy have been excised.[52]

Genetics embraced a paradox: everyone's nature is innate; yet it can be manipulated. So was Kant wrong when he uttered a dictum that had traditionally attracted a lot of emotional investment in the West: 'there is in man a power of self-determination, independent of any bodily coercion'? Without such a conviction, individualism would be untenable. Determinism would make Christianity superannuated. Systems of laws based on individual responsibility would crumble. Of course, the world was already familiar with determinist ideas that tied character and chained potential to inescapably fatal inheritances. Craniology, for instance, assigned individuals to 'criminal' classes and 'low' races by measuring skulls and making inferences about brain size (see p. 325). Nineteenth-century judgements about relative intelligence, in consequence, were unreliable. In 1905, however, searching for a way of identifying children with learning problems, Alfred Binet proposed a new method: simple, neutral tests designed not to establish what children know but to reveal how much they are capable of learning. Within a few years, the concept of IQ – age-related measurable 'general intelligence' – came to command universal confidence. The confidence was probably misplaced: intelligence tests in practice only predicted proficiency in a narrow range of skills. I can recall outstanding students of mine who were not particularly good at them. Yet IQ became a new source of tyranny. By the time of the outbreak of the First World War, policymakers used it, inter alia, to justify eugenics, exclude immigrants from the United States, and select promotion candidates in the US Army. It became developed countries' standard method of social differentiation, singling out the beneficiaries of accelerated or privileged education. The tests could never be fully objective, nor the results reliable; yet, even in the second half of the century, when critics began to point out the problems, educational psychologists preferred to tinker with the idea rather than jettison it.

The problem of IQ blended with one of the century's most politically charged scientific controversies: the 'nature versus nurture' debate, which pitted right against left. In the latter camp were those who thought that social change can affect our moral qualities and collective achievements for the better. Their opponents appealed to evidence that character and capability are largely inherited and therefore unadjustable by social engineering. Partisans of social radicalism contended with conservatives who were reluctant to make things worse by ill-considered attempts at improvement. Although the IQ evidence was highly unconvincing, rival reports exacerbated debate in the late 1960s. Arthur Jensen at Berkeley claimed that eighty per cent of intelligence is inherited, and, incidentally, that blacks are genetically inferior to whites. Christopher Jencks and others at Harvard used similar IQ statistics to argue that heredity plays a minimal role. The contest raged unchanged, supported by the same sort of data, in the 1990s, when Richard J. Herrnstein and Charles Murray exploded a sociological bombshell. In *The Bell Curve*, they argued that a hereditary cognitive elite rules a doomed underclass (in which blacks are disproportionately represented). They predicted a future of cognitive class conflict.

Meanwhile, sociobiology, a 'new synthesis' devised by the ingenious Harvard entomologist Edward O. Wilson, exacerbated debate. Wilson rapidly created a scientific constituency for the view that evolutionary necessities determine differences between societies, which can therefore be ranked accordingly, rather as we speak of orders of creation as relatively 'higher' or 'lower' on the evolutionary scale.[53] Zoologists and ethologists often extrapolate to humans from whatever other species they study. Chimpanzees and other primates suit the purpose because they are closely related to humans in evolutionary terms. The remoter the kinship between species, however, the less availing the method. Konrad Lorenz, the most influential of Wilson's predecessors, modelled his understanding of humans on his studies of gulls and geese. Before and during the Second World War he inspired a generation of research into the evolutionary background of violence. He found that in competition for food and sex the birds he worked with were determinedly and increasingly aggressive. He suspected that in humans, too, violent instincts would overpower contrary tendencies. Enthusiasm for Nazism tainted Lorenz. Academic critics disputed the data he selected. Yet he won a Nobel Prize, and exercised enormous influence, especially when his major work became widely available in English in the 1960s.

Whereas Lorenz invoked gulls and geese, ants and bees were Wilson's exemplars. Humans differ from insects, according to Wilson, mainly in being individually competitive, whereas ants and bees are more deeply social: they function for collective advantage. He often insisted that biological and environmental constraints did not detract from human freedom, but his books seemed bound in iron, with little spinal flexibility, and his papers close-printed without space for freedom between the lines. He imagined a visitor from another planet cataloguing humans along with all the other species on Earth and shrinking 'the humanities and social sciences to specialized branches of biology'.[54]

The human–ant comparison led Wilson to think that 'flexibility', as he called it, or variation between human cultures, results from individual differences in behaviour 'magnified at the group level' as interactions multiply. His suggestion seemed promising: the cultural diversity that intercommunicating groups exhibit is related to their size and numbers, and the range of the exchanges that take place between them. Wilson erred, however, in supposing that the genetic transmissions cause cultural change. He was responding to the latest data of his day. By the time he wrote his most influential text, *Sociobiology*, in 1975, researchers had already discovered or confidently postulated genes for introversion, neurosis, athleticism, psychosis, and numerous other human variables. Wilson inferred a further theoretical possibility, although there was and is no direct evidence for it: that evolution 'strongly selected' genes for social flexibility, too.[55]

In the decades that followed Wilson's intervention, most new empirical evidence supported two modifications of his view: first, genes influence behaviour only in unpredictably various combinations, and in subtle and complex ways, involving contingencies that elude easy pattern detection. Second, behaviour in turn influences genes. Acquired characteristics can be transmitted hereditarily. Mother rats' neglect, for instance, causes a genetic modification in their offspring, who become jittery, irritating adults, whereas nurturing mothers' infants develop calm characteristics in the same way. From debates about sociobiology, two fundamental convictions have survived in most people's minds: that individuals make themselves, and that society is worth improving. Nevertheless, suspicion abides that genes perpetuate differences between individuals and societies and make equality an undeliverable ideal. The effect has been to inhibit reform and encourage the prevailing conservatism of the early twenty-first century.[56]

For a while, the work of Noam Chomsky seemed to support the fight-back for the retrieval of certainty. He was radical in politics and linguistics alike. From the mid-1950s onward, Chomsky argued persistently that language was more than an effect of culture: it was a deep-rooted property of the human mind. His starting point was the speed and ease with which children learn to speak. 'Children', he noticed, 'learn language from positive evidence only (corrections not being required or relevant), and ... without relevant experience in a wide array of complex cases.'[57] Their ability to combine words in ways they have never heard impressed Chomsky. Differences among languages, he thought, seem superficial compared with the 'deep structures' that all share: parts of speech and the grammar and syntax that regulate the way terms relate to each other. Chomsky explained these remarkable observations by postulating that language and brain are linked: the structures of language are innately imbedded in the way we think; so it is easy to learn to speak; one can genuinely say that 'it comes naturally'. The suggestion was revolutionary when Chomsky made it in 1957, because the prevailing orthodoxies at the time suggested otherwise. We reviewed them in chapter 9: Freud's psychiatry, Sartre's philosophy, and Piaget's educational nostrums all suppose that upbringing is inscribed on a *tabula rasa*. Behaviourism endorsed a similar notion – the doctrine, fashionable until Chomsky exploded it, that we learn to act, speak, and think as we do because of conditioning: we respond to stimuli, in the form of social approval or disapproval. The language faculty Chomsky identified was, at least according to his early musings, beyond the reach of evolution. He jibbed at calling it an instinct and declined to offer an evolutionary account of it. If the way he formulated his thinking was right, neither experience nor heredity makes us the whole of what we are, nor do both in combination. Part of our nature is hard-wired into our brains. Chomsky went on to propose that other kinds of learning may be like language in these respects: 'that the same is true in other areas where humans are capable of acquiring rich and highly articulated systems of knowledge under the triggering and shaping effects of experience, and it may well be that similar ideas are relevant for the investigation of how we acquire scientific knowledge ... because of our mental constitution'.[58]

Chomsky rejected the notion that humans devised language to make up for our dearth of evolved skills – the argument that 'the richness and specificity of instinct of animals ... accounts for their remarkable achievements in some domains and lack of ability in others ... whereas humans, lacking such ... instinctual structure, are free to think, speak and discover'. Rather, he thought, the language prowess on which we tend to congratulate ourselves as a species, and which some people even claim as a uniquely human achievement, may simply resemble the peculiar skills of other species. Cheetahs are specialists in speed, for instance, cows in ruminating, and humans in symbolic communication.[59]

Dogmatism Versus Pluralism

I love uncertainty. Caution, scepticism, self-doubt, tentativeness: these are the toeholds we grope for on the ascent to truth. It is when people are sure of themselves that I get worried. False certainty is far worse than uncertainty. The latter, however, breeds the former.

In twentieth-century social and political thought, new dogmatisms complemented the new determinisms of science. Change may be good. It is always dangerous. In reaction against uncertainty, electorates succumb to noisy little men and glib solutions. Religions transmute into dogmatisms and fundamentalisms. The herd turns on agents of supposed change, especially – typically – on immigrants and on international institutions. Cruel, costly wars start out of fear of depleted resources. These are all extreme, generally violent, always risky forms of change, embraced for conservative reasons, in order to cleave to familiar ways of life. Even the revolutions of recent times are often depressingly nostalgic, seeking a golden and usually mythical age of equality or morality or harmony or peace or greatness or ecological balance. The most effective revolutionaries of the twentieth century called for a return to primitive communism or anarchism, or to the medieval glories of Islam, or to apostolic virtue, or to the apple-cheeked innocence of an era before industrialization.

Religion had a surprising role. For much of the twentieth century, secular prophets foretold its death. Material prosperity, they argued, would satiate the needy with alternatives to God. Education would wean the ignorant from thinking about Him. Scientific explanations of the cosmos would make God redundant. But after the failure of politics and the disillusionments of science, religion remained, ripe for revival, for anyone who wanted the universe to be coherent and comfortable to live in. By the end of the century, atheism was no longer the world's most conspicuous trend. Fundamentalisms in Islam and Christianity, taken together, constituted the biggest movement in the world and potentially the most dangerous. No one should find this surprising: fundamentalism, like scientism and brash political ideologies, was part of the twentieth-century reaction against uncertainty – one of the false certainties people preferred.

Fundamentalism began, as we have seen, in Protestant seminaries in Chicago and Princeton, in revulsion from German academic fashions in critical reading of the Bible. Like other books, the Bible reflects the times in which the books it comprises were written and assembled. The agendas of the authors (or, if you prefer to call them so, the human mediators of divine authorship) and editors warp the text. Yet fundamentalists read it as if the message were uncluttered with historical context and human error, winkling out interpretations they mistake for unchallengeable truths. The faith is founded on the text. No critical exegesis can deconstruct it. No scientific evidence can gainsay it. Any supposedly holy scripture can and usually does attract literal-minded dogmatism. The name of fundamentalism is transferable: though it started in biblical circles, it is now associated with a similar doctrine, traditional in Islam, about the Qur'an.

Fundamentalism is modern: recent in origin, even more recent in appeal. Counterintuitive as these assertions may seem, it is not hard to see why fundamentalism arose and throve in the modern world and has never lost its appeal. According to Karen Armstrong, one of the foremost authorities on the subject, it is also scientific, at least in aspiration, because it treats religion as reducible to matters of incontrovertible fact.[60] It is charmless and humdrum – religion stripped of the enchantment. It represents modernity, imitates science, and reflects fear: fundamentalists express fear of the end of the world, of 'Great Satans' and 'Antichrists', of chaos, of the unfamiliar, and above all of secularism.

Though they belong in different traditions, their shared excesses make them recognizable: militancy, hostility to pluralism, and a determination to confuse politics with religion. Militants among them declare war on society. Yet most fundamentalists are nice, ordinary people who make do with the wicked world and, like most of the rest of us, leave religion at the door of their church or mosque.

Nonetheless, fundamentalism is pernicious. Doubt is a necessary part of any deep faith. 'Lord, help my unbelief' is a prayer every intellectual Christian should take from St Anselm. Anyone who denies doubt should hear the cock crow thrice. Reason is a divine gift; to suppress it – as the eighteenth-century Muggletonian Protestants did in the belief that it is a diabolical trap – is a kind of intellectual self-amputation. Fundamentalism, which demands a closed mind and the suspension of critical faculties, therefore seems irreligious to me. Protestant fundamentalism embraces an obvious falsehood: that the Bible is unmediated by human hands and weaknesses. Fundamentalists who read justifications of violence, terrorism, and bloodily enforced moral and intellectual conformity in their Bible or Qur'an wantonly misconstrue their own sacred texts. There are fundamentalist sects whose ethic of obedience, paranoid habits, crushing effects on individual identity, and campaigns of hatred or violence against supposed enemies recall early fascist cells. If and when they get power, they make life miserable for everybody else. Meanwhile, they hunt witches, burn books, and spread terror.[61]

Fundamentalism undervalues variety. An equal and opposite response to uncertainty is religious pluralism, which had a similar, century-long story in the twentieth century. Swami Vivekananda, the great spokesman of Hinduism and apostle of religious pluralism, uttered the call before he died in 1902, when the collapse of certainty was still unpredictable. He extolled the wisdom of all religions and recommended 'many ways to one truth'. The method has obvious advantage over relativism: it encourages diversification of experience – which is how we learn and grow. It overtrumps relativism in its appeal to a multicultural, pluralistic world. For people committed to a particular religion, it represents a fatal concession to secularism: if there is no reason to prefer one religion over the others, why should purely secular philosophies not be equally good ways to follow? On the ride along the multi-faith rainbow, why not add more gradations of colour?[62]

Where religions dominate, they become triumphalist. In retreat, they perceive the advantages of ecumenism. Where they rule, they may persecute; where they are persecuted they clamour for toleration. After losing nineteenth-century struggles against secularism (see p. 328) rival Christian communions began to evince desire for 'wide ecumenism', bringing together people of all faiths. The Edinburgh Conference of 1910, which attempted to get Protestant missionary societies to co-operate, launched the summons. The Catholic Church remained aloof even from Christian ecumenism until the 1960s, when shrinking congregations induced a mood of reform. In the late twentieth century, extraordinary 'holy alliances' confronted irreligious values, with Catholics, Southern Baptists, and Muslims, for instance, joining forces to oppose relaxation of abortion laws in the United States, or collaborating in attempts to influence the World Health Organization policy on birth control. Interfaith organizations worked together to promote human rights and restrain genetic engineering. Ill-differentiated faith opened new political niches for public figures willing to speak for religion or bid for religious voters. US President Ronald Reagan, unaware, it seems, of the self-undermining nature of his recommendation, urged his audience to have a religion, but thought it did not matter which. The Prince of Wales proposed himself in the role of 'Defender of Faith' in multicultural Britain.

Religious pluralism has an impressive recent past. But can it be sustained? The scandal of religious hatreds and mutual violence, which so disfigured the past of religions, appears conquerable. With every inch of common ground religions find between them, however, the ground of their claims to unique value shrinks.[63] To judge from events so far in the twenty-first century, intrafaith hatreds are more powerful than interfaith love-ins. Shiite and Sunni dogmatists massacre each other. Liberal Catholics seem on most social questions to have more in common with secular humanists than with their ultramontane coreligionists or with conservative Protestants. Muslims are the victims of a Buddhist *jihad* in Myanmar. Christians face extermination or expulsion by Daeshist fanatics in parts of Syria and Iraq. Wars of religion keep spreading ruin and scattering ban, like Elizabeth Barrett Browning's cack-hoofed god, to the bafflement of the secular gravediggers who thought they had buried the gods of bloodlust long ago.

Religious pluralism has secular counterparts, with similarly long histories. Even before Franz Boas and his students began accumulating evidence for cultural relativism, early signs of a possible pluralist future emerged in a place formerly outside the mainstream. Cuba seemed behind the times for most of the nineteenth century: slavery lingered there. Independence was often proposed and always postponed. But with Yankee help the revolutionaries of 1898 finally cracked the Spanish Empire and resisted US takeover. In newly sovereign Cuba, intellectuals faced the problem of extracting a nation out of diverse traditions, ethnicities, and pigments. Scholarship – first by the white sociologist Fernando Ortiz, then, increasingly, by blacks – treated black cultures on terms of equality with white. Ortiz began to appreciate blacks' contribution to the making of his country when he interviewed prison internees in an attempt to profile criminals. Coincidentally, as we have seen, in the United States and Europe, white musicians discovered jazz and white artists began to esteem and imitate 'tribal' art. In French West Africa in the 1930s, 'Négritude' found brilliant spokesmen in Aimé Césaire and Léon Damas. The conviction grew and spread that blacks were the equals of whites – maybe in some ways their superiors or, at least, predecessors – in all the areas of achievement traditionally prized in the West. The discovery of black genius stimulated independence movements for colonized regions. Civil rights campaigners suffered and strengthened in South Africa and the United States, where blacks were still denied equality under the law, and wherever racial prejudice and residual forms of social discrimination persisted.[64]

In a world where no single system of values could command universal reverence, universal claims to supremacy crumbled. The retreat of white empires from Africa in the late 1950s and 1960s was the most conspicuous result. Archaeology and palaeoanthropology adjusted to postcolonial priorities, unearthing reasons for rethinking world history. Tradition had placed Eden – the birthplace of humankind – at the eastern extremity of Asia. There was nowhere east of Eden. By placing the earliest identifiably human fossils in China and Java, early-twentieth-century science seemed to confirm this risky assumption. But it was wrong. In 1959, Louis and Mary Leakey found remains of a tool-making, manlike creature 1.75 million years old in Olduvai Gorge in Kenya. Their find encouraged Robert Ardrey in a daring idea: humankind evolved uniquely in East Africa and spread from there to the rest of the world. More Kenyan and Tanzanian ancestors appeared. The big-brained *Homo habilis* emerged in the early 1960s. In 1984 a skeleton of a later hominid, *Homo erectus*, showed that hominids of a million years ago had bodies so like those of modern people that one might hardly blink to share a bench or a bus-ride with a million-year-old revenant. Even more humbling was the excavation Donald Johanson made in Ethiopia in 1974: he called his three-million-year-old bipedal hominid 'Lucy' in allusion to a currently popular song in praise of 'Lucy in the Sky with Diamonds' – lysergic acid, which induced cheap hallucinations: that is how mind-bending the discovery seemed at the time. The following year basalt tools two and a half million years old turned up nearby. Footprints of bipedal hominids, dating back 3.7 million years, followed in 1977. Archaeology seemed to vindicate Ardrey's theory. While Europeans retreated from Africa, Africans edged Eurocentrism out of history.

Most nineteenth-century theorists favoured 'unitary' states, with one religion, ethnicity, and identity. In the aftermath of imperialism, however, multiculturalism was essential for peace. Redrawn frontiers, uncontainable migrations, and proliferating religions made uniformity unattainable. Superannuated racism made homogenizing projects practically unrealizable and morally indefensible. States that still strove for ethnic purity or cultural consistency faced traumatic periods of 'ethnic cleansing' – the standard late-twentieth-century euphemism for trails of tears and pitiless massacre. Meanwhile, rival ideologies competed in democracies, where the only way of keeping peace between them was political pluralism – admitting parties with potentially irreconcilable views to the political arena on equal terms.

Large empires have always encompassed different peoples with contrasting ways of life. Usually, however, each has had a dominant culture, alongside which others are tolerated. In the twentieth century, mere toleration would no longer be enough. Enmity feeds dogmatism: you can only insist on the unique veracity of your opinions if an adversary disputes them. If you want to rally adherents for irrational claims, you need a foe to revile and fear. But in a multi-civilizational world, composed of multicultural societies, shaped by massive migrations and intense exchanges of culture, enmity is increasingly unaffordable. We need an idea that will yield peace and generate co-operation. We need pluralism.

In philosophy, pluralism means the doctrine that monism and dualism (see pp. 90, 96) cannot encompass reality. This claim, well documented in antiquity, has helped to inspire a modern conviction: that a single society or a single state can accommodate, on terms of equality, a plurality of cultures – religions, languages, ethnicities, communal identities, versions of history, value systems. The idea grew up gradually. Real experience instanced it before anyone expressed it: almost every big conquest-state and empire of antiquity, from Sargon's onward, exemplified it. The best formulation of it is usually attributed to Isaiah Berlin, one of the many nomadic intellectuals whom twentieth-century turbulence scattered across the universities of the world – in his case from his native Latvia to an honoured place in Oxford common rooms and London clubs. 'There is', he explained,

> a plurality of values which men can and do seek, and ... these values differ. There is not an infinity of them: the number of human values, of values that I can pursue while maintaining my human semblance, my human character, is finite – let us say 74, or perhaps 122, or 26, but finite, whatever it may be. And the difference it makes is that if a man pursues one of these values, I, who do not, am able to understand why he pursues it or what it would be like, in his circumstances, for me to be induced to pursue it. Hence the possibility of human understanding.

This way of looking at the world differs from cultural relativism: pluralism does not, for instance, have to accommodate obnoxious behaviour, or false claims, or particular cults or creeds that one might find distasteful: one might exclude Nazism, say, or cannibalism. Pluralism does not proscribe comparisons of value: it allows for peaceful argument about which culture, if any, is best. It claims, in Berlin's words, 'that the multiple values are objective, part of the essence of humanity rather than arbitrary creations of men's subjective fancies'. It helps make multicultural societies conceivable and viable. 'I can enter into a value system which is not my own', Berlin believed. 'For all human beings must have some common values ... and also some different values.'[65]

Ironically, pluralism has to accommodate anti-pluralism, which still abounds. In revulsion from multiculturalism in the early years of the twenty-first century, policies of 'cultural integration' attracted votes in Western countries, where globalization and other huge, agglutinative processes made most historic communities defensive about their own cultures. Persuading neighbours of contrasting cultures to coexist peacefully got harder everywhere. Plural states seemed fissile: some split violently, like Serbia, Sudan, and Indonesia. Others experienced peaceful divorces, like the Czech Republic and Slovakia, or renegotiated the terms of cohabitation, like Scotland in the United Kingdom or Catalonia and Euzkadi in Spain. Still, the idea of pluralism endured, because it promises the only practical future for a diverse world. It is the only truly uniform interest that all the world's peoples have in common. Paradoxically, perhaps, pluralism is the one doctrine that can unite us.[66]

Prospect

The End of Ideas?

Memory, imagination, and communication – the faculties that generated all the ideas covered in the book so far – are changing under the impact of robotics, genetics, and virtual socialization. Will our unprecedented experience provoke or facilitate new ways of thinking and new thoughts? Will it impede or extinguish them?

I am afraid that some readers may have started this book optimistically, expecting the story to be progressive and the ideas all to be good. The story has not borne such expectations out. Some of the findings that have unfolded, chapter by chapter, are morally neutral: that minds matter, that ideas are the driving force of history (not environment or economics or demography, though they all condition what happens in our minds); that ideas, like works of art, are products of imagination. Other conclusions subvert progressive illusions: a lot of good ideas are very old and bad ones very new; ideas are effective not because of their merits, but because of circumstances that make them communicable and attractive; truths are less potent than falsehoods people believe; the ideas that come out of our minds can make us seem out of our minds.

God protect me from the imps of optimism, whose tortures are subtler and more insidious than the predictable miseries of pessimism. Optimism is almost always a traitress. Pessimism indemnifies you against disappointment. Many, perhaps most, ideas are evil or delusive or both. One reason why there are so many ideas to tell of in this book is that every idea successfully applied has unforeseen consequences that are often malign and require more thinking in response. The web creates cyber-ghettoes in which the like-minded shut out or 'unfriend' opinions other than their own: if the habit spreads far enough, it will cut users off from dialogue, debate, and disputation – the precious sources of intellectual progress. The biggest optimists are so deeply self-traduced as to defy satire, imagining a future in which humans have genetically engineered themselves into immortality, or download consciousness into inorganic machines to protect our minds from bodily decay, or zoom through wormholes in space to colonize worlds we have, as yet, had no chance to despoil or render uninhabitable.[1]

Still, some pessimism is excessive. According to the eminent neuroscientist Susan Greenfield, the prospects for the future of the human mind are bleak. 'Personalization', she says, converts brain into mind. It depends on memories uneroded by technology and experience unimpeded by virtuality. Without memories to sustain our narratives of our lives and real experiences to shape them, we shall stop thinking in the traditional sense of the word and re-inhabit a 'reptilian' phase of evolution.[2] Plato's character Thamus expected similar effects from the new technology of his time (see p. 97). His predictions proved premature. Greenfield is, perhaps, right in theory, but, on current showing, no machine is likely to usurp our humanity.

Artificial intelligence is not intelligent enough or, more exactly, not imaginative enough or creative enough to make us resign thinking. Tests for artificial intelligence are not rigorous enough. It does not take intelligence to meet the Turing test – impersonating a human interlocutor – or win a game of chess or general knowledge. You will know that intelligence is artificial only when your sexbot says, 'No.' Virtual reality is too shallow and crude to make many of us abandon the real thing. Genetic modification is potentially powerful enough – under a sufficiently malign and despotic elite – to create a lumpen race of slaves or drones with all critical faculties excised. But it is hard to see why anyone should desire such a development, outside the pages of apocalyptic sci-fi, or to expect the conditions to be fulfilled. In any case, a cognitive master class would still be around to do the pleb's thinking for it.

So, for good and ill, we shall go on having new thoughts, crafting new ideas, devising innovative applications. I can envisage, however, an end to the acceleration characteristic of the new thinking of recent times. If my argument is right, and ideas multiply in times of intense cultural interchange, whereas isolation breeds intellectual inertia, then we can expect the rate of new thinking to slacken if exchanges diminish. Paradoxically, one of the effects of globalization will be diminished exchange, because in a perfectly globalized world, cultural interchange will erode difference and make all cultures increasingly like each other. By the late twentieth century, globalization was so intense that it was almost impossible for any community to opt out: even resolutely self-isolated groups in the depths of the Amazon rainforest found it hard to elude contact or withdraw from the influence of the rest of the world once contact was made. The consequences included the emergence of global culture – more or less modelled on the United States and Western Europe, with people everywhere wearing the same clothes, consuming the same goods, practising the same politics, listening to the same music, admiring the same images, playing the same games, crafting and discarding the same relationships, and speaking or trying to speak the same language. Of course, global culture has not displaced diversity. It is like a beekeeper's mesh, under which a lot of culture pullulates. Every agglutinative episode provokes reactions, with people reaching for the comfort of tradition and trying to conserve or revive threatened or vanished lifeways. But over the long term, globalization does and will encourage convergence. Languages and dialects disappear or become subjects of conservation policies, like endangered species. Traditional dress and arts retreat to margins and museums. Religions expire. Local customs and antiquated values die or survive as tourist attractions.

The trend is conspicuous because it represents the reversal of the human story so far. Imagine the creature I call the galactic museum-keeper of the future, contemplating our past, long after our extinction, from an immense distance of space and time, with objectivity inaccessible to us, who are enmeshed in our own story. As she arranges in her virtual vitrine what little survives of our world, ask her to summarize our history. Her reply will be brief, because her museum is galactic, and a short-lived species on a minor planet will be too unimportant to encourage loquacity. I can hear her say, 'You are interesting only because your history was of divergence. Other cultural animals on your planet achieved little diversity. Their cultures occupied a modest range of difference from one another. They changed only a little over time. You, however, churned out and turned over new ways of behaving – including mental behaviour – with stunning diversity and rapidity.' At least, we did so until the twenty-first century, when our cultures stopped getting more unlike each other and became dramatically, overwhelmingly convergent. Sooner or later, on present showing, we shall have only one worldwide culture. So we shall have no one to exchange and interact with. We shall be alone in the universe – unless and until we find other cultures in other galaxies and resume productive exchange. The result will not be the end of ideas, but rather a return to normal rates of innovative thinking, like, say, those of the thinkers in chapter 1 or 2 of this book, who struggled with isolation, and whose thoughts were relatively few and relatively good.

Notes

CHAPTER 1 *Mind Out of Matter: The Mainspring of Ideas*

1. B. Hare and V. Woods, *The Genius of Dogs* (New York: Dutton, 2013), p. xiii.
2. Ch. Adam and P. Tannery, eds, *Oeuvres de Descartes* (Paris: Cerf, 1897–1913), v, p. 277; viii, p. 15.
3. N. Chomsky, *Aspects of the Theory of Syntax* (Cambridge, MA: MIT Press, 1965), pp. 26–7.
4. F. Dostoevsky, *Notes from Underground* (New York: Open Road, 2014), p. 50.
5. A. Fuentes, *The Creative Spark: How Imagination Made Humans Exceptional* (New York: Dutton, 2017); T. Matsuzawa, 'What is uniquely human? A view from comparative cognitive development in humans and chimpanzees', in F. B. M. de Waal and P. F. Ferrari, eds, *The Primate Mind: Built to Connect with Other Minds* (Cambridge, MA: Harvard University Press, 2012), pp. 288–305.
6. G. Miller, *The Mating Mind: How Sexual Choice Shaped the Evolution of Human Behaviour* (London: Heinemann, 2000); G. Miller, 'Evolution of human music through sexual selection', in N. Wallin et al., eds, *The Origins of Music* (Cambridge, MA: MIT Press, 1999), pp. 329–60.
7. M. R. Bennett and P. M. S. Hacker, *Philosophical Foundations of Neuroscience* (Oxford: Blackwell, 2003); P. Hacker, 'Languages, minds and brains', in C. Blakemore and S. Greenfield, eds, *Mindwaves: Thoughts on Identity, Mind and Consciousness* (Chichester: Wiley, 1987), pp. 485–505.
8. This once fashionable faith now seems nearly extinct. I refer those who retain it to my *A Foot in the River* (Oxford: Oxford University Press, 2015), pp. 90–3 and the references given there, or R. Tallis, *Aping Mankind: Neuromania, Darwinitis and the Misrepresentation of Humanity* (Durham: Acumen, 2011), pp. 163–70.
9. I proposed this account briefly in a few pages of a previous book, *A Foot in the River*. Much of the rest of this chapter goes over the same ground, with updating and reformulation.

10. R. L. Holloway, 'The evolution of the primate brain: some aspects of quantitative relationships', *Brain Research*, vii (1968), pp. 121–72; R. L. Holloway, 'Brain size, allometry and reorganization: a synthesis', in M. E. Hahn, B. C. Dudek, and C. Jensen, eds, *Development and Evolution of Brain Size* (New York: Academic Press, 1979), pp. 59–88.
11. S. Healy and C. Rowe, 'A critique of comparative studies of brain size', *Proceedings of the Royal Society*, cclxxiv (2007), pp. 453–64.
12. C. Agulhon et al., 'What is the role of astrocyte calcium in neurophysiology?', *Neuron*, lix (2008), pp. 932–46; K. Smith, 'Neuroscience: settling the great glia debate', *Nature*, ccccIxviii (2010), pp. 150–62.
13. P. R. Manger et al., 'The mass of the human brain: is it a spandrel?', in S. Reynolds and A. Gallagher, eds, *African Genesis: Perspectives on Hominin Evolution* (Cambridge: Cambridge University Press, 2012), pp. 205–22.
14. T. Grantham and S. Nichols, 'Evolutionary psychology: ultimate explanation and Panglossian predictions', in V. Hardcastle, ed., *Where Biology Meets Psychology: Philosophical Essays* (Cambridge, MA: MIT Press, 1999), pp. 47–88.
15. C. Darwin, *Autobiographies* (London: Penguin, 2002), p. 50.
16. A. R. DeCasien, S. A. Williams, and J. P. Higham, 'Primate brain size is predicted by diet but not sociality', *Nature, Ecology, and Evolution*, i (2017), https://www.nature.com/articles/s41559-017-0112 (accessed 27 May 2017).
17. S. Shultz and R. I. M. Dunbar, 'The evolution of the social brain: anthropoid primates contrast with other vertebrates', *Proceedings of the Royal Society*, cclxxic (2007), pp. 453–64.
18. F. Fernández-Armesto, *Civilizations: Culture, Ambition, and the Transformation of Nature* (New York: Free Press, 2001).
19. V. S. Ramachandran, *The Tell-tale Brain* (London: Random House, 2012), p. 4.
20. M. Tomasello and H. Rakoczy, 'What makes human cognition unique? From individual to shared to collective intentionality', *Mind and Language*, xviii (2003), pp. 121–47; P. Carruthers, 'Metacognition in animals: a sceptical look', *Mind and Language*, xxiii (2008), pp. 58–89.
21. W. A. Roberts, 'Introduction: cognitive time travel in people and animals', *Learning and Motivation*, xxxvi (2005), pp. 107–9; T. Suddendorf and M. Corballis, 'The evolution of foresight: what is mental time travel and is it uniquely human?', *Behavioral and Brain Sciences*, xxx (2007), pp. 299–313.
22. N. Dickinson and N. S. Clayton, 'Retrospective cognition by food-caching western scrub-jays', *Learning and Motivation*, xxxvi (2005), pp. 159–76; H. Eichenbaum et al., 'Episodic recollection in animals: "if it walks like a duck and quacks like a duck ..."', *Learning and Motivation*, xxxvi (2005), pp. 190–207.
23. C. D. L. Wynne, *Do Animals Think?* (Princeton and Oxford: Princeton University Press, 2004), p. 230.

24. C. R. Menzel, 'Progress in the study of chimpanzee recall and episodic memory', in H. S. Terrace and J. Metcalfe, eds, *The Missing Link in Cognition: Origins of Self-Reflective Consciousness* (Oxford: Oxford University Press, 2005), pp. 188–224.
25. B. P. Trivedi, 'Scientists rethinking nature of animal memory', *National Geographic Today*, 22 August 2003; C. R. and E. W. Menzil, 'Enquiries concerning chimpanzee understanding', in de Waal and Ferrari, eds, *The Primate Mind*, pp. 265–87.
26. J. Taylor, *Not a Chimp: The Hunt to Find the Genes that Make Us Human* (Oxford: Oxford University Press, 2009), p. 11; S. Inoue and T. Matsuzawa, 'Working memory of numerals in chimpanzees', *Current Biology*, xvii (2007), pp. 1004–5.
27. A. Silberberg and D. Kearns, 'Memory for the order of briefly presented numerals in humans as a function of practice', *Animal Cognition*, xii (2009), pp. 405–7.
28. B. L. Schwartz et al., 'Episodic-like memory in a gorilla: a review and new findings', *Learning and Motivation*, xxxvi (2005), pp. 226–44.
29. Trivedi, 'Scientists rethinking nature of animal memory'.
30. G. Martin-Ordas et al., 'Keeping track of time: evidence of episodic-like memory in great apes', *Animal Cognition*, xiii (2010), pp. 331–40; G. Martin-Ordas, C. Atance, and A. Louw, 'The role of episodic and semantic memory in episodic foresight', *Learning and Motivation*, xliii (2012), pp. 209–19.
31. C. F. Martin et al., 'Chimpanzee choice rates in competitive games match equilibrium game theory predictions', *Scientific Reports*, 4, article no. 5182, doi:10.1038/srep05182.
32. F. Yates, *The Art of Memory* (Chicago: University of Chicago Press, 1966), pp. 26–31.
33. K. Danziger, *Marking the Mind: A History of Memory* (Cambridge: Cambridge University Press, 2008), pp. 188–97.
34. D. R. Schacter, *The Seven Sins of Memory* (Boston: Houghton Mifflin, 2001).
35. R. Arp, *Scenario Visualization: An Evolutionary Account of Creative Problem Solving* (Cambridge, MA: MIT Press, 2008).
36. A. W. Crosby, *Throwing Fire: Missile Projection through History* (Cambridge: Cambridge University Press, 2002), p. 30.
37. S. Coren, *How Dogs Think* (New York: Free Press, 2005), p. 11; S. Coren, *Do Dogs Dream? Nearly Everything Your Dog Wants You to Know* (New York: Norton, 2012).
38. P. F. Ferrari and L. Fogassi, 'The mirror neuron system in monkeys and its implications for social cognitive function', in de Waal and Ferrari, eds, *The Primate Mind*, pp. 13–31.
39. M. Gurven et al., 'Food transfers among Hiwi foragers of Venezuela: tests of reciprocity', *Human Ecology*, xxviii (2000), pp. 175–218.

40. H. Kaplan et al., 'The evolution of intelligence and the human life history', *Evolutionary Anthropology*, ix (2000), pp. 156–84; R. Walker et al., 'Age dependency and hunting ability among the Ache of Eastern Paraguay', *Journal of Human Evolution*, xlii (2002), pp. 639–57, at pp. 653–5.
41. J. Bronowski, *The Visionary Eye* (Cambridge, MA: MIT Press, 1978), p. 9.
42. G. Deutscher, *Through the Language Glass: Why the World Looks Different in Other Languages* (New York: Metropolitan, 2010); S. Pinker, *The Language Instinct* (London: Penguin, 1995), pp. 57–63.
43. E. Spelke and S. Hespos, 'Conceptual precursors to language', *Nature*, ccccxxx (2004), pp. 453–6.
44. U. Eco, *Serendipities: Language and Lunacy* (New York: Columbia University Press, 1998), p. 22.
45. T. Maruhashi, 'Feeding behaviour and diet of the Japanese monkey (*Macaca fuscata yakui*) on Yakushima island, Japan', *Primates*, xxi (1980), pp. 141–60.
46. J. T. Bonner, *The Evolution of Culture in Animals* (Princeton: Princeton University Press, 1989), pp. 72–8.
47. F. de Waal, *Chimpanzee Politics* (Baltimore: Johns Hopkins University Press, 2003), p. 19.
48. J. Goodall, *In the Shadow of Man* (Boston: Houghton Mifflin, 1971), pp. 112–14.
49. J. Goodall, *The Chimpanzees of Gombe: Patterns of Behaviour* (Cambridge, MA: Harvard University Press, 1986), pp. 424–9.
50. R. M. Sapolsky and L. J. Share, 'A Pacific culture among wild baboons: its emergence and transmission', *PLOS*, 13 April 2004, doi:10.1371/journal.pbio.0020106.

CHAPTER 2 *Gathering Thoughts: Thinking Before Agriculture*

1. R. Leakey and R. Lewin, *Origins Reconsidered: In Search of What Makes Us Human* (New York: Abacus, 1993); C. Renfrew and E. Zubrow, eds, *The Ancient Mind: Elements of Cognitive Archaeology* (Cambridge: Cambridge University Press, 1994).
2. M. Harris, *Cannibals and Kings* (New York: Random House, 1977).
3. A. Courbin, *Le village des cannibales* (Paris: Aubier, 1990).
4. P. Sanday, *Divine Hunger* (Cambridge: Cambridge University Press, 1986), pp. 59–82.
5. Herodotus, *Histories*, bk 3, ch. 38.
6. B. Conklin, *Consuming Grief: Compassionate Cannibalism in an Amazonian Society* (Austin: University of Texas Press, 2001).
7. L. Pancorbo, *El banquete humano: una historia cultural del canibalismo* (Madrid: Siglo XXI, 2008), p. 47.
8. D. L. Hoffmann et al., 'U-Th dating of carbonate crusts reveals Neanderthal origins of Iberian cave art', *Science*, ccclix (2018), pp. 912–15.

9. D. L. Hoffmann et al., eds, 'Symbolic use of marine shells and mineral pigments by Iberian Neanderthals 115,000 years ago', *Science Advances*, iv (2018), no. 2, doi:10.1126/sciadv.aar5255.
10. C. Stringer and C. Gamble, *In Search of the Neanderthals* (New York: Thames and Hudson, 1993); P. Mellars, *The Neanderthal Legacy* (Princeton: Princeton University Press, 1996); E. Trinkaus and P. Shipman, *The Neanderthals: Changing the Image of Mankind* (New York: Knopf, 1993).
11. C. Gamble, *The Paleolithic Societies of Europe* (Cambridge: Cambridge University Press, 1999), pp. 400–20.
12. I. Kant, *The Groundwork of the Metaphysics of Morals*, [1785] (Cambridge: Cambridge University Press, 2012), and A. MacIntyre, *A Short History of Ethics* (Indianapolis: University of Notre Dame Press, 1998), are fundamental. I. Murdoch, *The Sovereignty of Good* (London: Routledge, 1970), is a study of the problem of whether morals are objective, by a writer whose wonderful novels were all about moral equivocation.
13. C. Jung, *Man and His Symbols* (New York: Doubleday, 1964).
14. W. T. Fitch, *The Evolution of Language* (Cambridge: Cambridge University Press, 2010); S. Pinker and P. Bloom, 'Natural language and natural selection', *Behavioral and Brain Sciences*, xiii (1990), pp. 707–84.
15. J. Goody, *The Domestication of the Savage Mind* (Cambridge: Cambridge University Press, 1977), pp. 3–7.
16. L. Lévy-Bruhl, *Les fonctions mentales dans les sociétés inférieures* (Paris: Presses Universitaires de France, 1910), p. 377.
17. C. Lévi-Strauss, *The Savage Mind* (London: Weidenfeld, 1962); P. Radin, *Primitive Man as Philosopher* (New York: Appleton, 1927).
18. A. Marshack, *The Roots of Civilization* (London: Weidenfeld, 1972).
19. M. Sahlins, *Stone-Age Economics* (Chicago: Aldine-Atherton, 1972).
20. J. Cook, *Ice-Age Art: Arrival of the Modern Mind* (London: British Museum Press, 2013).
21. C. Henshilwood et al., 'A 100,000-year-old ochre-processing workshop at Blombos Cave, South Africa', *Science*, cccxxxiv (2011), pp. 219–22; L. Wadley, 'Cemented ash as a receptacle or work surface for ochre powder production at Sibudu, South Africa, 58,000 years ago', *Journal of Archaeological Science*, xxxvi (2010), pp. 2397–406.
22. Cook, *Ice-Age Art*.
23. For full references, see F. Fernández-Armesto, 'Before the farmers: culture and climate from the emergence of *Homo sapiens* to about ten thousand years ago', in D. Christian, ed., *The Cambridge World History* (Cambridge: Cambridge University Press, 2015), i, pp. 313–38.
24. L. Niven, 'From carcass to cave: large mammal exploitation during the Aurignacian at Vogelherd, Germany', *Journal of Human Evolution*, liii (2007), pp. 362–82.
25. A. Malraux, *La tête d'obsidienne* (Paris: Gallimard, 1971), p. 117.

26. H. G. Bandi, *The Art of the Stone Age* (Baden-Baden: Holler, 1961); S. J. Mithen, *Thoughtful Foragers* (Cambridge: Cambridge University Press, 1990).
27. P. M. S. Hacker, 'An intellectual entertainment: thought and language', *Philosophy*, xcii (2017), pp. 271–96; D. M. Armstrong, *A Materialist Theory of the Mind* (London: Routledge, 1968).
28. 'Brights movement', https://en.wikipedia.org/wiki/Brights_movement (accessed 22 June 2017).
29. D. Diderot, 'Pensées philosophiques', in *Oeuvres complètes*, ed. J. Assézat and M. Tourneur (Paris: Garnier, 1875), i, p. 166.
30. H. Diels and W. Kranz, *Die Fragmente der Vorsokratiker* (Zurich: Weidmann, 1985), Fragment 177; P. Cartledge, *Democritus* (London: Routledge, 1998), p. 40.
31. B. Russell, *The Problems of Philosophy* (New York and London: Henry Holt and Co., 1912), ch. 1.
32. M. Douglas, *The Lele of the Kasai* (London: Oxford University Press, 1963), pp. 210–12.
33. Radin, *Primitive Man as Philosopher*, p. 253.
34. T. Nagel, *Mortal Questions* (Cambridge: Cambridge University Press, 1980).
35. Aristotle, *De Anima*, 411, a7–8.
36. J. D. Lewis-Williams, 'Harnessing the brain: vision and shamanism in Upper Palaeolithic western Europe', in M. W. Conkey et al., eds, *Beyond Art: Pleistocene Image and Symbol* (Berkeley: University of California Press, 1996), pp. 321–42; J. D. Lewis-Williams and J. Clottes, *The Shamans of Prehistory: Trance Magic and the Painted Caves* (New York: Abrams, 1998).
37. Author's translation.
38. R. H. Codrington, *The Melanesians: Studies in Their Anthropology and Folklore* (Oxford: Oxford University Press, 1891), introduced the concept of mana to the world, and M. Mauss, *A General Theory of Magic* (London: Routledge, 1972), originally published in 1902, generalized it.
39. B. Malinowski, *Magic, Science and Religion* (New York: Doubleday, 1954), pp. 19–20.
40. H. Hubert and M. Mauss, *Sacrifice: Its Nature and Function* (Chicago: University of Chicago Press, 1972), pp. 172–4.
41. L. Thorndike, *A History of Magic and Experimental Science*, 8 vols (New York: Columbia University Press, 1958).
42. G. Parrinder, *Witchcraft* (Harmondsworth: Penguin, 1958), is a classic from a psychological point of view; J. C. Baroja, *The World of the Witches* (London: Phoenix, 2001), from that of anthropology, with a salutary emphasis on Europe.
43. E. E. Evans-Pritchard, *Witchcraft, Oracles and Magic among the Azande* (London: Oxford University Press, 1929).
44. B. Levack, ed., *Magic and Demonology*, 12 vols (New York: Garland, 1992), collects major contributions.

45. I. Tzvi Abusch, *Mesopotamian Witchcraft: Towards a History and Understanding of Babylonian Witchcraft Beliefs and Literature* (Leiden: Brill, 2002).
46. B. S. Spaeth, 'From goddess to hag: the Greek and the Roman witch in classical literature', in K. B. Stratton and D. S. Kalleres, eds, *Daughters of Hecate: Women and Magic in the Ancient World* (Oxford: Oxford University Press, 2014), pp. 15–27.
47. L. Roper, *Witch Craze: Terror and Fantasy in Baroque Germany* (New Haven: Yale University Press, 2004); Baroja, *The World of the Witches.*
48. Parrinder, *Witchcraft.*
49. G. Hennigsen, *The Witches' Advocate: Basque Witchcraft and the Spanish Inquisition* (Reno: University of Nevada Press, 1980).
50. A. Mar, *Witches of America* (New York: Macmillan, 2015).
51. I have in mind G. Zukav, *The Dancing Wu Li Masters* (New York: Morrow, 1979).
52. C. Lévi-Strauss, *Totemism* (London: Merlin Press, 1962); E. Durkheim, *The Elementary Forms of Religious Life* (London: Allen and Unwin, 1915); A. Lang, *The Secret of the Totem* (New York: Longmans, Green, and Co., 1905).
53. L. Schele and M. Miller, *The Blood of Kings: Dynasty and Ritual in Maya Art* (Fort Worth: Kimbell Art Museum, 1986).
54. E. Trinkaus et al., *The People of Sungir* (Oxford: Oxford University Press, 2014).
55. K. Flannery and J. Markus, *The Creation of Inequality* (Cambridge, MA: Harvard University Press, 2012); S. Stuurman, *The Invention of Humanity: Equality and Cultural Difference in World History* (Cambridge, MA: Harvard University Press, 2017).
56. M. Sahlins, *Culture and Practical Reason* (Chicago: University of Chicago Press, 1976); P. Wiessner and W. Schiefenhövel, *Food and the Status Quest* (Oxford: Berghahn, 1996), contrasts culture and ecology as rival 'causes' of the feast idea; M. Dietler and B. Hayden, *Feasts* (Washington DC: Smithsonian, 2001), is a superb collection of essays that cover the field; Hayden develops his theory of the feast as a means of power in *The Power of Feasts* (Cambridge: Cambridge University Press, 2014): M. Jones, *Feast: Why Humans Share Food* (Oxford: Oxford University Press, 2007), is an innovative archaeological survey.
57. Marshack, *The Roots of Civilization*, is a highly controversial but insidiously brilliant study of Palaeolithic calendrical and other notation; K. Lippincott et al., *The Story of Time* (London: National Maritime Museum, 2000), an exhibition catalogue, is the best survey of the whole subject. J. T. Fraser, *The Voices of Time* (New York: Braziller, 1966) and *Of Time, Passion and Knowledge* (Princeton: Princeton University Press, 1990), are fascinating studies of human efforts to devise and improve time-keeping strategies. As a general introduction, J. Lindsay, *The Origins of Astrology* (London:

Muller, 1971), has not been bettered, but the controversial work of J. D. North has cast much light on the subject, especially *Stars, Minds and Fate* (London: Hambledon, 1989). M. Gauquelin, *Dreams and Illusions of Astrology* (Buffalo: Prometheus, 1969), exposed the scientific pretensions of twentieth-century astrology.

58. Plato, *Timaeus*, 47c.
59. S. Giedion, *The Eternal Present* (Oxford: Oxford University Press, 1962), is a stimulating introduction; see E. Neumayer, *Prehistoric Indian Rock Paintings* (Delhi: Oxford University Press, 1983), for the evidence from Jaora. J. E. Pfeiffer, *The Creative Explosion* (New York: Harper and Row, 1982), is a stimulating attempt to trace the origins of art and religion in Palaeolithic people's search for order in their world.
60. K. Whipple et al., eds, *The Cambridge World History of Food*, 2 vols (Cambridge: Cambridge University Press, 2000), ii, pp. 1502–9.
61. M. Douglas, *Purity and Danger* (London: Routledge, 1984), includes the best available study of food taboos; M. Harris, *Good to Eat* (New York: Simon & Schuster, 1986), is a lively and engaging collection of studies from a materialist perspective.
62. F. Fernández-Armesto, *Near a Thousand Tables* (New York: Free Press, 2003).
63. C. Lévi-Strauss, *The Elementary Structures of Kinship* (Paris: Mouton, 1949), is the classic study, which, in essence, has withstood innumerable attacks; R. Fox, *Kinship and Marriage* (Cambridge: Cambridge University Press, 1967), is an excellent, dissenting survey. S. Freud, *Totem and Taboo* (Heller: Leipzig and Vienna, 1913), which traced incest prohibition to psychological inhibition, is one of those ever-admirable books: great but wrong.
64. K. Polanyi, *Trade and Economy in the Early Empires* (Glencoe: Free Press, 1957); J. G. D. Clark, *Symbols of Excellence* (New York: Cambridge University Press, 1986); J. W. and E. Leach, eds, *The Kula* (Cambridge: Cambridge University Press, 1983), is the best guide to the Melanesian island system.
65. K. Polanyi, *The Great Transformation* (New York: Rinehart, 1944), p. 43.
66. L. Pospisil, *Kapauku Papuan Economy* (New Haven: Yale University Press, 1967); B. Malinowski, *Argonauts of the Western Pacific* (London: Routledge, 1932).
67. M. W. Helms, *Ulysses' Sail* (Princeton: Princeton University Press, 2014); M. W. Helms, *Craft and the Kingly Ideal* (Austin: University of Texas Press, 1993).
68. A. Smith, *Wealth of Nations*, bk 1, ch. 4.

CHAPTER 3 *Settled Minds: 'Civilized' Thinking*

1. J. M. Chauvet, *Dawn of Art* (New York: Abrams, 1996); J. Clottes, *Return to Chauvet Cave: Excavating the Birthplace of Art* (London: Thames and Hudson, 2003).

2. A. Quiles et al., 'A high-precision chronological model for the decorated Upper Paleolithic cave of Chauvet-Pont d'Arc, Ardèche, France', *Proceedings of the National Academy of Sciences*, cxiii (2016), pp. 4670–5.
3. So thought E. Girard, *Violence and the Sacred* (Baltimore: Johns Hopkins University Press, 1979), which is an eccentric classic.
4. H. Hubert and M. Mauss, *Sacrifice: Its Nature and Function*, 1898 (Chicago: University of Chicago Press, 1968), set the agenda for all subsequent work. For a modern conspectus, see M. F. C. Bourdillon and M. Fortes, eds, *Sacrifice* (London: Academic Press, 1980). B. Ralph Lewis, *Ritual Sacrifice* (Stroud: Sutton, 2001), provides a useful general history, concentrating on human sacrifice.
5. T. Denham et al., eds, *Rethinking Agriculture: Archaeological and Ethnographical Perspectives* (New York: Routledge, 2016), p. 117.
6. I originally made this suggestion in *Food: A History* (London: Bloomsbury, 2000). Many tests of the hypothesis have followed, with inconclusive but suggestive results. See, for instance, D. Lubell, 'Prehistoric edible land snails in the Circum-Mediterranean: the archaeological evidence', in J. J. Brugal and J. Desse, eds, *Petits animaux et sociétés humaines: Du complément alimentaire aux resources utilitaires (XXIVe rencontres internationales d'archeologie et d'histoire d'Antibes)* (Antibes: APDCA, 2004), pp. 77–98; A. C. Colonese et al., 'Marine mollusc exploitation in Mediterranean prehistory: an overview', *Quaternary International*, ccxxxiv (2011), pp. 86–103; D. Lubell, 'Are land snails a signature for the Mesolithic-Neolithic transition in the Circum-Mediterranean?', in M. Budja, ed., *The Neolithization of Eurasia: Paradigms, Models and Concepts Involved, Neolithic Studies 11, Documenta Praehistorica*, xxi (2004), pp. 1–24.
7. D. Rindos, *The Origins of Agriculture: An Evolutionary Perspective* (Orlando: Academic Press, 1984); J. Harlan, *The Living Fields: Our Agricultural Heritage* (Cambridge: Cambridge University Press, 1995), pp. 239–40.
8. R. and L. Coppinger, *What is a Dog?* (Chicago: University of Chicago Press, 2016); B. Hassett, *Built on Bones: 15,000 Years of Urban Life and Death* (London: Bloomsbury, 2017), pp. 65–6.
9. M. N. Cohen, *The Food Crisis in Prehistory: Overpopulation and the Origins of Agriculture* (New Haven: Yale University Press, 1977); E. Boserup, *The Conditions of Agricultural Growth: The Economics of Agrarian Change under Population Pressure* (London: G. Allen and Unwin, 1965).
10. C. O. Sauer, *Agricultural Origins and Dispersals* (New York: American Geographical Society, 1952).
11. C. Darwin, *The Variation of Animals and Plants under Domestication* (New York: Appleton, 1887), p. 327.
12. F. Trentmann, ed., *The Oxford Handbook of the History of Consumption* (Oxford: Oxford University Press, 2014).
13. B. Hayden, 'Were luxury foods the first domesticates? Ethnoarchaeological perspectives from Southeast Asia', *World Archaeology*, xxxiv (1995),

pp. 458–69; B. Hayden, 'A new overview of domestication', in T. D. Price and A. Gebauer, eds, *Last Hunters–First Farmers: New Perspectives on the Prehistoric Transition to Agriculture* (Santa Fe: School of American Research Press, 2002), pp. 273–99.

14. Jones, *Feast: Why Humans Share Food*; M. Jones, 'Food globalisation in prehistory: the agrarian foundations of an interconnected continent', *Journal of the British Academy*, iv (2016), pp. 73–87.
15. M. Mead, 'Warfare is only an invention – not a biological necessity', in D. Hunt, ed., *The Dolphin Reader* (Boston: Houghton Mifflin, 1990), pp. 415–21.
16. L. H. Keeley, *War Before Civilization* (Oxford: Oxford University Press, 1996), presents an irresistibly convincing picture of the violence of humankind's remotest past.
17. B. L. Montgomery, *A History of Warfare* (London: World Publishing, 1968), p. 13.
18. J. A. Vazquez, ed., *Classics of International Relations* (Englewood Cliffs: Prentice-Hall, 1990), has some fundamental texts. R. Ardrey, *The Territorial Imperative* (New York: Atheneum, 1966), and K. Lorenz, *On Aggression* (New York: Harcourt, Brace and World, 1963), are the classic works on the biology and sociology of violence. J. Keegan, *A History of Warfare* (New York: Vintage, 1993), and J. Haas, ed., *The Anthropology of War* (Cambridge: Cambridge University Press, 1990), set the evidence in broad context.
19. R. Wrangham and L. Glowacki, 'Intergroup aggression in chimpanzees and war in nomadic hunter-gatherers', *Human Nature*, xxiii (2012), pp. 5–29.
20. Keeley, *War Before Civilization*, p. 37; K. F. Otterbein, *How War Began* (College Station: Texas A. and M. Press, 2004), pp. 11–120.
21. M. Mirazón Lahr et al., 'Inter-group violence among early Holocene hunter-gatherers of West Turkana, Kenya', *Nature*, dxxix (2016), pp. 394–8.
22. C. Meyer et al., 'The massacre mass grave of Schöneck-Kilianstädten reveals new insights into collective violence in Early Neolithic Central Europe', *Proceedings of the National Academy of Sciences*, cxii (2015), pp. 11217–22; L. Keeley and M. Golitko, 'Beating ploughshares back into swords: warfare in the Linearbandkeramik', *Antiquity*, lxxxi (2007), pp. 332–42.
23. J. Harlan, *Crops and Man* (Washington, DC: American Society of Agronomy, 1992), p. 36.
24. K. Butzer, *Early Hydraulic Civilization in Egypt: A Study in Cultural Ecology* (Chicago: University of Chicago Press, 1976).
25. K. Thomas, ed., *The Oxford Book of Work* (Oxford: Oxford University Press, 2001), is an endlessly entertaining and stimulating anthology. Sahlins, *Stone-Age Economics*, defined the notion of Palaeolithic affluence. On the transition to agriculture and its effects on work routines, Harlan, *Crops and Man*, is outstanding.

26. Aristotle, *Politics*, 1.3.
27. L. W. King, ed., *The Seven Tablets of Creation* (London: Luzac, 1902), i, p. 131.
28. L. Mumford, *The Culture of Cities* (New York: Harcourt, Brace, and Company, 1938), is an indispensable classic. P. Hall, *Cities in Civilization* (London: Phoenix, 1999), is essentially a collection of case studies. For Sumerian cities, see G. Leick, *Mesopotamia, the Invention of the City* (London: Allen Lane, 2001). A broad modern conspectus is Fernández-Armesto, *Civilizations*. P. Clark, ed., *The Oxford Handbook of Cities in World History* (Oxford: Oxford University Press, 2013), is a near-comprehensive survey. Hassett, *Built on Bones*, gallops through the disasters urban populations inflict on themselves.
29. Aristotle, *Politics*, 3.10.
30. S. Dalley, ed., *Myths from Mesopotamia: Creation, the Flood, Gilgamesh, and Others* (Oxford: Oxford University Press, 1989), p. 273.
31. M. Mann, *The Sources of Social Power*, vol. 1 (Cambridge: Cambridge University Press 1986), offers an original perspective on the origins of the state from a historically informed sociologist. T. K. Earle, *Chiefdoms* (New York: Cambridge University Press, 1991), collects useful essays.
32. See A. Leroi-Gourham, *Préhistoire de l'art occidental* (Paris: Mazenod, 1965), for a binarist interpretation of prehistoric art.
33. *Melanippe the Wise*, in August Nauck, ed., *Euripidis Tragoediae superstites et deperditarum fragmenta* (Leipzig: Teubner, 1854), Fragment 484; W. H. C. Guthrie, *A History of Greek Philosophy* (Cambridge: Cambridge University Press, 1962), i, p. 60.
34. Aristotle, *Physics*, 3.4, 203b.
35. Diels and Kranz, *Fragmente*, ii, Fragment 8.36–7.
36. F. Fernández-Armesto, *Truth: A History* (New York: St Martin's, 1997), p. 36.
37. Taoist Zhuangzi Fung Yu-Lan, *A History of the Chinese Philosophers*, trans. D. Bodde (Princeton: Princeton University Press, 1952), i, p. 223.
38. B. W. Van Nordern, *Introduction to Classical Chinese Philosophy* (Indianapolis: Hackett, 2011), p. 104.
39. D. W. Hamlyn, *Metaphysics* (Cambridge: Cambridge University Press, 1984), is a useful introduction. For some key texts, see E. Deutsch and J. A. B. van Buitenen, *A Source Book of Vedanta* (Honolulu: University Press of Hawaii, 1971). J. Fodor and E. Lepore, *Holism: A Shopper's Guide* (Oxford: Blackwell, 1992), traces a lot of philosophical and practical implications.
40. Evans-Pritchard, *Witchcraft, Oracles and Magic*, is the agenda-setting anthropological case study. M. Loewe and C. Blacker, *Oracles and Divination* (London: Allen and Unwin, 1981), covers a wide range of ancient cultures. C. Morgan, *Athletes and Oracles* (Cambridge: Cambridge University Press, 1990), is a superb, pioneering study of the oracles of

ancient Greece. On later phases in China, see Fu-Shih Lin, 'Shamans and politics', in J. Lagerwey and Lü Pengchi, eds, *Early Chinese Religion* (Leiden: Brill, 2010), i, pp. 275–318.

41. J. Breasted, *Ancient Records of Egypt* (Chicago: University of Chicago Press, 1906), iv, p. 55.

42. J. B. Pritchard, ed., *The Ancient Near East: An Anthology of Texts and Pictures* (Princeton: Princeton University Press, 2011), p. 433; M. Lichtheim, *Ancient Egyptian Literature: A Book of Readings, ii: The New Kingdom* (Berkeley: University of California Press, 1976).

43. Breasted, *Ancient Records of Egypt*, i, p. 747.

44. Pritchard, ed., *The Ancient Near East: An Anthology of Texts and Pictures*, p. 82.

45. P. Roux, *La religion des turcs et mongols* (Paris: Payot, 1984), pp. 110–24; R. Grousset, *The Empire of the Steppes* (New Brunswick: Rutgers University Press, 1970), remains unsurpassed on Central Asia generally, supplemented now by F. McLynn, *Genghis Khan* (Boston: Da Capo, 2015), and D. Sinor et al., eds, *The Cambridge History of Inner Asia*, 2 vols (Cambridge: Cambridge University Press, 1999, 2015).

46. Plato, *Phaedrus*, 274e–275b.

47. J. Goody, *The Interface between the Written and the Oral* (Cambridge: Cambridge University Press, 1987), is classic; J. Derrida, *Of Grammatology* (Baltimore and London: Johns Hopkins University Press, 1976), trans. G. C. Spivak, pursues the problem of what writing is; E. A. Havelock, *The Muse Learns to Write* (New Haven: Yale University Press, 1986), is a survey; Yates, *The Art of Memory*, is fascinating on mnemotechnics.

48. S. N. Kramer, *The Sumerians* (Chicago: University of Chicago Press, 1963), pp. 336–41; F. R. Steele, 'The Code of Lipit-Ishtar', *American Journal of Archeology*, lii (1948).

49. J. B. Pritchard, *Archaeology and the Old Testament* (Princeton: Princeton University Press, 1958), p. 211. M. E. J. Richardson, *Hammurabi's Laws* (London: Bloomsbury, 2004), is a good study of the text. H. E. Saggs, *The Babylonians* (Berkeley: University of California Press, 2000), and J. Oates, *Babylon* (London: Thames & Hudson, 1979), are excellent accounts of the historical background.

50. J. B. Pritchard, ed., *Ancient Near Eastern Texts Relating to the Old Testament* (Princeton: Princeton University Press, 1969), pp. 8–9; H. Frankfort et al., *The Intellectual Adventure of Ancient Man* (Chicago: University of Chicago Press, 1946), pp. 106–8; B. L. Goff, *Symbols of Ancient Egypt in the Late Period* (The Hague: Mouton, 1979), p. 27.

51. *Shijing*, 1.9 (Odes of Wei), 112.

52. J. Needham, *Science and Civilisation in China* (Cambridge: Cambridge University Press, 1956), ii, p. 105.

53. Pritchard, ed., *Ancient Near Eastern Texts*, pp. 431–4; Lichtheim, *Ancient Egyptian Literature: A Book of Readings, ii: The New Kingdom*, pp. 170–9.

54. The *Mahabharata*, bk 3, section 148.
55. *The Complete Works of Zhuangzi*, ed. B. Watson (New York: Columbia University Press, 2013), pp. 66, 71, 255–6.
56. Ovid, *Metamorphoses*, bk 1, verses 89–112.
57. R. Dworkin, *A Matter of Principle* (Cambridge, MA: Harvard University Press, 1985), and M. Walzer, *Spheres of Justice* (New York: Basic Books, 1983), treat equality from the perspective of jurisprudence. R. Nozick, *Anarchy, State and Utopia* (New York: Basic Books, 1974), and F. Hayek, *The Constitution of Liberty* (Chicago: University of Chicago Press, 1960), adopt an approach from political philosophy.
58. J. D. Evans, *Prehistoric Antiquities of the Maltese Islands* (London: Athlone Press, 1971), published the Tarxien evidence. The feminist interpretation was put forward by M. Stone, *When God Was a Woman* (New York: Barnes and Noble, 1976), M. Gimbutas, *The Civilization of the Goddess* (San Francisco: Harper, 1991), and E. W. Gaddon, *The Once and Future Goddess* (New York: Harper, 1989). See B. G. Walker, *The Woman's Dictionary of Symbols and Sacred Objects* (London: HarperCollins, 1988), for more evidence. M. Warner, *Alone of All Her Sex* (London: Weidenfeld and Nicolson, 1976), linked the Christian Mary cult to the goddess idea.
59. F. Nietzsche, *The Antichrist*, ch. 48; F. Nietzsche, *The Anti-Christ, Ecce Homo, Twilight of the Idols and Other Writings*, ed. A. Ridley and J. Norman (Cambridge: Cambridge University Press, 2005), p. 46.
60. Lichtheim, *Ancient Egyptian Literature: A Book of Readings, i: The Old and Middle Kingdoms*, p. 83; B. G. Gunn, *The Wisdom of the East, the Instruction of Ptah-Hotep and the Instruction of Ke'gemni: The Oldest Books in the World* (London: Murray, 1906), ch. 19.
61. Hesiod, *Theogony, Works and Days, Testimonia*, ed. G. W. Most (Cambridge: Cambridge University Press, 2006), pp. 67, 80–2.
62. Richardson, *Hammurabi's Laws*, pp. 164–80.
63. M. Ehrenberg, *Women in Prehistory* (Norman: University of Oklahoma Press, 1989), is the best introduction to the archaeological evidence. R. Bridenthal et al., eds, *Becoming Visible* (New York: Houghton Mifflin, 1994), is a pioneering collection on the rediscovery of the history of women. For the context of the Harappan figurines, B. and R. Allchin, *The Rise of Civilization in India and Pakistan* (Cambridge: Cambridge University Press, 1982), is the standard work. There is no good global study of marriage. P. Elman, ed., *Jewish Marriage* (London: Soncino Press, 1967), M. A. Rauf, *The Islamic View of Women and the Family* (New York: Speller, 1977), and M. Yalom, *History of the Wife* (London: Pandora, 2001), between them can provide a selective comparative conspectus.
64. Frankfort et al., *The Intellectual Adventure*, p. 100.
65. W. Churchill, *The River War* (London: Longman, 1899), ii, pp. 248–50.
66. Classic works are J. H. Breasted, *Development of Religion and Thought in Ancient Egypt* (New York: Scribner, 1912), and W. M. Watt, *Freewill*

and Predestination in Early Islam (London: Luzac and Co., 1948). For a general perspective on various kinds of determinist thinking, see P. van Inwagen, *An Essay on Free Will* (Oxford: Clarendon Press, 1983).

67. I. E. S. Edwards, *The Great Pyramids of Egypt* (London: Penguin, 1993), pp. 245–92.
68. Pyramid text 508. The translation I quote is from R. O. Faulkner, ed., *The Ancient Egyptian Pyramid Texts* (Oxford: Oxford University Press, 1969), p. 183.
69. Pritchard, ed., *Ancient Near Eastern Texts*, p. 36.
70. Frankfort et al., *The Intellectual Adventure*, p. 106.
71. R. Taylor, *Good and Evil* (New York: Prometheus, 1970), provides a general introduction. Pritchard, ed., *Ancient Near Eastern Texts*, prints a fascinating array of documents. H. Frankfort et al., *Before Philosophy* (Chicago: University of Chicago Press, 1946), is a richly reflective enquiry into ancient ethics. W. D. O'Flaherty, *Origins of Evil in Hindu Mythology* (Delhi: Motilal Banarsidass, 1976), is an interesting case study.
72. M. W. Muller, *The Upanishads* (Oxford: Clarendon, 1879), is the classic edition in translation, but the selections in J. Mascaró, *The Upanishads* (New York: Penguin, 1965), are brilliantly translated and accessible; M. W. Muller, *Rig-Veda-Sanhita* (London: Trübnew and Co., 1869), is still the standard translation, but the work can be appreciated in the anthology of W. Doniger, *The Rig Veda* (London: Penguin, 2005). N. S. Subrahmanian, *Encyclopedia of the Upanishads* (New Delhi: Sterling, 1985), and S. Bhattacharji, *Literature in the Vedic Age*, vol. 2 (Calcutta: K. P. Bagchi, 1986), are good modern critical surveys.
73. W. Buck, ed., *Mahabharata* (Berkeley: University of California Press, 1973), 196.
74. On the context of the Memphite theology, see S. Quirke, *Ancient Egyptian Religion* (London: British Museum Press, 1973).
75. Pritchard, ed., *The Ancient Near East: An Anthology of Texts and Pictures*, p. 2.
76. Swami Nikhilānanda, *The Upanishads: Katha, Iśa, Kena, and Mundaka* (New York: Harper, 1949), p. 264.
77. H. H. Price, *Thinking and Experience* (Cambridge, MA: Harvard University Press, 1953), is a good introduction to the problem of what it means to think. G. Ryle, *On Thinking* (Oxford: Blackwell, 1979), proposed a famous solution: thought is just physical and chemical activity in the brain. Cf. pp. 4–17 above.

CHAPTER 4 *The Great Sages: The First Named Thinkers*

1. R. Collins, *The Sociology of Philosophies* (Cambridge, MA: Harvard University Press, 1998); Guthrie, *A History of Greek Philosophy*, and Needham, *Science and Civilisation in China*, are multivolume works of

dazzling range that trace the relationship between styles of thinking in the civilizations concerned; G. E. R. Lloyd, *The Ambitions of Curiosity* (Cambridge: Cambridge University Press, 2002), and G. E. R. Lloyd and N. Sivin, *The Way and the Word* (New Haven: Yale University Press, 2002), compare Greek and Chinese thought and science directly.

2. H. Coward, *Sacred Word and Sacred Text* (Maryknoll: Orbis, 1988), and F. M. Denny and R. L. Taylor, eds, *The Holy Book in Comparative Perspective* (Columbia: University of South Carolina Press, 1985).
3. E. B. Cowell, ed., *The Jataka or Stories of the Buddha's Former Birth*, 7 vols (Cambridge: Cambridge University Press, 1895–1913), i, pp. 10, 19–20; ii, pp. 89–91; iv, pp. 10–12, 86–90.
4. H. Hasan, *A History of Persian Navigation* (London: Methuen and Co., 1928), p. 1.
5. D. T. Potts, *The Arabian Gulf in Antiquity* (Oxford: Oxford University Press, 1991).
6. F. Hirth, 'The story of Chang K'ien, China's pioneer in Western Asia', *Journal of the American Oriental Society*, xxxvii (1917), pp. 89–116; Ban Gu (Pan Ku), 'The memoir on Chang Ch'ien and Li Kuang-Li', in A. F. P. Hulsewe, *China in Central Asia – The Early Stage: 125 B.C.–A.D. 23* (Leiden: E. J. Brill, 1979), pp. 211, 219.
7. V. H. Mair, 'Dunhuang as a funnel for Central Asian nomads into China', in G. Seaman, ed., *Ecology and Empire: Nomads in the Cultural Evolution of the Old World* (Los Angeles: University of Southern California, 1989), pp. 143–63.
8. R. Whitfield, S. Whitfield, and N. Agnew, *Cave Temples of Mogao: Art and History on the Silk Road* (Los Angeles: Getty Publications, 2000), p. 18.
9. M. L. West, ed., *The Hymns of Zoroaster* (London: Tauris, 2010).
10. D. Seyfort Ruegg, 'A new publication on the date and historiography of the Buddha's decease', *Bulletin of the School of Oriental and African Studies*, lxii (1999), pp. 82–7.
11. D. R. Bandarkar, *Asoka* (Calcutta: University of Calcutta, 1925), pp. 273–336.
12. E. R. Dodds, *The Greeks and the Irrational* (Berkeley: University of California Press, 1951), pp. 145–6.
13. *Dao De Jing*, part 2, 78.1.
14. R. M. Gale, *Negation and Non-being* (Oxford: Blackwell, 1976), is a philosophical introduction. J. D. Barrow, *The Book of Nothing* (London: Jonathon Cape, 2000), is fascinating, wide-ranging, and good on the science and mathematics of zero. R. Kaplan, *The Nothing That Is* (Oxford: Oxford University Press, 1999), is an engaging, clear, and straightforward approach to the mathematics involved.
15. R. Mehta, *The Call of the Upanishads* (Delhi: Motilal Banarsidas, 1970), pp. 237–8.

16. R. M. Dancy, *Two Studies in the Early Academy* (Albany: SUNY Press, 1991), pp. 67–70.
17. P. Atkins, *On Being: A Scientist's Exploration of the Great Questions of Existence* (Oxford: Oxford University Press, 2011), p. 17. I owe the reference to R. Shortt, *God is No Thing* (London: Hurst, 2016), p. 42; D. Turner, *Thomas Aquinas: A Portrait* (New Haven: Yale University Press, 2013), p. 142.
18. D. L. Smith, *Folklore of the Winnebago Tribe* (Norman: University of Oklahoma Press, 1997), p. 105.
19. D. Cupitt, *Creation out of Nothing* (London: SCM Press, 1990), is a revisionist work by a radical Christian theologian. K. Ward, *Religion and Creation* (Oxford: Clarendon Press, 1996), takes an arresting comparative approach. P. Atkins, *Conjuring the Universe: The Origins of the Laws of Nature* (Oxford: Oxford University Press, 2018), attempts a materialist explanation.
20. J. Miles, *God: A Biography* (New York: Knopf, 1995).
21. E. E. Evans-Pritchard, 'Nuer time-reckoning', *Africa: Journal of the International African Institute*, xii (1939), pp. 189–216.
22. S. J. Gould, *Time's Arrow* (Cambridge, MA: Harvard University Press, 1987), is a brilliant study of the concept, with special reference to modern geology and palaeontology. G. J. Whitrow, *Time in History* (Oxford: Oxford University Press, 1989), and S. F. G. Brandon, *History, Time and Deity* (Manchester: Manchester University Press, 1965), are excellent comparative studies of different cultures' concepts of time. Lippincott et al., *The Story of Time*, is a comprehensive survey of theories of time.
23. K. Armstrong, *A History of God* (New York: Ballantine, 1994), is a wide-ranging survey of the history of the concept. L. E. Goodman, *God of Abraham* (Oxford: Oxford University Press, 1996), and R. K. Gnuse, *No Other Gods* (Sheffield: Sheffield Academic Press, 1997), study the origins of the Jewish concept. M. S. Smith, *The Origins of Biblical Monotheism* (Oxford: Oxford University Press, 2001), is a controversial revisionist version of the same subject.
24. M. J. Dodds, *The Unchanging God of Love* (Fribourg: Editions Universitaires, 1986), is a study of the doctrine in the form Aquinas gave it. The Mozi, a collection ascribed to the homonymous master, is available in many editions, most recently D. Burton-Watson, ed., *Mozi: Basic Writings* (New York: Columbia University Press, 2003).
25. *The Essential Samuel Butler*, ed. G. D. H. Cole (London: Cape, 1950), p. 501.
26. Frankfort et al., *The Intellectual Adventure*, p. 61.
27. C. P. Fitzgerald, *China: A Short Cultural History* (Cambridge: Cambridge University Press, 1961), p. 98.
28. A. Plantinga, 'Free will defense', in M. Black, ed., *Philosophy in America* (Ithaca: Cornell University Press, 1965); A. Plantinga, *God, Freedom and Evil* (The Hague: Eerdmans, 1978).

29. F. Fernández-Armesto, 'How to be human: an historical approach', in M. Jeeves, ed., *Rethinking Human Nature* (Cambridge: Eerdmans, 2010), pp. 11–29.
30. Needham, *Science and Civilisation in China*, ii, p. 23.
31. B. Russell, *History of Western Philosophy* (London: Routledge, 2009), p. 41.
32. See, for instance, T. Benton, *Natural Relations* (London: Verso, 1993); R. G. Frey, *Interests and Rights: The Case Against Animals* (Oxford: Oxford University Press, 1980); M. Midgley, *Beast and Man* (Hassocks: Harvester, 1980); P. Singer, *Animal Liberation* (New York: Avon, 1990).
33. A. Weber, *The Çatapatha-Brāhmaṇa in the Mādhyandina-Çākhā, with Extracts from the Commentaries of Sāyaṇa, Harisvāmin and Dvivedānga* (Berlin, 1849), i, 3.28.
34. Plato, *Republic*, 514a–520a.
35. Ibid., 479e.
36. Needham, *Science and Civilisation in China*, ii, p. 187.
37. Fernández-Armesto, *Truth: A History*, sets relativism in the context of a conceptual history of truth. R. Scruton, *Modern Philosophy* (London: Allen Lane, 1994), is a toughly argued defence against relativism. The most sophisticated modern apologia for relativism is R. Rorty, *Objectivity, Relativism and Truth* (Cambridge: Cambridge University Press, 1991).
38. Needham, *Science and Civilisation in China*, ii, p. 49.
39. H. Putnam, *Reason, Truth and History* (Cambridge: Cambridge University Press, 1981), pp. 119–20.
40. W. Burkert, *Lore and Science in Early Pythagoreanism* (Cambridge, MA: Harvard University Press, 1972), is a stimulating study; P. Benacerraf and H. Putnam, eds, *Philosophy of Mathematics* (Cambridge: Cambridge University Press, 1983), and J. Bigelow, *The Reality of Numbers* (Oxford: Oxford University Press, 1988), are clear and committed guides to the philosophical background of mathematical thinking.
41. Russell, *History of Western Philosophy*, p. 43.
42. Needham, *Science and Civilisation in China*, ii, p. 82.
43. Russell, *History of Western Philosophy*, p. 44.
44. Needham, *Science and Civilisation in China*, ii, p. 191.
45. Guthrie, *A History of Greek Philosophy*, ii, is the great authority – exhaustive and highly readable; Plato, *Parmenides*, is the dialogue that defined the debate; Dodds, *The Greeks and the Irrational*, was a pioneering exposé of the limits of Greek rationalism.
46. H. D. P. Lea, *Zeno of Elea* (Cambridge: Cambridge University Press, 1936); J. Barnes, *The Presocratic Philosophers* (London: Routledge, 1982), pp. 231–95.
47. W. H. C. Guthrie, *Aristotle* (Cambridge: Cambridge University Press, 1981), describes brilliantly the author's 'encounter' with Aristotle's thought.

48. I. Bochenski, *A History of Formal Logic*, trans. I. Thomas (Indianapolis: University of Notre Dame Press, 1961), is an excellent introduction; J. Lukasiewicz, *Aristotle's Syllogistic* (Oxford: Clarendon Press, 1957), is a valuable technical exposition; C. Habsmeier, *Science and Civilisation in China* (Cambridge: Cambridge University Press, 1998), vii, p. 1, helps set Greek logic in its global context.
49. Needham, *Science and Civilisation in China*, ii, p. 72.
50. *The Analects of Confucius*, trans. A. Waley (London: Allen and Unwin, 1938), p. 216.
51. Needham, *Science and Civilisation in China*, ii, p. 55.
52. A. Crombie, *Styles of Scientific Thinking* (London: Duckworth, 1994), is an unwieldy but invaluable quarry on the Western tradition. The same author's *Science, Art and Nature* (London: Hambledon Press, 1996) traces the tradition from medieval times.
53. N. Sivin, *Medicine, Philosophy and Religion in Ancient China* (Aldershot: Variorum, 1995), is a valuable collection of essays on the links between Tao and science. F. Capra, *The Tao of Physics* (Berkeley: Shambhala, 1975), is a maverick but influential work arguing for a Taoist interpretation of modern quantum physics.
54. J. Longrigg, *Greek Medicine* (London: Duckworth, 1998), is a useful source book. D. Cantor, ed., *Reinventing Hippocrates* (Farnham: Ashgate, 2001), is a stimulating collection of essays. For the history of medicine generally, R. Porter, *The Greatest Benefit to Mankind* (New York: W. W. Norton, 1999), is a vast, readable, and entertainingly irreverent account.
55. Needham, *Science and Civilisation in China*, ii, p. 27.
56. D. J. Rothman, S. Marcus, and S. A. Kiceluk, *Medicine and Western Civilization* (New Brunswick: Rutgers University Press, 1995), pp. 142–3.
57. L. Giles, ed., *Taoist Teachings, Translated from the Book of Lieh-Tzü* (London: Murray, 1912), p. 111.
58. For a critique of atheism, see J. Maritain, *The Range of Reason* (New York: Scribner, 1952). Classic apologias include L. Feuerbach, *Principles of the Philosophy of the Future* (1843), and B. Russell, *Why I Am Not a Christian* (New York: Simon & Schuster, 1967). J. Thrower, *Western Atheism: A Short History* (Amherst: Prometheus Books, 1999), is a clear, concise introduction.
59. W. K. C. Guthrie, *The Greek Philosophers from Thales to Aristotle* (London: Routledge, 2013), p. 63.
60. M. O. Goulet-Cazé, 'Religion and the early Cynics', in R. Bracht-Brahman and M. O. Goulet-Cazé, eds, *The Cynics: The Cynic Movement in Antiquity and Its Legacy* (Berkeley: University of California Press, 1996), pp. 69–74.
61. P. P. Haillie, ed., *Sextus Empiricus: Selections from His Major Writings on Scepticism, Man and God* (Indianapolis: Hackett, 1985), p. 189.
62. W. T. De Bary et al., eds, *Sources of Indian Tradition*, 2 vols (New York: Columbia University Press, 1958), ii, p. 43.

63. *The Epicurus Reader*, ed. L. Gerson (New York: Hackett, 1994), collects the main texts. H. Jones, *The Epicurean Tradition* (London: Routledge, 1992), traces Epicurus's influence in modern times. D. J. Furley, *The Greek Cosmologists*, vol. 1 (Cambridge: Cambridge University Press, 1987), is the standard work on the Greek origins of atomic theory. M. Chown, *The Magic Furnace* (London: Vintage, 2000), is a lively popular history of atomic theory. C. Luthy et al., eds, *Late Medieval and Early Modern Corpuscular Matter Theories* (Leiden: Brill, 2001), is a fascinating scholarly collection that fills in the gap between ancient and modern atomic theory.
64. Needham, *Science and Civilisation in China*, ii, p. 179.
65. C. P. Fitzgerald, *China: A Short Cultural History* (London: Cresset, 1950), p. 86.
66. P. Mathieson, ed., *Epictetus: The Discourses and Manual* (Oxford: Oxford University Press, 1916), pp. 106–7; Russell, *History of Western Philosophy*, p. 251.
67. A. A. Long, *Hellenistic Philosophy* (Berkeley and Los Angeles: University of California Press, 1974), is particularly good on Stoicism. J. Annas and J. Barnes, eds, *The Modes of Scepticism* (Cambridge: Cambridge University Press, 1985), collects the major Western texts. J. Barnes, *The Toils of Scepticism* (Cambridge: Cambridge University Press, 1990), is an engaging interpretative essay.
68. J. Legge, ed., *The Chinese Classics*, 5 vols (London: Trubner, 1861–72), ii, p. 190.
69. Needham, *Science and Civilisation in China*, ii, p. 19.
70. A. MacIntyre, *After Virtue* (London: Duckworth, 1981), is a fine introduction. E. O. Wilson, *On Human Nature* (Cambridge, MA: Harvard University Press, 1978), is one of the most materialist works on the subject ever written. The most defiantly optimistic is probably M. J. A. N. C. de Condorcet's *Progrès de l'esprit humain* (1794), written while he was awaiting execution by guillotine.
71. H. Wang and L. S. Chang, *The Philosophical Foundations of Han Fei's Political Theory* (Honolulu: University of Hawaii Press, 1986).
72. C. Ping and D. Bloodworth, *The Chinese Machiavelli* (London: Secker and Warburg, 1976), is a lively popular history of Chinese political thought. Detail and context appear in B. I. Schwartz, *The World of Thought in Ancient China* (Cambridge, MA: Harvard University Press, 1985), and Y. Pines, *Envisioning Eternal Empire: Chinese Political Thought of the Warring States Era* (Honolulu: University of Hawaii Press, 2009). A. Waley, *Three Ways of Thought in Ancient China* (Palo Alto: Stanford University Press, 1939), is a classic introduction. S. De Grazia, ed., *Masters of Chinese Political Thought* (New York: Viking, 1973), also prints essential texts in translation.
73. *Republic*, 473d.
74. K. Popper, *The Open Society and Its Enemies*, vol. 1 (Princeton: Princeton University Press, 1945), is the classic critique of Plato's theory. C. D. C.

Reeve, *Philosopher-Kings* ((Princeton: Princeton University Press, 1988), is a historical study of the ancient phenomenon. M. Schofield, *Saving the City* (London and New York: Routledge, 1999), studies the notion of philosopher-kings in ancient philosophy.

75. *The Book of Mencius*, 18.8; Legge, ed., *The Chinese Classics*, v, p. 357. On Mencius, K. Hsiao, *History of Chinese Political Thought* (Princeton: Princeton University Press, 2015), i, pp. 143–213, is especially good.
76. Aristotle, *Politics*, 4.4.
77. P. Pettit, *Republicanism* (Oxford: Oxford University Press, 1997), is a useful introduction. A. Oldfield, *Citizenship and Community* (London and New York: Routledge, 1990), and R. Dagger, *Civic Virtues* (Oxford: Oxford University Press, 1997), take broad looks at modern republicanism.
78. R. Cavendish, 'The abdication of King Farouk', *History Today*, lii (2002), p. 55.
79. The ancient context is well covered in T. Wiedemann, *Greek and Roman Slavery* (Baltimore: Johns Hopkins University Press, 1981). A. Pagden, *The Fall of Natural Man* (Cambridge: Cambridge University Press, 1986), sets in context the early modern evolution of the doctrine – on which the classic work is L. Hanke, *Aristotle and the American Indians* (London: Hollis and Carter, 1959).
80. A. Loombs and J. Burton, eds, *Race in Early Modern England: A Documentary Companion* (New York: Palgrave Macmillan), p. 77; Pagden, *The Fall of Natural Man*, pp. 38–41.
81. F. Bethencourt, *Racisms: From the Crusades to the Twentieth Century* (Princeton: Princeton University Press, 2013).

CHAPTER 5 *Thinking Faiths: Ideas in a Religious Age*

1. M. A. Cook, *Early Muslim Dogma* (Cambridge: Cambridge University Press, 1981), is an extremely important study of the sources of Muslim thought. M. A. Cook, *The Koran: A Very Short Introduction* (Oxford: Oxford University Press, 2000), is the best introduction to the text. The work of G. A. Vermes, in, for instance, *Jesus in His Jewish Context* (Minneapolis: Fortress Press, 2003), though much criticized as overdrawn, makes Christ intelligible as a Jew.
2. S. Rebanich, *Jerome* (London: Routledge, 2002), p. 8.
3. Augustine, *Confessions*, ch. 16.
4. R. Lane Fox, *Pagans and Christians: In the Mediterranean World from the Second Century AD to the Conversion of Constantine* (London: Viking, 1986).
5. N. G. Wilson, *Saint Basil on the Value of Greek Literature* (London: Duckworth, 1975), pp. 19–36.
6. Gregory the Great, *Epistles*, 10:34; G. R. Evans, *The Thought of Gregory the Great* (Cambridge: Cambridge University Press, 1986), p. 9.

7. B. Lewis, ed., *Islam* (New York: Harper, 1974), ii, pp. 20–1; W. M. Watt, *The Faith and Practice of Al-Ghazali* (London: Allen and Unwin, 1951), pp. 72–3.
8. S. Billington, *A Social History of the Fool* (Sussex: Harvester, 1984), is a brief attempt at a conspectus. V. K. Janik, *Fools and Jesters* (Westport: Greenwood, 1998), is a bibliographical compendium. E. A. Stewart, *Jesus the Holy Fool* (Lanham: Rowman and Littlefield, 1998), offers an entertaining sidelight on Christ.
9. W. Heissig, *The Religions of Mongolia* (Berkeley: University of California Press, 1980).
10. M. Rithven, *Historical Atlas of the Islamic World* (Cambridge, MA: Harvard University Press, 2004).
11. R. Bultmann, *Theology of the New Testament* (London: SCM Press, 1955), ii, p. 135.
12. See E. Leach and D. A. Aycock, eds, *Structuralist Interpretations of Biblical Myth* (Cambridge: Cambridge University Press, 1983), especially pp. 7–32; J. Frazer, *The Golden Bough* (New York: Macmillan, 1958), i, pp. 158, 405–45.
13. M. Moosa, *Extremist Shi'ites: The Ghulat Sects* (Syracuse: Syracuse University Press, 1988), p. 188.
14. G. O'Collins, *Incarnation* (London: Continuum, 2002), is a straightforward but stimulating account of the doctrine. B. Hume, *Mystery of the Incarnation* (London: Paraclete, 1999), is a touching meditation. S. Davis et al., *The Trinity* (Oxford: Oxford University Press, 2002), is an outstanding collection of essays.
15. *Patrologia Latina*, v, pp. 109–16.
16. W. H. Bright, ed., *The Definitions of the Catholic Faith* (Oxford and London: James Parker, 1874), is a classic work. H. Chadwick, *The Early Church* (London: Penguin, 1993), is the best historical survey, while J. Danielou, *A History of Early Christian Doctrine* (London: Darton, Longman, and Todd, 1977), gives the theological background.
17. J. Emminghaus, *The Eucharist* (Collegeville, MN: Liturgical Press, 1978), is a good introduction. R. Duffy, *Real Presence* (San Francisco: Harper and Row, 1982), sets the Catholic doctrine in the context of the sacraments. M. Rubin, *Corpus Christi* (Cambridge: Cambridge University Press, 1991), is a brilliant study of the Eucharist in late-medieval culture.
18. C. K. Barrett, *Paul* (Louisville: Westminster/John Knox, 1994), and M. Grant, *Saint Paul* (London: Phoenix, 2000), are excellent readable accounts of the saint. A. F. Segal, *Paul the Convert* (New Haven: Yale University Press, 1990), is particularly good on the Jewish background. Readers can now rely on J. G. D. Dunn, ed., *The Cambridge Companion to St Paul* (Cambridge: Cambridge University Press, 2003).
19. *The Fathers of the Church: St Augustine, the Retractions*, trans. M. I. Brogan, R.S.M. (Washington, DC: Catholic University Press, 1968), p. 32.

20. Augustine, *Confessions*, ch. 11.
21. W. Hasker, *God, Time and Knowledge* (Ithaca: Cornell University Press, 1989), is a good introduction. See also J. Farrelly, *Predestination, Grace and Free Will* (Westminster, MD: Newman Press, 1964), and G. Berkouwer, *Divine Election* (Grand Rapids: Eerdmans, 1960), for the theological implications.
22. G. Filoramo, *Gnosticism* (Oxford: Blackwell, 1990); E. Pagels, *The Gnostic Gospels* (London: Weidenfeld and Nicolson, 1980), and M. Marcovich, *Studies in Graeco-Roman Religions and Gnosticism* (Leiden: Brill, 1988), are equally indispensable guides.
23. *Contra Haereses*, 1.24.4; H. Bettenson and C. Maunder, eds, *Documents of the Christian Church* (Oxford: Oxford University Press, 2011), p. 38.
24. Augustine, *Confessions*, ch. 2.
25. J. Goody, *The Development of the Family and Marriage in Europe* (Cambridge: Cambridge University Press, 1983), pp. 49–60, 146. P. Brown, *The Body and Society* (New York: Columbia University Press, 1988), is a brilliant investigation of the early history of Christian celibacy. P. Ariès and A. Bejin, *Western Sexuality* (Oxford: Blackwell, 1985), has something like classic status, though it concentrates on challenges to conventional morality.
26. J. N. D. Anderson, *Islamic Law in the Modern World* (New York: New York University Press, 1959).
27. G. Fowden, *Qusayr 'Amra: Art and the Umayyad Elite in Late Antique Syria* (Berkeley: University of California Press, 2004).
28. L. Komaroff and S. Carboni, eds, *The Legacy of Genghis Khan: Courtly Art and Culture in Western Asia* (New York: Metropolitan Museum of Art, 2002), pp. 256–353.
29. R. Cormack, *Painting the Soul* (London: Reaktion, 1997), is a lively introductory survey. The same author's *Writing in Gold* (New York: Oxford University Press, 1985) is an excellent study of icons in Byzantine history. T. Ware, *The Orthodox Church* (London: Penguin, 1993), is the best general book on the history of orthodoxy.
30. S. Gayk, *Image, Text, and Religious Reform in Fifteenth-Century England* (Cambridge: Cambridge University Press, 2010), pp. 155–88.
31. Plotinus, *Enneads*, 2.9.16; J. S. Hendrix, *Aesthetics and the Philosophy of Spirit* (New York: Lang, 2005), p. 140.
32. On Aquinas's doctrines, I rely on Turner, *Thomas Aquinas*.
33. Thomas Aquinas, *Summa Contra Gentiles*, 7.1.
34. C. H. Haskins, 'Science at the court of the Emperor Frederick II', *American Historical Review*, xxvii (1922), pp. 669–94.
35. S. Gaukroger, *The Emergence of a Scientific Culture* (Oxford: Oxford University Press, 2006), pp. 59–76.
36. C. H. Haskins, *The Renaissance of the Twelfth Century* (New York: Meridian, 1957), was the pioneering work on the subject; A. Crombie, *Robert*

Grossteste (Oxford: Clarendon Press, 1953), is a controversial and engaging study of a major figure; D. C. Lindberg, *The Beginnings of Western Science* (Chicago: University of Chicago Press, 1992), admirably sets the general context.

37. E. Gilson, *History of Christian Philosophy in the Middle Ages* (New York: Random House, 1955), is the classic work; J. A. Weisheipl, *Friar Thomas d'Aquino* (New York: Doubleday, 1974), is still perhaps the best life of Aquinas, though now rivalled by Turner, *Thomas Aquinas*, which is insuperable on Aquinas's thought; M. M. Adams, *William Ockham* (Indianapolis: University of Notre Dame Press, 1987), is the best overall study of Ockham.
38. E. L. Saak, *Creating Augustine* (Oxford: Oxford University Press, 2012), pp. 164–6.
39. Augustine, *Confessions*, 11.3.
40. R. H. Nash, *The Light of the Mind* (Lexington: University Press of Kentucky, 1969), is a clear and shrewd study of Augustine's theory; D. Knowles, *What Is Mysticism?* (London: Burns and Oates, 1967), is the best short introduction to mysticism.
41. D. Sarma, *Readings in Classic Indian Philosophy* (New York: Columbia University Press, 2011), p. 40.
42. H. Dumoulin, *Zen Buddhism: A History*, 2 vols (Bloomington: World Wisdom, 2005), i, p. 85.
43. Dumoulin, *Zen Buddhism*, and T. Hoover, *Zen Culture* (New York: Random House, 1977), are good introductions; R. Pirsig, *Zen and the Art of Motorcycle Maintenance* (London: Vintage, 2004), is the classic story of the author's trans-American pilgrimage in search of a doctrine of 'quality'.
44. Pirsig, *Zen and the Art of Motorcycle Maintenance*, p. 278.
45. Ambrose, *Epistles*, 20:8.
46. B. Tierney, *The Crisis of Church and State 1050–1300* (Englewood Cliffs: Prentice Hall, 1964), p. 175; Bettenson and Maunder, *Documents of the Christian Church*, p. 121.
47. J. Maritain, *Man and the State* (Washington, DC: Catholic University of America Press, 1951), is the classic musing of a seminal modern thinker on Church–state relations. R. W. Southern, *Western Society and the Church in the Middle Ages* (London: Penguin, 1970), is the best introduction to medieval Church history. A. Murray, *Reason and Society in the Middle Ages* (Oxford: Clarendon Press, 1978), takes a fascinatingly oblique approach. O. and J. L. O'Donovan, *From Irenaeus to Grotius: A Sourcebook in Christian Political Thought* (Grand Rapids: Eerdmans, 1999), prints the most important sources with excellent commentary.
48. P. Brown, 'The rise and function of the holy man in late antiquity', *Journal of Roman Studies*, lxi (1971), pp. 80–101.
49. Bettenson and Maunder, *Documents of the Christian Church*, p. 121.

50. W. Ullmann, *The Growth of Papal Government in the Middle Ages* (London: Methuen, 1970), and *A History of Political Thought: The Middle Ages* (Middlesex: Penguin, 1965), distil the work of the greatest authority. E. Duffy, *Saints and Sinners* (New Haven: Yale University Press, 1997), is a lively, well-grounded history of the papacy.
51. G. E. R. Lloyd, *Aristotle: The Growth and Structure of His Thought* (Cambridge: Cambridge University Press, 1968), p. 255.
52. Aristotle, *Politics*, 4.3.
53. J. H. Burns and T. Izbicki, eds, *Conciliarism and Papalism* (Cambridge: Cambridge University Press, 1997), is an important collection. J. J. Ryan, *The Apostolic Conciliarism of Jean Gerson* (Atlanta: Scholars, 1998), is excellent on the development of the tradition in the fifteenth century. A. Gewirth, *Marsilius of Padua* (New York: Columbia University Press, 1951), is the best study of this thinker. The same author and C. J. Nedermann have produced a good translation and edition of Marsilius's *Defensor Pacis* (New York: Columbia University Press, 2001).
54. J. Mabbott, *The State and the Citizen* (London: Hutchison's University Library, 1955), is a good introduction to the political theory involved. J. Rawls, *A Theory of Justice* (Cambridge, MA: Harvard University Press, 1971), is an impressive attempt to bring social contract theory up to date.
55. See P. S. Lewis, *Essays in Later Medieval French History* (London: Hambledon, 1985), pp. 170–86.
56. Ibid., p. 174.
57. J. R. Figgis, *The Divine Right of Kings* (Cambridge: Cambridge University Press, 1922), and M. Wilks, *The Problem of Sovereignty in the Middle Ages* (Cambridge: Cambridge University Press, 2008), are outstanding studies. Q. Skinner, *The Foundations of Modern Political Thought*, 2 vols (Cambridge: Cambridge University Press, 1978), is an invaluable guide to all major themes of late-medieval and early modern politics.
58. M. Keen, *Chivalry* (New Haven: Yale University Press, 1984).
59. P. Binski, *The Painted Chamber at Westminster* (London: Society of Antiquaries, 1986), pp. 13–15.
60. F. Fernández-Armesto, 'Colón y los libros de caballería', in C. Martínez Shaw and C. Pacero Torre, eds, *Cristóbal Colón* (Valladolid: Junta de Castilla y León, 2006), pp. 114–28.
61. F. E. Kingsley, ed., *Charles Kingsley: His Letters and Memories of His Life*, 2 vols (Cambridge, Cambridge University Press, 2011), ii, p. 461. M. Girouard, *The Return to Camelot* (New Haven: Yale University Press, 1981), is a fascinating and stimulating account of the revival from the eighteenth century to the twentieth.
62. Keen, *Chivalry*, is the standard work; M. G. Vale, *War and Chivalry* (London: Duckworth, 1981), is an impressive investigation of the context in which chivalry had its greatest impact.

63. B. Lewis, *The Political Language of Islam* (Chicago: University of Chicago Press, 1988), pp. 73–4.
64. C. Hillenbrand, *The Crusades: Islamic Perspectives* (Edinburgh: Edinburgh University Press, 1999), and K. Armstrong, *Holy War* (New York: Anchor, 2001), are both highly readable and highly reliable. G. Keppel, *Jihad* (Cambridge, MA: Harvard University Press, 2001), is an interesting journalistic investigation of the holy-war idea in contemporary Islam. J. Riley-Smith, *What Were the Crusades?* (London: Palgrave Macmillan, 2009), is the best account of what crusaders thought they were doing.
65. Helpful essays by Maurice Keen are collected in M. Keen, *Nobles, Knights and Men-at-Arms in the Middle Ages* (London: Hambledon, 1986), especially pp. 187–221. The quotation from Marlowe is from *Tamburlaine the Great*, Act I, Scene 5, 186–90.
66. M. Rady, *Customary Law in Hungary* (Oxford: Oxford University Press, 2015), pp. 15–20.
67. P. O. Kristeller, *Renaissance Thought and Its Sources* (New York: Columbia University Press, 1979), is an unsurpassed brief introduction. R. Black, *Humanism and Education in Medieval and Renaissance Italy* (Cambridge: Cambridge University Press, 2001), is an exhaustive and powerful revisionist study, which should be set alongside R. W. Southern, *Scholastic Humanism and the Unification of Europe* (Oxford: Wiley-Blackwell, 2000).
68. R. W. Bulliett, *Conversion to Islam in the Medieval Period: An Essay in Quantitative History* (Cambridge, MA: Harvard University Press, 1979), pp. 16–32, 64–80.
69. *Selected Works of Ramon Llull*, ed. A. Bonner (Princeton: Princeton University Press, 1985), is a convenient introduction to his thought. The terms of debate on spiritual conquest were set, originally in work of the 1930s and 1940s, by R. Ricard, *The Spiritual Conquest of Mexico* (Berkeley: University of California Press, 1974). S. Neill, *A History of Christian Missions* (Harmondsworth: Penguin, 1964), is the best short overall account of the spread of Christianity.

CHAPTER 6 *Return to the Future: Thinking Through Plague and Cold*

1. A. W. Crosby, *The Columbian Exchange* (1972), is now best consulted in the 2003 edition (Santa Barbara: Greenwood).
2. There is no satisfactory overall study, though work in progress by J. Belich may yield it. Meanwhile, see W. McNeill, *Plagues and Peoples* (New York: Doubleday, 1976); M. Green, ed., 'Pandemic disease in the medieval world', *Medieval Globe*, i (2014).
3. H. Lamb, 'The early medieval warm epoch and its sequel', *Palaeogeography, Palaeoclimatology, Palaeoecology*, i (1965), pp. 13–37; H. Lamb, *Climate, History and the Modern World* (London: Routledge, 1995); G. Parker,

Global Crisis: Climate Change and Catastrophe in the Seventeenth Century (New Haven: Yale University Press, 2013).

4. The essays collected in F. Fernández-Armesto, ed., *The Global Opportunity* (Aldershot: Ashgate, 1998), and *The European Opportunity* (Aldershot: Ashgate, 1998), provide an overview.
5. H. Honour, *Chinoiserie: The Vision of Cathay* (New York: Dutton, 1968), p. 125.
6. The next paragraph is based on F. Fernández-Armesto, *Américo* (Madrid: Tusquets, 2008), pp. 28–31.
7. F. Fernández-Armesto, *Amerigo: The Man Who Gave His Name to America* (New York: Random House, 2007), pp. 6–7.
8. W. Oakeshott, *Classical Inspiration in Medieval Art* (London: Chapman, 1969).
9. J. Goody, *Renaissances: The One or the Many?* (Cambridge: Cambridge University Press, 2009).
10. F. Fernández-Armesto, *Millennium* (London: Bantam House, 1995), p. 59.
11. J. Winckelmann, *Reflections on the Painting and Sculpture of the Greeks* (London: Millar, 1765), p. 4; K. Harloe, *Winckelmann and the Invention of Antiquity* (Oxford: Oxford University Press, 2013). C. H. Rowland et al., eds, *The Place of the Antique in Early Modern Europe* (Chicago: University of Chicago Press, 2000), is an important exhibition catalogue. F. Haskell, *Taste and the Antique* (New Haven: Yale University Press, 1981), and *Patrons and Painters* (New Haven: Yale University Press, 1980), distil the work of the foremost scholar in the field.
12. *Bacon's Essays*, ed. W. A. Wright (London: Macmillan, 1920), p. 204.
13. The next few paragraphs are based on work cited in P. Burke, F. Fernández-Armesto, and L. Clossey, 'The Global Renaissance', *Journal of World History*, xxviii (2017), pp. 1–30.
14. F. Fernández-Armesto, *Columbus on Himself* (Indianapolis: Hackett, 2010), p. 223.
15. Useful books on Columbus are W. D. and C. R. Phillips, *The Worlds of Christopher Columbus* (Cambridge: Cambridge University Press, 1992); F. Fernández-Armesto, *Columbus* (London: Duckworth, 1996); and Martínez Shaw and Pacero Torre, eds, *Cristóbal Colón*. E. O'Gorman, *The Invention of America* (Westport: Greenwood, 1972), is a controversial and stimulating study of the idea.
16. D. Goodman and C. Russell, *The Rise of Scientific Europe* (London: Hodder and Stoughton, 1991), is a wonderful overview.
17. A. Ben-Zaken, *Cross-Cultural Scientific Exchanges in the Eastern Mediterranean, 1560–1660* (Baltimore: Johns Hopkins University Press, 2010).
18. G. Saliba, *Islamic Science and the Making of the European Renaissance* (Cambridge, MA: Harvard University Press, 2007).

19. D. C. Lindberg, *Theories of Vision from Al-kindi to Kepler* (Chicago: University of Chicago Press, 1976), pp. 18–32.
20. H. F. Cohen, *How Modern Science Came into the World. Four Civilizations, One 17th Century Breakthrough* (Amsterdam: Amsterdam University Press, 2010), especially pp. 725–9.
21. G. W. Leibniz, *Novissima Sinica* (Leipzig?, 1699).
22. S. Schapin, *The Scientific Revolution* (Chicago: University of Chicago Press, 1996).
23. R. Evans, *Rudolf II and His World* (Oxford: Oxford University Press, 1973).
24. F. Yates, *Giordano Bruno and the Hermetic Tradition* (Chicago: University of Chicago Press, 1964), and *The Art of Memory*, are fundamental; J. Spence, *The Memory Palace of Matteo Ricci* (New York: Penguin, 1985), is a fascinating case study.
25. F. Bacon, *Novum Organum*, in J. Spedding et al., eds, *The Works of Francis Bacon*, 4 vols (Cambridge: Cambridge University Press, 2011), iv, p. 237; L. Jardine and A. Stewart, *Hostage to Fortune: The Troubled Life of Francis Bacon* (New York: Hill, 1999).
26. T. H. Huxley, 'Biogenesis and abiogenesis,' in *Collected Essays*, 8 vols (London: Macmillan, 1893–8), viii, p. 229.
27. K. Popper, *The Logic of Scientific Discovery* (London: Routledge, 2002), pp. 6–19.
28. W. Pagel, *Joan Baptista van Helmont* (Cambridge: Cambridge University Press, 1982), p. 36.
29. R. Foley, *Working Without a Net* (New York and Oxford: Oxford University Press, 1993), is a provocative study of Descartes's context and influence. D. Garber, *Descartes Embodied* (Cambridge: Cambridge University Press, 2001), is an important collection of essays. S. Gaukroger, *Descartes' System of Natural Philosophy* (Cambridge: Cambridge University Press, 2002), is a challenging investigation of the philosopher's thought.
30. *The Philosophical Writings of Descartes*, ed. J. Cottingham, R. Stoothoff, and D. Murdoch (Cambridge: Cambridge University Press, 1984), i, pp. 19, 53, 145–50; ii, pp. 409–17; iii, p. 337; M. D. Wilson, *Descartes* (London: Routledge, 1978), pp. 127–30, 159–74, 264–70.
31. A. Macfarlane and G. Martin, *The Glass Bathyscaphe: Glass and World History* (London: Profile, 2002).
32. Saliba, *Islamic Science*.
33. J. M. Dietz, *Novelties in the Heavens* (Chicago: University of Chicago Press, 1993), is an engaging introduction. A. Koestler, *The Sleepwalkers* (London: Hutchinson, 1968), is a brilliant, spellbinding account of the early Copernican tradition. T. Kuhn, *The Copernican Revolution* (Cambridge, MA: Harvard University Press 2003), is unsurpassed on Copernicus's impact.
34. R. Feldhay, *Galileo and the Church: Political Inquisition or Critical Dialogue* (Cambridge: Cambridge University Press, 1995), pp. 124–70.

35. D. Brewster, *Memoirs of the Life, Writings, and Discoveries of Sir Isaac Newton*, 2 vols (Edinburgh: Constable, 1855), ii, p. 138. R. Westfall, *The Life of Isaac Newton*, 2 vols (Cambridge: Cambridge University Press, 1994), is the best biography, now rivalled in brief by P. Fara, *Newton: The Making of a Genius* (New York: Pan Macmillan, 2011). M. White, *The Last Sorcerer* (Reading, MA: Perseus, 1998), is a popular work intriguingly slanted toward Newton's alchemical interests. H. Gilbert and D. Gilbert Smith, *Gravity: The Glue of the Universe* (Englewood: Teacher Ideas Press, 1997), is an engaging popular history of the concept of gravity. Newton's self-description, reported by his fellow-member of the Royal Society, Andrew Ramsay, was reported in J. Spence, *Anecdotes, Observations and Characters, of Books and Men* (London: Murray, 1820), p. 54.
36. Needham, *Science and Civilisation in China*, ii, p. 142.
37. S. Lee, *Great Englishmen of the Sixteenth Century* (London: Constable, 1904), pp. 31–6.
38. J. Carey, ed., *The Faber Book of Utopias* (London: Faber and Faber, 1999), is a superb anthology, from which I draw my examples. K. Kumar, *Utopianism* (Milton Keynes: Open University Press, 1991), is a useful, simple, and short introduction.
39. N. Machiavelli, *The Prince*, ch. 18.
40. D. Wootton's translation of *The Prince* (Indianapolis: Hackett, 1995) is the best. H. C. Mansfield, *Machiavelli's Virtue* (Chicago: University of Chicago Press, 1998), is a profound and challenging reassessment of the sources of his thought. Q. Skinner, *Machiavelli* (Oxford: Oxford University Press, 1981), is a subtle short introduction.
41. J. G. A. Pocock, *The Machiavellian Moment* (Princeton: Princeton University Press, 1975), is the essential work. G. Q. Flynn, *Conscription and Democracy* (Westport: Greenwood, 2002), is an interesting study of the history of conscription in Britain, France, and the United States.
42. De Bary et al., eds, *Sources of Indian Tradition*, p. 7.
43. Ibid., pp. 66–7; T. De Bary, ed., *Sources of East Asian Tradition*, 2 vols (New York: Columbia University Press, 2008), ii, pp. 19–21.
44. De Bary, ed., *Sources of East Asian Tradition*, prints an invaluable selection of sources. L. Chi-chao, *History of Chinese Political Thought* (Abingdon: Routledge, 2000), is a good short introduction. F. Wakeman, *The Great Enterprise*, 2 vols (Berkeley and Los Angeles: University of California Press, 1985), is the best introduction to Chinese history in the period. L. Struve, *Voices from the Ming-Qing Cataclysm* (New Haven: Yale University Press, 1993), evokes the period in texts.
45. J. T. C. Liu, *Reform in Sung China: Wang-an Shih and His New Policies* (Cambridge, MA: Harvard University Press, 1959), p. 54.
46. De Grazia, ed., *Masters of Chinese Political Thought*, has some useful texts. On the consequences of Chinese universalism for China's external relations in what we think of as the Middle Ages, J. Tao, *Two Sons of Heaven* (Tucson:

University of Arizona Press, 1988), is extremely interesting. W. I. Cohen, *East Asia at the Center* (New York: Columbia University Press, 2001), is a useful survey of the history of the region in the context of a Sinocentric vision of the world. On the political connotations of maps I rely on J. Black, *Maps and Politics* (Chicago: University of Chicago Press, 1998).

47. H. Cortazzi, *Isles of Gold: Antique Maps of Japan* (New York: Weatherhill, 1992), pp. 6–38.
48. E. L. Dreyer, *Early Ming China: A Political History, 1355–1435* (Stanford: Stanford University Press, 1982), p. 120.
49. W. T. De Bary et al., eds, *Sources of Japanese Tradition*, 2 vols (New York: Columbia University Press, 2001–5), i, p. 467; M. Berry, *Hideyoshi* (Cambridge, MA: Harvard University Press, 1982), pp. 206–16.
50. I. Hirobumi, *Commentaries on the Constitution* (Tokyo: Central University, 1906). R. Benedict, *The Chrysanthemum and the Sword* (Boston: Houghton Mifflin, 1946), is the classic Western account of Japanese values. Cortazzi, *Isles of Gold*, is a splendid introduction to Japanese cartography. J. Whitney Hall, ed., *The Cambridge History of Japan*, 6 vols (Cambridge: Cambridge University Press, 1989–93), is outstanding. G. B. Sansom, *A Short Cultural History of Japan* (Stanford: Stanford University Press, 1978), is a helpful single-volume study.
51. K. M. Doak, *A History of Nationalism in Modern Japan* (Leiden: Brill, 2007), pp. 120–4; J. and J. Brown, *China, Japan, Korea: Culture and Customs* (Charleston: Booksurge, 2006), p. 90.
52. O'Donovan and O'Donovan, eds, *From Irenaeus to Grotius*, p. 728.
53. C. Carr, *The Lessons of Terror: A History of Warfare against Civilians* (New York: Random House, 2003), pp. 78–9.
54. H. Bull et al., *Hugo Grotius and International Relations* (Oxford: Clarendon Press, 1990), is a valuable collection. There is a selection of political writings of Vitoria in English translation, edited by J. Laurence and A. Pagden, *Vitoria: Political Writings* (Cambridge: Cambridge University Press, 1991).
55. C. Maier, *Once Within Borders* (Cambridge, MA: Harvard University Press, 2016), pp. 33–9.
56. L. Hanke, *The Spanish Struggle for Justice in the Conquest of America* (Philadelphia: University of Pennsylvania Press, 1949), p. 125.
57. C. Lévi-Strauss, *The Elementary Structures of Kinship* (Boston: Beacon, 1969), p. 46.
58. R. Wokler, 'Apes and races in the Scottish Enlightenment', in P. Jones, ed., *Philosophy and Politics in the Scottish Enlightenment* (Edinburgh: Donald, 1986), pp. 145–68. For a satirical sidelight on Lord Monboddo's theories, T. L. Peacock's novel *Melincourt* is one of the great comic achievements of English literature.
59. N. Barlow, ed., *The Works of Charles Darwin, vol. 1: Diary of the Voyage of the HMS Beagle* (New York: New York University Press, 1987), p. 109.

CHAPTER 7 *Global Enlightenments: Joined-Up Thinking in a Joined-Up World*

1. For sources of this and other materials on Maupertuis, see Fernández-Armesto, *Truth: A History*, pp. 152–8.
2. P. L. Maupertuis, *The Figure of the Earth, Determined from Observations Made by Order of the French King at the Polar Circle* (London: Cox, 1738), pp. 38–72.
3. J. C. Boudri, *What Was Mechanical about Mechanics: The Concept of Force between Metaphysics and Mechanics from Newton to Lagrange* (Dordrecht: Springer, 2002), p. 145 n. 37.
4. G. Tonelli, 'Maupertuis et la critique de la métaphysique', *Actes de la journée Maupertuis* (Paris: Vrin, 1975), pp. 79–90.
5. Parker, *Global Crisis*.
6. F. Fernández-Armesto, *The World: A History* (Upper Saddle River: Pearson, 2014).
7. L. Blussé, 'Chinese century: the eighteenth century in the China Sea region', *Archipel*, lviii (1999), pp. 107–29.
8. Leibniz, *Novissima Sinica*, preface; D. J. Cook and H. Rosemont, eds, *Writings on China* (Chicago and La Salle: Open Court, 1994).
9. I. Morris, in F. Fernández-Armesto, ed., *The Oxford Illustrated History of the World* (Oxford: Oxford University Press, 2019), ch. 7.
10. E. Gibbon, *The History of the Decline and Fall of the Roman Empire*, ch. 1.
11. Strabo, *Geography*, 3.1.
12. Gibbon, *Decline and Fall*, ch. 38.
13. P. Langford et al., eds, *The Writings and Speeches of Edmund Burke* (Oxford: Clarendon Press, 1981–), ix, p. 248.
14. D. Hay, *Europe: The Emergence of an Idea* (Edinburgh: Edinburgh University Press, 1957), is an excellent history of the concept. Long and short histories respectively can be found in N. Davies, *Europe: A History* (London: Bodley Head, 2014), and F. Fernández-Armesto, *The Times Illustrated History of Europe* (London: Times Books, 1995).
15. D. Diderot, 'L'Art', in *L'Encyclopédie* (1751), i, pp. 713–17.
16. D. Diderot, *Les Eleuthéromanes ou les furieux de la liberté*, in *Œuvres complètes* (Paris: Claye, 1875), ix, p. 16; E. A. Setjen, *Diderot et le défi esthétique* (Paris: Vrin, 1999), p. 78.
17. G. Avenel, ed., *Oeuvres complètes* (Paris: Le Siècle, 1879), vii, p. 184.
18. P. A. Dykema and H. A. Oberman, eds, *Anticlericalism in Late Medieval and Early Modern Europe* (Leiden: Brill, 1993), is an important collection of essays. S. J. Barnett, *Idol Temples and Crafty Priests* (New York: St Martin's, 1999), tackles the origins of Enlightenment anticlericalism in a fresh way. P. Gay, *The Enlightenment*, 2 vols (New York: W. W. Norton, 1996), is a brilliant work with a strong focus on the secular thinking of the *philosophes*, now challenged as the leading synthesis, at least on political thought, by J. Israel, *The Radical Enlightenment* (Oxford: Oxford University

Press, 2002). S. J. Barnett, *The Enlightenment and Religion* (Manchester: Manchester University Press, 2004), challenges the primacy of secularism in the Enlightenment as, most recently, does U. Lehner, *The Catholic Enlightenment: The Forgotten History of a Global Movement* (Oxford: Oxford University Press, 2016).

19. J. A. N. de Caritat, Marquis de Condorcet, *Sketch for an Historical Picture of the Progress of the Human Mind*, trans. J. Barraclough (London: Weidenfeld, 1955), p. 201.
20. J. B. Bury, *The Idea of Progress* (London: Macmillan, 1920), is an unsurpassed classic, stimulatingly challenged by R. Nisbet, *History of the Idea of Progress* (New Brunswick and London: Transaction, 1980), with an attempt to trace the idea back to Christian traditions of providence.
21. G. W. Leibniz, *Theodicy* (1710; new edn, London: Routledge, 1951), is the classic statement; G. M. Ross, *Leibniz* (Oxford: Oxford University Press, 1984), is the best short introduction to his philosophy generally.
22. M. Grice-Hutchinson, *The School of Salamanca* (Oxford: Oxford University Press, 1952), p. 96.
23. T. de Mercado, *Summa de tratos* (Book IV: 'De la antigüedad y origen de los cambios', fo. 3v) (Seville: H. Díaz, 1575).
24. K. Kwarteng, *War and Gold* (London: Bloomsbury, 2014).
25. L. Magnusson, *Mercantilism: The Shaping of an Economic Language* (London: Routledge, 1994), is a good introduction; I have not seen the heavily revised version, *The Political Economy of Mercantilism* (London: Routledge, 2015). I. Wallerstein, *The Modern World-System*, vol. 2 (Berkeley: University of California Press, 1980), is fundamental for the historical background, as is F. Braudel, *Civilization and Capitalism*, 3 vols (London: Collins, 1983).
26. Grice-Hutchinson, *The School of Salamanca*, p. 95.
27. Ibid., p. 94.
28. Ibid., p. 112. Other early sources are collected in A. E. Murphy, *Monetary Theory, 1601–1758* (London and New York: Routledge, 1997). D. Fischer, *The Great Wave* (Oxford: Oxford University Press, 1999), is a controversial but highly stimulating history of inflation.
29. A. Smith, *The Wealth of Nations*, bk 4, ch. 5. The standard edition is that edited by R. H. Campbell, A. S. Skinner, and W. B. Todd (Oxford: Oxford University Press, 1976).
30. A. Smith, *Wealth of Nations*, bk 5, ch. 2.
31. A. Smith, *Theory of Moral Sentiments* (London: Millar, 1790), 4.1, 10; *Selected Philosophical Writings*, ed. J. R. Otteson (Exeter: Academic, 2004), p. 74.
32. T. Piketty, *Capital in the Twenty-first Century* (Cambridge, MA: Harvard University Press, 2014).
33. F. W. Hirst, *Adam Smith* (New York: Macmillan, 1904), p. 236.
34. D. Friedman, *The Machinery of Freedom* (La Salle: Open Court, 1989),

sets Smith's work in the context of modern liberal economics. D. D. Raphael, *Adam Smith* (New York: Oxford University Press, 1985), is a good short introduction. P. H. Werhane, *Adam Smith and His Legacy for Modern Capitalism* (New York: Oxford University Press, 1991), traces his influence.

35. O. Höffe, *Thomas Hobbes* (Munich: Beck, 2010), is the best work. Hobbes's main work is usefully analysed in C. Schmitt, ed., *The Leviathan in the State Theory of Thomas Hobbes: Meaning and Failure of a Political Symbol* (Chicago: University of Chicago Press, 2008). A. Rapaczynski, *Nature and Politics* (Ithaca: Cornell University Press, 1987), sets Hobbes in the context of Locke and Rousseau. N. Malcolm, *Aspects of Hobbes* (Oxford: Clarendon Press, 2002), is a highly illuminating collection of searching essays. The quotation from Aristotle is from *Politics*, 1.2.
36. S. Song, *Voltaire et la Chine* (Paris: Presses Universitaire de France, 1989).
37. D. F. Lach, *Asia in the Making of Europe*, vol. 3 (Chicago: University of Chicago Press, 1993), is fundamental. Also important are J. Ching and W. G. Oxtoby, *Discovering China* (Rochester, NY: University of Rochester Press, 1992); W. W. Davis, 'China, the Confucian ideal, and the European Age of Enlightenment', *Journal of the History of Ideas*, xliv (1983), pp. 523–48; T. H. C. Lee, ed., *China and Europe: Images and Influences in Sixteenth to Eighteenth Centuries* (Hong Kong: Chinese University Press, 1991). The quotation from Montesquieu is from *L'Esprit des lois*, Book XVII, ch. 3.
38. N. Russell, 'The influence of China on the Spanish Enlightenment', Tufts University PhD dissertation (2017).
39. G. T. F. Raynal, *Histoire philosophique*, i, p. 124; quoted in Israel, *The Radical Enlightenment*, p. 112.
40. Fernández-Armesto, *Millennium*, pp. 458–9; *The Americas* (London: Phoenix, 2004), pp. 64–5.
41. P. Fara, *Sex, Botany and Empire* (Cambridge: Icon, 2004), pp. 96–126.
42. M. Newton, *Savage Girls and Wild Boys: A History of Feral Children* (London: Faber, 2002), pp. 22, 32; H. Lane, *The Wild Boy of Aveyron* (Cambridge, MA: Harvard University Press, 1975).
43. T. Ellingson, *The Myth of the Noble Savage* (Berkeley: University of California Press, 2001), is a useful introduction. H. Fairchild, *The Noble Savage* (New York: Columbia University Press, 1928), is an elegant history of the concept. M. Hodgen, *Early Anthropology* (Philadelphia: University of Pennsylvania Press, 1964), and Pagden, *The Fall of Natural Man*, are invaluable studies of the ideas generated by early modern ethnography.
44. Rousseau, *Discourse on the Origin of Inequality*, quoted in C. Jones, *The Great Nation* (London: Penguin, 2002), p. 29; M. Cranston, *Jean-Jacques: The Early Life and Work* (Chicago: University of Chicago Press, 1991), pp. 292–3; Z. M. Trachtenberg, *Making Citizens: Rousseau's Political Theory of Culture* (London: Routledge, 1993), p. 79.
45. Israel, *The Radical Enlightenment*, pp. 130–1, 700.

46. R. Wokler, *Rousseau, the Age of Enlightenment, and Their Legacies* (Princeton: Princeton University Press, 2012), pp. 1–28.
47. Rousseau, *Du contrat social*, bk 1, ch. 6. T. O'Hagan, *Rousseau* (London: Routledge, 1999), is particularly good at elucidating this text. Rousseau, *Discourse on the Origin of Inequality* (1754), is the fundamental text. A. Widavsky, *The Rise of Radical Egalitarianism* (Washington, DC: American University Press, 1991), is an excellent introduction. D. Gordon, *Citizens without Sovereignty* (Princeton: Princeton University Press, 1994), traces the concept in eighteenth-century French thought. R. W. Fogel, *The Fourth Great Awakening* (Chicago: University of Chicago Press, 2000), is a provocative work, linking radical American egalitarianism to the Christian tradition and arguing for a future in which equality will be attainable. A. Sen, *Inequality Reexamined* (Cambridge, MA: Harvard University Press, 1992), is an arresting essay that brings the story up to date and poses challenges for the future. On the general will, A. Levine, *The General Will* (Cambridge: Cambridge University Press, 1993), traces the concept from Rousseau to modern communism. P. Riley, *The General Will before Rousseau* (Princeton: Princeton University Press, 1986), is a superb study of its origins.
48. Rousseau, *Du contrat social*, bk 1, ch. 3.
49. J. Keane, *Tom Paine* (London: Bloomsbury, 1995), is a good biography. E. Foner, *Tom Paine and Revolutionary America* (New York: Oxford University Press, 1976), is a classic study. Rousseau's most influential works in the field were the *Discourse on Inequality* (1754) and *Émile* (1762).
50. O. de Gouges, *Déclaration des droits de la femme et de la citoyenne*, article x; there is a convenient edition (Paris: République des Lettres, 2012). De Gouges's views are curiously illuminated by her novel, *Maria or the Wrongs of Woman*. C. L. Johnson, ed., *The Cambridge Companion to Mary Wollstonecraft* (Cambridge: Cambridge University Press, 2002), is wide-ranging and helpful.
51. C. Francis and F. Gontier, eds, *Les écrits de Simone de Beauvoir: la vie-l'écriture* (Paris: Gallimard, 1979), pp. 245–81.
52. D. Diderot, *Encyclopédie méthodique* (Paris: Pantoucke, 1783), ii, p. 222.
53. J. C. D. Clark, *The Language of Liberty* (Cambridge: Cambridge University Press, 1994).
54. F. J. Turner, *The Frontier in American History* (New York: Dover, 1996); F. J. Turner, *Does the Frontier Experience Make America Exceptional?*, readings selected and introduced by R. W. Etulain (Boston: Bedford, 1999).
55. M. Cranston, *The Noble Savage: Jean-Jacques Rousseau, 1754–62* (Chicago: University of Chicago Press, 1991), p. 308.
56. E. Burke, *Reflections on the Revolutions in France*, ed. F. M. Turner (New Haven: Yale University Press, 2003), p. 80.
57. A. de Tocqueville, *Democracy in America*, introduction and vol. 1, ch. 17. A recent edition is by H. C. Mansfield and D. Winthrop (Chicago:

University of Chicago Press, 2000). J. T. Schneider, ed., *The Chicago Companion to Tocqueville's Democracy in America* (Chicago: University of Chicago Press, 2012), is comprehensive.

58. C. Williamson, *American Suffrage from Property to Democracy* (Princeton: Princeton University Press, 1960), traces the history of the American franchise. Fascinating light on the reception of American democratic ideas in Europe is cast by the influential J. Bryce, *The American Commonwealth* (London: Macmillan, 1888).
59. Locke, *An Essay Concerning Human Understanding*, bk 2, ch. 1.
60. A. J. Ayer, *Language, Truth and Logic* (London: Gollancz, 1936), is the baldest statement of logical positivism. For a critique, see Putnam, *Reason, Truth and History*. See pp. 363–5.
61. R. Spangenburg and D. Moser, *The History of Science in the Eighteenth Century* (New York: Facts on File, 1993), is a short popular introduction. A. Donovan, *Antoine Lavoisier* (Oxford: Blackwell, 1993), is a fine biography that sets the subject against a clear account of the science of the time. R. E. Schofield, *The Enlightenment of Joseph Priestley*, and *The Enlightened Joseph Priestley* (University Park: Pennsylvania State University Press, 1998, 2004), form an equally impressive biography of Lavoisier's rival.
62. L. Pasteur, *The Germ Theory and Its Applications to Medicine and Surgery* (1909).
63. R. W. Reid, *Microbes and Men* (Boston: E. P. Dutton, 1975), is a readable history of germ theory. A. Karlen, *Man and Microbes* (New York: Simon & Schuster, 1995), is a controversial, doom-fraught survey of the history of microbially inflicted plagues. L. Garrett, *The Coming Plague* (New York: Farrar, Straus and Giroux, 1994), is a brilliantly written admonition to the world about the current state of microbial evolution.
64. *Papers and Proceedings of the Connecticut Valley Historical Society* (1876), i, p. 56. M. J. McClymond and G. R. McDermott, *The Theology of Jonathan Edwards* (Oxford: Oxford University Press, 2012), is the most complete study.
65. *George Whitefield's Journals* (Lafayette: Sovereign Grace, 2000).
66. *Œuvres complètes de Voltaire*, ed. L. Moland (Paris: Garnier, 1877–85), x, p. 403.
67. T. Blanning, *The Triumph of Music* (Cambridge, MA: Harvard University Press, 2008).
68. Baron d'Holbach, *System of Nature*, quoted in Jones, *The Great Nation*, pp. 204–5.
69. Fernández-Armesto, *Millennium*, pp. 379–83.
70. I. Berlin, *The Roots of Romanticism* (Princeton: Princeton University Press, 2001), is a challenging collection of lectures. W. Vaughan, *Romanticism and Art* (London: Thames and Hudson, 1994), is a spirited survey. D. Wu, *Companion to Romanticism* (Oxford: Blackwell, 1999), is intended as an aid for the study of British romantic literature but is much more widely

useful. The final allusion is to a speech W. E. Gladstone made in Liverpool on 28 June 1886. P. Clarke, *A Question of Leadership* (London: Hamilton, 1991), pp. 34–5.

CHAPTER 8 *The Climacteric of Progress: Nineteenth-Century Certainties*

1. I. Kant, *Critique of Pure Reason*, ed. P. Guyer and A. W. Wood (Cambridge: Cambridge University Press, 1998).
2. *The Collected Works of William Hazlitt*, ed. A. R. Waller and A. Glover (London: Dent, 1904), x, p. 87.
3. T. R. Malthus, *Population: The First Essay* (Ann Arbor: University of Michigan Press, 1959), p. 5.
4. W. Hazlitt, *The Spirit of the Age* (London: Templeman, 1858), p. 93.
5. A. Pyle, ed., *Population: Contemporary Responses to Thomas Malthus* (Bristol: Thoemmes Press, 1994), is a fascinating compilation of early criticism. S. Hollander, *The Economics of Thomas Robert Malthus* (Toronto: University of Toronto Press, 1997), is an exhaustive and authoritative study. M. L. Bacci, *A Concise History of World Population* (Oxford: Blackwell, 2001), is a useful introduction to demographic history. A. Bashford, *Global Population: History, Geopolitics, and Life on Earth* (New York: Columbia University Press, 2014), puts population anxiety in perspective.
6. Langford et al., eds, *Writings and Speeches of Edmund Burke*, ix, p. 466.
7. Burke, *Reflections on the Revolution in France*, is the founding text of the tradition. The conservatism he established is brilliantly satirized – though perhaps rather caricatured – in T. L. Peacock's novel of 1830, *The Misfortunes of Elphin*. M. Oakeshott, *Rationalism in Politics* (London: Methuen, 1962), and R. Scruton, *The Meaning of Conservatism* (London: Macmillan, 1980), are outstanding modern statements. R. Bourke, *Empire and Nation: The Political Life of Edmund Burke* (Princeton: Princeton University Press, 2015), is masterly and vivid.
8. D. Newsome, *Godliness and Good Learning* (London: Cassell, 1988), p. 1.
9. E. Halévy, *The Growth of Philosophic Radicalism* (London: Faber, 1952), remains unsurpassed. See J. R. Dinwiddy, *Bentham* (Stanford: Stanford University Press, 2003), for a short introduction, and G. J. Postema, *Jeremy Bentham: Moral, Political, and Legal Philosophy*, 2 vols (Aldershot: Dartmouth, 2002), for a useful collection of important essays on the subject.
10. *The Collected Letters of Thomas and Jane Welsh Carlyle* (Durham: Duke University Press, 1970–in progress), xxxv, pp. 84–5.
11. A. Bain, *James Mill* (Cambridge: Cambridge University Press, 2011), p. 266; cf. J. S. Mill, *Utilitarianism* (London: Parker, 1863), pp. 9–10.
12. G. W. Smith, ed., *John Stuart Mill's Social and Political Thought*, 2 vols (London: Routledge, 1998), ii, p. 128.
13. H. H. Asquith, *Studies and Sketches* (London: Hutchinson and Co., 1924), p. 20.

14. J. S. Mill, *On Liberty* (London: Longman, 1867), p. 44. For a long-term view of the origins of liberalism, with roots in the Christian tradition, see L. Siedentop, *Inventing the Individual: The Origins of Western Liberalism* (Cambridge, MA: Harvard University Press, 2017).
15. A. Ryan, *The Philosophy of John Stuart Mill* (London: Macmillan, 1987), is an outstanding introduction. J. Skorupski, *John Stuart Mill* (London: Routledge, 1991), is useful and pithy. M. Cowling, *Mill and Liberalism* (Cambridge: Cambridge University Press, 1990), is a superb and cogent study.
16. E. O. Hellerstein, *Victorian Women* (Stanford: Stanford University Press, 1981), is a valuable collection of evidence. C. Heywood, *Childhood in Nineteenth-Century France* (Cambridge: Cambridge University Press, 1988), is a fine study of the problem of the labour laws. L. de Mause, ed., *The History of Childhood* (New York: Harper, 1974), is a pioneering collection of essays.
17. W. Irvine, *Apes, Angels and Victorians* (New York: McGraw-Hill, 1955).
18. S. Fraquelli, *Radical Light: Italy's Divisionist Painters, 1891–1910* (London: National Gallery, 2008), p. 158.
19. J. C. Petitfils, *Les socialismes utopiques* (Paris: Presses Universitaires de France, 1977). A. E. Bestor, *Backwoods Utopias, the Sectarian and Owenite Phases of Communitarian Socialism in America, 1663–1829* (Philadelphia: University of Pennsylvania Press, 1950), remains valid on US experiments in the tradition.
20. E. Norman, *The Victorian Christian Socialists* (Cambridge: Cambridge University Press, 1987), p. 141.
21. L. Kolakowski and S. Hampshire, eds, *The Socialist Idea* (London: Quartet, 1974), is an excellent, critical introduction. C. J. Guarneri, *The Utopian Alternative* (Ithaca: Cornell University Press, 1991), is a good study of backwoods socialism in America. C. N. Parkinson, *Left Luggage* (Boston: Houghton Mifflin, 1967), is perhaps the funniest-ever critique of socialism.
22. D. Ricardo, *On the Principles of Political Economy and Taxation* [1817] (London: Dent, 1911), is the basic work. G. A. Caravale, ed., *The Legacy of Ricardo* (Oxford: Blackwell, 1985), collects essays on his influence. S. Hollander, *The Economics of David Ricardo* (London: Heinemann, 1979), is an exhaustive study. A volume of the same author's collected essays, which brings his work up to date in some respects, appeared in *Ricardo: The New View*, i (Abingdon: Routledge, 1995).
23. *The Works and Correspondence of David Ricardo*, ed. P. Saffra (Cambridge, Cambridge University Press), ix, p. 29.
24. Ricardo, *On the Principles of Political Economy and Taxation*, chs. 1, 5, p. 61; *The Works of David Ricardo, Esq., MP* (London: Murray, 1846), p. 23.
25. The latter is the well-supported thesis of Piketty, *Capital in the Twenty-First Century*.

26. K. Marx and F. Engels, *The Manifesto of the Communist Party* (New York: International, 1948), p. 9.
27. Popper, *The Open Society and Its Enemies*, vol. 2, is a brilliant study and a devastating critique. D. McLellan, *Marx: Selected Writings* (Oxford: Oxford University Press, 2000), is a good introduction to Marx. F. Wheen, *Karl Marx* (New York: Norton, 2001), is a lively, insightful biography.
28. Berkeley's theory appeared in *The Dialogues between Hylas and Philonous* (1713). F. H. Bradley, *Appearance and Reality* (London: Swan Sonnenschein and Co., 1893), is a classic statement of an extreme form of idealism. G. Vesey, ed., *Idealism: Past and Present* (Cambridge: Cambridge University Press, 1982), treats the subject historically.
29. G. W. F. Hegel, *The Encyclopedia Logic*, ed. T. F. Geraets et al. (Indianapolis: Hackett, 1991); cf. *Grundlinien der Philosophie des Rechts oder Naturrecht und Staatswissenschaft im Grundrisse* (Berlin, 1833), p. 35; G. A. Magee, *The Hegel Dictionary* (London: Continuum, 2010), pp. 111 ff., does a good job of making Hegel's notions intelligible.
30. G. W. F. Hegel, *Lectures on the Philosophy of History*, trans. J. Sibree (London: Bell, 1914), p. 41.
31. S. Avineri, *Hegel's Theory of the Modern State* (Cambridge: Cambridge University Press, 1974), is a clear introduction to the key concepts. E. Weil, *Hegel and the State* (Baltimore: Johns Hopkins University Press, 1998), offers a sympathetic reading and an interesting discussion of some of the lineages of political thought Hegel fathered. R. Bendix, *Kings or People* (Berkeley and Los Angeles: University of California Press, 1978), is an important comparative survey of the rise of popular sovereignty.
32. *Thomas Carlyle's Collected Works* (London: Chapman, 1869), i, pp. 3, 14–15.
33. J. Burckhardt, *Reflections on History* [1868] (Indianapolis: Library Classics, 1943), pp. 270–96; many other editions.
34. T. Carlyle, *On Heroes, Hero-worship and the Heroic in History* [1840] (London: Chapman, n.d. [1857]), p. 2.
35. T. Carlyle, *Past and Present* (New York: Scribner, 1918), p. 249.
36. H. Spencer, *The Study of Sociology* (New York: Appleton, 1896), p. 34.
37. O. Chadwick, *The Secularization of the European Mind in the Nineteenth Century* (Cambridge: Cambridge University Press, 1975), is a brilliant study of the context.
38. Carlyle, *On Heroes*, is a representative text. F. Nietzsche, *Thus Spake Zarasthustra* [1883], ed. G. Parkes (Oxford: Oxford University Press, 2005), contains his thinking on the subject.
39. Nietzsche, *Thus Spake Zarathustra*, Prologue, part 3, p. 11. On Nietzsche as conscious provocateur see S. Prideau, *I Am Dynamite: A Life of Nietzsche* (New York: Duggan, 2018).
40. L. Lampert, *Nietzsche's Task: An Interpretation of Beyond Good and Evil* (New Haven: Yale University Press, 2001); F. Nietzsche, *Beyond Good and Evil*, ed. W. Kaufmann (New York: Random House, 1966), pp. 101–2, 198.

41. B. Russell, *History of Western Philosophy*, p. 690.
42. S. May, *Nietzsche's Ethics and His War on 'Morality'* (Oxford: Oxford University Press, 1999). A good English edition by K. Ansell, in translation by C. Diethe, is available of Nietzsche's *On the Genealogy of Morality* (Cambridge: Cambridge University Press, 1994). A useful collection of essays is R. Schacht, ed., *Nietzsche, Genealogy, Morality* (Berkeley: University of California Press, 1994).
43. F. Nietzsche, *The Will to Power* (New York: Vintage, 1968), p. 550.
44. A. Schopenhauer, *The World as Will and Idea* (1818), and Nietzsche, *The Will to Power*, are the fundamental texts. B. Magee, *The Philosophy of Schopenhauer* (Oxford: Oxford University Press, 1983), is the best introduction. J. E. Atwell, *Schopenhauer on the Character of the World* (Berkeley: University of California Press, 1995), focuses on the doctrine of the will. D. B. Hinton, *The Films of Leni Riefenstahl* (Lanham: Scarecrow, 1991), is a straightforward introduction to her work.
45. Quoted in W. Laqueur, *Guerrilla: A Historical and Critical Study* (New York: Little Brown, 1976), p. 135.
46. See F. Trautmann, *The Voice of Terror: A Biography of Johann Most* (Westport: Greenwood, 1980).
47. The slogan, first reported in English, as far as I can tell, by H. Brailsford, *Macedonia: Its Races and Their Future* (London: Methuen, 1906), p. 116, has passed into lore. See M. MacDermott, *Freedom or Death: The Life of Gotsé Delchev* (London: Journeyman, 1978), p. 348; W. Laqueur, *Terrorism: A Study of National and International Political Violence* (Boston: Little, Brown, 1977), p. 13. K. Brown, *Loyal unto Death: Trust and Terror in Revolutionary Macedonia* (Bloomington: Indiana University Press, 2013), covers Gruev's background superbly.
48. W. Laqueur, *The Age of Terrorism* (Boston: Little, Brown, 1987), is a fine introduction; W. Laqueur, ed., *The Guerrilla Reader* (London: Wildwood House, 1978), and *The Terrorism Reader* (London: Wildwood House, 1979), are useful anthologies. P. Wilkinson, *Political Terrorism* (London: Macmillan, 1974), is a practical-minded survey. J. Conrad, *The Secret Agent* (London: Methuen, 1907), and G. Greene, *The Honorary Consul* (New York: Simon and Schuster, 1973), are among the most perceptive novelistic treatments of terrorism.
49. P. Kropotkin, *Anarchism: A Collection of Revolutionary Writings*, ed. R. Baldwin (Mineola: Dover, 2002), p. 123.
50. C. Cahm, *Kropotkin and the Rise of Revolutionary Anarchism* (New York: Cambridge University Press, 1989). Kropotkin's memoirs are available in a translated version, *Memoirs of a Revolutionist* (New York: Dover, 1988). A. Kelly, *Mikhail Bakunin* (New Haven: Yale University Press, 1987), is probably the best book on Bakunin. D. Morland, *Demanding the Impossible* (London and Washington, DC: Cassell, 1997), studies nineteenth-century anarchism with a psychological perspective.

51. H. D. Thoreau, 'On the duty of civil disobedience', in D. Malone-France, ed., *Political Dissent: A Global Reader* (Lanham: Lexington Books, 2012), p. 37.
52. J. Rawls, *A Theory of Justice* (Cambridge, MA: Harvard University Press, 1971), pp. 364–88. See R. Bleiker, *Popular Dissent, Human Agency and Global Politics* (Cambridge: Cambridge University Press, 2000); J. M. Brown, *Gandhi and Civil Disobedience* (New York: Cambridge University Press, 1977).
53. E. E. Y. Hales, *The Catholic Church and the Modern World* (London: Eyre and Spottiswoode, 1958), makes a good starting point. B. Duncan, *The Church's Social Teaching* (Melbourne: Collins Dove, 1991), is a useful account of the late nineteenth and early twentieth centuries. D. O'Brien and T. Shannon, eds, *Catholic Social Thought: Encyclicals and Documents from Pope Leo to Pope Francis* (Maryknoll: Orbis, 2016), is a useful collection of documents. J. S. Boswell et al., *Catholic Social Thought: Twilight or Renaissance?* (Leuven: Leuven University Press, 2001), is a committed collection of essays, which covers the field.
54. A. R. Vidler, *A Century of Social Catholicism* (London: SPCK, 1964), is the single most important work, seconded by P. Misner, *Social Catholicism in Europe* (New York: Crossroad, 1991). L. P. Wallace, *Leo XIII and the Rise of Socialism* (Durham: Duke University Press, 1966), supplies important context. A. Wilkinson, *Christian Socialism* (London: SCM, 1998), traces Christian influence on labour politics in Britain. W. D. Miller, *Dorothy Day* (San Francisco: Harper and Row, 1982), is a good biography of a leading Catholic social activist of modern times.
55. Quoted in M. Hirst, *States, Countries, Provinces* (London: Kensal, 1986), p. 153.
56. N. Leask, 'Wandering through Eblis: absorption and containment in romantic exoticism', in T. Fulford and P. J. Kitson, eds, *Romanticism and Colonialism: Writing and Empire, 1730–1830* (Cambridge: Cambridge University Press, 1998), pp. 165–83; A. and N. Jardine, eds, *Romanticism and the Sciences* (Cambridge: Cambridge University Press, 1990), pp. 169–85.
57. E. Gellner, *Nations and Nationalism* (Ithaca: Cornell University Press, 2008), p. 47.
58. E. Gellner, *Nationalism* (London: Phoenix, 1998), is a superb introduction. B. Anderson, *Imagined Communities* (New York: Verso, 1991), is a pioneering study of nationalism and identity. E. Hobsbawm and T. Ranger, eds, *The Invention of Tradition* (Cambridge: Cambridge University Press, 1983), is an intriguing collection of essays on national self-extemporization. R. Pearson, ed., *The Longman Companion to European Nationalism, 1789–1920* (London: Longman, 1994), is a useful reference work. D. Simpson, *Romanticism, Nationalism and the Revolt against Theory* (Chicago: University of Chicago Press, 1993), is a good short conspectus.

L. Hagendoorn et al., *European Nations and Nationalism* (Aldershot: Ashgate, 2000), is an important collection of essays.

59. Quoted in Popper, *The Open Society and Its Enemies*, i, p. 300.
60. Davies, *Europe: A History*, p. 733.
61. J. G. Fichte, *Reden an deutsche Nation* (Berlin: Realschulbuchhandlung, 1808), is the basic text. A. J. P. Taylor, *The Course of German History* (London: Routledge, 2001), is a brilliant polemic. A. J. LaVopa, *Fichte, the Self and the Calling of Philosophy* (Cambridge: Cambridge University Press, 2001), makes Fichte's thought intelligible in context.
62. T. B. Macaulay, *Critical and Historical Essays*, 3 vols (London, 1886), ii, pp. 226–7.
63. T. B. Macaulay, *The History of England*, 2 vols (London: Longman, 1849), ii, p. 665.
64. Macaulay, *The History of England*, is the starting point of the nineteenth-century British myth; D. Gilmour, *Rudyard Kipling* (London: Pimlico, 2003), is the best biography of the greatest celebrant of Britishness. The quotation from Rhodes is at p. 137. N. Davies, *The Isles* (London: Macmillan, 2000), is the best, as well as the most controversial, single-volume British history.
65. In Act 1 of I. Zangwill's 1908 play, *The Melting Pot*.
66. R. Horsman, *Race and Manifest Destiny* (Cambridge, MA: Harvard University Press, 1990), is a lively and controversial enquiry. W. Cronon, ed., *Under an Open Sky* (New York: W. W. Norton, 1994), is a superb study of westward colonization and its ecological effects. W. Cronon, *Nature's Metropolis* (New York: W. W. Norton, 1992), is a gripping study of the growth of Chicago.
67. F. Fernández-Armesto, 'America can still save the world', *Spectator*, 8 January 2000, p. 18.
68. J. Farina, ed., *Hecker Studies: Essays on the Thought of Isaac Hecker* (New York: Paulist Press, 1983), is a good introduction. W. L. Portier, *Isaac Hecker and the Vatican Council* (Lewiston: Edwin Mellen, 1985), is a substantial study. J. Dolan, *The American Catholic Experience* (Indianapolis: University of Notre Dame Press, 1985), and P. Gleason, *Keeping Faith* (Indianapolis: University of Notre Dame Press, 1987), are good histories of US Catholicism.
69. Z. Sardar and M. Wynn Davies, *Why Do People Hate America* (London: Icon, 2005), is a brilliant summation. J. S. Nye, *The Paradox of American Power* (New York: Oxford University Press, 2002), is a searching and compelling study.
70. I. Jack, ed., *Granta 77: What We Think of America* (London: Granta, 2002), p. 9.
71. Han-yin Chen Shen, 'Tseng Kuo-fan in Peking, 1840–52: his ideas on statecraft and reform', *Journal of Asian Studies*, xxvi (1967), pp. 61–80 at p. 71.

72. I. Hsu, *The Rise of Modern China* (New York: Oxford University Press, 1999), is the best history of China throughout the relevant periods. S. A. Leibo, *Transferring Technology to China* (Berkeley: University of California Press, 1985), is an excellent study of one strand in the self-strengthening movement. R. B. Wong, *China Transformed* (Ithaca: Cornell University Press, 2000), is fundamental.
73. Quoted in C. Holcombe, *A History of East Asia* (Cambridge: Cambridge University Press, 2017), p. 245.
74. F. Yukichi, *Autobiography* (New York: Columbia University Press, 1966), is a fascinating memoir of one of Japan's 'discoverers of the West'. See also the works listed in chapter 6.
75. 'The man who was' (1889), in R. Kipling, *Life's Handicap* (New York: Doubleday, 1936), p. 91.
76. A. F. Salahuddin Ahmed, *Social Ideas and Social Change in Bengal, 1818–35* (Leiden: Brill, 1965), p. 37.
77. S. Chaudhuri, *Renaissance and Renaissances: Europe and Bengal* (University of Cambridge Centre for South Asian Studies Occasional Papers, no. 1, 2004), p. 4.
78. D. Kopf, *The Brahmo Samaj and the Shaping of the Modern Indian Mind* (Princeton: Princeton University Press, 1979), is a profoundly insightful work. G. Haldar, *Vidyasagar: A Reassessment* (New York: People's Publishing House, 1972), is an outstanding portrait. M. K. Haldar's introduction to Bankimchandra Chattopadhyaya's insider-essay, *Renaissance and Reaction in Nineteenth-Century Bengal* (Calcutta: Minerva, 1977), is brisk, perceptive, and provocative. M. Rajaretnam, ed., *José Rizal and the Asian Renaissance* (Kuala Lumpur: Institut Kajian Dasar, 1996), contains some suggestive essays.
79. N. Keddie, *Sayyid Jamal al-Din al-Afghani* (Berkeley: University of California Press, 1972). A. Hourani, *Arabic Thought in the Liberal Age* (Cambridge: Cambridge University Press, 1983), is fundamental. Z. Sardar is the current incarnation of Islamic tradition favourably disposed to the West. See, for instance, *Desperately Seeking Paradise: Journeys of a Sceptical Muslim* (London: Granta, 2005).
80. I. Duncan, 'Darwin and the savages', *Yale Journal of Criticism*, iv (1991), pp. 13–45.
81. C. Darwin, *On the Origin of Species* (London: Murray, 1859), p. 490.
82. *On the Origin of Species* (1859) and *The Descent of Man* (1872) set out the theory and placed humankind in its context. N. Eldredge, *Time Frames* (New York: Simon & Schuster, 1985), is the best modern critique. A. Desmond and J. Moore, *Darwin* (New York: W. W. Norton, 1994), is the best biography – exciting and challenging; more exhaustive and more staid are the two volumes of J. Browne, *Charles Darwin* (New York: Knopf, 1995).
83. R. C. Bannister, *Social Darwinism: Science and Myth in Anglo-American Social Thought* (Philadelphia: Temple University Press, 1989), p. 40.

84. H. Spencer, *An Autobiography*, 2 vols (London: Murray, 1902), i, p. 502; ii, p. 50.
85. M. Hawkins, *Social Darwinism in European and American Thought* (Cambridge: Cambridge University Press, 1997), pp. 81–6.
86. K. Taizo and T. Hoquet, 'Translating "Natural Selection" in Japanese', *Bionima*, vi (2013), pp. 26–48.
87. D. Pick, *Faces of Degeneration: A European Disorder, c. 1848–1918* (Cambridge: Cambridge University Press, 1993).
88. N. Stepan, *Picturing Tropical Nature* (Ithaca: Cornell University Press, 2001).
89. H. Krausnick et al., *Anatomy of the SS State* (New York: Walker, 1968), p. 13; Fernández-Armesto, *A Foot in the River*, p. 63.
90. Browne, *Charles Darwin*, i, p. 399.
91. G. Best, *Humanity in Warfare* (New York: Columbia University Press, 1980), pp. 44–5, 108–9.
92. G. W. F. Hegel, *Elements of the Philosophy of Right*, ed. A. Wood (Cambridge: Cambridge University Press, 1991), p. 361.
93. P. Bobbitt, *The Shield of Achilles* (New York: Knopf, 2002), is a spectacular, hawkish history of war in international relations. B. Heuser, *Reading Clausewitz* (London: Random House, 2002), explains his thought and surveys his influence. M. Howard, *Clausewitz* (Oxford: Oxford University Press, 2002), is a pithy and satisfying introduction.
94. C. von Clausewitz, *On War*, trans. J. J. Graham, 3 vols (London: Routledge, 1968), i, pp. 2; ii, p. 24.
95. G. Ritter, *The Sword and the Scepter*, 2 vols (Miami: University of Miami Press, 1969), is the classic study of German militarism. V. R. Berghahn, *Militarism* (Leamington Spa: Berg, 1981), and N. Stargardt, *The German Idea of Militarism* (Cambridge: Cambridge University Press, 1994), are helpful introductions for the period from the 1860s onward. S. Finer, *The Man on Horseback* (New York: Praeger, 1965), is an outstanding investigation of the social and political role of the military.
96. H. Pross, ed., *Die Zerstörung der deutschen Politik: Dokumente 1871–1933* (Frankfurt: Fischer, 1959), pp. 29–31.
97. A. Bowler, 'Politics as art: Italian futurism and fascism', *Theory and Society*, xx (1991), pp. 763–94.
98. B. Mussolini, *Doctrine of Fascism*, para. 3; C. Cohen, ed., *Communism, Fascism and Democracy: The Theoretical Foundations* (New York: Random House, 1972), pp. 328–39.
99. B. V. A. Rolling, 'The sin of silence', *Bulletin of the Atomic Scientists*, xxxvi (1980), no. 9, pp. 10–13.
100. K. Fant, *Alfred Nobel* (New York: Arcade, 1993), is the only really useful study of the man. L. S. Wittner, *The Struggle against the Bomb*, 2 vols (Stanford: Stanford University Press, 1995–7), is a comprehensive study of the nuclear disarmament movement. Stanley Kubrick´s movie of 1964, *Dr Strangelove*, is a delectable black-comic satire of the Cold War.

101. F. Galton, 'Hereditary talent and character', *Macmillan's Magazine,* xii (1865), pp. 157–66, 318–27; F. Galton, 'Eugenics: its definition, scope, and aims', *American Journal of Sociology*, x (1904), no. 1, pp. 1–25.
102. F. Galton, *Essays in Eugenics* [1909] (New York: Garland, 1985). M. S. Quine, *Population Politics in Twentieth-Century Europe* (London: Routledge, 1996), brilliantly sets out the context. M. B. Adams, ed., *The Well-Born Science* (New York: Oxford University Press, 1990), is a collection of important essays. M. Kohn, *The Race Gallery* (London: Jonathan Cape, 1995), studies the rise of racial science. C. Clay and M. Leapman, *Master Race* (London: Hodder and Stoughton, 1995), is a chilling account of one of Nazism's eugenics projects. Bashford, *Global Population,* is indispensable.
103. Bethencourt, *Racisms.*
104. A. Thomson, *Bodies of Thought: Science, Religion, and the Soul in the Early Enlightenment* (Oxford: Oxford University Press, 2008), p. 240.
105. A. de Gobineau, *The Inequality of Human Races* (New York: Howard Fertig, 1999), is the starting point. C. Bolt, *Victorian Attitudes to Race* (London: Routledge, 1971), and L. Kuper, ed., *Race, Science and Society* (Paris: UNESCO, 1975), are excellent modern studies.
106. Nietzsche, *Beyond Good and Evil,* p. 118.
107. D. Cohn-Sherbok, *Anti-Semitism* (Stroud: Sutton, 2002), is a balanced and rigorous history. N. Cohn, *Europe's Inner Demons* (Chicago: University of Chicago Press, 2001), is a classic and controversial investigation of the lineage of anti-Semitism. H. Walser Smith, *The Butcher's Tale* (New York: W. W. Norton, 2003), is a fascinating case study. P. Pulzer, *The Rise of Political Anti-Semitism in Germany and Austria* (Cambridge, MA: Harvard University Press, 1988), is well informed and convincing. S. Almog, *Nationalism and Antisemitism in Modern Europe* (Oxford: Pergamon Press, 1990), provides a short overview.
108. F. Adler, *The Religion of Duty* (New York: McClure, 1909), p. 108.
109. M. Knight, ed., *Humanist Anthology* (London: Barrie and Rockliff, 1961), is a useful collection of texts. Chadwick, *The Secularization of the European Mind,* is an excellent account of the nineteenth-century 'crisis of faith', echoed in A. N. Wilson, *God's Funeral* (New York: W. W. Norton, 1999).
110. Kristeller, *Renaissance Thought and Its Sources,* is a superb digest on the earlier, unrelated tradition, and can be helpfully supplemented by P. Burke, *Tradition and Innovation in Renaissance Italy* (London: Fontana, 1974).
111. See K. Armstrong, *The Battle for God: Fundamentalism in Judaism, Christianity and Islam* (New York: HarperCollins, 2000).

CHAPTER 9 *The Revenge of Chaos: Unstitching Certainty*

1. J. Chevalier, *Henri Bergson* (Paris: Plon, 1926), p. 40. L. Kolakowski, *Bergson* (Oxford: Oxford University Press, 1985), is the best introduction

to Bergson. A. R. Lacey, *Bergson* (London: Routledge, 1989), and J. Mullarkey, *Bergson and Philosophy* (Indianapolis: University of Notre Dame Press, 1999), go into more detail with less elegance.

2. Chevalier, *Henri Bergson*, p. 62.
3. H. Bergson, *Creative Evolution* (Boston, MA: University Press of America, 1983), p. 161.
4. H. Bergson, *Données immédiates de la conscience* [1889] in *Oeuvres* (Paris, 1959), p. 67; Chevalier, *Henri Bergson*, p. 53.
5. H. Bergson, *La perception du changement* (Oxford: Oxford University Press, 1911), pp. 18–37.
6. Ibid., pp. 12–17.
7. M. and R. Humphrey, *Stream of Consciousness in the Modern Novel* (Berkeley: University of California Press, 1954).
8. T. Dantzig, *Henri Poincaré, Critic of Crisis* (New York: Scribner, 1954), p. 11.
9. H. Poincaré, *The Foundations of Science* (Lancaster, PA: Science Press, 1946), p. 42.
10. Ibid., pp. 208, 321.
11. C. P. Snow, 'Einstein' [1968], in M. Goldsmith et al., eds, *Einstein: The First Hundred Years* (Oxford: Pergamon, 1980), p. 111.
12. J. A. Coleman, *Relativity for the Layman* (New York: William-Frederick, 1954), is an entertaining introduction. R. W. Clark, *Einstein* (New York: Abrams, 1984), and W. Isaacson, *Einstein's Universe* (New York: Simon & Schuster, 2007), are indispensable biographies. J. R. Lucas and P. E. Hodgson, *Spacetime and Electromagnetism* (Oxford: Oxford University Press, 1990), illuminates the physics and philosophy involved. D. Bodanis, *Einstein's Greatest Mistake* (Boston: Houghton, 2015), and M. Wazeck, *Einstein's Opponents* (Cambridge: Cambridge University Press, 2014), explain the decline of his influence.
13. W. James, *Pragmatism* (New York: Longman, 1907), p. 51.
14. R. B. Perry, *The Thought and Character of William James*, 2 vols (London: Oxford University Press, 1935), ii, p. 621.
15. James, *Pragmatism*, p. 115.
16. C. S. Peirce, *Collected Papers* (Cambridge, MA: Harvard University Press, 1965), and James, *Pragmatism*, are the fundamental texts. G. Wilson Allen, *William James* (New York: Viking, 1967), is the best biography, and J. P. Murphy, *Pragmatism from Peirce to Davidson* (Boulder: Westview, 1990), the best survey.
17. The essential guide is C. Saunders, ed., *The Cambridge Companion to Saussure* (Cambridge: Cambridge University Press, 2004).
18. J. Diamond, *Guns, Germs, and Steel* (New York: Norton, 1998), p. 2.
19. F. Boas, *The Mind of Primitive Man* (New York: Macmillan, 1911), pp. 113, 208–9.
20. B. Kapferer and D. Theodossopoulos, eds, *Against Exoticism: Toward the Transcendence of Relativism and Universalism in Anthropology* (New York:

Berghahn, 2016). Boas, *The Mind of Primitive Man*, is the fundamental text; G. W. Stocking, *A Franz Boas Reader* (Chicago: University of Chicago Press, 1974), is a useful collection. J. Hendry, *An Introduction to Social Anthropology* (London: Macmillan, 1999), is a good basic introduction.

21. F. Crews, *Freud: The Making of an Illusion* (New York: Metropolitan, 2017).
22. S. Freud, *Totem and Taboo* (London: Routledge, 2001), p. 171.
23. H. F. Ellenberger, *The Discovery of the Unconscious* (New York: Basic, 1981). P. Gay, *Freud: A Life for Our Time* (New York: Norton, 2006), should be contrasted with J. M. Masson, *The Assault on Truth* (New York: Harper, 1992), and F. Forrester, *Dispatches from the Freud Wars* (Cambridge, MA: Harvard University Press, 1997), as well as Crews, *Freud*.
24. E. Key, *The Century of the Child* (New York: Putnam, 1909).
25. J. Piaget, *The Child's Conception of Physical Causality* (New York: Harcourt, 1930), is fundamental. M. Boden, *Piaget* (New York: Fontana, 1994), is an excellent short introduction. P. Bryant, *Perception and Understanding in Young Children* (New York: Basic, 1984), and L. S. Siegel and C. J. Brainerd, *Alternatives to Piaget* (New York: Academic Press, 1978), are outstanding revisionist works. P. Ariès and G. Duby, *A History of Private Life* (Cambridge, MA: Harvard University Press, 1987–91), is a challenging, long-term, wide-ranging exploration of the background of the history of family relationships. De Mause, ed., *The History of Childhood*, is a pioneering collection of essays.
26. P. Conrad, *Modern Times, Modern Places* (New York: Knopf, 1999), p. 83.
27. M. Foot, *Aneurin Bevan: A Biography, Volume 1: 1897–1945* (London: Faber, 1963), p. 319.
28. E. Nolte, *Der europäische Burgerkrieg* (Munich: Herbig, 1997), is a brilliant history of modern ideological conflict. M. Blinkhorn, *Fascism and the Far Right in Europe* (London: Unwin, 2000), is a good brief introduction. S. J. Woolf, ed., *Fascism in Europe* (London: Methuen, 1981), is a useful compendium. C. Hibbert, *Benito Mussolini* (New York: Palgrave, 2008), is still the liveliest biography, but D. Mack Smith, *Mussolini* (New York: Knopf, 1982), is enjoyable and authoritative.

CHAPTER 10 *The Age of Uncertainty: Twentieth-Century Hesitancies*

1. M. J. Connelly, *Fatal Misconception: The Struggle to Control the World's Population* (Cambridge, MA: Harvard University Press, 2008); I. Dowbiggin, *The Sterilization Movement and Global Fertility in the Twentieth Century* (Oxford: Oxford University Press, 2008).
2. We now have a good history of the consumption explosion: F. Trentmann, *Empire of Things* (London: Penguin, 2015).

3. The term was originally Alvin Toffler's: see *Future Shock* (New York: Random House, 1970).
4. Fernández-Armesto, *A Foot in the River*, p. 197.
5. H. von Hofmannsthal, *Ausgewählte Werke, ii: Erzählungen und Aufsätze* (Frankfurt: Fischer, 1905), p. 445.
6. R. L. Carneiro, *Evolutionism in Cultural Anthropology: A Critical History* (Boulder: Westview, 2003), pp. 169–70.
7. 'Prof. Charles Lane Poor of Columbia explains Prof. Albert Einstein's astronomical theories', *New York Times*, 19 November 1919.
8. D. R. Hofstadter, *Gödel, Escher, Bach* (New York: Basic, 1979).
9. G. Boolos, 'Gödel's Second Incompleteness Theorem explained in words of one syllable', *Mind*, ciii (1994), pp. 1–3. I have benefited from conversations on Quine with Mr Luke Wojtalik.
10. Plato, *Republic*, X, 603.
11. R. Goldstein, *Incompleteness: The Belief and Paradox of Kurt Gödel* (New York: Norton, 2005), p. 76; see also L. Gamwell, *Mathematics and Art* (Princeton: Princeton University Press, 2015), p. 93. Hofstadter, *Gödel, Escher, Bach*, deals brilliantly with Gödel, albeit in service of an argument for artificial intelligence. M. Baaz et al., eds, *Kurt Gödel and the Foundations of Mathematics: Horizons of Truth* (Cambridge: Cambridge University Press, 2011), is now the leading work.
12. P. Levi, *Survival in Auschwitz and the Reawakening* (New York: Summit, 1986), p. 11.
13. A. Kimball Smith, *A Peril and a Hope: The Scientists' Movement in America* (Cambridge, MA: MIT Press, 1971), pp. 49–50.
14. J. P. Sartre, *Existentialism and Human Emotions* (New York: Philosophical Library, 1957), pp. 21–3.
15. C. Howells, ed., *The Cambridge Companion to Sartre* (Cambridge: Cambridge University Press, 1992), and S. Crowell, ed., *The Cambridge Companion to Existentialism* (Cambridge: Cambridge University Press, 2012), track origins and effects. N. Mailer, *An American Dream* (New York: Dial, 1965), recounts the horrors of an existential antihero who wreaks destruction in every life he touches except his own.
16. L. E. Hahn and P. A. Schlipp, eds, *The Philosophy of W. V. Quine* (Peru, IL: Open Court, 1986), pp. 427–31.
17. A. Orenstein, *W. V. Quine* (Princeton: Princeton University Press, 2002), is the best introduction. R. Gibson, ed., *The Cambridge Companion to W. Quine* (Cambridge: Cambridge University Press, 2004), makes it possible to trace all influences and effects. H. Putnam provides a telling critique in *Mind, Reality and Language* (Cambridge: Cambridge University Press, 1983), pp. 33–69.
18. B. Russell, *Autobiography*, 3 vols (London: Methuen, 1967), i.
19. L. Wittgenstein, *Philosophical Investigations*, trans. G. Anscombe et al. (Oxford: Blackwell, 2010), is the best edition. A. C. Grayling, *Wittgenstein:*

A Very Short Introduction (Oxford: Oxford University Press, 2001), combines succinctness, readability, and scepticism.

20. F. de Saussure, *Premier cours de linguistique générale (1907), d'après les cahiers d'Albert Riedlinger*, ed. and trans. E. Komatsu and G. Wolf (Oxford: Pergamon, 1996), is the starting point. *Of Grammatology* (Baltimore: Johns Hopkins University Press, 2016), is perhaps the clearest statement by the usually opaque J. Derrida; a good collection is *Basic Writings* (New York: Routledge, 2007).
21. This paragraph and the next two are adapted from F. Fernández-Armesto, 'Pillars and post: the foundations and future of post-modernism', in C. Jencks, ed., *The Post-Modern Reader* (Chichester: Wiley, 2011), pp. 125–37.
22. J. Jacobs, *The Death and Life of Great American Cities* (New York: Random House, 1961).
23. I. Hassan, *The Postmodern Turn* (Columbus: Ohio State University Press, 1987), p. 211.
24. H. Foster, *The Return of the Real: The Avant-Garde at the End of the Century* (Cambridge, MA, and London: MIT Press, 1996), pp. 205–6.
25. J. Monod, *Chance and Necessity* (New York: Vintage, 1972), pp. 169–70.
26. J. V. Mallow, *Science Anxiety* (Clearwater: H&H, 1986).
27. D. R. Griffin, *The Reenchantment of Science: Postmodern Proposals* (Albany: SUNY Press, 1988).
28. J. Prest, *The Garden of Eden: The Botanic Garden and the Re-Creation of Paradise* (New Haven: Yale University Press, 1981); R. Grove, *Green Imperialism: Colonial Expansion, Tropical Island Edens and the Origins of Environmentalism, 1600–1860* (Cambridge: Cambridge University Press, 1995).
29. J. McNeill, *Something New under the Sun* (New York: Norton, 2001).
30. A. Bramwell, *Blood and Soil: Richard Walther Darré and Hitler's 'Green Party'* (London: Kensal Press, 1985).
31. D. Worster, *Nature's Economy* (San Francisco: Sierra Club, 1977), is a brilliant history of environmentalist thinking, supplemented by A. Bramwell, *Ecology in the Twentieth Century* (New Haven: Yale University Press, 1989). McNeill, *Something New under the Sun*, is a wonderful, worrying history of twentieth-century environmental mismanagement.
32. T. Kuhn, *The Structure of Scientific Revolutions* [1962] (Chicago: University of Chicago Press, 1996), is fundamental. A. Pais, *Niels Bohr's Times* (Oxford: Oxford University Press, 1991), is an outstanding biography. Zukav, *The Dancing Wu-Li Masters*, is a controversial but suggestive attempt to express modern physics in the terms of Eastern philosophy.
33. P. W. Anderson, *More and Different: Notes from a Thoughtful Curmudgeon* (Singapore: World Scientific, 2011). J. Gleick, *Chaos: Making a New Science* (New York: Viking, 1987), is the brilliant, classic statement of chaos theory. J. Horgan, *The End of Science* (New York: Basic, 1996),

cleverly depicts science's successes as evidence of its limitations, on the basis of revealing interviews with scientists.

34. B. Hoff, *The Tao of Pooh* (London: Penguin, 1983).
35. D. Wilson, *Mao: The People's Emperor* (London: Futura, 1980), p. 265.
36. S. A. Smith, ed., *The Oxford Handbook of the History of Communism* (Oxford: Oxford University Press, 2014), p. 29.
37. Mao Zedong, *Selected Works*, 5 vols (Oxford: Pergamon, 1961–77), ii, p. 96.
38. P. Short, *Mao: The Man Who Made China* (London: Taurus, 2017), is the best study. J. Chang, *Wild Swans* (New York: Simon & Schuster, 1991) is a fascinating personal memoir by a participant in and survivor of the Cultural Revolution.
39. 'Songs of the Great Depression', http://csivc.csi.cuny.edu/history/files/lavender/cherries.html, accessed 25 November 2017.
40. F. Allen, *The Lords of Creation* (New York: Harper, 1935), pp. 350–1.
41. R. Skidelsky, *John Maynard Keynes* (New York: Penguin, 2005), is a grand biography. R. Lechakman, *The Age of Keynes* (New York: Random House, 1966), and J. K. Galbraith, *The Age of Uncertainty* (Boston: Houghton, 1977), are tributes to Keynes's influence. J. Schumpeter, *Capitalism, Socialism and Democracy* (New York: Harper, 1942), was an interesting and influential early answer to Keynes.
42. W. Beveridge, *Social Insurance and Allied Services* (London: HMSO, 1942), para. 458.
43. J. Harris, *William Beveridge* (Oxford: Oxford University Press, 1997), is a good biography. D. Fraser, *The Evolution of the British Welfare State* (New York: Palgrave, 2009), traces the relevant traditions in modern social and political thought. F. G. Castles and C. Pirson, eds, *The Welfare State: A Reader* (Cambridge: Polity, 2009), is a useful anthology. J. C. Scott, *Seeing Like a State* (New Haven: Yale University Press, 1999), is a brilliant, partisan indictment of state planning generally.
44. J. M. Keynes, *The End of Laissez-Faire* (London: Wolf, 1926), p. 6.
45. E. Burke, *Reflections on the Revolution in France* (London: Dent, 1910), para. 403, p. 242.
46. Ibid., p. 69.
47. J. Gray, *Hayek on Liberty* (London: Routledge, 1998), p. 59.
48. C. Kukathas, *Hayek and Modern Liberalism* (Oxford: Oxford University Press, 1989), and R. Kley, *Hayek's Social and Political Thought* (Oxford: Oxford University Press, 1994), are helpful. Gray, *Hayek on Liberty*, is brilliant and insightful; G. R. Steele, *The Economics of Friedrich Hayek* (New York: Palgrave, 2007), is outstanding in its field. On the Chicago School, there are helpful essays in R. Emmett, ed., *The Elgar Companion to the Chicago School of Economics* (Northampton, MA: Elgar, 2010). J. van Overfeldt, *The Chicago School: How the University of Chicago Assembled the Thinkers Who Revolutionized Economics and*

Business (Evanston: Agate, 2008), is interesting on the formation of the school.

49. A. M. Turing, 'Computing machinery and intelligence', *Mind*, lix (1950), pp. 433–60.
50. Hofstadter, *Gödel, Escher, Bach*, is the most brilliant – though ultimately unconvincing – apologia for 'artificial intelligence' ever penned. K. Hafner, *Where Wizards Stay Up Late* (New York: Simon & Schuster, 1996), is a lively history of the origins of the Internet. J. M. Dubbey, *The Mathematical Work of Charles Babbage* (Cambridge: Cambridge University Press, 2004), is probably the best book on Babbage.
51. F. Crick, *The Astonishing Hypothesis: The Scientific Search for the Soul* (New York: Scribner, 1994), pp. 6–7.
52. J. D. Watson, *The Double Helix* (New York: Atheneum, 1968), is the unabashedly personal account of one of the discoverers of DNA; it should be read alongside B. Maddox, *Rosalind Franklin* (New York: HarperCollins, 2002), which tells the fascinating story of Crick and Watson's rival. J. E. Cabot, *As the Future Catches You* (New York: Three Rivers, 2001), is brilliant on 'genomics' and 'genotechnics'.
53. I draw my account from my *A Foot in the River*.
54. E. O. Wilson, *Sociobiology* (Cambridge, MA: Harvard University Press, 1975), p. 547.
55. Ibid., p. 548.
56. Wilson, *Sociobiology*, is the classic statement. R. Hernstein and C. Murray, *The Bell Curve* (New York: Free Press, 1994), divided opinion by its chillingly reductionist logic. C. Jencks, *Inequality* (New York: Basic Books, 1972), is a good summary of the traditional liberal position.
57. N. Chomsky, *Knowledge of Language* (Westport: Praeger, 1986), p. 55.
58. Ibid., p. 272.
59. Ibid., p. 273.
60. Armstrong, *The Battle for God*, pp. 135–98.
61. M. E. Marty and R. S. Appleby, eds, *Fundamentalisms Observed* (Chicago: University of Chicago Press, 1991), and G. M. Marsden, *Fundamentalism and American Culture* (New York: Oxford University Press, 1980), are stimulating studies.
62. R. Rolland, *The Life of Vivekananda and the Universal Gospel* (Calcutta: Advaita Ashrama, 1953), is a sympathetic introduction to the swami.
63. E. Hillman, *The Wider Ecumenism* (New York: Herder and Herder, 1968), broaches the subject of interfaith ecumenism. M. Braybrooke, *Interfaith Organizations* (New York: Edwin Mellen, 1980), is a useful history.
64. G. Davis, *Aimé Césaire* (Cambridge: Cambridge University Press, 1997), is a study of the poet's thought. L. W. Levine, *Black Culture and Black Consciousness* (New York: Oxford University Press, 1978), is an interesting history of the movement in the United States. A. Haley, *Roots* (New York: Doubleday, 1976), was, in its day, an influential, 'factional' pilgrimage

by a black American, reconciling African identity with the American dream.

65. I. Berlin, in *New York Review of Books*, xlv, no. 8 (1998); H. Hardy, ed., *The Power of Ideas* (Princeton: Princeton University Press, 2013), pp. 1–23.

66. A. Lijphart, *Democracy in Plural Societies* (New Haven: Yale University Press, 1977), is a thoughtful, cogent, hopeful study of the problems. J. Gray, *Isaiah Berlin* (Glasgow: HarperCollins, 1995), is a stimulating and discerning study of the great apologist of modern pluralism. R. Takaki, *A Different Mirror* (New York: Little, Brown, 1993), is a vigorous and engaging history of multicultural America.

PROSPECT *The End of Ideas?*

1. M. Kaku, *The Future of Humanity: Terraforming Mars, Interstellar Travel, Immortality, and Our Destiny Beyond* (London: Allen Lane, 2018).

2. S. Greenfield, *Tomorrow's People: How 21st-Century Technology Is Changing the Way We Think and Feel* (London: Allen Lane, 2003).

Index